The Environmental Case
Translating Values into Policy

Second Edition

Judith A. Layzer
Massachusetts Institute of Technology

CQ PRESS

A Division of Congressional Quarterly Inc.
Washington, D.C.

CQ Press
1255 22nd Street, NW, Suite 400
Washington, DC 20037

Phone: 202-729-1900; toll-free, 1-866-427-7737 (1-866-4CQ-PRESS)

Web: www.cqpress.com

Cover design: Kimberly Glyder
Composition: BMWW
Maps drawn by Laris Karlis and International Mapping Associates

♾ The paper used in this publication exceeds the requirements of the American National Standard for Information Sciences—Permanence of Paper for Printed Library Materials, ANSI Z39.48-1992.

Printed and bound in the United States of America

09 08 07 06 05   1 2 3 4 5

Library of Congress Cataloging-in-Publication Data

Layzer, Judith A.
  The environmental case : translating values into policy / Judith A. Layzer. — 2nd ed.
    p. cm.
  Includes bibliographical references and index.
  ISBN 1-56802-898-9 (alk. paper)
  1. Environmental policy—United States—Case studies. I. Title.

GE180.L39 2006
363.7'0560973—dc22   2005032698

For Jean and David Layzer,
with love, gratitude, and admiration

Contents

Contents

Part 2   History, Changing Values, and Resource Management on Public Lands

Preface

The idea for this book was born when I was a graduate student in political science at the Massachusetts Institute of Technology (MIT) in the mid-1990s. My adviser, Stephen Meyer, and I were developing a new undergraduate course in environmental politics and policy, and, after searching extensively for material, we made an important discovery: although quite a few informative and readable texts on the history, substance, and efficacy of various environmental policies were available, few described environmental politics in action. Moreover, hardly any seemed to recognize the fundamental disagreements that make environmental controversies so intractable or the patterns that emerge as one looks at the policymaking process across a broad range of issues. I set out to craft a set of case studies that would simultaneously convey the drama and fascination of U.S. environmental politics and furnish useful insights into the policymaking process. My primary goal, then, was not to assess outcomes from a normative perspective but to make some provocative claims about how environmental policies are made, from the way we decide which problems are worthy of the government's attention to the mechanisms we choose to address them.

The organization of the book as a whole emerged as I added cases that captured new aspects of politics or policy, such as a new matter of concern—wetlands or species extinction, for example—or a novel political dynamic, such as the backlash against environmentalism or collaborative approaches to decision making. The division between pollution control and natural resource management was an obvious one; the other division—between common pool resources and innovative solutions—was less immediately apparent but reflects the most important contemporary puzzles in environmental policy scholarship. For the second edition, I added four new cases that extend the book's arguments to an even broader set of issues within each of the four categories.

In selecting which information to include in each case, I viewed the material through a particular lens—that of political science and, more specifically, one that focuses on the importance of problem definition in policymaking. Although I imposed a clear analytic structure, I tried to keep each narrative sufficiently self-explanatory so that economists, sociologists, historians, and others interested in using the book would not feel confined by my interpretation. Moreover, I sought to make the cases accessible not only to students and scholars but also to activists, policymakers, journalists, and others interested in environmental politics. Each case introduces the reader to fascinating characters and events and provides a foundation for more in-depth study of the issues raised. Taken as a whole, the book provides both a portrait of and an analytic framework for U.S. environmental policymaking, from the local level to the international level, that should be valuable to anyone concerned about the environment.

ACKNOWLEDGMENTS

Writing this book would not have been possible without the support of MIT and Middlebury College. MIT funded the initial development of the cases, and both institutions generously provided support for research assistants. In addition, many students labored to bring the book to fruition. The undergraduates—first at MIT and then at Middlebury—"who pilot tested the cases" gave enormously helpful feedback on them. At Middlebury, Katrina O'Brien, Lee Rowland, Sarah Weston, and Jess Widay provided research assistance for the first edition. As I revised chapters, Kelly Cavazos (MIT), Corey Ferguson (Bowdoin), Jessie Schaffer (MIT), and Anita Yip (Wellesley) helped with fact checking. MIT graduate students contributed to this endeavor as well. Xixi Chen and Kate Van Tassel tracked down sources and helped with proofreading. Abbie Emison earned my special gratitude for her cheerful willingness to hunt for obscure references and search out elusive information. Colleagues Christopher Bosso (Northeastern University) and Christopher Klyza (Middlebury College) read and made insightful comments on the introduction to the first edition. In addition, reviewers Gordon Bennett (University of Texas at Austin), Mark Lubell (Florida State University), Stuart Shulman (Drake University), and Stacy VanDeveer (University of New Hampshire) all provided detailed and thoughtful reviews of the original manuscript.

I would also like to thank the survey respondents who gave me feedback on the first edition with their students: Richard Andrews (University of North Carolina at Chapel Hill), Tina L. Bertrand (McMurray University), Brian Cook (Clark University), Irasema Coronado (University of Texas at El Paso), David L. Feldman (University of Tennessee), Mary Hague (Bucknell University), Timothy Lehman (Rocky Mountain College), Robert J. Mason (Temple University), Joseph Rish (King's College), and Frederick Van Geest (Dordt College).

At CQ Press, acquisitions editor Charisse Kiino has handled the book with great professionalism and an infectious optimism about its prospects. She managed the revision process—and particularly my propensity for endless editing—with great diplomacy. No one could ask for a more dedicated and scrupulous manuscript editor than Carolyn Goldinger, who not only trimmed my prose with care but also spotted numerous passages that needed clarification or explanation. Any remaining ambiguity or wordiness is solely my responsibility. Managing editor Steve Pazdan and production editor Belinda Josey graciously engineered a tight production schedule. And kudos to Kimberly Glyder for the cover design.

In addition to those who contributed directly, my colleagues, friends, and family helped by making my life wonderful while I was working on the book. Since I was a graduate student, Deborah Stone and Jim Morone have been generous beyond measure—with friendship, advice, encouragement, and a wonderful summer hiatus in Brookline—for which I am eternally grateful. My colleagues at Middlebury encouraged me throughout this process of putting together the original manuscript. At MIT, Bob Fogelson, Herman Karl, Lang Keyes, Larry Susskind, Larry Vale, and others have consistently been encouraging and have made my new department feel like home. In his effort to make me a world-class scholar, Steve Meyer has been my toughest critic and a valuable source of professional advice. Heather Boyer and Daphne Kalotay provided editorial advice as I struggled with a variety of storytelling challenges, and Lee Zamir took time out to take the photo that appears on the author page. I am especially grateful to two people who never saw *The Environmental Case* in print: Richard Marius, with his outsized passion, taught me to write sparingly and well; my sister, Daryl Layzer, showed me through her own grace and dignity how to live every day and take nothing for granted. My other siblings—Carolyn, Emily, Jon, and Nick—have been both cheerleaders and safety nets. Finally, I have dedicated the book to my parents, who instilled in me a passion for thinking, learning, and educating. But *The Environmental Case* is also for my nephew, Ian, whose magical presence makes the world a better place, and who will have to live with the consequences of our environmental policy decisions.

CHAPTER 1

Introduction

Defining Problems in U.S. Environmental Politics

Environmental politics concerns "how humanity organizes itself to relate to the nature that sustains it." [1] Because human life depends on what the earth provides, one might think environmental protection would be uncontroversial. Yet bitter disputes have erupted over proposals to preserve undeveloped land, save endangered species, protect or restore ecosystems, clean up toxic dumps and spills, reduce air and water pollution, conserve energy, mitigate human-caused changes in the global climate, and ensure an equitable distribution of environmental hazards. These issues have assumed positions of primacy in American politics, alongside the more conventional social, economic, and foreign policy concerns, and it is therefore essential to understand their political dynamics. And, although the policy process has many generic features, environmental policymaking, with a host of distinct attributes, warrants its own analytic niche. The goal of this book, then, is to illuminate the general attributes of the American political system as it grapples with the environment as a particular object of public action.

This introductory chapter begins by laying out my two-part argument that (1) environmental conflicts are fundamentally about differences in values and (2) the way problems are defined plays a central role in shaping how those values get translated into policies. The chapter goes on to describe the contributions of the system's major actors—policymakers, advocates, experts, and the media—in defining environmental problems, formulating solutions, and ultimately making decisions. It then introduces a number of concepts that help explain the process by which environmental policy is made. The result is a framework, the elements of which are treated in greater depth in the cases that follow. The chapter concludes by explaining the rationale behind the selection, organization, and presentation of the volume's sixteen case studies, each of which is interesting in its own right, but they also offer important lessons for anyone who wants to understand why environmental policy controversies turn out the way they do.

TWO CRITICAL FEATURES
OF U.S. ENVIRONMENTAL POLICYMAKING

Environmental policy disputes are, at heart, contests over values. To the casual observer, these conflicts may appear to revolve around arcane technical issues, but almost all of them involve a fundamental disagreement over how human beings ought to interact with the natural world. Even though environmental disputes are grounded in conflicting moral beliefs, the participants in environmental policy contests rarely make value-based arguments. Instead, they define problems in terms of the science, economics, and risks associated with environmental issues.

The Clash of Values at the Heart of Environmental Policymaking

The participants in environmental debates are divided into two broad camps based on entrenched differences in their beliefs about the appropriate relationship between humans and the natural world. Although each side incorporates a range of perspectives, for analytic purposes we can categorize them as environmentalists and cornucopians. Because value differences divide participants, environmental policy conflicts are rarely resolved by appeals to reason; no amount of technical information is likely to convert adversaries in such disputes.[2]

One Category: Environmentalists. Environmentalism is not a single philosophy but a congeries of beliefs with several roots. Environmental values, in one form or another, have been part of American culture and politics since before the arrival of white settlers on the North American continent. In fact, some contemporary environmentalists trace their values to the spiritual beliefs of Native Americans.[3] But most historians date the origins of American environmentalism to the late eighteenth- and early nineteenth-century Romantics and Transcendentalists, an elite community of artists and writers who celebrated wild nature as a source of spiritual renewal and redemption. They believed that only by preserving untrammeled wilderness could the nation ensure that landscapes remained to replenish the weary soul. In the 1830s George Catlin, a painter who traveled frequently in the West, was the first to plead for the establishment of a national park to preserve land in its "pristine beauty and wildness" for future generations.[4] Twenty years later, Henry David Thoreau deplored the wholesale clearing of land for farming, and he moved to a cabin at Walden Pond in search of a more "simple" and "natural" life. Thoreau also emphasized the importance of preserving wild nature for building character; in his famous essay "Walking," he wrote, "Hope and the future for me are not in lawns and cultivated fields, not in towns and cities, but in the impervious and quaking swamps."[5] In 1911 John Muir, founder of the Sierra Club and an ardent and prolific advocate of wilderness preservation, described nature as a "window opening into heaven, a mirror reflecting the Creator."[6] A half-century later, the federal government embedded the preservationist philosophy in laws such as the Wilderness Preservation Act (1964), the Wild and Scenic Rivers Act (1968), and the National Trails Act (1968).

A second form of environmental concern, conservationism, accompanied the Progressive movement that emerged at the turn of the twentieth century.

Unlike preservationists, who wanted to set aside swaths of undisturbed nature, conservationists advocated the prudent use of natural resources. As historian Samuel Hays points out, conservationists adhered to the "gospel of efficiency." [7] They were intent on managing the nation's coal, oil, timber, grassland, and water according to scientific principles to ensure their availability in the long run. (Most of the applied science disciplines that emerged during this period were geared toward increasing natural resource yields, not preserving ecosystem health.) Conservationists like Gifford Pinchot, for example, deplored the wasteful cut-and-run logging practices of private timber companies, and they feared that American industrialists would appropriate and squander the nation's natural resources unless government stepped in and planned for their orderly exploitation. It was this concern that drove the federal government to set aside forest reserves and in 1905 create the Forest Service to manage those lands for the public benefit.

Although strains of preservationist and conservationist thought pervade contemporary environmental debates, a divergent strand of environmentalism emerged after World War II—one more concerned with fighting pollution than with preserving pristine natural areas or managing natural resources efficiently. Ideas about the interdependence of human beings and nature derived from the scientific discipline of ecology, which focuses on the study of living organisms and their environment, and these ideas are the primary wellsprings of modern environmentalism.[8] In the late 1940s naturalist and forester Aldo Leopold sowed the seeds of the environmental movement with his book, *A Sand County Almanac*, which developed a "land ethic" based on principles of interrelatedness and stability. According to Leopold, "All ethics . . . rest upon a single premise: that the individual is a member of a community of interdependent parts." Therefore, "a thing is right when it tends to preserve the stability and beauty of the biotic community. It is wrong when it tends otherwise." [9]

Another philosophical foundation of mainstream environmentalism is the limits-to-growth thesis espoused by MIT biophysicist Donella Meadows and her coauthors in 1970. Based on a mathematical method called system dynamics, this perspective recognized the importance of relationships and feedback loops in complex systems.[10] According to the limits-to-growth argument, the human population is outrunning the earth's capacity to support it. Adherents of this view are not opposed to economic growth altogether; rather, they advocate growth that is "sustainable" and therefore does not come at the expense of future generations. An unregulated market system is anathema because it invariably leads to unsustainable levels of production and consumption.

The contemporary environmental movement is not monolithic. For example, deep ecologists distinguish themselves from mainstream environmentalists, whose environmental beliefs they regard as superficial. Deep ecology is ecocentric: whereas anthropocentric perspectives treat human beings as morally superior to other forms of life on the basis of our capacity for language and complex thought, ecocentric perspectives treat the world as "an intrinsically dynamic, interconnected web of relations in which there are no absolutely discrete entities and no absolute dividing lines between the living and the nonliving, the animate and the inanimate, or the human and the non-human." [11] As the quote makes clear, deep ecology rests on a premise of "bio-spherical egalitarianism"—that is, the inherent and equal value of all living things. Moreover, deep ecologists believe that human quality of life depends on maintaining a deep connection to, rather than simply a respectful rela-tionship with, other forms of life. It is worth noting that deep ecology is *not* logically derived from ecology; nor does it depend for substantiation on the results of scientific investigation.[12] Instead, as philosopher Arne Naess explains, "To the ecological field worker, the equal right to live and blossom is an intuitively clear and obvious value axiom." [13]

A Second Category: Cornucopians. Unlike environmentalists, cornucopians (or Prometheans) place a preeminent value on economic growth.[14] The term *cornucopian* suggests abundance, even limitlessness—in sharp contrast to environmentalism. Adherents of this perspective fear that environmental restrictions threaten their economic well-being or the economic health of their community.

Cornucopians have boundless confidence in humans' ability to devise tech-nological solutions to resource shortages.[15] Best known among the cornucopi-ans are economists Julian Simon and Herman Kahn, who say, "We are confi-dent that the nature of the physical world permits continued improvement in humankind's economic lot in the long run, indefinitely." [16] A theme of the cor-nucopian literature is that the kinds of doomsday forecasts made by environ-mentalists never come to pass. Resource shortages may arise in the short run, but the lesson of history, according to Simon and Kahn, is that "the nature of the world's physical conditions and the resilience in a well-functioning eco-nomic and social system enable us to overcome such problems, and the solu-tions usually leave us better off than if the problem had never arisen." [17]

In addition to being technological optimists, cornucopians place enormous value on individual liberty—defined as the freedom to do as one wishes with-out interference. Some proponents of this philosophy contend that envi-ronmentalists are actually Socialists disguising their rejection of markets and preference for government control over the means of production as concern about the environment.[18] Cornucopians criticize environmental regulations not only for limiting individual freedom but also for taking out of the economy resources that would otherwise be used productively. Reasoning that affluence leads to demands for better health and a cleaner environment, they propose that the best way to protect the environment is to ensure that individuals can pursue material prosperity.[19] The role of government, in such a world view, is simply to assign property rights in the earth's resources and let the market dic-tate allocations of the goods and services that flow from these resources.

Cornucopians regard their perspective as logical, rational, and optimistic; by contrast, they see environmentalists as sentimental and irrationally pessimistic. They particularly eschew ecocentric philosophies that elevate plants, animals, and even nonliving entities to the level of human beings, and instead adopt a view of the world in which "people may not sit above animals and plants in any metaphysical sense, but clearly are superior in their placement in the natural order." Therefore, "decent material conditions must be provided for all of the former before there can be long-term assurance of protection for the latter." [20]

In short, the schism between environmentalists and cornucopians arises out of different worldviews. That said, environmentalists are a diverse lot, ranging from those who believe that all life has value to those who yearn for simpler, less harried times to those with practical concerns about the impact of pollution on human health or quality of life. There is similar variation among cornucopians: some place a higher value on economic growth than they do on the aesthetic or moral importance of the natural world; others are avid out-doorsmen who simply have more faith in individuals' than in government's ability to protect natural amenities. But the heterogeneity of environmentalism and cornucopianism should not obscure the fundamental value differences underpinning environmental controversies. Only by recognizing such pro-found disagreements can we understand why environmental policymaking is rarely a straightforward technical matter of acknowledging a problem and devising an appropriate solution. Moreover, the extent to which participants' values diverge is the best clue to how intractable a conflict will be: controversies that involve consensual values like human health are typically less polarized than disputes over ecology, where value differences are often vast and sometimes irreconcilable.

How Participants Define Problems to Gain Political Support

Because the values of participants on both sides are entrenched, environmental politics consists largely of trying to gain the support of the unaware or undecided rather than trying to convert the already committed. As political scientist E. E. Schattschneider observed, "The outcome of every conflict is determined by the extent to which the audience becomes involved in it." [21] To attract sympathizers, advocates define problems strategically in ways they think will resonate with a majority of the public.[22] Defining a problem in politics is a way of simplifying a complex reality; it involves framing information to draw attention to some elements of a problem while obscuring or minimizing others.[23] Problem definition also entails explaining cause and effect, identifying victims and villains, and assigning responsibility for remediation.[24]

By changing which aspect of a problem the public focuses on, advocates can raise (or lower) its visibility and thereby get it onto (or keep it off of) the political agenda.[25] Participants in an environmental policy controversy compete ferociously to provide the authoritative explanation for a problem because "causal stories are essential political instruments for shaping alliances and for settling the distribution of benefits and costs." [26] Participants also compete to predict a problem's consequences because they know that fear of loss or harm is likely to galvanize the public. Finally, by authoritatively defining a problem, advocates can limit the range and type of solutions the public and policymakers are likely to regard as plausible. And, as Schattschneider also pointed out, "The definition of the alternatives is the supreme instrument of power." [27]

When polled, a large majority of Americans profess their support for the goals of the environmental movement.[28] These poll numbers make baldly antienvironmental rhetoric generally unacceptable in political discourse.[29] As a result, cornucopians know they must define environmental problems in ways that make their points in subtle and indirect ways, rather than proclaiming antienvironmental values. The competition between environmentalists and cornucopians to define an environmental problem thus revolves around three attributes: the scientific understanding of the problem, the economic costs and benefits of proposed solutions, and the risks associated with action or inaction. Because each of these is speculative, advocates can choose assessments and projections that are most consistent with their values. They then frame that information—using symbolic language, numbers, and causal theories—to emphasize either environmental or economic risk, depending on their policy objectives.

Translating Scientific Explanations into Causal Stories. The primary battleground in any environmental controversy is the scientific depiction of cause and effect. Scientists are often the first to identify environmental problems or to certify their seriousness. Furthermore, scientific claims carry particular weight because science has enormous cultural authority in the United States. Rather than providing a clear and authoritative explanation, however, science leaves considerable latitude for framing because, as a general rule, the scientific understanding of an environmental problem is uncertain. Most scientific research on natural systems involves practitioners in multiple disciplines, many of which are relatively new, working at the frontiers of scientific knowledge. Moreover, scientists' ability to measure the causes and consequences of environmental phenomena is limited, both technologically and financially, and, in the case of human health effects, by ethical considerations. Most important, few environmental problems can be simulated in laboratory experiments: they involve complex interactions among factors for which it is difficult or impossible to control. In the early stages of research, therefore, a wide range of uncertainty surrounds explanations of a problem's causes and consequences. Over time, even as additional research opens up further lines of inquiry and exposes new uncertainties, the boundaries of the original uncertainty tend to narrow.

An example of the process of building scientific knowledge about an environmental problem is the way that understanding of atmospheric ozone depletion has advanced since the 1970s. The stratospheric ozone layer absorbs UV-B radiation, thereby regulating the earth's temperature and protecting plants, animals, and people from excessive radiation. During the 1970s scientists developed several theories to explain the observed reduction in stratospheric ozone over the poles. Some scientists were concerned about aircraft emissions of nitrogen oxides; others suggested that nitrogen-based fertilizers or fallout from nuclear weapons tests might be the primary culprits. In 1974 chemists Sherwood Rowland and Mario Molina proposed that chlorine-containing compounds, such as chlorofluorocarbons, destroy the ozone layer through a series of complex, solar-induced chemical reactions. Over time this theory superseded its rivals and gained broad acceptance because it was consistent with evidence gathered using a variety of techniques. Subsequently, as researchers have learned more about stratospheric chemistry, estimates of ozone loss have become more accurate and the mechanisms by which it occurs more accurately specified.[30]

Unfortunately, the time period within which scientists converge on and refine an explanation is usually considerably longer than the time available to policymakers for choosing a solution. The reason is that the identification of a potential problem by scientists almost invariably prompts the mobilization of interests that are concerned about it and demand an immediate government response. The norms of scientific investigation—particularly those of deliberate and thorough study, rigorous peer review and criticism, and forthright expression of uncertainty—create opportunities for proponents of new policies, as well as for defenders of the status quo, to portray the problem in ways that are compatible with their own values and policy preferences. In most cases, advocates of more protective environmental policies publicize the worst-case scenarios hypothesized by scientists, overstate the certainty of scientific knowledge, and press for an early and stringent—or precautionary—policy response to avert catastrophe. By contrast, opponents of such policies typically emphasize the uncertain state of current knowledge or, if there is a strong scientific consensus that an environmental problem is genuine, highlight dissenting views within the scientific community as to its magnitude, causes, or consequences.[31]

Shifting Attention to the Economic Costs and Benefits. As the scientific consensus around the explanation for an environmental problem grows, opponents of protective policies turn to economic arguments. In particular, cornucopians emphasize (and environmentalists downplay) the economic costs of policies to address the problem. Like scientific explanations of cause and effect, the costs of regulation are highly uncertain, and projections vary widely depending on the assumptions used and the time horizon considered. For example, analysts disagree on the number of jobs likely to be lost as the direct result of an environmental regulation and diverge even more dramatically on the number of collateral jobs—in restaurants, banks, and other service industries—that will disappear. They make different assumptions about future levels of economic growth, the extent and pace of technological adaptation to a regulation, and the likelihood and extent of offsetting effects, such as the establishment or growth of new industries. As is true of scientists, given a choice among equally defensible assumptions, economists select premises that reflect their worldviews, so it is not surprising that industry projections of costs associated with a regulation tend to be much higher than projections made by environmentalists, with government estimates typically in the middle.[32]

In addition to debating projections of the cost of environmental policies, competing parties disagree over the desirability of cost-benefit analysis as a decision-making tool. Cost-benefit analysis entails determining the ratio of monetary benefits to costs of addressing a problem; by implication, government should undertake a program only if its benefits outweigh its costs—that is, if the ratio of benefits to costs is greater than one. Economists have developed a host of sophisticated techniques for assessing the costs and benefits of environmental policies, but many environmentalists contend that cost-benefit analysis is a political device for slowing the growth of regulation rather than a genuine analytic tool. They point out that estimates of the prospective costs and benefits of environmental policies are inherently biased against environmental protection because judgments about benefits, such as the value of saving wilderness or reducing the likelihood or severity of asthma attacks among sensitive populations, are difficult—if not impossible—to quantify, whereas immediate and tangible costs are easily figured. Moreover, they argue, using cost-benefit analysis as a decision rule eliminates ethical and moral considerations from the political calculus.[33] Regardless of how it is derived or how accurately it reflects a program's value, the number generated by a cost-benefit analysis constitutes a powerful frame because, as Deborah Stone observes, numbers have an aura of credibility and technical neutrality and therefore carry a great deal of political weight.[34]

Dramatizing the Risks of Action or Inaction. Finally, like scientific knowledge about a problem and the economic costs of addressing it, perceptions of the risk associated with it are subject to framing. Ordinary people do not assess risk based on objective analysis of statistical evidence; rather, they employ heuristics, or inferential rules—what political scientist Howard Margolis calls "habits of mind."[35] Psychologists have identified some inferential rules they believe shape the average person's perception of risks. Using the "availability" heuristic, for example, people judge an event as likely or frequent if instances of it are easy to recall. Therefore, they overestimate the risk of dramatic and sensational events, which tend to get abundant media coverage, while underestimating the risk of unspectacular events.[36] Psychologists also point out that the public incorporates factors besides expected damages—the measure used by experts—into their assessment of risk. Among those factors are: whether the risk is taken voluntarily, its immediacy, its familiarity, the extent of control one has over the risky situation, the severity of the possible consequences, and the level of dread the risk evokes.[37] The public's sensitivity to these factors explains why environmentalists are more successful at drawing attention to problems whose effects appear immediate, dramatic, and catastrophic than to those whose impacts are more remote and mundane.

Psychologists have found that other aspects of the way risk is framed can also have a dramatic impact on risk perceptions. First, people value the same gains differently, depending on the reference point. For instance, they value the increment from $10 to $20 more highly than the increase from $110 to $120. Second, people are more concerned about losses than about gains of the same magnitude; they fear losing $10 more than they value gaining $10. Third, people overweight low probabilities and underweight moderate and high probabilities, so they worry more about rare occurrences than common events.[38] Recognizing the importance of these elements of framing to the way the public perceives risk, both sides in an environmental contest define a problem as a loss from an already low status quo and overstate the likelihood of low probability but potentially disastrous outcomes. The difference is that environmentalists tend to emphasize the environmental or human health risks of inaction, whereas cornucopians minimize environmental risks and focus on a policy's potential economic costs.

In sum, the hallmark of a successful environmental policy campaign is the ability of its organizers to craft the dominant problem definition around the scientific explanation, the costs of regulation, and the risks associated with action or inaction. The side that succeeds in defining the problem authoritatively has an enormous advantage because the way people think and talk about a policy problem shapes what they are willing to do about it. In other words, those who furnish the prevailing problem definition are well-positioned to translate their values into policy.

MAJOR ACTORS IN ENVIRONMENTAL POLICYMAKING

Actors both inside and outside government have an impact on environmental policymaking. Government decision-makers must choose whether to address an environmental problem and, if so, how they will do it. Advocates on both sides try to influence that decision, adjusting their tactics to be consistent with the incentives and constraints of the institution making the decision. Their success depends heavily on both the support of experts and the media's coverage of the issue.

Government Decision-Makers

The decision-makers in the national environmental policymaking process are the president and members of Congress who formulate legislation, the executive branch officials who interpret and administer the laws, and the courts that review their implementation by agencies. In various combinations these actors determine whether, in response to a challenge launched by advocates, environmental policy becomes more protective or more permissive or remains the same. In making these decisions, policymakers are not only influenced by their values but also are responsive to the incentives and constraints inherent in their institutional settings.

Legislative Actors. Legislative actors, the president and Congress, decide which problems government will address and establish the basic goals of public policy. In reaching their decisions, members of Congress want to make good public policy and attain the respect of their peers.[39] But they are also deeply concerned with the views of their constituents, because, whether they are environmentalists or cornucopians at heart, they must be reelected if they hope to pursue their policy goals. Reelection concerns prompt legislators to support policies that distribute benefits to their constituents and oppose policies that threaten to impose direct, visible costs. Electoral considerations also create incentives for legislators to avoid positions likely to provoke controversy and to take positions they expect will garner them credit.[40]

Unlike rank-and-file members of Congress, the president and congressional leaders have powerful incentives to take on public policy issues of national, rather than simply district- or state-level, concern. The president, because he is elected by a national constituency and wants to establish a legacy, is attentive to broad public policy goals. He can initiate action by sending Congress a bill, by using the bully pulpit to convince the public, or by issuing an executive order. Similarly, legislative leaders (and aspirants) seek opportunities to demonstrate their stewardship. In addition, their visibility both among the public and the political elite tends to elicit a sense of responsibility for public affairs.[41] Legislative leaders also have the political resources to bring about policy change: they can enhance a bill's prospects by forging legislative coalitions and orchestrating negotiations as well as by mobilizing the public.

Both for leaders and rank-and-file legislators, the primary constraint on their desire to address an issue is its *salience*—that is, the extent to which the public cares about it.[42] Even if the president or a congressional leader thinks an issue is important, neither is likely to expend political resources on it unless he or she perceives it to be widely salient. Similarly, to calculate their wiggle room on an issue, rank-and-file legislators must ascertain its salience among their constituents. An issue's salience can be difficult to discern, but one straightforward indicator is polling data. (According to Riley Dunlap, "the mere expression of supportive opinion in a scientific survey or informal poll ... can be a vital resource" for groups hoping to bring about or block policy change.[43]) Although survey evidence can convey broad public preferences, it can also be misleading because the wording of questions and the order in which they are asked can yield different responses. Moreover, district- and state-level polling on individual issues is rarely available. Most important, however, surveys have difficulty detecting how much people actually care about a problem, their willingness to trade off one value for another, or the extent to which abstract values translate into support for concrete proposals.

Given the unreliability of survey data, politicians rely on a host of other indicators of an issue's salience. Because they garner media coverage, rallies and protests have been a mainstay of political activists; such public demonstrations are the simplest and most direct way for people with few political resources to transmit their concerns to elected officials. Other activities such as phoning, writing letters, and sending e-mails and faxes also convey salience. Note, however, that creating the perception that an issue is salient is not a one-way street that runs from the public to politicians; legislators who want to promote a particular policy shape their constituents' views using language that is crafted to generate public support. [44]

Administrators. Although less visible than legislators, administrators play a critical role in environmental policymaking because they implement the laws passed by Congress. Doing so involves choosing the scientific and economic models and projections that underpin administrative regulations, devising the regulations themselves, and monitoring and enforcing compliance. Throughout this process, administrators have substantial discretion to modify policy goals.[45] In exercising their discretion, they bring ample political resources to bear, including their longevity, expertise, and established relationships with organized interests and members of Congress.

At the same time, whether they are environmentalists or cornucopians, administrators' ability to pursue their preferred goals is constrained in several ways. One institutional feature that limits administrators' flexibility is the agency's mission and organizational culture.[46] An agency's mission is its original mandate, and its "organizational culture" consists of the norms and standard operating procedures that have evolved over time. For example, some agencies, such as the Forest Service and the Bureau of Land Management, were founded to conserve natural resources for human consumption. For a long time, such agencies were staffed by professionals, such as foresters and range managers, whose expertise lay in maximizing natural resource yields. As a result, these agencies' standard operating procedures emphasized resource extraction—often at the expense of environmental protection. On the other hand, the Environmental Protection Agency (EPA) was created to prevent and clean up pollution, and the orientation of its professionals as well as its standard operating procedures reflect this disposition. As a result, the EPA's decisions tend to be relatively protective and often impose substantial costs on industry.

Administrators do not simply act according to their missions and organizational cultures, however. The preferences of an agency's organized clientele, the nature and extent of its congressional oversight, and the direction given by the president and his political appointees also circumscribe bureaucratic choices.[47] For example, organized interests dissatisfied with an agency's behavior can lobby sympathetic members of Congress, who in turn can exert pressure on agency officials by holding hearings, threatening budget cuts or reductions in statutory authority, or simply contacting agency officials directly to express their disfavor. The president likewise can impose his will on agencies by appointing directors whose views are consistent with his own. In short, when implementing their statutory mandates, agency officials must navigate cautiously to avoid antagonizing powerful interests and their allies in Congress or the White House. Failure to do so almost always moves the battle to the courts.

The Judiciary. The federal courts have the authority to review agency decisions to determine whether they are consistent with congressional intent and, in this way, can circumscribe an agency's ability to pursue environmentally protective (or permissive) policies. The Administrative Procedures Act allows courts to invalidate decisions that lack "substantial evidence" or are "arbitrary and capricious." Moreover, many environmental statutes allow the courts to strike down agency decisions if they cannot discern a reasonable connection between the action and the supporting record. The courts increased the potential for environmental litigation substantially in the early 1970s when they expanded the concept of "standing" to permit almost any group to challenge agency regulations in federal court, regardless of whether its members are directly affected by the agency's activities.[48] Congress also encouraged environmentalists' use of the courts by inserting provisions in environmental laws explicitly granting citizens and citizen organizations the right to sue not only polluters that violate the law but also agencies that fail to implement or enforce their statutory mandates with sufficient zeal.

Like legislators and administrators, judges may be environmentalists or cornucopians, and they also face institutional constraints when evaluating an agency's decisions: they must base their reasoning on precedent, as well as on the wording and legislative history of a statute. Judges have debated how closely to scrutinize agency decisions—in particular, whether to examine the reasoning or simply the procedures followed—but regardless of the standard applied, the courts habitually require agencies to document a comprehensible justification for their decisions.[49] As a result, litigation has become "an especially potent resource for making transparent the values, biases, and social assumptions that are embedded in many expert claims about physical and natural phenomena." [50]

State and Local Decision-Makers. The discussion so far has focused on national policymaking, but the politics of an issue depends in part on whether it is addressed at the local, state, or national level. Although there are many similarities among them, each of these arenas has distinctive features, which in turn have implications for the balance of power among environmentalists and cornucopians. For example, environmental interests traditionally have felt disadvantaged at the state and local levels. One reason is that state and local officials tend to be deeply concerned with economic development and the need to attract and retain industry.[51] Another reason is that, historically, some states and most local governments have lacked the technical capacity necessary to analyze complex environmental problems and therefore to distinguish among effective and ineffective solutions. This situation appears to be changing, however. As environmental policy scholar Mary Graham points out, states' technical capacities have improved dramatically since the 1970s, as has their propensity to address environmental problems.[52] As a result, some environmentalists have become more interested in addressing environmental problems at the state and local levels. Proponents of devolution argue that place-based solutions are likely to be more effective and durable than approaches devised at the national level. In reality, environmental policymaking almost always involves multiple levels of government: because the United States has a federal system of government, most national policies are implemented by the states. And political events at one level often affect decisions made at another; for example, local or state activism may eventually prompt a national response.

Actors Outside of Government

Although politicians, administrators, and judges make environmental policy decisions, actors outside of government shape the context in which those decisions are made. In particular, organized interests that advocate for particular solutions play a major role because they make strategic choices about which venue to compete in, selecting the one they expect will be most hospitable to their goals.[53] Having chosen the arena, they select from a variety of tactics to influence government decision making. Critical to the success or failure of their efforts are experts, who provide the arguments and empirical support for advocates' positions, and the media, which may promote, reject, or modify the frames imposed by advocates.

Advocacy Organizations. Like government decision-makers, advocates in environmental policy debates generally fall into one of two camps: environmentalists, who support more environmentally protective policies, and cornucopians, who endorse less restrictive environmental policies. Advocacy groups on both sides are diverse in terms of funding sources and membership.[54] Some rely heavily on foundations or even the federal government for funding, while others raise most of their money from individual members. Some of the national environmental organizations, like the Sierra Club and the Wilderness Society, are well established. By contrast, community-based environmental groups may be somewhat ephemeral, springing up to address a single problem and then disbanding. Similarly, a host of long-standing organizations, such as the National Association of Manufacturers, oppose efforts to make environmental policies more protective, and myriad local groups have formed to challenge regulations that infringe on private property rights.

Although individual groups tend to specialize, advocates are most effective when they form broad coalitions. Such coalitions may be fleeting: they are united by common policy goals, but connections among them may not last beyond a single policy battle. The cohesiveness of a coalition over time is a major determinant of its political effectiveness. Coalitions that cannot maintain a united front tend to fare poorly, particularly in the legislative arena.[55]

As important as building coalitions is selecting the appropriate tactics for defining a problem in the venue of choice. Advocates know elected officials' perception that a problem is salient is an important determinant of whether they will attend to it. Conventional tactics, such as direct—or inside—lobbying and contributing money to a political campaign, remain important ways to exercise influence in the legislative arena, but "outside lobbying"—that is, raising public awareness of issues and stimulating grassroots mobilization—has grown in prominence as an advocacy tool.[56] Much of the public has only a vague understanding of individual environmental issues and relies on cognitive shortcuts and cues to know what to think.[57] Advocates therefore rely heavily on stories and symbols to define problems in ways that raise their salience. By contrast, in the administrative and judicial arenas, public opinion plays a lesser role and reasoned argument a larger one. To persuade bureaucrats and judges to adopt their preferred solution, advocates need to muster more sophisticated theoretical and empirical evidence in support of their definition of a problem.

Experts. Whatever tactics they adopt, advocates rely on experts and the research they generate to buttress their claims about the causes and consequences of an environmental problem. In environmental politics, experts include scientists, economists, lawyers, and policy analysts with specialized knowledge of environmental problems and policies. They work in academic departments, think tanks, foundations, interest groups, and government agencies. They are at the center of what political scientist John Kingdon calls "policy communities," where solutions to public policy problems are devised and the technical justifications for those solutions developed.[58] Both the public and policymakers tend to give greater weight to the views of experts than to those of outright advocates; as political scientist Benjamin Page and his coauthors observe, experts are considered credible because of their perceived objectivity, particularly when "complex technical questions affect the merits of policy alternatives." [59]

Experts, however, are not neutral purveyors of "facts." Most policy-relevant questions require experts to make value judgments based on uncertain data.[60] For example, policymakers might ask experts to ascertain a "safe" level of benzene in the environment. In conducting such a calculation, a chemical industry scientist is likely to make benign assumptions about benzene's hazards, consistent with her cornucopian values, while an academic scientist is likely to adopt more precautionary premises consistent with her environmental values.[61] Similarly, when asked about the economic impacts of benzene regulations, an industry economist is likely to base her projections on more pessimistic assumptions than is a government or academic economist.

The Media. Finally, the media—television, radio, newspapers, news magazines, and the Internet—are critical to determining the success or failure of competing advocates' efforts to define a problem. Writing more than eighty years ago, Walter Lippman likened news coverage to "the beam of a searchlight that moves restlessly about, bringing one episode and then another out of darkness into vision." [62] Evidence is steadily accumulating to suggest that "the media may not only tell [the public] what to think about, they may also tell us how and what to think about it, and even what to do about it." [63] For most people the media are the only source of information about the environment, so what the media choose to focus on and the nature of their coverage are crucial to shaping public opinion.[64] Scholars have also found that the way the media frame issues significantly affects how the public attributes responsibility for problems.[65] (Naturally, people are not mere sponges for views expressed in the press; they make sense of the news in the context of their own knowledge and experience.[66])

Media coverage of environmental issues affects policymakers—not just through its impact on the public but directly as well. There is little evidence that media-driven public opinion is a strong force for policy change, but news stories can prompt an elite response, even without a strong public reaction.[67] This reaction can occur when policymakers, particularly legislators, become concerned that media coverage *will* affect public opinion over time and so act preemptively. The relationship between the media and policymakers is not unidirectional: policymakers influence the media as well as react to it; in fact, policymakers are often more aware of their own efforts to manipulate media coverage than of the media's influence on their policy choices.[68]

Because the media have such a profound impact, the way they select and portray environmental news can have serious consequences for problem definition. Above all, the media focus on stories that are "newsworthy"—that is, dramatic and timely. Sudden, violent events with immediate and visceral consequences—such as oil spills, floods, and toxic releases—are far more likely to make the headlines than are ongoing problems such as species loss.[69] Furthermore, because journalists face short deadlines, they rely on readily available information from stable, reliable sources—such as government officials, industry, and organized interest groups—and the complexity of environmental science only reinforces this tendency.[70] Finally, in presenting the information gleaned from their sources, most reporters attempt to balance competing points of view, regardless of the relative support for either side; few journalists provide critical analysis to help readers sort out conflicting claims.[71] In their quest for balance, however, journalists tend to overstate extreme positions.[72]

THE ENVIRONMENTAL POLICYMAKING PROCESS

Many scholars have found it helpful to model the process by which advocates, experts, the media, and decision-makers interact to create policy as a series of steps:

- agenda setting—getting a problem on the list of subjects to which policymakers are paying serious attention;
- alternative formulation—devising the possible solutions to the problem;
- decision making—choosing from among the possible alternatives the approach that government will take to address the problem;

- implementation—translating a decision into concrete action; and
- evaluation—assessing those actions for their consistency with a policy's goals.[73]

Distinguishing among these steps in the policymaking process can be fruitful analytically. At the same time, scholars generally acknowledge that in reality the process is rarely so orderly or systematic.

That the policymaking process is not linear does not mean it is inexplicable; in fact, John Kingdon has developed a useful framework that captures its main attributes. He portrays policymaking as a process in which three "streams" flow independently. In the first stream, people in and around government concentrate on a set of problems; in the second, policy communities made up of experts, journalists, and bureaucrats initiate and refine proposals; and in the third, political events, such as a change of administration or an interest group campaign, occur.[74] In general, legislative and administrative policymakers engage in routine decision making; wary of major change, with its unpredictable political fallout, they tend to prefer making incremental modifications to existing policies.[75] A substantial departure from the status quo is likely only when the three streams merge, as a compelling problem definition and an available solution come together under hospitable political conditions. Such a convergence rarely just happens, however; usually a policy entrepreneur must link his or her preferred solution to a problem when a window of opportunity opens.

Windows of Opportunity and Major Policy Change

Major policy changes are likely to occur only when a window of opportunity opens for advocates to promote their pet solutions.[76] In environmental policymaking, an opportunity may occur as the result of a legal decision that forces legislators or administrators to reexamine a policy. A crisis or focusing event, such as an oil spill or the release of a major scientific report, can also create a chance for action by providing powerful new evidence of the need for a policy and briefly mobilizing public opinion. A recurring event that can alter the dynamics of an issue is turnover of pivotal personnel: the replacement of a congressional committee chair, Speaker of the House, Senate majority leader, president, or agency director. Even more mundane events, such as a legislative reauthorization or an administrative rulemaking deadline, occasionally present an opportunity for policy change.

Once a window has opened, policy may or may not change. Although some objective features define a policy window, advocates must recognize it to take advantage of it. And even if they accurately perceive an opportunity, advocates have a limited time to capitalize. A policy window may close because decision-makers enact a policy. Alternatively, action may stall, in which case advocates may be unwilling to invest additional time, energy, or political capital in the endeavor. Finally, newsworthy events in other policy realms may divert public attention, causing a window to shut prematurely. Opponents of policy change recognize that policy windows open infrequently and close quickly and that both participants and the public have limited attention spans, so they try to delay action by studying an issue or by another expedient until the pressure for change subsides. As Kingdon observes, supporters of the status quo take advantage of the fact that "the longer people live with a problem, the less pressing it seems." [77]

The Role of Policy Entrepreneurs in "Softening Up" and "Tipping"

Given the advantage held by supporters of the status quo, it is clear that advocates of policy change must do more than simply recognize an opportunity; they must also recruit one or more policy entrepreneurs to promote their cause. Policy entrepreneurs are individuals willing to invest their political resources—time, energy, reputation, money—in linking a problem to a solution and forging alliances among disparate actors to build a majority coalition.[78] Policy entrepreneurs must be adept at discovering "unfilled needs" and linking them to solutions, willing to bear the risks of investing in activities with uncertain consequences, and skilled at coordinating the activities of individuals and groups.[79] In addition, a policy entrepreneur must be ready to "ride the wave" when a policy window opens.[80] She must have lined up political allies, prepared arguments, and generated favorable public sentiment in preparation for the moment a decision-making opportunity presents itself.

Among the most important functions a policy entrepreneur performs while waiting for a policy window to open is "softening up" policy ideas, both in the expert communities whose endorsement is so important to the credibility of a policy solution and among the larger public. Softening up involves getting people used to a new idea and building acceptance for a proposal.[81] Policy entrepreneurs have a variety of means to soften up policy solutions: they can give speeches, write scholarly and popular articles, give briefings to policymakers, compose editorials and press releases, and teach the new approach in classrooms. Over time, a consensus emerges, particularly within a policy community, around a short list of ideas for solving a problem. Eventually, there is a broader convergence on a single idea, a phenomenon known as "tipping." At the tipping point, support for an idea is sufficiently widespread that it seems to take on a life of its own.[82]

The Importance of Process

To affect policymaking, solutions that have diffused through the policy community and the public must catch on among decision-makers as well. The way this happens in a traditional decision-making process is interesting: participants in a policy debate typically begin by staking out an extreme position and holding fast to it. At this point, bargaining and persuasion among coalitions commence, and participants try to build consensus by accommodating as many interests as possible. Once it becomes apparent that one side is going to prevail, even the holdouts recognize that, if they do not join in, they will have no say in the final decision. As Kingdon observes, "Once an issue seems to be moving, everybody with an interest in the subject leaps in, out of fear that they will be left out." [83]

In an adversarial process, a problem is never really solved, however; each decision is simply one more step in a never-ending contest.[84] To avoid protracted appeals, policymakers are turning with increasing frequency to non-adversarial processes—such as regulatory negotiation, mediation, and consensus building—to reach agreement on policy solutions. According to their proponents, such processes enhance the quality of participation by including a broader array of stakeholders and promoting deliberation, a search for common ground, and a spirit of cooperation. Proponents also believe that solutions arrived at collaboratively are likely to be more effective and enduring than those attained under adversarial processes.[85] On the other hand, critics fear that such approaches disadvantage environmentalists and result in watered-down solutions.[86]

CASE SELECTION

How these processes—adversarial or collaborative—translate values into policy is the subject of the next sixteen chapters. The cases in these chapters not only introduce a variety of environmental issues but also capture most aspects of the environmental policymaking process. They cover disputes from all regions of the country; offer examples of local, national, and international politics; and focus on problems that are of great concern to those who attend to this policy area. The cases are organized into four parts. These divisions reflect topical differences, but there are many similarities across cases as well. All of the cases illuminate the impact of participants' values and issue framing. In addition, each case highlights a small number of more particular attributes of environmental policymaking, expanding on various aspects of the framework briefly outlined above. As a whole, then, the cases provide a reasonably comprehensive foundation for understanding the way the American political system handles environmental issues.

Tackling the Issue of Pollution

When the issue of pollution burst onto the national political scene in the 1960s and early 1970s, the public responded with overwhelming interest in and concern about dirty air and water as well as toxic waste. Chapter 2, which describes the formation of the EPA and the passage of the Clean Air and Clean Water acts, explores the impact of widespread public mobilization on the legislative process. The case makes clear that when political leaders perceive an issue as salient, they may compete to craft a strong legislative response. Agencies trying to implement laws forged under such circumstances, however, are likely to encounter a host of practical obstacles. Chapter 3, which relates the story of toxic waste dumping at Love Canal, reveals the extent to which local and state governments historically have resisted confronting pollution issues because of technical incapacity and concerns about economic development. It also demonstrates the impact of media coverage on politics: alarming news stories can prompt citizen mobilization, and coverage of local groups' claims in turn can nationalize an issue and produce a strong policy response. In addition, this chapter makes clear that scientific experts rarely can resolve environmental policy controversies and may, in fact, exacerbate them.

"Government Secrets at Rocky Flats" (chapter 4) explores the government's role in polluting the environment. In particular, the case examines the military's use of national security to conceal sloppy environmental practices, the impenetrable relationship that developed between a government agency and its private contractors, the government's response to exposure, and the public's demands for environmental cleanup. The final case in this section, "Environmental Justice and Community Activism: The Dudley Street Neighborhood Initiative" (chapter 5), describes how citizens in a poor, predominantly minority community in Boston came together to revitalize a blighted urban neighborhood. The case highlights not only the value of social capital for bringing about such a transformation but also the myriad barriers that impede efforts by disadvantaged communities to improve the urban environment.

History, Changing Values, and Resource Management on Public Lands

Natural resource issues have a much longer history in American politics than do pollution issues; in fact, the distinctive feature of natural resource policymaking in the United States is that it is shaped by the legacy of past policies. The first chapter in this section, chapter 6, details the dynamics of the controversy over drilling for oil in Alaska's Arctic National Wildlife Refuge, illuminating the particularly intractable nature of conflicts between wilderness and natural resource development. It also illustrates the way competing advocates use language—particularly symbols and metaphors—to define problems. Chapter 7, which deals with federal grazing policy, takes up one of the nation's least publicized natural resource issues: how to manage the arid rangeland of the West. This case provides an opportunity to observe not only the impact of past policies on current decision making but also how the failure by advocates to arouse public concern about an issue helps to perpetuate the status quo. By contrast, chapter 8, "Jobs Versus the Environment: Saving the Old-Growth Forests of the Pacific Northwest," shows that attracting public attention to a natural resource concern using legal leverage and outside lobbying campaigns can overwhelm historically entrenched interests and change the course of policymaking on an issue, as well as an agency's approach to decision making. Finally, "Snowmobiles in Yellowstone" (chapter 9) looks at the bitter conflict over allowing motorized vehicles in order to explore how issues of recreational access can divide those who claim to value those lands.

Addressing Commons Problems

Common property resources, such as the oceans and the global atmosphere, present a unique challenge because the free-rider problem severely hampers efforts to protect them. That is, "Individuals have little or no incentive to . . . work for a collective good, since they will receive the benefit if others work for it and succeed in obtaining it (hence the term 'free ride')." [87] Issues of fisheries conservation, climate change, and international trade bring these concerns into particularly sharp relief. Chapter 10, "The New England Fisheries Crisis," illustrates how government's efforts to manage a commons (in this case, New England's cod, haddock, and flounder) can exacerbate the free-rider problem, especially when commercial interests dominate the regulatory process. In addition, the case outlines some of the novel approaches that governments are exploring to manage common-property resources more effectively, as well as the cultural sources of resistance to adopting such solutions. Chapter 11 examines one of the most complex and divisive commons problems facing the world today: climate change. The case reveals how the lack of an overarching global authority obstructs efforts to address the threat of global warming, explains how domestic politics has prevented U.S. leaders from acting more aggressively on this issue, and suggests that state-level policymaking may yet prompt a national-level shift. The section's final chapter (12) takes up the relationship between international trade and the environment by looking at disputes over U.S. restrictions on imports of tuna and shrimp caught using methods that kill other highly valued species. The case focuses on the challenge of reconciling national efforts to protect the global environment with the desire to prevent developing countries from bearing a disproportionate burden of economic globalization.

Antienvironmental Backlash and New Approaches

Chapter 13, the first case in part 4, takes up the backlash against environmentalism that began in the 1970s and flowered in the mid-1990s. This case illuminates the difficulties politicians face in ascertaining an issue's salience as well as the tools proponents of protective policies have for resisting policy reversals. Partly in response to the backlash, but also to critiques from within the environmental movement, some policy entrepreneurs have begun exploring new ways to address environmental problems. Therefore, the main theme underlying each of the remaining cases is that changing the problem-solving approach or offering novel solutions to address a problem can reshape the politics of that problem. Sometimes leaders can break a political logjam simply by offering a different policy tool, as was done with tradable sulfur dioxide permits in the case of acid rain (chapter 14). Alternatively, modifying the institutional structure within which a decision is made can have dramatic effects. As the case of the Florida Everglades restoration (chapter 15) illustrates, demands by scientists and environmentalists for ecosystem-level solutions, as well as the need to coordinate the activities of multiple agencies, have created a new kind of collaborative politics.

The book's two final cases concern innovative efforts by states and localities to manage the diffuse and complex issue of urban sprawl. Chapter 16 elucidates the process of constructing the Multiple Species Conservation Plan in San Diego, California. It illustrates how processes that build consensus among stakeholders can make possible otherwise inconceivable solutions, but it also explores the limits of such approaches. Chapter 17 investigates the origins of Oregon's land-use planning framework, the role of civic engagement in implementing that framework in the city of Portland, and the fragility of efforts to maintain stringent land-use controls in the face of a powerful ideological challenge. As all of the cases in part 4 make clear, many of the same political forces evident in previous cases are at play regardless of the decision-making approach adopted or the type of solution crafted. Institutionalized ideas and practices continue to limit the pace of policy change, and underlying value differences among participants remain, so the ability to define problems persuasively continues to be a critical source of influence.

GETTING THE MOST OUT OF THE CASES

This chapter has provided a cursory introduction to the burgeoning field of environmental politics and policymaking. The cases that follow deepen and make concrete the concepts introduced here, highlighting in particular how participants use language to define problems in ways consistent with their values. As you read, you will notice similarities and differences among cases. I encourage you to look for patterns, generate hypotheses about environmental politics, and test those hypotheses against the other instances of environmental policymaking that you study, read about in the newspaper, or become involved in. Questions posed at the end of each case may help you think more deeply about the issues raised in it and generate ideas for further research.

Notes

1. John S. Dryzek and David Schlosberg, eds., *Debating the Earth: The Environmental Politics Reader* (New York: Oxford University Press, 1998), 1.
2. Paul Sabatier makes this point about policy controversies more generally in Paul A. Sabatier, "An Advocacy Coalition Framework of Policy Change and the Role of Policy-Oriented Learning Therein," *Policy Sciences* 21 (1988): 129–168.
3. See, for example, Black Elk, "Native Americans Define the Natural Community," in *American Environmentalism,* 3d ed., ed. Roderick Frazier Nash (New York: McGraw-Hill, 1990), 13–16. Critics argue that environmentalists have romanticized Native Americans and other early peoples, pointing out that they too were capable of hunting species to extinction; that the Indians of eastern North America deliberately influenced the range and abundance of countless wild plant species through their food-gathering and land-use practices; and that Native Americans made great use of fire and, in doing so, altered the landscape on a sweeping scale. They contend that much of what we now see as "natural" is in fact the result of human alteration

during earlier time periods. See, for example, Stephen Budiansky, *Nature's Keepers: The New Science of Nature Management* (New York: Free Press, 1995).

4. George Catlin, "An Artist Proposes a National Park," in *American Environmentalism*, 31–35.

5. Henry David Thoreau, "Walking," in *Excursions, The Writings of Henry David Thoreau*, Vol. IX, Riverside edition, 11 vols. (Boston: Houghton Mifflin, 1893).

6. Quoted in Roderick Nash, *Wilderness and the American Mind*, 3d ed. (New Haven: Yale University Press, 1982), 125.

7. Samuel Hays, *Conservation and the Gospel of Efficiency* (Cambridge: Harvard University Press, 1959).

8. The relationship between ecology and environmentalism was reciprocal. According to historian Peter Bowler, although a distinct science of ecology emerged in the 1890s, ecology did not flower as a discipline until the 1960s with the proliferation of environmental concern. See Peter Bowler, *Norton History of Environmental Sciences* (New York: Norton, 1992).

9. Aldo Leopold, *A Sand County Almanac* (New York: Oxford University Press, 1948), 239, 262.

10. Donella Meadows et al., *The Limits to Growth* (New York: Universe, 1972).

11. Robyn Eckersley, *Environmentalism and Political Theory* (Albany: State University of New York Press, 1992), 49.

12. Arne Naess, "The Shallow and the Deep, A Long-Range Ecology Movement: A Summary," *Inquiry* 16 (1983): 95–100.

13. Ibid., 95.

14. Dryzek and Schlosberg coined the term *cornucopians* in *Debating the Earth*. In Greek mythology, Prometheus stole fire from Olympus and gave it to humans. To punish him for this crime, Zeus chained him to a rock and sent an eagle to eat his liver, which in turn regenerated itself each day. The term *Prometheans* therefore suggests a belief in the endless regenerative capacity of the earth.

15. Aaron Wildavsky and Karl Dake provide another label: *hierarchists*. They say, "Hierarchists ... approve of technological processes and products, provided their experts have given the appropriate safety certifications and the applicable rules and regulations are followed." See Aaron Wildavsky and Karl Dake, "Theories of Risk Perception: Who Fears What and Why?" *Daedalus* 119 (Fall 1990): 41–60.

16 Julian L. Simon and Herman Kahn, *The Resourceful Earth* (New York: Blackwell, 1984), 3.

17. Ibid.

18. Mary Douglas and Aaron Wildavsky, *Risk and Culture* (Berkeley: University of California Press, 1982).

19. See, for example, Aaron Wildavsky, *But Is It True?* (Cambridge: Harvard University Press, 1995); and Michael Fumento, *Science Under Siege* (New York: Quill, 1993), 370.

20. Gregg Easterbrook, *A Moment on the Earth* (New York: Viking, 1995), 649.

21. E. E. Schattschneider, *The Semisovereign People* (New York: Holt, Rinehart, and Winston, 1960), 189.

22. Political scientists use a variety of terms—*problem definition, issue definition*, and *issue framing*—to describe essentially the same phenomenon. Although I use the terms interchangeably, I refer readers to Deborah Stone's *Policy Paradox*, whose discussion of problem definition and its political impact is the most precise I have found. See Deborah Stone, *Policy Paradox: The Art of Political Decision Making*, rev. ed. (New York: Norton, 2001). See also David Rochefort and Roger Cobb, eds., *The Politics of Problem Definition* (Lawrence: University Press of Kansas, 1994).

23. Donald A. Schon and Martin Rein, *Frame Reflection: Toward the Resolution of Intractable Policy Controversies* (New York: Basic Books, 1994).

24. Stone, *Policy Paradox*.

25. Frank R. Baumgartner and Bryan D. Jones, *Agendas and Instability in American Politics* (Chicago: University of Chicago Press, 1993).

26. Stone, *Policy Paradox*, 189.
27. Schattschneider, *The Semisovereign People*, 66.
28. Deborah Guber, *The Grassroots of a Green Revolution: Polling America on the Environment* (Cambridge: MIT Press, 2003); Willett Kempton, James S. Boster, and Jennifer A. Hartley, *Environmental Values in American Culture* (Cambridge: MIT Press, 1995); Everett Carll Ladd and Karlyn H. Bowman, *Attitudes Toward the Environment* (Washington, D.C.: AEI Press, 1995).
29. Riley E. Dunlap, "Public Opinion in the 1980s: Clear Consensus, Ambiguous Commitment," *Environment*, October 1991, 10–22.
30. Although a few skeptics continue to challenge theories of ozone depletion, by the early 1990s most climatologists accepted the conclusions of the World Meteorological Association that "anthropogenic chlorine and bromine compounds, coupled with surface chemistry on natural polar stratospheric particles, are the cause of polar ozone depletion." See Larry Parker and David E. Gushee, "Stratospheric Ozone Depletion: Implementation Issues," CRS Issue Brief for Congress, No. 97003 (Washington, D.C.: Congressional Research Service, January 16, 1998).
31. On occasion, roles are reversed, particularly when the issue at stake is the impact of technology on human health or the environment. For example, scientists have been unable to detect a relationship between electromagnetic fields (EMFs) and cancer, and proponents of EMF regulation are the ones citing minority scientific opinions. This pattern recurs in the debates over nuclear power and genetically modified food.
32. Eban Goodstein and Hart Hodges, "Polluted Data," *American Prospect* 35, November–December 1997, 64–69.
33. Stephen Kelman, "Cost-Benefit Analysis: An Ethical Critique," in *The Moral Dimensions of Public Policy Choice*, ed. John Martin Gillroy and Maurice Wade (Pittsburgh: University of Pittsburgh Press, 1992), 153–164.
34. Stone, *Policy Paradox*.
35. Howard Margolis, *Dealing with Risk: Why the Public and the Experts Disagree on Environmental Risk* (Chicago: University of Chicago Press, 1996).
36. Paul Slovic, Baruch Fischhoff, and Sarah Lichtenstein, "Rating the Risks," in *Readings in Risk*, ed. Theodore Glickman and Michael Gough (Washington, D.C.: Resources for the Future, 1990), 61–75.
37. Ibid. Howard Margolis rejects this explanation for differences between expert and public assessments of risk. He argues instead that the difference turns on "habits of mind"; in particular, in some cases, the public stubbornly perceives only the costs of a technology or activity and is unable to see the benefits and therefore cannot make the appropriate trade-off between the two. See Margolis, *Dealing with Risk*.
38. Amos Tversky and Daniel Kahneman, "The Framing of Decisions and the Psychology of Choice," *Science*, January 30, 1981, 453–458.
39. Richard Fenno, *Congressmen in Committees* (Boston: Little, Brown, 1973).
40. David R. Mayhew, *Congress: The Electoral Connection* (New Haven: Yale University Press, 1974).
41. Timothy J. Conlan, Margaret Wrightson, and David Beam, *Taxing Choices: The Politics of Tax Reform* (Washington, D.C.: CQ Press, 1990); Martha Derthick and Paul J. Quirk, *The Politics of Deregulation* (Washington, D.C.: Brookings Institution, 1985).
42. John W. Kingdon, *Congressmen's Voting Decisions*, 3d ed. (Ann Arbor: University of Michigan Press, 1989).
43. Riley Dunlap, "Public Opinion in Environmental Policy," in *Environmental Politics and Policy*, ed. James P. Lester (Durham: Duke University Press, 1989), 87.
44. Lawrence R. Jacobs and Robert Y. Shapiro, *Politicians Don't Pander: Political Manipulation and the Loss of Democratic Responsiveness* (Chicago: University of Chicago Press, 2000).
45. Jeffrey L. Pressman and Aaron Wildavsky, *Implementation* (Berkeley: University of California Press, 1984).

46. James Q. Wilson, *Bureaucracy* (New York: Basic Books, 1989).

47. Herbert Kaufman, *The Administrative Behavior of Federal Bureau Chiefs* (Washington, D.C.: Brookings Institution, 1981).

48. "Standing" is the right to bring a lawsuit. Historically, the courts have granted standing to anyone who can demonstrate that he or she is personally affected by the outcome of a case. *Sierra Club v. Morton* (1972) laid the groundwork for the subsequent broadening of the courts' interpretation of the standing requirement.

49. Sheila Jasanoff, *Science at the Bar: Law, Science, and Technology in America* (Cambridge: Harvard University Press, 1995); David M. O'Brien, *What Process Is Due? Courts and Science-Policy Disputes* (New York: Russell Sage, 1987).

50. Jasanoff, *Science at the Bar*, 20.

51. Paul Peterson, *City Limits* (Chicago: University of Chicago Press, 1981).

52. Mary Graham, *The Morning After Earth Day: Practical Environmental Politics* (Washington, D.C.: Brookings Institution Press, 1999).

53. Baumgartner and Jones, *Agendas and Instability.*

54. For an extensive discussion of the funding, membership, tactics, and goals of major environmental interest groups, see Ronald G. Shaiko, *Voices and Echoes for the Environment* (New York: Columbia University Press, 1999); Christopher J. Bosso, *Environment Inc.: From Grassroots to Beltway* (Lawrence: University Press of Kansas, 2005).

55. Gary Mucciaroni, *Reversals of Fortune: Public Policy and Private Interests* (Washington, D.C.: Brookings Institution, 1995).

56. Ken Kollman, *Outside Lobbying: Public Opinion and Interest Group Strategies* (Princeton: Princeton University Press, 1998).

57. Shanto Iyengar argues that "people are exquisitely sensitive to context when they make decisions, formulate judgments, or express opinions. The manner in which a problem of choice is 'framed' is a contextual cue that may profoundly influence decision outcomes." See Shanto Iyengar, *Is Anyone Responsible? How Television Frames Political Issues* (Chicago: University of Chicago Press, 1991), 11.

58. John Kingdon, *Agendas, Alternatives, and Public Policies*, 2d ed. (New York: Harper-Collins, 1995).

59. Benjamin I. Page, Robert Y. Shapiro, and Glenn R. Dempsey, "What Moves Public Opinion," *Media Power in Politics*, 3d ed., ed. Doris A. Graber (Washington, D.C.: CQ Press, 1994), 132.

60. Alvin Weinberg, "Science and Trans-Science," *Minerva* 10 (1970): 209–222.

61. Frances M. Lynn, "The Interplay of Science and Values in Assessing and Regulating Environmental Risks," *Science, Technology, and Human Values* 11 (Spring 1986): 40–50.

62. Walter Lippman, *Public Opinion* (New York: Macmillan, 1922), 229.

63. Maxwell McCombs and George Estrada, "The News Media and the Pictures in Our Heads," in *Do the Media Govern?* ed. Shanto Iyengar and Richard Reeves (Thousand Oaks, Calif.: Sage Publications, 1997), 247.

64. Maxwell E. McCombs and Donald L. Shaw, "The Agenda-Setting Function of the Press," in *The Emergence of American Political Issues: The Agenda-Setting Function of the Press* (St. Paul: West Publishing, 1977), 89–105; Fay Lomax Cook et al., "Media and Agenda Setting Effects on the Public, Interest Group Leaders, Policy Makers, and Policy," *Public Opinion Quarterly* 47 (1983): 16–35.

65. Shanto Iyengar, "Framing Responsibility for Political Issues," in *Do the Media Govern?* 276–282.

66. Doris A. Graber, *Mass Media and American Politics*, 5th ed. (Washington, D.C.: CQ Press, 1997).

67. Ibid. Graber points out that the relative dearth of evidence supporting the claim that media-generated public opinion causes policy change is probably the result of using insufficiently sophisticated methods to detect such effects, not the absence of effects.

68. Kingdon, *Agendas.*

69. Michael R. Greenberg et al., "Risk, Drama, and Geography in Coverage of Environmental Risk by Network T.V.," *Journalism Quarterly* 66 (Summer 1989): 267–276.

70. Herbert Gans, *Deciding What's News* (New York: Pantheon, 1979); Dorothy Nelkin, *Selling Science*, rev. ed. (New York: Freeman, 1995).

71. Nelkin, *Selling Science*.

72. Eleanor Singer, "A Question of Accuracy: How Journalists and Scientists Report Research on Hazards," *Journal of Communication* 40 (Autumn 1990): 102–116.

73. See, for example, Charles O. Jones, *An Introduction to Public Policy*, 2d ed. (North Scituate, Mass.: Wadsworth, 1984).

74. In *Agendas*, Kingdon suggests that these three activities, or streams, proceed independently of one another. Gary Mucciaroni argues that changes in problem definition, solutions, and political conditions are actually quite closely linked. See Mucciaroni, *Reversals of Fortune*.

75. Incrementalism involves tinkering with policies at the margin rather than engaging in a comprehensive reexamination of each issue. See Charles E. Lindblom, "The Science of Muddling Through," *Public Administration Review* 14 (Spring 1959): 79–88; Aaron Wildavsky, *The Politics of the Budgetary Process*, 3d ed. (Boston: Little, Brown, 1979).

76. Kingdon, *Agendas*.

77. Ibid., 170.

78. Ibid.

79. Michael Mintrom and Sandra Vergari, "Advocacy Coalitions, Policy Entrepreneurs, and Policy Change," *Policy Studies Journal* 24 (1996): 420–434.

80. Kingdon, *Agendas*.

81. Ibid.

82. Malcolm Gladwell, *The Tipping Point: How Little Things Can Make a Big Difference* (Boston: Little, Brown, 2000).

83. Kingdon, *Agendas*, 162.

84. Stone, *Policy Paradox*.

85. Lawrence Susskind and Jeffrey Cruikshank, *Breaking the Impasse: Consensual Approaches to Resolving Public Disputes* (New York: Basic Books, 1987); Julia Wondolleck and Steven L. Yaffee, *Making Collaboration Work: Lessons from Innovation in Natural Resource Management* (Washington, D.C.: Island Press, 2000).

86. George Cameron Coggins, "Of Californicators, Quislings, and Crazies: Some Perils of Devolved Collaboration," in *Across the Great Divide: Explorations in Collaborative Conservation and the American West*, ed. Philip Brick, Donald Snow, and Sarah Van de Wetering (Washington, D.C.: Island Press, 2001), 163–171; Cary Coglianese, "Is Consensus an Appropriate Basis for Regulatory Policy?" in *Environmental Contracts*, ed. Eric W. Orts and Kurt Deketelaere (Boston: Kluwer Law International, 2001), 93–113.

87. Stone, *Policy Paradox*, 218.

Recommended Reading

Kingdon, John W. *Agendas, Alternatives, and Public Policies*. 2d ed. New York: HarperCollins, 1995.

Rosenbaum, Walter A. *Environmental Politics and Policy*. 6th ed. Washington, D.C.: CQ Press, 2005.

Stone, Deborah. *Policy Paradox: The Art of Political Decision Making*, rev. ed. New York: Norton, 2001.

Vig, Norman J., and Michael E. Kraft, eds. *Environmental Policy: New Directions for the Twenty-First Century*. 6th ed. Washington, D.C.: CQ Press, 2006.

CHAPTER 2

The Nation Tackles Pollution

The Environmental Protection Agency
and the Clean Air and Clean Water Acts

In the twenty-first century, Americans take for granted the importance of federal laws aimed at reducing air and water pollution. But less than four decades ago, the federal government was virtually uninvolved in pollution control. That changed abruptly on July 9, 1970, when President Richard Nixon established the Environmental Protection Agency. Shortly thereafter, Congress approved two of the nation's most far-reaching federal environmental laws: the Clean Air Act of 1970 and the Federal Water Pollution Control Act of 1972, commonly known as the Clean Water Act. Both laws shifted primary responsibility for environmental protection from the states to the federal government and required federal regulators to take prompt and stringent action to curb pollution.

The surge in environmental policymaking in the early 1970s was not a response to a sudden deterioration in the condition of the nation's air and water. In fact, while some kinds of pollution were getting worse in the late 1960s, other kinds were diminishing as a result of municipal bans on garbage burning and the phasing out of coal as a heating fuel.[1] Instead, what this case reveals is the profound impact that redefining, or reframing, an issue can have on policymaking. As political scientists Frank Baumgartner and Bryan Jones observe, "[If] disadvantaged policy entrepreneurs are successful in convincing others that their view of an issue is more accurate than the views of their opponents, they may achieve rapid success in altering public policy arrangements, even if these arrangements have been in place for decades." [2]

Their observation is accurate because if redefining an issue raises its salience—as manifested by widespread public activism, intense and favorable media coverage, and marked shifts in public opinion polls—politicians respond. In particular, a legislator who seeks a leadership role must take positions that appeal to a national constituency and demonstrate a capacity to build winning coalitions. The president—or anyone who aspires to be president—is the one most likely to embrace issues that promise broad public benefits; the president is also best equipped, in terms of political resources, to forge a winning coalition for a major policy change. It is therefore not surprising that competition among presidential candidates has been the impetus behind some of the nation's most significant environmental policies. Rank-and-file legislators are also moved by highly salient issues: they jump on the bandwagon in hopes of gaining credit, or at least avoiding blame, for addressing a problem about which the public is intensely concerned.

This case also shows how a focusing event—in this instance, Earth Day—can open a window of opportunity for a leader to promote policies that policy entrepreneurs have linked to a newly popular framing of an issue. The implementation of an ambitious new policy often encounters serious practical obstacles, however. While legislators are responsive to public enthusiasm about an issue, the implementing agencies must cater to "multiple principals"; that is, they must please the president and the congressional committees that oversee and fund them.[3] In addition, they must grapple with the demands of organized interests: agencies depend on the cooperation of those they regulate because they have neither the resources nor the personnel to enforce every rule they issue; moreover, organized interests provide agencies with political support in Congress.[4] The process of implementing environmental legislation is particularly complicated because the agencies administering it operate in a highly fractious context in which the participants have a propensity to take their disagreements to court. As a result of all these forces and regardless of provisions aimed at ensuring compliance with their lofty goals, policies that depart dramatically from the status quo rarely achieve the targets set forth in the legislation.

BACKGROUND

Until 1970 a patchwork of local, state, and federal laws and institutions aimed to reduce pollution in order to protect public health. Beginning in the mid-1950s the federal government expanded its funding and advisory roles in pollution control, but these policy changes were incremental, and the emphasis on state-level design and enforcement persisted. Because state and local officials were deeply concerned about fostering economic development, and because environmental activists in most states had insufficient clout to challenge economic interests, this arrangement meant that few states undertook serious pollution control programs.

Air Pollution

The earliest concerns about air pollution in the United States arose in response to the smoke emitted by factories that accompanied industrialization. Chicago and Cincinnati enacted the nation's first clean air laws in 1881. Chicago's ordinance declared that "the emissions of dense smoke from the smokestack of any boat or locomotive or from any chimney anywhere within the city shall be . . . a public nuisance." [5] By 1912, twenty-three of twenty-eight American cities with populations greater than 200,000 had passed similar laws, but these ordinances did little to mitigate air pollution.[6] During World War II, Los Angeles initiated the nation's first modern air pollution program in response to a public outcry about the odors of a wartime industrial plant. The city also placed severe curbs on oil refineries and backyard incinerators.

In 1948 toxic smog in Donora, Pennsylvania, killed 20 people and sickened almost 6,000, afflicting 43 percent of the city's population.[7] Similar incidents occurred in London and Los Angeles in the 1950s. These episodes attracted widespread media coverage, changed both the experts' and the public's perceptions of air pollution from a nuisance to a public health problem, and prompted the federal government to buttress state efforts with financial and research assistance. In 1955 Congress authorized the Public Health Service, a bureau within the Department of Health, Education and Welfare (HEW), to conduct air pollution research and to help states and educational institutions train personnel and carry out research and control. Upon taking office in 1961, President John F. Kennedy affirmed the importance of the federal government's role, asserting the need for an effective national program.

Then, in November 1962 a four-day inversion produced an air pollution episode in New York believed to have caused eighty deaths.[8] The event rekindled public interest in pollution control legislation; in response, Congress passed the Clean Air Act of 1963. This legislation expanded HEW's authority to enforce existing state laws, encouraged the development of new state laws, and regulated interstate air pollution. Two years later, the Motor Vehicle Air Pollution Control Act required HEW to establish regulations controlling emissions from all new motor vehicles. And in 1967 Congress passed the Air Quality Act, which required the National Air Pollution Control Administration, a small division within HEW, to designate regional air quality control areas, issue air quality criteria, and recommend pollution control techniques. But the new law lacked deadlines and penalties, and by 1970 the federal government had designated less than one-third of the metropolitan air quality regions projected in the statute, and no state had established a complete set of standards for any pollutant.[9]

Water Pollution

The federal government got involved in controlling water pollution as early as the late nineteenth century, but—as with air pollution—legal authority belonged almost entirely to states and localities. In 1899 Congress passed the Rivers and Harbors Act prohibiting the dumping of refuse that might impede travel in any navigable body of water. In 1912 Congress passed the Public Health Service Act, which authorized studies of waterborne diseases, sanitation, sewage, and the pollution of navigable streams and lakes. The 1924 Federal Oil Pollution Act prohibited ocean-going vessels from dumping oil into the sea. These laws were largely ineffectual, however, and by the 1940s every state had established its own agency responsible for controlling water pollution. The powers of these agencies varied widely, and states had no recourse when upstream users polluted rivers that crossed state borders.[10]

In an effort to create a more coherent water pollution policy, Congress passed the Federal Water Pollution Control Act in 1948. This law directed the surgeon general of the Public Health Service (PHS) to develop a comprehensive program to abate and control water pollution, administer grants-in-aid for building municipal waste treatment plants, conduct research, and render technical assistance to states. The law also authorized the surgeon general to enforce antipollution measures in interstate waters, but only with the consent of the affected states.[11] The PHS was unable to manage the federal water pollution program to the satisfaction of either conservation groups or Congress, however, and President Harry Truman further hampered the law's implementation by preventing the agency from distributing loans to states and localities for sewage treatment plants.

In order to redirect and strengthen HEW's efforts, Congress enacted the Federal Water Pollution Control Act of 1961, which transferred responsibility for water pollution control from the surgeon general to his superior, the secretary of HEW. The new law extended federal enforcement to all navigable waters, not just interstate waters, and called for an increase in appropriations for municipal treatment plants. Four years later, Congress went even further with the Water Quality Act of 1965, which officially created a separate agency, the Federal Water Pollution Control Administration, within HEW. The act gave the states until June 30, 1967, to develop individual water quality standards for drinking water, fish and wildlife, recreation, and agriculture on their interstate navigable waters. In addition, the bill established an explicit national goal: the "prevention, control, and abatement of water pollution." The following year, Sen. Edmund Muskie, D-Maine, proposed, and Congress passed, a bill that created a $3.5 billion sewage treatment plant construction fund.[12] Despite this expansion in federal jurisdiction, however, three consecutive bureaucratic reorganizations hampered the new water pollution control agency's ability to exercise its statutory authority, rendering its efforts more apparent than real.

THE CASE

The pace of federal air and water pollution control legislation accelerated during the 1960s, but it was the laws passed in the early 1970s that marked a substantial departure from the past. With these laws the federal government assumed primary responsibility for cleaning up the nation's air and water and instituted strict new pollution control standards. The impetus for this change was not a sudden or dramatic increase in the scale of the problem; rather, it was a redefinition of the pollution problem sparked by widely read environmental writers and the consequent emergence of environmental protection as a popular national cause. Public concern about pollution outran the incremental responses of the 1960s and culminated at the end of the decade in a massive Earth Day demonstration. That event, in turn, opened a window of opportunity for advocates of strict pollution control policies. Politicians, vying for a leadership role and recognizing the popularity of environmentalism, competed for voters' recognition of their environmental qualifications.

Environmentalism Becomes a Popular Cause

In 1962 Rachel Carson published *Silent Spring*, the book that many credit with lighting the fuse of the modern environmental movement. The *New York Times*'s Philip Shabecoff later described the impact of her work:

> What Carson did in *Silent Spring* . . . was to present the scientific evidence in clear, poetic, and moving prose that demonstrated how the destruction of nature and the threat to human health from pollution were completely intertwined. . . . The book synthesized many of the concerns of the earlier conservationists and preservationists with the warnings of new environmentalists who worried about pollution and public health. It made frighteningly clear that they were all skeins of a large web of environmental evil settling over the nation and the world. . . . She combined a transcendentalist's passion for nature and wildlife with the cool analytical mind of a trained scientist and the contained anger of a political activist. She touched an exposed wound.[13]

On the *New York Times* bestseller list for thirty-one weeks, Carson's book ignited a firestorm of environmental activism and was soon followed by an avalanche of antipollution literature, including a book by biologist and environmental popularizer Paul Ehrlich, *The Population Bomb*.

Then a series of highly publicized disasters hit. A Union Oil Company well blew out six miles off the coast of Santa Barbara, California, and for several weeks oil leaked into the Pacific Ocean at the rate of 20,000 gallons a day, polluting twenty miles of beaches. Cleveland's Cuyahoga River, heavily polluted with industrial chemicals, burst into flames. Mercury scares frightened people away from seafood, and coastal communities closed beaches when raw sewage washed up on shore.

Calls for environmental awareness in response to these episodes fell on receptive ears. The population was becoming younger and better educated: between 1950 and 1974, the percentage of adults with some college education rose from 13.4 percent to 25.2 percent.[14] Demographic change was coupled with a streak of unprecedented prosperity as the nation's economy rocketed out of World War II. The emerging generation, finding itself in the midst of this boom, began to worry about the pollution that accompanied rapid growth and urbanization. One indication of the growing public interest in environmental issues during this time was the explosion of citations under the heading "environment" in the *New York Times* index. In 1955 the word was not even indexed; in 1965 it appeared as a heading but was followed by only two citations; by 1970, however, there were eighty-six paragraphs under the heading.[15]

Earth Day 1970

The heightened environmental awareness of the 1960s culminated on April 22, 1970, in the national celebration of Earth Day. The demonstration was the brainchild of Sen. Gaylord Nelson, D-Wis., who had a long-standing interest in the environment but felt that few members of Congress shared his concern. After meeting with Paul Ehrlich, Nelson conceived of an environmental teach-in to raise public awareness. He hired Dennis Hayes, a twenty-five-year-old Harvard Law School student, to organize the event on a budget of $125,000.[16] Interestingly, the established preservation-oriented groups, such as the Sierra Club, the Audubon Society, and the National Wildlife Federation, played little or no role in Earth Day. In fact, as Shabecoff points out, they were surprised by and unprepared for the national surge in emotion.[17]

Despite the absence of the mainstream environmental groups, Earth Day was a resounding success—an outpouring of social activism comparable to the civil rights and Vietnam War protests. The *New York Times* proclaimed, "Millions Join Earth Day Observances Across the Nation." *Time* magazine estimated that 20 million people nationwide were involved.[18] Organizers claimed that more than 2,000 colleges, 10,000 elementary and high schools, and citizens' groups in 2,000 communities participated in festivities.[19]

Citizens in every major city and town rallied in support of the message. For two hours New York City barred the internal combustion engine from Fifth Avenue, and thousands thronged the fume-free streets; in Union Square, crowds heard speeches and visited booths that distributed information on topics such as air pollution, urban planning, voluntary sterilization, conservation, and wildlife preservation. In Hoboken, New Jersey, a crowd hoisted a coffin containing the names of America's polluted rivers into the Hudson. In Birmingham, Alabama, one of the most polluted cities in the nation, the Greater Birmingham Alliance to Stop Pollution (GASP) held a "right to live" rally. Washington's chapter of GASP passed out forms that pedestrians could use to report buses emitting noxious fumes or smoke to the transit authority.

Students of all ages participated in an eclectic array of events. Fifth graders at Charles Barrett Elementary School in Alexandria, Virginia, wrote letters to local polluters. Girls from Washington Irving High School in New York collected trash and dragged white sheets along sidewalks to show how dirty they became. University of New Mexico students collected signatures on a plastic globe and presented it as an "enemy of the Earth" award to twenty-eight state senators accused of weakening an environmental law. At Indiana University female students tossed birth control pills at crowds to protest overpopulation. And at the University of Texas in Austin, the campus newspaper came out with a make-believe April 22, 1990, headline that read: "Noxious Smog Hits Houston: 6,000 Dead."

Although it was the target of most Earth Day criticism, even the business community jumped on the Earth Day bandwagon in an effort to improve its image. Rex Chainbelt Inc. of Milwaukee announced the creation of a new pollution control division. Reynolds Metal Can Company sent trucks to colleges in fourteen states to pick up aluminum cans collected in "trash-ins" and paid a bounty of one cent for two cans. And Scott Paper announced plans to spend large sums on pollution abatement for its plants in Maine and Washington.

Republican and Democratic politicians alike tried to capitalize on the public fervor as well. Congress stood in recess because scores of its members were participating in Earth Day programs: Senator Muskie addressed a crowd of 25,000 in Philadelphia; Sen. Birch Bayh, D-Ind., spoke at Georgetown University; Sen. George McGovern, D-S.D., talked to students at Purdue University; and Sen. John Tower, R-Texas, addressed oilmen in Houston. Most audiences greeted politicians with suspicion, however. University of Michigan students heckled former interior secretary Stewart Udall until he promised to donate his $1,000 speaker's fee to the school's environmental quality group. Protestors at a rally held by Sen. Charles Goodell, R-N.Y., distributed a leaflet calling his speech "the biggest cause of air pollution." And organizers in the Environmental Action Coalition refused to allow politicians on their platform at all to avoid giving Earth Day a political cast.

The Polls

Public opinion polls confirm that Earth Day marked the emergence of environmentalism as a mass social movement in the United States. Before 1965 pollsters did not even deem pollution important enough to ask about, but by 1970 it had become a major political force. As Table 2-1 shows, over the five-year period leading up to Earth Day, the increase in public awareness of air

Table 2-1
Public Opinion on Air and Water Pollution, 1965–1970

Q: Compared with other parts of the country, do you think the problem of air/water pollution in your area is very serious or somewhat serious?

Year	Sample Size	Air (%)	Water (%)
1965	2,128	28%	35%
1966	2,033	48	49
1967	2,000	53	52
1968	2,079	55	58
1969	NA	NA	NA
1970	2,168	69	74

Source: John C. Whitaker, *Striking a Balance: Environment and Natural Resources Policy in the Nixon-Ford Years* (Washington, D.C.: AEI, 1976), 8. Reprinted with the permission of The American Enterprise Institute for Public Policy Research, Washington, D.C.

Table 2-2
Most Important Domestic Problems, 1969 and 1971

Q: Aside from the Vietnam War and foreign affairs, what are some of the most important problems facing people here in the United States?

Problem	May 1969 Survey	May 1971 Survey	Significant Changes
Inflation, cost of living, taxes	34%	44%	10%
Pollution, ecology	1	25	24
Unemployment	7	24	17
Drugs, alcohol	3	23	20
Racial problems	39	22	−17
Poverty/welfare	22	20	−2
Crime, lack of law and order	15	19	4
Unrest among young people	6	12	6
Education	5	8	3
Housing	NA	6	NA

Source: John C. Whitaker, *Striking a Balance: Environment and Natural Resources Policy in the Nixon-Ford Years* (Washington, D.C.: AEI, 1976), 8. Reprinted with the permission of The American Enterprise Institute for Public Policy Research, Washington, D.C.

and water pollution is striking: survey data gathered between 1965 and 1969 reflected public recognition of pollution, but most people did not identify it as a high priority issue. Then, between the summer of 1969 and the summer of 1970, the public's concern reached a tipping point, and the issue jumped from tenth to fifth place in the Gallup polls. By 1970 the American public perceived pollution as more important than race, crime, and teenage problems (see Table 2-2). In December 1970 a Harris survey showed that Americans rated pollution as "the most serious problem" facing their communities. According to another Harris poll, conducted in 1971, 83 percent of Americans wanted the federal government to spend more money on air and water pollution control programs.[20]

Writing in the spring of 1972, poll editor Hazel Erskine summed up the rapid growth of the environmental issue this way: "A miracle of public opinion has been the unprecedented speed and urgency with which ecological issues have burst into the American consciousness. Alarm about the environment sprang from nowhere to major proportions in a few short years." [21] According to historian Samuel Hays, this shift in public opinion was no transient phase but reflected a permanent evolution associated with rising standards of living and human expectations. "Environmental politics," he claims, "reflect major changes in American society and values. People want new services from government stemming from new desires associated with the advanced consumer economy that came into being after World War II." [22]

Politicians Respond

The emergence of broad-based public support for pollution control empowered proponents of more stringent policies, who pressed their demands on Congress and the president, citing the polls and Earth Day as evidence of the salience of environmental problems. To promote more ambitious policies, they capitalized on the competition between President Nixon and aspiring presidential candidate Muskie for control over the issue of environmental protection. The candidates, in turn, raised the stakes with their proposals.

Creating the Environmental Protection Agency. Reflecting their perception of the issue's low salience, neither of the major party presidential candidates in 1968 made the environment a campaign focus. Republican Richard Nixon and Democrat Hubert Humphrey concentrated on peace, prosperity, crime, and inflation. Only one of the thirty-four position papers and statements published in the compendium *Nixon Speaks Out* covers natural resources and environmental quality; in another Nixon campaign publication containing speeches, statements, issue papers, and answers to questions from the press, only 5 of 174 pages are devoted to the environment, natural resources, and energy. Nixon staff members do not recall even one question to the candidate about the environment.[23] The Humphrey campaign was equally silent on the subject.

Yet by 1970 Nixon's staff had grasped the growing salience of environmental protection and begun staking out the president's position. In his State of the Union address in January 1970, Nixon made bold pronouncements about the need for federal intervention to protect the environment, saying:

> Restoring nature to its natural state is a cause beyond party and beyond factions. It has become a common cause of all the people of this country. It is the cause of particular concern to young Americans because they more than we will reap the grim consequences of our failure to act on the programs which are needed now if we are to prevent disaster later—clean air, clean water, open spaces. These should once again be the birthright of every American. If we act now they can.[24]

Nixon went on to assert that the nation required "comprehensive new regulation." The price of goods, he said, "should be made to include the costs of producing and disposing of them without damage to the environment."[25] On February 10 Nixon delivered a special message to Congress on environmental quality in which he outlined a thirty-seven-point program encompassing twenty-three separate pieces of legislation and fourteen administrative actions.[26]

On July 9 the president submitted to Congress an executive reorganization plan that proposed the creation of the Environmental Protection Agency (EPA) and consolidated a variety of federal environmental activities within the new agency. The EPA's principal functions were to establish and enforce environmental protection standards, conduct research, gather and evaluate pollution information, strengthen environmental protection programs, recommend policy changes, and help control environmental pollution.[27] Ironically, the original impetus for the EPA came not from the environmental community but from a commission appointed by President Nixon to generate ideas for streamlining the federal bureaucracy. The President's Advisory Council on Executive Organization, known as the Ash Council, was composed primarily of business executives, but the staff included several environmental policy entrepreneurs. At first, council head Roy Ash favored vesting responsibility for both natural resources and pollution control in a single "super department," a department of natural resources. But council staff worried that such a plan would force environmentalists to compete with better-organized and better-financed natural resource development interests. They proposed instead an independent agency with jurisdiction over pollution control.[28] Council members also favored establishing an executive agency because creating a regulatory commission would require legislative action and subject the council's proposals to congressional politics. Furthermore, council members preferred the scientific and technical nature of executive agency decision making and were concerned that commissions tended to be dominated by legal and adjudicative experts.[29]

President Nixon did not accept all of the Ash Council's recommendations for the EPA, but he retained the central idea: to create an agency devoted to comprehensive environmental protection. The presidential message accompanying Reorganization Plan Number Three clearly reflects the extent to which ecological ideas permeated the political debate about pollution:

> Despite its complexity, for pollution control purposes, the environment must be perceived as a single, interrelated system. Present assignments of departmental responsibilities do not reflect this interrelatedness. . . . This consolidation of pollution control authorities would help assure that we do not create new environmental problems in the process of controlling existing ones.[30]

The Senate was hospitable to Nixon's proposal and introduced no resolution opposing it.[31] In spite of the objections of some prominent members, the House did not pass a resolution opposing the reorganization either, so on December 2, 1970, the EPA opened its doors.

The Clean Air Act of 1970. One of the first tasks of the new agency was to implement the Clean Air Act Amendments of 1970. This was a particular challenge for the fledgling bureau because the new legislation was much more than an incremental step beyond past policy experience; in fact, it was a radical departure from the approach previously taken by the federal government. Instead of helping the states design air pollution programs, the EPA was to assume primary responsibility for setting air quality standards and for ensuring that the states enforced those standards.

Congress and the president had begun work on the 1970 Clean Air Act months before the Nixon administration established the EPA. Recognizing the rising political cachet of environmentalism and wanting to launch a preemptive strike against Senator Muskie, his likely rival for the presidency, Nixon sent air pollution legislation to Congress in February 1970. Under the bill, HEW would issue stringent motor vehicle emissions standards and improve its testing procedures and regulation of fuel composition and additives. For stationary sources (factories and electric utilities), the bill established national air quality standards, accelerated the designation of air quality control regions, and set national emissions standards for hazardous pollutants and selected classes of new facilities.[32]

The administration's proposal fared well in the House of Representatives, where the chamber's bipartisan consensus reflected the rank-and-file members' sensitivity to the public mood. Under the guidance of Rep. Paul Rogers, D-Fla., the Commerce Committee's Subcommittee on Public Health and Welfare marked up the bill, and the full committee reported out a somewhat stronger version than the original. On June 10 the full House passed the bill 374–1.

The Senate received the administration bill less warmly because in that chamber Nixon's rival, Senator Muskie, was the undisputed champion of the environmental cause. On March 4, shortly after the president submitted his bill to the House, Muskie introduced an alternative, the National Air Quality Standards Act of 1970. His objective at the time was to prod agencies to strengthen their implementation of the 1967 act, rather than to initiate a radically different policy. Muskie had spent his Senate career characterizing pollution control as a state responsibility; as he understood it, the problem lay not in the design of the program but in its implementation.[33] Over the summer, however, Muskie changed his tune. He asked the Public Works Committee's Subcommittee on Air and Water Pollution to draft a new set of amendments containing stringent new provisions including national, rather than regional, standards for major pollutants.

Muskie's sudden change of heart was a clear attempt to reestablish his dominance in the environmental area. Despite Muskie's considerable record, not only Nixon but also some prominent environmental advocates had challenged the senator's commitment to environmental protection. A highly critical report by a Ralph Nader study group, released in May 1970, characterized Muskie as a weak and ineffectual sponsor of clean air legislation. The report, entitled *Vanishing Air*, assailed Muskie as

> the chief architect of the disastrous Air Quality Act of 1967. That fact alone would warrant his being stripped of his title as "Mr. Pollution Control." But the Senator's passivity since 1967 in the face of an ever worsening air pollution crisis compounds his earlier failure. . . . Muskie awakened from his dormancy on the issue of air pollution the day after President Nixon's State of the Union message. . . . In other words, the air pollution issue became vital again when it appeared that the President might steal the Senator's thunder on a good political issue.[34]

Media publicity of the Nader report's charges put Muskie on the defensive, and the Senate's environmental leader felt compelled to "do something extraordinary in order to recapture his [pollution control] leadership." [35]

In the end, Muskie's subcommittee drafted an air pollution bill more stringent than either the president's *or* the House of Representatives' proposals. It called for nationally uniform air quality standards that ignored economic cost and technological feasibility considerations and were based solely on health and welfare criteria; it required traffic control plans to eliminate automobile use in parts of some major cities; and it mandated a 90 percent reduction in automotive emissions of carbon monoxide, hydrocarbons, and nitrous oxides by 1975. In a clear manifestation of the burgeoning popularity of environmental protection, senators got on the bandwagon and endorsed this version of the clean air bill unanimously (73–0) on September 21, 1970.[36]

Because of substantial differences in critical sections of the bill, the House-Senate conference that ensued was protracted, involving at least eight long sessions over a three-month period. The Senate's eight conferees held an advantage over the five from the House because Muskie's prolonged attention to pollution issues had attracted several qualified and committed staffers who had amassed considerable expertise. As a consequence, the final conference report more closely resembled the Senate version of the bill than the House version.

On December 18 both chambers debated and passed the conference report, and on December 31 President Nixon signed the Clean Air Act of 1970 into law. Its centerpiece was the requirement that the EPA set both primary and secondary national ambient air quality standards.[37] The states were to submit state implementation plans (SIPs) outlining a strategy for meeting primary standards by 1975 and secondary standards "within a reasonable time." If the EPA determined a SIP to be inadequate, it had to promulgate a plan of its own. The act also targeted some polluters directly: it required automobile producers to reduce the emissions of new cars by 90 percent by 1975, and it required the EPA to set new source performance standards for all major categories of stationary sources.

The highly symbolic language, goals, and structure of the 1970 Clean Air Act clearly reflected the public's attentiveness to the problem of air pollution and its demand for federal action. As Helen Ingram points out, the new law

> set far more ambitious air pollution control goals, which were to be accomplished more quickly and under a more demanding regulatory regime than could possibly have been projected from previous policy evolution. . . . The understanding of clean air changed significantly through the legislative process in 1970. The pragmatic, functional definition of air quality, restricted to what was economically and technologically feasible, was abandoned, and clean air was legislated a fundamental national value.[38]

The Clean Water Act of 1972. President Nixon made not only air pollution but water pollution legislation a pillar of his February 10, 1970, special message to Congress. When Congress failed to address water pollution in that legislative session, the president moved administratively, using the permit authority granted by the Refuse Act of 1899 to control industrial pollution of waterways. By executive order, Nixon directed the EPA to require industries to disclose the amount and kinds of effluents they were generating before they could obtain a permit to discharge them into navigable waters.[39] When a polluter failed to apply for a permit or violated existing clean water regulations, the EPA referred an enforcement action to the Justice Department.

Neither the permit process nor the enforcement strategy was particularly effective at ameliorating water pollution, however. The president endorsed the permit program, but Congress was not pleased at being circumvented; state agencies were angry that federal rules superseded their own regulations; and many industries were furious at the sudden demands for discharge information.[40] Compliance was limited: on July 1, 1971, when the first 50,000 applications from water-polluting industries were due, only 30,000 had arrived, and many of them contained incomplete or inaccurate information. The enforcement process, which relied heavily on the overburdened federal court system, was slow and cumbersome.[41] Then, in December 1971 a district court in Ohio dealt the permit program its final blow: it held that the EPA had to draft an environmental impact statement for each permit issued in order to comply with the National Environmental Policy Act.[42]

While the EPA muddled through with its interim program, Congress began to debate the future of water pollution policy. In February 1971 President Nixon endorsed a proposal to strengthen a bill he had submitted to Congress the previous year. The new bill increased the administration's request for annual municipal waste treatment financing from $1 billion to $2 billion for three years and established mandatory toxic discharge standards. In addition, it requested authority for legal actions by private citizens to enforce water quality standards.

Refusing to be upstaged by the president, Muskie seized the opportunity to offer even more stringent legislation. The Senate began hearings in February, and eight months later Muskie's Public Works Committee reported out the Federal Water Pollution Control Act Amendments. Much to the administration's dismay, the price tag for the Senate bill was $18 billion, three times the cost of Nixon's proposal. Moreover, the administration found unrealistic the overarching objectives of the Senate bill: that "wherever attainable, an interim goal of water quality which provides for the protection and propagation of fish, shellfish, and wildlife and provides for recreation in and on the water should be achieved by 1981" and that "the discharge of all pollutants into navigable waters would be eliminated by 1985." Finally, the administration considered the Senate bill inequitable, claiming that it imposed a disproportionate burden on industry by singling out those that could not discharge into municipal waste treatment facilities. Nevertheless, on November 2, 1971, the Senate passed the bill by a vote of 86–0.

Having failed to shift the Senate, the administration focused on the House deliberations, with some qualified success: the House reported out a bill similar to the one proposed by the White House. In contrast to the Senate version, the House bill retained the primacy of the states in administering the program. After meeting forty times between May and September 1972, the House-Senate conferees overcame their differences and produced a bill satisfactory to both sides. In another extraordinary display of near unanimity, the Senate passed the conference bill by 74–0, and the House approved it by 366–11.

The compromise was too stringent for the administration, however. It retained the fishable, swimmable, and zero-discharge goals, as well as the financing provisions, that were so objectionable to the president. Furthermore, the bill's timetables and total disregard for economic costs offended the White House. So, in a tactical maneuver, Nixon vetoed the Clean Water Act on October 17, the day that Congress was scheduled to adjourn for the year. To Nixon's chagrin, however, Congress responded with unusual alacrity: less than two hours after the president delivered his veto message, the Senate voted to override the veto by 52–12.[43] The next afternoon the House followed suit by a vote of 247–23, and the Clean Water Act became law.

The New Environmental Regulations. The Clean Air and Clean Water acts reflected the prevailing definition of pollution, in which industrial polluters (not consumers) were the villains, and citizens (and only secondarily the environment) were the unwitting victims. They also reflected the public's skepticism of corporations' willingness and government bureaucrats' ability to address pollution. Concerns about "regulatory capture," whereby agencies become subservient to the industries they are supposed to monitor, had preoccupied academics for years, but in 1969 political scientist Theodore Lowi popularized the concept in his book *The End of Liberalism.* Lowi criticized Congress for granting agencies broad discretion in order to avoid making hard political tradeoffs. He argued that agencies, operating out of the public eye, strike bargains with the interest groups most affected by their policies, rather than making policies that serve a broader national interest. Led by Ralph Nader, reformers disseminated the concept of regulatory capture. Two reports issued by Nader's Center for the Study of Responsive Law, *Vanishing Air* in 1970 and *Water Wasteland* in 1971, attributed the failures of earlier air and water pollution control laws to agency capture. More important, they linked that diagnosis to Nader's preferred solution—strict, action-forcing statutes— reasoning that unambiguous laws would limit bureaucrats' ability to pander to interest groups.

Members of Congress got the message. In addition to transferring standard-setting authority from the states to the federal government, the Clean Air and Clean Water acts employed novel regulatory mechanisms—such as strict deadlines, clear goals, and uniform standards—that both minimized the EPA's discretion and restricted polluters' flexibility. For example, the Clean Air Act gave the EPA thirty days to establish health- and welfare-based ambient air quality standards. The states then had nine months to submit their SIPs to the EPA, which had to approve or disapprove them within four months of receipt. The agency was to ensure the achievement of national air quality standards no later than 1977. Similarly, the Clean Water Act specified six deadlines: by 1973 the EPA was supposed to issue effluent guidelines for major industrial categories; within a year it was to grant permits to all sources of water pollution;

by 1977 every source was supposed to have installed the "best practicable" water pollution control technology; by 1981 the major waterways in the nation were to be suitable for swimming and fishing; by 1983 polluting sources were to install the "best available" technology; and by 1985 all discharges into the nation's waterways were to be eliminated.

Congress also sought to demonstrate its commitment to preventing regulatory capture by incorporating public participation into agency decision making and thereby breaking up regulated interests' monopoly. For example, both the Clean Air and Clean Water acts required the EPA to solicit public opinion during the process of writing regulations. In addition, both laws encouraged public participation by explicitly granting citizens the right to bring a civil suit in federal court against any violator or "against the administrator [of the EPA] where there is alleged a failure of the administrator to perform any act or duty under [the Clean Air Act] which is not discretionary." The impact of the citizen suit provision was profound. As political scientist Shep Melnick explains:

> Previous statutes had required citizens wishing to sue administrators to show that they had suffered direct, concrete harm at the hands of an agency. Almost all the regulatory laws passed in the 1970s, though, authorized "any citizen" to file suit against administrators either for taking unauthorized action or for failing to perform "nondiscretionary" duties. Some statutes even reimbursed litigants in such suits for their trouble. When combined with detailed statutes these opportunities for judicial review provided fledgling environmental and consumer groups with powerful resources within the regulatory process.[44]

Finally, the Clean Air and Clean Water acts of the early 1970s reflected impatience with market forces and a desire to spur the development of new pollution control technology as well as to encourage businesses to devise innovative new production processes. Both laws included provisions that fostered technology in three ways: by prompting the development of new technology, by encouraging the adoption of available but not-yet-used technology, and by forcing diffusion of currently used technology within an industry. The motor vehicle provisions of the Clean Air Act, for example, forced the development of the catalytic converter. When Congress was debating the 90 percent emissions reduction, the automobile manufacturers strenuously objected that they did not have the technology to meet those standards, but Muskie responded with a flourish that this level of reduction was necessary to protect human health, so companies would have to devise a solution.[45] (As it turned out, car makers were able to meet the standards relatively easily.) The Clean Water Act, on the other hand, pushed polluters to adopt technology that was already available but not widely used by its initial deadline. In the second phase, however, the act required businesses to meet standards achievable with the best technology available, even if it was not in use at the time.

Implementation: Idealism Tempered

The Clean Air and Clean Water acts were sufficiently grandiose that they would have presented a challenge to any agency, but they were particularly onerous for a brand new one that drew staff from all over the federal government. Not surprisingly, because of the short time allowed for implementing these laws, combined with the haste in which the agency was designed, the EPA did not attain the ideal of interrelatedness outlined by President Nixon; instead, different offices continued to manage pollution in different media. Nor did the EPA fulfill the mandates of the Clean Air and Clean Water acts to virtually eliminate pollution in the nation's air and waterways. Although born in a period of great idealism, the EPA had to survive in the highly circumscribed world of practical politics. It had to establish relationships with and reconcile the demands of the president and Congress, and it had to navigate a course in a sea of competing interests, recalcitrant state and local officials, a skeptical media, and an expectant public. In all of these endeavors, the EPA was vulnerable to lawsuits because the statutes compelled it to act quickly and decisively, despite a dearth of scientific and technical information on which to base its decisions and, more important, with which to justify them.

Setting a Course. The new EPA was an organizational nightmare, as it comprised

> an uneasy amalgam of staff and programs previously located in 15 separate federal agencies. EPA had a total budget of $1.4 billion. Its 5,743 employees worked in 157 places, ranging geographically from a floating barge off the Florida coast to a water quality laboratory in Alaska. In Washington, D.C., alone there were 2,000 employees scattered across the city in 12 separate office buildings.[46]

The first EPA administrator, William Ruckelshaus, was a lawyer and former Justice Department official. He was confronted with the awesome tasks of coordinating the disparate offices of the new agency (it lacked a headquarters until 1973), establishing a set of coherent priorities, and carrying out the statutory mission of regulating polluters. From the outset, Ruckelshaus balanced his own approach against the conflicting preferences of the White House and Congress.

Dealing with the White House posed a considerable challenge. Although President Nixon created the EPA and introduced pollution control legislation, he did so more out of political opportunism than genuine environmental concern. He regarded environmentalism as a fad, but one that promised political rewards. "Elected with only 43 percent of the popular vote in 1968, Nixon needed to take bold steps to expand his ideological base in order to be reelected in 1972." [47] In truth, Nixon was hostile toward the federal bureaucracy and, as biographer Stephen Ambrose notes, wanted "credit for boldness and innovation without the costs." [48] Nixon instructed White House staff to scrutinize the EPA's activity, sought to block its rulemaking, and introduced legislation to curtail its authority. Most notably, he established a "quality of life" review under the Office of Management and Budget (OMB) to assess the legal, economic, and budgetary implications of EPA regulations—a mechanism that by 1972 "had become an administration device for obstructing stringent regulations, as the environmental groups had originally feared." [49]

Congress, on the other hand, was a mixed bag of backers and critics. Several members of Congress exhibited a genuine zeal for environmental protection. Members of the House and Senate subcommittees with jurisdiction over pollution control encouraged Ruckelshaus to enforce the law vigorously. Muskie, in particular, was dogged in his efforts to train national attention on pollution control and thereby hold the EPA's feet to the fire. His subcommittee convened frequent hearings that required Ruckelshaus to explain delays in setting standards. But other members on related committees were more conservative; for example, Rep. Jamie Whitten, D-Miss., chairman of the House Appropriations Subcommittee on Agriculture, Environment, and Consumer Protection, controlled the agency's purse strings and was a vocal opponent of strong environmental regulations. [50]

Squeezed between supporters and detractors in Congress and the White House, Ruckelshaus tried to build an independent constituency that would support the fledgling EPA. To establish credibility as an environmentalist and earn public trust, he initiated a series of lawsuits against known municipal and industrial violators of water pollution control laws. To reinforce his efforts, he promoted the agency in the media, giving frequent press conferences, appearing on talk shows, and making speeches before trade and business associations. According to John Quarles, the EPA's first assistant administrator for enforcement:

> Ruckelshaus believed in the strength of public opinion and public support. The organized environmental movement had been formed because of public pressure, and Ruckelshaus responded instinctively to that pressure. He did not seek political support for his actions in the established structures of political power. He turned instead directly to the press and to public opinion. . . . In doing so, he tied the fortunes of EPA to public opinion as the only base for political support. [51]

Ruckelshaus had to do more than file lawsuits and woo the media, however; he had to promulgate a series of regulations to meet statutory deadlines, notwithstanding the paucity of scientific and engineering information. Compounding the technical obstacles, the targeted industries resisted agency rulemaking. Although it had been ambushed by the regulatory onslaught of the late 1960s and early 1970s, business quickly adapted to the new political order. Corporations began to emphasize government relations as a fundamental part of their missions: between 1968 and 1978 the number of corporations with public affairs offices in Washington rose from 100 to more than 500. [52] In short, polluters sought to recapture their dominance over environmentalists at the implementation stage, and, with its almost bottomless resources, industry was able to challenge regulations administratively and in the courts.[53]

Implementing the Clean Air Act. Thanks to both their increased political involvement and a shift in public attention, the industries especially hard hit by regulation—automobile, steel, nonferrous smelting, and electric power—all succeeded in winning delays from the EPA. The automobile manufacturers were among those the Clean Air Act singled out most directly. Before the passage of the 1966 National Traffic and Motor Vehicle Safety Act, the automobile was completely unregulated by the federal government. Yet only four years later, the Clean Air Act required car makers to cut emissions of carbon monoxide, nitrogen oxides, and hydrocarbons by 90 percent within five years. Producers immediately applied for a one-year extension of the deadline, contending that the technology to achieve the standards was not yet available. Ruckelshaus denied their petition on the grounds that the industry had not made "good faith efforts" to achieve the standards. The manufacturers then took their case to the U.S. Court of Appeals for the District of Columbia, which overturned Ruckelshaus's decision, saying that the agency needed to give economic factors greater weight. Later that year, Ruckelshaus conceded and granted a one-year extension.

The power companies, automobile manufacturers, and coal and oil producers saw the 1973–1974 energy crisis as a window of opportunity to weaken the Clean Air Act requirements. Threatening widespread economic dislocation, these energy-related industries pressured Congress and the president into passing the Energy Supply and Environmental Coordination Act of 1974. The act included another one-year extension for hydrocarbon and carbon monoxide emissions and a two-year extension for nitrogen oxide emissions. When a controversy arose over the health effects of acid emissions from catalytic converters, Russell Train, who succeeded Ruckelshaus as EPA administrator in September 1973, granted the auto manufacturers a third extension.[54]

Meanwhile, however, the delays in achieving automotive emissions standards left the EPA in an awkward position: because of the extensions, states could not rely on cleaner cars to mitigate their pollution problems and had to reduce dramatically the *use* of automobiles, a politically unappealing prospect. Acknowledging the enormity of their task, Ruckelshaus granted seventeen of the most urbanized states a two-year extension on the transportation control portion of their implementation plans, giving states until 1977 to achieve air quality standards.[55] Although most state officials were pleased, disgruntled environmentalists in California filed suit in federal court to force the EPA to promulgate a transportation control plan (TCP) for Los Angeles. The plaintiffs charged that the Clean Air Act compelled the EPA to draft a plan for any state whose own plan the agency disapproved, not to grant extensions. The court agreed and ordered the agency to prepare a TCP for Los Angeles by January 15, 1973.

The pollution problem in Los Angeles basin was so severe that, to bring the region into compliance with air quality standards, the EPA had to write a TCP that included gas rationing and mandatory installation of emissions control devices on all cars. Needless to say, such measures were unpopular. Public officials who were supposed to enforce the plan ridiculed it: Mayor Sam Yorty called it "asinine," "silly," and "impossible." [56] State and local officials clearly believed that their constituents supported clean air in the abstract but would not give up their cars to get it.

Contributing to the agency's credibility woes, just two weeks after Ruckelshaus announced the Los Angeles TCP, a federal court found in favor of the Natural Resources Defense Council in its suit to overturn the two-year extensions for states' compliance with the air quality standards. To Ruckelshaus's chagrin, the court ordered him to rescind all seventeen extensions. The states again were faced with a 1975 compliance deadline to be achieved without the benefit of cleaner cars.

As a result, in late 1973 the EPA found itself forced to produce a spate of TCPs for states whose own TCPs the agency had rejected. State officials immediately challenged the plans in court, and in some cases judges were sympathetic, finding that the EPA plans lacked sufficient technical support. But many of the plans went unchallenged, and by spring 1974 the EPA was in another quandary: it had promulgated numerous TCPs the previous year, but the states were not implementing them. Although EPA lawyers believed they had the legal authority to require out-of-compliance areas to institute transportation controls, it was not clear how they would actually force recalcitrant states to do so, and the agency lacked the administrative apparatus to impose the control strategies itself. EPA officials decided to try enforcing a test case in Boston, a logical choice since it already had an extensive mass transit system.

The backlash in Massachusetts was severe, in part because the Boston plan was haphazard and incoherent—a reflection of the agency's lack of information. For example, one regulation required all companies with fifty or more employees to reduce their available parking spaces by 25 percent. The EPA planned to send enforcement orders to 1,500 employers but discovered that only 300 of those on the list actually fit the category, and many of those turned out to be exempt (hospitals, for example). In the end, only seven or eight of the twenty-five eligible employers responded to the EPA's request to cut parking spaces. As time went on, even northeast regional EPA officials became annoyed with the arbitrary assumptions and technical errors embedded in the Boston TCP. For example, EPA analysts had based the carbon monoxide reduction strategy for the entire city on an unusually high reading from an extremely congested intersection, and they based their ozone calculations on a solitary reading from a monitor that had probably malfunctioned.[57]

The city of Boston took the plan to court, and the judge remanded the plan to the agency for better technical justification. Eventually, a chastened EPA rescinded the Boston plan altogether and issued a replacement that dropped all mandatory traffic and parking restrictions and relied instead on stationary source controls and voluntary vehicle cutbacks. The EPA went on to abandon its attempts to force major cities to restructure their transportation systems, which in turn meant that many remained out of compliance with air quality standards. By 1975, the statutory deadline, not one state implementation plan had received final approval from the EPA.

Implementing the Clean Water Act. Like the Clean Air Act, the Clean Water Act required the EPA to take on powerful industries armed with only scant technical and scientific information. The law's cornerstone, the National Pollutant Discharge Elimination System, prohibited the dumping of any wastes or effluents by any industry or government entity without a permit. To implement this provision, the agency had to undertake a massive data collection task: it needed information about the discharges, manufacturing processes, and pollution control options of 20,000 different industrial polluters operating under different circumstances in a variety of locations.[58] To simplify its task, the EPA divided companies into 30 categories and 250 subcategories on the basis of product, age, size, and manufacturing process. The water program office then created the Effluent Guidelines Division to set industry-by-industry effluent guidelines based on the "best practicable technology" (BPT). The division collected and tabulated information on companies around the country. But it found sufficient variation to make generalizations about a single best technology highly uncertain. While the EPA wrestled with this problem, the Natural Resources Defense Council sued the agency for delay. The court, finding in favor of the plaintiffs, forced the EPA to release guidelines for more than 30 industry categories and 100 subcategories.

Although the permits granted to individual companies were supposed to be based on the BPT guidelines, as a result of delays in issuing those guidelines, the agency dispensed permits to almost all of the "major" polluters before the guidelines had even appeared![59] Industry seized on this discrepancy to contest the permits in the agency's adjudicatory proceedings. In addition, major companies brought more than 150 lawsuits to challenge the guidelines themselves: the very day the EPA issued guidelines for the chemical industry, DuPont hired a prestigious law firm to sue the agency.[60] Ultimately, the EPA was forced to adopt a more pragmatic and conciliatory relationship with out-of-compliance companies. In response, disappointed environmental groups began to file suits against polluters themselves.

The 1977 Clean Air and Water Act Amendments

Under pressure from newly mobilized industry groups and with the public's attention elsewhere, in 1977 Congress relaxed the stringent provisions of both the Clean Air and the Clean Water acts. The 1977 Clean Air Act Amendments postponed the healthy air goals (that had to be achieved by 1975 under the 1970 act) until 1982. In areas heavily affected by car emissions, such as California, the act gave the states until 1987 to achieve air quality goals. The amendments also extended the deadline for the 90 percent reduction in automobile emissions—originally set for 1975 and subsequently postponed until 1978—to 1980 for hydrocarbons and 1981 for carbon monoxide. Congress granted the EPA administrator discretionary authority to delay the achievement of auto pollution reduction objectives for carbon monoxide and nitrogen oxides for up to two additional years if the required technology appeared unavailable. In addition, the amendments required that the EPA take into account competing priorities: it had to grant variances for technological innovation and file economic impact and employment impact statements with all new regulations it issued.[61] Moreover, the amendments gave the governor of any state the right to suspend transportation control measures that required gas rationing, reductions in on-street parking, or bridge tolls.[62]

The 1977 Clean Water Act Amendments also extended a host of deadlines. The amendments gave industries that acted in "good faith" but did not meet the 1977 BPT deadlines until April 1, 1979, instead of July 1, 1977, to meet the standard. In addition, they postponed and modified the best available technology (BAT) requirement that industry was supposed to achieve by 1983. They retained the strict standard for toxic pollutants but modified it for conventional pollutants.[63] This change gave the EPA the flexibility to set standards less stringent than BAT when it determined that the costs of employing BAT exceeded the benefits. Finally, although the amendments retained the objective of zero discharge into navigable waters by 1985, changes in the law eviscerated that goal; the extension of the BPT target and the modification of the BAT target eliminated the connection between zero discharge and a specific abatement program.[64]

Despite these rollbacks, the EPA continued to have formidable regulatory powers. In January 1978, shortly after Congress passed the amendments, President Jimmy Carter submitted his 1979 budget. Although he called for an overall spending increase of less than 1 percent over 1978, he requested an increase of $668 million for EPA programs.[65] That allocation reflected an important shift that had taken place at the EPA: in the months prior to the budget announcement, the agency had made a concerted effort to recast its image from that of protector of flora and fauna to guardian of the public's health. The move was partly to deflect a threatened merger of the EPA with other natural resources agencies, but it also reflected shrewd recognition of congressional support for programs aimed at fighting cancer.[66] The agency's public relations campaign worked, and by the end of the 1970s the EPA had become the largest federal regulatory bureaucracy, with more than 13,000 employees and an annual budget of $7 billion.[67]

OUTCOMES

As a result of White House obstruction, business resistance, and the sheer magnitude of the task, the EPA's accomplishments have been neither as dramatic nor as far-reaching as the original air and water pollution statutes demanded. Moreover, a chorus of critics contends that what cleanup has been accomplished has cost far more than necessary because regulations were poorly designed and haphazardly implemented. Nevertheless, the nation has made enormous progress in cleaning up air pollution and has made some gains in addressing water pollution as well.

The EPA reports substantial reductions in air pollution for the six major "criteria" pollutants since the mid-1980s, even as the economy has more than doubled, energy consumption has increased 42 percent, and vehicle miles traveled have increased 155 percent. Between 1983 and 2002 emissions of nitrous oxide (NO_x) declined almost 15 percent; sulfur dioxide (SO_2) emissions decreased 33 percent (ambient concentrations dropped 54 percent); carbon monoxide (CO) emissions fell 21 percent (ambient concentrations decreased 42 percent); and airborne lead emissions dropped 93 percent. Between 1993 and 2002 direct emissions of particulates of 2.5 microns or less (small particulates) decreased 17 percent (concentrations vary widely because secondary particles account for a large percentage of the small particulates in the air). Progress has been slowest for ground-level ozone, which is not emitted directly but formed in the atmosphere by the reaction of volatile organic compounds and NO_x in the presence of heat and sunlight. Between 1993 and 2002, eight-hour ozone levels increased 4 percent nationally, while one-hour ozone levels decreased by 2 percent. Ozone concentrations varied over this ten-year period, but did not change overall. These achievements notwithstanding, the United States emits about 150 million tons of air pollution each year; furthermore, in 2002 about 146 million people lived in counties where monitored air was unhealthy at times because of high levels of at least one of the six main pollutants.[68]

Despite the gains in combating water pollution, the nation has not come close to realizing the lofty objectives of the 1972 Clean Water Act. It is difficult to assess progress in ameliorating water pollution because the EPA and the Council on Environmental Quality base their water quality indexes on only six pollutants, excluding important sources of water degradation such as heavy metals, synthetic organic compounds, and dissolved solids.[69] Moreover, according to the Government Accountability Office (GAO—formerly General Accounting Office), the states have assessed water quality for only about a third of total U.S. river miles, half of lake and three-quarters of estuarine square miles.[70] In 2000, the last time the EPA issued a water quality update, states reported that 39 percent of assessed river and stream miles, 45 percent of assessed lake acres, and 51 percent of assessed estuarine square miles were polluted—that is, not clean enough to allow fishing and swimming.[71] A majority of the population, 218 million people, live within ten miles of these impaired waters. Furthermore, the GAO has consistently found high levels of noncompliance with the discharge levels specified in their permits among both industrial and municipal polluters.[72]

Even more important from the perspective of many critics is that nonpoint source water pollution presents a significant and growing problem and continues to be virtually unregulated under the Clean Water Act.[73] Nonpoint sources include farmlands, city storm sewers, construction sites, mines, and heavily logged forests. Runoff from these sources contains silt, pathogens, toxic chemicals, and excess nutrients that can suffocate fish and contaminate groundwater. The act also fails to deal with groundwater, which supplies the drinking water for 34 of the nation's 100 largest cities.[74] The loss of wetlands, which according to the EPA continues at the staggering rate of nearly 60,000 acres per year, contributes to water quality problems as well.[75] Although the EPA and Army Corps of Engineers established a permit program for wetlands under Section 404 of the Clean Water Act, it has done little to stem the loss of these ecologically valuable places; moreover, a recent Supreme Court decision (*Solid Waste Agency v. Army Corps of Engineers*, 2001) cast doubt on the Corps' authority to regulate wetlands.[76]

Bearing in mind the deficiencies in measurement and the absence of controls on important pollution sources, water quality modeling by Resources for the Future suggests that the Clean Water Act has had only modest impacts on water quality. According to this group, between 1972 and the late 1990s the number of river miles meeting standards for swimming, fishing, and boating increased by only 6.3 percent, 4.2 percent, and 2.8 percent, respectively.[77] That said, the law has resulted in enormous investments in sewage treatment, and as a consequence many of the most seriously polluted water bodies have been substantially cleaned up.

CONCLUSIONS

As this case makes clear, public attentiveness, especially when coupled with highly visible demonstrations of concern, can produce dramatic changes in politics and policy. Front-page coverage of Earth Day demonstrations in 1970 both enhanced public awareness of and concern about environmental problems and convinced elected officials that environmental issues were highly salient. In response, aspiring leaders competed with one another to gain credit for addressing air and water pollution. Legislators' near-unanimous support for the Clean Air and Clean Water acts suggests that rank-and-file legislators also sought recognition for solving the pollution problem or, at a minimum, got on the bandwagon to avoid blame for obstructing such solutions.

The Clean Air and Clean Water acts that ensued departed dramatically from the status quo in both form and stringency. The command-and-control approach, which imposed uniform emissions standards on polluters, reflected the pollution issue's framing: industry had caused the problem, and neither they nor government bureaucrats could be trusted to address it unless tightly constrained by highly specific standards and deadlines. The laws' ambitious, symbolic goals reflected the initial urgency of public concern and the immediacy of the legislative response. The inchoate EPA was destined to fail when it tried to implement the laws as written, however. The agency encountered hostility from the president, who wanted to weaken implementation of the law, as well as from its overseers in Congress, who berated it for failing to move more quickly.

Equally challenging was the need to placate polarized interest groups on both sides of the issue. Citizen suit provisions designed to enhance public involvement in the regulatory process resulted in a host of lawsuits by environmentalists trying to expedite the standard-setting process. At the same time, newly mobilized business interests used administrative hearings and lawsuits to obstruct implementation of the new laws. Caught in the middle, the EPA tried to enhance its public image—first by cracking down on individual polluters and later by emphasizing the public health aspect of its mission. The agency hoped that by steering a middle course it could maintain its credibility, as well as its political support. On the one hand, therefore, the business backlash was effective, and by the late 1970s Congress had substantially weakened the requirements of the Clean Air and Clean Water acts. On the other hand, both laws survived, and they and the EPA continue to enjoy broad public support.[78]

QUESTIONS TO CONSIDER

- Critics charge that the Clean Air and Clean Water acts are classic examples of symbolic politics, in which politicians set goals that are clearly unattainable in order to placate the public. What do you think are the costs and benefits of adopting unrealistically ambitious legislative goals?
- In retrospect, what are the strengths and weaknesses of the particular approach to pollution adopted in the Clean Air and Clean Water acts?
- How have the creation of the EPA and passage of the Clean Air and Clean Water acts in the early 1970s affected the environment and our approach to environmental protection in the long run?

Notes

1. Mary Graham, *The Morning After Earth Day: Practical Environmental Politics* (Washington, D.C.: Brookings Institution, 1999).
2. Frank R. Baumgartner and Bryan D. Jones, *Agendas and Instability in American Politics* (Chicago: University of Chicago Press, 1993), 4.
3. Herbert Kaufman, *The Administrative Behavior of Federal Bureau Chiefs* (Washington, D.C.: Brookings Institution, 1981); Kenneth J. Meier, *Politics and the Bureaucracy* (North Scituate, Mass.: Duxbury Press, 1979).
4. Francis E. Rourke, *Bureaucracy, Politics, and Public Policy*, 3d ed. (Boston: Little, Brown, 1976).
5. Clarence J. Davies III, *The Politics of Pollution* (New York: Pegasus, 1970).
6. Council on Environmental Quality, *Environmental Quality: The First Annual Report of the Council on Environmental Quality* (Washington, D.C.: U.S. Government Printing Office, 1970).
7. John F. Wall and Leonard B. Dworsky, *Problems of Executive Reorganization: The Federal Environmental Protection Agency* (Ithaca: Cornell University Water Resources and Marine Sciences Center, 1971).
8. An inversion is an atmospheric condition in which the air temperature rises with increasing altitude, holding surface air down and preventing the dispersion of pollutants.

9. Gary Bryner, *Blue Skies, Green Politics: The Clean Air Act of 1990* (Washington, D.C.: CQ Press, 1993).

10. Davies, *The Politics of Pollution.*

11. Wall and Dworsky, *Problems of Executive Reorganization.*

12. Davies, *The Politics of Pollution.*

13. Philip Shabecoff, *A Fierce Green Fire: The American Environmental Movement* (New York: Hill and Wang, 1993), 109–110.

14. Marc K. Landy, Marc J. Roberts, and Stephen R. Thomas, *The Environmental Protection Agency: Asking the Wrong Questions,* expanded edition. (New York: Oxford University Press, 1994).

15. Charles T. Rubin, *The Green Crusade: Rethinking the Roots of Environmentalism* (Lanham, Md.: Rowman and Littlefield, 1998).

16. Graham, *The Morning After Earth Day.*

17. Shabecoff, *A Fierce Green Fire.* Although the environmental groups did not engineer Earth Day, their memberships grew in the 1960s, rising from 124,000 in 1960 to 1,127,000 in 1972. See Robert Mitchell, "From Conservation to Environmental Movement: The Development of the Modern Environmental Lobbies," in *Government and Environmental Politics: Essays on Historical Developments Since World War Two,* ed. Michael Lacey (Baltimore: Johns Hopkins University Press, 1989), 81–113.

18. Kirkpatrick Sale, *The Green Revolution: The American Environmental Movement 1962–1992* (New York: Hill and Wang, 1993).

19. The following Earth Day anecdotes are assembled from reports in the *New York Times* and the *Washington Post,* April 23, 1970.

20. Mary Etta Cook and Roger H. Davidson, "Deferral Politics: Congressional Decision Making on Environmental Issues in the 1980s," in *Public Policy and the Natural Environment,* ed. Helen M. Ingram and R. Kenneth Godwin (Greenwich, Conn.: JAI Press, 1985), 47–76.

21. Hazel Erskine, "The Polls: Pollution and Its Costs," *Public Opinion Quarterly* 1 (Spring 1972): 120–135.

22. Samuel P. Hays, "The Politics of Environmental Administration," in *The New American State: Bureaucracies and Policies Since World War II,* ed. Louis Galambos (Baltimore: Johns Hopkins University Press, 1987), 23.

23. John C. Whitaker, *Striking a Balance: Environment and Natural Resources Policy in the Nixon-Ford Years* (Washington, D.C.: American Enterprise Institute, 1976).

24. "Transcript of the President's State of the Union Message to the Joint Session of Congress," *New York Times,* January 23, 1970, 22.

25. Ibid.

26. Council on Environmental Quality, *Environmental Quality.*

27. Ibid.

28. Richard A. Harris and Sidney M. Milkis, *The Politics of Regulatory Change: A Tale of Two Agencies* (New York: Oxford University Press, 1989).

29. Ibid.

30. Council on Environmental Quality, *Environmental Quality.*

31. Congress may not amend an executive reorganization proposal; it must approve or disapprove the entire package. To stop a reorganization, either chamber must adopt a resolution disapproving it within sixty days of its introduction.

32. Charles O. Jones, *Clean Air: The Policies and Politics of Pollution Control* (Pittsburgh: University of Pittsburgh Press, 1975).

33. U.S. Congress, Senate, *Congressional Record,* 91st Cong., 2d sess., March 4, 1970, S2955.

34. John C. Esposito, *Vanishing Air* (New York: Grossman, 1970), 270, 290–291.

35. Jones, *Clean Air,* 192.

36. Alfred Marcus, "Environmental Protection Agency," in *The Politics of Regulation,* ed. James Q. Wilson (New York: Basic Books, 1980), 267–303.

37. Primary standards must "protect the public health" by "an adequate margin of safety." Secondary standards must "protect the public welfare from any known or anticipated adverse effects."

38. Helen Ingram, "The Political Rationality of Innovation: The Clean Air Act Amendments of 1970," in *Approaches to Controlling Air Pollution*, ed. Anne F. Friedlander (Cambridge: MIT Press, 1978), 14.

39. An executive order is a presidential directive to an agency that enables the president to shape policy without getting the approval of Congress.

40. John Quarles, *Cleaning Up America: An Insider's View of Environmental Protection* (Boston: Houghton Mifflin, 1976).

41. Alfred Marcus, *Promise and Performance: Choosing and Implementing an Environmental Policy* (Westport, Conn.: Greenwood Press, 1980).

42. The National Environmental Policy Act, which took effect in 1970, requires federal agencies to complete environmental impact statements before embarking on any major project.

43. Congress can override a presidential veto with a two-thirds majority in both chambers.

44. R. Shep Melnick, *Regulation and the Courts: The Case of the Clean Air Act* (Washington, D.C.: Brookings Institution, 1983), 8.

45. The industry mounted only weak resistance to Muskie's attacks on it. According to journalist Richard Cohen, Muskie later speculated that some industry leaders "could see what was coming" and therefore gave limited cooperation (or got on the bandwagon). The passive attitude of the car manufacturers probably also reflected its strong financial position at the time (imports represented only 13 percent of all U.S. auto sales) and its weak lobbying operation. General Motors, for example, did not even establish a Washington lobbying office until 1969. See Richard Cohen, *Washington at Work: Back Rooms and Clean Air* (New York: Macmillan, 1992).

46. Arnold Howitt, "The Environmental Protection Agency and Transportation Controls," in *Managing Federalism: Studies in Intergovernmental Relations* (Washington, D.C.: CQ Press, 1986), 116.

47. Graham, *The Morning After Earth Day*, 31.

48. Quoted in ibid., 53.

49. Howitt, "The Environmental Protection Agency," 125.

50. Marcus, *Promise and Performance*.

51. Quarles, *Cleaning Up America*, 61.

52. The number of business-related political action committees (PACs) also increased from 248 in 1974 to 1,100 in 1978. See David Vogel, "The Power of Business in America: A Reappraisal," *British Journal of Political Science* 13 (1983): 19–43.

53. More than 2,000 companies contested EPA standards within the first few years of its operation. See James T. Patterson, *Grand Expectations: The United States, 1945–1974* (New York: Oxford University Press, 1996).

54. Marcus, *Promise and Performance*.

55. Transportation control measures include creating bicycle paths and car-free zones, rationing gas, imposing gas taxes, building mass transit, creating bus lanes, encouraging carpooling, and establishing vehicle inspection and maintenance programs.

56. Quoted in Marcus, *Promise and Performance*, 133.

57. Howitt, "The Environmental Protection Agency."

58. Marcus, *Promise and Performance*.

59. The law required the EPA to grant permits to all industrial and government polluters, including 21,000 municipal sewage treatment facilities.

60. Marcus, *Promise and Performance*.

61. Recall that the original Clean Air Act did not allow the EPA to consider economic and technical factors.

62. Marcus, *Promise and Performance*.

63. Conventional pollutants are solids, biochemical oxygen demand (BOD) pollutants, pH, and fecal coliform.

64. Marcus, *Promise and Performance*.

65. Dick Kirschten, "EPA: A Winner in the Annual Budget Battle," *National Journal*, January 28, 1978, 140–141.

66. Ibid.

67. Paul R. Portney, "EPA and the Evolution of Federal Regulation," in *Public Policies for Environmental Protection*, 2d ed., ed. Paul R. Portney and Robert N. Stavins (Washington, D.C.: Resources for the Future, 2000), 11–30.

68. U.S. Environmental Protection Agency, *Latest Findings on National Air Quality: 2002 Status and Trends*, August 2003, EPA 454/K-03-001. The EPA estimates emissions based on actual monitored readings and engineering calculations of the amounts and types of pollutants emitted by different sources. The agency is continuously revising its estimation methods, so each year's estimates are slightly different from the previous year's.

69. Walter Rosenbaum, *Environmental Politics and Policy*, 5th ed. (Washington, D.C.: CQ Press, 2001).

70. U.S. GAO, *EPA: Major Performance and Accountability Challenges*, GAO-01-257 (January 2001). In 2000, EPA's National Water Quality Inventory reported somewhat lower numbers: 19 percent of rivers and streams; 43 percent of lakes, ponds, and reservoirs; and 36 percent of estuaries.

71. U.S. Environmental Protection Agency, "Water Quality Conditions in the United States," Fact Sheet, 2000. Available at www.epa.gov/305b/2000report/.

72. A. Myrick Freeman III, "Water Pollution Policy," in *Public Policies for Environmental Protection*, 169–213.

73. Nonpoint sources are regulated through the EPA's TMDL (total maximum daily load) rule, which requires states to develop TMDLs specifying the amount of each pollutant that a body of water can receive and still meet water quality standards and allocating pollutant loadings among point and nonpoint sources. Although the Clean Water Act has required TMDLs since 1972, until recently few states had developed them. In the 1990s, in response to a wave of citizen suits, states began preparing TMDLs.

74. Council on Environmental Quality, *Environmental Quality: The Fifteenth Annual Report of the Council on Environmental Quality* (Washington, D.C.: U.S. Government Printing Office, 1984).

75. Since the 1600s the lower forty-eight states have lost half of the nation's 220 million acres of wetlands. Development destroyed almost 460,000 acres per year in the 1970s, but since then the rate of loss has slowed. See www.epa.gov/owow/wetlands/facts/contents.htm. (Other organizations put the figure for current wetlands loss substantially higher.)

76. Rosemary O'Leary, "Environmental Policy in the Courts," in *Environmental Policy: New Directions for the Twenty-First Century*, 6th ed., eds. Norman J. Vig and Michael E. Kraft (Washington, D.C.: CQ Press, 2006), 148–168.

77. Freeman, "Water Pollution Policy," in *Public Policies for Environmental Protection*.

78. Americans continue to name air and water pollution as the world's most important environmental problems. Gallup poll release, "Despite Dire Predictions of Global Warming, Americans Have Other Priorities," www.gallup.com/poll/releases/pr010220.asp.

Recommended Reading

Graham, Mary. *The Morning After Earth Day: Practical Environmental Politics*. Washington, D.C.: Brookings Institution, 1999.

Landy, Marc K., Marc J. Roberts, and Stephen R. Thomas. *The Environmental Protection Agency: Asking the Wrong Questions.* Expanded edition. New York: Oxford University Press, 1994.

Shabecoff, Philip. *A Fierce Green Fire: The American Environmental Movement.* New York: Hill and Wang, 1993.

Web Sites

www.epa.gov (Environmental Protection Agency site)

CHAPTER 3

Love Canal

Hazardous Waste and the Politics of Fear

In the summer of 1978 Americans began to hear about a terrifying public health nightmare in Niagara Falls, New York. According to news reports, hundreds of families were being poisoned by a leaking toxic waste dump underneath their homes. Residents plagued by cancer, miscarriages, and birth defects were demanding to be evacuated and relocated. The episode, known simply as "Love Canal," became a national story because "it radicalized apparently ordinary people. [It] severed the bond between citizens and their city, their state, and their country."[1] Love Canal also shaped public attitudes about abandoned toxic dump sites—about the risks they pose and about government's responsibility for ensuring they are cleaned up. In addition, the incident was the catalyst for the nation's most expensive environmental law: the Comprehensive Environmental Response, Compensation, and Liability Act of 1980, popularly known as the Superfund Act.

The Love Canal case highlights the role of science and scientific experts in controversies over threats to human health. Experts' emphasis on detachment and objectivity can alienate a public that feels it has been harmed. Experts contend that the public is deeply concerned about environmental threats, such as hazardous waste, that pose relatively small risks, while more serious problems, such as climate change and wetlands loss, get short shrift. The reason is that experts and lay people perceive risks very differently. For experts, human health risk corresponds closely to statistical estimates of annual fatalities. Lay people, however, incorporate a much richer set of considerations—including voluntariness, immediacy, familiarity, and control—into their understanding of risk. The public particularly fears low probability catastrophic and "dread" risks. Moreover, because people's risk perceptions are based on general inferential rules (heuristics) that feel like common sense, they tend to be resistant to change, even in the face of compelling scientific evidence.[2]

Experts often unwittingly contribute to public alarm and confusion in other ways as well. For example, scientists calculate the cancer risk posed by prolonged exposure to small amounts of a chemical by extrapolating from the results of animal bioassays, epidemiological studies, and cellular analyses.[3] In doing so, they make a variety of assumptions that reflect their values—in particular their beliefs about the levels of risk to which the public *ought* to be exposed.[4] Because experts' values differ, they often arrive at divergent assessments. The resulting phenomenon of dueling experts breeds mistrust among the public, which lacks the wherewithal to sort out competing technical claims.

To enhance their technical competence, citizens have devised ways of acquiring information about environmental health risks using community-based participatory research, in which communities work collaboratively with scientists to investigate and address issues of local concern. One mode of participatory inquiry is popular epidemiology, a process by which laypersons gather scientific data and other information and marshal the knowledge of experts to understand the incidence of a disease.[5] Proponents of popular epidemiology believe that tools such as community health surveys bring to the fore environmental data and circumstances that traditional epidemiological studies otherwise would not elicit.[6] More important, they believe that putting information in the hands of citizens empowers them and enables them to transfer problems from the (inaccessible) technical realm to the political arena.

Even when armed with compelling information, however, citizens are likely to encounter tremendous resistance by state and local politicians to addressing environmental health threats. Those officials feel constrained by the need to foster economic development in order to retain high-income taxpayers.[7] In addition, because industry is mobile, officials tend to be cautious about taking on polluters for fear of alienating companies that employ citizens in the community.[8] They also may be reluctant to intervene because they want to avoid financial responsibility for problems that promise to be costly to solve.

Publicity can change this political dynamic in several ways. First, media coverage of a risk mobilizes citizens because people assume that the more attention the media pay to a risk the worse it must be. According to psychologist Baruch Fischhoff, "If scientists are studying it and the news reports it, people assume it must be worth their attention." [9] Moreover, because media coverage emphasizes dramatic, newsworthy events, the reports are likely to be alarming and hence effective at activating citizen groups. The media then amplify such groups' political influence by covering their activities. By focusing on human interest stories and anecdotes, journalists create victims, villains, and heroes. When such stories involve human health threats, particularly to children, they appeal to highly consensual values and have enormous potential to resonate with the broader public. Media attention galvanizes not only citizens but also elected officials, who fear the consequences of negative publicity.[10] Critical media coverage may put policymakers on the defensive, forcing them either to justify a problem or act to solve it.[11] In addition, policymakers use the extent of media coverage to gauge the intensity and nature of public opinion on that issue.[12]

BACKGROUND

Love Canal is the site of a forty-acre chemical landfill in the city of Niagara Falls, New York. In the late nineteenth century, entrepreneur William T. Love received permission from the New York State legislature to build a canal that would divert the Niagara River away from the falls for about seven miles, dropping nearly 300 feet before it reconnected to the river. The canal was the centerpiece of Love's scheme to construct a vast industrial city fueled by cheap and abundant hydropower.

Love dug a mile-long trench that was ten feet deep and about fifteen feet wide, then built a factory and a few homes alongside it. But his dream collapsed in the mid-1890s when a financial depression caused investors to withdraw their support. In any case, the 1910 advent of alternating current, which allowed power to be transported over long distances, rendered the notion of an industrial city near its power source less compelling. In a final blow, the U.S. Congress passed a law barring Love from diverting water from the Niagara because it wanted to preserve the falls. The abandoned canal soon became a popular fishing, swimming, and picnicking spot for residents.

In 1920 the canal was sold at public auction and became a municipal disposal site. Then, in 1942 the Niagara Power and Development Corporation gave the Hooker Chemical and Plastics Corporation permission to dispose of wastes in the abandoned canal, and in 1947 it sold the canal and sixteen acres of surrounding land to Hooker. Between 1942 and 1952 Hooker dumped about 22,000 tons of toxic chemical wastes at the site, widening or deepening the canal in places to accommodate its needs.[13] Company officials were aware that the materials they were dumping were dangerous to human health; residents recall workers at the site rushing to neighboring yards to wash their burns with water from garden hoses. As early as 1943, a letter to the *Niagara Gazette* claimed that the smell was unbearable and that the white cloud that came from the site "killed the grass and trees and burnt the paint off the back of the houses and made the other houses all black." [14] A favorite game of neighborhood children was to pick up phosphorous rocks, throw them against the cement, and watch them explode. In the hot weather, spontaneous fires broke out, and noxious odors wafted through open windows of nearby homes.[15] Nevertheless, from the company's perspective, the site was ideal: it was large, lined with walls of thick, impermeable clay and located in a thinly populated area. Furthermore, although Hooker took only minimal safety precautions— simply depositing drums or dumping the wastes directly into the pits and covering them with small amounts of topsoil—the company followed dumping practices that were legally acceptable at the time.

By 1952 the canal was nearly full. Hooker and the city of Niagara Falls covered the dumpsite with a protective clay cap and earth, and soon weeds and grasses began to sprout on its surface. In 1953, when city officials were looking for inexpensive land on which to build a school, Hooker obliged them by transferring the sixteen-acre site to the Board of Education for a token fee of one dollar. At that time, Hooker issued no detailed warnings about the possible hazards posed by the buried chemicals. The company did, however, include in the deed a disclaimer that identified the wastes in a general way and excused it from liability for any injuries or deaths that might occur at the site.[16] School board members toured the area with Hooker representatives and took test borings that showed chemicals in two locations only four feet below the surface. Yet the school board—apparently unconcerned about any potential health threat and despite the misgivings of its own architect—began to build an elementary school and playground at the canal's midsection. When workers started to excavate and discovered chemical pits and buried drums, the board simply moved the school eighty-five feet north and installed a drainage system to divert accumulating water into the Niagara River.

Not long after the 99th Street Elementary School was completed, the school board donated some unused property to the city to build streets and sidewalks. Then some homebuilders approached the board about trading part of the Love Canal site for parcels the board wanted. At a meeting in November 1957, representatives of Hooker strongly opposed the trade, saying they had made clear at the original transfer that the site was unsuitable for any construction that required basements and sewer lines. Apparently heeding Hooker's warnings, the school board voted against the trade, but developers began to build modest, single-family houses around the borders of the site anyway. During construction, contractors cut channels through the clay walls lining the hidden canal and used topsoil from the canal surface for fill. Because these houses were on land that was not part of the original transaction between the school board and Hooker, the property owners' deeds did not notify them of chemicals buried in the adjoining land.[17]

In 1960 the school board gave the northern portion of the site to the city, and in 1961 it sold the southern portion at auction. By that time, the city had already installed streets paralleling and crisscrossing the canal. In the late 1960s the state ran the LaSalle Expressway through the southern end of the site, necessitating relocation of a main street and uncovering chemical wastes that Hooker agreed to cart away.[18] By the early 1970s, the area around the canal was a working-class neighborhood; there were nearly 100 homes on 97th and 99th streets with backyards abutting a long, empty lot that should have been 98th Street but was really a chemical-filled trench (see Map 3-1, page 69).[19]

Individual residents around the Love Canal site throughout the 1950s and 1960s complained to the municipal government about odors and odd afflictions, including rashes and respiratory problems, as well as oily black substances in basements and exposed, rusting barrels in fields around their homes. Members of crews building streets in the area complained of itchy skin and blisters. In 1958 Hooker investigated reports that three or four children had been burned by debris on their former property, but the company did not publicize the presence of the chemicals even after this incident, probably because it feared liability.[20] Municipal records indicate that by 1969 building inspectors had also examined the Love Canal dumpsite area and reported that the conditions were hazardous: as the rusting barrels collapsed, holes appeared on the surface of the field, and chemical residues remained on the field after rainwater had evaporated.[21] Still, the city took no action to investigate the problem further or to remedy it.

THE CASE

The early history of Love Canal is more indicative of Americans' general faith in technology and complacency about chemical wastes during the postwar years than of venality on the part of municipal officials. Even in the 1970s, however, when it became apparent that there were potentially serious problems at the site, local officials continued to ignore them or tried to deal with them quietly, fearing not only the costs of cleanup but also the consequences of antagonizing a major employer and source of tax revenue. Addressing the possible hazards in the area threatened to inflict economic consequences and tarnish the city's image. Only when the media began to pay attention to the issue, in turn prompting residents to mobilize and demand a solution, did elected officials respond.

The City of Niagara Falls Stonewalls

In the mid-1970s, when a prolonged period of wet weather dramatically changed the area's hydrology, visible signs of a problem at Love Canal began to appear. The LaSalle Expressway along the canal's southern end blocked the groundwater from migrating southward to the Niagara River. In 1976 the built-up groundwater overflowed the clay basin holding the waste and carried contaminants through the upper silt layer and along recently constructed sewer lines. From there it seeped into yards and basements of nearby houses.

Trees and shrubs in the area began to turn brown and die. The field covering the canal site turned into a mucky quagmire dotted with pools of contaminated liquid. One family became alarmed when they noticed their swimming pool had risen two feet out of the ground. When they removed the pool, the hole quickly filled with chemical liquid, and soon their backyard was a wasteland. Local authorities pumped 17,500 gallons of chemical-filled water out of the yard in two days. The county's largest waste disposal company refused to handle it, and the waste water had to be trucked to Ohio and poured down a deep-well disposal site.[22]

In 1977 Michael Brown, a reporter from the *Niagara Gazette*, became interested in Love Canal after hearing an eloquent plea for help from a resident at a public meeting. When Brown began to investigate, it became clear to him that both the city manager and the mayor of Niagara Falls were stonewalling residents who tried to contact them or to speak up in city council meetings. Brown quickly ascertained that city officials had been aware for some time that the situation was serious.

Brown also discovered that a fellow reporter, David Pollack, had documented the history of chemical dumping at Love Canal in October 1976. When Pollack got a private company, Chem-Trol, to analyze the sludge from some Love Canal basements, the company found toxic chemicals and determined that Hooker was their source. Pollack also ascertained that in early 1976 the New York Department of Environmental Conservation (DEC) had begun testing houses around the canal site after tracing high levels of the pesticide Mirex in Lake Ontario fish to a dumpsite adjacent to the canal.[23] The DEC's investigation revealed that polychlorinated biphenyls (PCBs) and other highly toxic materials were flowing from the canal into adjoining sewers.[24] The DEC's study was proceeding slowly, however, because the agency lacked adequate funding, personnel, and equipment. Furthermore, the DEC got little cooperation: Hooker denied all responsibility, and municipal officials—uneasy about antagonizing the city's largest industrial employer and worried about the magnitude of the city's own liability—preferred to address the problem discreetly.

In April 1977 the city, with some funding from Hooker, hired the Calspan Corporation to develop a program to reduce the groundwater pollution at Love Canal. Calspan documented the presence of exposed, corroded drums and noxious fumes and notified officials that chemical contamination was extensive. That summer the *Niagara Gazette* published a summary of the Calspan report and urged the city to undertake the cleanup project recommended by its consultants. The city declined, however, and the story was insufficiently dramatic to capture residents' attention. In September a municipal employee concerned about the city's inaction contacted Rep. John LaFalce, D-N.Y., the district's member of Congress, and urged him to tour the area. Unable to get a response from the city manager, LaFalce asked the Environmental Protection Agency (EPA) to test the air in the basements along 97th and 99th streets. In October, soon after LaFalce's visit, the regional EPA administrator wrote in an internal memorandum that, based on what he had seen, "serious thought should be given to the purchase of some or all of the homes affected." [25]

By April 1978 New York health commissioner Robert Whalen had become sufficiently concerned that he directed Niagara County's health commissioner to remove exposed chemicals, build a fence around the dumpsite, and begin health studies of area residents.[26] In May the EPA released the results of its air-sampling studies. At a public meeting at the 99th Street School, agency officials told residents that they had found benzene in the air of their basements. At this point, Michael Brown, shocked by the EPA's reports and disturbed by the unwillingness of local officials to acknowledge the seriousness of the problem, undertook his own investigation.

The Local Media Raise Residents' Concern

Brown's story in the *Niagara Gazette* on the benzene hazard claimed that there was a "full fledged environmental crisis" under way at Love Canal. With local and county authorities unwilling to investigate further, Brown conducted an informal health survey and found a startling list of residents' ailments—from ear infections and nervous disorders to rashes and headaches. Pets were losing their fur and getting skin lesions and tumors; women seemed to have a disproportionate incidence of cancer; and several children were deaf.[27]

By repeating residents' claims about their health problems, Brown's reporting enhanced their perceptions of the threats posed by the buried chemicals. Until the spring of 1978 residents had been only dimly aware of the potential association between the fumes and chemical wastewater and their health problems. But as articles began to appear in the *Niagara Gazette* and then in the

Buffalo papers that May and June, some local people became alarmed. Lois Gibbs, a resident of 101st Street since 1972, made a frightening connection: Gibbs's son, Michael, had begun attending kindergarten at the 99th Street School and had developed epilepsy soon afterwards. Gibbs contacted her brother-in-law, a biologist at the State University of New York (SUNY) at Buffalo, and he explained the health problems that could be produced by chemicals dumped in the canal. Gibbs tried to transfer Michael to a different school, but school administrators resisted.

Disconcerted, the normally reticent Gibbs started going door-to-door with a petition demanding that the city address residents' concerns about the school. Talking day after day with neighbors, she discovered that some homeowners were worried that bad news about Love Canal would cause property values to decline and had formed a group to agitate for property tax abatement and mortgage relief. Gibbs also became deeply familiar with the health problems of canal area residents. To her,

> it seemed as though every home on 99th Street had someone with an illness. One family had a young daughter with arthritis. . . . Another daughter had had a miscarriage. The father, still a fairly young man, had had a heart attack. . . . Then I remembered my own neighbors. One . . . was suffering from severe migraines and had been hospitalized three or four times that year. Her daughter had kidney problems and bleeding. A woman on the other side of us had gastrointestinal problems. A man in the next house down was dying of lung cancer and he didn't even work in the [chemical] industry. The man across the street had just had lung surgery.[28]

Armed with this worrisome anecdotal evidence, Gibbs transformed herself into a highly effective policy entrepreneur. Although this was her first experience with political activism, Gibbs realized that she would need an organization behind her to wield any political clout. Following the strategic advice of her brother-in-law, she founded the Love Canal Homeowners Association (LCHA), which became the most visible and persistent of the citizen groups formed during this period. Gibbs devoted nearly all her waking hours to its activities. Her primary function was to promote a simple causal story—that Hooker had irresponsibly dumped dangerous chemicals that were making residents ill—and link it to her preferred solution: evacuation and compensation for all the families in the area.

Assessing (and Avoiding) Blame

The first response of government officials to LCHA activism was to try to shift responsibility to other levels of government. "It's a county health problem," said City Manager Donald O'Hara. "But if the state says the city has the authority to move them out and the people want to be moved, then we'll move them." Dr. Francis J. Clifford, the county health commissioner, responded: "Of course Don O'Hara says the responsibility is with the county. If I were him, I'd say the same thing. The lawyers will fight it out." [29] Everyone hoped to pin the blame on the federal government, with its deep pockets, especially upon hearing of witnesses' claims that the U.S. Army had also dumped wastes into the canal in the early 1950s. But after a brief investigation, the Department of Defense denied those allegations.

In the meantime, the county did little more than install a couple of inexpensive fans in two homes and erect a fence that children could still walk through without knocking it over. The municipal government was equally dilatory: the city council voted not to spend public money for cleanup because some of the site was owned by a private citizen living in Philadelphia. The city's tax assessor refused to grant any tax abatement on the homes, even though banks would not mortgage them and lawyers refused to title them.[30]

The city was also reluctant to pursue Hooker Chemical because it was an important employer and taxpayer in an area historically dependent on the chemical industry. At that time, Hooker employed about 3,000 workers from the Niagara area. The plant at Niagara Falls was the largest of Hooker's sixty manufacturing operations, and Hooker's corporate headquarters were there as well. Even more important, Hooker was planning to build a $17 million headquarters downtown. Municipal officials were offering Hooker a lucrative package of tax breaks and loans as well as a $13.2 million mortgage on a prime parcel of land.[31]

Hooker maintained from the outset that it had no legal obligations with respect to Love Canal. Once it began getting negative press coverage, the company retaliated with a concerted effort to redefine the problem: it launched a nationwide campaign involving thousands of glossy pamphlets and a traveling two-man "truth" squad to convince the media that the problems at Love Canal were not its fault. Hooker representatives emphasized that the canal had been the best available technology at the time. The company, they said, was merely acting as a good corporate citizen, not admitting guilt, when it contributed money toward the city-sponsored Calspan study and volunteered to share cleanup costs.

The National Media Expand the Scope of the Conflict

Normally, such a united front by industry and local officials would have squelched attempts at remediation, but citizens' mobilization—combined with sympathetic media coverage of their complaints and demonstrations—enhanced the residents' clout. Early August marked a turning point in the controversy because the arrival of *New York Times* reporter Donald McNeil on the scene transformed a local issue into a national one. In turn, national press coverage inflamed residents' passion and further escalated tensions.[32] Within a day of McNeil's first report on the situation, reporters from other national newspapers converged on Niagara Falls. The media's coverage of the ensuing confrontations was compelling because it conveyed the image of Hooker as, at worst, a malevolent villain and, at best, an irresponsible one, while depicting residents as ordinary citizens and innocent victims.

Meanwhile, the New York Department of Health (DOH) was collecting blood samples, surveying residents, and testing air samples in homes to ascertain the actual health threats posed by the buried waste. In early July 1978 residents received forms from the state indicating high levels of chemicals in their houses but providing little information about what those levels meant. On August 2 Commissioner Whalen announced the results of DOH's first large-scale health study of the area: researchers had found ten carcinogenic compounds in vapors in the houses at levels from 250 to 5,000 times as high as those considered safe. They also found that women living at the southern end of the canal suffered an unusually high rate of miscarriages and that their children were afflicted with an abnormally high rate of birth defects: a 29.4 percent miscarriage rate and five children out of twenty-four with birth defects. Four children in one small section of the neighborhood had serious birth defects: clubfeet, retardation, and deafness. The people who had lived in the area the longest had the most problems.[33]

Whalen declared a public health emergency and concluded that there was a "great and imminent peril" to the health of the people living in and around Love Canal.[34] He urged people to take precautionary measures to avoid contamination but offered no permanent solutions. He was unwilling to declare the neighborhood uninhabitable but did advise people to avoid spending time in their basements or eating vegetables from their gardens. Finally, he recommended that pregnant women and children under the age of two move out of the area.

On August 3, 150 residents—incensed by Whalen's announcement and fueled by the media coverage—met in front of their homes to collect mortgage bills and resolve not to pay them. They also planned to demand aid from the government or Hooker so they could relocate. Said one resident: "If they take my house, I owe $10,000 on it. . . . I couldn't sell it for ten. They won't kick me out for two years, and that's two years' taxes and payments I save to find someplace else." [35] The following evening, the first families began leaving the contaminated site, toting their cribs and suitcases past a scrawled sign that read: "Wanted, safe home for two toddlers."

As the summer wore on, public meetings became more acrimonious. Residents were frustrated because DOH scientists, in their attempts to conduct objective research, were reluctant to counsel fearful residents about the results of their medical tests. Furthermore, the government officials to whom the scientists deferred in decision making refused to act, awaiting definitive study results and, more important, a clear assessment of financial culpability. At one packed meeting in a hot, crowded school auditorium, sobbing young mothers stood up shouting out the ages of their children or the terms of their pregnancies and asked whether they would be moved out of their houses. As one journalist described the scene, "Angry young fathers, still in the sweaty T-shirts they had worn to work in local chemical factories, stood on chairs and demanded to know what would happen to their small children if their wives and infants were moved." [36]

Media coverage of their plight was particularly well-timed because Hugh Carey, the governor of New York, was facing an election in November 1978 and so felt compelled to respond to residents' highly publicized pleas. The state set up an office in a local school and provided rent vouchers, medical advice, and moving help for the thirty-seven families with pregnant women or infants under two years of age. Federal officials felt compelled to respond to the spate of newspaper stories as well: on August 6, 1978, William Wilcox of the Federal Disaster Assistance Administration inspected the site at the request of President Jimmy Carter. The following day, the president declared an emergency at Love Canal and approved federal relief funds for the area.[37]

Shortly after this announcement, Governor Carey toured Love Canal for the first time. During the visit, he pledged to relocate the 239 "inner ring" families and purchase their homes on 97th and 99th streets. Once these families were evacuated, he said, the state planned to raze the houses as well as the 99th Street School and begin a massive construction program to stop the leaching and seal the canal. The remediation plan, laid out in an engineering study sponsored jointly by the city and Hooker, called for ditches to be dug eight to ten feet deep along the periphery of the filled canal and drainage tiles to be laid and covered over. Chemical-laden water leaking out of the old clay canal bed would run down the tiles into a collecting basin, from which it would be pumped and taken for treatment or disposal.

The Outer Ring Residents Are Left Behind

The residents of the "outer ring" between 93d and 103d streets were enraged by this solution, feeling that the state was ignoring their predicament. They too had experienced health problems, and studies had detected high levels of chemicals in their houses as well. Under the supervision of Beverly Paigen, a biologist and cancer researcher who was helping residents interpret the information they received from the health department, the LCHA undertook one of the earliest efforts to do popular epidemiology—a telephone survey to ascertain the pattern of illnesses in the historically wet drainage areas around the canal. But when Dr. Paigen analyzed the data and presented her results, complete with qualifying statements about her methodology, the DOH dismissed her findings, saying that the study was meaningless because it was put together by a "bunch of housewives with an interest in the outcome of the study." [38]

Frustrated, Lois Gibbs and the LCHA continued to press the state to relocate the outer ring families, fearing their political leverage would decline after the gubernatorial election in November. By this point, Gibbs had become adept at raising the salience of her cause: she orchestrated dozens of public demonstrations and rallies, wrote letters and made phone calls to officials, submitted to interviews on talk shows and news programs, and even testified

before a congressional subcommittee. As a result, her version of events dominated national perceptions of the situation.

The state nevertheless continued to resist the idea of relocating the families
who lived on the outskirts of the contaminated area. Groups of angry, outer
ring residents began to picket the cleanup site, and on December 11 about fifty
people braved twelve-degree temperatures to stop workers' cars attempting
to enter the site. The police arrested six demonstrators for obstructing traffic.
Deepening the residents' desperation, the state announced it had discovered
dioxin at Love Canal. A *New York Times* report dramatized the lethal potential
of dioxin, a byproduct of herbicide production, by noting that "three ounces,
minced small enough into New York City's water supply, could wipe out the
city." [39]

To the disappointment of the LCHA, on January 29 the Federal Disaster
Assistance Administration rejected an appeal from the state to reimburse it for
the $23 million it spent removing the inner ring families and cleaning up the
site. This decision increased financial pressure on state officials and made
them even more reluctant to engage in a costly second relocation. The state's
own experts were not cooperating, however; a blue-ribbon panel appointed by
the governor concluded in early February that the site was hazardous, which
led David Axelrod, the newly installed health commissioner, to order that
pregnant women and families with children under the age of two be removed
temporarily from the area. This action only fueled Gibbs's rage: she pointed
out that if the place was dangerous for pregnant women and children, it posed
a threat to everyone else as well.[40] Although twenty-four families moved, hundreds more remained in limbo. By this time, according to Gibbs, reporters
were becoming impatient with the LCHA, and were beginning to ask, "If
you're so afraid, why don't you just leave?" Residents replied that they were
working people who had invested a lifetime of earnings in their homes. Where
would they go? they asked. What would they live on?

Experts Versus Citizens

For the families that remained, more uncertainty lay ahead. The $9.2 mil-
lion cleanup effort encountered frequent delays as people raised safety concerns and public officials quarreled over new health studies. By August 1979
Love Canal residents had endured another long, hot summer made more
oppressive by the fumes from the remedial construction site. For weeks people had been calling the LCHA office to say they were experiencing headaches,
difficulty breathing, and burning, itching eyes. The DOH scheduled a public
meeting for August 21, and residents again anticipated answers to questions
about their health and their future.

Instead, what turned out to be the final meeting between residents and the
commissioner of public health did little more than cement the antagonism
between them. During the meeting, Dr. Axelrod acknowledged that the department had found dioxin in the soil but said the remaining residents would have

to deal with the risks on their own. With that, what little remained of residents' faith in scientific experts and government officials evaporated. According to Lois Gibbs, the officials "offered no answers, no useful information. The residents' confidence was shaken time and again. They didn't trust the safety plan or the construction plan or the health department officials. People were more frustrated when they left than when they arrived." [41] Sociologist Adeline Levine describes in vivid terms the deepening alienation of residents:

> The more that officials met with residents, the more negative feelings and relationships developed. When professionals presented raw data, it confused people. When they tried to interpret the data in down-to-earth terms, describing risks as some number of deaths in excess of the usual number expected, people interpreted that to imply *their* deaths and their children's deaths. When they tried to calm people by saying that, despite all the serious possibilities, there was no evidence of serious health effects, the officials were seen as covering up, since no health studies had been done. Authorities trying to coordinate multiple governmental and private agencies were seen as wasting time in meetings. What the officials thought of as privileged advisory conferences were viewed as conclaves that excluded affected citizens. What officials saw as preliminary studies conducted to assess the situation were viewed by residents as wasting resources on repetitious research projects rather than doing something helpful. When they took action quickly or tried to do everything at once, for everyone, they overloaded facilities, made errors, and were faulted for bungling.[42]

At the end of August 1979 the Niagara Falls school board voted to close the 93d Street Middle School. Shortly thereafter, 110 families moved into hotels, taking advantage of an LCHA-initiated court settlement in which state officials agreed that, until the drainage ditches were complete, they would pay the hotel bills and a $13 per day meal allowance for those suffering medical problems because of fumes from the remedial construction site. The state emphasized that it was not paying for a permanent evacuation.

On November 6 the state finished construction of the multimillion-dollar drainage system at the dump site, and officials announced that the families could return to their homes. But a dozen of them refused. Challenging the cutoff of payments and asserting that their homes continued to be unsafe, the group vowed to stay at the motel until they were carried out.[43] As usual, Gibbs was hoping the motel sit-in would draw high-level attention to the situation facing the outer ring residents. She was well aware that Governor Carey had already signed legislation authorizing the state to spend $5 million to buy up to 550 additional homes in the outer ring, most of them to the west of the canal, including her own house. The buyout had been mired in political squabbles and red tape, however, as local officials continued to resist taking responsibility for the problem.

By the end of 1979 the money for relocating the outer ring families still was not forthcoming. As negotiations between the state and federal governments dragged on, skeptical residents feared that the public's interest was beginning to wane and that with it would go the pressure on politicians to act. Their fears were confirmed when, on February 24, 1980, the EPA announced that air monitors in two houses several hundred yards from the fence around the canal had detected four suspected carcinogens: benzene, chloroform, trichloroethylene, and tetrachloroethylene. To residents' dismay, that disclosure merited only a few paragraphs in the Metro section of the *New York Times*. Similarly, scant notice was taken of Attorney General Robert Abrams's filing, on April 28, of a lawsuit against the Occidental Petroleum Corporation and two of its subsidiaries, Hooker Chemical Corporation and Hooker Chemicals and Plastics Corporation, charging them with responsibility for the Love Canal disaster. With a presidential campaign in full swing, an influx of Cuban refugees, and the eruption of Mt. St. Helens, the focus of the national press had shifted.

Health Studies Breed Panic and More Publicity

Federal officials had, however, unwittingly set in motion the catalyst that would irrevocably change the fortunes of Love Canal residents. In early 1979 the EPA, hoping to bolster its tarnished public image on dealing with hazardous waste, had created the Hazardous Waste Enforcement Task Force, and the task force's first assignment was to collect information about Love Canal. On December 20 the Department of Justice, relying on evidence gathered by the task force, filed a lawsuit on behalf of the EPA against Hooker Chemical, the Niagara County Health Department, the city of Niagara Falls, and the city's board of education. The suit demanded $124.5 million, an end to the discharge of toxins in the Love Canal area, cleanup of the site, and relocation of residents if necessary. The lawsuit was remarkable because it asked the court to hold a private company retroactively liable for wastes it dumped many years ago in a site it no longer controlled.

To establish liability the Justice Department had to prove that the health damages suffered by residents were linked directly to Hooker's wastes. Evidence had shown that the area was contaminated by toxic chemicals and that residents had unusually high rates of health problems, but to link those damages unequivocally to Hooker required further evidence. The Justice Department and the EPA hired Biogenics of Houston, headed by Dr. Dante Picciano, to investigate chromosomal damage among the residents because such impairment indicates exposure to toxic chemicals. The lawyers intended this study to be purely exploratory: if the results were positive, the lawyers could order a full-blown epidemiological study.

From the outset Picciano's work was flawed in ways that jeopardized its credibility. First, Picciano was a controversial figure due to a much-publicized falling out with his former employer, Dow Chemical, over his tests of that company's workers. Second, and more critical, the study of Love Canal residents did not include a control group, apparently because the EPA did not wish to spend the time or money for one. And third, researchers selected study participants according to criteria that would maximize the chance of finding defects;

that is, they intentionally chose people who had had miscarriages or other health problems. Despite these methodological weaknesses, in spring 1980 the study moved forward, and in early May Biogenics made the preliminary results of its study available. Picciano reported that he had found chromosomal aberrations in eleven of the thirty-six individuals tested. He concluded that eight of them had a rare condition called "supernumerary acentric fragments," or extra pieces of genetic material.[44] According to Picciano, such abnormalities should occur in only 1 percent of individuals and might forewarn increased risk of miscarriages, stillborns, birth defects, or cancer.[45] Nevertheless, he advised prudence in using this data given the absence of a control group.

On May 17 someone leaked the Biogenics story to the *New York Times,* and media attention quickly returned to Love Canal. The EPA scrambled to control the damage, hastily scheduling a press conference in Niagara, preceded by private consultations with each of the residents in whom Picciano had detected abnormalities. The agency set aside half an hour for each family with a doctor who would explain the results and answer questions. Following the individual sessions, EPA representatives gave local and national press conferences. Even though officials were aware of the need to interpret the study results cautiously, especially as the investigation was exploratory and had not been designed to be scientifically valid, they were unable to control the ensuing media frenzy.

Love Canal residents were stunned by the news, and, as White House officials held strategy meetings in Washington, their dismay grew. Federal officials, recognizing the impact of the media coverage, raced to get the Biogenics study peer reviewed and decide on a course of action. In the meantime, the *New York Times* reported that Governor Carey and the White House were in an all-out feud over who would foot the bill for a large-scale relocation, which now appeared unavoidable.

At the LCHA offices on Monday, a crowd of anxious residents and the press gathered to await news of the government's next move. When the headline "White House Blocks Love Canal Pullout" appeared in the *Buffalo Evening News,* the crowd became agitated: people began stopping cars to spread the word, and one group set a fire in the shape of the letters "EPA" across the street. A few minutes later, a crowd of 200 blocked traffic on both ends of the street. Gibbs, hoping to defuse residents' ire, summoned the two EPA officials who were still in Niagara to address the crowd. Once she got them inside the LCHA building, however, Gibbs refused to let them leave, and for several hours residents held the officials hostage in a sweltering office. Gibbs explained that they were simply protecting the officials from a potentially violent mob. She moved back and forth between the crowd and the hostages, assuring each that the situation was under control. Finally, the FBI threatened to rush the crowd. Three FBI agents, four U.S. marshals, and six members of the Niagara Falls Police Department escorted the EPA officials from the LCHA office without further incident. Although it was resolved quietly, the episode left little doubt about residents' desperation.[46]

Figuring Out Who Will Pay

Ultimately it was the escalation of panic in Niagara Falls and across the nation—not the health studies, which continued to be inconclusive—that compelled politicians at the federal and state levels to support relocation for the remaining Love Canal homeowners. Officials had to work out the particulars, such as whether the move would be permanent or temporary and, most important, who would pay for it. Governor Carey, taking advantage of presidential election year politics, exerted continuous pressure on the Carter administration to finance a permanent move for residents living adjacent to the canal. He complained that the state had already shelled out $35 million for the initial evacuation and subsequent moves. Every day the press reported a new plea from the state to the federal government for relocation funds. Adding fuel to the fire, on May 21 the *New York Times* reported that a study had found nerve damage in twenty-eight of thirty-five Love Canal residents examined, whereas only two out of twenty in the Niagara Falls control group had similar ailments. Moreover, there was a qualitative difference in the nature of the impairment between the two groups.[47]

That afternoon, following media coverage of the latest study, President Carter declared a second federal emergency at Love Canal and urged the remaining families to move to temporary housing. The second Emergency Declaration Area was bound to the south by the LaSalle Expressway, to the east by uninhabited wooded wetlands, to the north by the Black and Bergholtz creeks, and to the west by 93d Street (see Map 3–1). The relocation was intended to last up to a year to give the EPA sufficient time to study the results of further medical tests of residents. The Federal Emergency Management Agency (FEMA), the successor to the Federal Disaster Assistance Administration, was to supervise the evacuation and relocation. When asked what finally prompted the federal government to act, EPA spokesperson Barbara Blum replied, "We haven't felt that we've had enough evidence before now." [48]

Five days after the president authorized the temporary relocation of 800 families, only 220 had registered for the move. Aware of their increasing leverage, many of the others said they would not leave until the government bought their houses. Residents also said they would refuse to participate in further health testing programs until an agreement was reached on the purchase of their homes. "We are not going to let the government use us as guinea pigs," said a spokesperson for the LCHA.[49] On May 23 Carey presented a detailed plan for the resettlement and estimated the cost at $25 million, of which the state was committed to paying one-fifth. The tug-of-war between the governor and the president dragged on as the state continued to demand money, while federal officials insisted that federal laws did not permit the purchase of homes under an emergency program. In mid-June Carey proposed that the federal government lend the state $20 million of the $25 million necessary to relocate outer ring residents.

Map 3-1 Love Canal Emergency Declaration Area

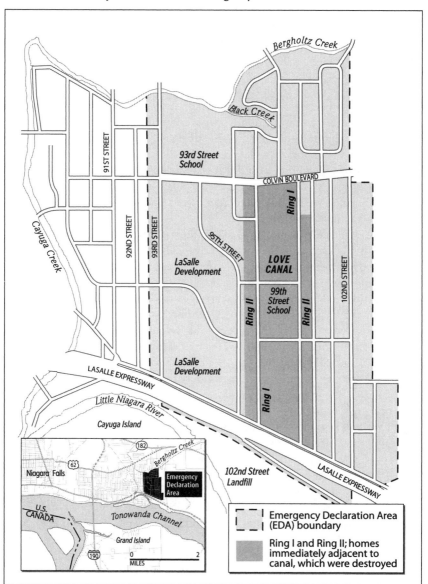

Emergency Declaration Area (EDA) boundary

Ring I and Ring II; homes immediately adjacent to canal, which were destroyed

Source: New York State Department of Health, www.health.state.ny.us/nysdoh/lcanal/lcdec88.pdf

As government officials struggled to resolve the financial issues, controversy continued to swirl around the health studies that had provoked residents' alarm. On June 14, nearly a month after the original Biogenics study's release, a scientific panel appointed by the EPA debunked its conclusions. Dr. Roy Albert of the New York University Medical Center, who headed the panel, called the results "indeterminate" and "really of no use," primarily because the study lacked contemporary controls.[50] The review panel also challenged Picciano's interpretation of the data based on its own analysis of photocopies of photographs of his chromosome preparations. (Cytogeneticists point out that detecting chromosome damage is subjective, more art than science.[51]) Adding to the confusion, two days later the EPA released another scientific review, and this one tended to support the Biogenics study. According to the second study group, headed by Dr. Jack Killian of the University of Texas, "Some individuals in the study had aberrations that were beyond the normal limits expected in 36 healthy people." [52]

On June 23 the DOH announced that in the early 1960s half the pregnancies of women living on a street bordering Love Canal had ended in miscarriage. (The normal miscarriage rate is 15 percent.) A report that compiled state studies performed in 1978, when the state first declared a health emergency, described unusual numbers of miscarriages and birth defects, as well as reduced infant weight. The health effects had peaked in the neighborhood about twenty years earlier, the report said, within a decade of most of the dumping. The journal *Science* rejected the report for publication, however, saying it was statistically unsound.[53]

Throughout the summer, as experts debated the technical merits of the health studies, the press perpetuated the causal story favored by Love Canal residents, portraying them as patriotic, working-class victims of corporate greed who had been abandoned by the government. "I can think of three or four [men] right off hand who say they'll never serve the country again for the simple reason that when they needed us, we were there," said one man. "Now they're turning their backs on us. It kind of makes you feel bad." [54] The *New York Times* ran stories headlined "For One Love Canal Family, the Road to Despair" and "Love Canal Families Are Left With a Legacy of Pain and Anger." Journalists reported that, along with a sense of betrayal, abandonment, and isolation, many in Love Canal were feeling enormous uncertainty and a loss of control over their lives. "They realize that this loss of control stems from long-ago decisions to bury chemicals and then to build homes near that spot, not from decisions they made," said Adeline Levine. "Now control rests in large measure on the decisions of distant political figures." [55]

Touching on issues sure to elicit public sympathy, reporters noted that the disaster had particularly acute consequences for many of the area's children. They interviewed one young pediatrician who had helped to bring about the closing of the 93d Street School because he had noticed in the mid-1970s that asthma and other respiratory diseases seemed to occur more frequently in Love Canal children than in his other patients. As the crisis unfolded, the children he saw began to manifest psychological problems, which he believed grew out of their intractable illnesses as well as the emotional hothouses in which they lived. "A lot of these kids are really upset that things might grow from their bodies, or that they might die prematurely," Dr. James Dunlop said.[56]

The Final Evacuation

The media portrait ultimately stirred a national political response: in September 1980, despite the ongoing controversy over the health studies, President Carter signed an agreement to lend the state of New York $7.5 million and provide a grant of another $7.5 million to purchase the homes of the relocated residents. To repay the loan, the newly formed Love Canal Area Revitalization Agency planned to rehabilitate the abandoned area and resell the homes. On October 2 the president signed the bill that made federal support for the Love Canal evacuation and renewal a reality.

Ironically, a week later a five-member panel of scientists that Carey had appointed in June told the press that "inadequate" scientific studies might have exaggerated the seriousness of the health problems caused by toxic wastes. Of the Biogenics study the panel said, "The design, implementation, and release of the EPA chromosome study has not only damaged the credibility of science, but exacerbated any future attempts to determine whether and to what degree the health of the Love Canal residents has been affected." The panel described Paigen's nervous system study as "literally impossible to interpret. . . . [It] cannot be taken seriously as a piece of sound epidemiological research." After reviewing government and private research from the previous two years, the panel concluded: "There has been no demonstration of acute health effects linked to exposure to hazardous wastes at the Love Canal site." But it added that "chronic effects of hazardous-waste exposure at Love Canal have neither been established nor ruled out as yet in a scientifically rigorous manner."[57]

Residents reacted bitterly to these findings because they feared that the report might allow the government to back out of its agreement to buy area homes. But the panel's eminent chairman, Dr. Lewis Thomas of the Memorial Sloan-Kettering Cancer Center, responded to residents' denunciations, saying that although claims of health effects were insupportable on scientific grounds, he believed that the anguish caused by the presence of chemicals and the possibility of future findings were reason enough not to live in the area.[58] In the end, the federal government did not renege on the buyout.

OUTCOMES

The crisis at Love Canal affected not only residents of the area but national politics as well, because the episode opened a window of opportunity for a new federal policy. As Daniel Mazmanian and David Morell write, "Love Canal was one of those rare catalytic events, one of those seemingly isolated incidents that so often throws an entire nation into turmoil. This unpredictable turning point in the late 1970s bared both the sensitive chemophobic nerve lurking just below the surface of American public consciousness and the growing lack of trust in both business and government expertise." [59] After Love Canal hit the headlines, the media expanded the scope of the conflict even further by covering similar horror stories across the nation.

The Superfund Law

Members of Congress, sensitive to the furor caused by Love Canal, responded quickly with an ambitious new law that established a system for identifying and neutralizing hazardous waste dump sites. In early December 1980 Congress passed the Comprehensive Environmental Response, Compensation, and Liability Act (CERCLA)—commonly known as the Superfund Act—and on December 11 President Carter signed the bill into law. The EPA had been pressing Congress for a hazardous waste cleanup law for some time, but the specter of an incoming Republican president—and hence the closing of the window of opportunity opened by Love Canal—prompted congressional Democrats to scale back their proposals sufficiently to garner majority support.[60]

CERCLA's structure clearly reflects the impact of Love Canal in defining the problem of abandoned hazardous waste dumps. To avoid the kind of delays experienced at Love Canal, the act authorized the EPA to respond to hazardous substance emergencies and clean up leaking chemical dump sites if the responsible parties failed to take appropriate action or could not be located. To speed up the process, CERCLA established a $1.6 billion trust fund, the Superfund, financed primarily by a tax on petrochemical feedstocks, organic chemicals, and crude oil imports. (In 1994 the legislation authorizing the trust fund income stream expired; as it has not been renewed, since 2004 the program has relied solely on appropriations from general revenues.) Congress also responded to the issues of corporate responsibility that were so painfully obvious at Love Canal by instituting retroactive, strict, joint, and several liability.[61] Strict, retroactive liability means that any company that disposed of hazardous waste, even if it did so legally and prior to CERCLA's passage, is automatically liable for the costs of cleanup. Joint and several liability means that one party may be held responsible for the entire cleanup cost, even if it dumped only some of the waste. Such an approach transfers the burden of proof from the victims of toxic pollution to the perpetrators; it also creates a powerful incentive for companies to dispose of waste in a precautionary way or to reduce the amount they generate out of fear of future liability.

Congress passed CERCLA by an overwhelming majority. Although the members of Congress had no real idea of the scope of the problem, they were clearly moved by the anecdotal evidence of human health effects from exposure to toxic waste and, more important, by public fears of such effects.[62] In passing Superfund, Congress ignored the wishes of the influential Chemical Manufacturers Association, which had opposed any cleanup legislation. Moreover, the chemical industry failed to get on the bandwagon as passage of the bill became imminent and missed an opportunity to weaken the law, which is one reason its provisions are so punitive.[63]

Legislators' near unanimity in passing CERCLA reflects not only heightened public attention combined with the industry's failure to cooperate, but also the widespread perception that the nation's hazardous waste problem was manageable: initial EPA studies had concluded that between 1,000 and 2,000 sites needed remediation at an estimated cost of $3.6 to $4.4 million. By the mid-1980s, however, it was obvious that the EPA had grossly underestimated the number of sites requiring cleanup. By 1986 the agency had identified more than 27,000 abandoned hazardous waste sites across the nation and had assigned almost 1,000 of the most dangerous to its National Priority List. In 1986 Congress passed the Superfund Amendments and Reauthorization Act, which increased funding and tightened cleanup standards. By fall 2005, 308 sites had been deleted from the priority list, while construction had been completed on 966 of the 1,200 remaining sites.[64] The EPA anticipated adding about 100 additional sites annually and expected the list eventually to reach 2,100. The EPA's Superfund expenditures regularly exceeded $1 billion per year, and in 1999 the U.S. General Accounting Office estimated that cleanups under the law would cost the federal government about $300 billion and the private sector hundreds of billions more.[65]

Remediation and Resettlement of Love Canal

With the passage of Superfund, public and legislative attention turned to other matters, but the cleanup of Love Canal quietly moved forward. By July 1989 a total of 1,030 families had left the area. Residents in all but two of the original 239 homes and all but 72 of the 564 outer ring families chose to move, as did most of the renters in the nearby housing project. Contractors razed the 99th Street Elementary School and the neat rows of houses adjacent to the six-block-long canal and then targeted their remediation efforts at containing the rubble in the forty-acre Love Canal landfill. In addition to the landfill, cleanup of the Emergency Declaration Area included decontaminating the area's storm sewers, dredging 3,000 feet of creek bed contaminated by rainwater runoff, returning to the landfill the 11,000 cubic yards of contaminated soil at the 93d Street Middle School that was transferred there in the 1960s, and excavating lesser amounts of soil from three "hotspots" created when former landowners stole fill from the canal before the problem was detected.[66]

Despite the massive restoration, the stigmatized Love Canal area remained deserted well into the 1990s. As of December 1991 only about twenty-five families had moved into the neighborhood after the federal government declared the area safe for resettlement. According to journalist Leslie Gruson:

Their refurbished homes sparkle[d] with new paint like oases in a sprawling desert of abandoned and decaying houses. Despite efforts to rejuvenate the area, it still [felt] and [looked] like a ghost town, or perhaps more accurately, a ghost suburb. The streets [were] silent, devoid of children. To prevent vandalism, most of the 200 still-abandoned houses [had] single burning porch lights, silent beacons of better times.[67]

The only visible reminder of the dump itself was a pasture, isolated by miles of cyclone fence covered with Day-Glo yellow warning signs reading: "Danger—Hazardous Waste Area—Keep Out." Stretching at exact intervals like distance markers on a driving range were brilliant orange pipes used to vent and monitor the landfill.[68]

CONCLUSIONS

Although it has been cleaned up, Love Canal remains a symbol of public fears about hazardous waste. Ironically, most experts believe those fears are greatly exaggerated. They lay blame for the public's misapprehension of the risks squarely at the feet of the media, which played a critical role in the cycle of activism and political response at Love Canal: through their coverage of scientific studies and residents' ailments, journalists raised local citizens' awareness of and concern about the threats posed by buried chemicals. Once local citizens mobilized, the media's extensive and sympathetic coverage of their complaints, and its framing of the story as a classic David and Goliath tale, attracted the sympathy of the national public.

Concerned about the potential liability, as well as costs likely to spiral, local and state officials put off responding to residents' complaints for as long as possible. They hoped instead to address the problem quietly in anticipation that the furor would die down. Then, once media coverage had raised the visibility of Love Canal, government officials expected that scientific analysis would clarify the dimensions of the problem and suggest an appropriate remedy. Instead, scientific studies—most of which were conducted hastily—only heightened tensions between residents and officials without pinpointing health effects. Ultimately, politicians at both the state and national levels felt compelled to respond—not because the scientific evidence confirmed the problem at Love Canal but because the media had created a strong sense of urgency among residents and the national public.

In hindsight, Governor Carey, Representative LaFalce, and other elected officials acknowledged that, although the first Love Canal evacuation was necessary, the second was probably an overreaction to citizen activism, particularly the "hostage-taking" event, rather than a product of careful evaluation. In the intervening years, some follow-up studies have confirmed the initial findings of adverse health effects at Love Canal, but reputable evaluators have been highly critical of their methodology. Other follow-up studies have shown few effects that can be decisively attributed to chemicals. A 1981 study, published in *Science*, concluded that people living near Love Canal had no higher cancer rates than other New York State residents.[69] In late 1982 the EPA and the U.S. Public Health Service released the results of a major assessment, which found that the Love Canal neighborhood was no less safe for residents than any other neighborhood in Niagara Falls. Less than a year later, the federal Centers for Disease Control reported that they too had found Love Canal residents no more likely to suffer chromosomal damage than residents living elsewhere in Niagara Falls.[70] Another follow-up study released by the DOH in August 2001 failed to find elevated cancer rates among Love Canal residents.[71]

In fact, it is notoriously difficult to prove the existence of residential cancer clusters like the one suspected at Love Canal. Among hundreds of exhaustive, published investigations of such clusters in the United States, not one has convincingly identified an environmental—as opposed to an occupational or medical—cause.[72] Michael Brown, one of the original journalists covering Love Canal for the *Niagara Gazette*, concludes that "perhaps science is simply not up to the task of proving a toxic cause and effect." He points out that "because residents move in and out, because families suffer multiple ailments, . . . because the effects of chemicals when they interact with one another are all but unknown, and because the survey populations are quite limited, attempts to prove a statistically significant effect may be doomed to failure." [73] Although the existence of neighborhood cancer clusters is suspect, however, public horror of them is real. As physician Atul Gawande points out, "Human beings evidently have a deep-seated tendency to see meaning in the ordinary variations that are bound to appear in small samples." [74]

The difficulty of documenting environmental and health effects of chronic exposure to toxic chemicals has rendered common law liability an ineffectual tool for addressing such problems. As Jonathan Harr's 1995 book *A Civil Action* makes vividly clear, individual citizens who believe they have been harmed by the activities of large, multinational corporations are at a severe disadvantage because legal liability in such cases is difficult to prove.[75] To prevail in a "toxic tort" case, plaintiffs must demonstrate not only that the alleged polluter was responsible for the harmful substance but also that the substance caused the injuries suffered. Both of these causal linkages can be enormously difficult to prove, and defendants have virtually unlimited resources with which to challenge the individual studies that constitute the building blocks of such arguments.

To avert this problem, Superfund shifts the burden of proof to polluters by establishing strict liability for hazardous waste dump sites. The Superfund mechanism also creates incentives for companies to behave in a precautionary way because complying with current disposal rules does not constitute a defense against liability in the future. Critics charge that, in practice, Superfund throws money at sites that pose negligible risks, unfairly penalizes small businesses that contributed little, if anything, to a site's toxicity, and constitutes little more than a subsidy for lawyers and hazardous waste cleanup firms.[76] In response to these criticisms, throughout the 1990s lawmakers proposed a barrage of legislative reforms (twenty-six in the 102d Congress, thirty-four in the 103d, and fifty-seven in the 104th).[77] Congress failed to pass any of these proposals, however, and in 1995 the Clinton administration instituted an administrative reform package that sought to make the distribution of cleanup costs among potentially responsible parties equitable (more in line with their contributions) and reduce the overall cost of remediation by linking cleanup levels to prospective land use at sites that are unlikely to become residential. When President George W. Bush took office in 2001, his EPA administrator, Christine Todd Whitman, expressed no interest in reversing the Clinton administration reforms.[78]

QUESTIONS TO CONSIDER

- Why did a local story about a toxic waste dump become a national crisis?
- Did the government react appropriately to the events at Love Canal? Why or why not?
- Ironically, some local officials (and even some residents) resist having abandoned toxic waste sites listed on the National Priority List. Why might that be, and what if anything should the federal government do about it?

Notes

1. Verlyn Klinkenborg, "Back to Love Canal: Recycled Homes, Rebuilt Dreams," *Harper's Magazine*, March 1991, 72.
2. Paul Slovic, Baruch Fischhoff, and Sarah Lichtenstein, "Rating the Risks," in *Readings in Risk*, ed. Theodore Glickman and Michael Gough (Washington, D.C.: Resources for the Future, 1990), 61–75.
3. Extrapolating from animal tests is difficult because species vary in their responses to chemicals; laboratory animals are often exposed to substances through different routes than are humans in the environment; and testers expose animals to massive doses of a substance. Epidemiological studies involve human subjects and larger samples, but it is notoriously difficult to isolate the effects of a single chemical. Moreover, such studies rely on statistical methods that may fail to detect the kinds of increases in lifetime cancer risks that regulators are concerned about. Finally, cellular analyses do not always reveal a substance's hazardous properties, nor do they quantify the low-dose risk of chemical carcinogens. For a detailed explanation of the shortcomings of these methods, see John D. Graham, Laura C. Green, and Marc J. Roberts, *In Search of Safety: Chemicals and Cancer Risk* (Cambridge: Harvard University Press, 1988).
4. Mark E. Rushefsky, *Making Cancer Policy* (Albany: State University of New York Press, 1986).
5. Phil Brown, "Popular Epidemiology and Toxic Waste Contamination: Lay and Professional Ways of Knowing," *Journal of Health and Social Behavior* 33 (September 1992): 267–281.
6. Frank Fischer, *Citizens, Experts, and the Environment* (Durham: Duke University Press, 2000).
7. Paul Peterson, *City Limits* (Chicago: University of Chicago Press, 1981); Kee Warner and Harvey Molotch, *Building Rules: How Local Controls Shape Community Environments and Economies* (Boulder: Westview Press, 2000).

8. Matthew Crenson, *The Un-Politics of Air Pollution: A Study of Non-Decisionmaking in the Cities* (Baltimore: Johns Hopkins University Press, 1971).

9. Quoted in Daniel Goleman, "Hidden Rules Often Distort Rules of Risk," *New York Times,* February 1, 1994, C1.

10. Martin Linsky, "Shrinking the Policy Process: The Press and the 1980 Love Canal Relocation," in *Impact: How the Press Affects Federal Policymaking,* ed. Martin Linsky (New York: Norton, 1986), 218–253.

11. David L. Protess et al., "The Impact of Investigative Reporting on Public Opinion and Policy Making," in *Media Power in Politics,* 3d ed., ed. Doris A. Graber (Washington, D.C.: CQ Press, 1994), 346–359.

12. David Pritchard, "The News Media and Public Policy Agendas," in *Public Opinion, the Press, and Public Policy,* ed. J. David Kennamer (Westport, Conn.: Praeger, 1992), 103–112.

13. The main components of the buried wastes were benzene hexachloride (a byproduct of the pesticide lindane), chlorobenzene, dodecyl mercaptan, sulfides, benzyl chloride, and benzoyl chloride. See Allan Mazur, *A Hazardous Inquiry: The Rashomon Effect at Love Canal* (Cambridge: Harvard University Press, 1998).

14. Quoted in Adeline Levine, *Love Canal: Science, Politics, and Public Policy* (Lexington, Mass.: Lexington Books, 1982), 11.

15. Michael Brown, *Laying Waste: The Poisoning of America by Toxic Chemicals* (New York: Washington Square Press, 1981).

16. Eric Zeusse, "Love Canal: The Truth Seeps Out," *Reason,* February 1981, 16–33.

17. Levine, *Love Canal,* 11.

18. Linsky, "Shrinking the Policy Process."

19. Andrew Danzo, "The Big Sleazy: Love Canal Ten Years Later," *Washington Monthly,* September 1988, 11–17.

20. Steven R. Weisman, "Hooker Company Knew About Toxic Peril in 1958," *New York Times,* April 11, 1979, B1.

21. Levine, *Love Canal.*

22. Donald McNeil, "Upstate Waste Site May Endanger Lives," *New York Times,* August 2, 1978, A1.

23. Mirex was used in the South to control ants and as a flame retardant and plasticizer until the Food and Drug Administration restricted its use.

24. PCBs, which are used to insulate electronic components, are known to kill even microscopic plants and animals.

25. Quoted in Levine, *Love Canal,* 19.

26. Mazur, *A Hazardous Inquiry.*

27. Brown, *Laying Waste.*

28. Lois Marie Gibbs, *Love Canal: My Story* (Albany: State University of New York Press, 1982), 15–16.

29. Quoted in Donald McNeil, "Upstate Waste Site: Carey Seeks U.S. Aid," *New York Times,* August 4, 1978, B14.

30. McNeil, "Upstate Waste Site May Endanger Lives."

31. Brown, *Laying Waste.*

32. Mazur, *A Hazardous Inquiry.*

33. Brown, *Laying Waste*; McNeil, "Upstate Waste Site May Endanger Lives."

34. Donald McNeil, "Health Chief Calls Waste Site a Peril," *New York Times,* August 3, 1978, A1.

35. Quoted in ibid.

36. Donald McNeil, "First Families Leaving Upstate Contamination Site," *New York Times,* August 5, 1978, 1.

37. Under an emergency declaration, the government can pay only for temporary relocation to save lives, protect public health, and protect property. A disaster declaration, by contrast, is intended to help a community recover after events such as

floods or earthquakes in which it is necessary to rebuild houses, schools, highways, and sewer systems.

38. Gibbs, *Love Canal*, 81.

39. Donald McNeil, "3 Chemical Sites Near Love Canal Possible Hazard," *New York Times*, December 27, 1978, B1.

40. Gibbs, *Love Canal*.

41. Ibid., 59.

42. Levine, *Love Canal*, 24.

43. "Love Canal Families Unwilling to Go Home Facing Motel Eviction," *New York Times*, November 8, 1979, B4.

44. Human beings have forty-six chromosomes in every cell. As new cells grow and reproduce by division, newly formed chromosomes and their genes are normally exact, complete replications of the originals. Ordinarily, environmental changes such as variations in temperature or barometric pressure, diet, or muscular activity have no effect on the process; moreover, a low level of mutation occurs spontaneously and is difficult to attribute to any specific cause. However, contact with radiation, chemicals, and other environmental hazards may cause abnormal changes in the structure of chromosomes. In some such cases, chromosome material may be missing; more rarely, additional material is detected.

45. It is important to note that everyone has some chromosome damage—probably from viral infections, medical X rays, or exposure to chemicals and medication. Although chromosome damage is an important test of exposure to toxic chemicals, not everyone with chromosome damage suffers ill effects. See Gila Kolata, "Chromosome Damage: What It Is, What It Means," *Science*, June 13, 1980, 1240.

46. Josh Barbanel, "Homeowners at Love Canal Hold 2 Officials Until F.B.I. Intervenes," *New York Times*, May 20, 1980, A1; Josh Barbanel, "Peaceful Vigil Resumed at Love Canal," *New York Times*, May 21, 1980, B1.

47. Dr. Paigen gave the following explanation: toxic chemicals, two of which—chloroform and trichloroethylene—have traditionally been used as operating room anesthetics, can act on the nervous system in two ways. They can attack the nerve fibers themselves or the fattier myeline sheath that encases the nerve fibers. "Chemicals which are soluble in fat, as the Love Canal chemicals tend to be, tend to concentrate in fatty tissues such as the nervous sheath," she said. Dr. Paigen said the damage showed up in two of the peripheral nervous systems tested. "These are the sensory nerves which control touch and feelings," she said. But she added that the findings probably meant that those who showed peripheral nervous system damage had also suffered some damage to the central nervous system. Dudley L. Clendinen, "New Study Finds Residents Suffer Nerve Problems," *New York Times*, May 21, 1980, B7.

48. Quoted in Irving Molotsky, "President Orders Emergency Help for Love Canal," *New York Times*, May 22, 1980, A1.

49. Quoted in Josh Barbanel, "Many at Love Canal Insist on U.S. Aid Before Moving," *New York Times*, May 27, 1980, B3.

50. Quoted in John Noble Wilford, "Panel Disputes Chromosome Findings at Love Canal," *New York Times*, June 14, 1980, 26.

51. Ibid.

52. Quoted in Irving Molotsky, "Love Canal Medical Study Backed," *New York Times*, June 18, 1980, B4. Although Killian had once supervised Picciano, he dismissed suggestions he might be biased, pointing out that he had no role in the Biogenics study and had participated in the evaluation of it at the request of the EPA.

53. Robin Herman, "Report Cites Miscarriage Rate at Love Canal in 60's," *New York Times*, June 24, 1980, D16.

54. Quoted in Georgia Dullea, "Love Canal Families Are Left With a Legacy of Pain and Anger," *New York Times*, May 16, 1980, A18.

55. Quoted in Constance Holden, "Love Canal Residents Under Stress," *Science*, June 13, 1980, 1242–4.

56. Quoted in Dudley L. Clendinen, "Love Canal Is Extra Tough on Children," *New York Times*, June 9, 1980, B1.

57. Quoted in Richard J. Meislin, "Carey Panel Discounts 2 Studies of Love Canal Health Problems," *New York Times*, October 11, 1980, 25.

58. Josh Barbanel, "Love Canal Skeptic Favors Relocation," *New York Times*, October 12, 1980, 39.

59. Daniel Mazmanian and David Morell, *Beyond Superfailure: America's Toxics Policy for the 1990s* (Boulder: Westview Press, 1992), 6.

60. John A. Hird, *Superfund: The Political Economy of Environmental Risk* (Baltimore: Johns Hopkins University Press, 1994).

61. Congress actually deleted the strict, joint, and several liability provision from the law immediately before its passage, but the courts subsequently reinstated the requirement through their interpretation of the statute. See Mazmanian and Morell, *Beyond Superfailure*.

62. Political scientist John Hird writes, "That the prospect of an incoming conservative Republican administration did not doom the Superfund effort entirely in 1980 is a testimony to the political appeal for both Republicans and Democrats of a hazardous waste cleanup program seen as vital by their constituents." See Hird, *Superfund*, 186.

63. Lawrence Mosher, "Environment," *National Journal*, December 30, 1980, 2130.

64. "NPL Site Totals by Status and Milestone," August 22, 2005. Available at www. epa.gov/superfund/sites/query/queryhtm/npltotal.htm.

65. U.S. GAO, *Superfund Program: Current Status and Future Fiscal Challenges*, GAO-03-850 (August 2004); U.S. GAO, *Superfund: Progress Made by EPA and Other Federal Agencies to Resolve Program Management Issues*, RCED-99-111 (April 1999).

66. Andrew Hoffman, "An Uneasy Rebirth at Love Canal," *Environment*, March 1995, 5–9, 25–30.

67. Leslie Gruson, "Home to Some Is Still Love Canal to Others," *New York Times*, December 9, 1991, B1.

68. Ibid.

69. Dwight T. Janerich et al., "Cancer Incidence in the Love Canal Area," *Science*, June 19, 1981, 1404–7.

70. Clark W. Heath Jr. et al., "Cytogenetic Findings in Persons Living Near the Love Canal," *Journal of the American Medical Association*, 251 (March 16, 1984): 1437–40.

71. New York State Department of Health, "Love Canal Follow-Up Health Study," August 2001, www.health.state.ny.us/nysdoh/lcanal/cancinci.htm.

72. Atul Gawande, "The Cancer-Cluster Myth," *New Yorker*, February 8, 1999, 34–37.

73. Michael Brown, "A Toxic Ghost Town," *Atlantic Monthly*, July 1989, 23–28.

74. Gawande, "The Cancer-Cluster Myth."

75. Jonathan Harr, *A Civil Action* (New York: Vintage, 1995).

76. See, for example, Marc K. Landy and Mary Hague, "The Coalition for Waste: Private Interests and Superfund," in *Environmental Politics: Public Costs, Private Rewards*, ed. Michael S. Greve and Fred L. Smith (New York: Praeger, 1992), 67–87.

77. Dianne Rahm, "Controversial Cleanup: Superfund and the Implementation of U.S. Hazardous Waste Policy," *Policy Studies Journal* 26 (1998): 719–734.

78. Robert T. Nakamura and Thomas W. Church, *Taming Regulation* (Washington, D.C.: Brookings Institution Press, 2003).

Recommended Reading

Gibbs, Lois Marie. *Love Canal: My Story.* Albany: State University of New York Press, 1982.

Hird, John A. *Superfund: The Political Economy of Environmental Risk.* Baltimore: Johns Hopkins University Press, 1994.

Levine, Adeline. *Love Canal: Science, Politics, and Public Policy.* Lexington, Mass.: Lexington Books, 1982.

Mazur, Allan. *A Hazardous Inquiry: The Rashomon Effect at Love Canal.* Cambridge: Harvard University Press, 1998.

Web Sites

www.epa.gov/superfund (EPA Superfund site)

www.epa.gov/history/topics/lovecanal/index.htm (EPA Love Canal site)

www.health.state.ny.us/nysdoh/lcanal/lcanal.htm (New York State Department of Health site)

ublib.buffalo.edu/libraries/projects/lovecanal (University of Buffalo site)

CHAPTER 4

Government Secrets at Rocky Flats

In March 1992 the federal government fined Rockwell International $18.5 million for horrific crimes against the environment, namely, letting toxic chemicals and radioactive plutonium wastes poison the soil and groundwater around Colorado's Rocky Flats nuclear weapons plant. Yet, according to members of the grand jury that heard the case, the penalty was far too lenient. The Department of Energy (DOE) never fully acknowledged its responsibility for allowing the facility and its surroundings to become contaminated, the jurors said; furthermore, the government and its contractors conducted substandard maintenance, concealed health statistics, and violated numerous environmental laws. The result was severe contamination of the environment around the plant and a breach of public trust that fueled the anger of citizens demanding cleanup of the facility. By summer 2005 that cleanup was nearly complete, and the DOE planned to turn the site into a wildlife refuge by 2007.

This case shares some features with the story of Love Canal. As in New York, local and state officials in Colorado were reluctant to sanction a major polluter, fearing the economic ramifications of doing so. Although initially complacent about the plant, residents eventually became alarmed by media coverage of scientific reports suggesting contamination and potential threats to their health and property values. Critical media coverage, combined with citizen activism, in turn, prompted elected officials, both locally and nationally, to look more closely at the plant's activities.

Beyond these similarities, however, the Rocky Flats case has some unique attributes, the most important of which is that the government, not a private firm, was the polluter. Rocky Flats was just one part of a massive weapons complex the federal government built during the cold war. For decades, the facilities in this complex operated according to a particular logic: weapons production was defined as an urgent concern, and all other considerations were secondary. With secrecy fostering an exclusive, symbiotic relationship between government agencies and their private contractors, plant managers took minimal precautions to protect workers and the environment. Members of Congress, theoretically guardians of the public interest, provided little oversight of the weapons production system because the military and its backers had formulated—and then institutionalized—a potent framing of the issue: the risk to national security of opening up nuclear weapons plants to scrutiny far outweighed the risk to the environment or workers' health posed by activities within the plants. As one commentator describes it, "For decades, the nuclear weapons enterprise functioned as a culture apart from society, holding absolute power made possible by secrecy. The weapons complex was run by a tiny elite, unconstrained by any democratic process."[1]

But such closed policy "subsystems," even when backed by powerful allies, are vulnerable to exposure because, although government transgressions can be suppressed for a long time, whistle-blowers inevitably come forward. When they do, challengers wielding alternative definitions of the problem capitalize on the new information to support their claims. If they can attract media attention, challengers often can get the problem onto the government's agenda. Over time, the feedback between negative media coverage and critical public reaction (or politicians' fear of it) can prompt a major policy response: while enthusiasm leads to the creation of new government institutions and subsystems, waves of criticism lead to their breakup and often to the creation of a new subsystem with different goals.[2]

Redirecting the nuclear weapons complex has not been simple, however. Repairing the environmental damage done by government polluters involves confronting two quandaries that face all toxic waste cleanup efforts. First, where does the waste go? And second, how clean is clean enough?

Local NIMBY (not-in-my-backyard) groups make transporting and disposing of hazardous waste more of a political than a technical problem because they limit the range of disposal options available. As one observer explains:

> Nimbys are noisy. Nimbys are powerful. Nimbys are everywhere. Nimbys are people who live near enough to corporate or government projects and are upset enough about them to work to stop, stall or shrink them. Nimbys organize, march, sue and petition to block the developers they think are threatening them. They twist the arms of politicians and they learn how to influence regulators. They fight fiercely and then, win or lose, they vanish.[3]

Initially, critics of the NIMBY phenomenon characterized such grassroots groups as emotional, uninformed, and unscientific. They accused NIMBYists of being motivated by selfish interests, such as concern about property values, and unwilling to bear the costs associated with their lifestyles. But as scholars have studied citizen opposition to noxious facilities, they have uncovered a more complex set of motives. Charles Piller argues that NIMBY groups unite disparate individuals to defy experts and technocrats who would impose risks on communities without consulting residents. According to Piller, members of NIMBY groups share a set of common characteristics: they perceive themselves as victims and are intensely focused on preserving their home environment.[4] Some studies have found that members of NIMBY groups think facilities in general impose serious health risks and are wary of government.[5] Others emphasize that citizens' perceptions of risks take into account a facility's psychological, emotional, or social effects on a community, whereas experts consider only the numerical probability of an accident.[6] In short, like members of more conventional environmental organizations, NIMBY activists are deeply concerned with the impact of toxic substances and new technologies on human health and the environment. But whereas the former are united for the longer term around shared ideals, the latter come together out of more immediate concerns and typically disband once the crisis passes.

The second dilemma that confronts every cleanup is: when is it finished? According to detractors, once a polluted area is designated a Superfund site, the law creates incentives for citizens to insist on "Cadillac cleanups." [7] Such demands, critics say, raise the cost of remediation and ignore the reality that resources are limited and excessive spending at one site means neglect at others. Furthermore, citizen resistance can lead to gridlock and delay action, further increasing costs. One way the DOE and other agencies have tried to get communities to be more modest in their cleanup demands and to ameliorate the tension between the public and government officials is to establish citizen advisory boards. Such boards increase opportunities for participation in decision making, although they may also perpetuate inequities in the distribution of environmental hazards if middle-class communities participate more effectively than their low-income counterparts.

BACKGROUND

As the following description makes clear, the Rocky Flats nuclear weapons plant was no ordinary industrial complex:

> Rolling ranch land dotted by clumps of pine trees line the road to Rocky Flats. In contrast to the scenic foothills of the Rocky Mountains that rise just over the next ridge, the plant is a nondescript mass of mostly windowless, aging industrial buildings, known by numbers, not names. Just inside the main gate, a huge safety-first billboard is followed by one that reads "National Security: Our Responsibility"—a deadly serious message. Rocky Flats is one of the nation's most closely guarded facilities. Coiled barbed wire tops each of two wire-mesh fences that surround the plutonium-processing buildings, about half the plant's area. Four guard towers, reminiscent of a high-security prison, loom overhead. Paramilitary security guards patrol the periphery in armored vehicles with mounted automatic weapons. The 250-member security force includes a SWAT team and is equipped with antiaircraft guns.[8]

Access to Rocky Flats was highly restricted, and until the early 1990s most activities there were shrouded in secrecy. As a result, accidents and leaks at the plant—many of which dated back to its very beginning—went unreported and their consequences undocumented.

Choosing a Site

The Rocky Flats facility was part of the full-scale nuclear weapons production program launched by President Harry Truman at the start of the cold war in the early 1950s. In 1951 the Atomic Energy Commission (AEC) initiated Project Apple, with the goal of finding a place to manufacture the plutonium triggers needed to detonate a new generation of atom bombs. The AEC hoped to have a plant built and operating by the end of the year, and it hired a consulting firm—the Austin Company of Cleveland, Ohio—to locate an appropriate site.

Project Apple principals decided that the ideal site would be no fewer than five and no more than twenty-five miles from a city of at least 25,000 in order to attract top-quality scientists and researchers. (This decision was striking: under the wartime Manhattan Project, Lt. Gen. Leslie Groves required that plutonium processing facilities be located *at least twenty miles away from* any city of more than 10,000 people, for safety reasons.[9]) Within two months, Austin had narrowed the search to Denver, Colorado, "the one location that [could] combine nationally known recreational facilities and the services of a large metropolitan center." [10] The consultants identified seven possible sites around Denver, but quickly eliminated five where the prevailing wind patterns were unfavorable. They ultimately settled on Rocky Flats, a mesa at the foot of the Rocky Mountains about fifteen miles northwest of the city. At the time, the land between the city and the proposed site was covered with sagebrush.

In making its decision, the AEC did not consider environmental or public health concerns, the site's underlying geological structure, or its suitability for radioactive waste disposal.[11] Nor, ironically, did the site-selection team study wind patterns.[12] Instead, the team simply assumed that most wind currents came from the south as they did at Stapleton Airport, twenty-seven miles from the foot of the Rockies. In fact, the winds at Rocky Flats rush down the mountain canyons and usually blow east or southeast—toward Denver.

Ignorant of possible hazards posed by a nuclear weapons manufacturing plant, and reflecting the generally incautious attitude of most Americans toward nuclear technology at the time, area residents welcomed the $45 million "A-plant," which promised employment and revenue for the modest city of 567,000. "There's Good News Today," reported the *Denver Post* on March 21, 1951.[13] Construction of the first permanent buildings began in July 1951, and by the following year the plant was on line, employing 200 workers in twenty buildings. By 1954 the plant was fully operational, and by the 1960s the number of workers had grown to 3,000.

Rocky Flats Operations

For most of the plant's life, decision making about Rocky Flats was restricted to a select few within a subsystem consisting of a private contractor, an agency, and a joint congressional committee. For the first fourteen years, Dow Chemical Company ran the plant's day-to-day operations under contract to the AEC. In 1975 Rockwell International replaced Dow. During Rockwell's tenure, the Energy Research and Development Administration superseded the AEC, and shortly thereafter the Energy Department took over as the responsible agency. In Congress, an unusual arrangement facilitated an extraordinarily closed system of nuclear weapons policymaking: the Joint Committee on Atomic Energy, made up of nine members from each chamber, had exclusive jurisdiction over "all bills, resolutions, and other matters in the Senate and the House of Representatives relating primarily to the [Atomic Energy] Commission or to the development, use, and control of atomic energy." [14]

Within the Rocky Flats plant itself, the need for secrecy shaped operations. The plant had two primary functions, both highly classified. First, workers made plutonium into first-stage fission bombs, the softball-sized pits that trigger the second-stage fusion reaction in hydrogen bombs. In addition, workers recovered and recycled plutonium from retired warheads and manufacturing residues using acids or high-voltage electrical currents to strip the metal from other materials.[15] Among the toxic substances emitted during these processes were: americium and plutonium (both radioactive carcinogens), beryllium (a probable inhalation carcinogen), carbon tetrachloride (a probable inhalation carcinogen), chloroform (a probable carcinogen), methylene chloride (a probable inhalation carcinogen), tetrachloroethylene, and trichloroethylene. Reflecting the secrecy surrounding the plant's mission, security "was so tight that only a handful of people had clearances to get into more than one building, and most employees had no idea what went on in areas of the plant other than their own. Plant employees were bussed from the front gate to their own buildings, since no personal vehicles were allowed on site." [16] The engineers who designed the plant were forbidden to discuss their work with anyone. Jim Stone, the mechanical engineer who designed the plutonium processing Building 771, never even saw the site or knew its orientation.[17]

Early Accidents, Leaks, and Cover-Ups

Secrecy surrounded not only the day-to-day operations at Rocky Flats but also the facility's poor safety record. The plant experienced numerous fires during its first two decades, the largest of which broke out in Building 771 late in the evening of September 11, 1957, when the plutonium inside a glove box ignited.[18] The boxes had been manufactured with flammable materials, and, because many had not been changed in four years, they contained large quantities of plutonium. In turn, the high-efficiency particulate aerosol filters designed to prevent plutonium from escaping the building caught fire, spewing plutonium dust and smoke into the atmosphere. After failing to put out the blaze with carbon dioxide, firefighters resorted to dousing it with water (which they had been reluctant to use, fearing a plutonium criticality chain reaction); in the meantime, however, they turned on the ventilation fans, spreading the flames throughout the building.[19]

Because the fire melted stack radiation monitors, plant managers had no idea how much plutonium escaped, and they could not monitor emissions until seven days later. Even then, the monitors detected levels of radioactive elements 16,000 times greater than the standards of the time.[20] Nevertheless, officials took no emergency action to protect the public or warn local residents, cities, or health agencies. Media coverage was minimal, so the public hardly reacted. A front-page story in the *Denver Post* reported the fire but provided little explanation; a story buried in the back pages of the *Rocky Mountain News* quoted AEC officials who said that "no spread of radioactive contamination of any consequence" had occurred; and the *Boulder Daily Camera* did not even report it.[21] Despite contamination of the building and the absence of filters to keep plutonium out of the environment, two days after the fire, Rocky Flats resumed limited production to meet a deadline.

Twelve years later, on May 11, 1969, another major fire occurred. This blaze began when plutonium kept in an open can within a glove box ignited spontaneously and burned for four hours, causing $45 million in damage (in 1969 dollars). A government report said that "the fire was out of the top of the [foundry] with flames about 18 inches high. One of the two firemen heard two loud reports (like rifle shots) and saw two fireballs (about basketball size) go to the ceiling." Firemen used so much water to douse the fire (again, carbon dioxide had no effect) that it flowed downhill through a 267-foot tunnel and into Building 771, the most dangerous building in the complex.[22] Critics estimated that the fire sent at least 2,200 pounds of plutonium into the atmosphere—enough for 220 warheads, but plant officials insisted that little or none had been released.[23] This time, Denver and Boulder papers reported the fire. The AEC, however, provided little concrete information about its origins or consequences, even though, according to its classified report on the fire, only the "heroic efforts of the firefighters" prevented a "major release of plutonium to the environment." [24]

In addition to these serious fires, Rocky Flats experienced hundreds of smaller blazes, as well as numerous other problems, the most notable of which stemmed from the practice of burning uranium-laden oil in open pits. Workers also buried more than 5,000 thirty- and fifty-gallon steel barrels containing plutonium-laden waste oil on a hillside behind the plant.[25] Dow company managers did not remove the barrels until 1967, even though they knew as early as 1959 that the barrels were leaking. The site was not capped until 1969, and in the interim, an estimated 5,000 gallons of plutonium-contaminated oil leaked into the soil and was scattered during windstorms.[26]

THE CASE

The tight control of information during the 1950s and 1960s and the scant press coverage meant that the public remained largely ignorant of the accidents and negligent practices at Rocky Flats. The 1969 fire galvanized a group of Boulder-area scientists, however, and in the early 1970s they conducted a series of studies that prompted a gradually intensifying cycle of negative media attention to and public criticism about the plant. Opponents of the facility took advantage of each new development to promote their view that it constituted an unacceptable public health threat. By the mid-1980s the cold war justification for concealment at Rocky Flats and other military installations had faded, replaced by an insistence on openness and accountability that extended even to nuclear weapons facilities. Just as the original framing of the problem, in which contamination was a minor side effect of national security, had allowed devastating levels of air, water, and soil pollution, the new definition prompted a hazardous waste cleanup on an unprecedented scale.

Scientists Sound the Alarm

Scientific reports of contamination at Rocky Flats released in the early 1970s opened a window of opportunity for advocates who wished to shut down the facility and dismantle the nation's nuclear arsenal. In 1969 a group of nuclear chemists, known as the Colorado Committee for Environmental Education, at the National Center for Atmospheric Research in Boulder had begun conducting soil tests around Rocky Flats. In 1970 they reported that plutonium contamination two miles east of the plant was up to 250 times higher than the levels attributable to fallout from nuclear tests worldwide. They found that eight miles east of the plant, in Westminster—which had become one of Denver's largest suburbs—the levels were ten times the normal level.[27] Then, in 1973 the Boulder scientists learned that the plant had accidentally released between 500 and 2,000 curies of tritium into the Great Western Reservoir one and a half miles to its east.[28] Alerted by their concern, in 1974 the Jefferson County Commission asked Carl Johnson, the county's Health Department director, to investigate the soil of a proposed housing development two and a half miles east of the plant. Johnson found that some of the area's soil exceeded the Colorado plutonium contamination standards by a factor of seven.[29] The media latched onto these studies, running stories that expressed skepticism of the AEC and its assurances of plant safety.[30]

Landowners who had hoped to develop property nearby were alarmed by Johnson's findings and filed lawsuits against Dow, Rockwell, and the DOE in 1975. They demanded $23 million in damages, claiming that fallout from the plant had rendered their land worthless. The lawsuits in turn prompted local and federal officials to reexamine development in the area, and in the mid-1970s the federal government established a 6,166-acre environmental and security buffer zone around the plant's 384-acre core. In 1978 the U.S. Department of Housing and Urban Development (HUD) temporarily stopped processing subdivisions, mortgage insurance, and other housing assistance within a seven-and-a-half-mile radius of Rocky Flats. Finally, in 1979, after repeated requests from the Environmental Protection Agency (EPA), HUD began to require that realtors issue warnings about plutonium contamination to all homebuyers purchasing federal mortgage insurance within a ten-mile radius of the plant.[31]

During this time, on his own initiative, Johnson had begun conducting the first major epidemiological study of the health effects of Rocky Flats on its neighbors. In the first of two controversial reports issued in the late 1970s, he concluded that Denver's overall cancer rates were higher than expected and higher still in neighborhoods near Rocky Flats. The pattern, he said, was consistent with soil contamination, which he measured at up to 380 times background levels at off-site locations. In the second study, Johnson found that infant mortality and adult cancer rates rose as one moved closer to the plant. He pointed out that leukemia deaths among Jefferson County children, which were below the national average before Rocky Flats opened, were above the national average shortly after the plant began operating and twice the national average after the 1957 fire.[32]

Advocates focusing on Rocky Flats as part of their nuclear disarmament campaign seized on Johnson's findings in their efforts to raise public concern and redefine nuclear weapons production there as a public health threat. The Rocky Flats Action Group, formed in 1974, conducted a public education campaign about the plant and advocated converting it to peaceful uses. The high point of their organizing efforts came in 1982, when more than 20,000 protesters rallied at the state capitol; a year later, an estimated 15,000 linked arms and tried to encircle the plant. Public attention to such activities was short-lived, however; in fact, many residents were hostile to these "outside agitators." As in the Love Canal case, local officials and many residents were reluctant to look too closely at the plant's operations because it was a mainstay of the local economy. With an annual budget of a half billion dollars, the plant represented 1 percent of the state's manufacturing economy and generated about 6,000 direct and thousands more indirect jobs.[33] (In 1981, after plant managers and even some scientists who opposed Rocky Flats criticized Johnson's statistical methodology, the county fired him.)

As media coverage of Johnson's and other studies waned, so did the prospects for closing Rocky Flats. In 1982 HUD retracted its order to warn prospective homebuyers on the grounds that the state had begun to distribute information on emergency procedures for homes within four miles of the plant. Soon afterward, the state—protecting its own economic development interests—also stopped giving out information. The government's definition of the plant as a crucial component of national security and the local economy held sway.

Health Threats Draw Renewed Attention to Rocky Flats

In the mid-1980s, however, a second window of opportunity for Rocky Flats opponents opened when another series of pollution problems came to light. Highly publicized scares about plutonium contamination of drinking water in 1985 and 1986 galvanized the plant's neighbors. The AEC had built the facility directly on top of a creek that feeds the Great Western Reservoir and immediately adjacent to a creek that flows to Standley Lake, another reservoir two miles away. After scientists first raised concerns in the 1970s, engineers built a series of holding ponds to catch runoff from the plant so it could be tested for radioactivity or toxic chemicals. That system did not prevent the eventual release of millions of gallons of polluted water, however, and in 1987 Rockwell International finally admitted that groundwater around Rocky Flats was contaminated.[34] The DOE then released some details about how several parts of the facility were dangerously contaminated with plutonium, uranium, and deadly solvents. The EPA identified 166 separate hazardous waste dumps on the reservation, contending that one of them—Hillside 881—was the most polluted site in America and posed a clear danger to the area's drinking water.

Even as public concern rose, the DOE steadfastly maintained its autonomy and need for secrecy. In 1985 Dow, Rockwell, and the DOE agreed to settle the

1975 lawsuit with the landowners out of court for nearly $10 million. The defendants devised a plan to minimize adverse publicity: as part of the settlement, the landowners agreed not to call any witnesses and to allow the defense's expert witnesses to testify unchallenged. In return, Rocky Flats agreed to reduce radioactivity to the 1973 Colorado standard for plutonium in soil. Remarkably, another provision of the settlement called for Jefferson County to purchase 800 acres of the contaminated property for $2 million (half its appraised value) and create a park.[35]

The Incinerator Prompts Citizen Mobilization

The settlement did not succeed in tamping down public concern, however. If the worrisome reports about drinking water constituted the fuse, then the incinerator proposal was the spark that ignited local citizen activism. Residents were already wary when, in January 1987, officials announced plans to incinerate thousands of tons of mixed radioactive and chemical wastes in a fluidized-bed incinerator.[36] If the state approved it, the plant would begin a ten-day trial incineration, the first burning of mixed radioactive and hazardous wastes in the country. Then, if state health officials determined the process was environmentally and technologically sound, managers intended to undertake full-scale incineration in the summer of 1987.

Rocky Flats officials argued that burning was necessary because there was no federally sanctioned disposal site for their mounting stockpiles of mixed wastes. "We have some 18,000 gallons of liquid wastes that are, in the main, machinery solvents resulting from activities involving depleted uranium metal," said Rockwell spokesman Gene Towne. "But by law, we cannot transport a hazardous liquid waste containing radioactive material." Plant engineers planned to seal the inert ash generated by the incinerator in concrete and ship it to a planned disposal site in Nevada. Towne emphasized that "maximum safeguards" had been taken, saying "there [would] be no health effects from this particular technology" and "the chances of anything getting out [were] minute."[37]

Despite Rockwell's assurances, many residents were alarmed and unwilling to put their faith in government experts' risk assessments. Richard E. Dryden, a thirty-five-year-old printer who lived with his family within view of the weapons facility, said, "Our reaction has gone from curiosity to concern to more recently panic." His wife, Charlene, said of Rockwell's safety promises, "I do not buy it. No way! They're testing us. We're the guinea pigs. Nobody knows what plutonium is going to do in the long term. My boys may not have healthy children some day."[38] Residents like the Drydens were particularly affronted by the incinerator proposal because they were already grappling with a Highway Department plan to build a new beltway, construction of which was expected to churn tons of dust into the air. High winds, which routinely closed Highway 93 on the plant's western edge, would disperse the dust widely.

The incinerator proposal, following on the heels of the drinking water scares and the highway plan, catalyzed local opposition to Rocky Flats. In early 1987 a group of Denver area citizens, led by veteran peace activist Jan Pilcher and homemaker Joan Seeman, established Citizens Against Rocky Flats Contamination (CARFC). Pilcher had been a member of the Rocky Flats Action Group in the 1970s and was well versed in lobbying, orchestrating public demonstrations, and arranging educational events. Reflecting the difference in risk standards employed by experts and laypeople, CARFC raised questions about the health and environmental effects of the incinerator, which had not been studied, and demanded that experts provide a worst case scenario. The organizers were well aware that the incinerator was only one of a multitude of potential health threats posed by the weapons plant, and perhaps not even the gravest one, but they also knew that few technologies motivate opposition as readily as toxic waste incineration.[39]

At a public meeting called by Rep. David Skaggs, D-Colo., irate neighbors shouted down Rocky Flats officials. The momentum generated at the meeting prompted residents to form additional smaller groups and keep the pressure on local politicians. Incinerator opponents inundated the Colorado Department of Health with 1,500 letters, and CARFC gathered more than 18,000 signatures on a petition to close down the facility. Municipal officials and small business owners spoke out against the test burn, and Democratic governor Roy Romer found himself besieged by mail from angry constituents.[40]

CARFC buttressed its opposition with evidence gathered by the Boulder scientists who claimed that the incinerator posed a major risk of explosion and that Rocky Flats managers had no means of monitoring or controlling emissions of vapors such as uranium hexafluoride. The scientists concluded, "The equipment, the plan, the monitoring, and the documentation are so flawed and deficient, so threatening to public safety that the application is beyond expectation of remedy." [41] Hoping to quell the controversy, Colorado politicians, all of whom had initially favored the incinerator, demanded health studies before consenting to the test burn.

Rocky Flats management reluctantly agreed to postpone the burn until July, but in the interim, a scientific panel convened by Representative Skaggs ascertained that the plant had already used the incinerator nine times since 1978 to burn twenty-four tons of unidentified and possibly radioactive waste.[42] CARFC and the Sierra Club then filed suit to prevent the test burn, arguing that it violated environmental laws, and Rocky Flats was forced to delay the test indefinitely to prepare an environmental impact assessment. Finally, amid unrelenting public opposition fueled by press reports of a small fire at the incinerator, the project ground to a halt.

Ironically, even as the public was becoming more fearful about Rocky Flats, local officials continued to annex nearby land for development. As a result of planned and actual acquisitions of adjacent land by surrounding cities and towns, the brush land between Rocky Flats and Denver was fast becoming a heavily populated stream of office buildings, businesses, and homes.[43] One consequence of this development was that in 1988 the U.S. General Accounting Office (GAO) ranked groundwater contamination at Rocky Flats the most serious environmental threat at any of the country's nuclear weapons facilities.[44]

Whither the Waste?

No sooner had they stopped the incinerator project than the residents of the rapidly growing Denver suburbs confronted another issue, the disposal of nuclear waste. Throughout the 1980s the nuclear industry—both its electric power and weapons divisions—faced the prospect of being overwhelmed by its radioactive byproducts. Each year Rocky Flats alone was generating about 16,000 tons of poisonous trash, including 75,000 cubic feet of transuranic radioactive clothing, glass, solvents, oils, and metals contaminated with plutonium or americium. From the beginning, the facility had shipped its refuse to the DOE's Idaho National Engineering Plant for "temporary storage," with its ultimate destination the government's Waste Isolation Pilot Plant (WIPP), a giant hole in a salt bed 2,150 feet beneath southeastern New Mexico. The plan was for WIPP to start receiving clothing and tools contaminated by radiation from Rocky Flats and nine other atomic plants in December 1988. But safety concerns and legal problems forced the government to postpone the dumpsite's opening date to the 1990s at the earliest.

The delay in opening WIPP triggered a posturing contest between Romer and Gov. Cecil Andrus, D-Idaho, both of whom hoped to get credit for being responsive to agitated constituents. At the time, Rocky Flats was producing less than its usual quota of trash because federal inspectors had shut down most of the facility in October 1988, after two unprotected employees and a DOE safety inspector had entered an unmarked room where workers were cleaning and repairing plutonium-contaminated equipment, and all three had inhaled radioactive particles. But, despite the closure, enough of the plant remained operational to generate nearly a boxcar of hazardous wastes each week. In late 1988, when it became clear that WIPP would not open on schedule, Andrus put his foot down and sent one of the boxcars back to Colorado, where it sat in the yard outside the plant beside six more boxcars and a sea of drums and crates packed with toxic waste.[45]

This arrangement was untenable, however, as Rocky Flats would be in violation of the federal Resource Conservation and Recovery Act (RCRA) if it stored more than 1,600 cubic yards of hazardous waste on site.[46] By May 1989 Rocky Flats was approaching this limit, and Romer could have ordered the plant to shut down. Instead, he tried to stave off the nuclear waste crisis by convening a meeting in Salt Lake City with Andrus, Gov. Garrey Carruthers, R-N.M., and top DOE officials. The group agreed on a tentative compromise: they would press Congress to pass a land-swap bill essential to opening WIPP while the DOE searched for an interim storage site and provided financial aid to the states.[47] This agreement did not resolve the immediate waste disposal problem, however.

In September 1989 White House chief of staff John Sununu appealed to the governors of the seven western states to accept Rocky Flats waste on a temporary, emergency basis so that the U.S. government could maintain its bomb production. With the collapse of communism, however, politicians found themselves unable to persuade their constituents to sacrifice on behalf of national security, and, fearing electoral repercussions, all seven governors refused. In desperation, the DOE prevailed upon Romer to store railcars filled with Rocky Flats waste at a U.S. Army training site in southern Colorado near the small town of Trinidad—one of the state's poorest municipalities, with a population of only 9,000. A private company offered to administer the waste at the new site, promising jobs, a new telephone system, hospital expansion, and other benefits as sweeteners to the town. The residents were not impressed: "About 500 angry Trinidadians attended a meeting to discuss the plan. They shouted down company representatives with cries of 'Get out of town! . . . Store it in your backyard!' "[48] Finally, the DOE acquired a supercompactor to reduce waste volume at Rocky Flats, thereby forestalling the waste crisis until some future date.

The EPA/FBI Investigation

Deepening the facility's woes, years of secrecy and arrogance by Rocky Flats managers and their overseers were beginning to take their toll. In 1987 former Rocky Flats engineer Jim Stone—frustrated with plant managers' unresponsiveness to his complaints about safety violations and inaction at the state level—tipped off the FBI about suspected violations of environmental laws at the site. Stone's whistle-blowing triggered a two-year investigation called Operation Desert Glow. On June 6, 1989, the investigation culminated in a raid in which more than seventy FBI and EPA agents spent three weeks searching the facility. Agents seized more than a million pages of internal documents and claimed to have found evidence to corroborate charges of improperly handled wastes and illegal use of outdated equipment.[49] The widely publicized search elevated the question of nuclear safety to the national level, especially because the entire nuclear weapons complex had come under scrutiny during the investigation.

Within a month, environmental officials had uncovered another mystery at the trouble-prone facility: there were traces of radioactive strontium and cesium that a nuclear chain reaction could produce, even though the site had no nuclear reactor.[50] The EPA demanded a study to determine how the mysterious isotopes got to Rocky Flats. Then, a month after the FBI raid, DOE officials conducted a week-long inspection and found ten radiation safety problems, including leaking boxes of radioactive waste. "The radiological protection program at Rocky Flats continues to be inadequate," wrote one inspector.[51]

The DOE responded by trying to salvage its image. In the summer of 1989, while continuing to insist that the plant was operating safely, newly appointed energy secretary James Watkins announced that he would end nearly fifty years of secrecy. To boost the agency's declining credibility with Congress and the public, Watkins declared that the DOE would allow state environmental officials to inspect its plants. If they uncovered any violations, Watkins said, the agency would fire operators. The DOE also announced its intention to have state safety teams conduct aerial surveillance. Signaling a substantial shift in federal priorities, Watkins assured the press that protecting health and the environment was as important as weapons output, and he announced plans to reward contractors for running safe plants.[52] To placate Governor Romer, who was threatening to close down Rocky Flats permanently, Secretary Watkins pledged $1.8 million to tighten environmental monitoring and $700,000 for the first year of a study of health effects on the area residents.[53] Shortly thereafter, to emphasize its openness, the DOE began to make available to independent researchers its storehouse of health information on workers in the bomb-making plants from the 1940s through 1990.

Successfully Redefining the Problem

Although they defused some of the political momentum behind reform, Watkins's efforts were insufficient to stem the tide of negative publicity. A rapid-fire series of revelations about mismanagement and contamination, combined with charges of a conspiracy between the DOE and Rockwell, enabled critics to redefine nuclear weapons production at the facility: no longer was Rocky Flats vital to national security; instead, it was a site at which a venal contractor, backed by a corrupt federal agency, was imposing deadly hazards on its unwitting neighbors. Substantiating this definition of the problem, a federal affidavit—based on the FBI investigation and brought before a grand jury in August 1989—alleged that Rockwell and the DOE had broken environmental laws, including RCRA and the Clean Water Act, in treating, storing, and disposing of both radioactive and toxic waste. It also charged that employees had falsified information to conceal the contamination. Finally, the FBI and EPA alleged that not only had the DOE failed to police Rockwell as it should have, but also that it had actually encouraged and then helped to cover up the contractor's mistakes.

During grand jury deliberations, the DOE continued to try to reopen Rocky Flats, despite the fact that in September the EPA had added the site to its Superfund National Priorities List. Impeding DOE efforts, however, was a series of damaging reports about plutonium contamination at the site. One report concerned the banks of filters in metal frames that in theory were protecting the public from plutonium. According to Dr. John Gofman, a former associate director of Lawrence Livermore Laboratory in California and a specialist on the health effects of low-level radiation, that was "not a happy thought for the residents of Colorado." Joe Goldfield, one of the chemical engineers who had helped to develop the filters, was similarly pessimistic: "People have the idea that all dangerous radioactive materials are protected from the public by steel and concrete walls. At Rocky Flats, the protection is fragile paper filters subject to cracking, fires, and being blown out in an explosion." [54] The condition of those filters' frames was also questionable, according to Goldfield and former plant workers.

In September 1989 the DOE terminated Rockwell's management contract and hired a new manager, EG&G of Wellesley, Massachusetts. A month later independent scientists reported finding several kilograms of plutonium in the plant's ventilation ducts, well beyond the point at which the high-efficiency particulate aerosol filters were supposed to stop such releases. In November the DOE closed the plant to conduct a $1 billion safety overhaul. Three months later, in early 1990, EG&G released a stunning piece of news: there were sixty-two pounds of plutonium—enough to make seven nuclear bombs—scattered along miles of ventilation ducts at the plant. In at least one building, filters whose frames had been replaced "did not seal properly, due to surface deterioration of the framework as a result of age." [55] Furthermore, that summer EG&G announced that it would remove only thirteen pounds of the plutonium before the plant reopened. Robert Nelson, the DOE plant manager, did not specify how much plutonium ultimately would be removed, saying only that "there will always be some amount of plutonium in the ducts." Another DOE spokesman said that "in all of the plutonium buildings, there are multiple stages of filters. . . . We will have no duct with more than 400 grams of plutonium in it. This is the quantity of plutonium that cannot go critical in any configuration." [56] Given the plant's history of fires, his words did not reassure people living in the area. Making matters worse, in May 1990 Germak Fletcher Associates, a consulting firm, released a study that cited serious management problems at the plant since EG&G had taken over in January.

In response to the spate of negative publicity, the Senate Armed Services Committee—which for years had backed Rocky Flats—changed its tune and began to question whether the DOE had completed enough of the safety improvements it had projected when it shut down the plant in 1989.[57] Throughout the following year, however, the departments of Defense and Energy continued to pressure Rocky Flats managers to reopen the plant, contending that the Pentagon's next generation of nuclear weapons, including advanced cruise missiles and the powerful 475-kiloton warhead for Trident II submarines, could not be manufactured as long as it was closed. Defending the rush to restart weapons production, Secretary Watkins said in an interview with the *New York Times* that "national security requires a prompt reopening of the plant but the reasons cannot be publicly discussed because they are classified." [58] This line of reasoning had lost its potency, however, and Sen. Tim Wirth, D-Colo., responded that the recent arms control treaty with the Soviet Union made weapons production *less* urgent, not more so. A Congressional Research Service report further undermined Watkins's rationale: it found that preventing Rocky Flats from operating for another two years would have only "modest consequences for national security." [59]

Further tarnishing the DOE's image were allegations of incompetence and corruption in the ongoing safety overhaul at Rocky Flats. A May 1991 department audit found that, although federal law requires that projects costing more than $1.2 million be paid for with specific congressional appropriations, contractors were stringing together the general plant project money to pay for construction projects that cost well over that amount. Some of the most egregious examples occurred at Rocky Flats, where EG&G had financed a $37.4 million project to improve the security of plutonium by allocating the cost of the project among at least thirty general plant construction accounts. Watkins rationalized the practice as a way of avoiding the delays plant managers feared might result from congressional review.[60]

Safety conditions at the plant continued to be an issue. In October 1990 EG&G replaced its plant manager amid employees' allegations that managers were risking unsafe conditions in their frenzy to restart the plant.[61] Nevertheless, in July 1991 the plant failed a readiness review after inspections that cost $1.5 million. In September an internal DOE report heavily criticized the work done to improve safety when an investigative team found numerous problems in the criticality safety program, which is meant to ensure that plutonium bomb fuel is never accidentally assembled in a critical mass that can set off a chain reaction. Investigators also found flaws in worker safety protection.[62]

Further exacerbating negative perceptions of the plant, in October 1991 two former Rocky Flats employees filed a civil suit against the facility in which they described plant management as bumbling and heavy-handed. In the suit, filed in Boulder County District Court, technicians Jaqueline Brever and Karen Pitts claimed that they were threatened, harassed, and forced out of their jobs because managers and coworkers feared they would supply evidence to federal agents that the incinerator had been running when plant officials vowed it was shut down. The technicians quoted the manager of plutonium operations as telling a staff meeting a few days after the FBI raid that "whistle-blowers will be dealt with severely and completely." [63]

Redefining the Problem Prompts Policy Change

The FBI investigation, combined with the exposés of the late 1980s and early 1990s, bolstered the Rocky Flats critics' definition of nuclear weapons production. Ultimately, that reframing of the problem prompted a massive policy shift. In his January 1992 State of the Union address, President George H. W. Bush announced the cessation of production at Rocky Flats. Shortly thereafter, Secretary Watkins formally transformed Rocky Flats' mission to decontamination and decommissioning. In March 1992 the grand jury delivered an explosive report in which it proposed to indict three DOE officials and five Rockwell employees. U.S. Attorney Michael Norton refused to sign the indictments, however, rendering them invalid, and instead announced that Rockwell had agreed to plead guilty to ten violations of environmental laws (five felonies and five misdemeanors) and pay a fine of $18.5 million. In exchange, the Justice Department promised not to indict any Rockwell employees.

The grand jury was furious with this plea agreement. Apparently, the prosecution had outlined for the jurors the charges to which Rockwell eventually pleaded guilty—charges that they considered too lenient. At the time, Norton told them it would be "inadvisable" for them to prepare a report. Nevertheless, the twenty-two members of the panel, inflamed by what they had heard in the courtroom, continued to meet and draft their own indictment, as well as a forty-two-page draft report under the leadership of a Denver lawyer on the panel. They even petitioned Congress for an investigation and wrote to president-elect Bill Clinton to ask for a special prosecutor.[64] When the plea bargain was announced in September, someone leaked the grand jury report to the press, and—in a breach of the secrecy surrounding grand jury proceedings— a Denver weekly newspaper, *Westword,* published a long account of the two- and-a-half-year investigation. In it, the grand jury depicted the DOE as incompetent and, at times, duplicitous, alleging that:

> For forty years, federal, Colorado, and local regulators and elected officials have been unable to make the Department of Energy and the plant's corporate operators obey the law. Indeed, the plant has been and continues to be operated by government and corporate employees who have placed themselves above the law and who have hidden their illegal conduct behind the cloak of "national security." Government and corporate employees have breached the public's trust by engaging in a continuous campaign of distraction, deception, and dishonesty. Little has changed at Rocky Flats since the FBI raid. Employees of the DOE and of EG&G continue to violate many federal environmental laws.[65]

Additional evidence of mismanagement surfaced as national investigative reporters took up the issue. In December 1992 a *U.S. News & World Report* article noted that the DOE had created five ponds at Rocky Flats for storing low-level radioactive and hazardous wastes. The idea was that contaminated liquid would evaporate. In 1985 DOE officials ordered Rockwell to clean up the sludge residue in the ponds. Rockwell's approach, which involved mixing the sludge with concrete and then disposing of the hardened blocks, failed miserably. As a result, the DOE's projected cleanup cost of $27 million escalated to $131 million, and possibly as high as $169 million; moreover, the agency did not expect the ponds to be cleaned up before 2009. In addition, the article pointed out, between 1990 and 1991 EG&G had awarded at least eleven "no bid" contracts to its own subsidiaries. Those contracts increased from an estimated $2.8 million to $10 million, and work on seven of the eleven contracts was completed behind schedule.[66]

Between the grand jury report and the ongoing media revelations, by the end of 1992 the environmental problems in the nuclear weapons complex had become sufficiently public that Congress felt compelled to act. Largely in response to the scandals at Rocky Flats, Congress passed the Federal Facilities Compliance Act, which held federal facilities to the same environmental standards as private companies. Moreover, in December the House Science, Space, and Technology Committee convened hearings on the Rockwell plea bargain. The committee's final report, issued in January 1993, charged that the Justice Department had given Rockwell too sweet a deal. The most benign interpretation, according to the report, was that the Justice Department regarded environmental crimes as unimportant; at worst, Justice may have gone out of its way to downplay the DOE's failure to oversee Rockwell's activities. Kenneth Fimberg, the government's lead prosecutor, defended the plea agreement saying that the fine against Rockwell was roughly five times as high as the previous record for a hazardous waste case and, in his opinion, taking the case to trial would have been extremely risky.[67] Prosecutors also felt that fairness prevented them from indicting individuals who had simply followed bad public policy.[68]

Cleaning Up Rocky Flats: How Clean Is Clean Enough?

Cleanup activities at Rocky Flats and throughout the nuclear weapons complex got off to an inauspicious start but accelerated in the mid-1990s. In 1994 the DOE renamed the Rocky Flats plant the Rocky Flats Environmental Technology Site to reflect its new objective of environmental restoration, waste management, decommissioning, decontamination, and economic development. In 1995 the DOE chose Kaiser-Hill as the new site contractor, and the following year the DOE, the EPA, and the Colorado Department of Public Health and Environment signed a new Rocky Flats Cleanup Agreement to replace the original signed in 1991.[69] Under the agreement, the state health department was to oversee cleanup in the former weapons production area, and the EPA was responsible for cleaning up the buffer zone. Early plans for the closure of Rocky Flats called for cleanup to be done and the DOE to withdraw by 2065 at an estimated cost of nearly $37 billion. But after designating Rocky Flats an Accelerated Closure site in 1997, the DOE drew up a new closure strategy that set 2006 as the target cleanup date, with a much lower price tag of approximately $7 billion.

The original plan for Rocky Flats was to leave the 6,200-acre buffer zone as open space, complete with hiking and biking trails, and to use the industrial core for open space or industrial redevelopment. But in 1999 and again in 2001 Sen. Wayne Allard, R-Colo., and Rep. Mark Udall, D-Colo., sponsored a bill to turn the entire site into a wildlife refuge. In defense of their proposal, they pointed out that about 250 species of wildlife use the high plains grassland, streams, and ponds that surround the site and that observers had documented the presence of twenty species of sparrows, nineteen species of ducks, and thirteen species of neotropical warblers. But some environmentalists, as well as officials from abutting towns, were concerned that the refuge designation would allow the DOE to embrace lower cleanup standards, and they refused to support the proposal.[70] To alleviate this fear, the bill's authors inserted language requiring the DOE to clean up the site to the levels established by the "regulators, the public, and interested state and federal agencies based on science, law and agreements reached with the public." [71] In other words, the bill—which passed in 2001—specifically prohibited using the wildlife refuge designation to avoid strict cleanup standards.

Yet many observers believe that is precisely what the EPA and the DOE proceeded to do. In an effort to defuse hostility toward the plant and improve public participation in the cleanup effort, in 1993 the DOE formed the Rocky Flats Citizen Advisory Board (RFCAB), which included representatives of local government, public interest groups, and academic institutions, as well as local citizens. In 1994 another DOE-funded advisory body, the Rocky Flats Local Impacts Initiative, created the Rocky Flats Future Site Use Working Group to advise the agency about the community's vision for the site. In June 1995 the working group submitted its consensus recommendation that the site be cleaned up so that only background levels of radiation remained, and both the Local Impacts Initiative and RFCAB endorsed this approach.[72] Nevertheless, the 1996 cleanup agreement established an interim "soil action level" of 651 picocuries of plutonium per gram of soil, which critics pointed out vastly exceeded levels for similar projects around the world.

To allay citizens' concerns, the DOE announced in 1997 that it would fund a citizen-directed scientific assessment of the soil standards. In February 2000 the independent contractor hired by the panel recommended soil cleanup levels of only 35 picocuries per gram and suggested that levels as low as 10 picocuries per gram might be necessary to ensure compliance with surface water standards. Nevertheless, in 2003 the DOE adopted revised cleanup standards that would allow a concentration of 50 picocuries per gram to remain in the top three feet of soil, up to 1,000 picocuries per gram at a depth of three to six feet, and no limit below six feet. (RFCAB had recommended more stringent standards.) Such an approach, the agency argued, would protect the "maximally exposed individual" on the site: a wildlife refuge worker. More important, however, it would enable Kaiser-Hill to limit cleanup costs to the agreed-on level.

OUTCOMES

The goal of closing Rocky Flats by 2006 presented a monumental task. In 2001 the GAO cited as a primary obstacle the difficulty of getting the necessary permits and the number of containers needed to transport and dispose of waste: the site had accumulated as much as twenty-one tons of nuclear materials—fourteen tons of plutonium and seven tons of enriched uranium—during its forty years of operation; in addition, there were hundreds of thousands of fifty-five-gallon drums of low-level radioactive waste, low-level mixed waste, transuranic waste, and hazardous wastes.[73] The process of demolishing equipment and buildings generated even more waste. The site had enough radioactive waste to fill a nineteen-story building the size of a football field, and all of it was to be shipped off site and across state lines to Nevada, New Mexico, Tennessee, and Utah.[74]

Despite its ambitious schedule, Kaiser-Hill is on track to complete the cleanup a year earlier than projected—by the end of 2005. As of summer 2005 workers had razed most of the original 805-building complex. Kaiser-Hill had also installed groundwater treatment systems to intercept contaminated plumes of groundwater before they could surface; the system instead funnels them through treatment cells that remove or reduce the contaminants.[75] As part of the cleanup, contractors had drained more than 4,000 gallons of volatile plutonium solutions from leaking pipes and tanks and unearthed another thirty tons of depleted uranium from outdoor trenches.[76] They had shipped thousands of pounds of plutonium pits to the Pantex facility near Amarillo, Texas, and removed all of the remaining weapons-grade plutonium from the site. In December 2004 Kaiser-Hill sent the last of the 1,457 glove boxes to Utah. In April 2005 the final shipment of high-level radioactive waste left Rocky Flats for disposal in New Mexico, and officials were predicting they would finish the cleanup in November.

Although faster cleanup saves money, critics argue that haste has led to sloppy and dangerous practices. In December 2000 plant officials disclosed that ten workers cleaning Building 771, the site's most contaminated building (often called "the most dangerous building in America"), had tested positive for exposure to radiation. More worrisome still, officials were unable to find the source of the radiation, and an earlier inspection had shown that at least one radiation monitor in the building had malfunctioned.[77] In January 2001 the DOE revealed that Rocky Flats had fourteen criticality incidents in 1999 and five in 2000. Kaiser-Hill, which had been fined $700,000 for safety violations since 1996, admitted that there were 138 worker-injury cases in 1999 and ninety-one in 2000.[78] In 2004 the DOE levied a fine of $522,000 against Kaiser-Hill for violations that led to the contamination of ten employees and involved improper storage of weapons-grade plutonium and combustible materials during 2002.[79]

CONCLUSIONS

The Rocky Flats case is unique in some respects, but secrecy and disregard for environmental laws have been endemic throughout the defense establishment. Historically, the Pentagon's vast enterprise produced well over a ton of toxic wastes every minute, a yearly output that some claimed was greater than that of the top five U.S. chemical companies combined. To make matters worse, the military branch of the federal government for decades operated almost entirely unfettered by environmental laws. The armed forces have contaminated virtually every one of their installations in the United States and, undoubtedly, hundreds more overseas. At the majority of the military's contaminated facilities, huge quantities of toxic wastes dumped into the ground have seeped beyond their fences and into local groundwater. As journalist Seth Shulman noted in the early 1990s, "[T]he military routinely [sanctioned] practices that [had] long been illegal for private firms operating in this country . . .

even in the face of hard evidence that pollutants [had] contaminated the drinking water of nearby residents, the Pentagon . . . tried to keep the dumping secret and thereby knowingly threatened the health of millions of U.S. citizens." [80]

Secrecy bred arrogance and carelessness among government officials: as Douglas Pasternak of *U.S. News & World Report* makes clear, the DOE bore much of the responsibility for the contractor violations at Rocky Flats. Because of personnel or budget constraints, DOE officials were sometimes incapable of assessing contractor performance, so they allowed companies to assess their own work. The DOE almost never challenged these evaluations; in fact, the agency used them to help determine the amount of contractors' fees and bonuses. At Rocky Flats, despite numerous problems, Rockwell filed a positive assessment of its management. That assessment was rewritten, with only modest changes, at the DOE's Rocky Flats office and typed on DOE letterhead. The department then passed the report on to the agency's Albuquerque field office, which sent it unchanged to Washington for approval.[81] Nor was Rocky Flats the only culprit: a December 1988 DOE report listed 155 instances of environmental contamination at its weapons plants and laboratories, many of which resulted from the disposal of nonradioactive toxic waste by using techniques that had been banned in private industry for more than a decade.[82]

Just as secrecy spawned recklessness, exposure enabled critics to redefine weapons production at Rocky Flats. New information disclosed by whistleblowers, government investigators, and journalists supported an alternative portrayal of the plant as an imminent threat to the health of surrounding residents, which in turn prompted a public outcry. Over time, the feedback that developed among public outrage, media coverage, and congressional investigations created incentives for Colorado politicians to challenge the federal government's "sovereign immunity" and take "a hard line on environmental health and safety standards at weapons plants once welcomed for their payroll." [83] Eventually, even the president and Congress got on the bandwagon in support of a massive nuclear weapons cleanup program.

NIMBY activism that blocks disposal of nuclear waste has complicated that cleanup, however. NIMBY groups pose a dilemma for some environmentalists because they embody the participatory ideal that many environmentalists cherish, yet they can thwart serious attempts to solve problems. One potential consequence of NIMBYism is that toxic waste has been accumulating at sites that are ill-prepared to manage it in the long term. Unlike sites specifically chosen for hazardous waste disposal, such locations have not been scrutinized for their hydrological and geological fitness. Nor have the containers in which toxic substances are placed been designed for long-term storage. On the other hand, journalist Matthew Wald argues that "with nuclear waste, procrastination may actually pay" because it allows time for the development of better storage technology.[84]

Another obstacle to the cleanup at Rocky Flats and other military installations is sharp disagreement over how clean is clean enough. The EPA, in conjunction with the DOE, is establishing separate cleanup standards at each federal installation. Many observers suggest that cleanup levels ought to be tied to future land uses, pointing out that "it makes little sense to impose the same cleanup standards on a future airport or industrial site as on a future playground." [85] But most acknowledge that future land uses are speculative. Moreover, it is difficult to ascertain the level of risk posed by a contaminated site, so even if participants agreed on the likely future use of the land, they would almost certainly still argue over what constitutes a safe level of cleanup. Such debates, which often pit citizens against experts, strain democratic decision-making procedures. At Rocky Flats, managers are making conspicuous efforts to link citizens and experts in cleanup decisions in hopes of averting gridlock. Ultimately, however, the citizen advisory groups created by the DOE seem to have had little impact on the final decision about soil cleanup levels there, affirming the worries of some observers that such boards are "little more than public relations vehicles." [86]

QUESTIONS TO CONSIDER

- Was the government justified in maintaining a veil of secrecy over nuclear weapons production? Why or why not?
- What safeguards, if any, do citizens have for ensuring that the government is not a major source of pollution?
- Are citizen advisory groups a good idea, and, if so, how can Congress ensure such groups have a genuine impact on agency decision making?

Notes

1. Charles Piller, *The Fail-Safe Society: Community Defiance and the End of American Technological Optimism* (New York: Basic Books, 1991), 75.
2. Frank R. Baumgartner and Bryan D. Jones, *Agendas and Instability in American Politics* (Chicago: University of Chicago Press, 1993).
3. William Glaberson, "Coping in the Age of 'Nimby,' " *New York Times,* June 19, 1988, Sec. 3, 1.
4. Piller, *The Fail-Safe Society.*
5. Susan Hunter and Kevin M. Leyden, "Beyond NIMBY: Explaining Opposition to Hazardous Waste Facilities," *Policy Studies Journal* 23 (Winter 1995): 601–619.
6. Paul Slovic, "Perceptions of Risk: Reflections on the Psychometric Paradigm," in *Social Theories of Risk,* ed. Sheldon Krimsky and Dominic Golding (Westport, Conn.: Praeger, 1992), 117–152; Gregory E. McAvoy, "Partisan Probing and Democratic Decisionmaking: Rethinking the Nimby Syndrome," *Policy Studies Journal* 26 (Summer 1998): 274–293.
7. See, for example, Marc Landy and Mary Hague, "The Coalition for Waste: Private Interests and Superfund," in *Environmental Politics: Public Costs, Private Rewards,* ed. Michael S. Greve and Fred L. Smith (New York: Praeger, 1992), 67–87.
8. Piller, *The Fail-Safe Society,* 39.
9. Bryan Abas, "Rocky Flats: A Big Mistake From Day One," *Bulletin of Atomic Scientists* 45 (December 1989): 19–24.
10. Ibid., 20.
11. Len Ackland, *Making a Real Killing: Rocky Flats and the Nuclear West* (Albuquerque: University of New Mexico Press, 1999).

12. Abas, "Rocky Flats," 20.

13. Mark Miller, "Trouble at Rocky Flats," *Newsweek*, August 14, 1989, 19.

14. The 1946 Atomic Energy Act, quoted in Ackland, *Making a Real Killing*, 33–34.

15. ChemRisk, "Reconstruction of Historical Rocky Flats Operations & Identification of Release Points." Report produced for the Colorado Department of Public Health, August 1992.

16. Ibid., 51.

17. Ackland, *Making a Real Killing*.

18. Glove boxes are enclosed, lead-lined containers that are filled with inert gases designed to prevent the spontaneous combustion that occurs when plutonium comes into contact with moist air. Glove boxes are sealed with protective rubber gloves. Workers put their hands in the gloves and reach through portholes to handle radioactive materials inside the boxes.

19. Colorado Department of Public Health and Environment, "Summary of Findings: Historical Public Exposure Studies on Rocky Flats," August 1999.

20. Abas, "Rocky Flats." Dow's official investigation report, which was classified until 1993, stated that 18.3 pounds of plutonium were unaccounted for after the fire, but health physicists have estimated the actual plutonium release at between 1.8 ounces and 1.1 pounds. See Ackland, *Making a Real Killing*.

21. Ackland, *Making a Real Killing*; Piller, *The Fail-Safe Society*.

22. Quoted in Mark Obmascik, "Price of Peace," *Denver Post*, June 25, 2000, A1.

23. Piller, *The Fail-Safe Society*; Colorado Department of Public Health, "Summary of Findings."

24. Quoted in Ackland, *Making a Real Killing*, 158.

25. Michael Janofsky, "Workers Cleaning Nuclear Arms Site for Wildlife Preserve Test Positive for Radiation," *New York Times*, December 8, 2000, A19.

26. Colorado Department of Public Health, "Summary of Findings."

27. The radioactivity released in atmospheric tests is dispersed in the upper atmosphere, whereas Rocky Flats' releases stay closer to the surface. See Abas, "Rocky Flats."

28. Tritium is the sole radioactive isotope of the element hydrogen.

29. Abas, "Rocky Flats."

30. Ackland, *Making a Real Killing*.

31. Piller, *The Fail-Safe Society*.

32. Carl Johnson, "Cancer Incidence in an Area Contaminated with Radionuclides Near a Nuclear Installation," *Ambio*, August 1981, 176–182; Carl Johnson et al., "Cancer Incidence and Mortality, 1957–1981, in the Denver Standard Metropolitan Area Downwind from the Rocky Flats Nuclear Plant," paper presented at the epidemiological section of the American Public Health Association (November 11, 1983).

33. Ackland, *Making a Real Killing*.

34. James Baker, "A New Scare at Rocky Flats," *Newsweek*, June 26, 1989, 60.

35. Abas, "Rocky Flats."

36. Such devices use 1,000-degree Fahrenheit smokeless, flameless chemical reactions to incinerate waste.

37. Quoted in Thomas J. Knudson, "Families Fear Test on Nuclear Waste," *New York Times*, April 23, 1987, A16.

38. Ibid.

39. Piller, *The Fail-Safe Society*.

40. Ibid.

41. Quoted in Piller, *The Fail-Safe Society*, 52.

42. Ibid.

43. Abas, "Rocky Flats."

44. U.S. GAO, "Nuclear Health and Safety: Summary of Major Problems at DOE's Rocky Flats Plant," RCED-89-53-BR (October 1988).

45. George J. Church, "Playing Atomic NIMBY," *Time*, December 26, 1988, 29.
46. Until 1984 the DOE managed the mixed hazardous and radioactive wastes generated by its facilities independent of any outside supervision. But that year a court ruling subjected DOE facilities to RCRA, which establishes a "cradle to grave" tracking system for such wastes and requires companies that handle hazardous waste to obtain a waste disposal permit from the EPA or an authorized state agency. Colorado established the 1,600-cubic-yard limit for on-site mixed and hazardous wastes. After initially resisting state control, in 1986 the DOE submitted to state jurisdiction over its hazardous and mixed wastes because it feared having to reveal "patently illegal" waste management practices at the plant. See Piller, *The Fail-Safe Society*. In 1988 Colorado Health Department officials cited Rocky Flats for nine violations of hazardous waste disposal laws, but a year later they had not determined the amount of the fine—it could have been as much as $25,000 for each violation—let alone collected any money. See Abas, "Rocky Flats."
47. Church, "Playing Atomic NIMBY."
48. Piller, *The Fail-Safe Society*, 74.
49. Miller, "Trouble at Rocky Flats."
50. "Colorado Nuclear Mystery," *Time*, June 26, 1989, 31.
51. Quoted in Abas, "Rocky Flats," 24.
52. Vicky Cahan, "Energy Czar—and Environmental Activist?" *Business Week*, July 24, 1989, 54.
53. Thomas Graf, "Safety Pact Reached on Rocky Flats," *Denver Post*, June 17, 1989, 1.
54. Minard Hamilton, "Papered Over," *Mother Jones*, November–December 1990, 29.
55. Ibid.
56. Quoted in ibid.
57. Congress abolished the Joint Committee on Atomic Energy in 1977 and transferred responsibility for nuclear weapons oversight to the Armed Services committees in each chamber, thereby creating opportunities for congressional critics of the nuclear weapons complex to become more involved in policymaking.
58. Quoted in Matthew L. Wald, "As U.S. Struggles to Restart Colorado Bomb Plant, Critics Question Its Need," *New York Times*, July 25, 1991, A18.
59. Ibid.
60. Keith Schneider, "New Irregularities Found at A-Weapons Plants," *New York Times*, May 24, 1991, A13.
61. "Manager of Troubled Arms Plant Is Removed," *New York Times*, October 21, 1990, 25.
62. Matthew L. Wald, "New Setbacks for Nuclear Arms Complex," *New York Times*, September 10, 1991, A17.
63. Quoted in Matthew L. Wald, "Plutonium Plant Accused in Civil Suit," *New York Times*, October 26, 1991, A6.
64. "The Rocky Flats Cover-up, Continued," *Harper's Magazine*, December 1992, 19–23.
65. Quoted in ibid., 19. In response to the report's publication, Judge Sherman Finesilver ordered the FBI to investigate whether jurors had violated federal grand jury secrecy laws, but that investigation eventually was dropped. In 2004 Wes McKinley, the grand jury foreman, published a book entitled *The Ambushed Grand Jury* that alleged the U.S. Justice Department covered up crimes by government officials and contractors.
66. Douglas Pasternak, "A $200 Billion Scandal," *U.S. News & World Report*, December 14, 1992, 34–47.
67. Michael Lemonick, "Sometimes It Takes a Cowboy," *Time*, January 25, 1993, 58.
68. Matthew L. Wald, "Nuclear Fingerprints All Over, But Try to Find the Hands," *New York Times*, June 7, 1992, E4.
69. In 1991 the DOE, the EPA, and Colorado's health and environment department had signed the Rocky Flats Interagency Agreement identifying 178 contaminated areas at the site and establishing a comprehensive plan for environmental restoration.

70. Theo Stein, "Flats Touted as Wildlife Refuge," *Denver Post*, February 22, 2001, B1; Kevin Flynn, "Arvada Backs Flats as Refuge," *Denver Rocky Mountain News*, August 29, 2000, 18A.

71. Rep. Mark Udall, "Introduction of Rocky Flats National Wildlife Refuge Act," U.S. Congress, House, *Congressional Record* 107th, Cong., 1st sess., March 1, 2001.

72. LeRoy Moore, "Rocky Flats: The Bait-and-Switch Cleanup," *Bulletin of the Atomic Scientists* 61 (January/February 2005): 50–57.

73. Rocky Flats Coalition of Local Governments et al., "Rocky Flats Closure" (April 2000).

74. U.S. GAO, *Nuclear Cleanup: Progress Made at Rocky Flats, but Closure by 2006 Is Unlikely, and Costs May Increase*, GAO-01-284 (February 2001).

75. The latest information is available at www.rfets.gov.

76. Obmascik, "Price of Peace."

77. Janofsky, "Workers Cleaning Nuclear Arms Site."

78. Stacie Oulton, "Flats Cleanup Violations Cited," *Denver Post*, January 9, 2001, B4.

79. Patricia Calhoun, "Toxic Shocker," *Westword*, March 11, 2004.

80. Seth Shulman, *The Threat at Home* (Boston: Little, Brown, 1992), xiii.

81. Pasternak, "A $200 Billion Scandal."

82. See Pat Towell, "Need for a Massive Cleanup May Slow Weapon-Building," *Congressional Quarterly Weekly Report*, January 20, 1990, 178–183.

83. Ibid., 178.

84. Matthew L. Wald, "A New Vision for Nuclear Waste," *Technology Review*, December 2004, 40. Wald argues that there are a host of technical problems with disposing of high-level nuclear waste at Yucca Mountain, Nevada, which was selected more for political than scientific reasons. He adds that storage technology is likely to improve in the next hundred years, and delay would allow the government to profit from those advances.

85. John A. Hird, *Superfund: The Political Economy of Environmental Risk* (Baltimore: Johns Hopkins University Press, 1994), 111.

86. Robert C. Lowry, "All Hazardous Waste Politics Is Local," *Policy Studies Journal* 26 (Winter 1998): 756.

Recommended Reading

Ackland, Len. *Making a Real Killing: Rocky Flats and the Nuclear West*. Albuquerque: University of New Mexico Press, 1999.

Shulman, Seth. *The Threat at Home*. Boston: Little, Brown, 1992.

Web Sites

www.energy.gov (DOE site)
www.rfcab.org (Rocky Flats Citizen Advisory Board site)
www.rfets.gov (Rocky Flats Environmental Technology site)

CHAPTER 5

Community Activism and Environmental Justice

The Dudley Street Neighborhood Initiative

In the late 1980s and early 1990s the city of Boston witnessed a near-miraculous transformation of one its most distressed neighborhoods. By 2005 the Dudley Street neighborhood—one and a half square miles once dominated by derelict buildings, vacant lots turned waste dumps, and streets lined with abandoned cars—was well on its way to becoming a vibrant urban village. Even more striking, this metamorphosis was not just another example of urban redevelopment orchestrated by the city in concert with a handful of developers; nor was it the result of gentrification, in which high-income professionals displace lower-income residents as renovations raise property values. Rather, the community itself—predominantly poor and minority—came together to take control of its own destiny.

The Dudley Street Neighborhood Initiative (DSNI) is a prominent example of grassroots organizations that aim for "environmental justice," a broad goal that includes objectives such as eliminating environmental hazards, enforcing environmental regulations equitably, gaining minority representation in environmental decision making, and creating safe, affordable housing and clean jobs.[1] The issue of environmental justice (EJ) appeared on the national political agenda in the early 1990s, and in 1994 President Bill Clinton issued Executive Order 12898, which required agencies to avoid inflicting disproportionate environmental harms on minorities and the poor. But EJ first gained widespread visibility in 1982, when citizens in Warren County, North Carolina, protested (unsuccessfully) a decision to dump PCB-laden hazardous waste in a county landfill.[2] Their actions prompted the U.S. General Accounting Office (GAO) to investigate the Environmental Protection Agency's (EPA) Region IV. The investigation revealed that three of the region's four hazardous waste facilities were in predominantly African American communities, and the fourth was in a low-income community.

Shortly thereafter, a series of quantitative assessments documented racial disparities in proximity to hazardous waste sites and in the enforcement of environmental laws around the country.[3] Although some critics challenged the methods used in these early analyses, dozens of subsequent studies confirmed the existence of race-based discrepancies in administering environmental regulations and choosing sites for dirty industries. In 2001 a comprehensive analysis of state-, county-, and city-level data confirmed the prevalence of inequities in the distribution of environmental hazards facing black and Hispanic Americans.[4] It has been trickier to pinpoint the causes of environmental injustice, which vary by site, but they probably include a combination of job and housing market forces, discriminatory real estate and financial practices, and exclusionary regulatory processes.

For mainstream environmentalists, the EJ movement initially appeared to pose a challenge because it expanded the definition of "the environment" to include not only the natural landscape but also the places "where [people] live, work, play, worship and go to school." [5] Furthermore, whereas mainstream environmentalism had come to rely heavily on professional, Washington, D.C.-based lobbying groups, the EJ movement united local organizations all over the United States that were striving to foster the sense of efficacy and the indigenous resources so essential to the success of social activism.[6] It aimed to build social capital—"social networks, norms of reciprocity, mutual assistance, and trustworthiness"[7]—to empower poor and minority populations. EJ activists believed that community-based organizations were more likely than professional environmental groups to meet the real needs of a particular place, have social and political legitimacy, and instill pride and hope in their participants.

Over time many environmentalists (albeit belatedly) embraced EJ. For some, this acceptance was part of a pragmatic effort to broaden the environmental coalition. For others, it came from the recognition that they shared with EJ activists a larger progressive and participatory vision. Still others understood that the urban revitalization many EJ activists pursue is an antidote to the widely recognized environmental problem of urban sprawl—the relentless spread of low-density development into rural landscapes. For example, a central EJ goal is to clean up urban brownfields—former industrial sites or abandoned lots, many of which are contaminated—and redevelop them as affordable housing, community meeting places, urban gardens, and parks. Most brownfields are located in older urban centers that, according to architect and planner Oliver Gillham "may represent the nation's best prospect for creating compact, walkable, mixed-use, transit-friendly communities." [8]

Despite its apparent desirability, comprehensive, citizen-led urban revitalization faces a host of legal, economic, and political barriers that are particularly formidable for low-income communities of color. Obstacles include control of property by absentee or indebted owners who may be hard to find or unwilling to relinquish the land; hazardous waste cleanup laws whose liability provisions make owners reluctant to dispose of, or even assess, contaminated land; local zoning and land use regulations that limit prospective developers' flexibility; and discriminatory real estate, lending, and insurance practices by institutions that perceive investment in poor, minority neighborhoods as financially risky. Other impediments include community skepticism, often born of disheartening experience, which makes it difficult to gain residents' trust and maintain their involvement; the challenge of piecing together funding from a complex web of public and private sources that may restrict how money can be used; and the daunting task of concurrently addressing distressed communities' multiple interrelated needs, from housing to economic development to social services.[9]

As the Dudley Street neighborhood story makes clear, these hurdles, though high, are not insurmountable. Overcoming them, however, depends heavily on a neighborhood's ability to gain clout within a city's political system. Many political scientists and sociologists have argued that disadvantaged city residents have little if any impact on urban policy, even if they are organized. According to "structuralist" or "economic constraint" theorists, the dynamics of the underlying socioeconomic system—in particular the resources and mobility of business and wealthy property owners—limit the capacity of a city to enact redistributive policies and force its leaders to focus instead on promoting economic growth.[10] From this perspective the interests of the private and public sectors are aligned: the role of city officials is to create a climate that is advantageous to business and well-to-do residents. Whatever benefits accrue to poor neighborhoods trickle down from vigorous urban cores. Structuralists "[highlight] the ways that private property, market competition, wealth and income inequality, the corporate system, and the stage of capitalist development pervasively shape the terrain on which political competition occurs." [11] But other scholars have pointed out that, despite constraints on a city's capacity to adopt progressive policies, considerable variation can be found in cities' responsiveness to poor and minority residents.[12] Political scientist Barbara Ferman argues that a neighborhood's success in making demands on city government depends on its ability to tailor its persuasive campaign to the particular combination of the city's culture and institutional arrangements.[13] In Boston, for example, where most important political decisions get made through elections and the political culture has a populist flavor, effective grassroots organizing can produce a response from the city's political system.

BACKGROUND

The deterioration of America's urban areas began in the late 1800s, as improved transportation and cheaper construction techniques enabled middle-income Americans to flee the cities for the leafy, streetcar-accessible suburbs. The process accelerated rapidly after World War II, when the construction of the national highway system (justified on the grounds of national defense) prompted an explosion of suburban development. In addition to the highway project, other federal programs created powerful incentives for sprawling, low-density development. For example, the Federal Housing Administration's insurance program for long-term housing construction and purchase loans, which made possible the widespread use of mortgages, strongly favored single-family homes over apartment projects.[14] Reinforcing the trend toward suburbanization was the introduction of shopping malls that could be reached only by car, and the exodus of manufacturing from the cities in response to the availability of trucking as a transportation option.

The incentives created by government-backed market forces do not fully explain the pattern of urban decline that occurred, however. Beginning in the

1950s and intensifying in the 1960s and 1970s, middle-class white Americans fled the cities in response to a wave of migration of blacks from the South and, later, school desegregation efforts. At the same time, low- and middle-income minorities found themselves excluded from the suburbs by discriminatory public and private lending and insurance practices collectively known as "redlining." With the out-migration of prosperous families and businesses, urban tax bases shrank, making it difficult for municipal governments to provide services to their hard-pressed residents. By the 1980s these patterns had become entrenched, and America's older cities were dotted with pockets of extreme poverty, crime, and physical deterioration. Despite the economic growth of that decade, the economic and social health of those areas grew worse.[15]

In the early 1980s Boston's Dudley Street neighborhood was a classic example of a blighted inner-city neighborhood with few prospects for renewal. Less than two miles south of downtown and once the location of wealthy Bostonians' country estates, by the 1800s the area at the intersection of Roxbury and Dorchester had become a thriving working-class immigrant community (see Map 5-1). Even as suburbanization began to drain the city, the Dudley Street neighborhood held on: in 1950 homes, business, municipal buildings, union halls, and social clubs lined Dudley Street and Blue Hill Avenue.[16] But during the 1950s the area underwent an abrupt transition. The population of what became the neighborhood's "core" area plummeted and shifted from predominantly white to mostly black. As realtors and banks redlined the area in response to the influx of minorities, owners who found themselves unable to improve or sell their property abandoned their buildings, which then deteriorated rapidly. Businesses vanished: the number of private enterprises on Dudley Street fell from 129 in 1950 to 26 in 1980; on Blue Hill Avenue the number dropped from 210 in 1950 to 47 in 1980.[17] Exacerbating the neighborhood's woes, arson ravaged the housing stock as residents tried to "burn their way out" of places where property values had declined precipitously.[18] The resulting vacant lots—an astonishing 1,300 in the one-and-a half-square-mile neighborhood—became dumping grounds for trash from all over the city.

Elected officials routinely ignored residents' pleas to clean up the mess. According to longtime community activist Robert Haas, "This part of Roxbury has really gotten the short end of the stick. When a street light breaks down, it takes an act of God to get it repaired." [19] There were several reasons for this situation. First, the neighborhood had neither cohesion nor leadership: a 1979 Boston Redevelopment Authority (BRA) report described the Dudley neighborhood as "typical of many lower income areas in that city services are inadequate, in part because of the lack of a well organized community. . . . Apathy seems pervasive among both residents and those responsible for street cleaning and garbage collection." [20] And second, the neighborhood lacked politically connected advocates. Kevin White, mayor from 1967 to 1983, although a liberal, was focused primarily on revitalizing the city's downtown to make

Map 5-1 Boston's Dudley Street Neighborhood

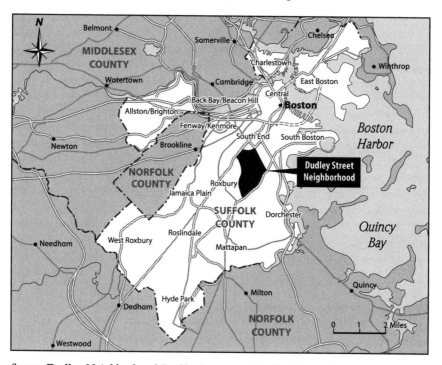

Source: Dudley Neighborhood Profile, June 2003. Dudley Street Neighborhood Initiative, www.dsni.org.

Boston a world-class city. At the state level Dudley's representation was diluted because the area was divided among several legislators. (Redistricting in the late 1980s changed the district lines.)

THE CASE

The Dudley Street Neighborhood Initiative, which formed in the mid-1980s, aimed to reverse Dudley's devastation by embarking on a citizen-led urban revitalization. Beginning with a massive cleanup campaign, DSNI mobilized residents and created the basis for sustained local participation in shaping the neighborhood's fate. DSNI proceeded to involve citizens in creating and implementing a plan for an urban village that included affordable housing, small businesses, parks, community gardens, and a town common. It also orchestrated a strategy to resuscitate the area's many brownfields by fostering urban agriculture. Thanks largely to DSNI's efforts, the neighborhood became "a national symbol of comprehensive community-based empowerment and development in depressed inner-city neighborhoods with moderate help from local government." [21]

Origins of the Dudley Street Neighborhood Initiative

By the mid-1980s, when DSNI was formed, the Dudley area had become one of the city's most depressed and appeared to outsiders to be unsalvageable. The neighborhood was poorer and younger than Boston as a whole; its population was nearly two-thirds black, whereas Boston's was two-thirds white. Compared to the city overall, Dudley's unemployment rate was at least twice as high, its per capita income was half, and the poverty rate was double (see Table 5-1). Furthermore, the Dudley area was isolated from the rest of the city, much of which had been gentrified. It had neither a supermarket nor a bank, and its prospects for renewal were grim: as with many such neighborhoods, investors' expectations of continued decline had become a self-fulfilling prophecy, as discriminatory lending policies reinforced investors' and residents' pessimism. Even more discouraging, previous redevelopment experiments, such as the federal Model Cities program, had failed to deliver on their promises.

The original impetus for DSNI was serendipitous: in spring 1984 Nelson Merced, the director of a nonprofit social service organization, La Alianza His-

Table 5-1
Demographic Data for the Dudley Street Neighborhood
and the City of Boston, 1990

	Dudley St. Neighborhood Initiative Area	City of Boston
Population	23,361	607,000
Race		
Asian	2%	5%
Black	63%	26%
American Indian	1%	0.3%
White	12%	63%
Other	23%	6%
Hispanic origin	23%	10%
Unemployment rate	15%	8%
Over 25 without high school diploma	39%	24%
Poverty rate	32%	19%
Households receiving public assistance	27%	12%
Female head-of-household with children	24%	9%
Median family income	$23,360	$36,256
Households	7,332	249,034
Housing units occupied by renters	74%	69%
Vacant housing units	12%	9%

Source: U.S. Government Accounting Office, *Community Development: Comprehensive Approaches Address Multiple Needs but Are Challenging to Implement*, GAO/RCED/ HEHS-95-69 (February 1995).

panica, approached the Boston-based Riley Foundation for funds to spruce up the group's deteriorating headquarters on Dudley Street. When the foundation's trustees visited to assess the organization's needs, Merced seized the opportunity to make a presentation on the area's decline, after which the trustees asked him to take them on a tour of the neighborhood's most devastated blocks. Trustee Robert Holmes Jr. described his shock at the realization that such an area—a "negative space, a place defined by neglect"—could exist in the middle of Boston.[22] Moved by what they saw, the trustees decided on a tactical shift from distributing small grants throughout the city to concentrating more of the foundation's resources on the Dudley Street neighborhood in hopes of encouraging redevelopment there.

That fall, the Riley Foundation convened a series of meetings at which representatives of Dudley area social service organizations discussed the neighborhood's problems and priorities. The group, which named itself the Dudley Advisory Group, decided to create a formal organization that would focus its energies on a 507-acre "core," over one-fifth of which consisted of vacant lots or abandoned buildings. In time, it would expand its activities to the secondary, surrounding area (see Map 5-2). The group also established a twenty-three-member governing board and in January 1985 named the new entity the Dudley Street Neighborhood Initiative. The founders explicitly aimed to make DSNI a planning and community organizing body, not a developer or service provider; from the outset the emphasis was on mediating among the various entities that already existed in the community.[23]

Hoping to gain the neighborhood's imprimatur on its anticipated two-year planning process, DSNI held its first communitywide meeting in St. Patrick's Church on Saturday, February 23, 1985. About 200 residents attended the meeting, many of them galvanized by a *Boston Herald* article reporting that the BRA had conceived a $750 million urban renewal scheme for nearby Dudley Square that called for an office and high-tech center, as well as retail space and new housing. Although the city promised the project would not displace anyone, current residents were distrustful. Many were refugees of the recent wave of gentrification in Jamaica Plain and the South End; others had already received offers from real-estate agents or had seen men in business suits surveying the neighborhood's vacant lots. They feared the booming downtown development would inevitably lead to their dislocation.[24]

The fledgling DSNI board had assumed it would gain the community's endorsement with relative ease, but instead, the initial meeting was tense and confrontational. Resident Che Madyun, suspicious of DSNI's motives, immediately challenged the proposed composition of the organization's governing board, which reserved only four of twenty-three slots specifically for residents. In a far-sighted move, the board quickly acknowledged its mistake and acceded to residents' demands; it created a new structure with thirty-one members, of which the majority (sixteen) would be residents. To prevent infighting, the board also decided on equal, rather than proportional, representation of each of the area's four main ethnic groups (black, white, Latino,

Map 5-2 The Core and Triangle Areas of the Dudley Street Neighborhood

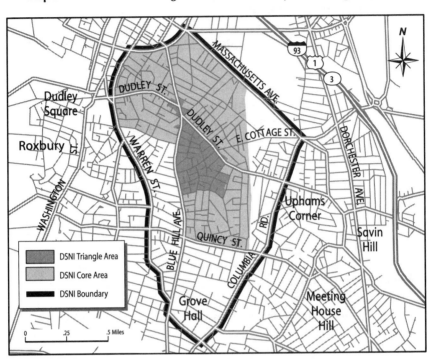

Source: Holly Sklar, "Dudley Street Neighborhood Initiative: Building on Success, 1984–2002," July 10, 2002.

and Cape Verdean).[25] And it established a participatory, bottom-up mission: "to empower Dudley residents to organize, plan for, create, and control a vibrant, diverse, and high quality neighborhood in collaboration with community partners." As the GAO explains, from the outset "the hallmarks of DSNI's operations and structure were set: resident control, cultural sensitivity, and collaboration with existing neighborhood organizations."[26]

With pro bono help from attorney and Riley Foundation trustee Robert Holmes, DSNI requested (and got) a $60,000 planning grant from the foundation, set up its office in a storefront, and set to work organizing residents and establishing partnerships with other local groups.[27] To defuse racial and ethnic tensions, DSNI began producing a multilingual newsletter—in English, Spanish, and Cape Verdean Creole—and acquired translation equipment for its public meetings. Attracting and retaining residents to this novel enterprise, as well as gaining the support of foundations and municipal agencies, required DSNI's leaders to redefine the neighborhood's problems in a variety of ways. Nelson Merced recalls that the new approach entailed transforming people's understanding of the area's ubiquitous vacant lots from a liability to an asset.[28] In addition, leaders had to reconceive urban renewal—shifting from a top-down process orchestrated by experts and implemented by city agencies to an exercise in bottom-up, citizen-led planning and development.

Cleaning Up: Don't Dump on Us

Long-term success depended not only on redefining the problem but also on demonstrating some tangible accomplishments. DSNI's first big project, led by newly hired executive director Peter Medoff, was the "Don't Dump on Us" campaign. According to environmentalist and attorney William Shutkin,

> The [Don't Dump on Us] campaign served as the critical link between the Dudley neighborhood's struggle for environmental quality and its effort to promote social and economic justice. DSNI conceived the community and environment as one and the same. The visibility and scale of the neighborhood's physical degradation made environmental action the most powerful lever for addressing overall community revitalization.[29]

DSNI based its decision to undertake the cleanup on the results of extensive door-to-door visits with community residents, most of whom complained bitterly about "illegal dumping on vacant lots and the city's dismal garbage collection and street cleaning." [30] In fact, entire blocks of vacant lots were strewn with old tires, junked furniture and appliances, and rotting garbage. Community organizer Ros Everdell points out that, although posted signs warned of fines for illegal dumping, people routinely drove into the neighborhood in broad daylight and dumped truckloads of debris.[31] Especially galling, some contractors dumped construction debris from apartments gutted for the very condo conversions that had driven tenants out of their homes in other parts of the city and into Dudley.[32]

DSNI's campaign entailed cleaning up the vacant lots, getting rid of the hundreds of abandoned cars, and closing down the illegal trash transfer stations sprinkled throughout the neighborhood.[33] As Everdell notes, some streets were so thinly populated they had no "eyes," so DSNI's short-run objective was to restore accountability for maintaining the streets. But as Medoff and his coauthor, Holly Sklar, explain in their book *Streets of Hope*, the long-range goal was to "transform people's thinking—from seeing the lots as health-threatening eyesores to seeing them as potential spaces for homes, businesses, community services, parks and playgrounds." [34]

Everyone was gratified by city officials' response to the Don't Dump on Us campaign's kickoff event, a community meeting held on June 18, 1986. Previous efforts to get high-level attention had met with derision, particularly under Mayor Kevin White, whose administration had ignored individual complaints and spurned a neighborhood revitalization campaign under the auspices of the Jesus Helps Baptist Church in the early 1980s.[35] But this time the city acknowledged residents' grievances—in part because DSNI could credibly claim to speak for the entire neighborhood, but also because Ray Flynn, the newly elected mayor, portrayed himself as a populist, neighborhood mayor. After an hour in which residents vividly described the impacts of dumping, Mayor Flynn arrived and made an impromptu speech promising to provide money and manpower to clean up the abandoned lots and vowing to close the illegal waste transfer stations.[36] The day after the meeting, the city's Public Works Department joined more than 100 residents—many of whom were children and young adults—to undertake a massive community cleanup. A week later the mayor's office issued a press release reiterating the city's intention to clean up the Dudley Street neighborhood.

Next, DSNI generated a list of the dozens of abandoned cars that littered the neighborhood's streets and asked the city to tow them away. When officials were slow to respond, DSNI adopted another tactic that involved making strategic use of the media: they approached the *Boston Globe*, which in early September 1986 ran a story about the problem. Shortly thereafter, the city began towing cars, though at a leisurely pace. The following summer, prompted by DSNI, the *Globe* again covered the problem of abandoned cars, saying: "Boston streets have become virtual parking lots for thousands of junked automobiles. In recent months, the cars have multiplied like rabbits while the city vainly scrambles to eliminate them." The article went on to note that at the corner of Dudley Street and Brook Avenue, the skeletons of thirteen "battered and burned vehicles" sat "like discarded toys among shards of broken glass and miscellaneous car parts." [37] Eventually, impatient with the city's continuing sluggishness, DSNI came up with an even more provocative approach. Capitalizing on the impending mayoral election, DSNI staff began plastering the abandoned vehicles with bumper stickers that read "Ray Flynn for Mayor." As they did in Love Canal, local officials responded with alacrity to the prospect of negative press coverage.

In the summer of 1987 DSNI also turned its attention to the illegal trash transfer stations, which were infested with rats, served as a breeding grounds for mosquitoes, and posed a threat to public health. The Dudley area was home to five transfer stations—more than in any other part of the city—among which three were unlicensed open-air facilities. One vacant lot lined with overflowing dumpsters backed up on private houses, and two of the illegal operations were close to the Mason Elementary School. According to resident Mayra Nieves, heavy trucks started rolling through the neighborhood at 4:00 a.m. and continued all day long: "We can't sit in [the kitchen] sometimes unless we close the windows, even when it's hot and humid and that's almost unbearable. The noise and that smell never goes away during the day." [38] Although the mayor had pledged to shut down the area's illegal trash transfer stations during his 1983 campaign and again at the June 1986 neighborhood meeting, the city—citing legal obstacles—was dragging its feet.

DSNI decided to launch a direct-action campaign: organizers enlisted residents to stage a mid-morning demonstration on July 8, in which participants blocked the entrance to one trash station and then marched to the two other sites. Again, the city's media covered the protest, and again the mayor responded to the negative publicity by taking a public stand over the objections of his lawyers. On July 23 he and a team of city officials padlocked the gates to the illegal transfer stations after they refused to cease operations on their own. Residents were energized by this unexpected victory, and the *Boston Globe* ran an editorial praising the mayor for his actions.

Imagining (and Creating) an Urban Village

Cleaning up abandoned lots was only the first step in attaining DSNI's broader goal of a rejuvenated urban neighborhood; the next step was redevelopment of the area's physical infrastructure. In 1986, using money from foundation grants and with the advice of MIT planner Tunney Lee, DSNI put out a request for proposals (RFP) from consultants to develop a comprehensive plan for the area. The RFP explicitly stated that "neighborhood participation in the process is a prerequisite to an acceptable plan." [39] After choosing DAC International, a Washington, D.C.-based firm, DSNI began a nine-month, resident-driven process of imagining an "urban village." As Medoff and Sklar explain, many members of the DSNI resident planning committee had little experience or technical background in development. But they worked hard to master the details and soon were willing to challenge the professionals on issues they cared deeply about. Furthermore, DAC planners trained DSNI staff to elicit stories from residents about their experiences—such as traveling long distances on irregular buses simply to shop at a supermarket or go to a bank—an approach that both generated useful information and cemented residents' trust in the process.[40] In short, as Sklar observes, "DSNI . . . turned the traditional top-down urban planning process on its head." [41]

The vision that emerged from this exercise was a village that featured affordable housing, community centers, a town common, gardens, playgrounds, green spaces, and thriving local businesses.[42] To translate these ideas into an actual blueprint, designers and architects held a series of charrettes, or design workshops, throughout the spring of 1987. In July DAC delivered a seventy-five-page draft of the comprehensive plan, which prescribed rehabilitating the "triangle," a central part of the core bounded by Dudley Street, Blue Hill Avenue, and Brookford Street. The plan emphasized quality of life, not just construction; it called for a "village commons" that would be "a place for meeting, strolling, sitting, watching, and living." [43]

After making some revisions, the DSNI board and resident planning committee released the final, five-year, $135 million plan in late October at the neighborhood's annual multicultural festival. In presenting the plan, DSNI board president Che Madyun expressed the determination and optimism that DSNI hoped to foster, saying

> We intend to fight every step of the way to assure that this neighborhood remains a community that is diverse and affordable. We warn speculators. . . . You are not welcome here. At the same time, those developers who want to come in and produce housing we can afford and create jobs that go to this community, we welcome you and look forward to a rejuvenated neighborhood in the years to come.[44]

DSNI board member Cynthia Lopes-Jefferson added: "It is a very ambitious plan, but what makes it doable is that these are the hopes and aspirations of the residents. . . . In doing this we are not only rebuilding the neighborhood, but its spirit that has been down for a long time." [45]

Although enthusiasm ran high at this point, the obstacles to realizing the urban village plan were immense. The Triangle encompassed sixty-four acres of land, half of which was vacant. The city owned fifteen of the thirty acres of abandoned lots, and the other half consisted of 181 parcels owned by 131 different individuals, of whom 62 percent were absentee landlords and three-quarters owed back taxes. [46] To undertake a coherent redevelopment, DSNI had to persuade the city to donate its portion; figure out how to acquire the hundreds of privately owned lots; obtain financing for a construction project in a neighborhood that historically had been redlined by realtors, banks, and insurance companies; and ensure that the project created homes for, rather than displacing, the area's low-income residents. (DSNI also had to persuade the city to allow it to establish zoning codes independent of the ongoing process of rezoning Roxbury.) To help it navigate the complex political and economic system, the organization solicited the advice of lawyers, activists, and community developers, most of whom contributed their services free of charge.

In addition to surmounting these logistical barriers, DSNI had to navigate the process of building partnerships with other local organizations, each of which had its own mission and operating style. An early effort to collaborate with Local 26 of the Hotel and Restaurant Employees International Union foundered when the union began pursuing its own agenda without regard to DSNI's long-range planning process or its housing standards. A partnership between DSNI and Nuestra Comunidad caused the neighborhood's black residents to suspect a Latino conspiracy. And DSNI struggled early on to involve local human service agencies, many of whom had refused to cooperate in the planning process—either because they were reluctant to provide extensive information about their finances or because they simply lacked the resources to participate. [47]

Despite the challenges and setbacks, DSNI's leaders were determined, and their first major achievement came in October 1988, when the BRA delegated to DSNI its power of eminent domain under Massachusetts Chapter 121A—the first time in the nation's history that a community group had acquired this power. [48] Traditionally, government itself either uses eminent domain or delegates the power to wealthy development corporations to *remove* low-income populations. This time, as a *Boston Globe* editorial remarked, "[Chapter] 121A [was] at the service of poor people struggling to determine their future." [49] To mobilize local support for the idea, DSNI had organized a "Take a Stand, Own the Land" campaign that featured rallies and informational meetings to educate residents about how community control could help avert speculation and ensure comprehensive development. Nevertheless, because delegating eminent domain to a low-income community was unprecedented and DSNI had no track record, the proposition encountered skepticism from property owners who had bought the land on speculation and from some members of the BRA board. The mayor strongly supported it, however, as did Lisa Chapnick, his Public Facilities Department (PFD) director. Chapnick said her support arose out of the fact that "the Dudley Street neighbors have gone through a very long and very deep grass-roots process that's unprecedented. They've unified a community that was dispirited and created a plan that will give people a whole lot of hope." [50]

Armed with the power of eminent domain, in late 1988 DSNI formed Dudley Neighbors, Incorporated (DNI), an urban redevelopment corporation and community land trust.[51] DNI's mission was to facilitate "development without displacement." To this end, it aimed to acquire the fifteen acres of privately owned vacant lots through eminent domain, combine them with city-owned parcels, and lease the land to developers during the construction period. Once a project was completed, DNI would then issue ninety-nine-year ground leases to homebuyers and cooperative housing corporations. This mechanism would enable DNI to ensure its properties were used in ways consistent with the community's vision; it would also allow the organization to control the prices of new or renovated houses and keep them affordable for residents.

Once established, DNI hoped to move quickly to begin buying up the property of people who owned land but did not live in the Triangle. Unfortunately DSNI was in the midst of an organizational transition: in December 1988 it had hired a new director, Gus Newport, and had recently lost its development specialist. In addition the number of paid staff had declined from twelve to four.[52] As a result, the DSNI board's Development Committee, which met weekly, had to solve the difficulties associated with locating the disparate owners, determining the appropriate criteria for selecting developers, and financing purchases from willing sellers. Crucial assistance came from the Ford Foundation, which—after lengthy negotiations that relied heavily on the pro bono work of local law firms—announced in October 1989 that it would lend the DNI $2 million for nine years at a 1 percent interest rate. (The foundation did not actually close on the loan until March 1992, by which time the original three-year period of eminent domain authority had expired and been extended by the BRA through 1994.) This loan, an act of faith by the foundation, enabled the DNI to acquire those privately owned parcels that the city had not foreclosed on. The DNI's efforts were also bolstered by the real-estate market crash of the late 1980s, which not only reduced the cost of land acquisition but also enabled the community to move deliberately, rather than hastily, and thereby avoid potentially disastrous early mistakes.

Despite the Ford Foundation grant, DSNI lacked the resources and the expertise to effect its ambitious restoration plan alone, and in January 1990 PFD director Lisa Chapnick signed a memo of understanding that established a partnership between the DNI and the PFD to develop the Dudley area. The memo formally designated a joint disposition committee to identify parcels for development, craft RFPs for developer selection, and designate developers for city-owned lots. It also set up a system whereby the Public Facilities

Commission would oversee the DNI's exercise of its eminent domain authority. It established cooperation between the DNI and the city to identify and obtain money that would enable them to meet the guidelines specifying that 51 percent of new housing units must go to low- and moderate-income households. And it required that land acquired through eminent domain and combined with city-owned land be advertised or designated for development within two years of title transfer to DNI.[53] As DSNI community organizer Andrea Nagel observes, the partnership merged the community energy and ideas mobilized by DSNI with the institutional, financial, and technical resources of the city.[54] But it also involved a delicate balancing act, in which DSNI needed to cooperate with the city without compromising the community control that gave it standing in the neighborhood.

Preparations to build the Triangle's first two housing projects got under way in late 1989. In the spring of that year DSNI hired a local architecture consultant to complete a build-out plan for the Triangle that specified residents' desire (determined through three community meetings) for lower-density housing, safe areas for children to play, community facilities, and open spaces. During this process the original goal of 500 housing units was reduced to 364 units, most of which were town houses with yards. (This figure was later reduced to 296, as some sites turned out to be unsuitable for housing and some owners refused to sell their property.[55]) In August the city's PFD and the DNI jointly issued a request for qualifications from developers, and in December— after a community meeting to review proposals—they approved the nonprofit Nuestra Comunidad Development Corporation to build fifty-one limited-equity cooperative units (Stafford Heights) and Triangle Development Associates to construct forty-eight single- and two-family townhouses (Winthrop Estates). Most of the units were earmarked for low- and moderate-income first-time homebuyers, and DSNI painstakingly assembled a package of subsidies, tax credits, and grants from federal, state, and local sources to cover the projected $15 million cost.[56]

The process of getting construction going was agonizingly slow, however, hampered by political, financial, and bureaucratic impediments that reflected each participant's concerns about the risks involved with such an unprecedented undertaking. The pace of development created friction between DSNI and the PFD because the latter was compelled by the mayor's 1987 campaign pledge to develop all 747 of the city-owned buildable lots by 1990. Despite the delays, by the mid-1990s DSNI's urban village plan had begun to take shape. In late 1993 contractors finished the first Winthrop Estates homes: consistent with residents' vision, these three- and four-bedroom semi-attached units featured unfinished basements, off-street parking, porches, and backyards. With subsidies from the city of Boston, DSNI sold for $90,000 houses that had cost $150,000 to build; qualified buyers faced total monthly housing costs of between $495 and $800 per month. The same year, the Dorchester Bay Economic Development Corporation completed the Alexander/Magnolia Cooperatives, consisting of thirty-eight three-bedroom homes. Two years later, Nuestra Comunidad completed Stafford Heights, a forty-one-unit cooperative that targeted house-holds with incomes of $15,000 and below, at a cost of nearly $7 million.[57]

In addition to getting houses built, DSNI faced the challenge of enabling low-income residents to assemble the financing to purchase them. As Egidio Teixeira, who had opened a sub shop on Dudley Street in 1986, told the authors of the book *Better Together*: "There was no such thing as a loan in this neighborhood. We all had a good job and we couldn't get a forty-thousand-dollar loan from any bank at all."[58] To address this problem, in early 1989 DSNI joined the Community Investment Coalition, which included the Greater Roxbury Neighborhood Authority, the Massachusetts Affordable Housing Alliance Home Buyers Union, and the Hotel and Restaurant Work-ers Union Local 26, to urge Boston banks and insurance companies to estab-lish a lending pool for low-income borrowers and neighborhood-based com-munity developers. To generate publicity for its cause, the coalition organized residents to picket the banks. Bolstering the coalition's case were a series of studies documenting the discriminatory pattern of home lending in Bos-ton and the United States in general. In August 1989 the Federal Reserve announced that, even after accounting for income differences, whites in Boston were twice as likely as blacks to receive mortgages. Then in December economist Charles Finn released an analysis conducted for the BRA showing that between 1981 and 1987 Boston's white neighborhoods received home loans at nearly three times the rate of black neighborhoods of comparable income. According to the Finn report, the neighborhood with the worst lend-ing rate of all was Dudley.[59]

From that point on, as journalist Steven Marantz asserted, "The fact of racial lending patterns [was] no longer debated."[60] But the question of how to reverse the trend remained. After all, the discriminatory practices documented in these studies had occurred despite a 1977 federal law, the Community Rein-vestment Act, which required banks to service all neighborhoods equally.

Throughout the fall of 1989, Boston banks negotiated with city officials and community advocates in hopes of coming up with a way of remedying the lending disparities. The process broke down in late 1989, when Mayor Flynn announced he would not accept a plan that did not include mortgage rates 1 percent to 2 percent below the standard rate for low-income families, a con-dition that several banks opposed on the grounds that they would lose money. In early 1990, after Federal Reserve Bank of Boston president Richard Syron intervened to broker a deal, the mayor, banks, and activists announced a $400 million reinvestment plan that included at least $30 million for below-market mortgages.[61]

Recognizing that high-level bank policy does not always translate into lending practice, DSNI set about ensuring that Dudley area residents had the confidence, skills, and knowledge to actually obtain the newly available low-cost mortgages. In 1992 DSNI also began offering free classes and counseling for prospective homebuyers. (Another Federal Reserve study released that year underscored the need for DSNI's assistance in qualifying homeowners for mortgages: the authors found that black and Latino applicants in the Boston area were about 60 percent more likely to be turned down than whites, after controlling for the variety of financial and employment variables that lenders consider.[62])

In addition to facilitating the construction and purchase of new houses, DSNI orchestrated the creation of the Dudley Town Common. In November 1994 newly elected Boston mayor Thomas Menino announced funding for the common: $700,000 from the state for design and construction and $500,000 from the city in capital funds for streetscaping.[63] Completed in June 1996, the common consists of a small cement amphitheater surrounded by colorful metalwork and a two-story clock. Across the street is a beautifully landscaped courtyard surrounded by a low wall on which is inscribed DSNI's inspirational mission statement. The common, which serves as a gateway to the neighborhood, quickly became the heart of the community, hosting the farmer's market, celebrations, and art, music, and dance performances.

In July 1997 DSNI began its next phase: transforming seven blocks of Dudley Street beginning at Blue Hill Avenue into Dudley Village. An urban village visioning exercise in 1996 to update the comprehensive revitalization plan of 1987 yielded the idea of a multiethnic neighborhood populated by small stores, bookshops, cafes, and pushcarts.[64] Residents imagined the village would become a major tourist attraction, offering a variety of restaurants and shops as well as multicultural art and performances. "If we can establish some new cafes and expand some old ones, that will get some evening foot traffic started," mused DSNI executive director Greg Watson. "If we can get things like a hardware store, a pharmacy, and grocery stores that are buying the locally made produce, people can keep their money in the neighborhood and begin to create a web of dependency." [65]

The second phase got under way in April 1998 with the completion of the thirty-six-unit Brook Avenue Cooperative Homes project.[66] As with previous projects, DSNI had to assemble a complex package to finance this $7 million venture, which combined $5 million in low-income housing tax credit equity with money from State First Mortgage, the Federal Reserve, the Massachusetts Housing Innovation program, and the City of Boston Housing Trust Fund.[67] Although pleased with their accomplishments to date, the organization's leaders envisioned that future homes in the village would be models of "resource-efficient" housing, solarized and superinsulated and therefore less expensive to maintain.[68]

Cleaning Up Brownfields and Fostering Urban Agriculture

By the mid-1990s DSNI had developed 300 of the neighborhood's 1,300 vacant parcels, but the Dudley area still contained an inordinate amount of vacant, contaminated land. The Massachusetts Department of Environmental Protection estimated the neighborhood had at least fifty-four hazardous waste sites. Many toxic chemicals—including chromium, mercury, and benzene—

polluted these sites, but perhaps the worst threat came from lead, which poses a well-documented risk to children's health and development. Not only had federal and state laws failed to facilitate cleanup of these brownfields, they may have exacerbated the problem by making rural land cheaper and less complicated to develop relative to urban land. As the environmental justice movement gained the national spotlight under the Clinton administration, however, regional EPA administrator John DeVillars moved to address urban environmental issues—and environmental racism in particular—in New England. After visiting the Dudley Street neighborhood in 1994, DeVillars concluded, "No citizens anywhere face greater public health consequences from environmental neglect than those who live in our cities." [69] In fact, 50 percent of the Dudley neighborhood children were at risk of lead poisoning, and the neighborhood's rates of asthma and bronchitis were five times the national average.[70]

DSNI adopted a variety of tactics to address the area's pollution. In 1992 the organization initiated a campaign to discourage people from dumping oil and other toxics into storm drains. Backed by the Massachusetts Water Resources Authority, they recruited youth volunteers to paint the drains with a stencil of a fish and the message (in three languages): "Don't Dump: Drains to Boston Harbor." [71] DSNI used more confrontational methods as well. In December 1994 the Boston Bar Association joined with ten other groups to found the Massachusetts Environmental Justice Network, which aimed to provide free legal services to poor and minority communities fighting illegal waste dumping and other pollution sources. The network's first three cases were based on complaints lodged by DSNI. The first case challenged trash dumping and chemical storage on four properties; the second involved an illegal trash transfer station abutting private homes; and the third concerned noxious odors from a business where workers were allegedly dumping white, foamy liquids down a storm drain.[72]

Another way DSNI sought to address the threat from sites containing hazardous waste was to landscape the area's open spaces. In 1991 DSNI established Dudley PRIDE (People and Resources Investing in Dudley's Environment), a campaign to establish neighborhood greening programs, such as creating community gardens and planting trees and shrubs provided by the City Parks and Recreation Department. In 1992, together with the Massachusetts Horticultural Society and the Boston Natural Areas Fund, DSNI created the "Green Team" to hire neighborhood youths to supervise and staff two landscaping crews that worked in the area's four community gardens as well as on street beautification.

In the mid-1990s DSNI's Ros Everdell and Trish Settles began exploring the prospects for urban agriculture as a way of simultaneously combating lead poisoning and spurring economic development. For Settles, agriculture offered a way of linking residents from rural backgrounds, such as the Cape Verdeans, with the environment. She believed that urban farming would allow residents to affirm their cultural identities in ways that would contribute to the Dudley Street neighborhood's sense of place.[73] Settles and Everdell joined forces with the Drumlin Farm Food Project, which in 1993 had begun recruiting Dudley area youth to work on its farm in Lincoln, Massachusetts. In 1995 the Food Project opened a farmers' market in the Dudley area and began reclaiming a half-acre lot at the corner of Langdon and George Streets for food production. By the summer of 1996 lead tests showed the land was clean enough to grow crops on. In 1997 the Food Project began work on a nearby 1.4-acre parcel (West Cottage), and in 2001 it began restoring a third lot nearby.[74]

Another agricultural prospect arose when the EPA's New England regional office approached DSNI with an offer to have the Massachusetts Highway Department fund a hazardous waste cleanup operation as part of a settlement for illegally disposing of hazardous waste at its equipment yards. Settles jumped on the opportunity: she chose a site close to the DSNI's Dudley Street offices that residents had identified as an important brownfield and a prime location for a possible greenhouse or bioshelter.[75] In 1995 the EPA and the highway department approved the project. Even though the department had agreed to subsidize the Brook Avenue greenhouse/bioshelter, transforming the polluted land into a productive agricultural operation faced numerous impediments. DSNI had to address questions of liability for contamination caused by former uses and obtain low-cost loans and grants for assessing and cleaning up the site. If it succeeded in building the structure, DSNI would have to devise a marketing strategy to promote its locally grown produce.[76]

Shutkin contends that the arrival of DSNI's new executive director, Greg Watson, ensured that urban agriculture in Dudley would have a chance to succeed. Well-versed in environmental issues, Watson had also been commissioner of the Massachusetts Department of Agriculture under Gov. Michael Dukakis and was firmly committed to urban agriculture. Echoing the problem definition of DSNI's founders, Watson explained, "Urban agriculture will make a significant contribution to our local, village-scale economy and, by focusing on abandoned lots and brownfields, gardens, farms, and greenhouses will play a key role in transforming current liabilities into community assets." [77] Under Watson's leadership DSNI launched the Urban Agriculture Strategy (UAS) in spring 1997. As Shutkin describes it, "The UAS's mission is to clean up the dozens of brownfield sites and vacant lots in the neighborhood and redevelop them for food production or value-added food enterprises such as prepared foods—smoked fish, preserves, dried mushrooms." [78] The Ford Foundation contributed $172,000 to this initiative, and the Jessie Smith Noyes Foundation gave another $60,000.

Sustaining the Momentum

In addition to neighborhood cleanup, redevelopment, and urban agriculture, DSNI launched other activities to build and institutionalize the neighborhood's civic capacity, which is critical to its long-term success. About 200 residents typically attend DSNI's annual meetings. To encourage diverse participation, DSNI furnishes earphones and translates information into Spanish and Cape Verdean; it also provides refreshment$ and child care. DSNI regularly hosts community meetings, workshops, and conferences and distributes its trilingual newsletter to 3,100 residents as well as posting it on the DSNI Web site. In 1998 DSNI established the Resident Development Institute, which aims to perpetuate knowledge of the community's history and provide formal training in leadership, innovative thinking, planning, community organizing, and problem solving.

Another crucial aspect of DSNI's effort to institutionalize its civic capacity is its extraordinary commitment to incorporating and nurturing the area's youth. Among DSNI's first projects was the effort to rid the Mary Hannon Park of drug dealers and make it a safe place for children to play. In addition, the board decided early on—after challenges from some prominent youth members—to give residents voting rights in DSNI at age fifteen and to allow them to run for board membership at seventeen. As Jose Barros, who has lived in the Dudley Street neighborhood for many years, explains, the DSNI board's willingness to listen to his children gave them the confidence to become leaders.[79] In 1995 DSNI hired a full-time youth organizer. Four years later members elected as the organization's president John Barros—the first youth elected to DSNI's board and founder of the Nubian Roots Committee in 1991.

Finally, DSNI is committed to helping the area develop its economic base to ensure that longtime residents, not just newcomers, benefit from the neighborhood's revival. In 1993 DSNI hosted a summit with residents, labor, business, and government leaders called Economic$ with People in Mind. Three years later, DSNI launched the Buck$ Stop Here campaign to keep money in the community. As part of this effort, local businesses distributed frequent buyer tickets to customers, who were then entered in a raffle to win prizes at DSNI's 1997 annual meeting. At the 1998 meeting residents and staff performed a skit to demonstrate how purchasing local goods and services could help improve the neighborhood economy.[80] The same year DSNI began promoting the earned income tax credit, reckoning that if all eligible families took the credit on their tax returns the neighborhood would gain $5 million in economic power. To carry out the campaign, DSNI formed a partnership with the Tax Equity Alliance of Massachusetts, Community Tax Aide, and the Jewish Community Relations Council. The Internal Revenue Service trained Dudley resident volunteers to provide preliminary tax credit screenings; the Dudley Library provided tax assistance; and volunteers used a tax assistance Web site to help 400 residents file tax returns.[81]

OUTCOMES

As of 2005 DSNI had more than 3,700 voting members, although in conjunction with the DNI it employed only ten full-time staff. Its numerous accomplishments included getting rid of the illegal trash transfer stations and converting almost half of the neighborhood's ubiquitous vacant lots into affordable housing, a town common, a community garden, an orchard, and a playground. It had also overseen construction of two new community centers (Orchard Gardens and Vine Street) and was developing a third. The 10,000-square-foot Brook Avenue greenhouse was complete and ready to start producing cash crops to generate revenue to be used to finance more neighborhood revitalization.[82] In addition to rebuilding the neighborhood's physical infrastructure, over the course of twenty years DSNI had organized annual multicultural festivals and neighborhood cleanups; created an agency collaborative to help integrate local social service providers; trained and employed local youth in asset-mapping, landscaping, environmental cleanup, and mentoring; and matched residents with local employment opportunities. The results of DSNI's work are plainly evident. A walk through the once dilapidated Dudley Street neighborhood reveals unexpected delights: block after block of brightly colored townhouses with neat lawns and gardens and well-tended parks and playgrounds. Crime in the area fell, and the number of businesses rose from 425 in 1992 to more than 650 in 2000.[83]

But decades of disinvestment are not easy to reverse: in the late 1990s, 21 percent of the land in the Dudley area was still blighted, and the neighborhood's residents remained poor, with a per capita income of just $7,600, compared to nearly $16,000 for the city as a whole.[84] The median family income was less than $21,000, and the unemployment rate was nearly 14 percent. Almost one-third of the population remained below the poverty level, twice Boston's rate. Although reduced, crime continued to be a problem, and the Boston police did not maintain a sufficiently consistent presence to discourage drug dealing in the area. As Sklar observes, it is a serious challenge to maintain the neighborhood for those who fought for it in the absence of genuine economic improvement. Recognizing this, in 2000 DSNI turned its attention to the difficult task of bringing commercial activity back to the Dudley neighborhood. And in 2004 the city's Department of Neighborhood Development designated the Dorchester Bay Economic Development Corporation the developer of nineteen city-owned plots that will become Dudley Village, a two-phase development of fifty affordable rental units and 9,600 square feet of commercial space.

CONCLUSIONS

During its twenty-year life, DSNI has managed to engage in urban renewal while avoiding the speculation and displacement that typically accompanies it. Partly as a result of its concrete achievements, DSNI "has transformed despair, disinvestment, and political powerlessness into visionary optimism, community control, and public-private partnerships." [85] To achieve their goals in the face of a host of structural constraints, DSNI members, like other EJ activists, have drawn successfully on a number of tactics that environmentalists employed in the 1970s. First, DSNI members organized to have a greater impact, and they have been especially effective because they can credibly claim to represent the community. Getting favorable media coverage has enabled DSNI to put pressure on local politicians not only by creating costs for ignoring the community's plight but also by presenting opportunities to take credit for addressing the neighborhood's concerns. DSNI members have cemented their gains by building coalitions with other nonprofit organizations and reaching out to business interests. And they have devised creative ways to institutionalize the civic engagement on which their long-term success depends.

It should be noted, however, that DSNI's intense, decades-long struggle has yielded the kinds of amenities—decent homes and safe, clean streets—that most middle-class Americans take for granted. Furthermore, as Shutkin points out, the same forces that left Roxbury with a legacy of brownfields remain operative and continue to impede efforts at change. DSNI's Everdell observes that the problem often is not an absence of policies to overcome those obstacles but a lack of political will or private sector commitment to implement existing policies. By the same token, although lack of funding and inattention from elected officials hamper community-based redevelopment in long-neglected neighborhoods, an equally serious challenge is building and maintaining residents' sense of hope.

Although environmentalists were slow to embrace EJ, some have recognized that organizations like DSNI embody many of the ideals that originally animated the modern environmental movement. For example, the multiple, concurrent needs of minority communities forced DSNI to be holistic in its approach, while the numerous low-level chronic threats led members to focus on the cumulative impacts of pollution. Moreover, DSNI's approach rests on a genuine recognition that the continuing social and economic vitality of a place depends on its ecological health. Above all, DSNI dispels the notion that environmental quality is an elite concern. Dudley residents made clear from the outset that revitalizing their neighborhood would entail more than bringing jobs and economic development; it would also involve creating bike paths, apple orchards, outdoor cafes, community gardens, fountains, art programs, concerts, and town commons. As it turns out, even people who are struggling economically imagine lives that are richer than mere survival. As Gus Newport, former DSNI director, observed:

A lot of these urban programs do only housing, but that's not all there is to a community. Where's the culture? The commerce? That's why we have community gardens here, why we have flowers. I think planners take it for granted that poor people don't need culture, vital businesses, or beauty. If you had those things in inner cities, you'd have less crime. You have to get inside the heads of the people who live here, see what they want. They want more than houses. Beauty—no matter how small it is, just a few flowers—is what matters most.[86]

QUESTIONS TO CONSIDER

- Critics have argued that environmentalism is losing its effectiveness because the movement's aims do not resonate with ordinary Americans. Does environmental justice activism offer hope for or a challenge to mainstream environmentalism?
- What does this case suggest to you about the appropriate balance between local and federal environmental initiatives, and why?

NOTES

1. Luke W. Cole and Sheila R. Foster, *From the Ground Up: Environmental Racism and the Rise of the Environmental Justice Movement* (New York: New York University Press, 2001).
2. Robert D. Bullard, *Dumping in Dixie: Race, Class, and Environmental Quality* (Boulder: Westview Press, 1990).
3. See, for example, United Church of Christ, Commission for Racial Justice, *Toxic Waste and Race in the United States* (New York: Public Data Access, 1987); Marianne Lavelle and Marcia Coyle, "Unequal Protection: The Racial Divide in Environmental Law," *National Law Journal*, September 21, 1992.
4. James P. Lester, David W. Allen, and Kelly M. Hill, *Environmental Justice in the United States: Myths and Realities* (Boulder: Westview Press, 2001). In 2005 political scientist Evan Ringquist conducted a meta-analysis of environmental inequity and found that both polluting facilities and pollution emissions are concentrated in minority communities. See Evan J. Ringquist, "Assessing Evidence of Environmental Inequities," *Journal of Policy Analysis and Management* 24 (2005): 223–248.
5. Robert D. Bullard, "Environmental Justice for All," *The New Crisis* 110 (2003): 24–26.
6. Douglas McAdam, *Political Process and the Development of Black Insurgency, 1930–1970* (Chicago: University of Chicago Press, 1982).
7. Robert D. Putnam and Lewis M. Feldstein, *Better Together: Restoring the American Community* (New York: Simon and Schuster, 2003).
8. Oliver Gillham, *The Limitless City* (Washington, D.C.: Island Press, 2002), 187.
9. U.S. GAO, *Community Development: Comprehensive Approaches Address Multiple Needs but Are Challenging to Implement*, GAO/RCED/HEHS-95-69 (February 1995).
10. In the 1970s and 1980s scholars working within a variety of analytic traditions converged on this conclusion, although they offered different explanations for, and extent of the dominance of, the economic growth imperative. See, for example, Harvey Molotch, "The City as Growth Machine," *American Journal of Sociology* 82 (September 1976): 309–332; Paul Peterson, *City Limits* (Chicago: University of Chicago Press, 1981); Clarence Stone, *Economic Growth and Neighborhood Discontent* (Chapel Hill: University of North Carolina Press, 1976).
11. John Mollenkopf, "How to Study Urban Political Power," in *The City Reader*, 3d ed., ed. Richard T. LeGates and Frederic Stout (New York: Routledge, 1996), 238.
12. John R. Logan and Harvey Molotch, *Urban Fortunes: The Political Economy of Place* (Berkeley: University of California Press, 1987); Todd Swanstrom, "Urban Populism: Uneven Development and the Space for Reform," in *Business Elites and Urban Development: Case Studies and Critical Perspectives*, ed. Scott Cummings (Albany: State University of New York Press, 1988), 121–152.
13. Barbara Ferman, *Challenging the Growth Machine: Neighborhood Politics in Chicago and Pittsburgh* (Lawrence: University Press of Kansas, 1996).
14. Gillham, *The Limitless City*.
15. U.S. GAO, *Community Development*.

16. Peter Medoff and Holly Sklar, *Streets of Hope: The Fall and Rise of an Urban Neighborhood* (Boston: South End Press, 1994).

17. Ibid.

18. As Medoff and Sklar explain, arson in such areas is the result of a tension between appreciating and depreciating forces. Housing values and services are declining for long-term, low-income residents, while speculators stand to make a profit by selling to moderate- and high-income people as the neighborhood gentrifies.

19. Quoted in Norman Boucher, "The Death and Life of Dudley," *Boston Globe Magazine*, April 8, 1990, 9.

20. Quoted in Medoff and Sklar, *Streets of Hope*, 35.

21. Diego Ribadeneira, "Roxbury's New 'Progressive Populist,' " *Boston Globe*, December 21, 1988, 2.

22. Quoted in Medoff and Sklar, *Streets of Hope*, 42.

23. As DSNI community organizer Andrea Nagel notes, this focus on mediation appeased the area's social service agencies, which were concerned about competition. Andrea Isabel Nagel, *The Dudley Street Neighborhood Initiative: A Case Study in Community-Controlled Planning*, Thesis for Master in City Planning, Department of Urban Studies and Planning (Cambridge: MIT, 1990).

24. Charles E. Claffey, "Roxbury's Turn for Renewal; Minority Groups Want More Input into Dudley Station Revitalization Plan," *Boston Globe*, February 17, 1985, A21; Nagel, *The Dudley Street Neighborhood Initiative.*

25. The final governing structure was as follows: twelve community members, five non-profit agencies based in the core area, two community development corporations from the core, two small businesses from the core, two members of the broader business community, two representatives of the core area religious communities, two others (determined by the board), representatives of two nonprofit organizations from the secondary area, one city official, and one state official. This structure remains today.

26. U.S. GAO, *Community Development.*

27. Nagel, *The Dudley Street Neighborhood Initiative.*

28. Medoff and Sklar, *Streets of Hope.*

29. William A. Shutkin, *The Land That Could Be* (Cambridge: MIT Press, 2000), 148.

30. Medoff and Sklar, *Streets of Hope.*

31. Ros Everdell, DSNI Community Organizer, personal communication, April 20, 2005.

32. Boucher, "The Death and Life of Dudley."

33. Trash transfer stations are permanent structures that link garbage collection and disposal. Garbage trucks collect trash and dump it at transfer stations, and tractor trailers pick it up to haul it to landfills.

34. Medoff and Sklar, *Streets of Hope*, 70.

35. Nagel, *The Dudley Street Neighborhood Initiative.*

36. Bonnie V. Winston, "Roxbury Residents Tell the City They Want Dumping to Stop," *Boston Globe*, June 19, 1986.

37. Alexander Reid, "Hub Can't Keep Up With Junked Autos; Many Neighborhoods Fall Victim," *Boston Globe*, June 3, 1987, 1.

38. Quoted in Alexander Reid, "Hub Trash Causing a Stink; Residents Angered by Illegal Garbage Yards," *Boston Globe*, July 11, 1987, 1.

39. Quoted in Medoff and Sklar, *Streets of Hope*, 96.

40. Medoff and Sklar, *Streets of Hope.*

41. Holly Sklar, "Creating a Sustainable Urban Village," *Orion*, Autumn 1996, 30.

42. Ibid.

43. Quoted in Boucher, "The Death and Life of Dudley," 44.

44. Quoted in Medoff and Sklar, *Streets of Hope*, 113.

45. Quoted in Diego Ribadeneira, "Plan Maps Future of Dudley St.; Report Says Area Residents Should Control Land Use," *Boston Globe*, October 26, 1987, 19.

46. Medoff and Sklar, *Streets of Hope.*

47. Ibid.; Jose Antonio Alicea, *Dancing With the City: The Dudley Street Neighborhood and Land Control in Roxbury,* Thesis for Master in City Planning, Department of Urban Studies (Cambridge: MIT, 1991).

48. Eminent domain is "the power of the state to take property for public use without the public's consent upon making just compensation." The genesis of the idea for DSNI to apply for eminent domain status is murky. According to one story, BRA director Stephen Coyle proposed the idea on a visit to the neighborhood; a second version suggests the idea came from the real estate firm that was providing DSNI with pro bono legal advice.

49. "A Dudley Street Transformation," *Boston Globe,* October 6, 1988, 20.

50. Quoted in Peter S. Canellos, "Neighborhood Hopes to Wield Eminent Domain," *Boston Globe,* October 28, 1988, 1.

51. Chapter 121A requires that such a corporation hold the power of eminent domain.

52. Nagel, *The Dudley Street Neighborhood Initiative.*

53. Alicea, *Dancing With the City.*

54. Nagel, *The Dudley Street Neighborhood Initiative.*

55. Medoff and Sklar, *Streets of Hope.*

56. Brian C. Mooney, "City Panel Names Two Developers to Begin Dudley Triangle Projects," *Boston Globe,* December 22, 1989, 62; Medoff and Sklar, *Streets of Hope.*

57. Diana A. Meyer et al., "On the Ground With Comprehensive Community Initiatives," The Enterprise Foundation, March 2000. Available at www.enterprisefoundation. org/model%20documents/1272.pdf.

58. Putnam and Feldstein, *Better Together,* 77.

59. Boucher, "The Death and Life of Dudley."

60. Steven Marantz, "Boston Banks, City Officials Divided over Remedy for Lending Disparity," *Boston Globe,* December 24, 1989, 27.

61. Steven Marantz, "$400m Investment Plan for Hub," *Boston Globe,* January 11, 1990, 1.

62. Medoff and Sklar, *Streets of Hope.*

63. Originally, the state had promised $1 million for the project, but Gov. William Weld's administration reneged on that promise. After heavy lobbying by DSNI, the governor approved a $700,000 grant.

64. Derrick Z. Jackson, "Dudley Street's Vision for a Village," *Boston Globe,* July 16, 1997, A19; Alan Lupo, "A Roxbury Development Plan Gains Currency," *Boston Globe,* September 7, 1997, 1.

65. Quoted in Jackson, "Dudley Street's Vision."

66. Tasha Robertson, "Dudley Street Neighborhood Sees a Rebirth," *Boston Globe,* April 12, 1998, B3.

67. Meyer et al., "On the Ground."

68. Dudley Street Neighborhood Initiative, "Welcome to Dudley Village." Available at http://www.dsni.org/dudley_village.htm.

69. Usha Lee McFarling, "Turning Back a Toxic Tide on Dudley Street," *Boston Globe,* November 13, 1994, 1.

70. Meyer et al., "On the Ground."

71. Medoff and Sklar, *Streets of Hope.*

72. Scott Allen, "Environmental Lawyers Unite to Help Low-Income Communities," *Boston Globe,* December 1, 1994, 36.

73. Shutkin, *The Land That Could Be.*

74. Ibid.; The Food Project, "History of the Land—Urban." Available at www.thefood project.org/agriculture/internal1.asp?ID=107.

75. Bioshelters are similar to greenhouses but have additional features, such as aquaculture systems.

76. Shutkin, *The Land That Could Be.*

77. Quoted in ibid., 155.

78. Ibid., 155.

79. Jose Barros, personal communication, May 16, 2005.
80. Meyer et al., "On the Ground."
81. Ibid.
82. Brian Ballou, "Saviors of Dudley St.: Residents Work Together to Save Their Neighborhood," *Boston Herald*, February 27, 2005.
83. Holly Sklar, "Dudley Street Neighborhood Initiative: Building on Success, 1984–2002," July 10, 2002. Available at www.sibleyconsulting.com/dsni/archives/2002buildingonsuccess.htm.
84. Shutkin, *The Land That Could Be.*
85. Sklar, "Dudley Street Neighborhood Initiative."
86. Quoted in Jay Walljasper, "The Dudley Street Example," *Conscious Choice*, June 2000.

RECOMMENDED READING

Medoff, Peter, and Holly Sklar. *Streets of Hope: The Fall and Rise of an Urban Neighborhood.* Boston: South End Press, 1994.

WEB SITES

www.dsni.org (DSNI Web site)
www.thefoodproject.org/agriculture (The Food Project Web site)

CHAPTER 6

Oil Versus Wilderness
in the Arctic National Wildlife Refuge

The controversy over drilling for oil on the Coastal Plain of Alaska's Arctic National Wildlife Refuge (ANWR, pronounced "anwar") began shortly after the passage of the Alaska National Interest Lands Conservation Act (ANILCA) in 1980, and it has raged ever since. The conflict pits those who want to explore for oil and gas in the refuge against those who want to see the area off-limits to all development. Ordinarily, decisions about oil and gas development on public lands are made administratively, but an unusual statutory provision in ANILCA requires legislative approval for oil exploration, so combatants have waged this battle almost entirely in Congress. Over the years, the contest has featured fierce public relations campaigns by advocates on both sides, as well as a variety of parliamentary maneuvers by legislators. Nearly two decades after the issue first arose, oil and gas development in the refuge was the major environmental issue in the 2000 presidential campaign, and it soon became the centerpiece of President George W. Bush's national energy policy. In spring 2005 the Senate—historically the last bastion of refuge protection—voted by a narrow margin to allow oil exploration in ANWR as part of the budget process.

The ANWR dispute epitomizes the divide between proponents of natural resource extraction and advocates of wilderness preservation. Such controversies are particularly intractable because the two sides are separated by fundamental and irreconcilable value differences. Unlike disputes over human health, which involve relatively consensual values, debates about developing wilderness tap into ecological values, about which differences are often so wide as to be unbridgeable. For wilderness advocates, compromise is unthinkable: any development in a pristine area constitutes a complete loss, a total violation of the spiritual and aesthetic qualities of the place. For development proponents, such an attitude reflects a lack of concern about human economic needs. The chasm between the two sides also grows out of their differing views about what constitutes "security." [1] Environmentalists believe that security lies in pursuing lifestyles that are sustainable in the long run and preserving wild places, while cornucopians believe that security depends on short-run economic growth and job creation.

Both sides have used tactics that reflect their strategic focus on the legislative arena, where the battle over ANWR has been fought. Development interests prefer to pursue their policy goals out of the limelight, in the administrative arena if possible. Even in Congress, in the absence of public attention, an influential industry or local economic development interest can almost always have its way. In this case, however, wilderness advocates have managed to expand the scope of the conflict by using symbols and metaphors to transform an apparently local battle into a national contest, thereby dramatically changing the dynamics of the legislative process. Forced to respond, development advocates have enlisted symbols and metaphors of their own to appeal to widely held values such as economic growth, national security, and local control. In support of their definitions of the problem, both sides interpret technical and scientific information in ways consistent with their own values. And both sides latch onto focusing events to shape public perceptions and open windows of opportunity for policy change.

Government officials also use information selectively and frame it in ways consistent with their values. Experts within administrative agencies choose among plausible assumptions to formulate the official models and projections on which policy decisions are based. Complicating matters, the crafting of official reports often reveals tension between how an agency's professionals define the problem and the preferred framing of its political appointees. While the former are primarily driven by professional norms and standards, the latter share the ideology of the White House. Not surprisingly, the two are sometimes incompatible.

This case also features an unusual twist on typical natural resource policymaking: wilderness advocates in the ANWR debate have the advantage because *not* drilling is the status quo, and it is always much easier to block policy change than to bring it about. The legislative complexity of energy policymaking has enhanced this advantage. At least two committees in each chamber, and as many as seven in the House, claim jurisdiction over energy decisions. Traditionally, a single committee has jurisdiction over a bill; however, since the 1970s, multiple referral—or referral of a bill to more than one committee—has become more common, particularly in the House. Multiple referral, which can be simultaneous or sequential, complicates the legislative process because a bill must clear all of the committees of reference before it can go to the floor.[2] Legislating a national energy policy is also daunting because so many organizations mobilize in response to the myriad provisions that threaten to impose costs or promise to deliver benefits. The involvement of multiple interests creates the possibility of antagonizing one or more of them, something legislators prefer to avoid. To get around this obstacle, drilling proponents have repeatedly tried to attach refuge-opening riders to budget bills, which have the additional benefit of being immune to Senate filibusters.[3]

BACKGROUND

The ANWR debate is the most recent manifestation of a century-old conflict over both Alaska's resource-based economy and the state's relationship to the federal government. The battle over the trans-Alaska pipeline, in particular, set the stage for the passage of ANILCA in 1980, which, in turn, created the legal and institutional context for the protracted struggle over ANWR. Shortly after ANILCA's passage, two distinct coalitions formed—one to advocate wilderness designation for the newly established refuge and the other to promote oil and gas development in the area.

A History of Resource Exploitation in Alaska

Alaska has long been a battleground between development interests and environmentalists. From the time the United States acquired the Alaska territory from Russia in 1867, American adventurers seeking to make their fortunes have exploited the area's natural attributes. The first terrestrial resource to attract attention was gold. Discovery of the Klondike gold fields in 1896, when the territory's white population was little more than 10,000, precipitated an influx of prospectors and others hoping to profit from the boom. Development there from the late 1800s to the mid-1900s conformed to the boom-and-bust cycle typical of natural resource–based economies. Prior to Alaska attaining statehood in the late 1950s, the federal government tried to mitigate this trend by setting aside millions of acres of land to conserve natural resources—including coal, oil, gas, and timber—in order to ensure their orderly development. Environmentalists also have longstanding interests in Alaska's natural endowments. As early as the 1930s, forester and outspoken wilderness advocate Bob Marshall began pleading for the preservation of Alaskan wilderness.[4] While the U.S. Navy was searching for oil and gas, the National Park Service began to investigate Alaska's recreational potential, and in 1954—after surveying the Eastern Brooks Range—it recommended that the federal government preserve the northeastern corner of the state for its wildlife, wilderness, recreational, scientific, and cultural values.

Fearing inroads by environmentalists, boosters such as Robert Atwood—editor and publisher of the *Anchorage Daily Times*—and Walter Hickel—millionaire real estate developer, contractor, and hotelier—advocated statehood to support greater economic development. In 1957 a prostatehood pamphlet declared, "If Alaska becomes a state, other people, like ourselves, will be induced to settle here without entangling federal red tape and enjoy an opportunity to develop this great land." [5] On January 3, 1959, after more than a decade of debate, Congress made Alaska a state, and for the next twenty years, the state and its native tribes jockeyed to select lands for acquisition. In 1966 Stewart Udall, secretary of the Department of the Interior (DOI), froze applications for title to Alaska's unappropriated land until Congress could settle outstanding native claims. The same year, however, Hickel was elected governor. With his swearing-in a long period of development got under way in the state, best symbolized by the rush to develop the Prudhoe Bay oil field that began with Atlantic Richfield's strike in the winter of 1967–1968.[6]

The Trans-Alaska Pipeline Controversy

In 1969 President Richard Nixon appointed Hickel to head the DOI, a position from which he was well placed to act as a policy entrepreneur for his pet project, the trans-Alaska pipeline. On February 10, 1969, the "big three" companies that had been developing oil reserves on Alaska's North Slope came together into a loose consortium called the Trans-Alaska Pipeline System (TAPS), which announced plans to build a 798-mile-long pipeline from the oil fields at Prudhoe Bay to the port of Valdez. This announcement coincided with a surge in national environmental consciousness, however, making a clash inevitable. At first, opponents were able to delay the project by citing technical impediments, administrative and legal requirements, and native claims. The history of the oil industry's destructive practices in the Arctic also fueled public skepticism about TAPS. Resistance crystallized in 1970, and national environmental groups filed three lawsuits to stop the pipeline, citing the Mineral Leasing Act and the National Environmental Policy Act (NEPA).[7] But in January 1971 a DOI staff report recommended building the pipeline, even though it would cause environmental damage.

By this time, President Nixon had replaced Hickel with Rogers C. B. Morton, who was dubious about the pipeline and wanted more information. Interior Department hearings held in February 1971 "became a showcase of unyielding positions" in which environmentalists warned that the pipeline would destroy pristine wilderness, while oil interests claimed that Alaskan oil was economically essential and that the environmental risks were minimal.[8] Environmental activists subsequently formed the Alaska Public Interest Coalition to coordinate and intensify the public campaign against the pipeline.[9] Complicating matters for the coalition, however, was the December 1971 passage of the Alaska Native Claims Settlement Act (ANCSA), which had been strongly supported by oil and gas interests. ANCSA transferred to native Alaskans ownership of 44 million acres and proffered a settlement of nearly $1 billion, half of which was to be paid from oil production royalties, thereby giving native Alaskans a powerful financial stake in oil development. At the same time, the act prohibited the state of Alaska or its native tribes from selecting lands within a proposed oil pipeline corridor as part of that 44 million acres, which ensured that neither the state nor a native tribe could use its property rights to block the project.

In March 1972 Interior released its final environmental impact statement (EIS) on the pipeline, and the document stressed the need to develop Alaskan oil to avoid increasing dependence on foreign sources.[10] Environmentalists immediately challenged the EIS in court, arguing that it was based on unreliable data and failed to consider transportation alternatives. Later that year Secretary Morton declared the pipeline to be in the national interest, but public sentiment remained strongly against it until the summer of 1973, when forecasts of an energy crisis opened a window of opportunity for development advocates. The oil industry capitalized on the specter of an oil shortage to generate legislative interest in the pipeline, and in July the Senate narrowly passed an amendment offered by Mike Gravel, D-Alaska, which declared that Interior's EIS fulfilled all the requirements of NEPA, thus releasing the project from further legal delay.[11] Just before the end of its 1973 session, Congress passed the Trans-Alaska Pipeline Authorization Act (361–14 in the House and 80–5 in the Senate), and on November 16 President Nixon signed it into law.[12]

The Alaska National Interest Lands Conservation Act (ANILCA)

Although development interests prevailed in the pipeline controversy, environmentalists in the 1960s and 1970s also succeeded in staking some claims to Alaska. On December 9, 1960, Interior Secretary Fred Seaton set aside 8.9 million acres as the Arctic National Wildlife Range. Then, acting under Section 17d(2) of ANCSA, which authorized the secretary to set aside "national interest" lands to be considered for national park, wilderness, wildlife refuge, or national forest status, Seaton added 3.7 million acres to the range. In the late 1970s environmentalists began campaigning to get formal protection for the lands Seaton had set aside. Their campaign ended in 1980 when Congress enacted ANILCA, which placed 104 million acres of public domain land under federal protection.[13] The act reclassified the original 8.9-million-acre Arctic National Wildlife Range as the Arctic National Wildlife Refuge, adding to the refuge all lands, waters, interests, and submerged lands under federal ownership at the time Alaska became a state. In addition, ANILCA expanded the original refuge by adding 9.1 million acres of adjoining public lands, extending it west to the pipeline and south to the Yukon Flats National Wildlife Refuge.

ANILCA made significant compromises, however, such as excluding from federal protection areas with significant development potential, thereby setting the stage for another showdown over resource development in Alaska. The provision of particular consequence was Section 1002, which instructed the DOI to study the mineral and wildlife resources of the refuge's 1.5 million-acre Coastal Plain to determine its suitability for oil and gas exploration and development. Although the House of Representatives had favored wilderness designation for this area, often called the "ecological heart" of the refuge, the Senate had resisted in the absence of a thorough assessment of its oil and gas potential. As a compromise, Section 1002 prohibited leasing, development, and production of oil and gas in the refuge unless authorized by Congress.[14]

At first glance, oil and gas development might appear out of place in a wildlife refuge; after all, the statutory purpose of the refuge system, established in 1966, is "to provide, preserve, restore, and manage a national network of lands and waters sufficient in size, diversity, and location to meet society's needs for areas where the widest possible spectrum of benefits associated with wildlife and wildlands is enhanced and made available." [15] Furthermore, ANILCA specifies that ANWR is to be managed:

(i) to conserve fish and wildlife populations and habitats in their natural diversity including, but not limited to, the Porcupine caribou herd (including the participation in coordinated ecological studies and management of this herd and the Western Arctic caribou herd), polar bears, grizzly bears, muskox, Dall sheep, wolves, wolverines, snow geese, peregrine falcons, and other migratory birds and arctic char and grayling; (ii) to fulfill the international treaty obligations of the United States with respect to fish and wildlife and their habitats; (iii) to provide, in a manner consistent with purposes set forth in subparagraphs (i) and (ii), the opportunity for continued subsistence uses by local residents; and (iv) to ensure, to the maximum extent practicable and in a manner consistent with the purposes set forth in subparagraph (i), water quality and necessary water quantity within the refuge.[16]

A provision of Section 4(d) of the act that establishes the refuge system, however, authorizes the use of a refuge for any purpose, including mineral leasing, as long as that use is "compatible with the major purpose for which the area was established." [17] And, in fact, private companies hold mining leases as well as oil and gas leases on many of the nation's wildlife refuges, and oil and gas exploration and development has occurred in about 25 percent of them (155 of 575).[18] Currently, 4,406 oil and gas wells—1,806 of which are active—are sprinkled throughout 105 refuges. Although there is little systematic documentation of the environmental impact of resource development in wildlife refuges, in 2003 the U.S. General Accounting Office (GAO) found that those effects varied from negligible to substantial and from temporary to long term.[19] In a 1991–1992 survey, a substantial number of managers in the U.S. Fish and Wildlife Service, which administers the refuge system, described oil and gas operations in their refuges as incompatible with wildlife protection.[20] But with funding of only $2 per acre, compared to $13 per acre for the Park Service and $7 per acre for the Forest Service, the Fish and Wildlife Service has limited resources with which to resist or mitigate the effects of such incursions.[21]

THE CASE

Vast and extremely remote, ANWR is the most northerly unit, and the second largest, in the National Wildlife Refuge System. ANWR encompasses about 19.6 million acres of land in northeast Alaska, an area almost as large as New England. It is bordered to the west by the trans-Alaska pipeline corridor, to the south by the Venetie-Arctic Village lands and Yukon Flats National Wildlife Refuge, to the east by Canada, and to the north by the Beaufort Sea. Fairbanks, the nearest city, is about 180 miles south of the refuge boundary by air. Two native villages, Kaktovik on Barter Island and Arctic Village on the south slope of the Brooks Range, abut the refuge (see Map 6-1).

The refuge is diverse. It contains a full range of boreal forest, mountain, and northern slope landscapes and habitats, as well as the four tallest peaks and the largest number of glaciers in the Brooks Range. The refuge's northern edge descends to the Beaufort Sea and a series of barrier islands and lagoons, and the valley slopes are dotted with lakes, sloughs, and wetlands. In the southeastern portion, the Porcupine River area, groves of stunted black spruce grade into tall, dense spruce forests. In addition to portions of the main calving ground for the 130,000-member Porcupine caribou herd and critical habitat for the endangered peregrine falcon, ANWR is home to snow geese, tundra swans, wolves, wolverines, arctic foxes, lynx, marten, and moose. The rivers,

Map 6-1 The Arctic National Wildlife Refuge

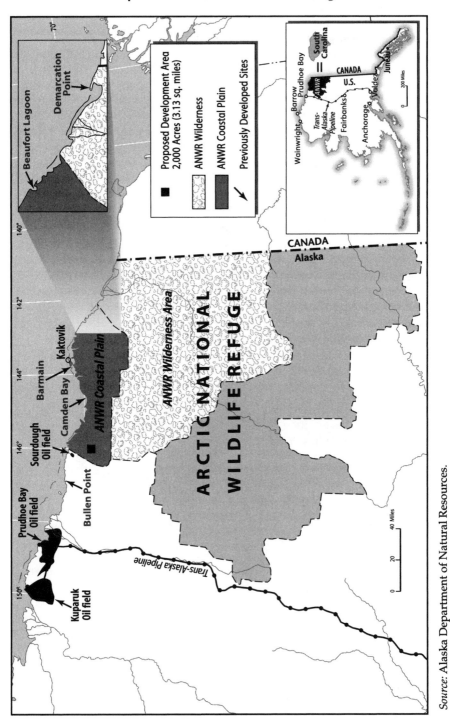

Source: Alaska Department of Natural Resources.

lakes, and lagoons contain arctic grayling, lake trout, whitefish, northern pike, turbot, arctic cod, and several varieties of salmon. The waters offshore harbor summering bowhead whales, and the coastal lagoons provide year-round habitat for polar bears and ringed and bearded seals.

Although a quintessential wilderness seldom visited by humans, ANWR is an unusual poster child for the preservationist cause: it is not among the most spectacular of America's wild places. Yet advocates of preservation have created a powerful image of the refuge as the nation's last remaining true wilderness, a symbol of the American frontier. Their opponents have also crafted a compelling case, however, one in which oil development in the Coastal Plain will enhance the country's economic and military security while posing only a marginal risk to an uninspiring landscape.

The ANWR Coalitions

Spearheading the movement to preserve ANWR's Coastal Plain is the Alaska Coalition, a consortium of seventy-five Alaskan, national, and international environmental groups. Among the most influential members are the Sierra Club, the Wilderness Society, the Natural Resources Defense Council, the National Wildlife Federation, the Audubon Society, and the Trustees for Alaska. Backing the environmentalists are the Gwich'in Eskimos, a subgroup of the Athabascan tribe that for thousands of years has relied on the Porcupine caribou herd for its survival. The government of Canada, another player on this side, also opposes opening the refuge to development because the Porcupine caribou and other wildlife regularly migrate across the Canadian border.

The primary force behind the campaign to open up ANWR to development is the oil industry, which has always been a formidable presence in U.S. politics. The industry is particularly influential in Alaska because the state's economy is dependent on oil; the state government derives about 85 percent of its revenues from oil royalties.[22] Furthermore, instead of paying income tax, Alaskans receive an annual dividend of approximately $1,000 from oil revenues. Taking no chances, the oil and gas industry also contributes heavily to the campaigns of the state's elected officials, as well as to members of Congress around the country.[23] Supporting the oil companies are the Inupiat Eskimos, who live in Kaktovik and are represented by the Arctic Slope Regional Corporation. Not only have oil revenues brought prosperity to the small community of Inupiat living within the refuge, but also, in an effort to build native support for development, Congress authorized the regional corporation to acquire 92,160 acres of subsurface mineral interests underlying the Inupiat's claim, should Congress ever open the refuge to oil and gas development. In 1987 the corporation formed the Coalition for American Energy Security (CAES), which subsequently grew to include motorized recreation, agriculture, labor, maritime, transportation, and other interests and quickly became the primary lobbying arm on behalf of ANWR development.

The Battle to Frame the Problem, 1986–1992

From the outset, the parties in this debate framed the problem in contrasting ways, describing scientific and economic risks and uncertainties in terms that were consistent with their values. Proponents of drilling argued that the nation needed to develop its domestic oil reserves to preserve national security and boost the economy, and they asserted that the supply available in ANWR was significant enough to justify the minimal risk of environmental harm. Opponents of development argued that the amount of oil that ANWR was likely to hold would satisfy just a tiny fraction of total domestic demand and therefore would only marginally reduce the nation's dependence on foreign oil. Moreover, they said, development would certainly create air and water pollution, generate toxic wastes, disturb wildlife habitat, and, most important, destroy the wilderness character of the landscape. By the late 1980s, when the conflict was in full swing, both sides had developed elaborate arguments about the national interest in ANWR and had marshaled and interpreted scientific and economic evidence to support their claims and rebut those of their opponents.

The Potential Benefits of Oil and Gas Development. The Interior Department has developed the authoritative models predicting the amount of oil that lies under the refuge's Coastal Plain.[24] The first of these, the 1987 *Arctic National Wildlife Refuge, Alaska, Coastal Plain Report*, known as the "1002 Report," concluded that there was a 19 percent chance of finding economically recoverable oil reserves. The report judged it possible to recover between 600 million and 9.2 billion barrels of oil, with a mean of 3.2 billion barrels. If that average were correct, the Coastal Plain would be the third largest oil field in U.S. history. According to the report's mean case scenario, ANWR would produce 147,000 barrels per day by the year 2000, peak at 659,000 barrels per day in 2005, fall over the next decade to 400,000 barrels per day, and continue to decline for the remaining thirty- to fifty-year life of the field. At its peak, ANWR's production would equal 4 percent of U.S. consumption, 8 percent of domestic production, and about 9 percent of imports, while increasing the gross national product (GNP) by $74.9 billion and reducing the annual trade deficit by approximately $6 billion.[25]

Wielding these official estimates, proponents of development advanced the argument that drilling in the Coastal Plain would enhance national security. They cited the country's growing dependence on imported oil, noting that of the 17.3 million barrels per day consumed in 1990, an average of 7.6 million barrels per day was imported, with 2.1 million of those coming from the politically unstable Middle East. In 1990 the Energy Department predicted that, without changes in the nation's energy policy, imports would account for 65 percent of the U.S. oil supply by 2010. With chilling language, drilling advocates stressed America's vulnerability to reliance on foreign oil: "Remember that two million barrels of oil a day coming down that pipeline from Alaska's

Prudhoe Bay played a major role in breaking OPEC's grip. And recall how that grip felt, with its lines at the gasoline pumps and aggravated inflation." [26] Sen. Ted Stevens, R-Alaska, warned that "without the Arctic Wildlife Range resources, this nation faces the threat of a precarious future in which OPEC nations would be able to hold another and perhaps more serious oil embargo over our heads." [27]

Environmentalists used the same information but framed it differently to argue that the amount of recoverable oil that *might* lie within the refuge was unlikely to enhance the nation's energy security; they noted that it would most likely amount to "less than 200 days worth of oil at current consumption rates" and "less than 3 percent of our daily demand." [28] Environmentalists also contended that the nation's need for additional oil supplies was more apparent than real. They pointed out that the rise in U.S. petroleum imports in the late 1980s was accompanied by a decline in conservation, which was not surprising because the price of oil was low and federal incentives to conserve had atrophied. Environmentalists had official data to support their claims as well: the Congressional Research Service estimated that energy conservation research and development expenditures in real dollars fell from $322 million in 1981 to $129 in 1989. Funding for renewable energy research and development also dropped dramatically, from $708 million in 1981 to $110 million in 1990, before rising to $157 million in 1991.[29] Reflecting the low oil prices and lack of conservation incentives, automotive fuel efficiency fell in the late 1980s for the first time since 1973. Daniel Lashof, senior scientist for the Union of Concerned Scientists, concluded: "There is simply no way we can produce our way to energy security. [Oil from ANWR] cannot significantly affect the world market prices or the world markets for oil. The only way we can insulate our economy from price shocks is by improving our efficiency and reducing our total consumption of oil." [30]

Drilling advocates had a subsidiary argument about the benefits of drilling in the refuge, however: they claimed that opening ANWR to development would ease the federal deficit and create jobs. In 1990 the prodevelopment CAES suggested that if the DOI's high-end estimates of the refuge's oil potential were correct, the GNP could rise by $50.4 billion by 2005 and the trade deficit could decline by billions of dollars. Citing a 1990 study by Wharton Econometrics Forecasting Associates, CAES contended that developing a 9.2-billion-barrel oil field (the high-end estimate, on which they again chose to focus) would create 735,000 jobs by 2005.[31] CAES produced literature that reinforced its claims. At the height of the controversy, the organization was distributing a glossy, eight-page monthly newsletter with articles such as "Leasing ANWR Could Ease Budget Woes" and "Rising Oil Prices Push Up U.S. Trade Deficit," as well as a postcard-sized map of the United States showing the dollar amounts generated in each state by existing oil development in the North Slope area.

Environmentalists responded to the deficit argument in turn, pointing out that non-DOI analysts, using different oil price projections and revised tax and financial assumptions, had generated quite different total expected present values of developing ANWR. In 1990 those values ranged from $0.32 billion to $1.39 billion, compared to the DOI's $2.98 billion.[32] Furthermore, they pointed out, GNP figures disguised the allocation of oil revenues, most of which would go to oil companies. To highlight the self-interested motives of the prodrilling coalition, environmentalists noted that the oil industry reaped more than $41 billion in profit from North Slope oil development and transportation between 1969 and 1987, according to a study done for the Alaska Department of Revenue.[33]

Antidrilling advocates also rebutted the Wharton study's job creation figures, citing a Congressional Research Service analysis that characterized the estimates as "generous" and based on the "most optimistic of underlying scenarios."[34] They added that developing photovoltaics, wind, and other alternative energy sources would yield new jobs as well. Such jobs, they contended, would have the advantage of being local and stable, not subject to the boom-and-bust cycles that in the past had ravaged Texas, Oklahoma, and Alaska. Finally, environmentalists reiterated that conservation measures could have a much bigger impact on domestic oil consumption, and therefore on the trade deficit, than increased domestic oil production. For example, they said, an increase in fuel economy standards to 40 mpg for new cars and 30 mpg for light trucks could save more than 20 billion barrels of oil by 2020—more than six times the total amount the government believed lay under ANWR's Coastal Plain.

The Environmental Costs of Oil and Gas Development. Not only did environmentalists contest estimates of the economic and security value of ANWR reserves, they also raised the specter of certain and catastrophic ecological impacts of oil development in the refuge. Most important, they emphasized, because ANWR's Coastal Plain is so windy, it provides relief from insects and provides safe calving grounds for the Porcupine caribou herd, the second largest caribou herd in Alaska and the seventh largest in the world. They pointed out that most biologists believe the cumulative disturbance resulting from North Slope oil field activity had prevented many Central Arctic herd caribou from feeding optimally, resulting in reduced summer weight gain, decreased pregnancy rates, and increased mortality. Biologists forecast similar effects on the Porcupine caribou herd in the event of Coastal Plain development.

Antidrilling advocates also highlighted biologists' concern about the effect of oil exploration on the approximately 2,000 polar bears that roam the land from northwestern Alaska to the Northwest Territories in Canada. Studies showed that pregnant polar bears habitually use the Coastal Plain and the refuge lands to the east as sites for onshore denning during the winter. Although only a relatively small number of female bears use Section 1002 for dens, the area is nonetheless important: researchers found that the productivity of land dens in the Beaufort Sea polar bear population from 1981 to 1989 was significantly higher than that of dens on the offshore ice pack. Furthermore, biologists believed that the Beaufort Sea polar bear population could sustain little, if any, additional mortality of females; the number of animals dying annually was already equal to the number born each year.[35]

Supporting environmentalists' position was the Interior Department's own 1002 Report, which warned of poor long-term prospects for wildlife in a developed Coastal Plain based on wildlife studies at Prudhoe Bay:

> Post-development studies indicate an absence of calving near the coast of Prudhoe Bay during 1976–85, possibly due to avoidance of the area by caribou. Despite apparent changes in distribution, the populations of both caribou herds have been increasing. At some point, however, incremental loss and modification of suitable calving habitat could be expected to result in population declines. Similarly, at some time, cumulative habitat loss within the region potentially could result in changes in habitat distribution or population reductions of other species including muskoxen, wolves, wolverines, polar bears, snow geese, and arctic grayling.[36]

Further buttressing environmentalists' position was the Canadian government's stance that because the Porcupine caribou herd migrates between the United States and Canada neither country owned it exclusively, and each had an obligation to protect its habitat. [37]

Not surprisingly, the oil industry and its allies rejected environmentalists' assertion that oil development would disturb wildlife, emphasizing the uncertainty surrounding scientific estimates of likely wildlife impacts. A BP Exploration publication portrayed environmentalists as unscientific and misanthropic, saying, "Claims of serious adverse effects on fish and wildlife populations are simply not supported by scientific data and may in fact represent an objection to the presence of humans in a wild area." [38] Prodrilling advocates got a boost when Interior Secretary Donald Hodel wrote an editorial in the *New York Times* saying, "We do not have to choose between an adequate energy supply on the one hand and a secure environment on the other. We can have both." [39]

The two sides also disputed the size of the footprint that would be made by oil development on the Coastal Plain. CAES pointed out that oil operations on the Coastal Plain would occupy only nineteen square miles, an area roughly the size of Dulles Airport outside of Washington, D.C. Environmentalists responded that, although the Prudhoe Bay complex covered a mere 9,000 acres, that acreage was spread out over 800 square miles. The Office of Technology Assessment concurred with environmentalists, saying:

> Although the industry argues—correctly—that the actual coverage of the surface is likely to be less than one percent of the coastal plain, the physical coverage would be spread out like a spiderweb, and some further physical effects, like infiltration of road dust and changes in drainage patterns, will spread out from the land actually covered.[40]

Environmentalists added that the oil industry had a poor record of both estimating likely environmental impacts and repairing damage. To support this charge they cited a Fish and Wildlife Service report comparing the actual and predicted impacts of the trans-Alaska pipeline and the Prudhoe Bay oil fields. The report concluded that the actual area of gravel fill and extraction was 60 percent greater than expected; gravel requirements surpassed predictions by 400 percent; and road miles exceeded the planned number by 30 percent.[41]

Finally, environmentalists argued that, although it did support a host of wildlife, ANWR's Coastal Plain is a fragile ecosystem that is more vulnerable than temperate ecosystems to damage from industrial activity. To support this claim, they pointed out that ANWR is an Arctic desert that receives an average of only seven inches of moisture a year. Its subsoil, permafrost, remains frozen year round, and only the top few inches to three feet of ground thaw in the summer. They noted that the combination of low temperatures, short growing season, and restricted nutrients limit the area's biological productivity. Because plants grow slowly, any physical disturbance—even driving vehicles across the terrain in winter—can scar the land for decades, and regrowth could take centuries. They added that, like other Arctic areas, ANWR contains large concentrations of animal populations but relatively low diversity. Mammal populations, in particular, gather in large numbers, thereby heightening their vulnerability to catastrophe. They warned that arctic plants are more sensitive to pollutants than are species that grow in warmer climates; toxic substances persist for a longer time in cold environments than in more temperate climates; and the severe weather and complex ice dynamics of the Arctic complicate both environmental protection and accident cleanup.[42]

In addition to proffering different causal stories and numbers in the debate, the two sides adopted contrasting symbols that revealed the chasm separating their values. Environmentalists characterized the refuge as the last great American wilderness, a vast expanse of untrammeled landscape that provides a home for increasingly rare Arctic wildlife. They likened opening the refuge to "destroy[ing] America's Serengeti" for a few weeks' supply of oil.[43] Development proponents described the area as a barren, marshy wilderness in the summer and a frozen desert the rest of the year. "ANWR's Coastal Plain is no Yellowstone," scoffed a *Wall Street Journal* editorial.[44]

The Political Contest, 1986–1992

These competing arguments had a profound impact on legislative politics. By nationalizing the issue, environmentalists enabled non-Alaskan legislators to claim credit with their environmentalist constituents for protecting the refuge. Development interests responded by trying to persuade uncommitted legislators that opening the refuge would provide their constituents with tangible benefits, including jobs, cheap oil, and international security. Both sides tried to capitalize on focusing events to gain the upper hand. Protection advocates had the advantage for several reasons. First, not drilling is the status quo, and it is easier to block a policy change in Congress than to enact one. Second, ANWR falls under the jurisdiction of multiple committees in Congress, which also makes obstructing policy change easier. Third, the sheer complexity of national energy policy makes it contentious and therefore unattractive to most legislators, who prefer to avoid provoking opposition.

ANWR Gets on the Congressional Agenda. In late 1986 Trustees for Alaska and other environmental groups learned that the Interior Department planned to circulate for public review the EIS it had prepared for oil leasing in ANWR at the same time it submitted its recommendation to Congress. Representing the Reagan administration's position, William Horn, the assistant DOI secretary for fish and wildlife, justified releasing the draft report to the public and Congress simultaneously on the grounds that the refuge might contain "a supergiant oil field that does not exist anywhere else in the United States." [45] The environmentally oriented Alaska Coalition promptly filed a lawsuit against the department, arguing successfully that NEPA requires public participation in the preparation of an EIS *prior* to its release to Congress. Compelled by the court, the Fish and Wildlife Service held public hearings in January 1987.

On June 1, after incorporating public comments and responses, Secretary Hodel submitted a final report on the oil and gas potential of the Coastal Plain, the projected impacts of development, and a recommendation that Congress authorize oil and gas leasing in Area 1002. In the report's introduction, Hodel said, "The 1002 area is the nation's best single opportunity to increase significantly domestic oil production." He embraced a national security argument in support of his conclusions, saying production from the area would "reduce U.S. vulnerability to disruptions in the world oil market and could contribute to our national security." [46] After projecting only minimal impacts on caribou and muskoxen, the report assured readers that oil development and wildlife could coexist.

The Natural Resources Defense Council and the Steering Committee for the Gwich'in immediately filed lawsuits against the Interior Department, alleging that the report failed to properly evaluate potential environmental damage. The Gwich'in suit also claimed that the DOI had overestimated the revenues to be gained from drilling by using unrealistically inflated assumptions about oil prices. The plaintiffs requested that a new EIS be prepared that was based on realistic revenue projections and addressed the survival of Gwich'in culture.

Congressional Action, 1987–1989. Concurrently with the legal battles over the adequacy of the 1002 EIS, Congress began debating the merits of developing the refuge. In 1987 sponsors introduced seven bills concerning ANWR, five of which would have opened up the 1.5-million-acre Coastal Plain to oil and gas exploration, development, and production. In the House, two committees—Merchant Marine and Fisheries and Insular and Interior Affairs—held extensive but inconclusive hearings.

In the Senate, William Roth, R-Del., introduced S 1804, an ANWR wilderness designation bill, while Frank Murkowski, R-Alaska, introduced S 1217, a bill to open up the refuge. Two Senate committees, Energy and Natural Resources and Environment and Public Works, held hearings but failed to report bills to the floor. S 1217 was stopped at least in part because of a series of scandals that broke in 1987. First, in July, the press revealed that the DOI had begun dividing the Coastal Plain among Alaskan native corporations for leasing to oil companies without congressional approval. Shortly thereafter, environmentalists discovered that the DOI had excluded the conclusion of one of its own biologists that oil development would result in a 20 percent to 40 percent decline in the Porcupine caribou population.[47] What the DOI claimed was an editing error environmentalists attributed to political censorship. Either way, the controversy was sufficient to derail the bill's progress.

The following year, the House Subcommittee on Fisheries and Wildlife Conservation and the Environment, chaired by Don Young, R-Alaska, approved (28–13) HR 3601, which favored leasing. The subcommittee considered but did not adopt several environmentally oriented amendments. Instead, the bill attempted to soften the impact of drilling by requiring oil and gas development to impose "no significant adverse effect" on the environment; establishing a three-mile-wide coastal "insect relief zone" for caribou; and allowing only "essential facilities" within 1.5 to 3 miles of the coast. The House took no further action on the legislation, however, because the Interior Committee, under Morris "Mo" Udall, D-Ariz., claimed equal jurisdiction over the matter and failed to report out a bill. The Senate also debated the wilderness and oil leasing issue, and advocates of protection on the Environment Committee were able to thwart supporters of drilling on the Energy Committee.[48]

With the inauguration of George H. W. Bush as president in 1989, environmentalists hoped their prospects might improve because as a candidate Bush had tried to distance himself from President Reagan's antienvironmental record. In January the Alaska Coalition sent a petition signed by 100 environmental groups and local civic associations to the new president and his designated interior secretary, Manuel Lujan Jr. (a former member of Congress who had introduced legislation to open the refuge), requesting that they protect the refuge from development.[49] But the letter, although it affected the administration's language, did not prompt a shift in its position: in February President Bush called for "cautious development" of ANWR. Backed by the approval of the Bush administration, the Senate Energy and Natural Resources Committee reported S 684 favorably on March 16, 1989, by a vote of 12 to 7.[50]

The House Merchant Marine and Interior committees also had been holding ANWR hearings, and a week after the Senate committee's report, Rep. Walter Jones, D-N.C., introduced a companion bill (HR 1600) to open up the refuge.[51] But House deliberations were interrupted in March by what was for environmentalists a serendipitous focusing event: the *Exxon Valdez* oil spill, which inundated Alaska's Prince William Sound with nearly 11 million gallons of oil. Environmentalists capitalized on the devastating impact of the spill and subsequent news coverage of oil-soaked wildlife. Jones reluctantly conceded the issue, citing hysteria. "We hoped before the oil spill to come out with a bill in July," he said, "but due to the emotional crisis this spill has created, we think it is best to put it on the back burner for the time being until the emotionalism has subsided." Even the prodevelopment Bush White House acknowledged that "it will be some time before [ANWR legislation] is considered." [52] Within Alaska, where support for drilling had run high, the oil industry and its supporters were chastened: the Democratic governor, Steve Cowper, expected the spill to "cause a permanent change in the political chemistry in Alaska." [53]

At least in the short run, the *Valdez* spill helped environmentalists derail industry's arguments that reserves could be developed without threatening environmental harm. Lodwrick Cook, the chairman and chief executive of ARCO, confessed that "ARCO and the [oil] industry have lost a certain amount of credibility because of this spill, and we're going to have to work toward recapturing that." [54] On the advice of Secretary Lujan, the oil industry launched a major public relations campaign. It was confident that approval of an oil-spill preparedness bill, combined with the passage of time, would defuse public ire over the *Valdez* fiasco.[55] In fact, within a year, visible signs of damage to Prince William Sound had disappeared, and supporters of oil exploration in ANWR prepared to revisit the issue.

Congressional Action, 1990–1992. In the summer of 1990 international events opened a window of opportunity for drilling advocates. The threat of war in the Persian Gulf following the invasion of Kuwait by Iraqi forces sparked renewed debate over U.S. dependence on foreign oil and bolstered support for drilling in ANWR. Rep. Billy Tauzin, D-La., expressed his contempt for environmental values when he said, "It's amazing to me how we could put caribou above human lives—our sons and daughters." [56] Although the Bush administration insisted that the subsequent U.S. invasion (in January 1991) did not constitute a "war for oil," proponents of domestic oil and gas development seized on the event to revive drilling proposals. By September the oil industry and its backers in the Bush administration were again pressing Congress to open the Coastal Plain to drilling. As one House aide remarked, "The Middle East crisis wiped the *Exxon Valdez* off the ANWR map as quickly as the *Exxon Valdez* wiped ANWR off the legislative map." [57]

Pressing its advantage, in April 1991 the Bush administration's development-friendly DOI released a revised estimate of the probability of finding oil in ANWR, raising it from 19 percent to 46 percent—a level almost unheard of in the industry—and estimating peak production of 870,000 barrels per day by the year 2000. Based on 1989 data, which included more accurate geological studies and test wells drilled on the periphery of the refuge, the DOI's Bureau of Land Management now estimated that the Coastal Plain most likely contained between 697 million and 11.7 billion barrels of oil.[58]

In the 102d Congress prodrilling senators Bennett Johnston, D-La., and Malcolm Wallop, R-Wyo., introduced S 1120, the Bush administration's "National Energy Security Act of 1991," Title IX of which permitted development of ANWR's Coastal Plain. In an effort to win over several Democratic senators who had denounced the plan because it was not accompanied by higher automotive fuel economy standards, Johnston's bill included a provision directing the secretary of transportation to raise CAFE (corporate average fuel economy) standards substantially, although it did not specify how much. In a further effort to appease proenvironment legislators, Johnston proposed that federal proceeds from ANWR oil be used to fund energy conservation and research. Although Johnston touted the bill as a compromise, the bill's preamble made its purpose clear: "to reduce the Nation's dependence on imported oil" and "to provide for the energy security of the Nation."

Again, however, antidrilling advocates were able to take advantage of unforeseen developments to bolster their depiction of the oil industry as greedy profiteers. In January 1991 the *New York Times* reported that in the last quarter of 1990 oil industry profits had jumped dramatically as oil prices skyrocketed in anticipation of the Gulf War. Net income for Exxon, the world's largest oil company, had more than tripled, and Mobil's profits had climbed 45.6 percent; Texaco's, 35 percent; and Amoco's, 68.6 percent. "In fact," journalist Thomas Hayes reported, "each of these quarterly earnings might have been much larger, but each of the top five lowered their reported profit with bookkeeping tactics that oil giants often employ legally to pare taxes in periods when profits—and public resentment—are on the rise." [59] Furthermore, instead of an oil shortage, the world was experiencing a glut, as Saudi Arabia increased its output and demand slumped.

Although these developments weakened prodrilling arguments, the Senate Energy Committee nevertheless was persuaded by the DOI's revised estimates of the probability of finding oil in the refuge and the promise of jobs in the deepening recession, and in late May 1991 the committee approved S 1120 by a vote of 17 to 3. The sheer comprehensiveness of the energy bill undermined its prospects in the chamber as a whole, however, as its myriad provisions prompted the mobilization of a host of interests. Energy consumer groups joined environmentalists, fearing that measures to restructure the utility industry would raise electricity rates. The auto industry, which opposed the CAFE standards, as well as small utilities disadvantaged by some provisions in the bill, opposed the bill. The prodrilling coalition gained the support of large electric utilities that stood to benefit from the bill, as well as the nuclear power industry lobby. Coalitions on both sides waged an all-out war for public opinion and the votes of uncommitted members of Congress, resulting in a cacophony of competing messages.

Further hampering the bill's chances of passing, in October 1991 the Senate Environment and Public Works Committee approved legislation that would prohibit oil and gas drilling in ANWR; and six Democratic senators pledged to filibuster S 1120 if it came up for a vote on the floor.[60] On November 1 Johnston called for a vote on cloture, which would have ended the filibuster, but failed by ten votes to get the necessary three-fifths majority. The bill's complexity had simply created too much highly charged opposition for senators to risk the political fallout that accompanies a controversial decision. The Senate eventually passed a national energy bill in 1992, by a vote of 94 to 4, but it contained neither ANWR nor automobile fuel efficiency provisions.

The House also considered bills authorizing oil and gas leasing in the refuge in 1991 and 1992. In 1991 the House postponed consideration of an ANWR drilling bill after allegations surfaced that Alyeska, operator of the Trans-Alaska Pipeline System, had coercively silenced its critics. Mo Udall reintroduced his ANWR wilderness bill, but it did not make it to the floor for a vote. On May 2, 1992, the House passed (381–37) an energy bill similar to S 1120, but, like the Senate bill, it lacked provisions on ANWR or fuel efficiency standards. In October 1992 the president signed the ANWR-free Energy Policy Act into law.

ANWR Proposals on the Quiet, 1993–1999

The election of Bill Clinton to the presidency in 1992 temporarily punctured the hopes of drilling advocates, as the newly installed administration made clear its staunch opposition to oil development in the refuge. Based on more conservative geologic and economic assumptions than those made by its predecessor, the Clinton administration's Interior Department in June 1995 reduced its estimate of economically recoverable oil in the refuge to between 148 million and 5.15 billion barrels. The department's 1995 *Coastal Plain Resource Assessment* also affirmed that "there would be major environmental impacts from oil and gas development on the coastal plain" and documented even greater dependence of the Porcupine caribou herd on the 1002 area than had earlier reports.[61]

Nevertheless, in 1995, after two years of relative quiescence, congressional sponsors resumed their efforts to open up the refuge, hoping that the ascension of the Republican-controlled 104th Congress had presented a new opportunity for a prodrilling policy. A chief difference between 1995 and preceding years was that two ardent proponents of drilling (both Alaskans) had acquired positions of power on the very committees that previously had obstructed efforts to open the refuge. Murkowski became chairman of the Senate Environment and Natural Resources Committee, and Young took over the House Resources Committee (previously the House Interior Committee). Both chairmen promptly announced their intention to attach ANWR drilling provisions to the omnibus budget reconciliation bill in the fall.[62] Such a strategy was promising because small riders attached to major bills tend to attract less public notice than individual pieces of legislation and, perhaps more important, the budget reconciliation bill cannot be filibustered. Moreover, the president was less likely to veto omnibus legislation than a less significant bill.

By the middle of the legislative session, Sen. Joseph Lieberman, D-Conn., an ANWR defender, was expressing his concern that a majority in both houses favored opening the refuge. Sure enough, the fiscal 1996 budget resolution

(H Con Res 67), approved by the House and adopted by the Senate in May, assumed $1.3 billion in revenue from ANWR oil leases. Furthermore, the day before passing the resolution, the Senate voted 56–44 to kill an amendment that would have prohibited exploration in the Coastal Plain. But environmentalists had an ally in the White House. Clinton's interior secretary, Bruce Babbitt, voiced the administration's resistance to the congressional proposal and chastised prodrilling legislators as greedy. "In effect, we are being asked to jeopardize an irreplaceable piece of our national heritage over a three-year difference in budget projections by the people in green eyeshades," Babbitt said.[63] Citing the ANWR provision as one of the chief reasons, President Clinton vetoed the 1996 budget bill, and, after a week-long standoff during which the federal government shut down altogether, the provision's sponsors backed down and removed that rider.

Undaunted, drilling advocates continued their campaign to open the refuge. In 1997 the *Washington Post* reported that Arctic Power, a group formed in 1992 to promote drilling in the refuge, had contracted with a Washington, D.C.–based lobbying group (Decision Management Inc.) to target Democratic senators John Breaux and Mary Landrieu of Louisiana with information about the economic ties between Alaska and their state.[64] Drilling proponents also forged an alliance with the Teamsters Union based on their claim that opening the refuge would produce hundreds of thousands of jobs, even though several analyses refuted that assertion.[65] In support of their national security argument, drilling advocates touted an Energy Department finding that, while domestic oil production had been declining, the percentage of U.S. oil that was imported rose from 27 percent in 1985 to nearly 50 percent in 1997. In 1998 revised U.S. Geological Survey (USGS) estimates also bolstered drilling advocates' claims: based on new geological information, technological advances, and changes in the economics of North Slope drilling, agency experts said there was a 95 percent chance that more than 5.7 billion barrels of oil would be technically recoverable and a 5 percent chance of extracting more than 16 billion barrels from the refuge. At a price of $20 per barrel, the mean estimate of the amount of economically recoverable oil was 3.2 billion barrels.[66] A fact sheet from the House Resources Committee embraced the new figures and said, "The fact is, ANWR will help balance the budget, create jobs, increase domestic production, reduce oil import dependence and the trade deficit." [67]

Despite concerted efforts by congressional proponents, the Clinton administration's unwavering opposition stymied efforts to open the refuge for the remainder of the decade. Although sponsors introduced bills in the 105th Congress (1997–1998), neither chamber debated the issue. In the 106th Congress (1999–2000), sponsors again introduced both wilderness designation and energy development bills. In addition, assumptions about revenues from ANWR were originally included in the FY2001 budget resolution as reported by the Senate Budget Committee. The House-Senate conference committee rejected the language, however, and it was excluded from the final budget passed in April 2000.

The 2000 Presidential Campaign and President Bush's Energy Policy

In the summer of 2000 the debate over ANWR's fate again captured the national spotlight when presidential candidate George W. Bush expressed his support for oil development there. The issue subsequently became a main point of contention between Bush and Vice President Al Gore, the Democratic candidate. Gore adopted the rhetoric of environmentalists about the superior benefits of conservation and the importance of preserving wilderness, while Bush cited the nation's need for energy independence and the slowing economy's vulnerability to higher energy prices. When Bush won the election, drilling advocates again felt certain their opportunity had arrived.

Hoping to boost support for drilling, a spokesman for ARCO—which would be a major beneficiary of permission to drill in the refuge—testified at a House Resource Committee hearing that the company had learned a lot about environmentally friendly oil development over the years. "We can explore without leaving footprints," he said, "and the footprint required for new developments is a tenth of what it once was." [68] BP Amoco, another leading player in Alaska, contended that technological advances enabled it to extract oil with minimal environmental impact: thanks to cutting-edge technology for steering drill bits, the newest wells occupy a much smaller area than older wells; pipelines are built higher, to let caribou pass beneath them, and feature more elbows, which reduce the amount of oil spilled in an accident; and often, rather than constructing roads, companies airlift workers to the site.[69]

To enhance its credibility, BP spent much of the 1990s trying to transform its image from black to green by acknowledging the threat of climate change and embracing alternative fuels. (Taking no chances, the company also donated tens of thousands of dollars to the prodevelopment lobbying group Arctic Power, as well as to Republican politicians, including Bush.[70]) The company's British CEO wrote in a memo to employees that BP's values "may be manifested in different ways, but they have much in common: a respect for the individual and the diversity of mankind, a responsibility to protect the natural environment." [71] Environmentalists remained skeptical, however: the World Wildlife Fund's Francis Grant-Suttie said that "on the PR level they have been successful at differentiating themselves from others, but by virtue of what they're doing on the coastal plain, you can see it's sheer rhetoric." [72]

Reflecting the issue's high priority for his administration, during his first month in office Bush said, "I campaigned hard on the notion of having environmentally sensitive exploration at ANWR, and I think we can do so." [73] Claiming that the nation faced an energy crisis, at the end of January President Bush created a task force headed by Vice President Dick Cheney to devise ways to reduce America's "reliance upon foreign oil" and to "encourage the development of pipelines and power-generating capacity in the country." [74] Drilling advocates were confident, and opponents worried, that a sympathetic president and his allies in Congress would be able to capitalize on concerns about a spike in energy prices and California's energy deregulation fiasco to win passage of a drilling bill.[75]

The Bush administration's rhetoric set in motion yet another ferocious lobbying campaign featuring Arctic Power, which hired the law firm Patton Boggs, the public relations firm Qorvis, and media consultant Alex Castellanos to create a series of radio and television ads. In late March Arctic Power announced the formation of a new coalition, the Energy Stewardship Alliance. At the same time, the Audubon Society launched its own ad campaign, and Audubon and Defenders of Wildlife began mobilizing citizens to send e-mails and faxes to Congress.

The arguments employed by both sides had changed little over the years. Proponents of drilling emphasized increasing economic security and reducing dependence on foreign sources. They cited the high end of USGS oil estimates (16 billion barrels, an estimate that included state waters and Native lands in addition to the ANWR 1002 area), neglecting to note the low odds associated with that number, and they claimed that technological improvements would dramatically minimize the footprint and environmental impact of oil and gas development. And they disparaged the aesthetic qualities of the refuge, making sure to fly uncommitted legislators over the area in winter to emphasize its barrenness. Opponents responded by citing the low end of the range of USGS oil estimates (3.2 billion barrels) and reminding the public that such an amount would hardly put a dent in U.S. reliance on foreign energy sources. They rejected drilling advocates' arguments about environmentally sound exploration, noting that serious hazardous waste spills were continuing to occur at Prudhoe Bay. They argued that conservation, not exploration, was the solution to the nation's energy woes. For example, in a *New York Times* editorial, Thomas Friedman cited the Natural Resources Defense Council's estimate that increasing the average fuel efficiency of new cars, SUVs, and light trucks from 24 mpg to 39 mpg in a decade would save 51 billion barrels of oil, more than fifteen times the likely yield from ANWR. And they touted the spiritual importance of untrammeled wilderness: likening the refuge to a cathedral, Friedman compared drilling to online trading in church on a Palm Pilot, saying, "It violates the very ethic of the place." [76]

The two sides also continued their fierce debate over the impact of drilling on the refuge's wildlife. Late winter snows in 2001 caused one of the worst years for the Porcupine caribou herd in the thirty years scientists had been observing them. Thousands of newborn calves died because their mothers gave birth before reaching the Coastal Plain. Antidrilling advocates pointed out that industrial development would have a similar effect by keeping calving mothers off the Coastal Plain. But drilling proponents retorted that this occurrence was a natural pattern that had little to do with whether oil exploration should be allowed. They pointed out that the Central Arctic herd continued to flourish despite Prudhoe Bay development (dismissing the caveat that most of the Central Arctic herd had moved away from its historic calving grounds, something that might not be possible in ANWR).[77] In spring 2002 the USGS released a study warning that caribou "may be particularly sensitive" to oil exploration in ANWR. But a week later, after Interior Secretary Gale Norton asked scientists to plug two "more likely" scenarios into its model, the agency issued a more sanguine two-page follow-up. In response to the ensuing uproar, one biologist who worked on the study acknowledged, "The truth is, we just don't know what the impact would be." [78]

Journalists often reinforced environmentalists' message by using poetic language to describe the refuge. For example, *Los Angeles Times* reporter Kim Murphy rhapsodized: "The Alaskan Arctic is a place where the dawning summer is transcendent, an Elysian landscape trembling with tentative new life after a dark winter of vast frosts and howling winds." [79] Charles Seabrook wrote in the *Atlanta Journal and Constitution*, "It is a raw, elemental land, a place of exquisite beauty and enormous geometry—one of the Earth's last great wild places. The hand of man is hardly known here. The cutting edges of light, water and wind predominate. Grizzly bears roam the wide-open spaces, and great herds of migrating caribou appear in the summer and fall." Creating a stark contrast, he observed, "Prudhoe lights up the tundra for miles with powerful industrial lights. Steam erupts from eight-story buildings. More than 500 roads link 170 drilling sites along the coast." [80]

In a blow to the Bush administration's plans, the House Budget Committee released a budget for 2002 that did not include anticipated oil revenue from drilling in the refuge, saying that it would provoke too much controversy. The chairman of the Senate Budget Committee indicated he was likely to follow suit. Although the administration continued to emphasize increasing the supply of fossil fuels rather than conserving and developing alternative fuels, by the end of March, it seemed to be backing away from ANWR drilling proposals.[81] And by the summer of 2001, despite Cheney's roadtrip to promote an energy plan that focused on developing domestic supplies, the context of the issue had once again changed. Oil prices were falling, supplies had stabilized, and the sense of crisis—so critical to passing major legislation—had vanished. As a result, although the House passed energy bills containing ANWR drilling provisions in 2001 and 2002, opponents in the Senate were able to block them.

OUTCOMES

In 2003 and 2004 the debate seesawed, as both sides seized on expert reports and fortuitous events to bolster their claims about drilling in the refuge. Just prior to the 2003 Senate energy bill debate, the National Academy of Sciences released its two-year study of the impacts of oil development in Prudhoe Bay. The panel, which included several oil company experts and Alaskan organizations, concluded that, even though oil companies had greatly improved their practices in the Arctic, decades of drilling on the North Slope had produced a steady accumulation of environmental damage that would probably increase as exploration spread and would heal only slowly, if at all. The report concluded that industrial development had "reduced opportunities for solitude and [had] compromised wild-land and scenic values over large areas" and that "[c]ontinued expansion will exacerbate existing effects and create new ones." The panel stopped short of making a recommendation, saying, "Whether the benefits derived from oil and gas activities justify acceptance of the foreseeable and undesirable cumulative effects is an issue for society as a whole to debate and judge." [82] Environmentalists felt the report supported their position, but in August, a massive blackout across the Midwest and Northeast briefly buoyed Republican lawmakers' hopes of turning public opinion in their favor. But environmentalists were vindicated when a GAO report released in October found that the Fish and Wildlife Service's record of protecting wildlife refuges from the environmentally damaging effects of oil and gas drilling had been spotty and that refuge managers lacked the resources and training to properly oversee oil and gas activities. [83]

Aware that they lacked the votes to stop a filibuster, Senate leaders tried instead to amend the budget resolution, which required only 51 votes to pass, wooing Senate holdouts by trading local benefits for votes. For example, in 2003 they offered Norm Coleman, R-Minn.—normally an opponent of drilling—up to $800 million in federal loan guarantees to build a power plant in one of his state's most economically depressed regions. [84] Although this approach failed, prospects for drilling brightened dramatically in the fall of 2004, when President Bush was reelected, and Republican gains in the Senate appeared to net drilling advocates three new seats. [85] Although environmentalists again geared up for a major grassroots lobbying effort, this time their efforts were insufficient: in March 2005, by a vote of 51 to 49, the Senate approved a budget that included instructions allowing the Energy and Natural Resources Committee to lift drilling prohibitions in order to collect $2.4 billion in revenues from ANWR leasing over five years. [86]

The House budget, which passed, 218 to 214, the same week did *not* include revenues from drilling in ANWR, and environmentalists hoped to persuade members to prevent those revenues from being included in the conference report. But in late April House and Senate conferees agreed on a budget that did include revenues from ANWR drilling, and both chambers approved the deal. The budget resolution did not mention ANWR specifically, however, so it shielded members from accountability on the issue. By contrast, the reconciliation process would compel the authorizing committees in each chamber to approve explicit drilling language, depriving legislators of any political cover for their vote. Environmentalists were doing their best to dissuade members of the House Resources Committee from including such language, and when Hurricane Katrina struck in late August they hoped to capitalize on the delay to shore up support for their position. But many observers believed that high gas prices, which rose even higher in Katrina's aftermath, would make the political climate more hospitable to drilling in ANWR and other environmentally sensitive areas.

CONCLUSIONS

This case starkly illuminates the polarization between advocates of natural resource development and proponents of wilderness protection. Advocates of drilling in ANWR see little value in saving a place that few people will visit; for them, preserving the refuge is tantamount to placing the welfare of animals above the security and comfort of human beings. True cornucopians, they believe that technological innovation will solve any environmental problems drilling might cause.[87] By contrast, those who value wilderness take satisfaction in simply knowing that it exists. As one biologist says, "There are a lot of people who will never go to the refuge, but I get some peace of mind knowing that there is an area of naturalness on such a scale." [88] Wilderness advocates are adamant in their opposition to any kind of development in ANWR; for them, compromise is defeat. According to Tim Mahoney, chairman of the Alaska Coalition, for example, "To say that we can have oil and caribou is akin to saying that we can dam the Grand Canyon and still have rocks." [89] Assurances that oil companies now have the technological capability to minimize the environmental impact of drilling makes little impression on wilderness advocates. As Deborah Williams, executive director of the Alaska Conservation Foundation, concludes, "The one thing you can't get away from is that in the end, even with all this technology, you've got a massive industrial complex." [90]

Given the chasm separating the two sides, it is clear that the massive amounts of information generated and rhetoric employed during the nearly two decades of debate over ANWR are not aimed at changing the minds of the opposition. Instead, advocates direct evidence and arguments at the public and uncommitted members of Congress, with the goal of shaping legislators' perceptions of public opinion on the issue and the likely electoral consequences of their vote. Drilling advocates have tried to capitalize on focusing events—the Gulf War in the 1980s, rising energy prices in the 1990s, and the war in Iraq—to cast the issue of ANWR drilling as a source of economic and military security, just as they used the energy crisis of 1973 to get approval for the Alaskan pipeline. They have tried to take advantage of windows of opportunity, such as the turnover in congressional leadership in the mid-1990s and the elections of George Bush in 2000 and 2004.

That environmentalists fended off development interests' efforts for nearly twenty years is a tribute to their ability to generate national support, which they did by using the refuge's "charismatic megafauna"—particularly caribou and polar bears—to reinforce the symbolism of the last remaining wilderness. In addition, environmentalists exploited the fact that *not* drilling was the status quo: they used multiple jurisdiction (in the House), filibusters (in the Senate), and the threat of a presidential veto to thwart ANWR exploration bills. And they benefited from the complexity of energy policy, which prompted diverse interests to mobilize. Interest group activity in turn stymied congressional decision making because legislators feared the electoral repercussions of antagonizing attentive constituents. Even some of the major oil companies found the level of controversy daunting, and by early 2005 BP and Conoco-Phillips had retreated from publicly supporting legislative efforts to open up the refuge.[91]

Despite environmentalists' advantages, by fall 2005 approval of ANWR drilling appeared virtually certain, prompting many to ponder the implications of that decision. For critics, the legislative shift on ANWR exemplified the environmental movement's irrelevance to the American public and its inability to articulate a broad vision. But others disputed this interpretation, noting that a 2005 Gallup Poll found only 42 percent of respondents favored opening the refuge, while 53 percent opposed it.[92] Still others regarded the vote as a simple reflection of the change in the balance of seats in the 2004 election, which could hardly be attributed to candidates' positions on ANWR drilling. Sierra Club president Carl Pope's assessment was blunt: "If we lose this battle, it means we have lost an incredible place," he said. "It is not the end of the environmental community." [93]

QUESTIONS TO CONSIDER

- Why do you think the conflict over ANWR has been so intractable?
- Did opponents of drilling in ANWR neglect any arguments or tactics that might have helped them fend off the powerful proponents of developing oil and gas in the refuge? If so, what sorts of arguments might they have made, or what kinds of tactics should they have tried?
- Why did drilling proponents' prospects for success improve so dramatically in the 2000s? What changed, and why?

NOTES

1. As political scientist Deborah Stone observes, apparently universal values such as "security" mean different things to different people. See Deborah Stone, *Policy Paradox: The Art of Political Decision Making* (New York: Norton, 1997).
2. For more detail on the impact of multiple referral on the legislative process, see Garry Young and Joseph Cooper, "Multiple Referral and the Transformation of House Decision Making," in *Congress Reconsidered*, 5th ed., ed. Lawrence C. Dodd and Bruce J. Oppenheimer (Washington, D.C.: CQ Press, 1993), 211–234.
3. A filibuster is a tactic that is available only in the Senate and involves employing "every parliamentary maneuver and dilatory motion to delay, modify, or defeat legislation." Walter Oleszek, *Congressional Procedures and the Policy Process*, 4th ed. (Washington, D.C.: CQ Press, 1996), 249.
4. Roderick Nash, *Wilderness and the American Mind*, 3d ed. (New Haven: Yale University Press, 1982).
5. Quoted in Peter A. Coates, *The Trans-Alaska Pipeline Controversy: Technology, Conservation, and the Frontier* (Bethlehem: Lehigh University Press, 1991), 84.
6. John Strohmeyer, *Extreme Conditions: Big Oil and the Transformation of Alaska* (New York: Simon and Schuster, 1993).
7. The first suit charged that TAPS was asking excessive rights of way under the Mineral Leasing Act of 1920. A second suit joined one filed by native villagers that did not want the pipeline to cross their property. The third claimed that the DOI had not submitted an environmental impact statement, as required by NEPA. See Strohmeyer, *Extreme Conditions*.
8. Ibid., 83.
9. The Alaska Public Interest Coalition comprised a diverse set of interests, including the Sierra Club, the Wilderness Society, the National Wildlife Federation, the National Rifle Association, Zero Population Growth, Common Cause, the United Auto Workers, and others.

10. NEPA requires federal agencies to prepare an EIS for any major project. L. J. Clifton and B. J. Gallaway, "History of Trans-Alaska Pipeline System." Available at http://tapseis.anl.gov/documents/docs/Section_13_May2.pdf.

11. Coates, *The Trans-Alaska Pipeline Controversy*. Congress had already amended the Mineral Leasing Act of 1920 to make environmentalists' other legal challenge to the pipeline moot.

12. Strohmeyer, *Extreme Conditions*.

13. Public domain land is federally owned land that has not been designated for a specific purpose and is still eligible for withdrawal under federal land laws.

14. This provision is unusual; ordinarily, the Fish and Wildlife Service can allow oil development in a wildlife refuge without congressional approval.

15. U.S. DOI, *Arctic National Wildlife Refuge, Alaska, Final Comprehensive Conservation Plan, Environmental Impact Statement, Wilderness Review, Wild River Plans* (Washington, D.C.: U.S. Government Printing Office, 1988), 12.

16. P.L. 96-487; 94 Stat. 2371.

17. P.L. 89-669; 80 Stat. 926.

18. U.S. GAO, *Opportunities to Improve the Management and Oversight of Oil and Gas Activities on Federal Lands*, GAO-03-517 (August 2003).

19. Ibid.

20. Douglas Jehl, "Wildlife and Derricks Coexist, but the Question Is the Cost," *New York Times*, February 20, 2001, A1.

21. Ted Williams, "Seeking Refuge," *Audubon*, May–June 1996, 34–45, 90–94.

22. As part of its statehood deal, Alaska received title to 90 percent of the revenues from oil development within its borders.

23. According to the Center for Responsive Politics, between 1990 and 2004 oil and gas interests gave more than $178 million to congressional candidates, three-quarters to Republicans. See www.opensecrets.org/industries/indus.asp?lnd=E01.

24. Estimates of the recoverable amount of oil vary depending on the price of oil and the costs of extraction. Projections of the former depend on a host of variables; the latter depend on technological developments, geography, and environmental regulations.

25. U.S. DOI, *Arctic National Wildlife Refuge, Alaska, Coastal Plain Resource Assessment: Report and Recommendation to the Congress of the United States and Final Legislative Environmental Impact Statement* (Washington, D.C.: U.S. Fish and Wildlife Service, 1987).

26. Peter Nulty, "Is Exxon's Muck-up at Valdez a Reason to Bar Drilling in One of the Industry's Hottest Prospects?" *Fortune*, May 28, 1989, 47–49.

27. Quoted in Philip Shabecoff, "U.S. Proposing Drilling for Oil in Arctic Refuge," *New York Times*, November 25, 1986, A1.

28. Lisa Speer et al., *Tracking Arctic Oil* (Washington, D.C.: Natural Resources Defense Council, 1991), 30.

29. "National Energy Policy," *Congressional Digest*, May 1991, 130–160.

30. Quoted in ibid., 153.

31. Isabelle Tapia, "Time for Action on Coastal Plain Is Now," Newsletter, Coalition for American Energy Security, March 1991.

32. Speer et al., *Tracking Arctic Oil*.

33. Ibid.

34. Bernard Gelb, "ANWR Development: Analyzing Its Economic Impact," Congressional Research Service, February 12, 1992.

35. U.S. House of Representatives, Committee on Merchant Marine and Fisheries, "ANWR Briefing Book," April 1991.

36. U.S. DOI, *Arctic National Wildlife Refuge*, 163–164.

37. In 1987 Canada and the United States signed the Agreement on the Conservation of the Porcupine Caribou Herd. See www.canadianembassy.org/environment/

coastal-en.asp. In 1995 the Fish and Wildlife Service concluded that oil drilling in ANWR might violate an international agreement, signed in 1973, to protect polar bears. See Michael Grunwald, "New Species Enters Debate on Arctic Oil," *Washington Post*, October 30, 2001, A3.

38. BP Exploration (Alaska) Inc., *Major Environmental Issues*, 3d ed. (Anchorage: BP Exploration, 1991).

39. Donald P. Hodel, "The Need to Seek Oil in Alaska's Arctic Refuge," *New York Times*, June 14, 1987, Sec. IV, 25.

40. U.S. Office of Technology Assessment, *Oil Production in the Arctic National Wildlife Refuge: The Technology and the Alaskan Context* (Washington, D.C.: Office of Technology Assessment, 1989), OTA-E-394, 13.

41. U.S. Fish and Wildlife Service, *Comparison of Actual and Predicted Impacts of the Trans-Alaska Pipeline Systems and Prudhoe Bay Oilfields on the North Slope of Alaska* (Fairbanks: U.S. Fish and Wildlife Service, 1987).

42. Gail Osherenko and Oran Young, *The Age of the Arctic: Hot Conflicts and Cold Realities* (New York: Cambridge University Press, 1989).

43. Shabecoff, "U.S. Proposing Drilling."

44. Anonymous, "Energy Realism," *Wall Street Journal*, May 30, 1991, A1.

45. Quoted in Shabecoff, "U.S. Proposing Drilling."

46. U.S. DOI, *Arctic National Wildlife Refuge*, vii, 186.

47. Joseph A. Davis, "Alaskan Wildlife Refuge Becomes a Battleground," *Congressional Quarterly Weekly Report*, August 22, 1987, 1939–43.

48. Joseph A. Davis and Mike Wills, "Prognosis Is Poor for Arctic Oil-Drilling Bill," *Congressional Quarterly Weekly Report*, May 21, 1988, 1387.

49. Philip Shabecoff, "Bush Is Asked to Ban Oil Drilling in Arctic Refuge," *New York Times*, January 25, 1989, A16.

50. Joseph A. Davis, "Arctic-Drilling Plan Clears Committee," *Congressional Quarterly Weekly Report*, March 18, 1989, 578.

51. The House considered three other bills to open the refuge and one to designate the area as wilderness in 1989.

52. Quoted in Philip Shabecoff, "Reaction to Alaska Spill Derails Bill to Allow Oil Drilling in Refuge," *New York Times*, April 12, 1989, A17.

53. Quoted in Richard Mauer, "Oil's Political Power in Alaska May Ebb With Spill at Valdez," *New York Times*, May 14, 1989, A1.

54. Quoted in Richard W. Stevenson, "Why Exxon's Woes Worry ARCO," *New York Times*, May 14, 1989, Sec. 3, 1.

55. Philip Shabecoff, "Oil Industry Gets Warning on Image," *New York Times*, April 4, 1989, B8.

56. Quoted in Phil Kuntz, "ANWR May be Latest Hostage of Middle East Oil Crisis," *Congressional Quarterly Weekly Report*, September 8, 1990, 2827–8.

57. Ibid.

58. U.S. DOI, Bureau of Land Management, *Overview of the 1991 Arctic National Wildlife Refuge Recoverable Petroleum Resource Update*, Washington, D.C., April 8, 1991. For comparison, experts estimated that the Prudhoe Bay oil field, North America's largest, contained about 14 billion barrels of recoverable oil.

59. Thomas Hayes, "Oil's Inconvenient Bonanza," *New York Times*, January 27, 1991, A4.

60. Christine Lawrence, "Environmental Panel Sets Up Floor Fight over ANWR," *Congressional Quarterly Weekly Report*, October 19, 1991, 3023.

61. U.S. DOI, *Arctic National Wildlife Refuge, Alaska, Coastal Plain Resource Assessment: Report and Recommendation to the Congress of the United States* (Washington, D.C.: U.S. Government Printing Office, 1995).

62. The budget reconciliation bill reconciles tax and spending policies with deficit reduction goals.

63. Quoted in Allan Freedman, "Supporters of Drilling See an Opening," *Congressional Quarterly Weekly Report*, August 12, 1995, 2440–1.
64. Bill McAllister, "Special Interests: Lobbying Washington," *Washington Post*, October 30, 1997, 21.
65. See, for example, Bernard Gelb, "ANWR Development: Economic Impacts," Congressional Research Service, October 1, 2001; Dean Baker, "Hot Air Over the Arctic: An Assessment of the WEFA Study of the Economic Impact of Oil Drilling in the Arctic National Wildlife Refuge," Center for Economic Policy and Research, September 5, 2001.
66. U.S. DOI, U.S. Geological Survey, "Arctic National Wildlife Refuge, 1002 Area, Petroleum Assessment, 1998, Including Economic Analysis," USGS Fact Sheet FS-028-01, April 2001; U.S. Geological Survey, news release, May 17, 1998.
67. On file with the author. For a more recent version of the ANWR fact sheet, see http://resourcescommittee.house.gov/issues/emr/anwrrpt.htm.
68. Quoted in Andrew Revkin, "Hunting for Oil: New Precision, Less Pollution," *New York Times*, January 30, 2000, D1.
69. Neela Banerjee, "Can BP's Black Gold Ever Flow Green?" *New York Times*, November 12, 2000, Sec. 3, 1; Revkin, "Hunting for Oil."
70. In 2000 BP contributed $50,000 to Arctic Power, $34,421 to candidate Bush (compared to $4,250 to candidate Gore), and $613,870 to the Republican Party. See Banerjee, "Can BP's Black Gold Ever Flow Green?"
71. Quoted in ibid.
72. Quoted in ibid.
73. Quoted in Joseph Kahn and David E. Sanger, "President Offers Plan to Promote Oil Exploration," *New York Times*, January 30, 2001, A1.
74. Ibid.
75. Andrew Revkin, "Clashing Opinions at a Meeting on Alaska Drilling," *New York Times*, January 10, 2001, A1.
76. Thomas Friedman, "Drilling in the Cathedral," *New York Times*, March 2, 2001, A23.
77. Kim Murphy, "Caribou's Plight Intersects Oil Debate," *Los Angeles Times*, July 5, 2001, 1.
78 Quoted in Michael Grunwald, "Warnings on Drilling Reversed," *Washington Post*, April 7, 2002, 1.
79. Murphy, "Caribou's Plight."
80. Charles Seabrook, "Alaska," *Atlanta Journal and Constitution*, July 22, 2001, 1.
81. Katharine Q. Seelye, "Facing Obstacles on Plan for Drilling for Arctic Oil, Bush Says He'll Look Elsewhere," *New York Times*, March 30, 2001, A13.
82. Quoted in Andrew C. Revkin, "Experts Conclude Oil Drilling Has Hurt Alaska's North Slope," *New York Times*, March 5, 2003, A1; Andrew C. Revkin, "Can Wilderness and Oil Mix? Yes and No, Panel Says," *New York Times*, March 11, 2003, F2.
83. U.S. GAO, *Improvement Needed in the Management and Oversight of Oil and Gas Activities on Federal Land*, GAO-04-192T, October 2003.
84. Dan Morgan and Peter Behr, "Energy Bill Add-Ons Make It Hard to Say No," *Washington Post*, September 28, 2003, A10.
85. Helen Dewar, "GOP Gains Boost Chance of Alaska Drilling," *Washington Post*, December 16, 2004, A02.
86. As part of the budget process, each chamber's budget resolution can include reconciliation instructions that require authorizing committees with jurisdiction over particular spending and revenue policies to make legislative changes in those programs to ensure a specific budgetary goal is reached. Although the budget committees write these instructions based on specific assumptions about which policies will be changed, the authorizing committees have complete discretion over the specific changes and must only meet the spending or revenue targets given in the budget resolution. Once the budget resolution is approved by both chambers, the

relevant authorizing committees report their legislation to the budget committees, which then combine those recommendations into omnibus packages—largely an administrative task, as the Budget Act prohibits budget committees from making substantive changes in the legislation. The House and Senate vote separately on their respective omnibus packages, which are then sent to conference committee to be unified. Both chambers must approve the final version of the reconciliation bill before it goes to the president for signature.

87. For a classic exposition of this argument, see Gale A. Norton, "Call of the Mild," *New York Times*, March 14, 2005, 21.
88. Quoted in Banerjee, "Can BP's Black Gold Ever Flow Green?"
89. Quoted in Davis, "Alaskan Wildlife Refuge Becomes a Battleground."
90. Quoted in Revkin, "Hunting for Oil."
91. Arctic Power and oil executives acknowledge that the prospect of trying to drill in the refuge is not particularly attractive in business terms because of the threat of litigation and policy reversal. Further complicating matters for the oil industry, rising Arctic temperatures in the last three decades have cut the frozen season, the only period oil prospecting convoys are allowed to cross the tundra, from 200 days to 100 days. See Brad Knickerbocker, "Clash Over Policies on Energy Pollution," *Christian Science Monitor*, February 10, 2005; Neela Banerjee, "BP Pulls Out of Campaign to Open Up Alaskan Area," *New York Times*, November 26, 2002, C4; Neela Banerjee, "Oil Industry Hesitates Over Moving Into Arctic Refuge," *New York Times*, March 10, 2002, Sec.1, 39; Andrew C. Revkin, "Alaska Thaws, Complicating the Hunt for Oil," *New York Times*, January 13, 2004, F1.
92. Ben Geman, "ANWR Vote Spurs Debate Over Environmentalists' Clout," *Greenwire*, March 24, 2005. On the other hand, the poll also showed that people's views were not strongly held—a result that probably led some legislators to conclude they had leeway on the issue.
93. Quoted in Ben Geman, "ANWR Lobbying Furious as Senate Vote Draws Near," *Greenwire*, March 16, 2005.

RECOMMENDED READING

Speer, Lisa, et al. *Tracking Arctic Oil*. Washington, D.C.: Natural Resources Defense Council, 1991.
Strohmeyer, John. *Extreme Conditions: Big Oil and the Transformation of Alaska*. New York: Simon and Schuster, 1993.

WEB SITES

www.r7.fws.gov/nwr/arctic (FWS site)
agdc.usgs.gov/data/projects/anwr/webhtml (USGS site)
www.anwr.org (prodevelopment Web site)
www.dog.dnr.state.ak.us/oil/products/maps/maps.htm (State of Alaska site, with oil development maps)

CHAPTER 7

Federal Grazing Policy

Some Things Never Change

When President Bill Clinton took office in January 1993, he declared his intention to raise fees for grazing livestock, end below-cost timber sales, and charge royalties for mining on the nation's public lands. Within six months, however, the president had retreated, marking the latest in a century-long series of failed attempts to curtail the prerogatives of resource users on federal lands. As a result of these privileges, ranchers with permits to graze sheep and livestock have transformed much of the arid public rangelands, which once featured a diverse array of ecosystems, into desert. Yet the nation's two largest land managers, the Forest Service and the Bureau of Land Management, have been reluctant to implement policies to restore the range. And when they have tried to institute protective practices, ranchers' congressional supporters have stymied their efforts.

Federal grazing policy exemplifies the extent to which policy history constrains current debates and decisions. The legacies of past policies influence the present in several ways. First, the ideas embedded in its authorizing statute(s), along with subsequent interpretations by the courts, shape an agency's view of its mandate; an agency is likely to resist adopting practices that seem contrary to its founding mission.[1] Second, congressional reactions to administrative decisions create a sense of what is appropriate and legitimate behavior among agency employees. Therefore, over time, congressional oversight molds the agency's organizational culture and standard operating procedures. And third, as sociologist Theda Skocpol observes, past policies "affect the social identities, goals, and capabilities of interest groups that subsequently struggle or ally in politics."[2] Interest groups privileged by past policies in turn create the context for current decisions and constrain an agency's choices among alternatives.[3]

With respect to grazing, for example, past policies deferential toward ranchers have created a sense that they have vested property rights in the resource and must be compensated if those claims are terminated.[4] The critical factor responsible for this outcome has been the ability of a minority of members of Congress to use their positions on committees that deal with public lands to exert a virtual monopoly on lawmaking and agency oversight. In general, members of Congress concerned about local development interests try to protect them by gaining positions on the authorizing committees and appropriations subcommittees with jurisdiction over the issues most relevant to those interests.[5] From that vantage point, lawmakers can stave off legislative changes perceived as damaging to their constituents in a variety of ways. Authorizing committees set the congressional agenda because they have gatekeeping power; in addition, they craft legislation and get a second crack at the bills after the conference committee does its work. Authorizing committees also exercise control over agencies under their jurisdiction through informal oversight and carefully structured administrative procedures.[6] Appropriations subcommittees guide an agency's policy implementation by determining whether it has sufficient resources—both in terms of budget and capable staff—for the tasks it has been asked to do. (In fact, political scientist Herbert Kaufman finds that appropriations subcommittees, particularly in the House, are among the most zealous superintendents of every bureau.[7])

Some political scientists argue that the constraints and incentives created by Congress "stack the deck" in agency decision making in favor of constituencies important to its congressional overseers.[8] In practice, the extent to which a single interest can dominate policymaking on an issue varies, depending on the intensity of congressional interest and the number of committees with jurisdiction.[9] Internally simple, autonomous, and unified Congress-agency "subsystems"—such as the grazing policy subsystem—are especially difficult for reformers to infiltrate. To break a minority's grip on such a subsystem, challengers must raise public concern sufficiently to give congressional leaders outside the subsystem incentives to expend their political capital on disrupting the status quo. They must also make a case salient enough to persuade uncommitted legislators to get on the bandwagon. Doing so typically involves redefining a problem to highlight an aspect the public heretofore had not considered, such as an activity's environmental costs. A successful campaign can shift not only the public's attention but also that of election-conscious legislators to the issue.[10] Reframing an issue is not simple, however; challengers need a compelling political story, complete with villains and victims and the threatened loss of something the public values. Advocates of grazing policy reform have struggled to come up with a story that generates widespread public concern. Faced with the potent symbols wielded by supporters of the status quo, reformers have had little success in their efforts to disrupt the grazing policy subsystem or make federal grazing policy more environmentally protective.

BACKGROUND

"There is perhaps no darker chapter nor greater tragedy in the history of land occupancy and use in the United States than the story of the western range," lamented associate Forest Service chief Earl H. Clapp in 1936 in *The Western Range*.[11] Although the public domain rangeland was in deplorable condition when federal managers assumed control in the early 1900s, policies to regulate its use in the first two-thirds of the twentieth century did little to restore it.[12] The Forest Service and the Bureau of Land Management (BLM) established grazing lease and permit systems during this period, but federal land managers faced enormous resistance when they tried to restrict grazing. Legal scholar Charles Wilkinson describes the essence of range policy during the twentieth century as "a series of attempts to resuscitate the range from the condition it reached in the late 1800s . . . [that] proceeded in the face of ranchers who continue to assert their 'right' to graze herds without regulation." [13] Because the original grazing policy subsystem was so tightly controlled, ranchers' congressional allies were consistently able to thwart efforts to restore the range, establishing a pattern that proved exceedingly difficult for contemporary environmentalists to break.

Introducing Grazing in the West

The introduction of cattle onto the western range began during the century following the Revolutionary War, as the federal government sought to dispose of its landholdings west of the Mississippi. Large portions of the West were too dry for homesteaders to cultivate, but the vast, grassy rangelands beckoned to cattle- and sheep-raisers. Because homesteading laws forbade any single claimant to acquire more than 160 acres, an area considered uneconomical for stockraising in the arid West, ranchers devised creative methods to gain control of larger expanses of prairie and grasslands.[14] One commonly used approach was to find and claim a 160-acre plot with access to water and timber (perhaps supplementing this acreage with dummy claims bought from other homesteaders or family members); build a base ranch there with a residence, hay pastures, corrals, and barns; and then establish informal control over a much larger area by illegally fencing the surrounding public domain. In the spring, summer, and fall, ranchers would turn their stock loose to graze on tens of thousands of acres of public lands (see Map 7-1).[15]

By the 1870s and 1880s stockmen had spread across the West. Between 1865 and 1885 the cattle population skyrocketed from an estimated 3 million to 4 million, mostly in Texas, to about 26 million, along with 20 million sheep. Unregulated use of the western range by livestock wrought ecological havoc, however: grazing depleted or degraded more than 700 million acres of grassland during this early period, and massive cattle die-offs occurred periodically in the late 1800s and early 1900s. Although stockmen blamed these disasters on severe weather, the cattle were clearly vulnerable to natural fluctuations because overgrazing had so debased the range.[16]

The Origins of Grazing Regulation

Federal regulation of grazing began in 1906, when the first Forest Service director, Gifford Pinchot, announced his intention to require stockmen whose cattle or sheep grazed on national forests to obtain a permit and pay a fee. The proposed charge was $0.05 per animal unit month (AUM—one unit equals one horse or cow, or five sheep or goats). Although this charge was less than one-third of the forage's market value, stockmen rebelled, insisting that the

Map 7-1 The Western Range

Source: Debra L. Donahue, *The Western Range Revisited* (Norman: University of Oklahoma Press, 1999), 8.

agency could not tax them through administrative fiat. Eventually, however, the stockmen acquiesced to Forest Service regulation, recognizing that restricting access would protect their own interests in the range. Permittees soon began to exploit their "permit value" by adding it to the sale price of their ranches.[17]

Not surprisingly, the combination of low fees and lax congressional homesteading policies increased the demand for national forest range. At the same time, the onset of World War I prompted the Forest Service to issue temporary grazing permits and allow stock numbers far greater than the carrying capacity of the range. As a result, between 1908 and 1920, stockraising on the national forests rose from 14 million AUMs to an all-time high of 20 million AUMs.[18] In 1919 the House Appropriations Committee began insisting on more substantial grazing fee increases, mostly in hopes of raising revenue to offset war debts, but Sen. Robert Stanfield, R-Ore.—a rancher and permittee himself—orchestrated a full-scale revolt. In hopes of deterring the appropriators, he held hearings on the fee system and the general administration of rangelands and traveled throughout the West to stir up ranchers' complaints.

Stanfield's "stage managed senatorial attack on Forest Service policy" infuriated forestry experts and conservationists, who promptly retaliated.[19] Representatives of the Society of American Foresters and the American Forestry Association toured the country and criticized the livestock industry in editorials and press releases. The eastern press also struck back: the *New York Times* charged that western senators were resisting the "march of civilization" and called for their assaults to be checked; the *Saturday Evening Post* ran an article by Chief Forester William Greeley condemning the demand by stockmen to secure special privileges for a few users.[20] Despite the spirited defense by conservationists, however, the Forest Service ultimately retreated from its proposal to increase fees.

While Forest Service permittees were resisting efforts to raise grazing fees, those who ran their livestock on the remaining public domain continued to fend off attempts to regulate *those* lands as well. But by the mid-1930s a series of droughts and the precipitous fall in livestock prices during the Great Depression had caused a crisis in ranching, and some leading ranchers began to believe that a government leasing program on the public domain could stabilize the industry. They opposed turning the program over to the Forest Service, however, afraid the agency would charge them the economic value of the forage and reduce the number of cattle permitted on the land. To placate the stockmen, President Franklin D. Roosevelt's interior secretary, Harold Ickes, promised ranchers favorable terms if they supported keeping the public domain under his department's jurisdiction.[21]

In 1934, with the backing of the largest public domain ranchers, Congress passed the Taylor Grazing Act, named for its sponsor Edward Taylor, D-Colo., a Forest Service critic. The act created the Division of Grazing within the Department of the Interior and established a system of grazing permits for public domain land akin to the one administered by the Forest Service. To avoid the vitriolic criticism ranchers had leveled at the Forest Service over the years, the new division set grazing fees at $0.05 per AUM, even though by this time Forest Service fees were three times that amount. And to avoid the perception that the grazing division was a distant bureaucratic organization centered in Washington, Secretary Ickes established a decentralized administration that drew its chief officers not, as the Forest Service did, from a pool of trained professionals but from men with "practical experience" who had been residents of public lands states for at least a year. Finally, the Taylor Grazing Act and its early amendments required the secretary to define regulations for grazing districts "in cooperation with local associations of stockmen." These grazing advisory boards quickly became the dominant force in administering the system, particularly because the division was chronically underfunded and understaffed.[22]

Grazing Policy Controversies, 1940–the Late 1960s

By the time the Taylor Grazing Act was passed, the public domain grasslands of the West were already severely depleted. When federal land managers in the new division tried to regulate grazing, however, ranchers' congressional allies intervened. In 1944, when Director Clarence Forsling proposed tripling the grazing fee from $0.05 to $0.15 per AUM, the congressional response was "immediate and harsh." [23] Sen. Pat McCarran, D-Nev., head of the Public Lands Committee, held a series of inflammatory hearings in the West, and shortly thereafter Congress essentially dismantled the division, which by then had been renamed the Grazing Service.[24] In 1946 President Harry S. Truman combined the remnants of the service with the General Land Office to form the Bureau of Land Management. Thus, the BLM began its life with no statutory mission, yet with responsibility for administering 2,000 unrelated and often conflicting laws enacted over the previous century. It had only eighty-six people to oversee more than 150 million acres of land, and its initial budget was so deficient that the grazing advisory boards paid part of some administrators' salaries.[25]

The Forest Service also ran afoul of the stock industry in the mid-1940s. In 1945, when Forest Service grazing permits were due for a decennial review, the agency planned to reduce the number of livestock on the range, shorten the grazing season, and exclude stock altogether in some areas in an effort to rejuvenate the land.[26] Rep. Frank Barrett, R-Wyo., who felt such a move warranted a punitive response, gained authorization to investigate the agency's grazing policies. Emulating McCarran and Stanfield before him, Barrett held hearings throughout the West soliciting criticism of the Forest Service.

Conservationists again were outraged at what they called "the great land grab." Bernard DeVoto, a noted western historian, used his *Harper's Magazine* column to dissent, writing in one essay that:

> A few groups of Western interests, so small numerically as to constitute a minute fraction of the West, are hellbent on destroying the West. They are stronger than they otherwise would be because they are skillfully manipulating in their support sentiments that have always been powerful in the West—the home rule which means basically that we want federal help without federal regulation, the "individualism" that has always made the small Western operator a handy tool of the big one, and the wild myth that stockgrowers constitute an aristocracy in which all Westerners somehow share.[27]

The *Atlantic Monthly* rushed to defend the land management agencies with an article by Arthur Carhart that claimed the Barrett hearings were "rigged" and designed to "throw fear into the U.S. Forest Service," as evidenced by the "transparent manipulations of the meetings, the bias displayed by the chairman ... the very odor of the meetings."[28] Articles critical of the livestock industry also appeared in *The Nation, Colliers, Reader's Digest,* and hundreds of daily newspapers.

But again, although conservationists managed to stir up the eastern establishment sufficiently to block rancher-friendly legislation, the incendiary hearings caused the land management agencies to retreat from their reform efforts. To improve relations with the stockmen, for example, the Forest Service agreed to cut fees in return for range improvements and to hold hearings on reducing cattle numbers at the request of the affected rancher. As scholars Samuel Dana and Sally Fairfax note:

> The events of 1945–1950 ... amply demonstrated that congressional supporters of the reactionary cattle operators were quite prepared to destroy an agency that did not meet their peculiar set of goals—through budget cuts, legislative enactment, and simple harassment. Obviously, the ability of a McCarran or a Barrett to hold "hearings" year after year and to tie up the time of BLM and Forest Service officials testifying, gathering data, and defending themselves is a tremendous weapon that members of Congress used to bring recalcitrant officials into line.[29]

In the 1950s, under the Eisenhower administration, the Forest Service became even more deferential to ranchers, providing its permittees fencing, stock driveways, rodent control, poisonous and noxious plant control, revegetation of grass and shrubs, water development, corrals and loading facilities, and brush control. In the opinion of Forest Service critic William Voigt, "No changes in Forest Service policy with respect to grazing have been more critical than those which ... shifted so much of the burden of rehabilitating the damaged forest ranges from individual permittees to the taxpayer at large."[30] In addition, Forest Service and BLM grazing fees, although they rose occasionally during this period, fell even further below the real market value of the forage.

Little changed in the 1960s. In 1961 President John F. Kennedy raised the stakes when he delivered a message on natural resources that trained a spotlight on the issue of public lands user fees. The only concrete result, however, was more studies. Then, touting an interdepartmental report showing that fees were well below their economic value, in 1969 President Lyndon Johnson's Bureau of the Budget announced what would have been the most progressive grazing policy shift in history: both the BLM and the Forest Service were to raise their fees to a market-value $1.23 per AUM and then index fees to the rates on private lands, phasing in the increase over a ten-year period. Grazing fees did rise during the following years, but not as much as Johnson wanted. The stockmen—with the help of their congressional allies—were once again able to stave off a substantial portion of the planned increase.[31]

THE CASE

With the advent of the environmental era in the late 1960s and early 1970s came a spate of new environmental laws that affected public lands management, most notably the National Environmental Policy Act (NEPA), the Clean Air and Clean Water acts, and the Endangered Species Act. At the same time, conservation biologists and range ecologists were beginning to provide the scientific basis for a challenge to the existing range management regime. Encouraged by these developments, environmentalists tried to use their new-found political clout to challenge ranchers' dominance over federal grazing policy. But each push for reform encountered the legacy of past policies: agencies intimidated by entitled ranchers, who were backed by their well-positioned congressional allies. Unable to redefine the grazing issue in a way that captured public attention, environmentalists could not mount a successful legislative or administrative challenge and so over the next thirty years made only marginal gains.

Environmentalists' Arguments

The environmentalists' case was (and remains) that livestock overgrazing was destroying the western range and that federal land management practices were exacerbating rather than ameliorating this trend. Some environmentalists wanted to remove cattle from the western public lands altogether; others argued that at a minimum ranchers' prerogatives ought to be severely curtailed and the range restored to ecological health.

The Effect of Grazing on the Range. Environmentalists charged that when ranchers grazed extremely large numbers of livestock, the animals inflicted serious, long-term, and sometimes permanent damage to the range. Environmentalists cited several reasons for the damage. First, cattle eat the most palatable and digestible plants before eating anything else. Such selective grazing, combined with the limited tolerance of some plant species for grazing, can prompt shifts in the composition of plant communities.[32] Second, cows are heavy consumers of water, which is in short supply west of the 98th meridian. Beyond that line, precipitation drops below twenty inches a year, the lower limit for many nonirrigated crops, and even more important, it falls irregularly, leading to frequent droughts. Third, herds of cattle compact the soil, making rainwater run off, which causes erosion, gullying, and channel cutting.

Environmentalists added that cattle were particularly destructive to the West's precious riparian zones, the lush, vegetated areas surrounding rivers and streams. According to Barry Reiswig, manager of the Sheldon Wildlife Refuge in Nevada and Oregon, "You'll hear lots of [range conservationists], even people on my staff, crowing about how 99 percent of the range is in good or excellent condition, but they ignore the fact that the one percent that is trashed—the riparian zones—is really the only part important for most wildlife species." [33] Riparian zones are important ecologically because they sustain a much greater quantity of species than the adjoining land, providing food, water, shade, and cover for fish and wildlife. They also benefit humans by removing sediment from the water table, acting as sponges holding water and stabilizing both streamflow and the water table, and dissipating flood waters. Cattle degrade riparian zones by eating tree seedlings, particularly the cottonwoods, aspen and willow on which species such as bald eagles and great blue herons rely. Cattle trampling on and grazing streamside vegetation also cause streambanks to slough off, channels to widen, and streams to become shallower, so they support fewer and smaller fish.[34]

To support their allegations about overgrazing, environmentalists cited evidence that more than half of private and public rangeland was in fair or poor condition.[35] They also referred to data collected by the U.S. General Accounting Office (GAO) confirming that most of the West's riparian areas were in poor condition and a 1990 Environmental Protection Agency (EPA) report that stated: "Extensive field observations in the late 1980s suggest riparian areas throughout much of the West are in the worst condition in history." [36] And they highlighted Texas Tech soil scientist Harold Dregne's finding that, by the mid-1970s, 98 percent of the arid lands in the western United States—some 464 million acres of privately and publicly owned rangeland—had undergone some degree of desertification.[37] Although some traditionally trained range scientists disputed environmentalists' claims about the ecological impact of livestock grazing, particularly on rangeland plants, most conservation biologists agreed that past overgrazing had eroded soil, destroyed watersheds, and extinguished native grasses and other vegetation on which wildlife feed.[38]

The Failure of Range Management. Environmentalists also charged that federal grazing policy had failed to restore, and in some cases had further depleted, a range already badly damaged by early ranching practices. According to their critics, the BLM and Forest Service allowed too many cattle to graze with too few restrictions on the roughly 31,000 allotments these agencies administer. Critics cited a 1988 GAO finding that, on about 18 percent of the BLM's allotments and 21 percent of Forest Service allotments, the authorized grazing levels exceeded the carrying capacity of the land.[39] Moreover, critics claimed that, by undercharging ranchers for grazing, federal land managers encouraged overgrazing, a claim supported by numerous studies that found federal grazing fees were well below rates charged on comparable private lands.

Environmentalists also contended that a third aspect of grazing policy, range improvement—a euphemism for developing water supplies, fencing, seeding, and making other investments to enhance the forage supply—had serious ecological consequences. They pointed out that fences limited the movement of wildlife; water development reduced the supply of water for wildlife and depleted aquifers; predator control had extirpated species such as wolves, mountain lions, and bears from their historic ranges; and vegetation controls—such as herbicide spraying and plowing and seeding—had reduced plant species diversity. Environmentalists noted that ranchers generally condoned such operations while opposing riparian restoration projects—those most important to environmentalists—because the latter involved prohibiting access to stream banks.[40]

In an effort to undermine the cowboy symbolism deployed by ranchers, environmentalists alleged that low grazing fees, overstocking, and range improvements constituted a subsidy to wealthy hobby ranchers, not the rugged individuals that the word "rancher" connoted. While acknowledging that some of the approximately 23,000 western BLM and Forest Service permittees were small ranchers, environmentalists pointed out that the main beneficiaries were large ranchers with historical ties to the public lands. As evidence, they cited GAO studies saying that 3 percent of livestock operators in the West used 38 percent of the federal grazing land, while less than 10 percent of federal forage went to small-time ranchers (those with fewer than 100 head of cattle); only 15 percent of BLM permittees had herds of 500 or more animals, but they accounted for 58 percent of BLM's AUMs; and stockmen with more than 500 animals comprised only 12 percent of Forest Service permittees but accounted for 41 percent of the agency's AUMs.[41] To make their argument more concrete, environmentalists named the wealthy individuals, partnerships, and corporations that worked many of the largest allotments: Rock Springs Grazing Association of Wyoming, for example, controlled 100,000 acres; J. R. Simplot, said to be the wealthiest man in Idaho, ranched 964,000 acres; the Metropolitan Life Insurance Company had permits for 800,000 acres; and the Zenchiku Corporation of Japan controlled 40,000 acres. Union Oil and Getty Oil, as well as the Mormon Church, were also large permit holders.[42]

Although some environmentalists advocated eliminating grazing on BLM and Forest Service land, others had more modest goals. First and foremost, they demanded that public lands ranchers pay grazing fees equivalent to the market value of the forage, noting that existing fees covered only 37 percent of BLM and 30 percent of Forest Service program administration costs.[43] They also insisted that federal land managers reduce the number of cattle to a level the land could comfortably support. And they asked for more opportunities for public participation in rangeland management decisions.

Ranchers' Resistance to Reform

Public lands ranchers did not take environmentalists' assaults lying down. They responded that public and private fees were not comparable because it cost more to run cattle on public lands. Those who ranch on public lands, they argued, had to provide capital improvements such as fencing and water that owners supplied on private lands. Moreover, they pointed out, the value of their lease or permit had long ago been capitalized into the cost of the associated ranch, and a cut in cattle numbers would therefore devalue their ranches. Permittees portrayed themselves as an important part of the livestock industry, even though public lands supply only about 2 percent of the forage consumed by beef cattle.[44] They further contended that because many of them were marginal, family operations, an increase in grazing fees could put them out of business and destabilize the communities in which they operated. Ranchers' most formidable rhetorical weapons were not reasoned arguments, however, but the iconographic symbols they wielded: cowboys, rugged individualism, and freedom from control by a distant and oppressive federal government.

In any case, permittees' influence derived less from their public arguments than from their historic ties to members of Congress who sat on the public lands authorizing committees and appropriations subcommittees. Legislators from the Rocky Mountain states in particular had secured positions on the House and Senate Interior (now Resources and Energy and Natural Resources) committees, from which they fended off efforts at grazing policy reform. As a result, in spite of their small numbers and their minority status in the livestock industry as a whole, public lands ranchers retained substantial power. As journalist George Wuerthner marveled, "There are more members of the Wyoming Wildlife Federation than there are ranchers in the entire state of Wyoming, but it is ranchers, not conservationists, who set the agenda on public lands." [45]

Permittees' influence was enhanced by their association with the academic community in western land grant colleges and universities. As one commentator observed, "This community specializes in rangeland management and has, with few exceptions, been solidly allied with ranching interests, which, in turn, have the political power to determine higher education budgets and sometimes serve as regents of various schools." [46] The permittees' clout also derived in part from their ties to allies in banking and real estate. According to Charles Wilkinson:

> Ranches are usually valued for loan purposes based on AUMs, and the appraised value will drop if the AUMs drop. A decrease in AUMs thus will reduce a rancher's ability to raise capital and will weaken the security on existing loans. . . . As Charles Callison, longtime observer of range policy, has told me: "It's one thing when western congressmen hear from the ranchers. But they really leap into action when the bankers start getting on the telephone." [47]

Finally, many prominent stockmen affected policy directly by taking an active role in Republican Party politics or actually holding elected or appointed office: former president Ronald Reagan's BLM director, Robert Burford, was a millionaire BLM rancher; Wyoming's former senators Clifford Hansen and Alan Simpson, as well as New Mexico representative Joe Skeen, were cattlemen; former Nevada senator Paul Laxalt was a sheep rancher; and Reps. Robert Smith of Oregon and Jim Kolbe of Arizona came from ranching families.

The Federal Land Policy Management Act

Although their track record was not encouraging, in the early 1970s environmentalists hoped to capitalize on the window of opportunity opened by Earth Day and began to press Congress for grazing policy reform. The most obvious route by which to alter grazing policy was through the organic act that BLM had been prodding Congress to pass for a decade.[48] Between 1971 and 1974 the Senate approved several bills granting BLM statutory authority, but proposals foundered in the House, primarily on the issue of grazing fees. Finally, in the 94th Congress (1975–1976), the Senate approved a bare-bones authorization bill sponsored by Henry Jackson, D-Wash., and supported by the Ford administration. The House managed to settle on a bill as well, although its version clearly favored ranchers: it gutted BLM law enforcement authority and increased local control over BLM and Forest Service planning.[49] It also contained four controversial grazing provisions, all beneficial to ranchers. First, it established a statutory grazing fee formula based on beef prices and private forage costs, with a floor of $2.00 per AUM. Second, it improved ranchers' tenure by making ten-year permits the rule, rather than the exception. Third, it required the BLM to compensate ranchers for improvements they had made to the land if it canceled their permits. And fourth, it resurrected and prescribed the composition of local grazing advisory boards, which Congress had replaced with multiple-use advisory boards one year earlier.[50] The Interior Committee narrowly approved the bill, 20–16; and the full House—deferring to the committee—also approved it, 169–155.

Because the House and Senate versions were substantially different, it was unclear whether the conference committee could reconcile them. House negotiators offered to implement the rancher-friendly fee formula for two years but in the meantime conduct a study of the issue, a deal Senate conferees refused. House members then offered to drop the grazing fee formula altogether but freeze current fees, an option also unpalatable to Senate conferees. Finally, the Senate conferees made a counteroffer that the House conferees accepted: a one-year freeze on grazing fees, accompanied by a one-year study of the fee issue conducted jointly by the Agriculture and Interior departments.[51] Once the study was completed, Congress could take up the issue again. The conference bill passed the House on September 30, 1976, and the Senate on October 1, just hours before the 94th Congress adjourned. Grazing interests objected to the deletion of their preferred grazing fee formula and encouraged the president to pocket veto the bill, but President Gerald Ford signed the Federal Land Policy and Management Act (FLPMA) into law on October 21. Although disappointed about the grazing fee provision, overall, livestock interests were satisfied with the outcome.

The Carter Administration, 1977–1981

The following year, the expiration of the grazing fee freeze and the election of a proenvironmental president offered another opportunity for reformers, and a flurry of legislative activity ensued. In the autumn of 1977 President Jimmy Carter's Agriculture and Interior departments released their congressionally mandated study of grazing fees and proposed raising fees administratively to a uniform $1.89 per AUM for the 1978 season. The fees would rise thereafter no more than 12 percent per year until they reached a market value of $2.38 per AUM. Livestock groups called the proposal "unfair and unrealistic" and, worried about the Carter administration's propensity for reform, opted for their favorite tactic: deferral. They urged the administration to let Congress decide the grazing fee question. The administration responded by freezing fees at the 1977 level, while ranchers pressured Congress to adopt another one-year moratorium on increases.[52]

By the fall of 1978 Congress had produced a new grazing bill, the Public Rangelands Improvement Act (PRIA), which had two major provisions: range improvement funding, which met with near-universal support, and a statutory grazing fee formula, which was highly controversial. Environmentalists, as well as both the BLM and the Forest Service, supported a market value-based fee similar to the one that had technically been in place since 1969 (even though, as noted earlier, fee increases had rarely taken effect in practice); livestock interests agitated for a fee with built-in profits (based on forage costs and beef prices). After bitter debates in the House and Senate, both chambers passed the PRIA with the rancher-approved formula and a provision prohibiting annual fee increases or decreases of more than 25 percent of the previous year's fee. Its language reflected the authorizing committees' rationale: "To prevent economic disruption and harm to the western livestock industry, it is in the public interest to charge a fee for livestock grazing permits and leases on the public lands which is based on a formula reflecting annual changes in the cost of production." [53] President Carter signed the bill on October 25, 1978.

Although constrained by the PRIA, Carter's BLM nevertheless embarked on a program of intensive, conservation-oriented range management in which Director Frank Gregg encouraged agency staff to conduct range inventories and cut grazing permit allocations if they found forage supplies insufficient to support assigned levels. The reduction program was short-lived, however. Public lands ranchers sounded the alarm about what they regarded as the agency's heavy-handed tactics, and rancher ally Sen. James McClure, R-Idaho, succeeded in attaching an amendment to the 1980 appropriations bill that mandated a two-year phase-in for any stock reduction of more than 10 percent.[54]

Despite McClure's amendment, the BLM initiative fueled ranchers' antagonism toward federal land managers, and they instigated the Sagebrush Rebellion, a vocal but disjointed attempt to persuade Congress to transfer ownership of federal lands to western states. The rebels did not accomplish the transfer (nor is it clear the majority even wanted to), but they did succeed in drawing attention to their plight.[55] Their cause was sufficiently visible that, in the 1980 presidential campaign, Republican candidate Ronald Reagan declared himself a sagebrush rebel.

The Reagan Administration, 1981–1989

In the early 1980s federal grazing fees, now indexed to ranchers' costs and expected returns, fell to $1.37 as a consequence of sluggish beef prices (see

Table 7-1). In the meantime, reformers and livestock interests mustered their forces for another confrontation when the PRIA expired in 1985. Although the battle lines were drawn in Congress, the position of the White House had shifted considerably. In contrast to his predecessor, newly elected President Reagan made no secret of his sympathy for public lands ranchers.[56] Upon taking office, he appointed livestock industry supporters to prominent positions in the Interior Department. Secretary James Watt was a lawyer with the Mountain States Legal Foundation, which litigates on behalf of ranchers and other resource extraction interests. BLM director Robert Burford was a Colorado rancher "who had jousted repeatedly with the BLM, most often over his own grazing violations," and believed there was a tremendous capacity for increasing beef production on America's rangeland.[57]

The administration drew on all its resources to alter BLM's range management agenda, changing the mix of professionals (including laying off ecologists), the budget, and the structure of the agency. In addition, Burford used informal rulemaking processes to increase ranchers' security. The centerpiece of his approach was the Cooperative Management Agreement (CMA) program. In theory, the program provided exemplary ranchers with CMAs, which allowed them to manage their allotments virtually unimpeded. In 1985, however, a federal district court declared that the CMA approach illegally circumvented BLM's statutory obligation to care for overgrazed public rangeland. Although forbidden to transfer authority for the public range to ranchers formally, the Interior Department managed to accomplish the same result through neglect: under pressure from Reagan's political appointees, BLM range managers abandoned the stock reductions and range restoration projects begun by the Carter administration.

Rebuffed by the administration, environmentalists could only hope to make inroads into grazing policy when the grazing fee issue returned to the congressional agenda in 1985. By that time, environmental groups, fiscal conservatives in the administration, and some BLM and Forest Service officials had formed a loose coalition to press for higher grazing fees. Reformers launched an all-out campaign in the media, labeling public lands ranchers as "welfare cowboys" and deploring low grazing fees as a subsidy in an era of high deficits and fiscal austerity. Hoping to shame public officials and reduce the influence of livestock interests, journalists investigated stories about BLM or Forest Service officials who had been fired or transferred for trying to implement environmental reforms.[58]

Buttressing reformers' case were the results of yet another grazing fee analysis. In March 1985 the BLM and Forest Service completed a four-year study in which twenty-two professional appraisers collected data for every county in the West that had rangeland. The researchers discovered that fees on private lands averaged $6.87 per AUM, nearly five times higher than fees for comparable public land, and that the fees charged by other federal agencies averaged $6.35 per AUM.[59] The study presented for congressional consideration five alternative fee formulas, all involving a fee hike.

Table 7-1
Annual Grazing Fees for the Bureau of Land Management
and the Forest Service, 1940–2005

Year	BLM Fee ($ per AUM)	Forest Service Fee ($ per AUM)
1940	$0.05[a]	$0.15
1945	0.05	0.25
1950	0.10	0.42
1955	0.15	0.37
1960	0.22	0.51
1965	0.30	0.46
1970	0.44	0.60
1975	1.00	1.11
1976	1.51	1.60
1977	1.51	1.60
1978	1.51	1.60
1979	1.89	1.93
1980	2.36	2.41
1981	2.31	2.31
1982	1.86	1.86
1983	1.40	1.40
1984	1.37	1.37
1985	1.35[b]	1.35[b]
1986	1.35	1.35
1987	1.35	1.35
1988	1.54	1.54
1989	1.86	1.86
1990	1.81	1.81
1991	1.97	1.97
1992	1.92	1.92
1993	1.86	1.86
1994	1.98	1.98
1995	1.61	1.61
1996	1.35	1.35
1997	1.35	1.35
1998	1.35	1.35
1999	1.35	1.35
2000	1.35	1.35
2001	1.35	1.35
2002	1.43	1.43
2003	1.35	1.35
2004	1.43	1.43
2005	1.79	1.79

Source: U.S. Forest Service and Bureau of Land Management.

a. The BLM began charging fees in 1936, and from 1936 to 1946 the fee was 5 cents per AUM.
b. The Public Rangeland Improvement Act of 1978 set a minimum fee of $1.35 per AUM.

But Congress failed to come up with grazing legislation that satisfied both environmentalists and ranchers, and, when the PRIA formula expired at the end of 1985, authority to set the fee reverted to the Reagan administration. Although environmentalists directed their best efforts at influencing President Reagan, they never had a chance. On December 13, 1985, Senator Laxalt, a close friend of the president's, delivered a letter from a group of mainly western, Republican senators urging the president to freeze the grazing fee. Eventually, twenty-eight senators and forty representatives joined the lobbying effort.

In the face of this assault, in late January 1986 the Office of Management and Budget (OMB) pulled out of its alliance with environmentalists. OMB director James Miller wrote to President Reagan that he was backing off in recognition of the political sensitivity of the issue, but he did recommend freezing fees for no more than one year in order to pressure Congress to act.[60] To the dismay of environmentalists, Reagan ignored Miller's advice and issued Executive Order 12548 extending the PRIA fee formula indefinitely. The executive order effectively hamstrung BLM and Forest Service efforts to rehabilitate the range because the cost of administering the grazing program substantially exceeded revenues from grazing fees under the PRIA system, and the enormity of the federal deficit precluded any additional funding for either agency.

The Bush Administration, 1989–1993

In 1988 advocates of higher grazing fees began to prepare a run at the 101st Congress, hopeful that changes in the composition of the House Interior Committee, which had been a major obstacle to reform, would improve their prospects. In the 1970s Phillip Burton, a reform-minded California Democrat, had taken over the committee chairmanship and recruited environmentally oriented members. For a brief period, ranching allies were in the minority; by 1991 only nine of the committee's twenty-six Democrats hailed from the West, and three of those were from urban areas of Los Angeles, Oakland, and Salt Lake City. Despite these changes, however, livestock interests' allies continued to stave off proenvironmental reforms.

In 1990 the House adopted (251–155) an amendment to the Interior Department's appropriations bill that would have increased the grazing fee sharply. But the provision was deleted in conference with the Senate, where proranching western senators narrowly prevailed on the issue in return for rescinding their opposition to oil exploration in the Outer Continental Shelf. The same year, Rep. Bruce Vento, D-Minn., tried to attach his BLM authorization bill, which contained a grazing fee increase, to the budget reconciliation bill in an effort to circumvent western senators. The bill did not promise enough deficit reduction to satisfy the Budget Committee, however, and was dropped.[61]

In 1991 opposition from westerners on the House Interior Committee forced Rep. George "Buddy" Darden, D-Ga., to abandon an amendment to a BLM reauthorization bill that would dramatically increase grazing fees. Darden and Rep. Mike Synar, D-Okla., then took their case to the Appropriations Committee, where they were more successful, and in late June the full House voted 232–192 to quadruple grazing fees, bringing them up to market rates over a four-year period. (New information from the GAO had bolstered the claims of fee-increase advocates: the GAO reported that the existing formula double-counted ranchers' expenses, so that when ranchers' expenses went up, the fee went down. As a result, the fee was 15 percent lower in 1991 than it had been in 1975, whereas private grazing land lease rates had risen 17 percent in the same period.[62]) Then, in July the House voted overwhelmingly to add a grazing fee amendment to the BLM reauthorization bill despite Interior Committee opposition. These votes signaled changes in the proportion of proenvironmental western representatives in the chamber, which in turn reflected the shifting demographics of the West: as the region urbanized, environmentalists, recreation advocates, and tourism interests were gaining a political voice. But despite these changes in the House, a handful of western senators, who continued to speak primarily for the traditional economic interests, managed to deflect attempts to raise grazing fees, and the BLM reauthorization bill simply disappeared in the Senate without a hearing. The negotiation over the appropriations bill was more convoluted, but the result was the same.[63]

The Early Clinton Years, 1993–1994

With the election of Bill Clinton to the presidency and Al Gore to the vice presidency, environmentalists believed they finally had a genuine chance to reform the federal grazing policy. President Clinton confirmed their expectations when, immediately upon taking office, he announced his plan to cut subsidies for grazing, as well as logging, mining, and water development on the public lands. Bruce Babbitt, Clinton's secretary of interior, also adopted a markedly different tone from that of his recent predecessors, and he was well received by proenvironmental park rangers, biologists, and other land managers who had suffered through years of political pressure to favor industrial uses of the land. Babbitt got a standing ovation from a roomful of federal employees when he proclaimed, "I see us as the department of the environment. . . . We are about the perpetual American love affair with the land and the parks." [64] Clinton also delighted environmentalists with his appointment of Jim Baca as head of the BLM. Baca had been New Mexico's public land commissioner and was a former board member of the Wilderness Society.

Some members of Congress found Clinton's position refreshing as well. George Miller, D-Calif., head of the House Interior Committee, claimed that most westerners embraced the changes that Clinton was proposing. According to Miller, "Reagan and Bush were just holding back the future. They were the last gasp of an outdated philosophy." [65] But others were not so optimistic about prospects for reform, especially when ranchers banded together with other resource users into what they called the Wise Use movement, an amalgamation whose objective was to promote unfettered access to public lands (see chapter 13). These interests continued to have fiercely protective and influential congressional sponsors, particularly in the Senate.

Although he favored reform, Clinton was wary of alienating these pro-ranching western senators; given his precarious electoral coalition, he was loath to antagonize influential western Democrats whose support was essential to passing his legislative agenda. On March 16, capitalizing on the president's frail majority, seven western senators led by Democrat Max Baucus of Montana met with Clinton to discuss trading their support for his economic stimulus and deficit reduction program for his dropping public land management reform. Two weeks later, the president backed off his initial proposal to raise fees for commercial uses of public resources as part of the budget but promised instead to pursue an increase administratively.

In August 1993—after a series of public hearings on the issue throughout the West—Secretary Babbitt proposed to add to the Interior appropriations bill a provision that more than doubled grazing fees on federal lands over a three-year period and imposed tough environmental standards on ranchers. In response, Sen. Pete Domenici, R-N.M., and Sen. Harry Reid, D-Nev., proposed an amendment placing a one-year moratorium on Babbitt's ability to spend any money to implement his grazing policy. Because of the issue's low salience outside the West, the Senate deferred to Domenici and Reid, 59–40. The House instructed its negotiators on the bill to reject the Senate moratorium, however. In response, Reid—hoping to put the grazing policy issue to bed—worked out a compromise with Babbitt and House Democrats to resolve the differences between the two chambers by increasing grazing fees (to $3.45, far short of the $4.28 Babbitt wanted, well below most state lands' fees, and barely one-third of the average on private lands in the West) but imposing fewer land management requirements than the original proposal. Babbitt agreed, and the House and Senate conferees approved Reid's amendment.[66]

In late October the full House approved the bill containing Reid's grazing compromise, but the Senate was unable to muster the sixty votes necessary to head off a filibuster by Domenici, who viewed the bill as too proenvironment. Republicans achieved near-perfect unity in support of Domenici's filibuster, and five western and northern plains Democrats joined them. "This proposal threatens a rural way of life," said the embattled Domenici. "If we lose we'll go down with every rule in the Senate to protect our people." [67] After failing three times to invoke cloture (54–44 on the final try), Reid agreed to drop the grazing compromise, Domenici stopped stalling the bill, and on November 9 the Senate and House sent the revised version without grazing fee language to President Clinton.[68] Again, ranching interests had averted reform.

Following this series of highly publicized congressional debacles, Babbitt vowed to raise grazing fees and institute management reforms administratively. Faced with the prospect of a lawsuit and extremely hostile press coverage in the West, however, Babbitt adopted a conciliatory stance. In February 1994 he ousted his outspoken BLM director, Baca, to placate western governors and senators who had complained about his aggressive approach to rangeland management. Then in April, after traveling extensively throughout the West to gain local buy-in and defuse a second Sagebrush Rebellion that was bubbling up in several western counties, Babbitt unveiled a proposal that retained some of the protectiveness of the original plan but made several concessions to ranchers. The proposal called for creating local "resource advisory councils" to develop range management plans. The councils, designed to operate by consensus, would consist of five permittees or other commodity interests, five environmentalists, and five representatives of other public land uses and state and local government. The proposal also allowed environmental groups to purchase grazing permits for conservation, a practice that was prohibited under the existing rules; made grazing permits good for ten years, compared with five years in the initial plan; rendered decisions by BLM field officers effective immediately; and allowed any member of the public—not just those directly affected—to participate in and appeal BLM decisions. Although the modified proposal doubled grazing fees over three years, Babbitt sought to increase its palatability by adding a two-tier fee structure that charged small ranchers less and offered a 30 percent discount to ranchers who improved the land.

Despite the grazing fee increase, environmentalists sharply criticized the administration for backpedaling. "This appears to be a complete reversal from the proposal we saw in August [1993]. It's headed away from reform," said Nancy Green, a specialist on federal lands issues at the Wilderness Society.[69] Babbitt defended his position, saying it reflected his view that "those closest to the land, those who live on the land, are in the best position to care for it."[70] But no one expected a system of local advisory councils dominated by ranchers to result in any serious scaling back of grazing privileges. Meanwhile, ranchers also rejected the compromise rules: after issuing his revised proposal, Babbitt held a second round of public hearings that were, once again, dominated by ranchers who denounced the proposal as an attack on rural westerners. "The government is trying to take our livelihood, our rights, and our dignity," testified one Nevada rancher. "This is the most threatening ordeal our family has faced in five generations," said another.[71] Confirming environmentalists' worst fears, in December 1994 Babbitt, after encountering serious opposition by powerful Republican members of Congress, retracted the grazing fee increase altogether and delayed the effective date of many of the proposed environmental regulations to allow Congress to vote on them. Ironically, in 1995, under the existing formula, grazing fees dropped from $1.98/AUM to $1.61 and fell again to $1.35 in 1996 (see Table 7-1).

The Republican Congress Retaliates, 1995–1997

Ranchers saw a chance to expand their privileges when the Republicans assumed control of Congress in 1995. In the early spring Senator Domenici introduced the Public Rangeland Management Act (S 852), a bill designed to preempt Secretary Babbitt's proposed rule changes. The bill raised grazing fees by a nominal amount, thereby heading off the substantial increase sought by Babbitt and the majority of members of Congress, and enhanced permittees' control over federal grazing allotments. Most important, the bill excluded from land management decisions anyone but ranchers and adjacent property owners by creating 150 advisory boards consisting solely of ranchers. In July the Senate Energy and Natural Resources (formerly Interior) Committee approved the bill over the objections of the BLM, whose acting director, Mike Dombeck, fumed, "This bill takes the public out of public lands. It returns land management to an era of single use at taxpayers' expense." [72] Domenici's proposal stalled, however, when it became clear it could not garner the sixty votes necessary to break an anticipated filibuster supported by Democrats and moderate Republicans.

In the House, the Resource Subcommittee on Public Lands approved a similar bill (HR 1713), which barred the Interior secretary from setting national rangeland standards; gave ranchers proportional title to improvements, such as fencing, landscaping, and ponds; and lengthened the term of a grazing lease from ten years to fifteen years. Like Domenici's failed effort, however, HR 1713 never reached the floor, thanks to a parliamentary maneuver by New Mexico Democrat Bill Richardson. Sponsors of both bills then tried to insert a modest fee increase provision into the budget reconciliation bill, again in hopes of averting a much more substantial one, but that rider was dropped before the bill went to the president. In a final attempt at an end-run around Babbitt's rules, the Senate attached a provision to Interior's appropriations bill to postpone the rules' implementation, but President Clinton vetoed the bill.

In the meantime, in August 1995 Babbitt finally issued his new grazing package, which did not contain the most controversial element, a grazing fee increase. The regulations did, however, set federal standards for all rangelands and allowed the federal government to claim title to all land improvements and water developments made by ranchers on public lands. They also established regional resource advisory councils, with guaranteed spots for environmentalists, to help the BLM devise grazing guidelines for each state and write comprehensive plans for preserving rangeland ecosystems. And they limited ranchers' rights to appeal BLM decisions to reduce the number of animals on an allotment. Not surprisingly, environmentalists applauded the regulations, and ranchers were enraged.

Ranchers' Senate allies were resolute, and in 1996 they managed to pass a bill (S 1459) similar to S 852 aimed at replacing Babbitt's initiative with a more rancher-friendly version. The House Resources (formerly Interior) and Senate Energy and Natural Resources committees approved a similar bill, but it met resistance in the full House from a coalition of environmentalists and fiscal conservatives and faced a certain presidential veto. The bill died at the end of the session. Frustrated westerners in the House also attempted to insert pro-grazing provisions into the omnibus parks bill by holding hostage funding for New Jersey's Sterling Forest, a priority for many easterners. In September western representatives abandoned that effort as well, recognizing, according to Republican James Hansen of Utah, that pressing forward would carry an unacceptable political price.[73]

Although their legislative efforts to thwart Babbitt stumbled, ranchers got a boost from the courts. Scheduled to go into effect in March 1996, the new rules had been held in abeyance until legal challenges by five livestock groups were resolved. In June Judge Clarence Brimmer of the U.S. District Court in Wyoming rejected several of the reforms on the grounds that they would "wreak havoc" on the ranching industry and exceed the BLM's legislative authority. Brimmer ruled that the provision to weaken ranchers' rights to renew federal grazing permits was illegal because the Taylor Grazing Act specified "grazing preference" to ensure that ranchers and their creditors had some certainty about their tenure. The judge also rejected the rules giving the government title to future range improvements and allowing conservationists to acquire grazing permits. He did uphold the agency's right to check on permittees' compliance with regulations and to suspend or cancel a permit if the lessee was convicted of violating environmental laws. (Ranchers' judicial victory was short-lived, however. In September 1998 the Tenth Circuit Court of Appeals rejected major parts of the Brimmer ruling: it affirmed the BLM's authority to reduce the number of cattle allowed by permits and retain title of range improvements on public lands, but concurred with Brimmer's rejection of conservation-use permits. In 2000 the Supreme Court unanimously upheld the appeals court's ruling.[74])

In October 1997 the House passed a "grazing reform" measure (HR 2493) that raised grazing fees by 15 percent—again in hopes of deflecting attempts to raise fees more substantially—lengthened ranchers' lease terms and eased restrictions on ranching permits. The bill's passage was a victory for ranching advocates, as the House had been a "major burial ground for grazing bills" in the 104th Congress.[75] The Senate Energy and Natural Resources Committee marked up and reported HR 2493 without amendment on July 29, 1998, but the bill did not reach the Senate floor. At that point legislative efforts to make grazing policy less restrictive retreated to the back burner, while environmental reformers once again focused on the administrative arena.

Administrative Policymaking Redux

Finding their efforts to impose across-the-board reforms temporarily waylaid by the courts, the Forest Service and the BLM began targeting individual sites on which to implement ecological improvement measures. For example, in an uncharacteristically bold move, BLM officials proposed in July 1997 to reduce grazing by one-third across 1.3 million acres in Owyhee County, Idaho, and to restrict off-road vehicles to marked trails. In addition, lawsuits filed by the Santa Fe-based Forest Guardians and the Tucson-based Southwest Center for Biological Diversity against both the Forest Service and the BLM prompted the agencies to review the environmental impacts of grazing on hundreds of allotments throughout the Southwest and reduce cattle numbers on many of them.[76] Although some ranchers adapted to land managers' conservation efforts, others were aghast and vowed to resist. Revealing the depth of some locals' antipathy toward federal regulators, Owyhee Sheriff Gary Aman warned that federal agents risked being thrown in jail if they ventured into the county to enforce grazing reductions.[77] In another high-profile skirmish, Nevada ranchers reacted with fury to a 2001 BLM roundup of the cattle of two ranchers who refused to pay hundreds of thousands of dollars in back grazing fees and fines. Ranchers and their supporters employed a variety of tactics to thwart land managers, including intimidation and violence (see chapter 13). Nor were incendiary tactics limited to ranchers: radical environmentalists began cutting fences and otherwise sabotaging ranching operations.[78]

Ranchers hoped that with the presidency of George W. Bush in 2001 they would regain some of their privileges, particularly after Bush expressed his solidarity with ranchers who resented the interference of land managers in their efforts to make a living and appointed rancher-friendly officials to the Interior Department.[79] To ranchers' delight, in 2003 the BLM began considering grazing policy changes that, reflecting the Bush administration's anti-regulatory stance, "would provide more management flexibility and promote innovative partnerships." [80] The new approach, called the "Sustaining Working Landscapes" initiative, would encourage ranchers to make voluntary improvements to their grazing allotments. An additional set of rules, proposed in late 2003, sought to limit BLM's discretion and enhance ranchers' security by giving permit holders part ownership of any fences or wells they install, allowing them five years to comply with a request to remove more than 10 percent of their cattle, and prohibiting the BLM from improving damaged rangeland in the absence of extensive monitoring data.

In mid-June 2005 the BLM released its new grazing rules, which would take effect at the end of the summer. The rancher-friendly rules retained the provision giving ranchers an ownership share in fences or other "improvements" to their allotments; required managers to consider the social, economic, and cultural effects of their decisions on communities; required the agency to carry out detailed monitoring before asserting that an allotment does not meet rangeland standards and then allow up to twenty-four months before demanding any change in damaging grazing practices; and phased in over five years any decreases (or increases) of more than 10 percent in the number of livestock allowed on an allotment. Public lands watchdog groups complained that the new rules made life easier for ranchers while making it more difficult for the public to have a say in federal range management. BLM spokesman Tom Gorey responded: "We believe the changes are going to improve our working relationships with public land ranchers." [81]

But the administration's credibility was severely damaged after reports that in preparing its environmental impact statement (EIS) the BLM had ignored or excised criticisms of the rules from its own as well as Environmental Protection Agency and Fish and Wildlife Service (FWS) scientists. According to a sixteen-page FWS report, "The proposed revisions would change fundamen-

tally the way the BLM lands are managed, temporally, spatially and philo-
sophically. These changes could have profound impacts on wildlife
resources." [82] The BLM's own internal report warned: "The proposed action
will have a slow, long-term adverse impact on wildlife and biological diversity
in general." [83] By contrast, the final EIS said that the rule changes would, at
worst, harm wildlife only in the short run and only in a few cases. In some
cases, it asserted, wildlife would benefit from the change. The report also
claimed that riparian areas would remain in the same condition or even
improve slightly under the new rules—a finding that directly contradicted
concerns expressed by both BLM and EPA experts in their reviews.

OUTCOMES

The ability of ranching allies to prevent major curtailments in public lands
grazing is reflected in the annual AUM levels, which have been relatively stable since around 1970 at between 8 million and 9 million on national forest
land and around 10 million on BLM land.[84] It is difficult to assess the environmental impacts of these numbers, or of periodic efforts to improve the ecological health of the range, however. In the 1990s the agencies moved away from
the "excellent/good/fair/poor" system of evaluating rangeland because they
said it was too simplistic and controversial; instead, they began focusing on
"ecosystem function" relative to management objectives. Based on the ecosystem function criterion, *Rangeland Reform '94: Draft Environmental Impact Statement*, still the most comprehensive evaluation, described the condition of vegetation on BLM lands in the following way: of the 86 percent of its land that
had been assessed, 67 percent was static or had reached management objectives; 20 percent was moving toward management objectives; and 13 percent
was moving away from management objectives.[85] Using the same classification scheme, a Forest Service assessment in 2000 found that by 1997, 49 percent
of the allotments it had evaluated met its management objectives; 38 percent
were moving toward those objectives; and 13 percent were failing.[86]

Although these reports portray BLM and Forest Service rangelands as stable
or improving, both agencies acknowledged they lacked the funding and the
personnel to evaluate their allotments systematically or to repair past damage.
The BLM's *Rangeland Reform '94* asserted that "there is still much progress to be
made. Rangeland ecosystems are still not functioning properly in many areas
of the West. Riparian areas are widely depleted and some upland areas produce
far below their potential. Soils are becoming less fertile." [87] The report concluded that the all-important public land riparian areas "have continued to
decline and are considered to be in their worst condition in history." [88] Moreover, the Forest Service's *2000 RPA Assessment* pointed out the agency lacked
the necessary information, both historical and current, to evaluate broad ecological processes. In November 2004 the Forest Guardians released the results
of its own study of more than 6,000 Forest Service records for 1999–2003. The
group looked at how often the agency was completing the required monitoring

and how many allotments were being overgrazed. It found that one-half to three-quarters of all Arizona and New Mexico allotments were out of compliance during that five-year period, either because they were not monitored or because monitoring turned up violations.[89] Frustrated with the pace and contentiousness of attempts to promote rangeland conservation and discouraged by the polarization between ranchers and environmentalists, some groups have begun cautiously experimenting with a variety of alternative approaches. The National Public Lands Grazing Campaign has been promoting the Voluntary Grazing Permit Buyout Act, which would compensate public lands ranchers who agreed to relinquish their grazing permits at a price of $175 per AUM. (Under this program a rancher with a federal permit to graze 500 cows for five months—2,500 AUMs—would receive $437,500.) The federal government would then retire the permits and manage the land for its biodiversity values. If passed, the law would formalize an approach that conservation groups such as the Grand Canyon Trust, the National Wildlife Federation, and the Oregon Natural Desert Association have employed for years. In fact, by 2005 the Conservation Fund alone had purchased permits covering 2.5 million acres.[90] Although some ranchers supported such buyouts, traditional ranching associations, such as the National Cattlemen's Beef Association, the Public Lands Council, and the American Farm Bureau Federation, vehemently opposed them, fearing they would lead to the eviction of ranchers from the public lands altogether. "We've never objected to any transfer of ownership of allotments," said Doc Lane of the Arizona Cattle Growers Association. "Now if for some reason Grand Canyon Trust decides they're not going to use the allotments as the law says they're supposed to, then we'd have a problem." [91] To appease these groups, some land managers have required conservation groups who have acquired permits to run cattle on the land, at least at first.

Other environmentalists have endorsed a different approach that involves collaborating with ranchers to enhance ecological values on their land. One of the earliest and best known of these, the Malpai Borderlands Group, began in the mid-1990s on an 800,000-acre territory in southern Arizona and New Mexico along the U.S.-Mexican border. The group is a nonprofit organization with nine members, eight of whom are ranchers, dedicated to restoring and maintaining "the natural processes that create and protect a healthy, unfragmented landscape to support a diverse, flourishing community of human, plant, and animal life in our Borderlands region." [92] A pivotal member of the group is a representative of the Nature Conservancy, which in 1990 bought the Gray Ranch, in southern New Mexico, as part of its Last Great Places campaign. The group has assembled scientists, as well as federal and state land managers, to help it stake out what it calls "the radical center." Among other land management mechanisms, the Malpai Borderlands Group uses controlled burns to rejuvenate the range. It also created the concept of grass banking, a means by which ranchers can trade a promise to protect their land from suburban development in exchange for the right to graze their livestock on grass-rich land during dry years.

The notions of controlled burns, grass banking, and collaborative management more generally have since spread throughout the West, and other organizations—including the Six-Six Group, the Northern Lights Institute, and the Quivira Coalition—have sprung up to promote these ideas. In fall 2000 the Conservation Fund, the Northern New Mexico Stockmen's Association, the U.S. Forest Service, the Cooperative Extension Service of New Mexico State University, the Quivira Coalition, and the Malpai Borderlands Group sponsored a conference to introduce the grass bank concept to ranchers and community organizers from seven states. Some groups on both sides of the issue remain suspicious of collaborative problem solving, however. Caren Cowan, executive director of the 2,000-member New Mexico Cattle Growers' Association, did not attend the conference, saying, "We don't oppose grass banks as a tool per se, but we don't want anyone to tell us how to run our business." [93] Four years later Cowan remained skeptical that nonranchers could understand the land or that collaboration could be applied broadly.[94] Similarly, hardline environmental groups, such as the Forest Guardians of Santa Fe and the Southwest Center for Biodiversity, did not attend the conference and continue to oppose livestock grazing on public lands altogether.

A third idea that has caught on among environmental groups is paying ranchers to preserve the private lands to which federal grazing allotments are attached. Most ranchers are land rich and cash poor, and their heirs may struggle to pay inheritance taxes. But environmentalists have taken to buying development rights, an approach that gives ranchers money while reducing the value of their ranches—and hence their taxes. The number of land trusts has ballooned in recent years, although as journalist Jon Christensen warns, "the tributaries of the land trust movement are being overwhelmed by the great tidal force of development in the West." [95]

It is this threat of suburban development, which has been steadily encroaching on the West's open spaces, that has motivated many former adversaries to consider alternatives to litigation and legislative battles. Wildlife biologist Richard L. Knight points out that "As ranches fold and reappear [as] ranchettes, 20 miles from town and covering hillsides, people of the West and beyond increasingly wonder what this New West will look like." [96] But environmental writer John Horning rejects the notion that the only two alternatives for the western landscape are ranching or sprawl. He points out that ranchers have been selling out to developers for decades, not because of environmental rules but because the ranching business is economically marginal. He proposes a third vision of the West, one that "embraces the West's wild heart, its droughts, fires, wolves and all of the extremes of this stark and beautiful land that we call home." [97]

CONCLUSIONS

The 100-year history of federal grazing policymaking has been a tug-of-war between environmentalists and ranchers. The overall pattern that emerged over the first sixty-five years of grazing management was one in which western members of Congress were able to stave off most reforms and blunt the impacts of those that did pass. In the absence of widespread public concern about and scrutiny of federal grazing policy, which might prompt legislators from outside the West to expend their political capital on the issue, western members found myriad ways to insulate their ranching constituents from short-term economic harm. In the statutes that govern BLM and Forest Service grazing policy, they mandated a rancher-friendly approach to planning and management, empowering rancher-dominated advisory boards and keeping grazing fees low. When land managers got out of line, ranchers' congressional allies on agency oversight committees used intimidation to promote greater deference—holding hearings to embarrass agency officials; delaying administrative action by moratoria, studies, and reports; and threatening to cut the agencies' budgets. In a more subtle exercise of control, congressional supporters of the livestock industry contacted agencies' Washington staff and urged them to discipline or even transfer aggressive range managers.

The repeated use of such tactics over time established the context in which environmentalists launched modern grazing policy reform efforts. By the early 1970s ranchers' congressional allies had achieved firm control over the public lands authorizing and appropriations subcommittees in both chambers. They had cowed BLM and Forest Service range managers with their punitive responses to efforts at environmentally protective range management, their unwillingness to raise grazing fees, and their minimal budgetary allocations. As a result, when environmentalists challenged the permissive grazing policy regime, they encountered a dispirited federal bureaucracy and a well-guarded congressional fortress. Unable to provoke widespread public outrage about the deterioration of the western range, and lacking focusing events that might attract public attention, environmentalists consistently found themselves foiled.

The tenacity with which western members of Congress continue to protect their constituents reflects both their convictions and the intense electoral pressure they face. Sen. Malcolm Wallop, R-Wyo., himself a rancher, articulated the rationale for western senators' ardent defense of grazing privileges when he said: "The public lands were reserved for the expansion of the economy. The variety of uses on public lands provides for economic stability." [98] Others were more circumspect, acknowledging the force of constituency pressure. For instance, proenvironment representative Morris "Mo" Udall, D-Ariz., abandoned his proposal to raise grazing fees in the early 1980s saying, "I haven't seen the light, but I have felt the heat." [99] Apparently, Udall judged ranchers' electoral clout accurately; the National Cattlemen's Association lobbied heavily against Representatives Synar and Darden after they tried to raise grazing fees, and both lost their seats in 1994.

The political power of ranchers is not immutable, however. Over the years, reformers have infiltrated the House and Senate public lands oversight committees, traditionally the bastions of those interested in protecting public lands users. And demographic changes in the Rocky Mountain West have reduced the electoral consequences of opposing ranching interests for representatives in some districts. As the region urbanizes, constituents' demands for outdoor recreation and for environmental quality have intensified.[100] Moreover, as the timber and mining industries decline in the face of worldwide competition and mechanization, the recreation and tourism businesses have begun to supersede extractive industries in jobs and revenues generated. Still, unless environmentalists can muster sufficient political influence in the public lands states to counteract the clout of resources users, the institutions of Congress will provide myriad opportunities to stymie reform. For this reason, perhaps, some of the most promising recent developments in rangeland management are not the result of traditional congressional, or even administrative, reforms; instead, they have grown out of the voluntary, collaborative ventures springing up in the Rocky Mountain West.[101]

QUESTIONS TO CONSIDER

- How do you think federal land management agencies should deal with the issue of grazing on federal land, given the history of congressional intervention?
- Is overgrazing a sufficiently important environmental problem to warrant environmentalists' attention?
- What should environmentalists be doing if they want to bring about changes in grazing on the western range, and why?

Notes

1. Judith Goldstein, "Ideas, Institutions, and American Trade Policy," *International Organization* 42 (Winter 1988): 179–217; Christopher M. Klyza, *Who Controls Public Lands? Mining, Forestry, and Grazing Policies, 1870–1990* (Charlotte: University of North Carolina Press, 1996).
2. Theda Skocpol, *Protecting Soldiers and Mothers: The Political Origins of Social Policy in the United States* (Cambridge: Harvard University Press, 1992), 58.
3. Francis Rourke points out that agencies try hard to cultivate client groups because the ability to command strong political support is an important source of agency power. Francis E. Rourke, *Bureaucracy, Politics, and Public Policy*, 3d ed. (Boston: Little, Brown, 1976).
4. Charles F. Wilkinson, *Crossing the Next Meridian: Land, Water, and the Future of the West* (Washington, D.C.: Island Press, 1992).
5. Richard F. Fenno Jr., *Congressmen in Committees* (Boston: Little Brown, 1973); Kenneth A. Shepsle, *The Giant Jigsaw Puzzle: Democratic Committee Assignments in the Modern House* (Chicago: University of Chicago Press, 1978).
6. Kenneth A. Shepsle and Barry R. Weingast, "The Institutional Foundations of Committee Power," *American Political Science Review* 81 (March 1987): 85–104; Randall L. Calvert, Matthew D. McCubbins, and Barry R. Weingast, "A Theory of Political Control and Agency Discretion," *American Journal of Political Science* 33 (August 1989): 588–611.

7. Herbert Kaufman, *The Administrative Behavior of Federal Bureau Chiefs* (Washington, D.C.: Brookings Institution, 1981).

8. See, for example, Matthew D. McCubbins, Roger G. Noll, and Barry R. Weingast, "Administrative Procedures as Instruments of Political Control," *Journal of Law, Economics, and Organization* 3 (1987): 243–277.

9. Keith Hamm, "The Role of 'Subgovernments' in U.S. State Policy Making: An Exploratory Analysis," *Legislative Studies Quarterly* 11 (August 1986): 321–351; James Q. Wilson, *Bureaucracy* (New York: Basic Books, 1989). Wilson argues that the extent to which Congress can constrain a bureaucracy also depends on the type of task the agency performs and the level of support in its political environment.

10. Bryan D. Jones, *Reconceiving Decision-Making in Democratic Politics: Attention, Choice, and Public Policy* (Chicago: University of Chicago Press, 1994).

11. Quoted in Debra L. Donahue, *The Western Range Revisited: Removing Livestock to Conserve Native Biodiversity* (Norman: University of Oklahoma Press, 1999), 2.

12. The term "public domain" refers to land that the federal government had neither disposed of nor set aside in federally managed reserves.

13. Wilkinson, *Crossing the Next Meridian*, 90.

14. Congress established the 160-acre limit with the Land Ordinance of 1785, which divided western land into 6 x 6–mile townships, subdivided into one-mile squares containing four 160-acre plots. The goal was to create a system of small freeholders that would ultimately become a prosperous republican society. According to historian Richard White, "It was an ideal more suited to the East than to the West and more appropriate for the American past than the American future." Richard White, *"It's Your Misfortune and None of My Own": A New History of the American West* (Norman: University of Oklahoma Press, 1991), 142.

15. Wilkinson, *Crossing the Next Meridian*.

16. Ibid.

17. William D. Rowley, *U.S. Forest Service Grazing and Rangelands: A History* (College Station: Texas University Press, 1985).

18. William Voigt Jr., *Public Grazing Lands: Use and Misuse by Industry and Government* (New Brunswick: Rutgers University Press, 1976).

19. Samuel T. Dana and Sally K. Fairfax, *Forest and Range Policy*, 2d ed. (New York: McGraw-Hill, 1980), 137.

20. Rowley, *U.S. Forest Service Grazing*.

21. At the time, the Interior Department was responsible for disposing of the public domain but did not have any regulatory authority over unclaimed lands. Like any good bureau chief, Ickes wanted to retain control of his "turf" and therefore sought ways to avoid turning over public domain land to the Agriculture Department's Forest Service. Getting the support of ranchers, through rancher-friendly policies, was the key to retaining Interior Department control.

22. Phillip Foss, *Politics and Grass* (Seattle: University of Washington Press, 1960).

23. E. Louise Peffer, *The Closing of the Public Domain* (Stanford: Stanford University Press, 1951), 264.

24. Easterners, disgruntled with the extent to which grazing fees subsidized ranchers (fee receipts were one-fifth of program expenditures) unwittingly collaborated with western, anti–Grazing Service interests to slash the agency's budget. See William L. Graf, *Wilderness Preservation and the Sagebrush Rebellions* (Savage, Md.: Rowman and Littlefield, 1990).

25. Dana and Fairfax, *Forest and Range Policy*.

26. Ibid.

27. Bernard DeVoto, *The Easy Chair* (Boston: Houghton Mifflin, 1955), 254–255.

28. Quoted in Paul W. Gates and Robert W. Swenson, *History of Public Land Law Development* (Washington, D.C.: U.S. Government Printing Office, 1968), 629.

29. Dana and Fairfax, *Forest and Range Policy*, 186.

30. Voigt, *Public Grazing Lands*, 132.

31. Klyza, *Who Controls Public Lands?*

32. Reed F. Noss and Allen Y. Cooperrider, *Saving Nature's Legacy: Protecting and Restoring Biodiversity* (Washington, D.C.: Island Press, 1994).

33. Quoted in George Wuerthner, "How the West Was Eaten," *Wilderness* (Spring 1991): 28–37.

34. Ibid.

35. U.S. GAO, *Rangeland Management: Comparison of Rangeland Condition Reports*, GAO/RCED-91-191 (July 1991). One prominent dissenter, Thadis Box, pointed out that two issues confound our understanding of range conditions. First, he claimed that data on range conditions were old or nonexistent. Second, he argued that range conditions must be evaluated with respect to some management objective. If the goal was to provide better forage for cattle, the trend for rangelands had, on average, been upwards over a number of decades, and the range was in the best condition of the twentieth century. See Thadis Box, "Rangelands," in *Natural Resources for the 21st Century* (Washington, D.C.: American Forestry Association, 1990), 113–118. In 1994 a National Academy of Sciences panel concluded that because many reports on range conditions depended on the judgment of field personnel, rather than on systematic monitoring data, they could not determine whether livestock grazing had degraded western rangelands. See National Research Council, *Rangeland Health: New Methods to Classify, Inventory, and Monitor Rangelands* (Washington, D.C.: National Academy Press, 1994).

36. U.S. GAO, *Public Rangelands: Some Riparian Areas Restored but Widespread Improvement Will be Slow*, GAD/RCED-88-105 (June 1988); EPA report cited in Wuerthner, "How the West was Eaten."

37. Harold E. Dregne, "Desertification of Arid Lands," *Economic Geography* 3 (1977): 322–331.

38. Some of the disagreements among scientists over the impact of grazing on the arid western range arise out of differences in their orientation. For decades, range scientists were trained at land grant colleges whose programs were closely affiliated with, and often funded by, the ranching industry. Studies of rangeland ecology, to the extent they existed, were primarily concerned with forage quality and availability. By contrast, conservation biologists are primarily concerned with maximizing biodiversity. For conservation biologists' perspective, see Noss and Cooperrider, *Saving Nature's Legacy;* Thomas L. Fleischner, "Ecological Costs of Livestock Grazing in Western North America," *Conservation Biology* 8 (September 1994): 629–644. For arguments over whether intensively managed grazing is actually beneficial for rangeland (the "herbivore optimization" theory), see E. L. Painter and A. Joy Belsky, "Application of Herbivore Optimization Theory to Rangelands of the Western United States," *Ecological Applications* 3 (1993): 2–9; M. I. Dyer et al., "Herbivory and Its Consequences," *Ecological Applications* 3 (1993): 10–16; S. J. McNaughton, "Grasses, Grazers, Science and Management," *Ecological Applications* 3 (1993): 17–20; Allan Savory, "Re-Creating the West . . . One Decision at a Time," in *Ranching West of the 100th Meridian*, ed. Richard L. Knight, Wendell C. Gilgert, and Ed Marston (Washington, D.C.: Island Press, 2002), 155–170.

39. U.S. GAO, *Rangeland Management: More Emphasis Needed on Declining and Overstocked Grazing Allotments*, GAO/RCED-88-80 (June 1988).

40. U.S. GAO, *Public Rangelands: Some Riparian Areas Restored.*

41. U.S. GAO, *Rangeland Management: More Emphasis Needed;* U.S. GAO, *Rangeland Management: Profile of the Forest Service's Grazing Allotments and Permittees*, GAO/RCED-93-141FS (April 1993).

42. William Kittredge, "Home on the Range," *New Republic*, December 13, 1993, 13–16.

43. U.S. Congress, House, Committee on Government Operations, *Federal Grazing Program: All Is Not Well on the Range* (Washington, D.C.: U.S. Government Printing Office, 1986).

44. Private lands in the East, which are far more productive per acre, support 81 percent of the livestock industry, and private lands in the West sustain the remaining 17 percent. The small western livestock industry is quite dependent on public grazing privileges, however; about one-third of western cattle graze on public land at least part of the year.
45. Wuerthner, "How the West Was Eaten," 36.
46. Philip L. Fradkin, "The Eating of the West," *Audubon,* January 1979, 120.
47. Wilkinson, *Crossing the Next Meridian,* 108.
48. An organic act articulates an agency's mission. Recall that the BLM was created as part of an executive reorganization, so it did not have an overarching, congressionally defined purpose.
49. Irving Senzel, "Genesis of a Law, Part 2," *American Forests,* February 1978, 32–39.
50. Klyza, *Who Controls Public Lands?*
51. Ibid.
52. Ibid.
53. PL 95-514; 92 Stat. 1803; 43 USC Section 1901 *et seq.*
54. Wilkinson, *Crossing the Next Meridian.*
55. Robert H. Nelson, "Why the Sagebrush Revolt Burned Out," *Regulation,* May–June 1984, 27–43.
56. The Reagan administration's primary goal for the public lands was to make the nation's resources more accessible to those who wished to exploit them. (More generally, the administration aimed to reduce government intervention in the economy.) See Robert F. Durant, *The Administrative Presidency Revisited: Public Lands, the BLM, and the Reagan Revolution* (Albany: State University of New York Press, 1992).
57. Ibid., 59.
58. For example, the *New York Times, High Country News,* and *People* magazine all covered Forest Service district ranger Don Oman's story. When Oman, a twenty-six-year veteran of the Forest Service, tried to regulate grazing in the Sawtooth Forest in southern Idaho, ranchers threatened to kill him if he was not transferred. Instead of accepting a transfer, Oman filed a whistleblower's complaint with the inspector general's office of the Agriculture Department. See Timothy Egan, "Trouble on the Range as Cattlemen Try to Throw Off Forest Boss's Reins," *New York Times,* August 19, 1990, 1.
59. Klyza, *Who Controls Public Lands?*
60. Cass Peterson, "OMB Urges Freezing Fees for Grazing Federal Land," *Washington Post,* January 28, 1986, 4.
61. "BLM Reauthorization Died in Senate," *1991 CQ Almanac* (Washington, D.C.: Congressional Quarterly, 1992), 216.
62. U.S. GAO, *Rangeland Management: Current Formula Keeps Grazing Fees Low,* GAO/RCED-91-185BR (June 1991).
63. Phillip A. Davis, "After Sound, Fury on Interior, Bill Signifies Nothing New," *Congressional Quarterly Weekly Report,* November 2, 1991, 3196.
64. Quoted in Timothy Egan, "Sweeping Reversal of U.S. Land Policy Sought by Clinton," *New York Times,* July 21, 1995, 1.
65. Ibid.
66. Catalina Camia, "Administration Aims to Increase Grazing Fees, Tighten Rules," *Congressional Quarterly Weekly Report,* August 14, 1993, 2223.
67. Quoted in Steve Hinchman, "Senate Dukes It Out With Babbitt," *High Country News,* November 15, 1993.
68. Catalina Camia, "The Filibuster Ends; Bill Clears; Babbitt Can Still Raise Fees," *Congressional Quarterly Weekly Report,* November 13, 1993, 3112–3.
69. Quoted in Associated Press, "Local Control of Rangeland Touted by U.S.," *Boston Globe,* February 15, 1994, 7.
70. Ibid.

71. Steve Hinchman, "The West's Grazing War Grinds On," *High Country News,* June 27, 1994.
72. Quoted in Timothy Egan, "Grazing Bill to Give Ranchers Vast Control of Public Lands," *New York Times,* July 21, 1995, 1.
73. "Grazing Rules Bill Fizzles in House," *1996 CQ Almanac* (Washington, D.C.: Congressional Quarterly, 1997), Sec. 4, 14–16.
74. Pamela Baldwin, *Federal Grazing Regulations: Public Lands Council v. Babbitt* (Washington, D.C.: Congressional Research Service, 2000).
75. "House Backs Grazing Fee Increase," *1997 CQ Almanac* (Washington, D.C.: Congressional Quarterly, 1998), Sec. 3, 32.
76. The plaintiffs charged that federal grazing programs were jeopardizing endangered species such as the laoch minnow and the willow flycatcher, a songbird.
77. Hal Bernton, "Grazing-Cutback Proposal Meets Trouble on the Range," *Seattle Times,* July 6, 1997, B8.
78. James Brooke, "It's Cowboys vs. Radical Environmentalists in New Wild West," *New York Times,* September 20, 1998, 31.
79. Michael Grundwald, "BLM Attacked for Inaction on Tortoise Land," *Washington Post,* May 12, 2001, 3.
80. See www.blm.gov/nhp/news/releases/pages/2003/pro30325_grazing.htm.
81. Quoted in Joe Bauman, "Battle Brewing Over BLM's New Grazing Rules," *Deseret Morning News,* June 23, 2005.
82. Quoted in Julie Cart, "Federal Officials Echoed Grazing-Rule Warnings," *Los Angeles Times,* June 16, 2005, 14.
83. Quoted in Tony Davis, "New Grazing Rules Ride on Doctored Science," *High Country News,* July 25, 2005.
84. U.S. Forest Service, *2000 RPA Assessment of Forest and Range Lands* (Washington, D.C.: U.S. Department of Agriculture, 2001).
85. Donahue, *The Western Range Revisited.*
86. John E. Mitchell, *Rangeland Resource Trends in the United States,* Report No. RMRS-GTR-68 (Fort Collins, Colo.: U.S.D.A. Forest Service, Rocky Mountain Research Station, 2000).
87. Quoted in Donahue, *The Western Range Revisited,* 58–59.
88. Ibid., 59.
89. Tania Soussan, "Report: Federal Land Overgrazed," *Albuquerque Journal,* November 10, 2004, B3.
90. April Reese, "The Big Buyout," *High Country News,* April 4, 2005.
91. Quoted in ibid.
92. Jake Page, "Ranchers Form a 'Radical Center' to Protect Wide-Open Spaces," *Smithsonian,* June 1997, 50–60.
93. Quoted in Sandra Blakeslee, "On Remote Mesa, Ranchers and Environmentalists Seek Middle Ground," *New York Times,* December 26, 2000, F4.
94. Carrie Seidman, "Not His Father's Ranch," *Albuquerque Journal,* December 3, 2004, 1.
95. Christensen observes that the amount of developed land in the thirteen western states rose from 20 million acres in 1970 to 42 million acres in 2000 and that developers prefer the same land that is best for ranching and wildlife: the mid-elevation, well-watered area. See Jon Christensen, "Who Will Take Over the Ranch?" *High Country News,* March 29, 2004.
96. Richard L. Knight, "The Ecology of Ranching," in *Ranching West of the 100th Meridian,* 123.
97. John Horning, "Ranching Advocates Lack a Rural Vision," *High Country News,* December 9, 2002.
98. Quoted in Phillip A. Davis, "Cry for Preservation, Recreation Changing Public Land Policy," *Congressional Quarterly Weekly Report,* August 3, 1991, 2151.

99. Ibid.
100. The 2000 census showed that the West is now nearly as urban as the Northeast, with more than three-quarters of its residents living in cities.
101. For testimonials about collaborative environmental problem solving in the West, see Phil Brick et al., *Across the Great Divide: Explorations in Collaborative Conservation and the American West* (Washington, D.C.: Island Press, 2001).

Recommended Reading

Dana, Samuel T., and Sally K. Fairfax. *Forest and Range Policy*, 2d ed. New York: McGraw-Hill, 1980.
Donahue, Debra L. *The Western Range Revisited: Removing Livestock to Conserve Native Biodiversity*. Norman: University of Oklahoma Press, 1999.
Noss, Reed F., and Allen Y. Cooperrider. *Saving Nature's Legacy: Protecting and Restoring Biodiversity*. Washington, D.C.: Island Press, 1994.
Wilkinson, Charles F. *Crossing the Next Meridian: Land, Water, and the Future of the West*. Washington, D.C.: Island Press, 1992.

Web Sites

www.blm.gov/nhp/index.htm (BLM site)
www.fs.fed.us (Forest Service site)
www.grazingactivist.org (Public Lands Grazing Activist site)

CHAPTER 8

Jobs Versus the Environment

Saving the Northern Spotted Owl

In the late 1980s the federal government became embroiled in one of the most notorious environmental controversies in the nation's history. At issue was the government's obligation to protect the northern spotted owl, a creature that makes its home almost exclusively in the old-growth forests of the Pacific Northwest. But the debate transcended disagreement over the fate of a particular species; instead, it was yet another eruption of the long-standing confrontation between fundamentally different philosophies about the relationship between humans and nature. It pitted those determined to preserve the vestiges of a once-abundant forest ecosystem against those who feared losing their way of life and the region's historical economic base.

This case vividly illustrates the evolving role of science and environmental values in decision making by the nation's natural resource management agencies. Each federal bureau with jurisdiction over the environment has a distinctive orientation that arises out of its founding principles and subsequent development. Congress created many of these agencies, including the U.S. Forest Service and the Bureau of Land Management (BLM), to pursue the dual objectives of conserving natural resources for future generations and maintaining the stability of the industries and communities that depend on revenues from exploiting those resources. Such missions predisposed the agencies to treat resources as commodities and pay little attention to their aesthetic or ecological values. As the grazing policy case in chapter 7 shows, pressure from members of Congress sympathetic to industries that extract resources reinforced this orientation, as did the fact that for many years agency personnel dealt almost exclusively with ranching, timber, and mining interests in formulating policy. In addition, the agencies relied on experts trained in forestry and range sciences, both of which were rooted in the utilitarian goal of maximizing resource yields. And a variety of agency socialization practices—such as hiring from one profession, promoting from within, and conducting frequent lateral transfers—further increased the homogeneity of agency professionals.[1]

In the 1970s, however, the Forest Service and the BLM began incorporating environmental science and values into their decision making. The change occurred in part because new laws required both agencies to hire more environmental scientists; to collect biological data on species, water quality, and other ecosystem amenities; and to put more emphasis on considerations such as fish, wildlife, and watershed health. In addition, by the 1980s the agencies were employing a new generation of workers who were more diverse demographically and had grown up in an era when environmentalism was part of mainstream American culture.[2] In the Forest Service, for example, even though many professional foresters continued to adhere to a timber philosophy, the infusion of environmentally oriented personnel, combined with directives to take factors other than resource extraction into account in decision making, contributed to a gradual shift in district rangers' and forest supervisors' attitudes and values and hence to changes in the agency's organizational culture.[3] Some agency employees, particularly scientists, began to make more ecologically risk-averse assumptions when generating information on which decisions were based.

Enhancing the influence of environmentally oriented employees on agency decision making was the increasing number, growing vigilance, and expanding clout of environmental groups. Just as the grazing policy case exemplifies the way members of Congress can constrain agencies on behalf of commodity interests, the spotted owl case shows how environmentalists can successfully challenge the dominance of extractive interests in administrative decision making. In hopes of raising the salience of threats to the spotted owl and old-growth forest, advocates of more protective policies transformed scientific claims into a compelling story. Frustrated with the slow pace of BLM and Forest Service responses to the owl's plight, environmentalists resorted to a tactic that has become a staple of the environmental movement: litigation.

Judicial involvement changes the dynamics of bureaucratic decision making by raising the level of scrutiny to which an agency's calculus is exposed. During the 1970s the courts became more activist in reviewing regulations, justifying their behavior on the grounds that congressional delegation of vast authority to agencies made them more susceptible to "capture" by particular interests and that judicial intervention was necessary to ensure fairness.[4] Since then, scholars and judges have debated the merits of reviewing the substance or merely the procedures of agency decision making. But both approaches have the same goal: getting agencies to "elaborate the basis for their decisions and to make explicit their value choices in managing risks."[5] That requirement, in turn, has elevated environmentally oriented scientists who can provide solutions to the challenges posed by new statutory requirements.

In addition to forcing agencies to justify their decisions, lawsuits raise an issue's public visibility, which in turn often prompts intervention by high-level political appointees. Such officials, if part of an administration sympathetic to commodity interests, may try to suppress an agency's efforts to incorporate environmental values. But when visibility opens up narrow subsystems, it generally benefits previously excluded groups wielding public-spirited arguments. Naturally, defenders of the status quo have not simply acquiesced in the face of environmentalists' challenges to their prerogatives. Forced into the limelight, resource extraction interests have retaliated with arguments about the reliance of regional economies on extractive jobs, the importance of low-cost resources for the nation's well-being, and the tradeoff between economic growth and environmental protection. In response, environmentalists generate economic projections of their own. As with scientific predictions, the two sides make very different assumptions about the likely impact of regulations and therefore reach divergent conclusions.[6] As previous cases have made clear, neither side is persuaded by the other's evidence; rather, the purpose of both sides' efforts is to win over the uncommitted public and persuade elected officials to see the problem (and therefore its solution) the way they do.

BACKGROUND

In the eighteenth, nineteenth, and early twentieth centuries, timber companies, railroads, and homesteaders cleared most of the nation's primeval forest as they moved westward. But for many years the enormity and impenetrability of the nearly 20 million acres of the Pacific Northwest's old-growth forest daunted explorers. To facilitate westward expansion and economic development, in the late 1800s the federal government gave most of the West's grandest old-growth forest—the biggest trees on the flattest, most fertile land—to timber companies and railroads. (In all, states and the federal government gave railroads about 223 million acres. The rationale was that the railroads would enhance the value of the surrounding, government-owned land, and subsequent purchasers would pay more for it.) The government also transferred western forestland to the states and to Native Americans. At the same time, Congress began setting aside some acreage in forest reserves, in hopes of averting a repeat of the timber industry's cut-and-run practices in the Midwest. In 1905 Congress established the Forest Service within the Department of Agriculture to administer these newly created national forests.[7] Forest Service chief Gifford Pinchot established the agency's founding principle: "The continued prosperity of the agricultural, lumbering, mining, and livestock interests is directly dependent upon a permanent and accessible supply of water, wood, and forage, as well as upon the present and future use of these resources under businesslike regulations, enforced with promptness, effectiveness, and common sense."[8]

Although the national forests were open to logging, timber harvesting in the Pacific Northwest did not begin in earnest until the lumber requirements of World War I pushed a railroad out to the farming village of Forks, Washington. Then, after World War II demand for northwest timber skyrocketed. By the mid-1980s, when the spotted owl controversy was coming to a head, private companies had virtually denuded the region's privately owned old growth. (In the early 1980s the upheaval in New York's financial markets had spurred a spate of corporate takeovers, and timber companies with uncut assets became prime takeover targets for raiders, who then clear-cut their holdings to pay off debts). State land management agencies, responding to state policies to manage their forests for maximum dollar benefits, logged most of the state-owned old growth during the 1980s as well.

As a result of these logging practices, when the spotted owl controversy erupted, nearly 90 percent of the remaining old-growth forest was on federal lands. Federally managed lands fall under a variety of designations and receive varying degrees of protection. The law prohibits logging in national parks and monuments, which are managed by the National Park Service. Congress also has designated roadless portions of the land managed by the U.S. Forest Service and the BLM as wilderness and therefore off-limits to timber companies. The protected old growth in both the parks and wilderness areas tends to be on rocky, high-altitude lands, however, so nearly all of the remaining low-elevation old growth was on Forest Service and BLM lands that were eligible for logging.[9]

By the mid-1980s many observers were noting with alarm that the old-growth forests on Forest Service and BLM land were going the way of those on state and private property. Despite a host of federal laws passed in the 1960s and 1970s requiring those agencies to incorporate recreation, watershed, and wildlife concerns into their land management, logging remained the dominant use of federal forests in the region. The primary reason was that the timber industry had become inextricably bound up with the region's economy: in 1985 the industry accounted for almost 4 percent of the workforce in western Oregon and 20 percent of the area's total manufacturing sector employment; in 1988 the Forest Service estimated that 44 percent of Oregon's economy and 28 percent of Washington's were directly or indirectly dependent on national forest timber.[10] In many small communities and some entire counties the timber industry was central not only to the economy but to the culture. In 1990 a journalist described the integral role of logging in Douglas County, Oregon, saying: "Oregon produces more lumber than any state, and Douglas County boasts that it is the timber capital of the world. . . . There one can tune in to KTBR, feel the roads tremble beneath logging trucks, and watch children use Lego sets to haul sticks out of imaginary forests." [11]

The enormous old-growth trees occupied a particular niche within the logging economy of the Pacific Northwest. Timber companies use huge, scissors-like machines called "fellerbunchers" to log second-growth forests (which have been harvested and replanted and thus contain smaller trees), whereas harvesting old-growth stands is labor-intensive and relies on highly skilled cutters. Many of the region's small, independent mills use old-growth logs to make specialty products. And old-growth timber is highly profitable; it provides long stretches of clear-grained lumber and therefore sells for triple what similar second-growth timber is worth. In the 1980s, in about seventy towns in the two states, the local sawmill was the largest single private taxpayer and employer.[12] In addition to providing jobs in the private sector, logging on federal lands generates revenues for local governments. The federal government returns 25 percent of revenues derived from timber sales on federal lands to the county in which the forest is located. These revenues are earmarked primarily for schools and roads. In the late 1980s, ten Oregon counties earned between 25 percent and 66 percent of their total income from federal timber sales.[13]

Federal law requires the Forest Service and the BLM to harvest trees at a sustainable pace—that is, by the time the last tree of the virgin forest is cut, the first tree of the regrown forest should be big enough to harvest.[14] During the 1980s, however, under pressure from Reagan administration appointees, the agencies accelerated the rate at which timber companies were allowed to cut, and logging substantially exceeded new growth. Congress, hoping to preserve community stability, forced the Forest Service to cut even more than the agency itself deemed sustainable.[15] As the rate of cut increased during the 1980s, environmentalists became alarmed that not only were federal land managers ignoring the principles of sustainable yield but that all the trees over 200 years old would be gone in less than thirty years.

THE CASE

Conflict over preserving the spotted owl raged during a fifteen-year period from the mid-1980s through the 1990s, but the issue actually arose a decade earlier when agency scientists first sounded the alarm. In 1968 a twenty-two-year-old Oregon State University student named Eric Forsman and his adviser, Howard Wight, began to study the biology and ecology of the owl, and they quickly became concerned about Forest Service harvesting practices. By the early 1970s Forsman was pestering anyone who might be able to help him protect spotted owl habitat: the Corvallis City Council, the Audubon Society, the Forest Service, and the BLM. Although federal land management agencies were gradually becoming more receptive to scientists' ecological concerns, their long-standing timber bias circumscribed their willingness to act protectively. Eventually, environmentalists—impatient with the pace of policy change—took the agencies to court to force their hands. The result was a national controversy that pitted protecting species against preserving regional economies.

Land Managers Try to Solve the Problem Quietly

Reacting to Forsman's inquiries and spurred by the imminent passage of the federal endangered species protection law, the director of the Oregon State Game Commission established the Oregon Endangered Species Task Force. At its first meeting, on June 29, 1973, the task force formally acknowledged the importance of the old-growth forest for wildlife and expressed concern about its disappearance from Oregon. The group also arrived at a minimum habitat recommendation of 300 acres per nest for northern spotted owls—an estimate based on Forsman's best guess, as no one knew much about either the nongame animals on Forest Service land or the extent of the old-growth forest.[16] But neither the Forest Service—which holds about 68 percent of the owl's habitat in northern California, Oregon, and Washington (see Map 8-1)—nor the BLM was particularly interested in the task force's recommendations; agency managers feared the precedent that setting aside areas for individual

Map 8-1 Spotted Owl Habitat

Source: U.S. Forest Service.

species might establish. So when the task force sent plans around, the agencies responded that there were insufficient scientific data on which to base a management decision with such potentially devastating economic consequences.

A number of statutory changes in the mid-1970s complicated matters for the agencies, however. In December 1973 Congress passed the Endangered Species Act (ESA), and the Fish and Wildlife Service (FWS) included the spotted owl on a list of potentially endangered species. In addition, the Sikes Act, passed in 1974, required federal land managers to help states protect state-listed sensitive species. Finally, the 1976 National Forest Management Act

(NFMA) and Federal Land Policy and Management Act required the agencies to develop comprehensive forest- and district-level management plans and formally designated wildlife as a major use of both Forest Service and BLM lands. Thus, in October 1977, when the task force recommended that land managers protect 400 pairs of owls (290 on Forest Service land, 90 on BLM land, and 20 on state and private land) by setting aside 300 acres of contiguous old growth for each pair, both agencies reluctantly agreed. They hoped by doing so to avert a decision to list the owl as an endangered species, which would severely curtail their management options.

Local environmentalists were dissatisfied with the degree of owl protection in the agencies' spotted owl plans, however. Led by the Oregon Wilderness Coalition, they filed an administrative appeal with the Forest Service in February 1980 on the grounds that the plan was implemented without preparing an environmental impact statement (EIS) as required by the National Environmental Policy Act (NEPA).[17] The regional forester, whose decision was supported by the chief forester, rejected the appeal on the grounds that the agency had not taken a major federal action (which would require an EIS) but simply an affirmative step to protect the owls until a formal management plan, as required under the NFMA, was complete. The agency declared its intent to conduct a "proper biological analysis" in preparing the official regional plan.

Shortly thereafter, in spring 1981, the BLM became embroiled in a controversy over its owl management plan for the Coos Bay district.[18] When environmentalists appealed the plan, the timber industry retaliated with a local media campaign portraying spotted owl protection as a threat to industry and the region's economy. Under the leadership of Reagan appointees, the BLM was disposed to side with timber, but local agency officials were acutely aware that environmentalists could escalate their demands by petitioning to list the spotted owl as an endangered species. Facing intense pressure from the Oregon Department of Fish and Wildlife, in 1983 the BLM engineered a compromise in which it agreed to manage the land to maintain habitat sufficient for ninety pairs of spotted owls and revisit the issue within five years.[19]

The Emerging Science of Owls and Old-Growth Forests

Even as Forest Service and BLM managers were wrangling with environmental and timber interests over their owl protection guidelines, agency scientists were requesting more acreage for the owl. In developing the Region 6 (Pacific Northwest) Guide, which would direct forest-level planning, the Forest Service had designated the spotted owl as the indicator species for the old-growth forest ecosystem, and government biologists had begun grappling with analyses of its viability.[20] Additional research had clarified the owl's habits; for example, radio telemetry data—gathered by fitting radio transmitters into tiny backpacks strapped on owls—suggested that it required a much more extensive habitat area than Forsman had suspected. By 1981 scientists were suggesting that the agencies expand their owl reserves from 300 acres to 1,000 acres.

In addition to studying the owl, government biologists were learning more about the ecological value of the old-growth forest and biological diversity in general. Forest Service ecologist Jerry Franklin was among the first to draw attention to the potential value of old growth. In 1981 he released the first comprehensive ecological study of the Pacific forest. His research defined a "classic" old-growth forest as one that is more than 250 years old, with enormous trees, big downed logs, and standing snags (dead trees). Franklin noted that some trees in these forests had survived 1,000 years or more and reached heights of 300 feet and diameters of six feet. He found that in late-succession forests there was also a healthy understory, a mixed and layered canopy, and light-filled gaps, as well as an abundance of ferns, moss, lichens, and other epiphytic plants.[21]

Franklin discovered that old growth, once thought to be a biological desert because it lacked big game, was actually teeming with life. He described a system rich with symbiotic links: lichen and moss on the trees are not parasites, but metabolize nitrogen from the air and feed the trees that support them. Some tree voles eat truffles buried in the forest humus, excreting the undigested spores throughout the forest. The truffles are fungus colonies that, in turn, enable the roots of trees to extract nutrients from the soil. Woodpeckers rely on standing dead trees because the wood of young trees is too hard and gums their beaks with sap. Fallen dead wood houses a multitude of amphibians. And the wider spacing of trees in old-growth stands provides flying room for predators and sunlight for a second layer of young trees.[22] Finally, Franklin suggested that, in addition to storing carbon and thereby serving as a hedge against global warming, old growth plays an integral role in regulating water levels and quality, cleaning the air, enhancing the productivity of fisheries, and enriching and stabilizing the soil. While recognizing its ecological significance, however, Franklin and his colleagues were uncertain about how much old-growth forest was needed to sustain the intricate ecosystem of the Pacific Northwest; in fact, they were not even sure how much viable old growth existed.

The Forest Service Region 6 Guide

Notwithstanding these scientific advances, in 1984 the Forest Service produced a Final Region 6 Guide that, according to environmental policy scholar Steven Yaffee,

> clearly looked like it had not fully incorporated information generated in the previous four years, and . . . was walking a line between what was seen as biologically legitimate and what was seen as politically and economically correct. . . . The level of owl protection at the forest level remained fairly minimal and dependent on the benevolence of the individual forest managers.[23]

Environmental groups filed another administrative appeal in the fall of 1984, challenging the methodology of and management measures contained in the Region 6 Guide. The forestry chief again supported the regional forester's rejection of the appeal, but this time the deputy assistant secretary of agriculture overruled him and required the region to prepare a supplemental environmental impact statement (SEIS) on spotted owl management.

With its plans already behind schedule, the Forest Service conducted its assessment relatively quickly. After intense negotiations among factions within the agency, in July 1986 the service released its two-volume draft SEIS. Within months, the Forest Service had received 41,000 comments on the report, only 344 of which supported its owl recommendations.[24] Environmentalists, aware that they needed powerful scientific ammunition, not just rhetoric, to press their case, had recruited eminent Stanford population biologist Paul Ehrlich and population geneticist Russell Lande of the University of Chicago to create alternative owl viability models. The Forest Service tried a modest revision of the plan, hoping to satisfy both environmentalists and timber interests, but the final SEIS—released in April 1988—did little to quell rumblings on either side.

The Pressure Mounts to List the Owl as Endangered

Although many within the agencies were beginning to see the value of the old-growth forest and the spotted owl, to environmentalists and concerned scientists the rate of actual policy change seemed glacial. As scientific knowledge advanced, it became clear that federal managers' actions fell far short of what was needed to protect the owl and its habitat. In fact, forest managers—under pressure from the White House and members of Congress—more than doubled the federal timber harvest between 1982 and 1988 from less than 3 billion to more than 5 billion board feet. Although mainstream national environmental groups, such as Audubon and the Sierra Club, were concerned about the rapid demise of the old-growth forests, they were reluctant to confront directly the biggest industry in the Pacific Northwest. They believed there was little public support in the region for their cause, and they did not want to provoke a backlash against the ESA or the environmental movement more generally. Andy Stahl of the Sierra Club Legal Defense Fund (SCLDF) even made a special trip to northern California to dissuade a pair of earnest environmentalists from petitioning the FWS to list the owl as endangered.[25]

In October 1986, however, GreenWorld, an obscure environmental organization based in Cambridge, Massachusetts, requested that the FWS list the northern spotted owl. After finding further action might be warranted, the FWS Region 1 (Pacific Northwest) director assigned three biologists to prepare a status report. But less than a year after the process began, under pressure from the Reagan administration and against the advice of its own biologists, the Region 1 director signed a finding that, although declining in number, the spotted owl was not endangered. Mainstream environmentalists, who joined the fray after GreenWorld submitted its petition, were livid at what they charged was a political rather than a science-based decision. In May 1988 the SCLDF sued the Interior Department and FWS on the grounds that the agency had ignored scientific evidence clearly showing the owl to be endangered in the Olympic Peninsula and Oregon Coast Range. Six months later, Judge Thomas Zilly of the U.S. District Court for the Western District of Washington found that the FWS had acted in an "arbitrary and capricious" manner by failing to demonstrate a rational connection between the evidence presented and its decision. The court gave the agency until May 1, 1989, to provide additional evidence.

Affirming Judge Zilly's ruling and further arming environmentalists, in February 1989 a review of the listing process by the U.S. General Accounting Office (GAO) found that "Fish and Wildlife Service management substantively changed the body of scientific evidence. . . . The revisions had the effect of changing the report from one that emphasized the dangers facing the owl to one that could more easily support denying the listing petition." [26] The GAO found that two of the three scientists had concluded the owl was already endangered, but FWS management had ignored them. Administrators also had deleted a section warning that Forest Service logging would lead to the owl's eventual extinction and had excised a twenty-nine-page scientific appendix supporting this conclusion, replacing it with a new report prepared by a forest industry consultant. Finally, although the decision-making process was largely undocumented, the Region 1 director admitted that his decision was based in part on a belief that top FWS and Interior Department officials would not accept a decision to list the owl as endangered. According to the GAO, "These problems raise serious questions about whether FWS maintained its scientific objectivity during the spotted owl petition process." [27]

Interest Group Confrontations: Lawsuits and PR Campaigns

While the FWS struggled with the listing question and federal land managers tried to navigate a middle course in planning, environmental activists pressed ahead on other fronts. They had already persuaded both Washington and Oregon to designate the owl as a state-listed endangered species, and they were gumming up the timber sales process by appealing hundreds of individual sales.[28] Now they began pursuing injunctions against logging on the federal lands inhabited by the owl, claiming that neither the Forest Service nor the BLM had satisfied its obligations under NEPA, NFMA, the O&C Lands Act, the Migratory Bird Treaty Act, and other laws.[29] In late 1987 the SCLDF represented the Portland Audubon Society and other environmental groups in a lawsuit challenging the BLM's logging of spotted owl habitat in Oregon (*Portland Audubon Society v. Lujan*). In 1988 Portland judge Helen Frye issued a temporary injunction that halved timber harvesting on BLM lands in Oregon. Also in 1988 the Seattle chapter of the National Audubon Society, the Oregon Natural Resources Council, and more than a dozen other plaintiffs also filed suit challenging the adequacy of the Forest Service's plans to safeguard the owl (*Seattle Audubon Society v. Robertson*). The plaintiffs convinced federal district judge William Dwyer to enjoin the Forest Service from conducting timber sales scheduled for 1989. These injunctions had dramatic effects: they temporarily halted more than 150 timber sales throughout the Pacific Northwest, slashing the amount of timber available for harvesting on federal lands in 1989 from 5.4 billion board feet to 2.4 billion board feet.[30]

Environmentalists recognized that, in the long run, they would need more than legal support for their position. Furthermore, they knew the battle could not simply be waged in Oregon and Washington, where timber was a pillar of the economy. Ultimately, they would have to create a vocal, national constituency for the old-growth forest by persuading millions of Americans that, even if they did not live in the Pacific Northwest, they needed to protect the old-growth forest because it was a national treasure. So they initiated a multifaceted national public relations campaign: they coined the term "ancient forest" to describe the area; sponsored hikes, tours, and flyovers to capitalize on the shocking visual impacts of clear-cutting; wrote articles for national magazines from the *New Yorker* to *National Geographic;* and toured the country with a giant redwood in tow to dramatize the plight of the Northwest's trees.

While mainstream environmental groups pursued these conventional means, more radical groups engaged in guerrilla tactics. Earth First! members, for instance, camped out on plywood platforms in trees scheduled to be cut down. They sat on boxes of company dynamite to prevent blasting, spiked trees, set their feet in cement-filled ditches, chained themselves to timber equipment, and buried themselves in rocks to stop bulldozers from moving up logging roads. Their approach did not always engender sympathy for their cause, but it made mainstream environmentalists appear reasonable by comparison.

Although the timber industry would have preferred to resolve the conflict locally, where its influence was greatest, it did not react passively to environmental activism. Timber workers quickly organized themselves into coalitions, such as the 72,000-member Oregon Lands Coalition. Like the environmentalists, these groups recognized the power of rhetoric and display. On July 1, 1989, the First Annual American Loggers Solidarity Rally came to Forks, Washington, the self-proclaimed timber capital of the world. A reporter for *Audubon* magazine described the scene, as hundreds of logging trucks rolled into town honking their horns:

> Yellow balloons and flags and legends. "No timber, no revenue, no schools, no jobs." Over a picture of a mechanical crane: "These birds need habitats, too." On the side of a truck: "Enough is enough!" In the hands of a child: "Don't take my daddy's job." On a sandwich board: "Our Ancient Trees are Terminally Ill." [31]

Speaker after speaker at the rally derided environmentalists as frivolous and selfish.

Political organization was less straightforward for the timber industry than for loggers, however, because the timber industry consists of at least two components with different economic needs and political agendas. Six large timber companies led by Weyerhauser had already logged the old growth on the more than 7 million acres they owned in the Northwest, and their future in the region lay in harvesting managed stands of smaller trees. Therefore, although some leading timber companies had a stake in ensuring access to the old-growth forests, the companies most affected were the small sawmills that were entirely dependent on federal timber for their log supply.

Ultimately, big timber—fearing their lands would be scrutinized next—joined the smaller operators in working aggressively behind the scenes to counteract environmentalists' pressure. They made substantial campaign contributions to candidates supporting their position and worked through their lobbying organizations, the American Forest Resource Alliance and the National Forest Products Association, to assemble evidence supporting their argument that the government should not protect the owl unless and until scientists were certain the bird was endangered. (Forest industry consultants insisted that they were finding northern spotted owls on cutover lands, not just in old growth, but most scientists believed those findings were relevant to only a handful of forests in Northern California.[32]) To mobilize popular sentiment, industry groups submitted editorials and took out advertisements in local newspapers. Because environmentalists had nationalized the issue, logging supporters also worked to transform the issue into a concern of carpenters, builders, and consumers nationwide. They activated allies in industries that relied on cheap wood, such as the National Homebuilders Association, which ran a full-page ad in national newspapers blaming the spotted owl for "soaring lumber prices."

The Region's Elected Officials Get Involved

With the BLM and Forest Service paralyzed by court-ordered injunctions and interest groups up in arms, politicians from California, Oregon, and Washington began to seek legislative solutions to the impasse. Members of Congress wanted to appease voters interested in timber, but they were loath to propose modifying existing environmental laws, recognizing that such actions would attract negative publicity and therefore garner little support from members outside the region. So in the summer of 1989, as the controversy was heating up, Sen. Mark Hatfield, R-Ore., and Neil Goldschmidt, Oregon's Democratic governor, convened a meeting of timber industry representatives, environmentalists, and federal officials. After some acrimonious debate, Hatfield offered a one-year compromise plan that protected some areas of the forest while allowing old-growth harvesting to continue in others. A major provision prohibited anyone from seeking injunctions to prevent logging. Hatfield and Sen. Brock Adams, D-Wash., discreetly introduced the "compromise" as a rider to the Interior Department appropriations bill, and President George H. W. Bush signed it into law in October 1989.[33]

The Hatfield-Adams amendment forced Judge Dwyer in Seattle to rescind his temporary injunction and allow timber sales to proceed. It also compelled Judge Frye in Portland to dismiss the pending case against the BLM. During the subsequent nine months, while the SCLDF appealed those rulings to the

Ninth Circuit Court of Appeals, more than 600 timber sales went forward, leaving only 16 fiscal year 1990 sales that could be challenged. Congress had found a short-term solution while avoiding the generic problem of reconciling habitat protection with timber harvesting—a strategy legislators hoped would placate timber advocates without unduly arousing environmentalists.

The Thomas Committee Report

The Hatfield-Adams amendment was clearly inadequate as a long-term solution, however, especially because in June 1989 the FWS reversed itself and announced its intention to designate the northern spotted owl a threatened species, which compelled the federal government to protect the bird and its habitat. Complying with a provision in the Hatfield-Adams amendment requiring the agencies to develop a scientifically credible plan, in October 1989 the secretaries of agriculture and Interior named an interagency scientific committee to formulate a strategy to save the owl. To enhance the group's legitimacy, the agency heads chose veteran Forest Service biologist Jack Ward Thomas as its chair, and thereafter the group was known as the Thomas Committee. Thomas selected for his core team the five foremost spotted owl experts in the world, including Eric Forsman and Barry Noon, a specialist in mathematical modeling of bird populations.

After six months of study, the Thomas Committee recommended a system of habitat conservation areas on federal lands that constituted a radical departure from previous conservation management. The plan prohibited logging in these areas and allowed cutover lands within the reserves to return to old-growth status. It preserved 7.7 million acres of habitat, of which 3.1 million acres was timberland designated for harvest. The remainder was already in national parks or wilderness areas or otherwise too remote, steep, high, or scenic for logging.[34] Although the plan incorporated up-to-date principles of conservation biology, Thomas was a pragmatist and therefore avoided the explosive issue of old-growth preservation. He made it clear that in its deliberations the committee did not consider "how much old growth shall be preserved, where, and in what form."[35] In fact, 41 percent of the land within the habitat conservation areas consisted of recent clear-cuts, nonforested lands and deciduous areas, and private lands (most of which had been logged). The committee also acknowledged that its plan constituted a minimum, not an optimal, strategy to prevent the owl's extinction; it would still result in a 40 percent to 50 percent reduction in the owl population over the next century. After a panel of scientists convened by the Bush administration conceded they could not challenge the report's merits, the Forest Service announced its intention to be consistent with the report's recommendations and halted tree sales in the area.

The Argument Shifts to Economic Costs

With an authoritative scientific document like the Thomas Committee report on the table, the only recourse open to owl-protection opponents was to demonstrate that implementation costs would be astronomical. Timber industry groups hastened to project the potential impact of the plan on timber-harvest levels and employment in the region. On July 9, 1990, the American Forest Resource Alliance sponsored a gathering at the National Press Club in Washington, D.C., at which a panel of statisticians contended that over the next decade the Thomas Plan would cost the region 102,757 jobs. By contrast, the Wilderness Society, the U.S. Forest Service, and the Scientific Panel on Late-Successional Forest Ecosystems—known as the Gang of Four, or G4, and assembled by two congressional subcommittees in 1991—estimated the region would lose between 30,000 and 35,000 jobs as a result of technological change, federal forest plans, and Thomas Committee recommendations combined. The Bush administration quoted a Forest Service projection of 28,000 jobs lost for all three spotted owl states, and some members of Congress cited a figure of only 13,000.[36]

Two factors accounted for most of the differences among these job-loss estimates. First, each group independently estimated the extent of the timber-harvest reductions that forest protection measures would cause. Some analysts assumed that mid-1980s harvest levels would continue in the absence of environmental restrictions, while others recognized that such levels were unsustainable even in the absence of regulations. Second, groups used different estimates to translate changes in the harvest level into changes in employment. For example, most analysts agreed that for every billion board feet of timber harvested, an estimated 9,000 jobs were created in direct woods work, milling, and production. But there was less consensus on how many indirect jobs, such as work in restaurants and stores, resulted. Some put the ratio at 1:1, while others put it at 4:1 or 5:1. As a result, the estimates of job impact for each billion-board-foot change ranged from 18,000 to 50,000.[37]

Moreover, the American Forest Resource Alliance concluded that ESA restrictions would result in significant timber-harvest reductions on private lands, eliminating more than 62,000 additional jobs. In contrast, the Forest Service, the G4, and the Wilderness Society predicted an *increase* in private timber-harvest levels, as well as a reduction in log exports, in response to public lands harvest declines and rising timber prices. Finally, groups that opposed spotted owl protection predicted a smaller number of jobs lost to technological change in the timber industry (8,000) than did groups supporting owl protection (12,000).

Regardless of which projections they believed, many commentators foresaw economic and social catastrophe for the region if the government undertook preservation measures. A reporter for *Time* magazine speculated that

> Real estate prices would tumble, and states and counties that depend on shares of the revenue from timber sales on federal land could see those funds plummet. Oregon would be the hardest hit, losing hundreds of millions of dollars in revenue, wages and salaries, say state officials. By decade's end the plan could cost the U.S. Treasury $229 million in lost timber money each year.[38]

A joint Forest Service-BLM study predicted the very fabric holding some communities together would unravel and claimed that "in severe cases of community dysfunction, increased rates of domestic disputes, divorce, acts of violence, delinquency, vandalism, suicide, alcoholism and other social problems are to be expected." [39]

Congress Takes Up the Issue

By 1990 the spotted owl was front-page news across the country, and, in the legislative session that followed, some ambitious members of Congress crafted measures to protect the old-growth forest in hopes of capitalizing on national environmental concern. The House Interior Subcommittee on National Parks and Public Lands and the House Agriculture Subcommittee on Forests, Family Farms, and Energy each debated forest protection bills in 1990. Neither pleased environmentalists, who argued the timber levels were too high, or timber lobbyists, who argued they were too low. Unable to move a bill out of committee, it appeared likely that Congress would once again pass a one-year measure specifying timber levels and limiting judicial review.

But on September 19, 1990, plans to attach another rider to the appropriations bill were scrapped when the Ninth Circuit Court of Appeals in San Francisco sided with environmentalists and declared the judicial review provision in the Hatfield-Adams amendment unconstitutional. Judge Harry Pregerson wrote for a unanimous panel that the amendment "does not establish new law, but directs the court to reach a specific result and make certain factual findings under existing law in connection with two cases pending in federal court," which contravenes the principle of separation of powers.[40] It was the first time in 120 years that an act of Congress had been overturned on such grounds, and the unexpected ruling—coming only twelve days before the previous year's timber harvest bill was to expire—left Congress in a bind. Should it waive environmental laws for a year and risk provoking a public furor? Or should it approve a package that would conform to environmental laws but antagonize timber interests?

On September 21 the Bush administration unveiled a plan to do the former. An administration study group, which included the secretaries of agriculture and Interior, as well as representatives of the Environmental Protection Agency and the Office of Management and Budget, called for a 20 percent reduction in the 1991 timber harvest. The group recommended that Congress approve a timber-sale program of 3.2 billion board feet in Forest Service Region 6 but permit no timber sales from the habitat conservation areas designated by the Thomas Committee. It also proposed to exempt timber sales in the Pacific Northwest from the two major laws (NFMA and NEPA) governing Forest Service behavior and requested that Congress convene an endangered species committee, or God Squad, to conduct a full review of federal timber sales and land management plans.[41] In yet another sign of the parties' polarization, the plan inflamed both environmentalists and timber interests.

Congress had only ten days from receipt of the administration's proposal to pass a timber program for the next fiscal year. Congressional leaders chose instead to rely on the advice of federal scientists and devise their own proposal to allow harvesting of about 3 billion board feet annually, one-third less than the amount offered in 1990. By the end of the session, however, the congressional proposal's sponsors had failed to gain majority support, and yet another year passed with no resolution to the controversy. During the winter and spring of 1991, Congress considered another slew of proposals, but opponents managed to tie them up in committees, and the courts continued to be the arbiters of the agencies' timber policy.

The Crisis Escalates

At this point, two events outside of Congress increased the urgency of the spotted owl issue even further. First, on April 26, 1991, the FWS announced plans to designate as critical habitat, and thus ban logging on, 11.6 million acres of forest in the Pacific Northwest to ensure the owl's survival.[42] Three million of those acres were on private land and included not only old growth but land where old growth might exist in the future to link up habitat areas. Furthermore, unlike the Thomas Committee's plan, the FWS's set-aside did not even include the nearly 4 million acres already reserved in parks and wilderness areas. The federal government had never proposed anything so sweeping in its entire history. Although the FWS later reduced its figure to a little less than 7 million acres—under pressure from the timber industry and the BLM to exclude private, state, and Native American lands—the protected area remained considerable.

Second, the courts stopped both agencies' old-growth timber sales. In May 1991 environmentalists filed another lawsuit in Judge Dwyer's court to block all new Forest Service timber sales in the old-growth forest until the service could present an acceptable plan to protect the spotted owl habitat. In October, still unable to engineer a long-term solution, Congress acceded to Interior Secretary Manuel Lujan's request to convene the God Squad, composed of seven cabinet-level officials, to review forty-four BLM timber sales in spotted owl habitat in Oregon. On May 14, 1992, the God Squad voted to allow logging on thirteen of the forty-four disputed tracts. The BLM was unable to implement the committee's decision, however, because Judge Frye issued an injunction against the agency until it submitted a credible plan to protect the owl. Compounding the problem for policymakers, in July Judge Dwyer made his injunction against the Forest Service permanent. He ordered the service to draft plans protecting not only the owl but a number of other species dependent on the ancient forest. Basing his ruling more on the NFMA than on the controversial ESA, Dwyer left the environmentalists in a temporarily impregnable legal position from which they had little incentive to compromise.

To lift the injunctions, the Forest Service and the BLM had to revise their spotted owl protection plans to satisfy the criteria of the NFMA and NEPA, or

Congress had to pass new legislation to override existing land management laws. The Bush administration offered no salvation. In mid-May Secretary Lujan had released the FWS's official owl recovery plan, which—as mandated by the ESA—sought to revive the owl's population to levels high enough that it could be removed from the list of threatened species. Lujan estimated the revised plan, although more modest than the agency's original proposal, would cost up to 32,000 jobs—a level he called unacceptable. He simultaneously released his own "preservation plan," prepared by an ad hoc committee, which emphasized saving regional timber jobs: it proposed setting aside only 2.8 million acres of timberland and 2 million acres of parks and wilderness. Lujan's plan protected an area that could support only 1,300 pairs of owls, a level most biologists regarded as unsustainable.[43]

Neither the FWS plan nor Lujan's alternative received much support in Congress. Environmentally oriented legislators argued that neither would protect the owl or the old-growth forest, while industry supporters complained that both plans would cost too many jobs. In the meantime, for the third successive year, subcommittees of the House Interior and Agriculture committees were working on ancient forest protection bills. None of those bills emerged from their respective committees, however, and Congress failed yet again to pass a comprehensive forest management plan.

The Clinton Plan

By 1992 the spotted owl controversy had become sufficiently visible to be a campaign issue in the presidential race, and the election of Bill Clinton gave encouragement to environmentalists hoping to gain permanent protection for the old-growth forests. In April 1993, as they had promised on the campaign trail, President Clinton and Vice President Al Gore held a summit in Portland, Oregon, with four cabinet members, as well as scientists, environmentalists, timber workers, and industry officials. The administration aimed to bypass Congress and resolve the spotted owl problem by devising a forest plan that not only would satisfy the warring parties but also would serve as the environmental impact statement required by Judge Dwyer.

In the meantime, environmentalists got an unexpected boost in early May, when the Society of American Foresters urged a dramatic departure from the century-old practices of the U.S. timber industry. In an uncharacteristically pointed report, the society said that cutting trees at their rate of regrowth would not protect the forests over time; instead, the society recommended an "ecosystem approach" to forestry that would base logging decisions on protection of wildlife, water quality, and overall ecological health. Frances Hunt, a forester for the National Wildlife Federation, said of the report, "If you read between the lines, what it is saying is what the profession was taught, and what it helped teach, has turned out to be wrong and we are going to have to make amends for past mistakes." [44]

On July 1 President Clinton unveiled his long-awaited Northwest Forest Plan. Of the variety of forest management options considered, the one he endorsed—Option 9—allowed annual timber harvests of 1.2 billion board feet from old-growth forests on 24.5 million acres of federal lands, down from a high of more than 5 billion board feet per year in 1987 and 1988, and considerably less than the approximately 3 billion board feet per year of the early 1980s. Option 9 also set up reserve areas for the owl in which logging was limited to some salvage of dead or dying trees and some thinning of new trees, but only if it posed no threat to the species. It established ten "adaptive management" areas of 78,000 acres to 380,000 acres each for ecological experiments. And it tried to protect entire watersheds in an attempt to head off controversies over endangered salmon and other fish species.

In addition to its owl protection measures, the Northwest Forest Plan provided $1.2 billion over five years to assist workers and families in Oregon, Washington, and northern California. It also supported retraining or related logging activities, such as cleaning up logging roads and streams. The White House estimated that 6,000 jobs would be lost immediately under its plan but anticipated that employing displaced timber workers to repair streams and roads would create more than 15,000 new jobs over five years. Most elements of the plan could be implemented administratively, without congressional approval. Thus, the plan shifted the status quo: if Congress wanted to raise timber harvest levels from those designated in the plan, it would have to change existing environmental laws.

Not surprisingly, critics on both sides immediately lambasted the plan: environmentalists thought it was insufficiently protective and objected in particular to the provision allowing salvage in owl reserves; timber advocates believed it was overly restrictive. Then, in December 1993 about four dozen scientists released a report providing strong evidence that the spotted owl population was declining and the trend was accelerating. Of particular concern, the scientists said, was that the survival rate of adult females had declined 1 percent per year between 1985 and 1993, a time when capturing and banding of individual owls provided reliable data.[45] According to the report, new data suggested that "the Northwest's old-growth forest ecosystems may already be approaching the extinction threshold for the northern spotted owl" and cast serious doubt on whether the population could survive any additional habitat loss. Moreover, the report's authors argued that "political compromise and scientific uncertainty should not be used to justify overexploitation for short-term economic and political gain at the cost of future sustainability." [46]

Scientists' reservations and the timber industry outcry notwithstanding, in early March 1994 the administration affirmed Option 9 as the final blueprint for timber cutting in the Pacific Northwest and announced its intention to present the plan to Judge Dwyer. For the plan to pass muster, the judge had to find it scientifically sound, so the question before the court was whether the plan represented a scientific consensus or a politically expedient compromise. Dwyer approved Option 9 in December. Although either side could appeal, his seventy-page opinion addressed every substantive objection raised by environmentalists and the timber industry and left little room for legal challenge. At the same time, Dwyer made his reservations plain: "The question is not whether the court would write the same plan," he said, "but whether the agencies have acted within the bounds of the law." [47] He also said that any more logging sales than the plan contemplated would probably violate environmental laws and admonished the government to monitor owl populations carefully in the future. Notwithstanding the judge's caution, the Northwest Forest Plan was finally clear of legal hurdles, and it took effect in early 1995.

The Timber Salvage Rider

Protection advocates' triumph was not only limited but short-lived because Republicans assumed control of Congress in 1995, giving renewed hope to the timber industry. Sen. Larry Craig, R-Idaho, introduced a bill to accelerate logging in areas where trees had been damaged by fire or insects but still retained some commercial value. The bill eliminated citizens' rights of administrative and judicial appeal and suspended provisions of the ESA and NEPA.[48] It also promoted logging in roadless areas and opened up sections of the forest that had been closed because of spotted owl restrictions. Rep. Charles Taylor, R-N.C., a tree farmer and staunch property rights advocate, hastily assembled a similar bill in the House. Taylor's bill directed the Forest Service to triple its current salvage timber volume over a two-year period, requiring the sale of an unprecedented 6.2 billion board feet of "salvage" timber over two years—an amount approximately double the 1994 yield from the entire national forest system.[49] In tacit recognition that no such quantities of salvage existed, the bill authorized the Forest Service to sell not just dead or dying trees but any "associated" green trees.

The premise of these initiatives was that there was a forest health crisis that needed to be addressed. At hearings on the bill, however, many scientists disputed the existence of such an emergency and challenged the appropriateness of thinning and salvage logging as a remedy for forest ills in any case.[50] Professional organizations, such as the American Fisheries Society, the Society for Conservation Biology, the Wildlife Society, and the Ecological Society of America, protested the salvage program as it was rushed through Congress as a rider to the 1995 Emergency Supplemental Rescissions Act. But according to journalist Kathie Durbin, congressional Republicans used the specter of wildfires to alarm constituents who were largely ignorant of forest ecology, and even skeptical members were concerned about jeopardizing the seats of western Democrats by voting against the rider.[51]

After years of efforts to protect the spotted owl and old-growth forest, federal land managers were stunned by the potential impact of the timber salvage rider.[52] On March 11, 1995, Lydon Werner, head of the BLM timber sale program for western Oregon, wrote a memo to BLM state director Elaine Zielinski saying that the BLM "would suffer a severe setback in the implementation of the Northwest Forest Plan [if the rider passed]. We support the need to improve forest health and expedite the salvage of diseased, infested, or dead and dying timber; however we are opposed to this amendment. . . . We believe [the sales] should occur in compliance with existing laws and management plans." [53] Even agency officials who supported salvage logging were dubious about the scale of the program Congress envisioned. "Physically, there's no way we could get it done," said Walt Rogers of the Lowman Ranger District in Idaho.[54]

Responding to a deluge of mail from forest activists and a spate of editorials opposing the timber salvage provision, President Clinton vetoed the Budget Rescissions Act on June 7, citing as one reason the antienvironmental riders. In a series of backroom negotiations orchestrated by Senator Hatfield, however, Clinton reached an agreement with Congress on a budget-cutting bill that included the timber salvage rider. Despite the vehement opposition of top advisers, including Vice President Gore, Clinton signed the measure on July 27. In doing so, he assured environmental activists that his administration would adhere to environmentally sound practices when implementing the rider.

But the bills' congressional sponsors had no intention of allowing that to happen. The day Clinton signed the rescissions act, a group of three senators and three representatives sent a letter to Agriculture Secretary Dan Glickman and Interior Secretary Bruce Babbitt reminding them that the rider applied to all unawarded timber sales in western Oregon and western Washington, regardless of their status as endangered species habitat. When President Clinton sent a directive to his department heads to begin implementing the provision in an "environmentally sound manner," Senate authors of the rider went on the attack, berating administration representatives in a hearing and threatening to cut off the agencies' funding. In a series of rulings issued throughout the fall of 1995, U.S. District Judge Michael Hogan affirmed the congressional sponsors' interpretation of the law, dismissing challenges to timber sales released under the rider.

Bowing to congressional pressure, the Forest Service began ramping up timber sales east of the Cascade Range, in the Rockies, the Great Lakes, and the Southeastern Coastal Plain. Initially, the response from the timber industry was anemic: the Forest Service did not get a single purchase bid in the first three months after the law was signed. But timber companies responded enthusiastically to the opening up of old-growth stands west of the Cascades. There, logging proceeded on several previously closed stands, over the objections of government and university scientists as well as environmental protestors. On June 14, 1996, however, the Ninth Circuit Court of Appeals overturned the decision by Judge Hogan, ruling that in the absence of clear direction from Congress, the Forest Service and BLM must use scientific criteria to determine where ESA-listed marbled murrelets were nesting.[55] The ruling saved several thousand acres of coastal old growth, as well as stopping four hotly contested sales in the Umpqua and Siskiyou national forests.[56]

By summer, there were signs that environmentally damaging timber sales were slowing down, although congressional advocates continued to push for more liberal fire salvage policies. The prognosis for the owl and the old-growth forest it inhabits was improving but still tenuous. Tom Tuchmann, the Clinton administration's choice to direct the implementation of its Northwest Forest Plan, insisted that the timber sales associated with the timber salvage rider would have a minimal ecological impact in the long run. "What we're talking about is less than 600 million board feet of the last of the old sales," he said. "It's less than one percent of all late-successional and old-growth habitat." [57]

Although they received relatively little attention in the national press, the sales initiated under the timber salvage rider stimulated tremendous concern in the Pacific Northwest, where environmental activists were up in arms about what they dubbed "logging without laws." [58] Events in the Pacific Northwest in February 1996 made the environmentalists' case even more credible, as flooding caused devastating mudslides in heavily logged parts of Idaho, Montana, Oregon, and Washington. The floods ripped out logging roads, triggered massive landslides, and dumped soil, debris, and giant conifers into streams. During a tour of the Pacific Northwest, after being greeted in Seattle by more than 1,000 demonstrators protesting the timber salvage rider, Clinton called the rider "a mistake" and advocated its repeal.[59]

Manifesting the change in its orientation, the Forest Service resisted congressional efforts to promote logging, and in July 1996 Agriculture Secretary Glickman acknowledged that the Forest Service had suffered a severe loss of credibility over the timber salvage rider. He announced strict new guidelines that restricted logging in roadless areas and cutting of healthy trees as part of its "forest health" treatments. The agency subsequently withdrew some of its largest and most controversial roadless area sales, restrictions that were expected to reduce 1996 timber sale levels by 12 percent in Oregon and Washington alone. In June 1997 Forest Service Chief Mike Dombeck announced that the agency was shifting its focus: "We are in the midst of a profound change—a change of values and priorities. . . . Our challenge is to make watershed health, ecosystem health, the health of the land—whatever you wish to call it—our driving force." [60] In January 1998, after the timber salvage rider had expired, Dombeck announced an eighteen-month moratorium on logging in roadless areas in the national forests, explaining that the Forest Service was changing its emphasis from timber extraction to stewardship. (Furious, congressional Republicans threatened to reduce the Forest Service to a "custodial role" if it did not manage the national forests primarily for logging.) President Clinton was unperturbed, however, and in 1999 announced his intention to ban road building on 43 million acres of undeveloped national forestland. On November 13, 2000—shortly before leaving office—the administration issued a final rule banning virtually all commercial logging from 54 million national forest acres.[61] (The Bush administration refused to defend this rule in court and in May 2005 formally repealed it and replaced it with a rule giving governors discretion over decisions concerning inventoried roadless areas in their states.)

The Bush Administration Relaxes Timber Harvest Restrictions

Although the agencies resisted, congressional allies of the timber industry showed no signs of giving up on their efforts to open old-growth forests to logging; between 1996 and 2000, they introduced dozens of "fire salvage" and "forest health" bills. Scalded by the timber salvage rider experience, however, Democrats and moderate Republicans resisted, suspecting these bills were thinly veiled efforts to increase logging in the national forests. So timber industry supporters were delighted when newly elected president George W. Bush reinvigorated the "war in the woods" by introducing his Healthy Forests Initiative and pledging to double the amount of logging on federal lands in the Pacific Northwest.

When President Bush took office, the Forest Service and BLM were harvesting less than half the 1.2 billion board feet projected by the Northwest Forest Plan. In early 2002 the administration announced its intent to raise logging levels in the region by relaxing two rules that hampered timber sales: the plan's "survey and manage" rule, which required the agencies to safeguard about 350 species linked to old growth, including fungi, lichens, and bugs; and its mandate that the agencies maintain extrawide buffers along streams and rivers to protect salmon. Combined, Forest Service Chief Dale Bosworth argued, these provisions led to lawsuits and "analysis paralysis." Scientists reacted furiously to the administration's proposals, and in April 2002, 200 prominent biologists and ecologists sent a letter to the White House saying that logging on national forests should be banned altogether. Three months later six scientists fired off a letter to the House Subcommittee on Forests and Forest Health denouncing Bosworth's claims that unwieldy procedures and questionable science were bogging down timber sales. Instead, the scientists wrote, the Forest Service had caused the delays by ignoring the best available science, which supported fire prevention by thinning small trees and reducing roads, and instead pursuing controversial post-fire salvage sales.[62] Nevertheless, in March 2004 the administration officially terminated the survey-and-manage provision and adjusted river and stream protections.

At the same time, the agencies began implementing the Healthy Forests Restoration Act, which had been passed by Congress and signed by the president in December 2003. Over scientists' objections, the new law allowed logging of big trees to finance thinning of smaller ones; it also limited judicial review of timber sales. Thanks to these provisions, in the five months after the law's passage the government won seventeen straight court cases favoring timber cutting over environmental challenges.[63] In late December 2004 the Bush administration issued comprehensive new rules for managing the national forests. The new rules gave economic activity and preserving ecological health equal priority in management decisions. They also eliminated the requirement that managers prepare an EIS with each forest management plan or use numerical counts to ensure the maintenance of "viable populations" of fish and wildlife. Instead, say Bush administration officials, federal managers will focus on the forest's overall health—although it is unclear how they will measure this.

Even the administration's best efforts were not enough to reverse the trend in the Pacific Northwest toward protecting old growth, however. Environmentalists did not simply acquiesce to the Bush administration's policy changes but instead initiated a new publicity campaign. For example, over the summer and fall of 2003 two former BLM employees toured the country with a 500-pound, six-foot-wide slab of a 400-year-old tree in tow to protest the Healthy Forests Initiative. And environmental groups persisted in challenging timber sales in roadless areas and endangered species habitat. The courts continued to be sympathetic to their arguments. In August 2004 the Ninth Circuit Court of Appeals ruled unanimously that, in formulating its biological opinions on Forest Service and BLM timber sales, the FWS had to apply a stricter standard to protect habitat for the spotted owl and other listed species than merely gauging the "impact on species' survival." The judges pointed out that the ESA was enacted "not merely to forestall the extinction of species . . . but to allow a species to recover to the point where it may be delisted." [64] In August 2005 U.S. District Court judge Marsha Pechman in Seattle rejected the Bush administration's elimination of the Northwest Forest Plan's "survey and manage" rules. And finally, timber companies' response to proposed logging sales was pallid; for example, by summer 2005 the largest and most controversial postfire timber salvage plan, following the 500,000-acre Biscuit fire in Oregon's Siskiyou National Forest, had not come close to generating the 370 million board feet anticipated.[65] Meanwhile, in the midst of the gridlock, an innovation emerged that promised to defuse some of the conflict over logging in old-growth forests. Several timber sales in the Corvallis-based Siuslaw National Forest and in the Mount Hood National Forest employed stewardship contracts. These agreements, which Congress approved in 2002, allow loggers to thin trees as long as they simultaneously undertake environmental restoration by erasing deteriorated roads, replacing failed stream culverts, or making other improvements for fish, wildlife, and water quality.[66]

OUTCOMES

The combined impact of the spotted owl injunctions, the Northwest Forest Plan, the timber salvage rider, and the Healthy Forests Restoration Act on the ecological health of the Pacific Northwest forest ecosystem remains unclear. As judges began imposing injunctions in response to environmentalists' lawsuits, timber harvests on federal lands in Washington and Oregon dropped by more than 50 percent—from more than 5 billion board feet in 1987, 1988, and 1989 to just over 2 billion board feet in 1992 (see Table 8-1). The timber harvest dwindled steadily from then on: by 2000 the annual harvest had fallen to 409 million board feet (mbf), and between 2001 and 2004 it ranged from 277 mbf to 500 mbf. In fact, a FWS survey of owl habitat lost to logging, completed in January 2002, showed that logging had removed only 0.7 percent of the 7.4

Table 8-1

Forest Service Timber Sales in the Pacific Northwest, 1981–2004
(in millions of board feet)

Year	Timber Offered	Timber Sold	Timber Harvested
1981	5488	5482	3382
1982	4857	4642	2264
1983	4746	4915	3868
1984	4926	4962	4539
1985	5367	4753	4760
1986	5271	5060	4965
1987	5271	5273	5597
1988	5056	4919	5408
1989	4413	2811	5231
1990	5048	3997	3879
1991	1094	2106	3166
1992	684	741	2140
1993	630	787	1666
1994	436	434	1127
1995	777	401	877
1996	908	940	776
1997	951	871	768
1998	790	652	662
1999	419	434	570
2000	255	242	409
2001	317	269	307
2002	335	306	277
2003	438	400	321
2004	506	491	500

Source: U.S. Forest Service.

million acres set aside under the Northwest Forest Plan, well under the 2.5 percent the plan had projected.[67] "If you're using habitat as a basis for judgment," said Joan Jewett of the FWS, "there hasn't been much effect on the spotted owl." [68] (As of late 2005 the impact of the Bush administration rule changes and the Healthy Forests Restoration Act on this trend was uncertain.)

Despite a dramatic reduction in logging of its habitat, however, the spotted owl population continued to decline at a rate faster than forecast in the Northwest Forest Plan. As of 1998 the owl population was declining at a rate of 3.9 percent annually, not the 1 percent predicted in the plan.[69] A review of the spotted owl's status completed in 2004 reported that between 1998 and 2003 owl numbers declined only slightly in Oregon and California (about 2.8 and

2.2 percent per year, respectively) but fell so fast in Washington (7.5 percent per year) that the population as a whole fell by 4.1 percent.[70] The review, conducted by the Sustainable Ecosystems Institute of Portland, examined the more than 1,000 scientific reports published on the owl since it was listed. The report noted that, although the hazard posed by habitat loss had been reduced by federal protection, other threats loomed: the barred owl, an invader from the Midwest, was preying on spotted owls; West Nile virus could spread to spotted owls; and Sudden Oak Death could attack tanoak, a tree favored by spotted owls in southern Oregon and northern California.[71] After reviewing the institute's synthesis and other policy-relevant information, the FWS concluded in fall 2004 that the spotted owl still warranted ESA protection.

Although the spotted owl's long-term prospects remain uncertain, the economic impacts of reducing the timber harvest are less murky. When the courts ordered restrictions on logging, Oregon mill owner Michael Burrill said, "They just created Appalachia in the Northwest."[72] Many commentators envisioned the timber communities of Oregon and Washington turning into ghost towns, and at first it seemed as though the bleak forecasts were coming true. In April 1990 a *U.S. News & World Report* article on the town of Mill City reported that those loggers who found jobs often had to travel across the state to keep them; their wives were taking jobs for the first time; and there were increases in teenage pregnancy, spouse abuse, the number of calls to suicide hotlines, and the number of runaway children. Between 1989 and 1996 the region lost 21,000 jobs in the forest products industry, but, because the spotted owl injunctions hit at about the same time as a national economic recession, many analysts found it difficult to separate the effects of the two.[73]

Many commentators argued that two major structural changes in the industry that had begun more than a decade before the spotted owl controversy erupted were largely responsible for job losses in the region. First, throughout the 1980s the timber industry had been shifting its operations from the Pacific Northwest to the Southeast: the seven largest forest-products companies reduced their mill capacity by about 35 percent in the Pacific Northwest while raising it by 121 percent in the South.[74] Second, automation reduced the number of timber jobs in the Northwest: timber employment in Oregon and Washington fell by about 27,000 jobs between 1979 and 1989, even though the harvest was roughly the same in both years.[75] Other factors affected the region's timber employment as well. Exports of raw (unmilled) logs overseas, particularly to Japan and China, cost the region local mill jobs.[76] And during the 1980s and early 1990s urban and suburban development encroached on an average of 75,000 acres of timberland each year in Washington and Oregon.[77]

Other changes in the Pacific Northwest suggested that it was a region in transition away from a timber-based economy toward a more diversified one. Between 1988 and 1994 the total number of jobs in the Pacific Northwest grew by 940,000, and earnings rose 24 percent, according to a 1995 study endorsed by dozens of Northwest economists.[78] After a slowdown in the early 2000s, mirroring the national recession, by 2004 the region's economy was picking up again, and economists were forecasting a rosy future.

Oregon, the most timber-dependent of the spotted owl states, offers some instructive lessons about the complexity of economic projections based on the fortunes of a single industry. In October 1995, three years into a drastic curtailment of logging on federal land, Oregon posted its lowest unemployment rate in more than a generation—just over 5 percent. The state gained nearly 20,000 jobs in high technology, with companies such as Sony opening up factories and Hewlett Packard expanding in the state. By early 1996, for the first time in history, high technology surpassed timber as the leading source of jobs in Oregon. Even some of the most timber-dependent counties in southern Oregon reported rising property values and a net increase in jobs. In fact, only two of the thirty-eight counties in the spotted owl region experienced a decline in total employment between 1990 and 1996.[79]

Even more startling, as the number of logging jobs fell, the average wage in Oregon rose. In 1988, the peak year for timber cutting, per capita personal income in Oregon was 92 percent of the national average, but in 1999 it was more than 94 percent of the national average.[80] Conditions continued to improve through the 1990s, and even places like the remote Coos Bay, once the world's largest wood-products shipping port, cashed in on the high-tech boom.[81] The state made these gains without sacrificing its role as the nation's timber basket, producing 5 billion board feet of mostly second-growth lumber a year. Even though numerous mills closed because they could no longer get the big trees, by the mid-1990s operations like Springfield Forest Products had retooled and were hiring.[82]

There were some costs associated with the transition from a resource-based to a service-based economy, however. In isolated pockets, such as Burns, Oregon, and Hoquiam, Washington, poverty intensified. Inflation in some rural counties was in double digits through the 1990s. And while the service economy produced a cleaner industrial base, it also had a dark side: the gap between rich and poor widened. The wealthy bought enormous luxury homes as well as SUVs—which by the late 1990s made up more than half the new vehicles sold in the Northwest—trends that threatened to undermine the environmental gains associated with reduced natural resource extraction.[83]

CONCLUSIONS

The spotted owl challenge was a litmus test for federal land managers trying to adjust to environmentalism. With its spectacular old-growth forests, combined with a historic economic dependence on timber, the region was a powder keg waiting to be ignited, and the spotted owl provided the spark. For more than a decade, the Forest Service and BLM—the two agencies primarily responsible for managing the owl's habitat—wrestled quietly with protecting the bird while maintaining timber harvest levels. Although agency scientists accumulated compelling evidence suggesting the owl and its dwindling old growth habitat were in trouble, the agencies' long-standing commitments to timber harvesting, as well as political pressure from the region's elected officials, made a dramatic departure from the status quo unlikely. Scientists and environmentally oriented managers found themselves isolated, as political appointees tried to steer policy in directions determined by political expediency rather than science. (To provide personal and professional support for dissenters, as well as to increase their political clout, forester Jeff DeBonis formed the Forest Service Employees for Environmental Ethics in 1990 and Public Employees for Environmental Responsibility in 1993.)[84]

Frustrated with the agencies' slow response to science indicating the ecological value of the old-growth forest, environmentalists filed lawsuits in hopes of changing the political dynamics of the issue. Court rulings in Washington and Oregon shifted the status quo radically, from extensive logging to virtually no logging of old-growth forests. They also elevated ecosystem protection relative to timber harvesting and raised the status of agency biologists, who had been overruled in the 1970s and early 1980s but now offered the only way through the impasse at which the agencies found themselves. Court-ordered injunctions also helped environmentalists raise the national salience of preserving old-growth forests, a phenomenon that was manifested in the candidates' attention to the issue during the 1992 presidential campaign, as well as in a burgeoning number of congressional proposals to protect the region's forests.

The national campaign that ensued revealed the political potency of "environment versus economy" rhetoric. Whenever environmental regulations are proposed, advocates of natural resource development publicize projections of massive job losses and dire economic repercussions, and the spotted owl controversy was no exception. Wielding studies conducted at the region's universities, as well as by government agencies and the timber industry, opponents of spotted owl protection measures crafted a powerful case about the human costs of such interventions. Environmentalists responded with their own studies suggesting that owl protection measures were not the primary culprit behind lumber price increases or job losses in the region's timber industry. Neither side took into account the broader changes in the economy of the Pacific Northwest or the industry's dynamic response to the new restrictions, however. Over time, the relationship between environment and economy has proven to be more complicated than either side portrayed it. According to Bill Morisette, mayor of Springfield, Oregon, "Owls versus jobs was just plain false. What we've got here is quality of life. And as long as we don't screw that up, we'll always be able to attract people and businesses." [85]

QUESTIONS TO CONSIDER

- Why do you think the northern spotted owl gained such national prominence?
- Have the Forest Service and the BLM done a good job of handling the demands that they take environmental, and not just extractive, considerations into account when managing the nation's land and natural resources? If not, how might they have done better?
- What strategies should environmentalists focus on in trying to redirect the nation's land management agencies?

Notes

1. Reed F. Noss and Allen Y. Cooperrider, *Saving Nature's Legacy: Protecting and Restoring Biodiversity* (Washington, D.C.: Island Press, 1994); Herbert Kaufman, *The Forest Ranger: A Study in Administrative Behavior* (Baltimore: Johns Hopkins University Press, 1960); Ben Twight and Fremont Leyden, "Measuring Forest Service Bias," *Journal of Forestry* 97 (1989): 35–41.

2. Greg Brown and Charles C. Harris, "The Implications of Work Force Diversification in the U.S. Forest Service," *Administration & Society* 25 (May 1993): 85–113.

3. Ibid.; Paul A. Sabatier, John Loomis, and Catherine McCarthy, "Hierarchical Controls, Professional Norms, Local Constituencies, and Budget Maximization: An Analysis of U.S. Forest Service Planning Decisions," *American Journal of Political Science* 39 (February 1995): 204–242; Greg Brown and Chuck Harris, "Professional Foresters and the Land Ethic Revisited," *Journal of Forestry* 96 (January 1998): 4–12.

4. Agency capture refers to the situation in which agencies are responsive to a particular interest rather than considering the public interest in decision making (see chapter 2).

5. David M. O'Brien, *What Process Is Due?* (New York: Russell Sage Foundation, 1987), 159.

6. As legal scholar David Driessen points out, however, both conduct their analyses within a "static efficiency" framework—that is, they do not consider the economy's dynamic response to changes in the regulatory climate. For example, predictions rarely capture the impacts of technological innovation or how communities and industries adapt to changes in external conditions. See David M. Driessen, *The Economic Dynamics of Environmental Law* (Cambridge: MIT Press, 2003).

7. Congress actually passed the Forest Service's Organic Act in 1897, but did not establish a management system until it transferred the national forests from the Interior Department to the Agriculture Department in 1905.

8. The Pinchot Letter, quoted in Charles F. Wilkinson, *Crossing the Next Meridian: Land, Water, and the Future of the American West* (Washington, D.C.: Island Press, 1992), 128.

9. Forest Service Region 6 (the Pacific Northwest) comprises twelve national forests: the Olympic, Mt. Baker-Squonalmie, and Gifford Pinchot National Forests in western Washington; the Mt. Hood, Willamette, Umpqua, Rogue River, Suislaw, and Siskiyou National Forests in western Oregon; and the Klamath, Six Rivers, and Shasta-Trinity National Forests in northern California. The BLM oversees forestland in six management districts. In Oregon and California, the BLM manages land reclaimed by the federal government during the Great Depression from the O&C Railroad. These lands are exempt by statute (the O&C Lands Act of 1937) from much of the restrictive legislation governing the national forests and are heavily logged.

10. Jeffrey T. Olson, "Pacific Northwest Lumber and Wood Products: An Industry in Transition," in *National Forests Policies for the Future*, vol. 4 (Washington, D.C.: The Wilderness Society, 1988); U.S. Department of Agriculture-Forest Service, *Final Supplement to the Environmental Impact Statement for an Amendment to the Pacific Northwest Regional Guide, Vol. 1, Spotted Owl Guidelines* (Portland: Pacific Northwest Regional Office, 1988).

11. Ted Gup, "Owl vs. Man," *Time*, June 25, 1990, 60.

12. Roger Parloff, "Liti-slation," *American Lawyer*, January–February 1992, 82.

13. Ibid.

14. A sustainable-yield harvest is one that can be regenerated in perpetuity. Sustainable yield is not a static concept, however; as scientists learn more about the factors that affect forest health, they revise their ideas about what harvest levels are sustainable.

15. Research by the Portland *Oregonian* showed that in 1986 Congress ordered the Forest Service to sell 700 million board feet more than the agency proposed; in 1987 it

ordered an extra billion board feet; in 1988 the increase was 300 million; and in 1989 it was 200 million. (A board foot is an amount of wood fiber equivalent to a one-inch thick, one-foot wide, one-foot long board. A billion board feet of lumber is enough wood for about 133,000 houses.) See William Dietrich, *The Final Forest: The Battle for the Last Great Trees of the Pacific Northwest* (New York: Simon & Schuster, 1992).

16. Steven L. Yaffee, *The Wisdom of the Spotted Owl: Policy Lessons for a New Century* (Washington, D.C.: Island Press, 1994).

17. An administrative appeal is the first stage in the formal process by which a citizen can force an agency to reexamine and explicitly justify a decision.

18. BLM timber management plans are revised every ten years. The plans due in the early 1980s had to conform to the Sikes Act, the Federal Land Policy and Management Act, and the Endangered Species Act. See Yaffee, *The Wisdom of the Spotted Owl.*

19. Ibid.

20. NFMA regulations require the Forest Service to identify indicator species, whose health reflects the condition of the entire forest ecosystem, and to determine the viability of those species' populations.

21. An epiphytic plant is one that grows on other plants. See Jerry F. Franklin et al., "Ecological Characteristics of Old-Growth Douglas-Fir Forests," General Technical Report PNW-118 (Portland: Pacific Northwest Forest and Range Experiment Station, 1981).

22. Ibid. Scientists are uncertain about the extent to which various species depend exclusively on old-growth tracts. Research has yielded ambiguous information, mostly because wildlife biologists have compared young and old "natural" forests but have not systematically compared the robustness of species in natural and managed stands. Recent research suggests that for many species it is not the age of the stand but its structural components that are critical.

23. Steven L. Yaffee, "Lessons About Leadership From the History of the Spotted Owl Controversy," *Natural Resources Journal* 35 (Spring 1995): 392.

24. Yaffee, *The Wisdom of the Spotted Owl.*

25. Dietrich, *The Final Forest.*

26. U.S. GAO, *Endangered Species: Spotted Owl Petition Evaluation Beset by Problems,* GAO/RCED-89-79 (February 1989).

27. Ibid.

28. David Seideman, "Terrorist in a White Collar," *Time,* June 25, 1990, 60.

29. Courts issue injunctions on timber sales if a plaintiff proves that "irreparable harm" will occur and if there is a "substantial likelihood" that the plaintiff will prevail at trial.

30. Michael D. Lemonick, "Showdown in the Treetops," *Time,* August 28, 1989, 58–59.

31. John G. Mitchell, "War in the Woods II," *Audubon,* January 1990, 95.

32. Tom Abate, "Which Bird Is the Better Indicator Species for Old-Growth Forest?" *Bioscience* 42 (January 1992): 8–9. For a political interpretation of these scientists' results, see James Owen Rice, "Where Many an Owl Is Spotted," *National Review,* March 2, 1992, 41–43.

33. A rider is an amendment that is not germane to the law. Sponsors of such amendments use them to avoid public scrutiny.

34. Kathie Durbin, "From Owls to Eternity," *E Magazine,* March–April 1992, 30–37, 64–65.

35. Quoted in ibid.

36. Sylvia Wieland Nogaki, "Log Industry Fears Major Loss of Jobs—Others Dispute Study's Claims," *Seattle Times,* July 10, 1990, D4; Bill Dietrich, "Experts Say Owl Plan Omits Other Species," December 18, 1991, D3; David Schaefer and Sylvia Wieland Nogaki, "Price to Save Owl: 28,000 Jobs?" *Seattle Times,* May 4, 1990, 1.

37. Neil Samson, "Updating the Old-Growth Wars," *American Forests,* November–December 1990, 17–20.

38. Gup, "Owl vs. Man," 57.

39. Quoted in ibid., 58.

40. Quoted in Parloff, "Liti-slation," 82.

41. The ESA provides for the creation of a cabinet-level endangered species committee (informally known as the God Squad) to grant exemptions from the act's provisions for economic reasons. Congress can pass legislation to convene the God Squad only if an agency can prove to the Interior secretary that it has exhausted all other alternatives. (Otherwise, the law requires the federal government to come up with a plan based on science.) In the seventeen years prior to the spotted owl controversy, Congress had convened the God Squad only twice.

42. The ESA requires the designation of critical habitat for any species listed as threatened or endangered.

43. Manuel Lujan Jr., "Bush Plan Protects Both Owl and Logging," *New York Times*, September 28, 1992, 14.

44. Quoted in Scott Sonner, "In Switch, Foresters Push Ecosystem Policy," *Boston Globe*, May 2, 1993, 2.

45. John H. Cushman Jr., "Owl Issue Tests Reliance on Consensus in Environmentalism," *New York Times*, March 6, 1994, 28.

46. Quoted in ibid.

47. Quoted in John H. Cushman Jr., "Judge Approves Plan for Logging in Forests Where Rare Owls Live," *New York Times*, December 22, 1994, 1.

48. More precisely, the bill required the Forest Service to consider the environmental impacts of the sale program but specified in advance that the sales satisfied the requirements of various environmental laws. See U.S. Congress, Senate, *Hearing Before the Subcommittee on Forests and Public Land Management of the Committee on Energy and Natural Resources*, 104th Congress, March 1, 1995 (Washington, D.C.: U.S. Government Printing Office, 1995).

49. Tom Kenworthy and Dan Morgan, "Panel Would Allow Massive Logging on Federal Land," *Washington Post*, March 3, 1995, 1.

50. Most scientists concurred that many western forests were in trouble, particularly the dry, low- to medium-elevation forests once dominated by fire-dependent species like ponderosa pine and western larch. A history of fire suppression, combined with timber harvesting practices, had dramatically altered such forests. But although in some forests thinning and salvage logging may have been appropriate, scientists maintained that there was no "one size fits all" prescription. See Tom Kenworthy, "Forests' Benefit Hidden in Tree Debate," *Washington Post*, April 18, 1995, 1.

51. Kathie Durbin, *Tree Huggers: Victory, Defeat, and Renewal in the Ancient Forest Campaign* (Seattle: Mountaineers, 1996).

52. The Forest Service had undertaken a comprehensive environmental study of the ten national forests in the area and, pending completion of that study, recommended interim protection for the remaining patches of old-growth trees. The agency's scientific panel wanted a comprehensive study of the effectiveness of thinning and salvage before undertaking such a program. See Kenworthy, "Forests' Benefit Hidden."

53. Quoted in Durbin, *Tree Huggers*, 255.

54. Quoted in Kenworthy, "Forests' Benefit Hidden."

55. The marbled murrelet, a seabird, also relies on old-growth forest and was listed as threatened in 1992.

56. Durbin, *Tree Huggers*.

57. Quoted in ibid., 263. Only about half of the total national forest harvest in the Pacific Northwest between 1995 and 1997 came from the western forests covered by the Northwest Forest Plan.

58. Brad Knickerbocker, "The Summer of Discontent for Greens, Monks in West," *Christian Science Monitor*, July 24, 1995, 3.

59. Timothy Egan, "Clinton Under Attack by Both Sides in Renewed Logging Fight," *New York Times,* February 29, 1996, 10.

60. Remarks of Mike Dombeck, Outdoor Writers Association of America Public Lands Forum, June 25, 1997.

61. Between the draft and the final rule, the administration added roadless areas in the Tongass National Forest in Alaska to the ban. See Hal Bernton, "Forest Chief Asks Reduced Logging," *Oregonian,* March 30, 1999 B1; Douglas Jehl, "Expanded Logging Ban Is Proposed for National Forests," *New York Times,* November 14, 2000, 8.

62. Michael Milstein, "Scientists Chastise Forest Service Chief," *The Oregonian,* July 27, 2002, B01.

63. Matthew Daly, "Forest Cases Going Cutters' Way Under New Law," Associated Press, May 20, 2004.

64. Quoted in Joe Rojas-Burke, "Ruling on Spotted Owl May Hinder Logging," *The Oregonian,* August 8, 2004, D03.

65. Jeff Barnard, "Three Years After, Salvage From Biscuit Fire Limping Along," Associated Press, July 13, 2005.

66. Jim Kadera, "Timber Sale Has Potential for Peace," *The Oregonian,* December 30, 2004, 01.

67. Michael Milstein, "Federal Forests in Line to See More Logging," *Seattle Times,* January 16, 2002, 1.

68. Quoted in ibid.

69. Associated Press, "Owl Disappears," July 10, 2000, ABCNews.com.

70. "Analysis Shows Northern Spotted Owl Still Declining," Associated Press, May 12, 2004.

71. Timber industry spokespeople seized on these threats to argue that harvest restrictions were not scientifically justified given the other threats to the owl's survival. See Hal Bernton, "Spotted Owl Faces Nonlogging Threats," *Seattle Times,* June 23, 2004, B1.

72. Quoted in Timothy Egan, "Oregon Foiling Forecasters, Thrives as It Protects Owl," *New York Times,* October 11, 1994, 1.

73. Ed Niemi, Ed Whitelaw, and Andrew Johnston, *The Sky Did NOT Fall: The Pacific Northwest's Response to Logging Reductions* (Eugene: ECONorthwest, 1999). Niemi and his coauthors estimate that about 9,300 workers in Washington and Oregon lost their jobs between 1990 and 1994 as a consequence of spotted owl restrictions. See also William R. Freudenburg, Lisa J. Wilson, and Daniel J. O'Leary, "Forty Years of Spotted Owls? A Longitudinal Analysis of Logging Industry Job Losses," *Sociological Perspectives* 41 (February/March 1998): 1–26. Freudenburg and his coauthors find no statistical evidence for a spotted-owl effect on timber employment in the Pacific Northwest.

74. "Log On," *Economist,* November 5, 1992, 26.

75. Niemi et al., *The Sky Did NOT Fall.* Moreover, because industry had forced the timber workers' unions to take a pay cut during the 1980s, in 1989 timber workers received paychecks that were less than two-thirds of those they had received a decade earlier.

76. Recognizing the severe impact of raw log exports, the federal government banned such exports from federal and state lands in the West, but timber companies circumvented the ban by substituting logs from private land for export and cutting national forest timber for domestic sale. See Michael Satchell, "The Endangered Logger," *U.S. News and World Report,* June 25, 1990, 27–29.

77. Dietrich, *The Final Forest.*

78. Thomas M. Power, ed., "Economic Well-Being and Environmental Protection in the Pacific Northwest: A Consensus Report by Pacific Northwest Economists" (Economics Department, University of Montana, December 1995). Another study found 27 percent and 15 percent increases, respectively, in the region's total employment and per capita income. See Niemi et al., *The Sky Did NOT Fall.*

79. Niemi et al., *The Sky Did NOT Fall.* Sociologist William Freudenburg and his coauthors note that "the period since the listing of the spotted owl has . . . been one of soaring job growth in the Northwest." See Freudenburg et al., "Forty Years of Spotted Owls?"
80. State of Oregon, Bureau of Economic Analysis, "Oregon Per Capita Personal Income" (May 2001), www.olmis.org/pubs/single/pcpi.pdf.
81. Sam Howe Verhovek, "Paul Bunyan Settling into His New Cubicle," *New York Times,* August 21, 2000, 1.
82. Egan, "Oregon Foiling Forecasters."
83. Alan Thein Durning, "NW Environment Hurt by Raging Consumerism," *Seattle Post-Intelligencer,* July 13, 1999, 9.
84. The FSEEE seeks to make the Forest Service's land management philosophy more sustainable. PEER is even more ambitious; it aims to persuade all agencies, federal and state, to adopt environmentally friendly land management policies.
85. Quoted in Egan, "Oregon Foiling Forecasters."

Recommended Reading

Dietrich, William. *The Final Forest: The Battle for the Last Great Trees of the Pacific Northwest.* New York: Simon & Schuster, 1992.
Durbin, Kathie. *Tree Huggers: Victory, Defeat, and Renewal in the Ancient Forest Campaign.* Seattle: Mountaineers, 1996.
Yaffee, Steven L. *The Wisdom of the Spotted Owl: Policy Lessons for a New Century.* Washington, D.C.: Island Press, 1994.

Web Sites

www.fs.fed.us/r6/welcome.htm (Forest Service, Pacific Northwest Region site)
www.fs.fed.us/pnw (Forest Service Pacific Northwest Research Station site)
www.reo.gov (Northwest Forest Plan site)

CHAPTER 9

Playground or Paradise?

Snowmobiles in Yellowstone National Park

In the winter of 1963 Yellowstone National Park staff allowed the first snow-mobiles to enter the park. By the mid-1990s the Park Service was reporting that wintertime air quality in some parts of the park was the worst in the nation and that the drone of snowmobiles was perpetually audible at Old Faithful, the park's premiere attraction. In fall 2000, after five years of study-ing the issue, the Clinton administration decided to phase in a ban on snow-mobiles in Yellowstone and most other national parks on the grounds that allowing them was inconsistent with the Park Service mission as well as with laws and regulations governing park management. Just a day after his inau-guration in 2001, however, President George W. Bush suspended the Clinton-era ban, and the following year he substituted a plan that limited the maxi-mum number of snowmobiles entering the park but allowed an increase in their daily average number.

The case of snowmobiles in Yellowstone exposes one of the schisms that have arisen among self-described environmentalists. Both sides claim to appreciate the amenities nature provides—wildlife, scenic beauty, and open space—but their values are actually quite different. For motorized recreation enthusiasts, the nation's public lands, including the parks, are playgrounds; nature is theirs to enjoy, and improved technology can resolve any problems posed by human use. By contrast, those who prefer passive recreation value nature for its own sake and believe managers should limit the form and amount of access to ensure the health of the parks' flora and fauna. This divi-sion poses a serious dilemma for environmentalists: on the one hand, they espouse the view that contact with nature fosters appreciation and concern; indeed, that is part of the rationale for establishing such preserves. On the other hand, they worry that overly intensive use by large numbers of people threatens the integrity and long-term survival of natural areas.

In many respects this debate resembles the spotted owl and grazing cases. As is true in nearly all cases of natural resource policymaking, efforts to pro-tect ecological values—even in national parks—face enormous obstacles. Once a resource-dependent activity becomes entrenched, its beneficiaries believe they have rights to the resource. Furthermore, the businesses that pro-vide services to resource-users claim that the local economy depends on their prosperity. Elected officials feel compelled to support those with a direct eco-nomic stake, who—although often a minority numerically—tend to be orga-nized and mobilized. Protection advocates hoping to overcome these forces rely heavily on the courts' willingness to interpret agencies' statutory mandates—which are often ambiguous—in protective ways, and on scientific evidence that the activity they hope to curb or eliminate damages human health or the environment.

In addition to exemplifying the dynamics of natural resource politics, this case illustrates both the importance of agency rules as policy instruments and the extent to which presidents and their appointees can use their rulemaking power to influence the content of public policy. Many scholars emphasize the difficulties presidents face in trying to change policy and bureaucratic behavior. Richard Neustadt, one of the most influential writers on presidential power, asserts that in the fragmented U.S. government system a president's power lies in the ability to persuade, not command.[1] Political scientists Harold Seidman and Robert Gilmour emphasize the difficulty for political appointees of steering agencies, which have "distinct and multidimensional personalities and deeply ingrained cultures and subcultures reflecting institutional history, ideology, values, symbols, folklore, professional biases, behavior patterns, heroes, and enemies."[2]

But more recent scholarship suggests that presidents have more influence over administrative decision making than once believed. Working in the tradition of "new institutionalism," political scientist Terry Moe argues that, because they can make unilateral decisions, presidents actually have considerable power over the bureaucracy: "If [the president] wants to develop his own institution, review or revise agency decisions, coordinate agency actions, make changes in agency leadership, or otherwise impose his views on government he can simply proceed—and it is up to Congress (and the courts) to react."[3] Other scholars have noted that presidents have "important and practical legal powers, and the institutional setting of the presidency amplifies these powers by enabling presidents to make the first move in policy matters, if they choose to do so."[4] And political scientist William Howell describes the varied ways that presidents historically and with increasing frequency have used their "powers of unilateral action" to shape policy in substantial ways.[5]

The case also demonstrates how advocates on both sides of environmental policy disputes use the courts strategically to challenge administrative decisions. After environmentalists and other public interest groups achieved many of their early successes through lawsuits in the 1960s and 1970s, conservative groups quickly mobilized and adopted the same tactic.[6] As a result, "a wide range of groups regularly resort to the judicial arena because they view the courts as just another political battlefield, which they must enter to fight for their goals."[7] Advocates on both sides cite procedural requirements to challenge agency decisions they disagree with; for example, opponents of environmentally protective regulations have begun using the National Environmental Policy Act, the darling of environmentalists, to delay or block administrative decisions. To the extent possible, advocates also engage in forum shopping—that is, selecting the court in which they expect to fare best—because they recognize that judges' attitudes are important predictors of how they will rule.[8] Precedent, statutory language, and how lawyers frame an issue all constrain the way judges can rule. In addition, judges are sensitive to the political context; because they cannot enforce their own rulings, they need to make decisions that are likely to be carried out in order to maintain their legitimacy. But judges' decisions also reflect their values and ideology. In short, as political scientist James Gibson explains, "Judges' decisions are a function of what they prefer to do, tempered by what they think they ought to do, but constrained by what they perceive is feasible to do." [9]

BACKGROUND

Yellowstone National Park, established in 1872, is the nation's oldest park and among its most spectacular. But from its inception the purpose of Yellowstone was unclear: was it to be a playground or a shrine for nature? More than forty years after founding Yellowstone, Congress created the National Park Service (NPS) to manage the nation's inchoate park system and, in the process, reinforced this tension by endowing the agency with an ambiguous—and potentially contradictory—mandate: to encourage visitation while at the same time protecting the parks' natural amenities in perpetuity. After World War II, as the number of people using the national parks surged, the parks' condition began to decline precipitously.

The Origins of Yellowstone National Park

The Yellowstone region, which spans Wyoming, Montana, and Idaho, was occupied for thousands of years before Europeans "discovered" it. Although little is known about how the area's early human inhabitants modified the landscape, it is clear that they affected it in a variety of ways: they set fires to manipulate vegetation and animals, used the plentiful obsidian left over from volcanic activity to make arrowheads, and hunted large game animals. At the same time, as former Yellowstone park ranger and historian Paul Schullery notes, there is "overwhelming evidence that most of the tribes that used the Yellowstone area . . . saw it as a place of spiritual power, of communion with natural forces, a place that inspired reverence." [10]

Reports from some early white visitors to the region suggest that, like the native people, they were awed by its spectacular and peculiar geological features. The first white man known to have visited Yellowstone was John Coulton, a member of the Lewis and Clark Expedition, who traveled there in 1807–1808. Subsequently, trappers and a handful of explorers spent time in the area, followed by prospectors looking for gold. Although few of these visitors kept records of their experience, a handful of later explorers did. For example, in a retrospective account of the 1870 Washburne-Langford-Doane Expedition, published in 1905, Nathaniel Langford described the region in the following way: "I do not know of any portion of our country where a national park can be established furnishing visitors more wonderful attractions than here. These

Map 9-1 Yellowstone National Park

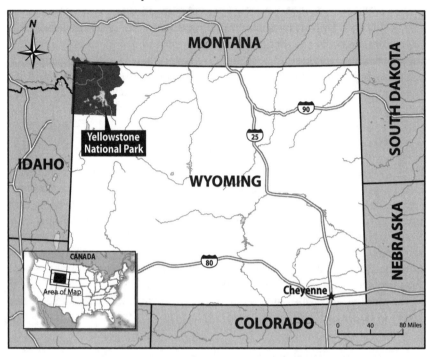

Source: National Park Service, U.S. Department of the Interior.

wonders are so different from anything we have seen—they are so various, so extensive—that the feeling in my mind from the moment they began to appear until we left them has been one of intense surprise and incredulity." [11] According to Schullery, in other early depictions of the region: "The weirdness fascinates and attracts us, and then the beauty rises to awe and stun. All is brilliant light and ominous shadow, alternative dazzling prismatic displays with the 'dark, dismal, diabolical aspect' of each place." [12]

The official NPS myth is that the idea for a park at Yellowstone emerged during a Washburne expedition camping trip. According to a sign at the park's Madison Junction, the members of the expedition "were grouped around a campfire discussing their explorations when Cornelius Hedges suggested the region be set apart as a national park." [13] In March 1872, after a year in which the members of the Washburne expedition energetically promoted the idea, President Ulysses S. Grant signed the bill establishing Yellowstone National Park, the world's first national park. From the outset the park's purpose embodied two contradictory ideals. Congress decreed that 2.2 million acres be "reserved and withdrawn . . . dedicated and set apart as a public park or pleasuring ground for the benefit and enjoyment of the people" (see Map 9-1). The area was to be managed for "preservation from injury or spoliation" and

retained in its "natural condition." At the same time, however, the act authorized the construction of "roads and bridle paths" in the park. And in 1906 Congress enlarged and extended the Interior secretary's authority to allow leases
for the transaction of business in Yellowstone "as the comfort and convenience
of visitors may require" as well as to permit the construction of buildings in
the park.[14]

The National Park Service Is Born

In 1910, nearly forty years after the creation of Yellowstone and after the
designation of several other scenic areas, proponents began lobbying Congress to authorize a bureau to manage the entire park system. In 1912 President William Howard Taft urged Congress to create a bureau to oversee the
parks, saying it was "essential to the proper management of those wonderful
manifestations of nature, so startling and so beautiful that everyone recognizes the obligation of the government to preserve them for the edification
and recreation of the people." [15] When Congress finally established the NPS
in August 1916, the agency's Organic Act again contained dual, and potentially contradictory, aims: it required the NPS to manage the parks "to conserve the scenery and the natural and historic objects and the wildlife therein,"
while at the same time providing for "the enjoyment of the same in such manner and by such means as will leave them unimpaired for the enjoyment of
future generations." [16]

According to Park Service historian Richard West Sellars, the park system's
founders simply assumed that most natural areas would be preserved. Visitation was modest relative to the scale of the parks, and nature seemed resil-
ient.[17] From the outset, however, NPS officials aggressively promoted park
visitation because the agency's first director, Stephen Mather, recognized that
tourists would form the base of public support that would allow the system to
expand and thrive. As longtime Park Service observer Michael Frome writes,
Mather was well aware that "bears and trees don't vote and wilderness preserved doesn't bring revenue to the federal treasury." [18] In hopes of raising the
parks' profile and thereby establishing a secure place for the NPS in the federal bureaucracy, Mather encouraged the development of roads, hotels, concessions, and railroad access. Congress condoned the NPS's evolving management philosophy by sanctioning road building within and outside the
parks and by failing to require (or fund) scientific research by the service.

Despite Mather's best efforts, the political constituency he envisioned
never materialized. Instead, as political scientists Jeanne Clarke and Daniel
McCool observe, summer visitors to the parks remained "diverse, unorga-
nized, and largely unaware of the political and funding problems facing the
Park Service." [19] Although the burgeoning numbers of park visitors did not
coalesce to lobby on behalf of the NPS, the parks' concessionaires, railroads,
and automobile organizations quickly became vocal clients of the agency. The
Organic Act allowed the NPS to "grant privileges, leases, and permits for the

use of the land for the accommodation of visitors in the various parks, monu-ments, or other reservations."[20] The act placed minimal restrictions on con-cessionaires' twenty-year leases, and its provisions, taken together, "placed substantial qualifications on what Congress meant when it required the parks to be 'unimpaired.' "[21] The 1965 Concessions Policy Act modified concession-aires' mandate somewhat, allowing them to provide only those services deemed "necessary and appropriate." But it also cemented concessionaires' privileges by giving them a "possessory interest"—that is, all the attributes of ownership except legal title—to any capital improvements they erected on park land.

The consequences were predictable: it became virtually impossible to limit concessions in and around the parks, and the overall trend was toward allow-ing more access to more types of tourists. As Frome explains, over time, polit-ical necessity forced the parks to emphasize recreation "complete with urban malls, supermarkets, superhighways, airplanes and helicopters sightseeing overhead, snowmobiling, rangers who know they can get ahead by being policemen, and nature carefully kept in its place. Park service visitors expect comfort, convenience, and short-order wilderness served like fast food."[22] The rise in tourism took its toll, and from the 1950s and through the 1980s observers decried the parks' deterioration. In 1953 Bernard DeVoto wrote a piece in *Harper's*, "Let's Close the National Parks," in which he expressed dismay at the parks' inadequate staff and funding and their decrepit infrastructure. A fifteen-part series published by the *Christian Science Monitor* in spring and summer 1968 entitled "Will Success Spoil the National Parks?" deplored overcrowding and fantasized about policies to reduce the intrusiveness of park visitation.[23] In 1980 the NPS issued a report that identified thousands of threats to the integrity of the park system, including air and water pollution, overuse, over-crowding, and unregulated private development at or near park boundaries. A 1980 General Accounting Office (GAO) investigation looked at twelve of the most popular parks and found they were in extreme disrepair. A 1986 article in *U.S. News & World Report* argued that America's 209 million acres of forests, parks, and wildlife refuges were in the greatest peril since being saved from the robber barons during the conservation era at the turn of the twentieth cen-tury.[24] The same year a *Newsweek* article noted that the exponential growth in human ability to dominate nature presents the national parks with their great-est challenge ever.[25] A 1994 article in *National Geographic* ruminated on the problems facing the parks, from deteriorating air quality to invasive species to overcrowding and budget woes.[26] And another investigation by the GAO in 1994 reported on damage to the parks outside their borders.[27]

THE CASE

As with many of the activities that threatened the parks by the mid-1990s, the introduction of snowmobiles into Yellowstone National Park at first seemed innocuous. Within a decade, however, manufacturers were advertising bigger, faster machines; outfitters were aggressively promoting the sport; and affluent baby boomers were responding. By the mid-1990s the tiny gateway town of West Yellowstone, Montana (population 761) was billing itself as "the snowmobile capital of the world," and more than 1,000 snowmobiles were entering the park on peak weekend days. After failing to get a response to their requests, in 1997 environmentalists sued the NPS to force it to address the issue of exploding snowmobile use in Yellowstone. The lawsuit in turn triggered a series of administrative and judicial decisions that highlighted the intense differences between those who value the parks for their serenity and those who regard them as playgrounds.

Allowing Snowmobiles in Yellowstone

During the park's first 100 years, managing wildlife was park staff's chief concern, but they also had to regulate human visitation. In 1915 Yellowstone officially allowed automobiles into the park after several years of public debate, in which local automobile organizations pressed resistant park managers for admittance. The number of visitors arriving in cars increased dramatically thereafter: in 1915 more than 80 percent of the park's 52,000 visitors arrived on trains, but by 1930 only about 10 percent of the park's 227,000 visitors came by rail. In 1940 the number of visitors rose to half a million, almost all of whom drove, and, with the exception of the war years, the number climbed steadily thereafter. One million visitors toured the park in 1949, and 2 million came in 1965.[28]

These visitors came in the summer, however, and the park's long winter months remained a time of snowy silence. All that changed in the early 1960s, when a few businessmen from West Yellowstone persuaded park officials to allow snowmobiles into the park as a way of creating some winter business. The number of snowmobilers remained modest through the 1960s, with only 10,000 riders entering the park during the winter of 1968–1969.[29] And, as journalist Todd Wilkinson points out, those intrepid early snowmobilers "encountered no open hotels or restaurants, no gas stations or warming huts, no grooming machines or fleets of vehicles used to shuttle skiers to the interior."[30]

In 1971, however, the NPS started grooming the park's snow-covered roads, and from then on the number of visitors began to increase: during the winter of 1973–1974, 30,000 snowmobilers entered the park; nearly 40,000 did so in the winter of 1986–1987.[31] Snowmobile outfitters were thrilled with the growing numbers: "People think it's great," said Joel Gough, an employee at the Flagg Ranch, "It's Yellowstone, it's the middle of winter, and they're on a snowmobile. They seem to thrive on it." But others were concerned. Park officials talked about the ecological stresses imposed by the soaring snowmobile population, and ranger Gerald Mernin fretted, "Sometimes it seems like you see more snowmobiles en route from West Yellowstone to Old Faithful than you do cars on a busy day in the summer."[32] In addition, the park was feeling the financial pinch of having to groom and patrol 180 miles of roads all winter.

In early spring 1987 officials began preparing a plan for managing winter operations that would address how much of the park should be accessible to snowmobiles. At the time, however, management assistant Judy Kuncl acknowledged that "politically, limiting snowmobiles or other visitation to the park is not a viable option." [33] Even so, the plan, released in 1990, forecast that the park would have to consider limiting snowmobile access when the number of winter visitors reached an arbitrary threshold of 140,000, which it expected would be around 2000. Within just two years of making this projection, however, the number of winter visitors topped 143,000, and 60 percent of them used snowmobiles. Yellowstone had become "a premier snowmobiling destination." [34]

The Origins of the Snowmobile Ban

By the mid-1990s the effects of increased snowmobile use in Yellowstone were unmistakable. At Old Faithful, the park's most popular destination, the wait for gasoline at the service station reached forty-five minutes, and exhaust smell permeated the parking lots. In 1994 the park received 110 letters from winter visitors, almost all complaining about congestion and related air pollution and harassment of wildlife.[35] In early 1995, after employees complained of headaches and nausea during heavy snowmobile-traffic days, Yellowstone park officials set up monitors to gauge carbon monoxide levels in the West Yellowstone entrance booths. They also pressed superintendent Bob Barbee to come up with a comprehensive monitoring program that would quantify the hazards facing the employees and the biological resources.

In January 1995 the park began a two-year study to determine the effects of over-snow traffic. The following month park officials reported that during the President's Day weekend air pollution levels at West Yellowstone violated federal air quality standards.[36] In early 1996 the NPS reported that fourteen months of measurement revealed that the nation's highest carbon monoxide (CO) levels occurred in Yellowstone on busy winter days.[37] In March researchers riding a snowmobile rigged with an air monitoring device had recorded CO levels of 36 parts per million (ppm) along the well-traveled fourteen-mile stretch between West Yellowstone and Madison Junction. The federal CO limit is 35 ppm, and the highest level recorded anywhere else in the nation in 1995 was 32 ppm in Southern California's Imperial County.[38]

Environmentalists and park officials expressed concerned not just about emissions but also about snowmobiles' impact on bison and other wildlife. In the winter of 1996–1997 Montana livestock officials killed 1,084 bison out of a herd of 3,500 when they wandered out of the park on roads groomed for snow machines.[39] (State livestock officials worried the bison carried brucellosis, a disease that can contaminate cattle herds and cause pregnant cows to miscarry.) According to research biologist Mary Meagher, grooming the roads removed the natural fence of snow depth and caused a population explosion among the bison. "We have screwed up the system royally," she told journalist Bryan Hodgson.[40]

Although its own staff members were disgruntled, park officials feared the political repercussions of limiting snowmobile access to the park. But their delays infuriated environmental activists, who had been warning NPS for more than a year that they would sue if the agency did not conduct an environmental impact statement (EIS) for winter uses, and in May 1997 the Fund for Animals and the Biodiversity Legal Foundation filed a lawsuit against the NPS. Having spent two years studying the impact of motorized recreation in winter, the groups alleged that the park's existing winter use plan violated the National Environmental Policy Act and the Endangered Species Act. Four months later the NPS announced a settlement in which it agreed to start work on an EIS to consider a full range of winter uses for Yellowstone, Grand Teton National Park, and the John D. Rockefeller Memorial Parkway. The agency also agreed to consider closing a fourteen-mile stretch of road to see what effect it had on the bison—a decision that provoked fury among local economic interests. "I'm beyond upset," said Vikki Eggers of the Wyoming Chamber of Commerce, "I'm purple with rage." Sen. Conrad Burns, R-Mont., expressed his intent to weigh in on behalf of his development-oriented constituents, claiming that "By caving in to a radical group . . . the Park Service has unnecessarily placed a lot of small businesses and the families that rely on them in jeopardy." [41]

Framing the Snowmobile Debate

The looming prospect of limits on snowmobile use in Yellowstone sparked a fierce debate that reflected the two sides' vastly different views on the appropriate use of the nation's parks. Environmentalists focused on snowmobiles' harmful impacts on air quality and wildlife and their inconsistency with the park's legal mandates. For them Yellowstone was a place where visitors should be able to wander through a landscape that had changed little since the 1800s and appreciate nature for its own sake. They regarded peace and quiet as central components of that experience. Scott Carsley, who guides skiers and hikers in Yellowstone, said, "There are just too many snowmobiles. They're loud. They stink. They ruin people's trips." [42] "There's no question the winter experience is diminished [by snowmobiles]," according to Jim Halfpenny, a Gardiner, Montana, scientist and guide.[43] Journalist Ben Long, who went to Yellowstone to try a snowmobile and see what the fuss was about, wrote:

> No matter how fast or far we went, we couldn't outrun the other snowmobilers. In three days of trying, we did not escape their racket. The engine noise muffled the earthy gurgles of the geysers and hot pots around Old Faithful. When we skied across wolf tracks along the Firehole River, we cocked our ears to listen for them. The only howling packs we heard were mechanical. We stopped to gaze at the haunting beauty of a trumpeter swan, swimming against the steaming current of the Madison River, as snowflakes showered down. But to do so we had to dodge a steady flow of rushing snowmobiles, like city pedestrians trying to cross against a traffic light.[44]

Long concluded that the biggest problem was "the carnival atmosphere that comes along with hundreds of zippy little machines. They quickly overshadow nature. The machine becomes the point of the visit. To snowmobile is to out-muscle nature, not enjoy it." [45]

Others deplored the snowmobiling "culture." For example, Bob Schaap, a native of the area, said he lost his taste for snowmobilers as a result of his experience owning a motel in West Yellowstone, where they roared drunkenly through town after the bars closed. Some critics spoke of snowmobilers who ignored private property and wilderness area boundaries and were unconcerned with fragile winter ecology and traffic laws.[46] As the machines became faster and more powerful, snowmobilers were able to ride deeper into wilderness, and illegal routes multiplied and further tempted trespassers. Mike Finley, the outspoken former Yellowstone superintendent, said of snowmobilers: "They are not bad people, but they think they have a God-given right to engage in an activity that has adverse effects on human health and the environment. They are either in denial about the extent of their actions or they don't really care." [47]

By contrast, snowmobilers focused on Yellowstone's recreational value and asserted the right to experience it in whatever way they chose. Adena Cook of the Idaho-based off-road advocacy group, the Blue Ribbon Coalition, said, "It's a public place, just like Niagara Falls. It's a natural phenomenon, but natural doesn't equate to wild." She added, "If at certain times things are a little crowded, that means you're doing something right. I really resist people telling us something is for our own good, especially when it's the federal government." [48] Jeff Vigean, a Bostonian, said, "If we're banned from the park, they're taking away my right to bring my kids here someday, to show them Yellowstone in the wintertime." From this perspective, efforts to limit snowmobile access were exclusive and unfair. Clark Collins, executive director of the Blue Ribbon Coalition, said of environmentalists: "Theirs is a very selfish, biased and elitist viewpoint. Where do they get off deciding what types of access is appropriate?" [49] "Face it, there are a lot of folks who just don't have the time to go cross-country skiing to Old Faithful," said one Midwestern visitor. "It's our park too, and this is the only way we can see it in winter." [50]

Snowmobile boosters touted the freedom the machines allow. As one snowmobiler pointed out, "You can't see much of the park on cross-country skis. We saw coyotes, moose, buffalo, elk." [51] Entrepreneur Jerry Schmier suggested anti-snowmobiling sentiment was nothing more than jealousy because snowmobilers could get to areas that cross-country skiers would never see. "In their minds, they'd like to get back into a quiet, pristine forest," he said. "They don't want to hear anything but the birds. But by the same token, many of these people never get more than a mile away from civilization. And the truth of the matter is they never will. With the snowmobiles you have freedom. You can go anywhere you want." [52] According to Brad Schmier of Yellowstone Adventures: "A snowmobile lets you be at one with the elements on your own little vehicle. The majority of the people who come here like that independence, being able to go at their own schedules—that will be a hard thing to take away from us Americans." He added, "Do I want to climb in a coach with 10 other people and somebody's whiny kid and sit there shoulder to shoulder with everybody and climb in and out when the driver decides we're going to stop? It doesn't sound like fun to me." [53]

Snowmobilers portrayed themselves as responsible, family-oriented people, pointing to industry surveys that said the average snowmobile rider was forty-one and married with children.[54] Jim Grogan, a real estate agent from Florida, described himself and his friends: "We're not yahoos; we're responsible people. We've got families and jobs and we're responsible. I'd call myself an environmentalist." [55] Many others depicted themselves as environmentalists as well, citing the trail work that snowmobile clubs perform. Ted Chlarson, a cattle trucker from Utah, said that environmentalists wanted to know how he could enjoy Yellowstone's beautiful scenery with all the noise from his snowmobile. He answered: "Well, I may not hear it, but I can see it. I can be riding on this noisy thing and I got my solitude." [56] To boost its image, the industry promoted safety standards, distributed rules of good conduct, and encouraged snowmobile clubs to get involved in local charities.

Snowmobile supporters also minimized the human health and environmental risks associated with the vehicles. Industry officials contended that snowmobile emissions occurred in remote areas and were dispersed by the wind. "There is no evidence to support the claim that snowmobile exhaust emissions cause damage to flora, fauna or the land or water," according to these officials. Roy Muth, who retired in late 1994 as president of the International Snowmobile Industry Association (ISIA), called the claims that a single snowmobile generates as much air pollution as 1,000 automobiles (a figure based on a California Air Resources Board study conducted in the 1980s) "irrational." [57] Snowmobile advocates also gleefully cited a study that showed cross-country skiers frightened elk and moose more than snowmobilers because they came upon them quietly and startled them, whereas the animals could hear a snowmobile a quarter of a mile away.[58]

While disparaging the claims of environmental impacts, snowmobile advocates emphasized the consequences of limiting the vehicles. Employing a slippery slope argument, some suggested that imposing a ban on snowmobiles in Yellowstone would lead inevitably to a prohibition of all forms of recreation on public lands. Ed Klim, president of the snowmobile manufacturers association, warned: "This may be happening to snowmobiles today, but I tell you tomorrow it will be campers and the next day it will be sport utility vehicles." [59] But advocates' most potent threat was the prospect of local economic decline. To reinforce their claims, they cited the money snowmobilers poured into the regional economy, claiming, for example, that in the late 1980s snowmobilers in Canada and the United States spent more than $3.2 billion on their sport each year.[60] Proponents also cited the "happiness" factor: "Snowmobile tourists spend a ton of money—between $200 and $300 a day for a family of four," said David McCray, manager of Two Top Snowmobile Inc. "And most of them come back saying it was the best day of their trip, even the best day of their lives." [61]

Motorized Recreation Versus Protection

The controversy over snowmobiles in Yellowstone was part of a larger debate over the explosion in motorized recreation on public lands. As legal scholar Robert Keiter observes, although once welcomed as an alternative to extractive industries, the new tourism-recreation economy posed environmental threats of its own.

> Rather than clearcuts and open pit mines, its legacy is suburban-like sprawl, new ranchettes, and mega-resorts that chop once pastoral landscapes into smaller and smaller fragments. As new homes and secondary roads spread across vacant agricultural lands, open space begins to disappear, winter wildlife habitat is lost, seasonal migration routes are disrupted, and erosion problems are exacerbated. . . . Unlike the site-specific impacts associated with a mine or timber sale, recreationists are ubiquitous; the mere presence of more people will generate more human waste, create more unauthorized travel routes, and disturb more wildlife. Motorized recreational users often compound those problems, particularly as they demand more roads and trails into undisturbed areas. The cumulative impact of myriad recreational users and related sprawling development places the very environmental qualities that lured them in the first place at risk. [62]

Conflicts among users became more intense in the 1980s and 1990s as people had more leisure time and money to pursue happiness outdoors, and the development and sale of motorized recreational vehicles boomed. In 1972 an estimated 5 million Americans used off-road vehicles; personal watercraft, such as JetSkis, and all-terrain vehicles did not exist. By 2002 the Forest Service estimated 36 million people used these machines. Between 1992 and 2001 annual sales of all-terrain vehicles rose from 169,000 to 825,000. Snowmobile registration increased more than 60 percent during the same period. [63]

Federal agencies had the legal authority to restrict motorized recreation but rarely invoked it, choosing instead to ignore the most egregious abuses on their lands and watch passively as surrounding communities built their economic futures on such activities. As a result, by the 1990s motorized vehicles were pervasive throughout the nation's public lands, and relations between hikers and off-road vehicles were strained. Environmentalists pointed out that recreational machines had a range of negative impacts, from scarring the landscape to causing erosion and noise, air, and water pollution to disturbing wildlife and carving up habitat. They wanted public lands closed to motorized recreational use except for specifically designated trails. They argued that the national obsession with extreme sports increased the likelihood that some off-road vehicle users would break the rules if they had access to remote areas; they pointed to commercials for trucks that showed vehicles cutting across streams and fragile meadows or driving onto beaches. "The message is this is something you ought to be doing, and it doesn't matter what the damage to the land," said Jerry Greenberg of the Wilderness Society.[64]

By contrast, proponents of motorized recreation portrayed the conflict as a dispute between average families and a small number of privileged athletes. Rep. Ron Marlenee, R-Mont., argued: "Mom and pop and their ice-cream-smeared kids have as much right to prime recreational opportunities as the tanned, muscled elitists who climb in the wilderness." [65] Proponents also portrayed their adversaries as extremists and said there was little prospect for cooperation as long as environmentalists wanted to turn large tracts of the West into federal wilderness areas.

The Evolution of the Snowmobile Ban

Throughout 1998, as the NPS collected data and met with local officials about the winter use plan, the controversy bubbled, and momentum built nationally for curbing snowmobiles. An editorial in *USA Today* on February 19, 1998, suggested eliminating snowmobiles from Yellowstone altogether: "Throughout the winter, there are days when the Yellowstone plateau looks and sounds more like Daytona than a national park. Thousands of snowmobiles cover its trails like swarms of two-stroke hornets, producing a chain-saw howl and leaving a pall of blue-white haze in the air." The editorial acknowledged that snowmobiles can be fun to ride but argued they should be banned from the park because "The noxious fumes and obnoxious noise quickly can destroy the contemplative park experience sought by millions of others." The editorial added that although "it sometimes seems [Yellowstone] has been deeded over to narrow local interests," Yellowstone's mission is to preserve the natural beauty, not ensure local economic development.

On January 21, 1999, the Bluewater Network—a coalition of sixty environmental groups—filed a petition with the NPS to ban snowmobiles from all U.S. national parks, saying, "They're killing our wildlife, ruining our air and water quality, poisoning the health of rangers exposed to snowmobiles' carbon monoxide exhaust, and destroying the solitude and peace cherished by other winter visitors." [66] Bluewater cited "adverse impacts to park wildlife, air and water quality, vegetation, park ecology, and park users." The network pointed to its analysis of government data, which showed that snowmobiles dumped about 50,000 gallons of raw gasoline into the snow pack in 1998.[67] The petition claimed that snowmobiles created more pollution around Old Faithful in one weekend than an entire year's worth of automobile traffic. Manufacturers objected to such assertions, which they called "unscientific," but they had no data to refute them. Instead, they disparaged the litigants and tried to shift attention to the economic consequences of a snowmobile ban. Ed Klim described the lawsuit as "a rather extreme move by a small group that wants to limit access to the parks." And West Yellowstone businessman Brad Schmier said, "A ban would put me out of business. Snowmobiling is our community's only winter economy." [68]

In response to environmentalists' petition, in July the park released a draft EIS that contained seven alternatives, ranging from unrestricted snowmobiling to restricted use. None of the options eliminated snowmobiles or trail grooming. Nevertheless, at public meetings held around the West, the NPS raised the possibility of prohibiting snowmobiles from the park, and in mid-March 2000 Yellowstone officials told state and local officials that the agency was leaning toward a ban. They conceded that, although the agency had originally favored phasing in cleaner machines over ten years, and representatives of local governments had also proposed converting the fleet over time, neither approach seemed to resolve the park's legal obligations. NPS officials pointed out that the Yellowstone Act requires the NPS to preserve "from injury or spoliation" the "wonders" of the park and ensure "their retention in their natural condition"; the National Park Service Organic Act of 1916 directs superintendents to conserve scenery, national and historic objects, and wildlife and to "leave them unimpaired for future generations"; and the Clean Air Act requires national parks to preserve, protect, and enhance their air quality. In addition, two executive orders require the NPS to limit motorized recreation: No. 11644, signed by President Richard Nixon in 1972, mandated that each agency establish regulations designating specific zones of use for off-road vehicles and that such chosen areas be located to "minimize harassment of wildlife and significant disruption of wildlife habitats." No. 11989, signed by President Jimmy Carter in 1977, strengthened the 1972 order, stating that if an agency head determined the use of off-road vehicles will cause "considerable adverse effects on the soil, vegetation, wildlife, wildlife habitat or cultural or historic resources of particular areas or trails of the public lands" the agency head shall "immediately close such areas or trails to off-road vehicles." Furthermore, NPS regulations prohibit the disturbance of any wildlife from their "natural state" and prohibit the use of snowmobiles "except where designated and when their use is consistent with the park's natural, cultural, scenic and aesthetic values, safety considerations, and park management objectives, and will not disturb wildlife or damage park resources."

As a ban began to appear imminent, newspapers around the country came out in support of it: an editorial in the Portland *Oregonian* on November 18, 1999, described "a slow-but-sure desecration of one of Nature's crown jewels. Just imagine some 60,000 snowmobiles belching blue smoke as they slice through white powder, bound over the hills and along streambanks, sounding like a reunion of jackhammer operators." (An outraged reader rightly retorted that 60,000 snowmobiles are not all in the park at once.) As winter approached, editorials in the *Omaha World Herald*, the *New York Times*, and the *San Francisco Chronicle* likewise lined up behind the proposed ban.

The NPS's inclination reflected not only the agency's legal constraints and public sentiment but also the values of the Interior Department's political appointees. A flurry of similarly protective verdicts on mechanized recreation in the parks accompanied the announcement that the NPS was seriously considering a snowmobile ban. On March 15, 2000, Congress passed a bill banning tourist flights over Rocky Mountain National Park and requiring all national parks to complete air-tour management plans in cooperation with the Federal Aviation Administration. On March 21 the NPS issued a rule banning personal watercraft from all but 21 of its 379 parks and recreation areas. Previously, the watercraft had been allowed in eighty-seven parks.[69] Two days later Interior Secretary Bruce Babbitt unveiled a plan to reduce auto congestion in Yosemite. The plan called for tearing out several parking lots inside the park, reducing the number of parking spaces from 1,600 to 550, and having visitors park in lots at the edges of the park and take shuttle buses into the valley. The following day President Bill Clinton announced new restrictions on sightseeing flights over Grand Canyon National Park.

In line with this trend, in April the NPS issued a memo directing parks that currently allowed snowmobiling to review their regulations and within a year amend or replace them with regulations that complied with existing laws and regulations. The announcement specifically excluded Denali and eleven other parks in Alaska where snowmobiling is explicitly permitted by law; Voyageurs, where the law establishing the park permitted snowmobiling; and Yellowstone, Grant Teton, and the John D. Rockefeller Memorial Parkway, for which the NPS was in the midst of crafting a winter use plan. In the other parks that snowmobilers used, the agency planned to allow them only on small sections to gain access to adjacent lands. Announcing the ban, Donald Barry, assistant secretary of Interior for fish and wildlife and parks said, "Snowmobiles are noisy, antiquated machines that are no longer welcome in our national parks. The snowmobile industry has had many years to clean up their act, and they haven't." [70]

An approving editorial in the *New York Times* of April 29, 2000, said:

> What Mr. Barry's announcement underscores is the simple principle that America's national parks should lead the nation in adherence to environmental law. Recreation is not incompatible with strict adherence. It is enhanced. For years snowmobiling has been tolerated even though it violated the law, and its environmental impacts had scarcely been monitored until recently. But now that the impact of snowmobiling is clearly understood and the extent of its pollution clearly documented, overlooking the law has become intolerable.

Editorials in the *Denver Post* and *Seattle Times* also endorsed the decision. Nevertheless, in hopes of prompting Congress to pass a law preventing the NPS from phasing out snowmobiles in the parks, in late May legislative opponents of a ban convened hearings in the House and Senate. At those hearings, and in a flurry of press releases that accompanied them, environmentalists emphasized the NPS's legal obligation to protect the park's resources, the scientific evidence that snowmobiles harmed those resources, and the public's overwhelming support for a snowmobile ban. Defenders of the status quo disputed and downplayed the scientific evidence and highlighted the economic importance of snowmobiling to the region.

Debating the Science. In testimony before the Senate Energy Committee's Subcommittee on National Parks, Historic Preservation, and Recreation, Barry described the pollution caused by snowmobiles' two-stroke engines:

> First, up to one-third of the fuel delivered to the engine goes straight through and out the tailpipe without being burned. Second, lubricating oil is mixed directly into the fuel, and is expelled as part of the exhaust. Third, poor combustion results in high emissions of air pollutants as well as several toxic pollutants, such as benzene and aromatic hydrocarbons that the EPA classifies as known probable human carcinogens. When compared to other emissions estimates, a snowmobile using a conventional two-stroke engine, on a per-passenger mile basis, emits approximately 36 times more carbon monoxide and 98 times more hydrocarbons than an automobile.[71]

Barry added that winter meteorological conditions—particularly cold temperatures, stable atmospheric conditions, and light winds—exacerbated the accumulation of pollutants in the air. He cited the NPS study, *Air Quality Concerns Related to Snowmobile Usage*, which found that "although there are 16 times more cars than snowmobiles in Yellowstone, snowmobiles generate between 68 and 90 percent of all hydrocarbons and 35 to 68 percent of all carbon monoxide released in [the park]." [72]

In addition to detailing air pollution impacts, Barry referred to noise studies showing that the "relentless whine" of snowmobiles was persistent and inescapable in the park. For example, in March 2000, two environmental groups, the Greater Yellowstone Coalition and the National Parks Conservation Association, had released a study providing data that substantiated complaints about snowmobiles' noise. Using methods established by the NPS, volunteers had listened at a variety of often-used places in the Old Faithful area. Of the thirteen spots chosen, they documented eleven where the sound of snowmobiles was audible 70 percent of the time or more. At Old Faithful itself listeners heard snowmobiles 100 percent of the time. They found that only one place, the most remote location in the sample, was free of snowmobile sound. (Vikki Eggers responded to the study by saying that the park's mandate was not to preserve quiet, pointing out that motorcycles in the summer are noisy too.[73]) And Barry warned of the possibility that unburned gasoline could reach park streams and lakes as snow melted. And he pointed out that snowmobilers regularly harass bison, noting that winter is already the most stressful time for Yellowstone's wildlife. He concluded that the new machines, although cleaner and quieter were neither clean nor quiet and in any case did not eliminate the problem of wildlife harassment. In short, he said, snowmobiling "is not an essential, or the most appropriate, means for appreciating park resources in winter." [74]

Testifying before the Senate subcommittee, Mark Simonich, director of Montana's environmental quality department, disputed the NPS claim that air quality standards had been exceeded in the park. He added that there were short-term technological solutions—including the use of ethanol blend fuels and biodegradable lubrication oils—to the environmental problems posed by two-stroke-engine snowmobiles and claimed that cleaner, quieter four-stroke-engine vehicles would soon be available.[75] Although snowmobile groups did not contest the park's air pollution figures, they accused the NPS of rushing the study to comply with the lawsuit and fanning the flames of controversy by comparing Yellowstone's particulate concentrations with those of a Los Angeles suburb.

Local Economic Impacts. Snowmobilers and their supporters said they felt as though their concerns had been ignored, and they raised the specter of economic disaster if the ban were implemented. Kim Raap, trail-system officer with the Wyoming Department of Commerce, pointed out that snowmobiles contributed between $100 million and $150 million to the state's economy.[76] The Jackson Hole Chamber of Commerce said the move would devastate the local economy, claiming that snowmobile outfitting in Jackson Hole brought in $1.3 million annually and that nearly 20 percent of West Yellowstone's total resort taxes were collected during the winter season.[77] Adena Cook of the Blue Ribbon Coalition claimed the ban would cost neighboring communities 1,000 jobs and $100 million a year in tourism revenues.[78] Testifying July 13, 2000, before the House Small Business Committee's Tax, Finance, and Exports Subcommittee, Clyde Seely, owner of the Three Bear Lodge in West Yellowstone, warned: "Cuts will have to be made. The first cut would be employee insurance. The second cut would be employees."

But Kevin Collins of the National Parks Conservation Association pointed out that the mission of the Park Service was to preserve places in their original condition so they would be available for future generations, not provide economic benefits for nearby communities and businesses. Collins added that the economic impact of a snowmobile phaseout had been "greatly exaggerated," noting that the economist who assessed the rule's likely impact on West Yellowstone found it to be negligible—approximately $5 million—and temporary. And he concluded that in the long run the region's economy depended on the park's ecological health.[79]

To the chagrin of western lawmakers who were intent on demonstrating the adverse local impacts of a snowmobile ban, some residents of West Yellowstone went to Washington to make clear to Congress that locals were not monolithic on the issue. One resident carried a petition signed by 160 people (the town's entire population was still less than 1,000) asking lawmakers to protect the park and help the town diversify. Craig Mathews, a West Yellowstone native who supported the ban, said people in town had stopped waving at or greeting him. He accused those people of being more concerned with making a profit than with the "air our kids breathe" and said that they were developing an "NRA [National Rifle Association] mentality, contending that a successful ban on snowmobiling in national parks will eventually lead to bans on walking, hiking, fishing, and camping on public lands."[80] Other local supporters of the ban said it was necessary to restore the pristine glory of Yellowstone, noting that, should it be lost, tourists would not come anymore.

Still others said they were fed up with the constant roar of snowmobiles at all hours of night on the city streets. (Earlier in the year a group of West Yellowstone High School students had petitioned city hall to pass an ordinance banning recreational snowmobile use in town between 11:00 p.m. and 5:00 a.m., but the town declined to take any action.)

A New Ideology and a New Rule

In October 2000 the NPS issued a final EIS on the winter use plan for Yellowstone and Grand Teton national parks. The plan selected the environmentally preferred alternative, which phased out snowmobile use altogether by 2003–2004 and restricted winter access to snowcoaches, snowshoes, and skis. Rep. Barbara Cubin, R-Wyo., charged the process was a "farce" whose "outcome was predestined by the Clinton-Gore administration and its extremist environmental cohorts" and vowed to use every regulatory and legislative means necessary to achieve a compromise.[81] Nevertheless, in November the NPS signed a record of decision, and in December the agency issued a proposed rule. The snowmobile industry immediately sued to block the new rule, saying it was not supported by the facts, and all three members of the Wyoming delegation denounced the ban. In response to the plea of Sen. Craig Thomas, R-Wyo., Congress approved a two-year delay in the phaseout, giving the newly elected president, George Bush, an opportunity to block it.

The Bush administration's ideology, which was diametrically opposed to that of the Clinton administration, manifested itself in a dramatic turnaround vis-á-vis snowmobiles. Just hours after he was sworn in, President Bush signed an executive order imposing a sixty-day moratorium on the ban in order to review it. That winter snowmobilers entered Yellowstone in record numbers. The number of sleds coming in through the west entrance jumped nearly 37 percent in January to 21,742.[82] (There was also a 32 percent increase in the number of people coming in by snowcoach, to 2,042.) On President's Day weekend a total of 4,339 snowmobilers poured into the park—at a rate of one every ten seconds.[83] In mid-February Senator Thomas introduced legislation to rescind the snowmobile ban altogether.

In late April, as Earth Day neared, the Bush administration tried to shore up its environmental credentials by announcing that it would allow the snowmobile ban to stand. At the same time, however, the Interior Department was actively negotiating with snowmobile manufacturers, and in June 2001 the NPS settled the manufacturers' lawsuit by agreeing to conduct a supplemental environmental impact statement (SEIS) that considered data on new snowmobile technologies. In the meantime, the park would allow unlimited access in winter 2002–2003, but limit entries in 2003–2004 to 493 snowmobiles per day. Defending its decision not to defend the Clinton-era rule, Interior Department spokesman Mark Pfeifle said: "This administration feels strongly that greater local input, new information, scientific data and economic analysis and wider public involvement can only lead to better, more informed decisions." [84] Yellowstone Superintendent Mike Finley pointed out, however, that in formulating the settlement administration officials had not consulted anyone working in the park.

In February 2002 the NPS released its draft SEIS. The new impact statement did not furnish any evidence that contradicted the Clinton administration's decision; instead, it characterized the information submitted by the snowmobile industry about technology designed to cut noise and air pollution as "speculative and insufficient for analysis purposes." [85] It added that banning snowmobiles would reduce jobs and the local economy by less than 1 percent.[86] Nevertheless, the agency carefully avoided recommending proceeding with the ban, and in late June the Bush administration announced at a meeting with local state and county governments that it would allow snowmobiling in the park to continue but would restrict traffic volume and address noise and air pollution concerns. (In early July Democrats and eastern Republicans introduced legislation to restore the ban, but the move was pure politics; although the bill quickly garnered 100 cosponsors, the Republican-controlled House had no intention of letting the chamber vote on it.)

During the comment period, the NPS received more than 350,000 reactions to the SEIS, 80 percent of which supported the ban.[87] Nevertheless, on November 18, 2002, the NPS released a final rule delaying the implementation of a phaseout for another year. The agency also announced the administration's plan to allow 950 snowmobiles per day into the park, a 35 percent increase over the historical average of 840 per day—though well below the number that entered the park on peak weekend days. To soften the blow, the plan required that rented machines conform to best available technology standards and required that, beginning in the winter of 2003–2004, 80 percent of snowmobiles entering the park be accompanied by a guide. The administration justified its plan by saying there had been major improvements in snowmobile technology—in particular the introduction of the four-stroke engine, which according to a park spokesman cut noise from 79 to 73 decibels and emissions by 90 percent.[88] The administration called its approach a "balanced" one that would allow the public to continue using the park in winter and the nearby tourism industry to survive.

A critical editorial in the Minneapolis *Star Tribune* noted that the plan contained no clear standards for determining its own effectiveness. Instead, it set the number of snowmobiles and assumed that whatever noise and smoke that number of machines emits would be fine. "A more sensible approach," the editor urged, "would start with some management goals and work backward to policy," making sure that snowmobile use was consistent with a national park's "natural, cultural, scenic and aesthetic values, safety considerations, park management objectives, and will not disturb wildlife or damage park resources." The editorial noted that the park's new vision was about starting points, not outcomes, and that the Bush administration had "[spun] the giveaway to snowmobile clubs, companies and local businesses as stewardship for balanced use of the park." [89]

In February 2003 the NPS issued a final SEIS containing five alternatives, including an "environmentally preferred" option identical to the original phaseout. But this time the NPS selected Alternative 4, which had not been included in the draft SEIS but contained the administration's new approach, as its preferred alternative. The NPS signed the 2003 record of decision affirming the administration's plan in March, issued a proposed rule to accompany it in April, and published the final rule in December.[90]

Legal Challenges

It appeared as though the Bush administration would be thwarted, however, when just hours before the advent of the 2003–2004 snowmobiling season, Judge Emmet Sullivan of the U.S. District Court of the District of Columbia overturned the Bush rule and reinstated the Clinton-era snowmobile phaseout. In December 2002—after the Bush administration released its proposed rule for snowmobiles in Yellowstone and Grand Teton—a coalition of environmental groups had filed suit in Washington, D.C., claiming the new rule ignored requirements that national parks be preserved in a way that leaves them "unimpaired for the enjoyment of future generations." In his ruling on the case, Sullivan—a Reagan appointee—criticized the Bush administration's decision-making process, pointing to its reversal of the rule despite the fact that there had been no change in the scientific evidence supporting it. "The gap between the decision made in 2001 and the decision made in 2003 is stark," he said. "In 2001, the rule-making process culminated in a finding that snowmobiling so adversely impacted the wildlife and resources of the parks that all snowmobile use must be halted. A scant three years later, the rule-making process culminated in the conclusion that nearly 1,000 snowmobiles will be allowed to enter the park each day." Sullivan pointed out that the Park Service was "bound by a conservation mandate . . . that trumps all other considerations." He added that the NPS had not supplied a reasoned analysis for its changed position but only cited prospects of improved technology. But the original EIS had considered and rejected the argument that newer, cleaner machines would alleviate the problems associated with snowmobiles in the park. Sullivan concluded that in 2003 the NPS rejected the environmentally preferred alternative in favor of an alternative whose primary beneficiaries were the "park visitors who ride snowmobiles in the parks and the businesses that serve them." [91]

Locals reacted with desperation to the last-minute reinstatement of the ban. Jerry Johnson, mayor of West Yellowstone (and a motel owner and snowmobile outfitter) said, "It's out of control here. People are frantic not to have their vacation ruined." [92] Describing the week after the ruling came down, David McCray, owner of Two Top snowmobile rentals, said: "I saw three grown men in tears. This is their livelihood. This is their identity. This is how they're going to send they're kids to college. It's just so unbelievable that the judge would not take any of this into account." According to Marysue Costello, executive director of the West Yellowstone Chamber of Commerce: "The impact of [a ban] is going to be significant. The ripple effect of this, we're not just talking snowmobile people. It's the schools, the snowplows." [93] Since 1994, six new hotels had been built and at least 400 rooms added in anticipation of winter tourists.[94]

Environmentalists' celebration was short-lived, however: in February 2004 U.S. District Court judge Clarence Brimmer, in Wyoming, responded to the lawsuit originally filed by the manufacturers' association and the Blue Ribbon Coalition in 2000 challenging the snowmobile ban and reopened after Judge Sullivan issued his ruling. Brimmer issued a temporary restraining order requiring the NPS to suspend limits on snowmobiles in Yellowstone and Grand Teton. In overturning the limits, Brimmer ruled that the state of Wyoming and snowmobile touring companies would suffer irreparable harm that "far outweighed" any impact that would be suffered by the park's employees or wildlife. Brimmer credited a claim by Wyoming that the phaseout would cause millions of dollars in losses that could not be recovered or compensated, as well as its claim that, based on the revised (2003) rule, Wyoming outfitters had invested $1.2 million to convert their fleets, booked reservations, taken deposits, and contracted with employees for the 2003–2004 season. In addition, the judge was swayed by the manufacturer's association argument that some businesses were incurring catastrophic losses as a result of the rule and that many subsidiary businesses were threatened as well. In deciding on the balance of harms versus benefits, Brimmer agreed with the plaintiffs that any competing harm to park staff and visitors would be much reduced by new snowmobile technology. He ordered the park to adopt temporary rules to allow four-stroke snowmobiles into the park for the remaining five weeks of the winter. Defending his decision, Brimmer said: "A single Eastern district court judge shouldn't have the unlimited power to impose the old 2001 rule on the public and the business community, any more than a single Western district court judge should have the power to opt for a different rule." [95]

OUTCOMES

In August 2004 the Park Service proposed letting up to 720 guided snowmobiles enter the park each day through the winter of 2006–2007. In her defense of the agency's choice despite overwhelming public sentiment in favor of a ban, Yellowstone superintendent Suzanne Lewis said: "This is not a public opinion poll. This is not about majority votes." [96] The administration's "compromise" rule was bolstered by a ruling by Judge Brimmer in October 2004 striking down the snowmobile ban. Brimmer said the rule had been imposed without allowing for meaningful public participation. He also argued that the NPS had not adequately studied emissions, noise, and other impacts of an increased number of snowmobiles in the park. Turning Judge Sullivan's reasoning on its head, Brimmer argued the government had ignored proper procedures and arrived at a "prejudged political decision to ban snowmobiles from all the national parks." [97]

Just days after the NPS's announcement on November 4 that it would promulgate an interim (three-year) rule allowing 720 snowmobiles into Yellowstone and 140 machines per day into Grand Teton and the John D. Rockefeller Memorial Parkway, lawsuits began flying again. On November 10 the Wyoming Lodging and Restaurant Association filed suit in federal court in Wyoming saying its members wanted more traffic in the park. The Greater Yellowstone Coalition filed in federal court in Washington, D.C., asking the NPS to monitor snowmobiles' impact and reduce their numbers if pollution thresholds were exceeded. The Fund for Animals and Bluewater Network filed a separate suit in Washington charging that the NPS had failed to address the impacts of trail grooming which, according to Bluewater's Sean Smith, changed the dynamics of the entire ecosystem.

In February 2005 Interior Secretary Gale Norton toured the park by snowmobile, making a clear statement about her sympathies. Concluding her trip, Norton said: "We, I think, have a better understanding of what the experience is here and why people are so excited about the opportunity to snowmobile here." Norton also disparaged snowcoaches, saying they offered a "much more ordinary kind of experience" that is "not as special as a snowmobile." [98] Norton's enthusiasm notwithstanding, the number of snowmobiles passing through the park's west entrance in the winter of 2004–2005 was down about 70 percent from two winters earlier: 311 snowmobiles entered on the year's busiest day, and the average was about one-third of the 720 allowed.[99] Although the decline was partly because of the meager snowfall, the main reason was that more passengers were electing to travel by snowcoach. Largely as a result of the decreased snowmobile traffic, the monitors at the West Yellowstone entrance were registering a decrease of 90 percent in carbon monoxide.[100]

CONCLUSIONS

The decision about whether to allow snowmobiles in Yellowstone and other national parks turns on the simple question posed by former NPS director George Hartzog: what are the parks for? More concretely, a 1986 *Newsweek* magazine article asked, "Do the parks exist to conserve nature or to put it on display?" [101] Environmentalists contend that the NPS's highest duty is to protect the parks' unique and fragile natural resources for future generations. They tend to agree with the sentiment expressed by veteran national park observer Michael Frome, who writes: "National parks are sources of caring based on inner feeling, on emotional concern for wolf, bear, insect, tree, and plant, and hopes for the survival of all these species. National parks are schools of awareness, personal growth, and maturity, where the individual learns to appreciate the sanctity of life and to manifest distress and love for the natural world, including the human portion." [102] For protection advocates, as in the Arctic National Wildlife Refuge case, a compromise is a loss because even a small number of motorized vehicles can dramatically change the experience for everyone else.

By contrast, snowmobile proponents contend that the parks belong to all Americans, and that those who choose to enjoy them riding on a snowmobile have a right to do so. It is easier for advocates of motorized recreation to portray themselves as moderate (and environmentalists as extremists): by accepting limits on use advocates can claim to have compromised. Commentary on the issue by Nicholas Kristoff, the iconoclastic *New York Times* columnist, reflects the appeal of this position. He explains that limiting snowmobile access is a "reasonable" solution. He acknowledges that snowmobile manufacturers only developed cleaner, quieter machines when faced with eviction from the park but confirms that the new machines are, in fact, better. He concludes, "Some environmentalists have forgotten . . . that our aim should be not just to preserve nature for its own sake but to give Americans a chance to enjoy the outdoors." [103]

Michael Scott of the Greater Yellowstone Coalition describes the debate as a culture clash that pits "NASCAR vs. Patagonia," and under the Bush administration NASCAR is clearly winning. During the Clinton administration, backed by support from the top, many park superintendents devised plans to curb overcrowding and limit the types and extent of park use. For example, the NPS announced plans to rip up roads and parking lots in the Grand Canyon park and build a light rail system to carry visitors to the South Rim. Yosemite devised a plan to limit the number of cars entering the park. Poll after poll showed public support for such changes: in a 1998 survey conducted by Colorado State University, 95 percent of 590 respondents said the NPS should limit the number of visitors if overuse was harming park resources; 92 percent said they would be willing to ride a shuttle bus to ease traffic congestion rather than drive; and 92 percent said they would be willing to make reservations to visit a popular park to reduce crowding.[104]

But opposition to these limitations was intense and well organized, and advocates of unlimited access found sympathetic allies in the Bush administration, which moved quickly to reverse many of the Clinton-era reforms. For example, in February 2002 the Forest Service delayed closing Montana's Mount Jefferson to snowmobiles even though scientific studies had documented that the vehicles disturbed wolverine and other wildlife, and the public favored closure by two to one. After local politicians demanded that the Forest Service delay decision making in order to take snowmobilers' views into account and see if new information was available, forest supervisor Janette Kaiser acquiesced. In 2003 the Bureau of Land Management reversed a Clinton-era plan to put about 50,000 acres of California's Imperial Sand Dunes Recreation Area off-limits to off-road vehicles, even though these vehicles clearly damage sensitive plants and gatherings of their users have on occasion turned violent. The administration also made it easier for local and state authorities to claim rights-of-way through millions of acres of federal land, potentially opening vast areas to off-road vehicle use. And the NPS began drawing up plans to allow personal watercraft in several western lakes and eastern seashores, undoing a Clinton-era trend to ban their use.

Throughout the Clinton and Bush administrations, advocates who were excluded from or disadvantaged in the decision-making process turned to other venues, particularly the courts. Both sides chose their courts strategically: snowmobile advocates sought recourse in local courtrooms, where judges presumably were more sympathetic to local economic considerations, while environmentalists turned to D.C. judges, who they believed were more dispassionate. The judiciary has both advantages and disadvantages as a forum for resolving disputes over agency decision making. On the one hand, relative to other policymakers, judges are more insulated from public opinion and can—in theory at least—deliberate on the public interest without considering the short-term political ramifications. At the same time, they can take particular situations into account; they do not need to design a policy that is appropriate for every case. And the adversarial structure of judicial decision making creates incentives for both sides to bring forward information, so decisions are likely to be well-informed. On the other hand, judges are limited to reacting to issues in the ways that lawyers have defined them. Moreover, the legalization of issues allows judges to avoid hard questions and tackle the tractable ones—for example, by focusing on a procedural rather than a substantive aspect of the case. And judges are not experts in the areas they are making decisions about and may fail to anticipate consequences of a ruling. The most vocal critics of "adversarial legalism" have focused not on these drawbacks, however, but on the win-lose aspect of judicial decision making, saying it promotes resistance, backlash, and endless appeals. But defenders of the courts point out that most court cases are settled and that judges spend a great deal of time trying to get the two sides to negotiate with one another.

QUESTIONS TO CONSIDER

- What do you think is the appropriate role for motorized recreation on public lands and waters, and why?
- Would a collaborative process have produced a better outcome than the adversarial one did? If so, why, and in what respects? If not, why not?

Notes

1. Richard E. Neustadt, *Presidential Power and the Modern Presidents* (New York: Free Press, 1990).
2. Harold Seidman and Robert Gilmour, *Politics, Position, and Power: From the Positive to the Regulatory State*, 4th ed. (New York: Oxford University Press, 1986), 166–167.
3. Terry Moe, "The Presidency and the Bureaucracy: The Presidential Advantage," in *The Presidency and the Political System*, ed. Michael Nelson (Washington, D.C.: CQ Press, 1995), 412–413.
4. Kenneth Mayer, *With the Stroke of a Pen: Executive Orders and Presidential Power* (Princeton: Princeton University Press, 2001), 10.
5. William G. Howell, *Power Without Persuasion: The Politics of Direct Presidential Action* (Princeton: Princeton University Press, 2003).

6. Karen O'Connor and Bryant Scott McFall, "Conservative Interest Group Litigation in the Reagan Era and Beyond," in *The Politics of Interests*, ed., Mark P. Petracca, (Boulder: Westview Press, 1992), 263–281.

7. Lee Epstein, *Conservatives in Court* (Knoxville: University of Tennessee Press, 1985), 148.

8. For example, advocates appealing a federal agency decision can often choose between the Washington, D.C., court and a potentially more hospitable local court.

9. James L. Gibson, quoted in Christopher E. Smith, *Courts and Public Policy* (Chicago: Nelson-Hall Publishers, 1993), 17.

10. Paul Schullery, *Searching for Yellowstone: Ecology and Wonder in the Last Wilderness* (Boston: Houghton Mifflin, 1997), 29.

11. Quoted in Paul Schullery and Lee Whittlesey, *Myth and History in the Creation of Yellowstone National Park* (Lincoln: University of Nebraska Press, 2003), 9.

12. Cornelius Hedges, quoted in Schullery, *Searching for Yellowstone*, 55.

13. Quoted in Schullery and Whittlesey, *Myth and History in the Creation of Yellowstone National Park*, 4. Note that historians have challenged the NPS myth and, in particular, have challenged the notion that the original promoters of the park idea were motivated by altruism rather than commercial ambitions.

14. George B. Hartzog Jr., *Battling for the National Parks* (Mt. Kisco, N.Y.: Moyer Bell Limited, 1988), 6.

15. Quoted in Michael Frome, *Regreening the National Parks* (Tucson: University of Arizona Press, 1992), 8.

16. Quoted in Hartzog, *Battling for the National Parks*, 6.

17. Richard West Sellars, "The Roots of National Park Management," *Journal of Forestry*, January 1992, 15–19.

18. Frome, *Regreening the National Parks*, 8.

19. Jeanne Nienaber Clarke and Daniel C. McCool, *Staking Out the Terrain: Power and Performance Among Natural Resource Agencies*, 2d ed. (Albany: SUNY Press, 1996), 7.

20. Quoted in Hartzog, *Battling for the National Parks*, 6.

21. Sellars, "The Roots of National Park Management."

22. Frome, *Regreening the National Parks*, 11.

23. Robert Cahn, "Will Success Spoil the National Parks" *Christian Science Monitor*, May 1–August 7, 1968.

24. Ronald A. Taylor and Gordon Witkin, "Where It's Nature vs. Man vs. Machines," *U.S. News & World Report*, April 28, 1986, 68.

25. Jerry Adler, "Can We Save Our Parks?" *Newsweek*, July 28, 1986, 48–51.

26. John Mitchell, "Our National Legacy At Risk," *National Geographic*, October 1994, 18–29, 35–55.

27. U.S. GAO, *National Park Service: Activities Outside Park Borders Have Caused Damage to Resources and Will Likely Cause More*, GAO/RCED-94-59 (January 1994).

28. Schullery, *Searching for Yellowstone*.

29. Robert B. Keiter, *Keeping Faith with Nature: Ecosystems, Democracy, and America's Public Lands* (New Haven: Yale University Press, 2003).

30. Todd Wilkinson, "Snowed Under," *National Parks*, January 1995, 32–37.

31. Thomas J. Knudson, "Yellowstone and Staff Are Strained as Winter Visitors Swell," *New York Times*, March 24, 1987, 16.

32. Quoted in ibid.

33. Quoted in ibid.

34. Kevin McCullen, "Snowmobiles Kick Up Concern," *Rocky Mountain News*, March 7, 1994.

35. Lynne Bama, "Yellowstone Snowmobile Crowd May Hit Limit," *High Country News*, March 6, 1995.

36. James Brooke, "A Quiet, Clean, Solitary Winter in Yellowstone Park? Vroom! Cough! Think Again," *New York Times*, February 18, 1996, Sec. 1, 16.

37. Dan Egan, "Yellowstone: Geysers, Grizzlies and the Country's Worst Smog," *High Country News*, April 1, 1996.
38. Ibid. Note, however, that the Montana Department of Environmental Quality disputed the method park officials used to measure air quality.
39. "Parks to Study Snowmobiles' Effect on Bison," *New York Times*, September 28, 1997, 30.
40. Quoted in Bryan Hodgson, "Snowmobile Eruption: Vehicles Packing Yellowstone in Winter, Too," *Cleveland Plain Dealer*, February 27, 1995, 5E.
41. Quoted in Scott McMillion, "Snowmobiles Remain an Issue," *High Country News*, October 27, 1997.
42. Quoted in Ben Brown, "Snowmobile! Machines of Winter a Necessity for Some, a Nuisance to Others," *USA Today*, January 18, 1990, 8C.
43. Quoted in Kevin McCullen, "Winter Crowds Threaten Yellowstone," *Rocky Mountain News*, March 7, 1994, 6.
44. Ben Long, "Yellowstone's Last Stampede," *High Country News*, March 12, 2001.
45. Ibid.
46. Brown, "Snowmobile!"
47. Quoted in Blaine Harden, "Snowmobilers Favoring Access to Yellowstone Have Found an Ally in Bush," *New York Times*, March 6, 2002, 16.
48. Quoted in Egan, "Yellowstone: Geysers, Grizzlies and the Country's Worst Smog."
49. Quoted in Bill McAllister, "Snowmobiles Can Stay; Park Service Says Yellowstone Decision Strikes Balance," *Denver Post*, February 21, 2003, 2.
50. Quoted in Bryan Hodgson, "Environmentalists Decry Use of Snowmobiles in Yellowstone National Park," *Tampa Tribune*, February 19, 1995, 5.
51. Quoted in Brooke, "A Quiet, Clean, Solitary Winter in Yellowstone Park?"
52. Quoted in Brown, "Snowmobile!"
53. Quoted in Katharine Q. Seelye, "Bush May Lift Park's Snowmobile Ban," *New York Times*, June 24, 2001, 15.
54. Donald A. Manzullo, Chairman, Remarks Before the U.S. House of Representatives Small Business Committee, Subcommittee on Tax, Finance, and Exports, July 13, 2000.
55. Quoted in William Booth, "At Yellowstone, the Din of Snowmobiles and Debate," *Washington Post*, February 6, 2003, 3.
56. Quoted in Harden, "Snowmobilers Favoring Access to Yellowstone Have Found an Ally in Bush."
57. Quoted in Joseph B. Verrengia, "Thin Snowpack Revs Up Arguments over Snowmobiles," *Rocky Mountain News*, January 19, 1995, 64.
58. Brooke, "A Quiet, Clean, Solitary Winter in Yellowstone Park?"; Tim Wade, Chairman, Park County, Wyoming, Commission, Testimony Before the U.S. Senate Energy Committee, Subcommittee on National Parks, Historic Preservation, and Recreation, May 25, 2000.
59. Quoted in Douglas Jehl, "National Parks Will Ban Recreational Snowmobiles," *New York Times*, April 27, 2000, 12.
60. Brown, "Snowmobile!"
61. Quoted in Hodgson, "Environmentalists Decry Use of Snowmobiles in Yellowstone National Park."
62. Keiter, *Keeping Faith with Nature*, 262.
63. Tom Kenworthy, "Parkland Debate Keeps Trekking," *USA Today*, April 25, 2003, 3.
64. Quoted in Kim Cobb, "Invasion of Off-Road Vehicles," *Houston Chronicle*, July 23, 2000, 1.
65. Quoted in Taylor and Witkin, "Where It's Nature vs. Man vs. Machines."
66. Quoted in Reuters, "Snowmobile Ban Sought," *The Gazette* (Montreal, Quebec), January 22, 1999, 10.
67. Veronica Gould Stoddart, "Green Groups Fuming over Park Snowmobiles," *USA Today*, February 12, 1999, 4D.

68. Quoted in Stoddart, "Green Groups Fuming over Park Snowmobiles."

69. Shortly thereafter, Bluewater Network sued the NPS to exclude personal watercraft (PWC) from the twenty-one parks where they were permitted, and the Personal Watercraft Industry Association countersued to preserve access. On April 12, 2001, a federal judge agreed with Bluewater and required NPS to undertake park-specific EISs on PWC use. In April 2002 the NPS announced that five of the twenty-one remaining parks would ban PWC permanently; the other sixteen parks put temporary bans in place while they conducted environmental assessments and came up with regulations.

70. Quoted in Jehl, "National Parks Will Ban Recreational Snowmobiles."

71. Donald J. Barry, Assistant Secretary for Fish and Wildlife and Parks, Department of the Interior, "Testimony Before the Senate Energy Committee, Subcommittee on National Parks, Historic Preservation, and Recreation," May 25, 2000.

72. Ibid.

73. Jim Hughes, "Snowmobiles Shatter the Sounds of Silence," *Denver Post*, March 10, 2000, 1.

74. Barry, "Testimony Before the Senate Subcommittee on National Parks, Historic Preservation, and Recreation."

75. Mark Simonich, Director, Montana Department of Environmental Quality, "Testimony Before the Senate Energy Committee, Subcommittee on National Parks, Historic Preservation, and Recreation," May 25, 2000.

76. Jim Hughes, "Snowmobile Ban Favored," *Denver Post*, March 15, 2000, 1.

77. Rachel Odell, "Parks Rev Up to Ban Snowmobiles," *High Country News*, March 27, 2000.

78. Theo Stein, "Snowmobile Ban Set for 2003 at Two Parks," *Denver Post*, November 23, 2000, B1.

79. Kevin Collins, Legislative Representative, National Parks Conservation Association, "Testimony Before the House Small Business Committee, Subcommittee on Tax, Finance, and Exports," July 13, 2000.

80. Kit Miniclier, "Town Roaring Mad Over Snowmobiles' Future," *Denver Post*, May 21, 2000, B6.

81. Quoted in Bill McAllister, "Snowmobiles to Get Boot in Yellowstone, Teton," *Denver Post*, October 11, 2000, B01.

82. Kit Miniclier, "Noise vs. Nature: Record Number of Snowmobilers in Yellowstone," *Denver Post*, February 18, 2001, B1.

83. Kit Miniclier, "Park Snowmobile Phase-Out Delayed; Yellowstone Anticipates Record Crowds," *Denver Post*, February 6, 2002, B6; Todd Wilkinson, "Snowmobile Buzz Echoes in White House," *Christian Science Monitor*, February 21, 2001, 3.

84. Quoted in Katharine Q. Seelye, "U.S. to Reassess Snowmobile Ban in a Park," *New York Times*, June 30, 2001, 10.

85. Miniclier, "Park Snowmobile Phase-Out Delayed."

86. Katharine Q. Seelye, "Snowmobilers Gain Against Plan for Park Ban," *New York Times*, February 20, 2002, 14.

87. Kit Miniclier, "Winter Ban in Parks Eased; Snowmobiles Still OK in Yellowstone, Teton," *Denver Post*, June 26, 2002, 1.

88. Gary Gerhardt, "Proposal for Parks Unveiled," *Rocky Mountain News*, November 9, 2002, 14.

89. "Yellowstone: Status Quo on Snowmobiles," (Minneapolis) *Star Tribune*, November 14, 2002, 20.

90. In addition to relaxing the restrictions on snowmobiles in the park, the Bush administration undermined the EPA's ability to regulate pollution from snowmobiles. New standards released in April 2002 required a 30 percent reduction in emissions by 2006 and a 50 percent reduction by 2010. But snowmobile industry officials appealed to John Graham of the Office of Regulatory Affairs to eliminate the 50 percent limit. In response to this plea, Graham asked the EPA to conduct a full cost-benefit analysis

of its snowmobile rule (the "nonroad" rule). See Arthur Allen, "Where the Snow-mobiles Roam," *Washington Post Magazine*, August 18, 2002, W15.

91. *Fund for Animals v. Norton*, 294 F. Supp. 2d 92-117, D.D.C. (2003).

92. Quoted in Jim Robbins, "New Snowmobile Rules Roil Yellowstone," *New York Times*, December 22, 2003, 22.

93. Quoted in Steve Lipsher, "The Brink of Beauty, the Edge of Ruin," *Denver Post*, January 11, 2004, 1.

94. Ibid.

95. *International Snowmobile Manufacturers Association v. Norton*, 304 F. Supp. 2d 1278, D. Wyo. (2004).

96. Quoted in Michael Janofsky, "U.S. Would Allow 720 Snowmobiles Daily at Yellowstone," *New York Times*, August 20, 2004, 14.

97. Quoted in Felicity Barringer, "Judge's Ruling on Yellowstone Keeps It Open to Snowmobiles," *New York Times*, October 16, 2004, 9.

98. Quoted in Felicity Barringer, "Secretary Tours Yellowstone on Snowmobile," *New York Times*, February 17, 2005, 18.

99. Becky Bohrer, "Official: Snowmobile Average Falls Below Daily Cap," Associated Press, April 20, 2005.

100. Barringer, "Secretary Tours Yellowstone."

101. Adler, "Can We Save Our Parks?"

102. Frome, *Regreening the National Parks*, 7.

103. Nicholas Kristoff, "Yellowstone in Winter a Snowmobiler's Paradise," *New York Times*, December 26, 2002, 21.

104. John H. Cushman Jr., "Priorities in the National Parks," *New York Times*, July 26, 1998, Sec. 5, 11.

Recommended Reading

Schullery, Paul. *Searching for Yellowstone: Ecology and Wonder in the Last Wilderness*. Boston: Houghton Mifflin, 1997.

Hartzog, George B., Jr. *Battling for the National Parks*. Mt. Kisco, N.Y.: Moyer Bell Limited, 1988.

Frome, Michael. *Regreening the National Parks*. Tucson: University of Arizona Press, 1992.

Web Sites

www.nps.gov (National Park Service site)
www.yellowstone.net (Yellowstone National Park site)
www.nps.gov/yell/planvisit/winteruse (Yellowstone National Park's Winter Use Plan)

CHAPTER 10

Crisis in the New England Fisheries

In early 1994 many New Englanders were startled to learn of a crisis in the cod, flounder, and haddock fisheries. Apparently the region's groundfish stocks were on the verge of collapse, and federal regulators intended to institute strict new rules to try and save them.[1] In the meantime, regulators were shutting down for an indefinite period Georges Bank—a 6,600-square-mile area more than 100 miles offshore that was once the most prolific fishing grounds in the world. The fishers were in an uproar, and many charged that the federal management regime instituted in 1976, not overfishing, was the culprit. Regulators held firm, however, pointing out that government scientists had been warning of the groundfish's demise for well over a decade. Since the mid-1990s fishery rules have been tightened substantially, and some groundfish species are recovering, but a long-term response to the overfishing problem remains elusive.

The New England fisheries case illuminates the complexity of managing common pool resources. Garrett Hardin captured the special challenges of such management in a model he popularized in a 1968 *Science* magazine article entitled "The Tragedy of the Commons." According to Hardin's model, when a resource is open to everyone, those who use it will inevitably overexploit it. "The logic of the commons remorselessly generates tragedy," he wrote."[2] The tragedy of the commons applies to fisheries in the following way: as more fishers enter a fishery, each one eventually experiences declining yields for the same unit of effort. As the margin of profit shrinks, each rational fisher redoubles his efforts, recognizing that if he cuts back for the good of the resource, someone else will catch the fish. In doing what is individually rational, however, fishers produce a result that is collectively disastrous.

From Hardin's perspective, the only way to head off the destruction of a common resource is for an authoritarian state to regulate its use or convert it into private property. In the latter regime, owners of the resource theoretically have a stake in conserving it because they now have the sole rights to the "economic rents" it generates. As political scientist Elinor Ostrom points out, however, "neither the state nor the market [has been] uniformly successful in enabling individuals to sustain long-term, productive use of natural resource systems."[3] Furthermore, Ostrom cites numerous examples of creative institutional arrangements devised by communities to solve the problems of managing common property resources. In doing so, Ostrom draws our attention to the various factors that can complicate or simplify common property resource management—from a community's culture, history, and tradition to the political system in which decisions are made—making it clear that no single solution will apply.

This case also illustrates the challenges posed by management schemes in which regulated interests play a major role in devising and implementing government policy. Federal law mandates that regional fishery councils, made up of members who are familiar with the resource, formulate the rules under which fisheries operate. In theory, such an approach enables regulators to take into account the perspectives of the regulated sector and therefore to make rules that are both fair and sensible. If they are *not* involved in decision making, regulated interests often perceive rules as arbitrary and coercive and resist complying with them. As is true of every policy—from provisions in the tax code to antitheft laws—regulators cannot simply institute and enforce a set of rules; they rely heavily on the voluntary cooperation of those who must abide by them. If regulated interests dominate the rulemaking process, however, they are likely to generate policies that benefit themselves rather than the public.

Finally, this case increases our understanding of the pivotal role of litigation in bringing about major environmental policy shifts. As both the grazing policy and spotted owl cases (chapters 7 and 8) reveal, once a single interest has become entrenched in a subsystem, it is difficult to dislodge. Attempts to alter policy from both outside and within an agency encounter resistance from its clientele, congressional overseers, and even its own personnel who have become accustomed to a particular routine. A successful legal challenge can, however, shift the internal balance of power, giving those who previously were isolated—in this case, agency scientists—more authority. Moreover, by requiring an agency to move in a particular direction, the courts can also narrow the range of options available to managers.

BACKGROUND

The history of New England is inextricably tied to the fish found off its shores. In the year 1500 explorer John Cabot described the Grand Banks area off Northeast Canada as so "swarming with fish [that they] could be taken not only with a net but in baskets let down with a stone." [4] From Canada to New Jersey, the waters teemed with cod, supporting a relatively stable fishing industry for 450 years. Groundfish—not just cod but also yellowtail flounder, haddock, American plaice, and pollock—were the backbone of the region's fishing trade. In fact, the "sacred cod," a commemorative wooden plaque, still hangs in the Massachusetts State House, symbolizing the state's first industry and the source of its early wealth. For many years, the ports of Gloucester and New Bedford were among the nation's most prosperous.

At the beginning of the twentieth century, the introduction of steam-powered trawlers that drag nets across the ocean floor prompted concern among scientists about bottom-dwelling animals and plants. Then, in 1930 the fleet engaged in sufficiently intensive fishing that it caused a crash in the Georges Bank haddock fishery. Still, fishing in New England remained a small-scale affair, and after fishers shifted their effort northward, the haddock stocks recovered. The same pattern repeated itself for other species: because of the modest harvests overall, there was no persistent recruitment overfishing, so depleted stocks could rebound when fishers moved on to other species.[5]

In the mid-1950s, however, huge factory ships from Europe and the Soviet Union began to roam the North Atlantic just beyond U.S. coastal waters. Some of those boats exceeded 300 feet in length, brought in as much as 500 tons of fish in a single haul, and could process and deep-freeze 250 tons a day. They operated around the clock in all but the worst weather and stayed at sea for a year or more.[6] Called "factory-equipped freezer stern trawlers," or factory trawlers for short, the fleet was "a kind of roving industrial complex."[7] As fisheries expert William Warner describes the scene, the ships "paced out in long diagonal lines, plowing the best fishing grounds like disk harrows in a field."[8] Between 1960 and 1965 North American groundfish landings increased from 200,000 metric tons to 760,000 metric tons.[9]

For many years after the first factory trawler invasion, Canadian and American fishery officials clung to the hope that the fleets of both countries could withstand the assault. Some hoped that the International Commission for Northwest Atlantic Fisheries might reverse the trend of overfishing in the early 1970s when it instituted a management system allocating quotas by country, with the sum for each species equal to the total recommended catch. But by the time those quotas took effect enormous damage had already been done: between 1963 and 1974, groundfish populations declined almost 70 percent, and by 1974 many species had fallen to the lowest levels ever recorded.[10] Haddock was at an all-time low throughout its Northwest Atlantic range; the species was so rare, in fact, that biologists feared the end of a commercially viable fishery, if not extinction. Even the bountiful cod was showing signs of decline, as were the redfish, yellowtail flounder, and many other prime market fish.

The turning point came in 1974 when 1,076 fishing vessels swarmed across the Atlantic to fish North American waters. Their total catch of 2.176 million metric tons was ten times the New England and triple the Canadian catch.[11] Although the total was huge, the catch per vessel was down, and the fish were running smaller than before, despite the fact that the foreign vessels were fishing longer hours with improved methods over a larger range for a greater part of the year. In fact, the foreign catch had been better for five of the preceding six years—slowly declining from a peak of 2.4 million metric tons in 1968—with fleets of equal or lesser size.[12] American fishers charged that the international commission was ineffectual and demanded the United States assert control over the offshore fishery.[13]

In response to fishers' complaints about the foreign fleets and scientists' concern about the precarious status of fish stocks, in 1976 Congress passed the Magnuson Fisheries Conservation and Management Act, named after its sponsor, Sen. Warren Magnuson, D-Wash. The act had two goals: to rejuvenate the American fishing fleet and to restore and conserve fish stocks. It unilaterally asserted U.S. jurisdiction over fisheries within an exclusive economic zone that extended 200 miles from the coast and authorized the National Marine

Fisheries Service (NMFS, pronounced "nymphs"), a line office of the U.S. Department of Commerce's National Oceanic and Atmospheric Administration (NOAA), to administer the nation's resources between 3 miles and 200 miles off the coast.[14] The Magnuson Act also established eight regional councils to work with the five regional NMFS offices to develop management plans for the offshore fisheries.

The act directed that regional councils comprise federal and state officials, as well as "individuals who, by reason of their occupation or other experience, scientific expertise, or training are knowledgeable regarding the conservation and management of the commercial and recreational harvest." [15] Although the act vests final authority for rulemaking with the secretary of commerce, Congress clearly intended the councils to play the dominant role. According to the legislative history of the act:

> The regional councils are, in concept, intended to be similar to a legislative branch of government. . . . The councils are afforded a reasonable measure of independence and authority and are designed to maintain a close relation with those at the most local level interested in and affected by fisheries management.[16]

THE CASE

The Magnuson Act allows the Department of Commerce to reject, accept, or partially approve a council's fishery management plan (FMP) but not to change it, an arrangement that from the beginning encouraged acceptance of lax plans. NMFS was reluctant to try to impose its own plan over council objections, as the rules would be nearly impossible to enforce without fishers' compliance. Exacerbating NMFS's weak position was the tendency of members of Congress to intervene on behalf of fishing interests whenever the agency threatened to institute strict rules. Finally, although the region's fishing industry was not unified, it managed to dominate policy because it encountered little opposition; aside from scientists from the Northeast Fisheries Science Center (NEFSC), few voices spoke out on behalf of fishery conservation and precautionary management. Most environmental groups were not paying attention to fisheries—they were far more interested in marine mammals and ocean pollution—nor were they alerting the public to the impending groundfish collapse.

Scientists' Assessments of New England's Groundfish

Like range management and forestry science, both of which historically were dominated by resource extraction rather than ecosystem health, fisheries science historically has been concerned with determining the "maximum sustainable yield" of a fishery. In practice, this emphasis has meant developing expedient indicators, primary among which are fish stock assessments. A stock assessment includes estimates of the abundance of a particular fish stock (in weight or number of fish) and the rate at which the fish are being removed as a result of harvesting and other causes (mortality). It also includes one or more reference estimates of the harvesting rate or abundance at which the stock can maintain itself in the long term. Finally, a stock assessment typically contains one- to five-year projections for the stock under different management scenarios.

Because they cannot actually count the fish, scientists use a variety of data to estimate the abundance of each stock and its population trends. They rely primarily on two sources: reports on the commercial fish landing and NMFS resource surveys. The landing reports include the number of fish caught, their size, and the ratio of fish caught to the time spent fishing (catch per unit of effort). Landing data tell only part of the story, however, because many fish caught are discarded because they are too small to sell, exceed the catch limit, or belong to a species whose catch is prohibited. (These discards, known as bycatch, comprise a large portion of fishing mortality worldwide.[17]) Unlike fishing boats, which search for the largest aggregations of fish, NMFS's research trawlers conduct stratified random sample surveys of a wide range of locations. Such "fishery-independent" surveys are especially important for schooling species because fishers can maintain high catch rates on them by selectively targeting areas where the fish congregate. The New England groundfish survey, which began in 1963, is the nation's oldest and most reliable and provides the longest time-series data.[18]

Although they acknowledged that their stock assessments and projections were uncertain and their understanding of groundfish biology and life history incomplete when the Magnuson Act took effect at the end of 1976, NEFSC scientists nevertheless issued strong warnings about the need to cut back fishing of the region's groundfish. They advised the New England Fishery Management Council to set 1977 Gulf of Maine and Georges Bank commercial cod catches at approximately half the levels reached between 1970 and 1974. Scientists feared that fishing beyond the recommended level would lead to a precipitous decline. They also noted a pronounced decline in haddock since 1967 and found yellowtail flounder stocks "severely depressed." They recommended strict catch limits to enable these stocks to recover as well.[19]

Establishing a "Cooperative" Management Regime

The council was reluctant to follow scientists' advice, however. In theory, the cooperative management regime mandated by the Magnuson Act would ensure that managers took both the best available science and the needs and expertise of fishers into account when developing conservation measures. But the councils soon became a focal point for controversy because their members know a lot more about catching and marketing fish than about marine biology or natural resource stewardship. The New England Council, in particular, was dominated by current or former commercial fishers, who were understandably reluctant to impose stringent controls on their peers.[20] One former council member explained, "As members of the community, it's difficult for them to divorce themselves from the consequences of their actions." [21]

In response to scientists' warnings about decimated stocks, the newly appointed council did put some restrictions in place. Modeling its approach on the regulatory regime of the International Commission for Northwest Atlantic Fisheries, the council imposed catch quotas, prohibited fishing in spawning areas, required large-holed mesh (to allow young fish to escape), enacted minimum fish size requirements, and limited the amount of yellowtail flounder that could be caught per trip. In its first year of operation, however, fishers often exceeded total catch quotas, so NMFS often had to close the fishery abruptly. As a result, "the trip limits were perceived as unfair; many fish were mislabeled and handled illegally; and the closures were extremely unpopular." [22] In addition, public council meetings were unfocused and chaotic; council members vacillated and were reluctant to make difficult choices, which tarnished their image as decision makers. An editorial in a 1978 issue of the *National Fisherman* magazine exemplified fishers' antipathy toward managers:

> Years ago, the fish business was pretty simple. There was the fish, fishermen, the buyers and sellers of fish, and people who ate fish. Everything seemed t'go along fairly well. There were just enough fishermen to catch just the amount of fish that fish eaters would eat. Everybody made their fair share of money.
>
> Then along came the first fishcrat. . . . He made a pitch to his brother bureaucrat f'some funds. There want no trouble in getting the dough cause everybody knows that bureaucrats control all the purse strings.
>
> Well, the first fishcrat was so successful, he hired a bureau, the first fishcrat bureau. They went all over hell telling people things they didn't want t'know, how not t'do something right n' talkin' in a strange language nobody could understand, especially dumb fishermen.[23]

Making matters worse for the council, many fishers simply did not believe scientists' claims that the groundfish were in trouble. Fishers had a host of complaints about stock assessments. They criticized the NEFSC for using ancient gear that did not detect or catch fish as effectively as modern gear. (NEFSC scientists explained that they had standardized the survey in a variety of ways, from using the same boats and gear to survey methods, to ensure a consistent time-series of comparable data.) Fishers also regarded fishery science as inaccessible because it relied heavily on complex mathematical models that few but the most specialized scientists could understand. Finally, fishers pointed out that fishery science was weakest in an area that was crucial for fishery management: understanding fish behavior, life history, and interaction with other species. This, they noted, was where their own anecdotal knowledge—which scientists historically have dismissed—was likely to be most valuable.

The underlying reason for the disjuncture was that unlike scientists, who were precautionary, the fishers' perspective was cornucopian: they preferred to believe in the ocean's resilience and near-limitless bounty. Seeming to justify that view, high groundfish landings in the early part of 1977 belied scientists' pessimism. According to one observer,

> codfish landings throughout New England were nearly twice what they [had been] the previous spring (13.4 million pounds compared to 7.3 million pounds). . . . Piers in Gloucester and New Bedford were groaning under the load of spring landings and there was much concern that the processing houses for frozen fish were going to be grossly inadequate. Processors were running their facilities seven days a week in June and adding extra shifts, and still they could not keep up with the boats.[24]

The surge in landings was probably the fruit of the international commission's quota system; nevertheless, the credibility gap between scientists and fishers began to widen.

Although unified by their distrust of scientists and contempt for fishery managers, New England's fishers were deeply split in other respects, which complicated fishery management even further. The fishers were divided by gear type, vessel size, vessel ownership, fishing style and port of origin. Large trawlers accused small boats of taking advantage of loopholes in the laws and lax enforcement of fishery regulations to fish out of season or use illegal nets. Small boat owners blamed trawlers with their advanced sonar tracking system for cleaning out the ocean. Gillnetters pointed out that, unlike trawlers, they did not catch juvenile fish and did not tear up the ocean bottom. Longliners said their gear did not affect the bottom either, and was even more selective than gillnets. Both derided draggers for pounding the bottom with their heavy doors. The otter trawl, other gear users pointed out, had the greatest bycatch problem because unwanted fish were damaged in the net, brought up too quickly, or not thrown back soon enough. Draggers, on the other hand, complained about ghost-net fishing, lost lines, and hooks "souring" the bottom. The Maine Yankees disparaged the New Bedford Portuguese and the Gloucester Sicilians, who in turn criticized each other.[25] Unable to reconcile the many factions, the council simply tried to devise rules that would be perceived as "democratic"—that is, affecting everyone equally.

Devising a Multispecies Groundfish Fishery Management Plan

During the first two years of council operations, differences between scientists and fishers, uncertainty about the exact administrative procedures needed to ensure timely implementation of plans, apparent misunderstandings between the council and NMFS, the vagueness of the concepts on which the plans were supposed to be based, and the inexperience of many council members as fishery managers all lowered morale and undermined the fishery management process.[26] In hopes of moving away from the short-term, reactionary policymaking it had engaged in thus far, in summer 1978 the council set to work on a more comprehensive, long-term fishery management plan.

Ironically, in 1982—nearly four years after it began—the council submitted an Interim Groundfish FMP for Commerce Department approval that substantially *weakened* controls on fishing. Encouraged by apparent improvement in the stocks and under heavy pressure from fish processors, the council abandoned trip limits and quotas; instead, the plan allowed open fishing and required only "age-at-entry" controls in the form of minimum fish sizes and minimum mesh sizes. In a nod to conservation, the plan retained some spawning area closures (March to May) and instituted voluntary catch reporting as a data collection device.

After sustained pressure from several (though not all) fishing groups, NMFS agreed to forgo the usual four- to six-month comment period and implement the interim plan immediately under emergency regulations, a procedure normally reserved for a resource, not an industry, in jeopardy. The decision came after the commerce secretary and federal fisheries officials met in Washington with fish dealers and processors who spoke of the "disaster" that had befallen their businesses in the past two years. The dealers described falling employment in their industry, while the processors claimed that the quotas had prevented the boats from bringing in enough fish to meet operating costs or consumer demand.

In the years following implementation of the interim plan, federal scientists continued to urge the New England panel to institute more restrictive measures. Early on, it became apparent that age-at-entry controls were insufficient to protect fish stocks. Many fishers were not complying with minimum mesh size requirements, so juvenile fish were virtually unprotected. Making matters worse, in response to loan guarantee programs and generous depreciation and operating cost allowances added to the federal tax code, fishers had begun investing in new boats and high-tech equipment.[27] Because entry into the fishery was unlimited, the number of otter trawlers doubled between 1976 and 1984, even as the size and efficiency of the boats increased substantially.[28] The result was that by 1980 the New England fleet was catching 100,000 metric tons of cod, haddock, and yellowtail flounder—double the 1976 level—off Georges Bank, the Gulf of Maine, and Cape Cod. According to scientists, the industry was taking 50 percent to 100 percent more than the already weakened groundfish stocks could sustain, but, even though NEFSC cruises started to show stocks dropping, catches (and fishers' optimism) remained high until 1983, at which point they started to decline.[29]

The Northeast Multispecies Fishery Management Plan

Despite its apparent failure to curb fishing, the council proposed formalizing the interim plan's open fishing regime in 1985 as the Northeast Multispecies FMP. Initially, NMFS gave only conditional approval to the plan because agency officials, heeding their own scientists' advice, were concerned that the lack of direct controls on fishing mortality would lead to overfishing. In 1987, however, after fishers got the New England congressional delegation to weigh in heavily on the side of indirect controls, the agency approved the plan, requesting only modest adjustments to remedy its deficiencies.[30]

Not surprisingly, the new FMP did little to improve the prospects for New England's groundfish: stock assessments continued to show increases in mortality rates and corresponding decreases in stock sizes. This situation was not unique to New England, and NMFS officials were becoming increasingly frustrated with the regional councils' impotence. So, in response to the critical 1986 NOAA *Fishery Management Study*, NMFS scientists in 1989 revised a crucial section of the Magnuson Act regulations: the Section 602 Guidelines for National Standards to assist in the development of FMPs. The original guidelines had not defined the term *overfishing*, which appears in the Magnuson Act only once: "Conservation and management measures shall prevent overfishing while achieving, on a continuing basis, the optimum yield from each fishery for the U.S. fishing industry." [31] The 1989 guidelines mandated that each FMP define overfishing, a significant advance for fishery conservation.[32] The rationale for the change was clear: it was impossible to prevent overfishing if there was no standard against which to measure it and therefore no way of saying for certain that it was occurring. The second important revision to the guidelines read: "If data indicate that an overfished condition exists, a program must be established for rebuilding the stock over a period of time specified by the Council and acceptable to the Secretary." [33]

The 602 Guidelines revisions had an enormous, albeit not immediate, impact on New England. At the time, the New England Groundfish FMP—like most others—did not define overfishing; in fact, the plan did not even specify an optimal yield.[34] The council had eliminated optimal yield figures because they were too controversial and instead had begun defining optimal yield as "the amount of fish actually harvested by U.S. fishermen in accordance with the measures listed below." In other words, any size catch was optimal, by definition. The FMP also contained biological targets for stocks covered by the plan: the total catch should not exceed 20 percent of the maximum spawning potential. Although these targets were intended to ensure sufficient reproductive potential for long-term replenishment of stocks, the plan's management measures were, in fact, inadequate to achieve them. Seeking to comply with changes in the 602 Guidelines, the New England Council proposed that its overfishing definitions for groundfish be the targets already contained in the FMP: 20 percent of the maximum spawning potential. At the same time, the council acknowledged that it was not meeting those targets—in effect, admitting that it was allowing overfishing to occur.

Under such circumstances, the revised guidelines required the council to develop a recovery plan for the overfished stocks, but, because the guidelines did not specify a deadline, the council moved slowly. Among the many reasons for its tardiness, the most important was that representatives of the fishing industry remained dubious about the need for new fishing controls. Those council members who did perceive such a need anticipated strong resistance. The consequence was that "nineteen months after admitting that groundfish stocks were overfished, the council had not seriously begun to tackle the effort reduction that it had decided was necessary to end overfishing. Moreover, NMFS showed no signs of stepping in with a Secretarial plan." [35]

The Conservation Law Foundation Lawsuit

In early 1991 NMFS scientists reported that New England fishers were catching less than half as many groundfish as they had a decade earlier. The Massachusetts Offshore Groundfish Task Force estimated that lost landings were costing the region $350 million annually and as many as 14,000 jobs.[36] According to NEFSC scientists, spawning stocks were now less than one-twentieth what they had been when the Magnuson Act was passed. Despite the scientists' dire findings, council members remained reluctant to act, arguing that the series of halfway measures they had passed in the 1980s would, given time, enable stocks to rebound.

Frustrated with the council's inertia and hoping to force it to act, in June 1991 the Boston-based Conservation Law Foundation (CLF) filed a lawsuit against the secretary of commerce. CLF representatives had been attending council meetings for two years, but, although they had challenged the council's planning measures, they had lacked a legal basis to hold the council accountable until the issuance of the new 602 Guidelines. The CLF complaint charged that NMFS had failed to prevent overfishing, in violation of its statutory mandate. In August 1991 the CLF and NMFS settled the case by signing a consent decree that compelled the New England Council to develop a stock rebuilding plan. If it failed to do so by a specified deadline, the commerce secretary was required to devise a plan. In compliance with the settlement, the council began to develop Amendment 5 to the Northeast Multispecies FMP.[37]

The lawsuit had an important, if not immediately obvious, impact. Previously, fishing interests, despite their lack of cohesiveness, had managed to dominate fishery policy largely because neither environmentalists nor the general public was attentive to the issue of overfishing. By forcing the agency's hand, however, the lawsuit empowered conservation-oriented managers on the council and within NMFS to argue that they had no choice but to impose stringent regulations. NMFS was quick to use its new clout. On June 3, 1993, after receiving yet another report from its scientists that groundfish were severely depleted, NMFS issued an emergency order closing the eastern portion of Georges Bank to fishing for a month just two days after the area had opened for the season.[38]

Amendment 5

Hoping to eliminate the need for more emergency closures, on June 30, 1993, the beleaguered New England Council approved Amendment 5. The plan's ostensible goal was to reduce the groundfish catch by 50 percent in seven years. The plan included a moratorium on groundfishing permits and greatly limited the number of days fishers could catch groundfish. Before June 30 they were allowed to be out year-round, with the exception of periodic closures; now the number of days allowed was to go down each year until by 1998 large boats could fish only 110 days each year. The plan also limited fishers to 2,500 pounds of haddock each trip and increased the mesh size of nets in most areas to 5.5-inch diamonds or six-inch squares to allow young fish to escape. In addition, it required vessel owners and operators to possess valid fishing permits and to keep elaborate fishing logs detailing the species caught and bycatch.

As the council awaited Commerce Department approval of the plan, the bad news on groundfish stocks continued to roll in. During a two-day meeting in early December, Richard Roe, NMFS's northeast regional director, sought to ban haddock fishing indefinitely off the East Coast in response to reports of drastic declines in landings—from 40,000 metric tons per year in the early 1970s to only 90 metric tons in 1993. Still, the council resisted; it condoned emergency measures to preserve the dwindling stocks but stopped short of endorsing a complete ban. Instead, by a ten to four vote, the council recommended that NMFS impose a 500- to 1,000-pound limit on haddock catches by commercial fishing boats and close the portion of Georges Bank where haddock spawn.

As the crisis deepened, the council found itself with less and less wiggle room, however. Responding to warnings from its own scientists, at the beginning of Christmas week, Canada imposed sharp restrictions on haddock and other bottom feeders in nearly all of its Atlantic region. Following suit, on Thursday of that week NMFS ordered that New England boats be allowed no more than 500 pounds of haddock per trip and that haddock spawning grounds be closed in January, a month earlier than usual. Then, in late February 1994 federal regulators announced their intention to shut down even more valuable fishing grounds: in addition to Georges Bank, they planned to close a large swath of the Great South Channel and portions of Stellwagen Bank and Jeffreys Ledge.

Finally, on March 1 the provisions of Amendment 5 were scheduled to take effect. Fishers found this series of apparently arbitrary regulations, culminating in the imposition of Amendment 5 rules, infuriating; they believed that government bureaucrats had gotten out of hand. They contended that the days-at-sea limits would impose exorbitant costs on fishers: most fishing boat owners are independents who have high fixed costs—as much as $100,000 per month in loan payments—even if they never leave port. To attract public sympathy for their plight, an armada of more than 100 fishing vessels from Chatham, Gloucester, New Bedford, Provincetown, and elsewhere in the region jammed Boston Harbor.

Scientists Issue Another Warning

Making matters more uncomfortable for regulators, Amendment 5 began to look obsolete even before it took effect. In August 1994—only months after the council adopted it—NEFSC scientists released more bad news. In an advisory

Figure 10-1 Yellowtail Flounder, Georges Bank, East of Massachusetts

Metric tons (000s)

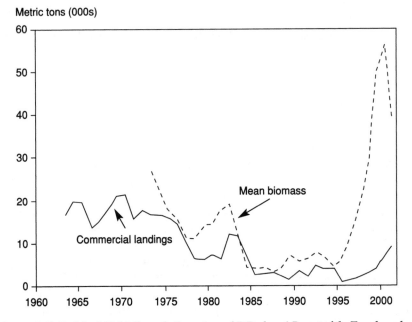

Source: S. X. Cadrin, J. D. Neilson, S. Gavaris, and P. Perley, *A Report of the Transboundary Resource Assessment Committee Meeting No. 3,* Northeast Fisheries Science Center. Reference Document 00-10, 2000; Report of the Multispecies Monitoring Committee, 2001, http://www.nefsc.noaa.gov/nefsc/publications.

report, they warned that reducing fishing by 50 percent over the next five to seven years, as Amendment 5 promised to do, probably would not be enough to save the groundfish. Of the yellowtail flounder, once the backbone of southern New England fishing ports, the report said: "The stock has collapsed! Fishing mortality on this stock should be reduced to levels approaching zero." [39] According to the report, of every 100 yellowtail flounder alive at the beginning of the year, only 8 survived the year. Under this pressure, the breeding population had declined to record lows (see Figure 10-1).

The report was also skeptical about the potential for recovery of the Georges Bank cod. In 1993 cod mortality in the fishing ground hit a record high, while the number of mature adults dropped to a record low (see Figure 10-2). Fishers had hoped that the relatively large cod harvests of 1989 and 1990 meant that this fish was weathering the crisis, but NEFSC researchers believed those years were an aberration. Scientists noted that two years previously the Canadians had closed their cod fishery off the Newfoundland coast expecting a quick recovery, but the cod population instead had dropped another 25 percent in the first year of the closure. By 1994 the Canadians were estimating that

Figure 10-2 Atlantic Cod, Georges Bank and South

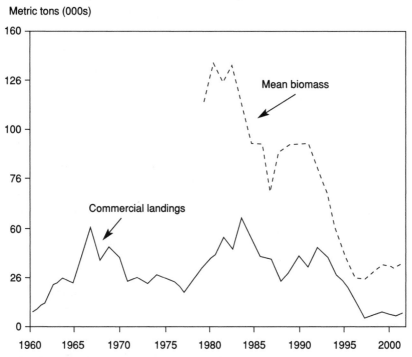

Metric tons (000s)

Source: L. O'Brien and N.J. Munroe, *Assessment of the Georges Bank Cod Stock for 2001*, Northeast Fisheries Science Center. Reference Document 01-10, 2001; Report of the Multi-species Monitoring Committee, 2001, http://www.nefsc.noaa.gov/nefsc/publications.

a recovery was not likely until the late 1990s. And Georges Bank was in even worse shape than the Canadian fisheries because fishers had been taking more than 70 percent of the cod swimming there each year. As a result, the Georges Bank catch had plummeted to its lowest level since the 1970s. Moreover, the cod's recovery was jeopardized because, as cod declined, predators, such as the spiny dogfish, were becoming an ever larger proportion of the fish.

Alan Peterson of the Northeast Fisheries Science Center at Woods Hole estimated that it would take ten to twelve years before the Georges Bank cod stock would be healthy enough that regulators could afford to increase the harvest. Even a twelve-year comeback was no sure thing, he said, because the cod's fate was complicated by natural cycles such as below-average ocean temperatures or increased salinity, which could reduce the survival of young cod. Peterson urged the New England Council to go even further than Amendment 5 and shut down almost all fishing. It could then selectively reopen fisheries that were still healthy and where nets did not accidentally catch cod or other vanishing species.

Fish Stocks Crash

On October 14, 1994, the council's groundfish committee, fearing that if it did not bite the bullet NMFS would institute its own plan, began work on Amendment 7. (Amendment 6 had simply made permanent the suite of emergency haddock measures enacted the previous year.) It had been less than six months since most of the Amendment 5 rules had taken effect, and fishers complained bitterly that the council had not waited long enough to assess their impact. Nevertheless, nearly two weeks later the council approved an emergency measure to close indefinitely vast areas of the Gulf of Maine, including Georges Bank, as well as 4,500 square miles of fishing grounds in southern New England. To prevent trawlers displaced by the ban from overfishing elsewhere, the council also proposed a quota system limiting catches closer to shore. Then on December 12 NMFS officially closed the entire 6,600-square-mile area of Georges Bank and announced its intention to lift the ban no earlier than March 1995.

Many fishers were, predictably, incensed. In their complaints a familiar refrain echoed: the scientists do not understand the condition of the fishery; they don't know where to look for the fish. "One scientist says one thing and another scientist says something else," scoffed Gloucester fisherman Jay Spurling. "They're not even out on the water; they don't see the things we see. . . . I think they're making a huge mistake." [40] Other fishers lamented the end of the only way of life they had ever known. "I've been a fisherman for 25 years," said Vito Seniti, also of Gloucester. "My father was a fisherman, and his father, and his father before. What am I gonna do now, deliver pizzas?" [41] Fishers' desperation notwithstanding, in January 1995 regulators extended the ninety-day closure indefinitely to give themselves time to come up with a real plan.

Bailing Out the Fishers

While the council wrangled over regulations, the formidable Massachusetts congressional delegation began seeking federal money to ameliorate the hardship, which was concentrated primarily around the ports of Boston, Gloucester, and New Bedford. Sen. John Kerry, D-Mass., and Rep. Gerry Studds, D-Mass., proposed legislation to create the New England Fisheries Reinvestment Program, which would disburse grants throughout the region. At the urging of New England's members of Congress, Commerce Secretary Ron Brown declared the Northeast fishery to be in an economic emergency and granted $30 million in aid to fishers and their families.

Even more important, after a year of lobbying by Massachusetts legislators, in March 1995 the Commerce Department initiated a $2 million Fishing Capacity Reduction Program—or boat buyout—to compensate fishers who retired their groundfish permits and fishing vessels and thereby reduced excess capacity in the fleet. Rather than embarking on a full-scale buyout, which could cost as much as $100 million, the department hoped to learn from the pilot program how to design an appropriate program. In August the department announced it would expand the buyout by $25 million but shrewdly made the money contingent on the New England Council showing progress on a groundfish stock rebuilding program, a potent incentive that NMFS hoped would entice fishermen to support new regulations.

Amendment 7 and Contrasting Problem Definitions

The buyout proposal came not a moment too soon. In mid-1995 the council received more alarming reports from NEFSC scientists: the measures taken under Amendment 5 and proposed since were insufficient to ensure stock recovery; in fact, things were getting worse. So the agency began to pressure the council to craft rules that would cut back fishing of groundfish by 80 percent rather than 50 percent. Fishers' reaction ranged from disbelief to fury as meetings on the new Amendment 7 got under way in fall 1995. The fishers had been blaming each other—different gear types, different ports—for the depletion of the fish, but the new proposals gave them a common foe: government regulators. As the council debated the terms of Amendment 7, the fishers continued to plead that changes to Amendment 5 were premature and that it was too early to tell whether the new rules had been effective.

Underlying these debates were the contrasting ways of defining the problem: scientists and environmentalists emphasized the ecological risks and espoused a precautionary approach. Fishers demanded proof that Amendment 5 was not working and that the stocks had, in fact, collapsed, and they argued that the risk lay in imposing strict new rules that would cause certain economic pain. As Maggie Raymond, spokeswoman for the Associated Fisheries of Maine, put it, if the plan takes effect "and then you realize you've gone too far, then it's too late. You've already put everybody out of business." [42]

Again the New England congressional delegation pressured the council on behalf of fishers. Rep. James Longley Jr., R-Maine, wrote: "Make some modifications if you must, but do not destroy Maine's groundfishing industry solely to accomplish faster recovery rates." [43] Sen. Olympia Snowe, R-Maine, encouraged the council to resist pressure from the NMFS to move more quickly. The Massachusetts delegation also weighed in. Democratic senator Ted Kennedy, Democratic representatives Barney Frank and Joseph Kennedy, and Republican representative Peter Torkildsen urged the NMFS to postpone further fishing restrictions until the socioeconomic impacts of the changes on fishing communities had been assessed.

The council was clearly in a bind. Empowered by the CLF lawsuit and backed by a coalition of environmental groups, NMFS regional director Andy Rosenberg insisted that the council make conserving the fish its primary concern. NEFSC scientists were convinced that the groundfish decline was continuing unabated, despite measures instituted the previous year. Even a handful of fishers doubted the wisdom of phased-in conservation rules and thought the fishers needed to take responsibility for the health of the fishery and stop resisting protective measures. John Williamson, a fisher from Kennebunkport, Maine, pointed out that the council's year-and-a-half-long deliberation constituted a sufficient phase-in for the plan.[44] With NMFS threatening to withhold the money for the boat buyout unless it reduced fishing dramatically and fishers, backed by their congressional delegations, undermining its attempts to do so, the council spent meeting after meeting trying to arrive at an amendment that everyone could live with.

The council rejected the option of banning groundfishing altogether, but then began to debate a mix of three alternatives: closing large fishing territories; reducing days at sea; and carving the fishery into inshore and offshore regions, each with its own quotas. Complicating the decision was the council's continuing concern that the rules affect all fishers equally, regardless of gear type or boat size. In late January 1996 the council agreed on Amendment 7 by a vote of eleven to three and sent its proposal to the commerce secretary for review. Bowing to congressional pressure, the proposal gradually phased in days-at-sea limits for cod, haddock, and yellowtail flounder and instituted "rolling" closures of 9,000 square miles of fishing grounds.[45] Under the plan, a typical boat was allowed 139 days at sea in 1996 and 88 in 1997, a considerable reduction from the 250–300 days previously allowed.[46] The plan also limited the total allowable catch for cod to 2,770 metric tons in 1996, about one-third of the 1993 catch, and reduced it further in 1997.[47] Despite the accommodations made to their industry, many fishers opposed Amendment 7, and congressional representatives notified Secretary Brown of their concerns about economic harm. Nevertheless, the Commerce Department approved the proposal, and it went into effect in July 1996.

Six months later, at the December 11–12 council meeting, the Multispecies Monitoring Committee (MMC) delivered its first assessment of Amendment 7.[48] The good news was that overfishing had been halted for all stocks except Gulf of Maine cod, and all were showing increases for the first time in years. The MMC remained cautious, however, noting that most stocks still needed to double or triple in size before they would reach minimum acceptable levels and that the measures contained in Amendment 7 would not be enough to accomplish this goal. It recommended an additional 62 percent cut in fishing for yellowtail and a 57 percent reduction in cod harvests on Georges Bank. Pressed by Andy Rosenberg, the council voted to begin drawing up additional rules and to consider drastic proposals such as reducing the number of days at sea for cod fishing to as few as fourteen for the 1997 season.[49]

Reauthorizing the Magnuson Act

While the New England Council was wrestling with Amendment 7, proponents of a more protective legislative mandate for fisheries had been raising the salience of overfishing nationally, using events in New England as well as problems in the Gulf Coast and Pacific Northwest as cautionary tales. Environmentalists identified several failings of the Magnuson Act that they wanted to see Congress address, but, most important, they contended it was vague in its fishery conservation mandate. In particular, although the 1989 revisions required each FMP to contain an objective and measurable definition of overfishing and a recovery plan in the event that overfishing occurred, some critics wanted to see those guidelines delineated in the statute itself. They also wanted the act to specify the period of time within which councils were to address overfishing once it had been identified. Finally, they hoped to refine the concept of optimum yield to emphasize the primacy of conservation, rather than economic and social considerations.

In 1996 Congress passed the Sustainable Fisheries Act (SFA), an amendment to the Magnuson Act that addressed that law's three biggest deficiencies: overfishing, bycatch, and habitat degradation. The SFA mandated that each fishery management plan include an explicit definition of overfishing for the fishery, a rebuilding plan for overfished stocks, a timetable of less than ten years for reaching recovery, conservation and management measures to avoid bycatch, and a description of essential habitats and management measures to protect them. The law gave the councils two years to amend their existing plans and prepare new ones where necessary.

The Focus Shifts to Gulf of Maine Cod

Although NEFSC reports in late 1997 confirmed that several groundfish species had begun to recover, they also made it clear that New England faced a crisis in the Gulf of Maine cod fishery. This news, combined with the new SFA requirements, severely restricted the council's options. In early January 1998, following yet another round of scientific reports documenting the cod's decline, the council announced that rules aimed at reducing the total cod catch by 63 percent would take effect in May 1998. Meanwhile, in April Framework Adjustment 24 limited Gulf of Maine cod landings to 1,000 pounds per day and total days at sea to fourteen.[50] A month later, Framework Adjustment 25 reduced the cod landing limit to 700 pounds per day and instituted a four-step rolling closure of inshore fisheries. By June, when half of the total allowable catch of 1,783 metric tons was reached, NMFS reduced the cod landing limit to 400 pounds. And by late summer the council had no choice but to consider closing the Gulf of Maine fishery entirely.

In December 1998 the council heard yet another bleak scientific presentation by the MMC documenting serious overfishing of Gulf of Maine cod, which were at a record low despite strict fishing restrictions. Because the SFA required that the cod population not drop below 7,500 metric tons, and scientists believed it was already down to around 8,300, the committee recommended an 80 percent catch reduction—to a total of 782 metric tons—in 1999.[51] "You want to get these [catches] as close to zero as possible," asserted MMC chair Steven Correia.[52] Accomplishing such a goal without creating new problems would be no mean feat, however. Extremely low catch limits exacerbate the problem of bycatch, as fishers are forced to throw away any fish above the limit. Furthermore, days-at-sea limits and ocean closures prompt fishers to shift their efforts to alternative species or new fishing grounds. Partly as a result of pressure from displaced groundfishers, shrimp, herring, and lobster fisheries were facing crises of their own.

In response to the MMC's recommendations, the council announced an emergency three-month closure, to begin in February 1999, of the cod fishery off the Massachusetts coast. The council's action, targeting the area where cod were concentrated, set off yet another round of protests. In January 1999, when the council took up proposals to address the Gulf of Maine cod problem more permanently, it faced an industry split by two major divides. First, Maine fishers insisted that Massachusetts and New Hampshire fishers needed to share the burden of rescuing the cod; second, small boat owners, which are limited to inshore fisheries, demanded regulations that did not discriminate between them and large boats, which have more flexibility to pursue fish off-shore. As the fishers lined up behind competing approaches, their congressional representatives echoed their concerns, further highlighting the tension among states.

The council had three proposals before it, all aimed at meeting the goals for cod established by the MMC: (1) expand the existing regulatory regime of days at sea and daily catch limits, combined with rolling closures; (2) ban groundfishing all spring and summer in waters within forty miles of the coast between Cape Cod and south of Portland; and (3) divide the gulf into inshore and offshore fisheries and require every boat to limit itself to one or the other. After a long and rancorous debate, the council rejected all three. According to journalist David Dobbs, by the final meeting, "no one trusted anyone. All the council members looked exhausted or scared or depressed or angry . . . and most of the audience appeared on the verge of rage or despair." [53] After the lunch break, security guards barely averted a violent confrontation between audience members and the council. At 1:00 a.m., the council finally came up with Framework Adjustment 27, which expanded the previous year's rolling closures and cut the daily catch limits to 100 pounds, while authorizing the administrator to cut trip limits to as low as five pounds if landings exceeded half the total allowable catch of 800 metric tons. [54]

Under pressure from Massachusetts and New Hampshire members and over the objections of members from Maine, the council opened inshore cod grounds off Portsmouth, New Hampshire, and Gloucester, Massachusetts. Thus, it was hardly surprising when, less than a month after the measures went into effect, fishers hit the 400 metric ton trigger point, and NMFS reduced the daily catch limit on cod to thirty pounds. Fishers were dumbfounded. "Fishermen all over the Gulf were catching cod no matter what they did to avoid them," Dobbs reports, describing one fisher who—despite his efforts to catch flounder without ensnaring cod—found that all he could do was catch the two in even proportions. [55] Fishers found the waste horrific and complained bitterly to NMFS that its scientific assessments were inaccurate. The agency held firm, however, continuing to defend its view by saying that the cod populations had not increased overall but had contracted into their core areas, so that when those areas reopened the fishers were right on top of them.[56]

Amendment 9 and a Second Lawsuit

As it was wrestling with what to do about Gulf of Maine cod, the council—having acknowledged that Amendment 7 did not meet the SFA's goals—began working on a new, even more stringent amendment. In September 1998 the council submitted, and in November 1999 NMFS approved, Amendment 9, which established biomass and fishing mortality targets consistent with the SFA's mandate to rebuild overfished stocks within ten years. But the following April, at the council's urging, NMFS implemented Framework Adjustment 33, which aimed to meet only the fishing mortality targets in Amendment 7, not the more ambitious ones contained in Amendment 9. A month later, four environmental groups, including the CLF, sued the agency for failing to institute rules consistent with the new overfishing definitions in Amendment 9 and for failing to minimize bycatch, as required by the SFA. Council officials admitted that Framework Adjustment 33 did not meet the standards set out by the SFA but said that, anticipating a time-consuming public review process, they wanted to get something in place by the deadline.[57]

In December 2001 U.S. district court judge Gladys Kessler issued her ruling. Citing "inaction and delay" by the council, she ordered NMFS to implement Amendment 9 so that groundfish stocks could rebuild by the statutory deadline of 2009. Four months later, after the council failed to come up with its own measures, Judge Kessler handed down a draconian set of rules for the 2002 fishing season and required the council to put in place a new set of restrictions by August 2003. The judge acknowledged that "the livelihood . . . of many thousands of individuals, families, small businesses, and maritime communities [would] be affected" by her decision, but she noted that "the future of a precious resource—the once rich, vibrant and healthy and now severely depleted New England Northeast fishery—[was] at stake." [58]

Ten days later, more than 100 fishing boats crowded into Gloucester for a rally to protest the judicial decree. Fishers and politicians denounced the new rules, saying, "To place further restrictions on fishermen at a time when the stocks are rebounding makes no sense." [59] Federal scientists and environmentalists responded that new data suggested fish stocks could rebound to a greater extent than once believed, and managers should impose sufficiently protective measures to allow fish populations to thrive. According to Eric Bilsky of Oceana, an environmental protection group, "[It] doesn't mean when fish show up things are OK. It just shows we are out of the critical care unit and into the intensive care unit." [60] (Judge Kessler subsequently softened her rules somewhat in response to fishers' objections.)

Disgruntled fishers seized another opportunity to disparage the science on which the rules were based when in September 2002 they discovered an improperly rigged survey net on one of the NEFSC's two research trawlers. A detailed report issued the following month concluded that, although two years of equipment problems had affected the nets' performance, it did not cause scientists to underestimate groundfish populations. But the findings did not appease disaffected fishers, who continued to refer to the incident as "Trawlgate." The NEFSC's Steve Murawski pointed out that even if the Albatross fish surveys were off by 100 percent, the overall picture would not change much. "We are so far from the goal post," he said, "that, even inserting a huge error in our computer models, the status does not change much." [61] But many fishers remained skeptical and asserted that cod, haddock, and other groundfish were more plentiful than scientific reports indicated. In early November, after yet another demonstration by angry fishers, the council asked Judge Kessler for a delay on new fishing rules in order to review the stock assessments. (Environmentalists supported the delay, hoping it would allow time to improve the public understanding of the science behind the rules.) In December the judge granted an eight-month delay but retained the 2009 rebuilding deadline.

In 2003, after another round of emotional and contentious public meetings, the council produced Amendment 13, a modified version of a proposal devised by an industry group, the Northeast Seafood Coalition, and the least stringent alternative of the five the council had considered. Instituted in May 2004, it cut days at sea by 25 percent, to an average of fifty-two days per year, but contained several provisions that worried environmentalists. First, it created a new category of fishing days ("B" days) that would allow fishers to go after rebounding and therefore relatively plentiful species, such as haddock. Second, it allowed fishers to lease fishing days from one another—a provision that environmentalists feared could undermine days-at-sea reductions. Oceana, the CLF, and the National Resources Defense Council immediately filed suit saying that Amendment 13 would not end overfishing of Georges Bank cod or four other significantly depleted groundfish stocks.

OUTCOMES

With a progressively more protective management regime in place since the mid-1990s, fishery scientists and managers are cautiously optimistic about the prognosis for most of the New England groundfish stocks. In June 2001 NMFS estimated that biomass levels for eleven groundfish stocks had increased almost 250 percent since 1994.[62] A 2002 report found that biomasses for seven groundfish stocks were 50 percent of the way toward rebuilt status and that, since 1995, nineteen of twenty stocks had improved, with a median stock size increase of 177 percent. At the same time, the report noted, fishing effort continued to be higher than the long-term sustainable rate for about half of the twenty stocks examined.[63] The following year, scientists reported that haddock and other populations were still rebounding, albeit not fast enough to comply with the SFA, but that other populations, such as Cape Cod yellowtail flounder, were still in danger of collapse.[64] In spring 2004 scientists reported the largest year-class of haddock ever recorded, a finding they interpreted as evidence that strict management measures were working. And in September 2005 the NEFSC told the council that fishing pressure had been reduced on most of the nineteen stocks it assessed between 2001 and 2004. Scientists found that overfishing was not occurring on ten of them, and population size increased for at least six. Since the 2001 assessment fishing rates had been lowered on thirteen stocks by an average of 50 percent.[65]

The news on cod was more perplexing, however. In early 2001 NMFS reported that the measures imposed to reduce the harvest of Gulf of Maine cod may have finally achieved the mortality rates scientists thought necessary to reverse the stock's decline. NMFS found that the total cod landings approached the target of 1,364 metric tons, compared to landings in 1996, 1997, and 1998 that had been double the target.[66] In September 2005, however, scientists reported that cod populations in the Gulf of Maine and around Georges Bank had plummeted nearly 23 percent between 2001 and 2004. According to University of Maine marine biologist Bob Steneck, this decline reflects the fact that cod are "remarkably fragile when they are in the early stages of rebuilding." [67] A study by Canadian scientists published in *Science* in June 2005 suggested the collapse of cod off Nova Scotia had changed the ecosystem so dramatically it may be impossible for cod to recover. The scientists documented an effect that has been observed in marine ecosystems around the world: as the population of large predators (in this case, cod) declines, species lower on the food chain proliferate. Those smaller species, in turn, eat their predators' eggs, larvae, and juveniles—preventing the predators from rebounding.[68]

In addition to their worries about cod, fishery managers remain concerned about the long term because the fleet still has a much greater capacity to catch fish than the waters of New England can sustain. Managers worry that any rebound in fish stocks will prompt fishers with permits to resume fishing, which could undermine recovery efforts. To address this concern, Congress authorized two $10 million buyout programs (in addition to the $25 million buyout implemented in 1996) to purchase latent groundfishing permits. Prior to this second round of buyouts, there were 1,732 groundfish permit holders in New England; combined, these boats were eligible to fish 154,286 days at sea, although only a fraction were used—for example, 51,880 in 1998.[69] The buyouts promised to eliminate only a fraction of these permits, however, and NMFS estimates that New England can support only 300 to 400 boats, even after fish populations rebound.

In the meantime, New England fishery managers hope that cooperative research initiatives undertaken by NMFS and the council will enhance understanding of the fish stocks and the effect of fishery management regimes and build mutual respect among fishers and scientists. In the Northeast, three main cooperative research programs are under way: bottom-up planning among scientists and fishers that aims to solve individual fishery management problems; the Research Partners program administered by the NMFS Northeast regional office; and the New England Consortium Cooperative Research, comprising the University of New Hampshire, the University of Maine, the Massachusetts

Institute of Technology, and the Woods Hole Oceanographic Institution. Although NEFSC scientists emphasize that such efforts cannot substitute for long-term, standardized resource surveys conducted by research vessels, they hope that they will make "valuable and unique contributions to the science underlying fishery management."[70]

CONCLUSIONS

Since 1976 New England fishery managers have spun their wheels trying to institute effective schemes to save the groundfish while simultaneously preserving the character of the New England fishery. For two decades, cooperative management—as mandated by the Magnuson Act—translated into trying to devise conservation policies that did not antagonize fishers. For the most part, the resulting policy consisted of reactionary measures prompted by crises; until recently, those measures did little more than slow the demise of the fishers at the expense of the fish. The eventual shift to a more restrictive fishing regime was not the result of a recognition by the council or fishers that scientists were right, however. In fact, as late as the early 1990s, exploitation rates of cod and yellowtail flounder were 55 percent and 65 percent of biomass, respectively, even though scientists recommended exploitation levels of 13 percent and 22 percent.[71] Rather, the CLF lawsuit empowered NMFS officials to force the council's hand.

Many observers believe that even the more stringent measures imposed in 2004 will fail to save the groundfish in the long run unless managers create private property rights in the fishery. Their pessimism stems from their adherence to the model of behavior embodied in the tragedy of the commons model. Certainly the actions of New England fishers since the early 1970s are consistent with that model: individual fishers reacted to whatever measures fishery managers put in place by expanding their effort in other ways. They pursued short-term economic gains at the expense of the long-term health of the fishery, and few seemed prepared to sacrifice their catch without assurances that others would do the same.

Some analysts have questioned the assumptions that underlie the tragedy of the commons model, however, arguing that people are not always as self-serving, individualistic, and short-sighted as the model posits.[72] They point to communities that have successfully managed their common property resources, such as the Maine lobster fishers, who have maintained a system of self-regulation for more than a century.[73] Although this and other examples suggest that the tragedy of the commons is not inevitable, they have limited applicability. As Elinor Ostrom explains, successful co-management is more likely to succeed where common pool resources have been managed by a settled, homogeneous population under long-enduring institutions, so that the populations believe they or their children will reap the benefits of conservation and are therefore more likely to adhere to agreements.[74] After examining unsuccessful experiments with co-management, such as the Canadian effort to establish a cooperative regime in the Bay of Fundy, anthropologist James McGoodwin concludes that co-management can generate new problems or heighten old ones: members' organizations may become embroiled in internal disputes or run into trouble if they have insufficient autonomy; unless they receive enough technical assistance, they may not be competent to carry out the responsibilities delegated to them.[75]

These caveats resonate. The fishermen of New England are not ideal candidates for co-management because they do not trust each other, do not communicate regularly, and have little experience forming binding agreements with one another. In addition, although some have joined in cooperative research projects sponsored by NMFS to improve relationships between scientists and fishers, others remain uneasy about the science on which management decisions are based. Workable solutions in New England are therefore likely to depend heavily on controlling access to the fishery rather than on cooperative schemes. But more than anything, New England fishers value their independence and their egalitarian view that "anyone should be able to go out and fish," so they adamantly oppose limiting entry into the fishery.[76]

The most popular approach to controlling access to fisheries involves distributing individual transferable quotas (ITQs) to individual fishers or fishing enterprises. Under an ITQ system, the owner of a quota share has exclusive rights to a particular fishery, to take a certain proportion or amount of fish in the fishery, and—in most instances—to sell or lease that right to others. ITQs are currently the most widely discussed solutions for overcrowded fisheries, but implementing an ITQ system can have broad and controversial social consequences; for example, such systems can concentrate the benefits of a fishery in the hands of a privileged few. Consolidation of the industry is not inevitable under an ITQ system, however; in Alaska's fishery, quotas for small boat owners are allocated in blocks, and no single owner can have more than five blocks.[77]

The Australian lobster fishing regime is another example of a successful ITQ system. Beginning in the 1960s the Australian government set a limit on the total number of lobster traps and then assigned licenses to working fishers. From then on, any newcomer had to buy a license from someone already working in the fishery, much the way the New York City taxi medallion system works. Australian lobster fishers now work 187 days a year (compared to as many as 240 days per year for Rhode Island lobster catchers), tending sixty traps apiece (versus as many as 800 as is typical in Rhode Island). Proponents of the Australian system point out that it has not only rejuvenated the stocks and enhanced the lives of the fishers (who make significantly more money than their American counterparts); it has also eased tension between fishers and scientists, who now work collaboratively to keep the fishery healthy.[78]

In 1996 Congress imposed a moratorium on ITQs under pressure from fishers who feared losing open access to the nation's fisheries. The National Academy of Sciences has endorsed ITQs, however, and Congress is considering lifting the ban. Although New England fishers would almost certainly resist the imposition of such a system, it is likely to be the first solution on the table when the next opportunity for policy change occurs.

QUESTIONS TO CONSIDER

- One explanation for why federal managers delayed acting to conserve the fishery, despite repeated warnings from scientists, is that there was a time lag between the receipt of scientific advice and action. Does that seem like an adequate explanation? Why or why not?
- What kind of regulation is most appropriate for New England to prevent the recurrence of overfishing? Does the political will exist to undertake the conservation measures you recommend?
- To what extent should those whose livelihoods depend on fish have a say in decisions about those regulations? What form should their participation take, how should their views be incorporated, and why?

Notes

1. Groundfish, or demersals, dwell at or near the bottom of the sea. The New England groundfish include members of the cod family (cod, haddock, hakes, pollock), flounders, dogfish sharks, and skates.
2. Garrett Hardin, "The Tragedy of the Commons," *Science*, December 13, 1968, 1243–8.
3. Elinor Ostrom, *Governing the Commons: The Evolution of Institutions for Collective Action* (New York: Cambridge University Press, 1990), 1.
4. Quoted in Carl Safina, "Where Have All the Fishes Gone?" *Issues in Science and Technology* (Spring 1994): 38.
5. Recruitment overfishing occurs when fishers reduce too many spawning adults and thereby affect the population's ability to reproduce. See Steven A. Murawski et al., "New England Groundfish," in National Marine Fisheries Service, *Our Living Oceans: Report on the Status of U.S. Living Marine Resources*, 1999, NOAA Technical Memo NMFS-F/SPO-41 (December 1999).
6. William Warner, *Distant Water: The Fate of the North Atlantic Fishermen* (Boston: Little, Brown, 1983).
7. Rodman D. Griffin, "Marine Mammals vs. Fish," *CQ Researcher*, August 28, 1992, 744.
8. Warner, *Distant Water*, viii.
9. A metric ton is equal to 1,000 kilograms, or approximately 2,200 pounds. See Murawski et al., "New England Groundfish."
10. National Marine Fisheries Service, *Our Living Oceans: Report on the Status of U.S. Living Marine Resources*, 1993, NOAA Technical Memo NMFS-F/SPO-15 (December 1993).
11. Warner, *Distant Water*.
12. Ibid.
13. Margaret E. Dewar, *Industry in Trouble: The Federal Government and the New England Fisheries* (Philadelphia: Temple University Press, 1983).
14. The coastal fisheries (zero to three miles off the coast) are managed by states and by interstate compacts.
15. PL 94-265, 90 Stat. 331; 16 USC sections 1801–1882.
16. Quoted in H. John Heinz III Center for Science, Economics, and the Environment, *Fishing Grounds: Defining a New Era for American Fisheries Management* (Washington, D.C.: Island Press, 2000), 87.

17. In 1996 the UN Food and Agriculture Organization estimated that 27 million metric tons of marine fish were killed as bycatch worldwide each year. In 2004 that bycatch estimate dropped to about 7.3 million tons, in part due to adoption of measures by fishers to avoid bycatch but also as a result of better use of the catch and improved reporting. See United Nations Food and Agriculture Organization, "New Data Show Sizeable Drop in Number of Fish Wasted," press release, September 14, 2004.

18. National Research Council, *Review of Northeast Fishery Stock Assessments* (Washington, D.C.: National Academy Press, 1998).

19. David E. Pierce, "Development and Evolution of Fishery Management Plans for Cod, Haddock, and Yellowtail Flounder" (Boston: Massachusetts Division of Marine Fisheries, 1982).

20. The New England Council has eighteen voting members: the regional administrator of the NMFS; the principal state officials with marine fishery responsibility from Connecticut, Maine, Massachusetts, New Hampshire, and Rhode Island; and twelve members nominated by the governor and appointed by the secretary of commerce. The council also has four nonvoting members: one each from the U.S. Coast Guard, the U.S. Fish and Wildlife Service, the U.S. Department of State, and the Atlantic States Marine Fisheries Commission.

21. Quoted in Heinz Center, *Fishing Grounds*, 88.

22. Eleanor M. Dorsey, "The 602 Guidelines on Overfishing: A Perspective from New England," in *Conserving America's Fisheries*, ed. R. H. Stroud (Savannah, Ga.: National Coalition for Marine Conservation, 1994), 181–188.

23. "Cap'n Sane Says," *National Fisherman*, May 1978.

24. Quoted in Pierce, "Development and Evolution of Fishery Management Plans," 13.

25. Madeleine Hall-Arber, " 'They' Are the Problem: Assessing Fisheries Management in New England," *Nor'Easter* (Fall-Winter 1993): 16–21.

26. Sonja V. Fordham, *New England Groundfish: From Glory to Grief* (Washington, D.C.: Center for Marine Conservation, 1996).

27. The standard investment tax credit was available to anyone, but was especially appealing to capital-intensive industries like fishing. The fishery-specific Capital Construction Fund program allowed fishing boat owners to set aside and invest pretax dollars for later use in upgrading or buying fishing boats. The Fishery Vessel Obligation Guarantee program provided government-guaranteed boat-building loans at lower interest rates and longer payback periods than traditional five-year loans. These and other incentives—such as fuel tax relief, gear replacement funds, and market expansion programs—attracted fishers into the industry and encouraged existing boat owners to expand and upgrade their boats. See David Dobbs, *The Great Gulf* (Washington, D.C.: Island Press, 2000); Heinz Center, *Fishing Grounds*.

28. Murawski et al., "New England Groundfish."

29. Dobbs, *The Great Gulf*.

30. Dorsey, "The 602 Guidelines."

31. PL 94-265, 90 Stat. 331.

32. Dorsey, "The 602 Guidelines."

33. Ibid.

34. In theory, optimal yield is the level of catch that will allow the stocks to sustain themselves, modified by any relevant economic, social, or ecological factor.

35. Dorsey, "The 602 Guidelines," 185.

36. Massachusetts Offshore Groundfish Task Force, *New England Groundfish in Crisis—Again*, Publication No. 16, 551-42-200-1-91-CR (December 1990).

37. Previous amendments had involved nongroundfish species.

38. In prior years NMFS had closed Area 2 of Georges Bank between February 1 and May 31 to protect spawning groundfish. The emergency order extended the closure

and enlarged the covered area. See John Laidler, "U.S. Emergency Order Shuts Part of Georges Bank to Fishing," *Boston Globe*, June 4, 1993, 31.

39. Northeast Fisheries Science Center, *Report of the 18th Northeast Regional Stock Assessment Workshop: Stock Assessment Review Committee Consensus Summary of Assessments*, 1994, NEFSC Ref. Doc. 94-22.

40. Quoted in Sam Walker, "Georges Bank Closes, Ending an Era," *Christian Science Monitor*, December 12, 1994, 1.

41. Ibid.

42. Quoted in Edie Lau, "Panel Backs Cutting Days for Fishing," *Portland Press Herald*, October 26, 1995, 1B.

43. Quoted in Linc Bedrosian, "Portland: Amendment 7 Is Sheer Lunacy," *National Fisherman*, December 1995, 17.

44. Edie Lau, "Council to Phase in Restraints," *Portland Press Herald*, December 15, 1995, 1.

45. Rolling closures are area closures that are instituted one after the other, as stocks migrate.

46. Andrew Garber, "Lawsuit Put on Fast Track," *Portland Press Herald*, August 9, 1996, 2B.

47. The actual 1996 cod catch was 6,957 metric tons, however. See Andrew Garber, "Report Calls for Deeper Cuts in Catches to Save Groundfish," *Portland Press Herald*, December 7, 1996, 1.

48. The monitoring committee includes scientists, managers, and a fisher.

49. Garber, "Report Calls for Deeper Cuts"; "New England Fisheries News" (Boston: Conservation Law Foundation, December 1996).

50. A framework adjustment can be implemented more quickly than a full-blown plan amendment.

51. John Richardson, "Panel to Vote on Drastic Cod Limits," *Portland Press Herald*, December 10, 1998, 4B.

52. Quoted in John Richardson, "Fishery Closure Also Lifts Hopes," *Portland Press Herald*, December 12, 1998, 1B.

53. Dobbs, *The Great Gulf*, 153.

54. "Closure and Trip Limits Are Part of Framework 27," *NMFS Northeast Region News*, April 30, 1999.

55. Dobbs, *The Great Gulf*, 174.

56. Ibid.

57. Associated Press, "Hard Line on Fishing Is Pushed in Lawsuit," *Portland Press Herald*, May 23, 2000, 2B.

58. Quoted in Susan Young, "Judge Sets Number of Fishing Days," *Bangor Daily News*, April 27, 2002, 1.

59. Quoted in Beth Daley, "New U.S. Fishing Rules Protested," *Boston Globe*, May 6, 2002, B1.

60. Quoted in ibid.

61. Quoted in David Arnold, "U.S. Study Say Fish Numbers Accurate," *Boston Globe*, October 26, 2002, B1.

62. Jerry Fraser, "Fix the Fisheries Act," *Boston Globe*, January 14, 2002, 11.

63. National Oceanic and Atmospheric Administration, "Groundfish Data Collected With Mismarked Gear Stand Up in Statistical Analysis," NMFS Northeast Fisheries Science Center News, October 25, 2002.

64. John Richardson, "Fishing Council Begins Its Process of Elimination," *Portland Press Herald*, July 17, 2003, 1B.

65. National Oceanic and Atmospheric Administration, "NOAA Issues Report on the Status of New England Groundfish Stocks," NMFS Northeast Fisheries Science Center News, September 13, 2005.

66. "Gulf of Maine Cod Near Landings Target for First Time," *NMFS Northeast Region News,* January 18, 2001.

67. Quoted in Tom Bell, "Report: Cod Rebound in Doubt," *Portland Press Herald,* September 14, 2005, 1.

68. Tom Bell, "Decline in Codfish Stocks May Not Be Reversible," *Portland Press Herald,* June 27, 2005, 1.

69. Beth Daley, "Still Hooked Despite Federal Efforts, Fishermen Await Return to Sea," *Boston Globe,* May 24, 2001, B1; John Richardson, "Fishermen Sell Back Permits to Government," *Portland Press Herald,* May 26, 2002, 1.

70. Michael Sissenwine, "On Fisheries Cooperative Research," Testimony Before the Committee on Resources Subcommittee on Fisheries Conservation, Wildlife and Oceans, U.S. House of Representatives, December 11, 2001.

71. National Research Council, *Sustaining Marine Fisheries* (Washington, D.C.: National Academy Press, 1999).

72. See, for example, James R. McGoodwin, *Crisis in the World's Fisheries* (Stanford: Stanford University Press, 1990).

73. James M. Acheson, "Where Have All the Exploiters Gone?" in *Common Property Resources: Ecology and Community-Based Sustainable Development,* ed. Fikret Berkes (London: Bellhaven Press, 1989), 199–217.

74. Ostrom, *Governing the Commons.*

75. McGoodwin, *Crisis in the World's Fisheries.*

76. Hall-Arber, " 'They' Are the Problem."

77. Peter Weber, *Net Loss: Fish, Jobs, and the Marine Environment* (Washington, D.C.: Worldwatch Institute, 1994).

78. John Tierney, "A Tale of Two Fisheries," *New York Times Magazine,* August 27, 2000, 38–43.

Recommended Reading

Dobbs, David. *The Great Gulf.* Washington, D.C.: Island Press, 2000.

Fordham, Sonja V. *New England Groundfish: From Glory to Grief.* Washington, D.C.: Center for Marine Conservation, April 1996.

H. John Heinz III Center for Science, Economics, and the Environment. *Fishing Grounds: Defining a New Era for American Fisheries Management.* Washington, D.C.: Island Press, 2000.

National Research Council. *Sustaining Marine Fisheries.* Washington, D.C.: National Academy Press, 1999.

Web Sites

www.nefmc.org (New England Fishery Management Council site)

www.heinzctr.org/Programs/SOCW/overview.htm (Heinz Center for Science, Economics, and the Environment site)

www.nmfs.noaa.gov (NMFS site)

www.nefsc.nmfs.gov (NEFSC site)

CHAPTER 11

Climate Change

The Challenges of International Environmental Policymaking

The possibility that human activity is changing the earth's climate gained the spotlight in the United States in June 1988, when James Hansen, a scientist for the National Aeronautics and Space Agency testified before Congress that he was "ninety-nine percent confiden[t]" that "the greenhouse effect has been detected, and it is changing our climate now." [1] Shortly thereafter, the United Nations established the Intergovernmental Panel on Climate Change (IPCC), comprising 2,000 leading experts from around the world, to assess the extent and likely impacts of climate change. Since 1990 the IPCC—the most distinguished international group of scientists ever assembled to address a policy question—has reported with increasing certainty that man-made emissions of greenhouse gases are causing rapid and potentially damaging changes in the global climate. Yet the United States has demonstrated little political will to deal with the problem.

The climate change case vividly confirms that political factors shape the relationship between science and policy. Like the New England fisheries (described in chapter 10), the global climate is a commons, so collective action problems hamper efforts to formulate policies to manage it—even in the face of scientific consensus. Because both responsibility for and the impacts of climate change are diffuse, individual nations have an incentive to free ride on the improvements made by others. The obstacles to collective action are likely to be even more formidable in the international arena than they are within or across regions of the United States because no international institution can enforce binding decisions on sovereign nations. Instead, nations must cooperate voluntarily, a prospect that some political scientists find improbable.

Traditionally, scholars who study international relations have portrayed nations as unitary actors with a single goal: survival. According to this "realist" perspective, countries do not cooperate with one another unless it is in their self-interest to do so. Furthermore, a nation's interest is self-evident: each wants to maintain its security and power relative to other countries. Therefore, "the potential for international cooperation is limited, and international laws and institutions are likely to be fragile and impermanent." [2] Extending this view, neorealists contend that international cooperation may occur if a single state with a preponderance of power (a "hegemon") is willing to use its resources to transform international relations.[3] By contrast, liberal theorists (and neoliberal institutionalists) argue that nations are interdependent and that their common interests lead them to work together. A third school of thought builds on the notion of interdependence and emphasizes the concept of international regimes, which consist of "principles, norms, rules, and decision making procedures around which participants' expectations converge in a given issue area." [4]

International environmental scholars adopting the latter perspective have turned their attention to how and why such regimes develop and persist. In particular, they argue that a nation's self-interest—and therefore its willingness to participate in an international process—is *not* a given but must be discovered. Political scientist Helen Milner offers an important insight into this process, noting that

> cooperation among nations is affected less by fears of other countries' relative gains or cheating than it is by the domestic distributional consequences of cooperative endeavors. Cooperative agreements create winners and losers domestically; therefore they generate supporters and opponents. The internal struggle between these groups shapes the possibility and nature of international cooperative agreements.[5]

From this perspective, forging international agreements involves what political scientist Robert Putnam has called a two-level game, in which policymakers try simultaneously to "maximize their own ability to satisfy domestic pressures while minimizing the adverse consequences of foreign developments." [6]

According to the two-level game logic, the way climate change is defined domestically is a primary determinant of the U.S. position on international agreements to address it. As the preceding cases in this book have made clear, environmentalists have had great success defining problems in ways that enable them to challenge policies favoring development interests. Enhancing their credibility have been highly reputable knowledge brokers—experts who translate scientific explanations into political stories—as well as the backing of authoritative scientific assessments. But conservative interests that oppose environmental regulation have not been passive; they have responded by forming interest groups and funding experts and think tanks of their own. As political scientists Darrell West and Burdett Loomis point out, well-heeled interests have become adept at generating information and embedding it in narratives. With their vast resources, industry coalitions can pay top lobbyists to craft storylines and disseminate them among legislators, their staffs, and opinion leaders. They can also inundate the public with their messages via television, radio, direct mail, telemarketing, and billboards.[7]

In response to conservatives' formidable climate change campaign, environmentalists have adopted some new tactics of their own. One approach has been to press for state-level policies to regulate carbon dioxide emissions and institute other climate-related policies. At one time, such unilateral efforts by individual states to address an environmental problem—particularly a transboundary problem such as climate change—would be unthinkable. In the 1960s few states had adopted strong measures to address air and water pollution (see chapter 2), and many observers theorized that, left to their own devices, states would engage in a race-to-the-bottom, competing to attract dirty industries and the economic benefits they bring. Environmentalists were also loath to fight on fifty fronts rather than one and so preferred federal policymaking to action at the state level. Since the late 1970s, however, states have greatly expanded their capacity to make and implement policy, and a growing chorus of scholars insists that states ought to play a larger role in solving the next generation of environmental problems.[8]

In addition to promoting state-level action, environmentalists have tried to persuade business leaders that mandatory federal greenhouse gas emissions limits are in their interest. Some groups have adopted confrontational tactics. Greenpeace and the Rainforest Action Network have used consumer boycotts and negative publicity campaigns to tarnish the reputations of big companies who oppose policies to curb global warming. Environmentalists and religious groups have joined forces to submit shareholder resolutions demanding that corporations reveal their global warming liability. But other groups, such as Environmental Defense and the World Wildlife Fund, have adopted a more conciliatory approach, working collaboratively to promote the environmentally friendly image of businesses that agree to reduce their emissions voluntarily.[9]

BACKGROUND

Modern scientific interest in climate change originated in the 1950s, but more than a century earlier scientists had discovered the "greenhouse effect" by which the earth's atmosphere keeps the planet warm. The process begins when the earth absorbs radiation from the sun in the form of visible light; that energy is then redistributed by the atmosphere and the ocean and re-radiated to space at a longer (infrared) wavelength. Most of that thermal radiation in turn is absorbed by greenhouse gases in the atmosphere, particularly water vapor, carbon dioxide (CO_2), methane, chlorofluorocarbons (CFCs), and ozone. The absorbed energy is then re-radiated both downwards and upwards. The result is that the earth's surface loses less heat to space than it would in the absence of greenhouse gases and therefore stays warmer than it would otherwise (see Figure 11-1).[10]

A series of discoveries in the nineteenth century laid the groundwork for subsequent investigations into the human impact on the climate. In 1827 French scientist Jean-Baptiste Fourier found that atmospheric gases help keep the climate warm by trapping thermal radiation in a fashion he likened to the role of glass in a greenhouse. In 1860 a British scientist, John Tyndall, measured the absorption of infrared radiation by CO_2 and water vapor. In 1896 Swedish scientist Svante Arrhenius estimated that doubling CO_2 concentrations would raise the average global temperature by 5 to 6 degrees Celsius. American geologist T. C. Chamberlin warned independently that the fossil fuel combustion that accompanied industrialization could lead to an out-of-control greenhouse effect. In 1938 British meteorologist G. D. Callendar calculated the actual

Figure 11-1 The Global Carbon Cycle

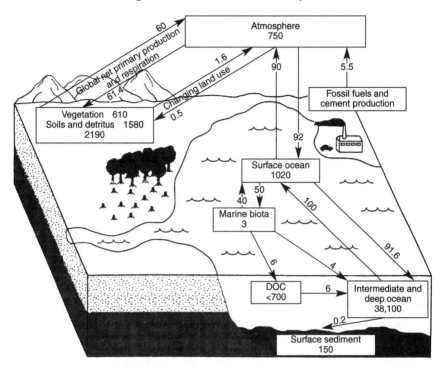

Source: IPCC, ed. J. T. Houghton, et al., *Climate Change 1994* (New York: Cambridge, 1995).

Note: The numbers in boxes indicate the size of GtC of each reservoir. On each arrow is indicated the magnitude of the flux in GtC/yr (DOC = dissolved organic carbon).

warming due to CO_2 from burning fossil fuels using data gathered from 200 weather stations around the world. Callendar's report was met with skepticism, however; the prevailing scientific view during the first half of the twentieth century was that climate remains constant, experiencing only short-term fluctuations.[11]

In the late 1950s scientists revisited the possibility that greenhouse gases might accumulate in the atmosphere and eventually cause a runaway greenhouse effect. In 1957 Roger Revelle and Hans Suess of the Scripps Institute of Oceanography published a paper to that effect after they discovered that the oceans had not absorbed as much CO_2 as previously assumed. Revelle and Suess coined an expression that subsequently became a catchphrase of climate change policy advocates; they claimed that human beings were carrying out a unique, "large scale geophysical experiment." [12] Prompted by these concerns,

Figure 11-2 Mauna Loa Annual Mean Carbon Dioxide

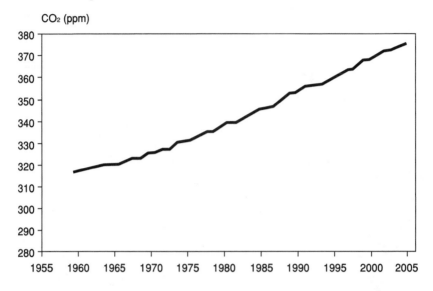

CO₂ (ppm)

Sources: Scripps Institution of Oceanography; National Oceanic and Atmospheric Administration.

Note: Atmospheric concentrations of CO_2 are expressed in parts per million (ppm) and reported in the 1999 SIO manometric mole fraction scale. Missing values are denoted by –99.99. In years where one monthly value is missing annual values were calculated by substituting a fit value (4-harmonics with gain factor and spline) for that month and then averaging the twelve monthly values.

in 1957 Revelle's graduate student, Charles David Keeling, instituted routine measurements of CO_2 at the observatory in Mauna Loa, Hawaii. By the early 1960s instruments at the observatory were detecting steady increases in CO_2 concentrations (see Figure 11-2). In 1963 the Conservation Foundation issued a report entitled *Implications of the Rising Carbon Dioxide Content of the Atmosphere*, one of the first to speculate on the possible consequences of this trend. Shortly thereafter, a group of White House science advisers led by Revelle concluded that a projected 25 percent increase in atmospheric CO_2 concentrations could cause marked changes in the earth's climate, with possibly deleterious consequences for humans.[13]

During the 1970s scientists debated whether changes in CO_2 concentrations were likely to produce global warming or global cooling, but over time scientific opinion converged on the warming hypothesis. In the United States the National Academy of Sciences (NAS) launched a series of efforts to assess the scientific understanding of CO_2 and climate, all of which warned about the potentially severe impacts of changes in the global climate. A 1979 NAS report advised that a "wait-and-see policy may mean waiting until it is too late" to avoid significant climatic changes.[14] Also in 1979 the World Meteorological Organization, which in 1974 had begun to examine the evidence, convened an international conference on the topic in Geneva and launched the World Climate Programme.[15] The final statement of the First World Climate Conference introduced the importance of factors besides greenhouse gas emissions and adopted a decidedly precautionary tone: "We can say with some confidence that the burning of fossil fuels, deforestation, and changes of land use have increased the amount of carbon dioxide in the atmosphere . . . and it appears plausible that [CO_2 increases] can contribute to a gradual warming of the lower atmosphere, especially at high latitudes." [16]

By the early 1980s scientists were becoming more outspoken about their concerns. Delegates to a 1980 international climate conference in Villach, Austria, issued alarms about global warming, and in 1983 the U.S. Environmental Protection Agency (EPA) released a report suggesting that global temperature increases could strain environmental, economic, and political systems.[17] In 1985 scientists from twenty-nine countries again met in Villach, where they agreed that human activity was causing increases in atmospheric concentrations of greenhouse gases and estimated that a doubling of atmospheric concentrations of CO_2 could lead to an increase in the global mean surface temperature of 1.5 to 4.5 degrees Celsius. Because such a temperature rise would be unprecedented in the period since the beginning of Holocene, they encouraged policymakers to begin considering responses.[18] More scientific consensus that humans were altering the global climate emerged from two subsequent climate workshops in 1987, one in Villach and the other in Bellagio, Italy.

THE CASE

Despite their unusually urgent tone, the periodic scientific bulletins of the 1970s and 1980s generated little social or political response in the United States. Instead, a number of severe weather episodes, combined with the activism of scientific knowledge brokers, briefly focused public attention on the issue of climate change. That attention in turn generated political support for UN-sponsored efforts to comprehend the phenomenon and its implications. But the improving scientific understanding that resulted did not translate into U.S. policy; rather, it prompted the mobilization of powerful interests opposed to international climate change policy. Those interests used their resources to emphasize scientific uncertainty and economic consequences and thereby undermine support for climate change policies among policymakers and the public. In the hopes of defusing domestic opposition, environmentalists have adopted a host of new tactics, from publicly challenging businesses that have resisted climate change policies to promoting market-based solutions and encouraging companies to adopt climate-friendly practices. Meanwhile, impatient with the lack of a national response, some states have begun to institute climate change policies of their own.

International Concern Leads to an Intergovernmental Panel

James Hansen's testimony is widely credited with triggering media attention to climate change in the United States. His highly publicized testimony asserted that human-induced global warming was imminent and that the phenomenon was sufficiently well understood that policymakers should act to address it. His appearance in June 1988 also coincided with one of the hottest and driest summers on record in North America. Hurricanes and other freak meteorological events around the world further enhanced the public's receptivity to the idea that the climate was changing. Although scientists were reluctant to attribute the severe weather to global warming, it provided an obvious hook for the media.

Two weeks after Hansen made his statement, government officials, environmentalists, and industry representatives from forty-eight countries assembled at a conference in Toronto to discuss the global security implications of climate change. Adopting an alarming version of Revelle and Suess's phrase, the Toronto Conference Statement concluded that "humanity is conducting an unintended, uncontrolled, globally pervasive experiment whose ultimate consequence could be second only to global nuclear war." [19] The statement recommended that governments begin negotiating a global convention as a framework to protect the atmosphere.[20] It further recommended that governments agree to reduce global emissions of CO_2 to 20 percent below 1988 levels by 2005 and create a "world atmosphere fund" from taxes on fossil fuel consumption in industrial countries.[21] Shortly after the Toronto conference, several world leaders—including Britain's prime minister, Margaret Thatcher, a former skeptic—made statements about the need for a government response to climate change.

As the scientific convergence grew, the United Nations Environment Programme and the World Meteorological Organization jointly sponsored the creation of the Intergovernmental Panel on Climate Change to provide policymakers with a scientific foundation for international negotiations. The IPCC met for the first time in November 1988, elected Swedish scientist Bert Bolin as its chair, and formulated a threefold mandate to: review the existing scientific literature on climate change and report on the scientific consensus (Working Group I), assess the environmental and socioeconomic impacts of climate change (Working Group II), and formulate response strategies (Working Group III).

The Bush Administration Demurs

Reflecting the heightened international attention, in 1989 the governing council of the UN Environmental Programme and the UN General Assembly adopted resolutions calling on governments to prepare a framework convention on climate change, as well as protocols spelling out concrete commitments based on scientific knowledge and taking into account the needs of developing countries. In July 1989 the statement of the Group of Seven major industrial democracies' annual summit called for "the early conclusion of an international convention to protect and conserve the global climate." [22] Rather than lead the charge, however, the Bush administration refused to propose or support climate policies, emphasizing instead the scientific uncertainties surrounding the issue.

To justify his position, President George H. W. Bush relied heavily on a paper issued by the conservative George C. Marshall Institute, entitled "Scientific Perspectives on the Greenhouse Problem," that downplayed the scientific consensus on climate change and concluded that it would be premature to impose policies to reduce greenhouse gas emissions. The president continued to tout the theme of scientific uncertainty in his April 1990 opening speech to a seventeen-nation White House Conference on Science and Economics Research Related to Global Climate Change, in which he said that before acting "what we need are facts." [23] In lieu of policy proposals, Bush called for further scientific investigation and a 60 percent increase in spending on research.

Hoping to pressure the administration, forty-nine Nobel Prize winners and 700 members of the NAS issued a public appeal, saying "there is broad agreement within the scientific community that amplification of the Earth's natural greenhouse effect by the buildup of various gases introduced by human activity has the potential to produce dramatic changes in climate. . . . Only by taking action now can we insure that future generations will not be put at risk." [24] The scientists' petition did not have much impact on President Bush, however. Nor was he moved to act by the May 1990 presentation by the IPCC of its interim findings, based on the work of 170 scientists from twenty-five countries, which concluded that:

- Emissions resulting from human activities are substantially increasing the atmospheric concentrations of the greenhouse gases: CO_2, methane, CFCs, and nitrous oxides (NO_x). For example, worldwide human-made emissions of CO_2, the main greenhouse gas, increased from less than 100 million tons per year before the industrial revolution to 6 billion tons per year in 1990. As a result, atmospheric concentrations of CO_2 rose from 280 parts per million (ppm) to more than 350 ppm and are continuing to climb.
- The evidence from modeling studies, observations, and sensitivity analyses indicate that the sensitivity of the global mean surface temperature to doubling CO_2 is unlikely to lie outside the 1.5 to 4.5 degrees Celsius range.
- There are many uncertainties in scientists' predictions, particularly with regard to the timing, magnitude, and regional patterns of climate change.
- Global mean surface air temperature has increased by 0.3 to 0.6 degrees Celsius over the last 100 years.
- The size of this warming is broadly consistent with predictions of climate models, but it is also of the same magnitude as natural climate variability.

Thus, the observed increase could be largely due to this natural variability; alternatively, natural variability combined with other human factors could have offset a still larger human-induced greenhouse warming.

- The unequivocal detection of the enhanced greenhouse effect from observations is not likely for a decade or more.[25]

The IPCC calculated that an immediate 60 percent reduction in CO_2 emissions would be needed to halt its buildup in the atmosphere.

The IPCC's Working Group II tried to forecast the consequences of climate change, acknowledging that its predictions were highly uncertain and based on a number of simplifying assumptions. Along with an increase in severe weather events and a higher incidence of infectious diseases, among the most serious potential consequences of a rapid increase in global temperatures projected by the panel was a rise in global sea level of between four and twelve inches in the next fifty years. Even at the low end of such a rise, coastal areas everywhere would be more vulnerable to flooding, and some regions would be partially submerged.

The IPCC's tentative tone notwithstanding, many European leaders responded with alacrity to its projections; between May and December 1990, fourteen of the Organization for Economic Cooperation and Development's twenty-four member countries initiated policies to stabilize or reduce emissions of greenhouse gases.[26] By contrast, the United States continued to equivocate. In August the American delegation clashed with other nations attending a meeting in Sweden to finalize the policymakers' summary of the IPCC report because the Americans insisted on amendments emphasizing scientific uncertainty and refused to establish any timetables or targets for the stabilization of greenhouse gas emissions.[27] Their primary objective was to ensure that any actions taken would not curtail economic growth. Despite U.S. resistance, however, the final conference statement reported that a clear scientific consensus had emerged on the extent of global warming expected during the twenty-first century. It added that if the increase of greenhouse gas concentrations was not stemmed, the predicted climate change would place stress on natural and social systems unprecedented in the past 10,000 years.

The January 1992 release of the Supplementary Report to the IPCC Scientific Assessment precipitated another round of publicity for the scientific consensus on climate change. Between 1990 and 1992 scientists had begun to incorporate the cooling effects of stratospheric ozone depletion and aerosols (airborne sulfur dioxide particles) into their models, resulting in a much greater consistency between those models and observed temperatures. The supplement reaffirmed the conclusions of the 1990 report and added several new findings, among which was that the anomalously high global temperatures of the 1980s had continued into 1990 and 1991, the warmest years on record.

In hopes of making progress on the policy front, the UN established the Intergovernmental Negotiating Committee to generate a convention in advance of the United Nations Conference on Environment and Development scheduled for June 1992 in Rio de Janeiro. The committee met at five two-week sessions between February 1991 and May 1992, during which the negotiators agreed on a process modeled after the one that produced the much acclaimed 1987 Montreal Protocol on Substances that Deplete the Ozone Layer: they would first establish a framework convention on the basic issues and then, at a later date, negotiate a protocol specifying the more concrete obligations of each country. During this period, however, President Bush made it clear that he would boycott the Earth Summit if negotiators produced a climate convention containing specific timetables or goals.

The United States' recalcitrance notwithstanding, at the UN conference in Rio, 154 governments signed the Framework Convention on Climate Change (FCCC), the primary goal of which is the "stabilization of greenhouse gas concentrations in the atmosphere at a level that would prevent dangerous anthropogenic [human] interference with the climate system." [28] The FCCC divided signatories into Annex I (developed) and Annex II (transitional and developing) nations, in recognition that the former were responsible for the bulk of the world's greenhouse gases, and created an obligation for Annex I nations to reduce their emissions to 1990 levels by 2000. The FCCC specified that policies devised under the convention should achieve equity through "common but differentiated responsibilities" and pay special attention to disproportionately burdened developing nations, such as small island states. Most notably, the FCCC stated that policies should be consistent with the "precautionary principle," which involves acting prudently in the absence of scientific certainty. The Bush administration signed the agreement reluctantly, with the understanding that it intended to encourage, but not mandate, emissions reductions. In October 1992 the U.S. Senate ratified the FCCC.

The Clinton Administration: Hopes for U.S. Leadership Bloom and Fade

With the inauguration of President Bill Clinton, advocates of climate change policies were hopeful that the United States would take a more proactive role in negotiations. Bolstering these expectations, Clinton announced his support for the FCCC and for CO_2 emissions reductions. After failing to get a national fossil fuel use tax through Congress, however, the president quickly retreated: the 1993 White House Climate Change Action plan included about fifty voluntary federal programs aimed at promoting energy conservation but did not address greenhouse gas emissions directly. Still, the administration projected that its plan would reduce emissions by about 109 million tons per year by 2000—enough to return them to their 1990 levels of 1.58 billion tons.

By the time government representatives gathered for the First Conference of the Parties (COP 1) in Berlin in spring 1995, however, it was clear the Clinton administration's plan was failing to stem the tide of U.S. CO_2 emissions, which were in fact almost 5 percent above 1990 levels. (The reason was partly that any gains achieved under the plan were offset by the declining average fuel efficiency of American cars, thanks largely to the boom in sport utility vehicles and an increase in the number of miles driven.[29]) In fact, only Germany and the United Kingdom were on target to reduce their emissions to 1990 levels by 2000. Two factors in addition to the general failure of voluntary emissions controls lent urgency to the talks. First, in 1994 IPCC chairman Bert Bolin had suggested that even if all Annex I governments met their commitments, it would not be sufficient to achieve the FCCC objective of preventing dangerous human interference with the climate system.[30] Second, in the spring and fall of 1994 negotiators had met five times to lay the groundwork for the upcoming COP, and each time the group was split by divisions between developed and developing nations.

Negotiators at COP 1 were therefore faced with two questions: whether Annex I countries should adopt binding emissions reductions and whether emissions reductions obligations should be extended to Annex II countries. The parties ultimately agreed on the Berlin Mandate, which specified that any legal instrument that resulted from formal negotiations scheduled to take place in Kyoto, Japan, would impose emissions reductions only on Annex I countries; the 134 developing nations, including China, India, and Mexico, would be exempt. They did not, however, resolve the issue of binding emissions reductions. The United States pressed for a "joint implementation" mechanism that would allow industrialized countries to earn credit if they financed emissions reductions in developing countries where, presumably, they could be made more cheaply. The parties ultimately agreed to a modest version of such a mechanism but, more important, committed themselves to a schedule for adopting a protocol at COP 3, to be held in Kyoto in December 1997.

In August 1995 the Ad Hoc Group on the Berlin Mandate began convening to establish the emissions targets for industrialized nations in advance of the 1997 Kyoto meeting. In December, in the midst of these meetings, the IPCC produced its Second Assessment Report. Since 1990 the IPCC had dramatically improved its climate models and was willing to make projections with greater confidence; it concluded that "the balance of the evidence suggests that there is a discernible human influence on global climate." [31] But the scientists downgraded their estimates of the magnitude of global warming, projecting that the mean global temperature would increase between 1 and 3.5 degrees Celsius (2–6 degrees Fahrenheit) by 2100, and most believed it would be in the lower half of that range. The IPCC forecast, however, that global mean sea level would rise between six inches and three feet, and that changes in spatial and temporal precipitation patterns would occur. Finally, the IPCC concluded that a 60 percent to 80 percent reduction in CO_2 emissions would be necessary just to stabilize atmospheric concentrations of greenhouse gases.[32]

Defining the Climate Change Problem in the United States

In the United States the 1995 IPCC report set the stage for a monumental battle to define the climate change problem—and thereby determine the U.S. position—in advance of the impending Kyoto meeting. Scientists had gotten the problem onto the public agenda, and environmentalists eagerly adopted a simplified version of the scientific story. Their most powerful weapon was the vocal support of prominent scientists and highly visible consensus panels. But the story science furnished was not particularly compelling: the villains were ordinary Americans, with their wasteful lifestyles; the victims were small island nations; and, rather than any imminent crisis, the effects were at least a generation away. Furthermore, powerful opponents, led by the oil and coal industries, retaliated with a well-financed lobbying campaign in the form of a four-pronged attack: they argued that models of climate change were highly uncertain; that a warmer earth would not be so bad, particularly for the United States; that imposing policies to avert climate change would cripple the American economy; and that imposing emissions limits on industrialized nations without holding developing countries to similar targets would unfairly disadvantage the United States. Both sides launched all-out public relations campaigns, well aware that whoever succeeded in defining the problem was likely to dictate the solution.

Environmentalists Use Scientists' Warnings. Among the earliest and most powerful proponents of policies to address climate change were members of the scientific community that studied the global climate. Throughout the 1980s scientific consensus reports indicating that global warming was real and a serious problem were accompanied by recommendations that the international community formulate policies *before* the effects became irreversible. Proponents of acting immediately portrayed such action as an "insurance policy against the potentially devastating and irreversible impacts of global warming." [33]

Environmentalists enthusiastically seized on these scientific warnings to advance their overarching goal of limiting human impact on the natural environment. As early as 1984, Environmental Defense's senior scientist Michael Oppenheimer had written an op-ed piece for the *New York Times* featuring the evocative language that environmentalists are so adept at employing:

> With unusual unanimity, scientists testified at a recent Senate hearing that using the atmosphere as a garbage dump is about to catch up with us on a global scale. . . . Carbon dioxide emissions from fossil fuels combustion and other "greenhouse" gases are throwing a blanket over the Earth. . . . The sea level will rise as land ice melts and the oceans expand. Beaches will erode while wetlands will largely disappear. . . . Imagine life in a sweltering, smoggy New York without Long Island's beaches and you have glimpsed the world left to future generations. [34]

For environmentalists, climate change conveniently linked a host of concerns, from deforestation to air pollution, and implicated industrial nations' demand for growth and luxury.

Opponents Challenge the Scientific Consensus. In the early 1990s a group of utility and coal companies created the Information Council on the Environment to promote arguments critical of climate change theory. The council ultimately disbanded when environmentalists exposed some of its unsavory tactics to the media, but its goal of creating public confusion about climate change had already been accomplished. More enduring was the Global Climate Coalition (GCC), which spun off from the National Association of Manufacturers in 1989. The GCC had fifty-four industry and trade association members, primarily from the coal, oil, and automobile industries, and spent heavily on its anti–climate change campaign.[35]

Opponents of climate change policies promoted the view that global warming, if it was occurring at all, was not the serious problem that hysterical scientists and environmentalists made it out to be. To support these views, they cited a handful of outspoken scientific skeptics who challenged the IPCC estimates of both the likelihood and the consequences of climate change. Among the most prominent of these skeptics were Pat Michaels, assistant professor of climatology at the University of Virginia; S. Fred Singer, professor of environmental science at the University of Virginia; Robert Balling, a geographer at the University of Arizona; and Richard Lindzen, an atmospheric physicist at Massachusetts Institute of Technology. Although few in number, skeptics took advantage of the media's adherence to the journalistic norm of presenting "both sides" of an issue, regardless of the relative merits of each side's argument. Further magnifying skeptics' impact, opponents invested heavily in disseminating their views—financing the publication and distribution of books, magazines, pamphlets, and press releases to undermine the credibility of climate change theories among the public.

The skeptics' primary argument was that scientists had only a rudimentary understanding of the feedbacks in the climate system. For example, they noted that early climate models contained only crude estimates of the effects of the ocean, yet ocean circulation is coupled with atmospheric circulation in a complex and critical way. Furthermore, skeptics highlighted the potential impact of aerosols (small particles) and clouds on climate change. They argued that the magnitude of observed warming to date was modest compared to the large, natural variability of the system. And they pointed out that scientists' predictions were based on theories and general circulation models (GCMs) that are difficult to confirm.[36]

In addition to emphasizing scientific uncertainty, some skeptics accused environmentalists of using science to achieve political ends—scaremongering to promote radical solutions to a problem for whose existence there was little evidence. They charged that environmentalists' messages were invariably apocalyptic; that the media published such stories to sell newspapers and television time; and that the resulting publicity abetted environmental groups' fundraising efforts.[37] According to the skeptics, warnings about climate change were part of a larger, coordinated effort to "establish international controls over industrial processes and business operations." [38]

Climate change skeptics also went after the IPCC and its members directly. In 1994 Frederick Seitz, director of the conservative Marshall Institute and former president of the National Academy of Sciences, attacked the authors of the IPCC scientific summaries, contending that they had distorted the views of participating scientists and created the impression of a consensus where none existed. (Defenders of the summary responded that the process of writing it was cautious and consensual, that participants agreed to the summaries at plenary meetings, and that none had expressed subsequent dissatisfaction with the final product.) In May 1996 opponents launched personal attacks on two eminent scientists, Benjamin Santer, a climate modeler at the Lawrence Livermore Laboratory, and Tom Wigley, a senior scientist at the National Center for Atmospheric Research. Seitz accused Santer of deleting references to scientific uncertainty from the 1995 IPCC report. The *Wall Street Journal* and *New York Times* published this allegation, although neither paper confirmed its veracity with any of the participants in the process. (In fact, not one IPCC scientist confirmed the charges against Santer, and forty-two signed a letter to the *Wall Street Journal* in his defense.[39])

Finally, some skeptics advanced the notion that climate change would be beneficial. Economist Thomas Gale Moore, the predominant exponent of this theme, pointed out that service industries could prosper as equally in a warm climate (with air conditioning) as a cold one (with central heating). In fact, Moore argued, higher temperatures combined with more CO_2 in the atmosphere would enhance plant and crop growth, thereby providing more food for the burgeoning global population.[40] In the early 1990s Western Fuels, a coal industry lobbying organization, spent $250,000 on a video entitled *The Greening of Planet Earth*, which argued that global warming would improve the lot of the human race and the United States in particular. Western Fuels also founded an organization called the Greening Earth Society to promote this perspective.

Opponents Shift the Focus to Costs. In addition to defining climate science as highly uncertain and ambiguous, opponents of climate change policies highlighted the costs of adopting policies to limit greenhouse gas emissions. Such policies, they argued, would be exorbitant and lead to "worldwide recession, rising unemployment, civil disturbances, and increased tension between nations as accusations of cheating and violations of international treaties inflamed passions." [41] Taking precautionary action, wrote one journalist in *Forbes*, could "spell the end of the American dream for us and the world." [42] The GCC's $13 million advertising campaign in advance of the Kyoto meeting in 1997 warned television viewers that

> strict reductions in greenhouse gases would have catastrophic economic consequences, endangering the lifestyle of every American. Gasoline would shoot up by fifty cents or more a gallon; heating and electricity bills would soar, while higher energy costs would raise the price of almost everything Americans buy. The livelihood of thousands of coal miners, auto-workers, and others employed in energy-related fields was on the line.[43]

Those hoping to prevent the imposition of greenhouse gas emissions limits seized on a 1990 study by the Bush administration's Council of Economic Advisors that estimated the cost of cutting carbon emissions by 20 percent by the year 2100 at between $800 billion and $3.6 trillion. The report concluded that until there was a solid scientific understanding of climate change, "there is no justification for imposing major costs on the economy in order to slow the growth of greenhouse gas emissions." [44] Opponents claimed that even a no-regrets policy, in which nations adopt such practices as conserving energy and increasing reliance on energy-efficient vehicles and public transit, would be nothing more than a "first, expensive, and ineffectual step down the road to programs that will cripple one of the most vital foundations of modern civilization—our energy supplies." [45]

The environmental Alliance to Save Energy responded with an analysis showing that U.S. carbon emissions could be cut by 25 percent by 2005 and by 70 percent by 2030 at a net *savings* of $2.3 trillion over forty years.[46] The 1991 NAS report, *Policy Implications of Global Warming*, concurred, arguing that the United States could reduce its greenhouse gas emissions between 10 percent and 40 percent of 1990 levels at low-cost, or even net savings, if the proper policies were implemented. And a 1992 study by William Cline of the Institute for International Economics suggested that "social benefit-cost ratios are favorable for an aggressive program of international abatement." [47] Cline pointed out that opponents of climate change policies failed to take into account the possibility of cost-effective energy efficiency measures and technological innovation.

But the opponents of climate change policies dismissed efforts to rebut their arguments and were adept at disseminating their competing perspective. At the Rio Earth Summit in 1992, the executive director of the GCC maintained that some of the proposals under consideration could cost the United States $95 billion and 550,000 jobs.[48] The Coalition for Vehicle Choice, financed by the U.S. auto industry and related groups, spent years trying to convince small business, labor, and local civic groups throughout the United States that the treaty would be "bad for America." In October 1997, immediately prior to the Kyoto meeting, the group ran an ad to that effect in the *Washington Post* featuring the endorsement of 1,300 groups.[49]

Opponents Raise the Equity Issue. The national media initially furthered environmentalists' cause by publicizing Hansen's 1988 congressional testimony. More important, the media linked scientists' climate change predictions to the heat, droughts, and freak weather events of 1988, thereby generating public alarm. But coverage of the science featured conflict among dueling scientists, a reflection of the effort by those supporting the status quo to reframe the debate. Moreover, by the early 1990s coverage of political debates and competing economic forecasts had begun to displace coverage of science.[50]

To cement their advantage, climate change policy opponents took a third tack: they began attacking the approach embodied in the Kyoto Protocol, framing it as inequitable—making the protocol, and not climate change, the problem. They insisted it would be unfair for developing countries to escape commitments to greenhouse gas emissions reductions because in the future they were likely to be the major emitters, while the industrialized nations' share of emissions would decline. They pointed out that several large developing countries—including China, India, Mexico, and South Korea—were already producing 44 percent of global fossil fuel emissions and were likely to surpass the emissions levels of the developed countries between 2020 and 2030. In addition, said critics, developing countries were responsible for much of the deforestation and other land-use practices that had eliminated carbon sinks.[51]

The developing nations and many environmentalists responded that the United States, with only 4 percent of the world's population, generated 25 percent of the world's greenhouse gas emissions and that industrialized nations were responsible for 70 percent of the human-made greenhouse gases currently in the atmosphere. Moreover, they noted that developing nations were likely to suffer the most serious consequences of climate change but were least well-positioned, financially or technologically, to mitigate, adapt to, or recover from those impacts. Dr. Mark Mwandosya of Tanzania, chairman of the developing country caucus at Kyoto, pointed out: "Very many of us are struggling to attain a decent standard of living for our peoples, and yet we are constantly told that we must share in the effort to reduce emissions so that industrialized countries can continue to enjoy the benefits of their wasteful life style." [52]

The Kyoto Protocol

As the Kyoto meeting drew near, the battle to shape the U.S. position intensified. In hopes of creating support for U.S. leadership, in June 1997 more than 2,500 American scientists endorsed the *Scientists' Statement on Global Climatic Disruption*. The statement claimed that:

further accumulation of greenhouse gases commits the earth irreversibly to further global climatic change and consequent ecological, economic, and social disruption. The risks associated with such changes justify preventive action through reductions in emissions of greenhouse gases. It is time for the United States, as the largest emitter of greenhouse gases, to . . . demonstrate leadership in a global effort.[53]

After receiving the statement, President Clinton told a special session of the UN General Assembly that "the science [of climate change] is clear and compelling," and he promised to bring to the Kyoto conference "a strong American commitment to realistic and binding limits that will significantly reduce our emissions of greenhouse gases." [54] The following month, Clinton launched an effort to convince the public that climate change was real by holding a conference of experts and a series of well-publicized regional panels.

The administration's international credibility was dubious, however, given that in 1996 alone U.S. emissions of greenhouse gases grew 3.4 percent, and by 1997 were about 7.4 percent greater than they had been in 1990.[55] At this rate of growth, U.S. greenhouse gas emissions promised to be an embarrassing 13 percent above 1990 levels by 2000.[56] Further hampering the administration's ability to negotiate was the unanimous (95–0) passage by the U.S. Senate, on June 12, 1997, of a nonbinding resolution (the Byrd-Hagel amendment) that it would not give its advice and consent to any agreement that did not require developing countries to reduce their emissions or that would result in "serious harm to the economy of the United States." Concerned about building domestic support for the treaty, Clinton began emphasizing the importance of cooperation by China and other developing nations. At the seventh Ad Hoc Group on the Berlin Mandate meeting in Bonn in October, U.S. negotiators pressed the other parties to commit both developing and industrialized nations to emissions reductions.

After meeting resistance in Bonn, the United States again raised the equity issue at the eighth and final Berlin Mandate session, which coincided with the third COP in Kyoto. Nearly 6,000 UN delegates from more than 160 countries attended the ten-day conference that opened on December 1, 1997. In addition, 3,600 representatives of environmental and industry groups and nearly 3,500 reporters poured into Kyoto. Leading the sixty-member U.S. delegation, Undersecretary of State Stuart Eizenstadt began by taking a hard line to appease domestic critics: "We want an agreement," he said, "but we are not going [to Kyoto] for an agreement at any cost." [57] Undaunted, the German and British ministers proposed substantial reductions in greenhouse gas emissions from their 1990 levels by 2010: Germany proposed a 15 percent cut; the United Kingdom, a 20 percent cut. Meanwhile, the latest computer models were projecting that greenhouse gas emissions would have to be lowered by 70 percent to prevent global warming.[58]

By the fourth day of the Kyoto meeting, a *New York Times* editorial declared that a "near miracle" would be required to salvage an agreement. The thorniest issue remained the degree to which developing countries would have to control their emissions. Led by the Chinese delegation, the developing countries adamantly resisted U.S. pressure, so, in a last-ditch effort to facilitate international agreement without provoking a domestic backlash, President Clinton dispatched Vice President Al Gore to give the American delegates more flexibility. On Monday, December 8, Gore told members of the conference that the president would allow the U.S. delegation to offer emissions reductions beyond those originally proposed (1990 levels between 2008 and 2012) in return for opening the door in Kyoto to language requiring emissions reductions by developing countries. COP chairman Raul Estrada proposed a compromise that would allow developing countries to reduce emissions voluntarily and give Annex I nations the option of accepting differentiated emissions reductions commitments for 2008–2012. In the negotiations that followed, the Chinese led a bloc of developing nations (the G77) that vigorously opposed the compromise. The resulting protocol, which emerged just as the meeting was closing, embodied the United States' worst case scenario: it went beyond the original target for U.S. reductions but provided no mechanism for making developing countries reduce their emissions.

The final version of the Kyoto Protocol required the European Union to reduce emissions of six greenhouse gases by 8 percent below 1990 levels by 2012. It set the U.S. emissions reduction target at 7 percent, Japan's at 6 percent, and twenty-one other industrialized nations at 5.2 percent. The protocol gave Annex I nations five options for meeting their obligations: (1) establish policies to lower national emissions; (2) enhance carbon sinks, such as forests; (3) take advantage of emissions-trading opportunities once the system is developed; (4) engage in joint implementation, which allows Annex I parties to earn credit for projects that lower emissions in other Annex I countries; and (5) employ "Clean Development Mechanisms," through which developed countries transfer energy-efficiency technology to developing countries. In addition, the protocol allowed developing countries to "opt in" to emissions controls but did not impose mandatory emissions reductions. Although delegates did not back a U.S. proposal that industrial nations be allowed to trade "emissions quotas," they did agree to consider such mechanisms in 1998.

Opponents of climate change policies were appalled by the agreement. In a press conference before leaving Kyoto, Sen. Chuck Hagel, R-Neb., coauthor of the Byrd-Hagel Amendment, vowed that there was "no way, if the president signs this, that the vote in the United States Senate will even be close. We will kill this bill." [59]

Promoting the Kyoto Protocol Back Home

Recognizing that he lacked Senate support, President Clinton decided not to submit the protocol for ratification but instead proposed a five-year, $6.3 billion package of tax breaks and research spending in pursuit of the protocol's emissions reductions goals—measures that most experts regarded as too modest to have much impact on America's $500 billion fossil fuel-based economy. By executive order, Clinton also directed the federal government, the world's largest energy consumer, to reduce petroleum use in federally owned cars to 20 percent below 1990 levels by 2005 and reduce greenhouse gases from federal buildings by 30 percent by 2010. At the same time, the administration continued its campaign to persuade the public that the science underpinning the protocol was valid.

Even as the Clinton administration struggled to generate public support for climate change policies, opponents geared up for the Senate ratification battle. Recognizing the political potency of the scientific consensus generated by the IPCC, by early spring 1998 a high-powered group including the American Petroleum Institute, Chevron, and Exxon had already planned a multimillion-dollar campaign to undermine that consensus. Aimed primarily at the public, the plan was to recruit a cadre of skeptical scientists and train them to convey their views persuasively to science writers, editors, columnists, and news-paper correspondents.[60] Some tactics adopted by opponents raised eyebrows: for example, Frederick Seitz circulated among thousands of scientists a peti-tion against climate change policies, accompanied by a letter on stationery designed to resemble National Academy of Sciences letterhead. The academy quickly disavowed the letter, which claimed to report on a scientific study con-cluding that CO_2 emissions did not pose a climatic threat.[61]

In response to industry's anti-climate change campaign, environmentalists undertook some new tactics of their own. They approached businesses directly and tried to persuade them to reduce their emissions voluntarily—to save money, improve their environmental credentials, and gain a seat at the table when the inevitable regulations were enacted. In May 1998, for example, the Pew Charitable Trusts established the Pew Center for Global Climate Change, funded by a $5 million annual grant from the foundation and administered by Eileen Claussen, former deputy assistant secretary of state for environmental affairs. One of the center's objectives is to bolster the credibility of climate change science. To this end, in an ad published in the *New York Times*, the cen-ter's members—including American Electric Power, U.S. Generating Com-pany, Maytag, Whirlpool, 3M, Toyota, Sunoco, United Technologies, Boeing, and Lockheed Martin—publicly accepted the views of most scientists that enough was known about the environmental impact of climate change to take steps to address the consequences, and they pledged to reduce their own emissions of greenhouse gases.[62] By the fall of 1998, twenty major U.S. com-panies, including three electric power companies and two oil companies, had joined the Pew Center. In October international oil companies Royal Dutch/ Shell and British Petroleum, both of which had defected from the Global Cli-mate Coalition, also committed themselves to substantial voluntary reduc-tions in their emissions.

Proponents of climate change policies also began publicizing a set of Clin-ton administration studies that downplayed the costs of cutting CO_2 emis-sions. A report by the Department of Energy buttressed environmentalists' position that the United States could reduce its fuel use by making fairly sim-ple and inexpensive changes that would have little impact on the economy.[63] A 1997 analysis by the Interlaboratory Working Group, a consortium of U.S. national labs, also concluded that large, low-cost energy savings were possible in the United States.[64] Finally, a 1998 report from Clinton's Council of Eco-nomic Advisors reiterated the NAS claim that if policies were designed cor-rectly, the effects on energy prices and the costs to the United States of meet-ing the Kyoto Protocol emissions targets could be extremely modest.[65] In response to this avalanche of information suggesting climate change policies would be affordable, the industry-sponsored Electric Power Research Institute commissioned its own economic studies concluding that agriculture, forestry, and outdoor recreation "are all projected to benefit from a slightly warmer, wetter, CO_2-enriched world."[66]

While factions in the United States sparred over the costs and benefits of implementing the Kyoto Protocol, scientists were debating whether the treaty would slow global warming, even if its obligations were fulfilled. In an analysis published in *Science* in January 1998, former IPCC chair Bert Bolin predicted that the CO_2 level in the atmosphere would climb to 382 parts per million (from 370) by 2010 even if countries strictly fulfilled their Kyoto commitments. Bolin noted that the Kyoto reductions would be "an important first step" but would be "far from what is required to reach the goal of stabilizing the concentration of CO_2 in the atmosphere." [67]

The Hague, 2000

This was the domestic context in which international talks to resolve outstanding issues from Kyoto resumed at the fourth COP in Buenos Aires, Argentina, which began in early November 1998. Hoping to facilitate consensus there, the Clinton administration had worked assiduously to forge bilateral agreements with developing countries on voluntarily limiting their CO_2 emissions. By the time negotiations got under way, however, only Argentina had agreed to join Annex I voluntarily and thereby accept emissions reductions obligations. (Thereafter, Kazakhstan and Bolivia announced their willingness to do the same.) In addition, on November 12 the United States signed the Kyoto Protocol, adding its name to the more than 150 signatories (only one of which, Romania, had actually ratified the treaty).

Nevertheless, little of substance was accomplished at the Buenos Aires meeting. At the close of COP 4, the role of developing nations and the status of international emissions trading were still unresolved. In a promising advance on emissions trading, the G77 was no longer monolithic: China and India were leading the faction opposed to emissions limits on developing countries, but African and Latin American countries were showing interest in making emissions reductions in exchange for aid. The second point was stickier: U.S. negotiators were tenacious about emissions trading because they thought it might defuse domestic opposition, but Europeans and many developing nations objected that the United States was trying to buy its way out of reducing its own emissions.

As officials around the globe struggled to find solutions everyone could agree on, the scientific evidence continued to pour in. In March 1999 a study published in *Nature* concluded that the growing season in the northern temperate zone, from the sub-Arctic to the Mediterranean region, had lengthened by about eleven days since 1970. The authors attributed the shift to a rise in daily temperatures caused by the general warming of the climate. Their findings were consistent with a series of studies reported in 1996 and 1997 that detected early spring and a longer growing season in the northern hemisphere.[68] Moreover, the effects of climate change were becoming increasingly visible and dramatic: in December scientists reported that 1999 had joined

1998 as one of the two warmest years on record. The following summer, eye-witness reports of open water from melting ice at the North Pole made head-lines. A scientist at the Applied Physics Laboratory at the University of Washington confirmed that polar ice thickness had decreased from an average of 10.2 feet in the 1960s and 1970s to 5.9 feet in the 1990s. Nor was the decrease an isolated phenomenon; it was widespread in the central Arctic Ocean and most pronounced in the eastern Arctic. Such findings confirmed climate model predictions that the Arctic would be among the first regions to respond to a global warming trend.[69]

Although the influx of worrisome scientific reports lent urgency to the climate change talks, COP 6 in the Hague in November 2000 foundered once again. The Hague conference was supposed to be the final meeting to establish greenhouse gas emissions reduction policies, and efforts to translate vague commitments into specific practices promised to be contentious. Prior to the meeting, the Clinton administration again made its precautionary view of the problem clear; testifying before the Senate Foreign Relations and Energy and Natural Resources Committees in September 2000, Frank Loy, undersecretary for global affairs, argued that:

> As policymakers, we must base our decisions on the best scientific evidence available. But we would fail in our duty to safeguard the health and well-being of our citizens and the environment they cherish if we waited to act until the details of the climate system have been fully understood. The science tells us that this would be a recipe for disaster, for we will only fully confirm the predictions of climate science when we experience them, at which point it will be too late. Instead, we should ask, "Are the risks great enough to justify taking action?" When it comes to the challenge of climate change, the answer is an emphatic "yes." [70]

At the same time, to placate its critics the administration continued to embrace the language of economic growth, efficiency, cost-effectiveness, and the primacy of markets. U.S. negotiators left for the Hague determined to obtain unlimited use of emissions-trading mechanisms and credit for land-use practices included in the agreement.

Although negotiators initially were hopeful, after eleven exhausting days of bargaining among the 170 countries in attendance, U.S. insistence that it be permitted to meet its greenhouse gas reduction obligations with forest and agricultural land management, rather than CO_2 emissions reductions, proved to be an insurmountable hurdle. Critics were dubious about relying on forests to curb CO_2, pointing out that research suggested the role of forests and soils in sequestering CO_2 was not straightforward.[71] Through the final night and into the early morning, environmental groups helped the European delegation analyze a variety of formulas for calculating carbon equivalents attributable to forest protection. At 3:00 a.m., a small cadre of British, American, and European diplomats shook hands on a deal; the following day, however, the complex formula turned out to be unacceptable to many in the European Union.

Jurgen Tritin, the German environment minister, explained that his country's opposition to forest credits was deeply rooted in his nation's values and derived from a sense that the United States and its collaborators were trying to get something for nothing.[72]

Observers were struck by the irony that previous talks had stumbled because of irreconcilable differences between developing and developed nations, or between environmentalists and industry, but the Hague negotiations fell apart primarily because of a schism within the environmental movement itself. While mainstream American environmental groups, as well as many climate change scientists, supported the business-friendly U.S. solutions of emissions trading and forest conservation credits, hard liners, such as Greenpeace, backed the German position. "We're better off with no deal than a bad deal," argued Bill Hare of Greenpeace moments after the negotiations ended.[73] The hard-line groups equated compromise with corruption and abdication to business interests but, ironically, found themselves allied with most of the business community in opposition to any treaty. For more moderate environmentalists, however, the failure to reach agreement at the Hague was particularly worrisome in light of the upcoming U.S. election. Michael Oppenheimer of Environmental Defense warned (presciently) that if George W. Bush became president, it would only become more difficult for American and European negotiators to find common ground.

The Bush Presidency

In early 2001 a series of reports detailed the latest scientific understanding of the magnitude and likely impacts of climate change, and the overall tone was one of foreboding. In January a new IPCC assessment confirmed that the global temperature had risen 1 degree Fahrenheit in the twentieth century, blamed part of that increase on fossil fuel combustion, and cautioned that it represented the most rapid change in ten millennia. The IPCC suggested that earlier climate change estimates may have been conservative and that the earth's climate could warm by as much as 10.5 degrees Fahrenheit by the end of the twenty-first century.[74] Then, in February the IPCC released a report entitled "Climate Change 2001: Impacts, Adaptations, and Vulnerability." Summarizing the work of 700 experts, the 1,000-page document concluded ominously that "projected climate changes during the 21st century have the potential to lead to future large-scale and possible irreversible changes in Earth systems," with "continental and global consequences." Among the likely outcomes were more "freak" weather conditions, such as cyclones, floods, and droughts; massive displacement of population in the most affected areas; greater risk of diseases like malaria; and extinction of entire species as their habitat disappeared. Over time, the report warned, global warming was also likely to cause large reductions in the Greenland and West Antarctic ice sheets and a substantial slowing of the circulation of warm water in the North Atlantic. Finally, changes in rainfall patterns due to climate change, combined with patterns of population growth, would likely lead to enormous pressure on water supplies.[75]

At conferences and in journals, researchers continued to document climate change effects that were already observable. At a meeting in San Francisco in February, scientists attributed the recently noted melting of equatorial glaciers in Africa and Peru to global warming. Scientists offered other evidence as well: thawing permafrost, delayed freezing, earlier break-up dates of river and lake ice, and longer growing seasons at mid- to high latitudes.[76] And a study reported in *Nature* suggested yet another potential impact: droughts caused by global warming could prompt northern soils to release CO_2 into the air, speeding up changes in the climate.[77]

Despite mounting concern among scientists, the election of President Bush and Vice President Dick Cheney, both former oilmen, dimmed hopes for U.S. leadership on a climate change agreement. Bush took office saying that more research on climate change was needed before any policies were undertaken, and in March 2001 he vowed not to seek CO_2 emissions reductions, thereby reneging on a campaign pledge to do so. He outlined his view in a letter to four prominent Republican senators:

> At a time when California has already experienced energy shortages, and other Western states are worried about price and availability of energy this summer, we must be very careful not to take actions that could harm consumers. This is especially true given the incomplete state of scientific knowledge of the causes of, and solutions to, global climate change and the lack of commercially available technologies for removing and storing carbon dioxide.[78]

Although justified as a response to an "energy crisis," Bush supporters attributed his change of heart to a last-minute lobbying campaign by congressional Republicans and top industry leaders.

As if to put an exclamation point on the president's position, the administration's 2002 budget proposal cut spending on energy efficiency programs by 15 percent.[79] Moreover, Bush's energy plan, released in May 2001, emphasized loosening environmental regulations and developing new fossil fuel supplies. After meeting with the president in early April and failing to change his mind about the Kyoto Protocol, European leaders announced their intention to move forward with the treaty even without American leadership. According to the European Union's environmental commissioner Margot Wallstrom, "Other countries [were] reacting very strongly against the U.S." [80]

The administration's position perplexed not only foreign leaders but other members of his own party, many of whom had solid environmental records. Furthermore, public opinion polls revealed substantial public support for action on global warming: a January 2001 Gallup poll found that 40 percent of Americans worried about global warming "a great deal," up five points since 1989 and much higher than the level of concern reported (27 percent) in 1997.[81] A July 2001 *New York Times*/CBS News Poll found that 72 percent of the public believed it was necessary to take immediate steps to counter global warming, and more than half thought the United States should abide by the Kyoto accord.[82]

Recognizing his political vulnerability, Bush commissioned an expert panel, convened by the NAS National Research Council, that could either legitimate his views or provide cover for a reversal on the issue. The panel—which comprised eleven prominent atmospheric scientists, including Richard Lindzen—"reaffirmed the mainstream scientific view that the earth's atmosphere was getting warmer and that human activity was largely responsible." [83] Although the president subsequently conceded the scientific point, he continued to inflame Europeans by opposing the Kyoto Protocol and rejecting mandatory emissions limits.

Bush's resistance notwithstanding, in November 2001 negotiators representing 178 countries hammered out the details of the Kyoto Protocol, and many large industrial countries said they intended to ratify the agreement. Although it was only a first step, environmentalists were pleased. "The parties have reached complete agreement on what's an infraction, how you decide a case, and what are the penalties," said David Doniger of the Natural Resources Defense Council. "That's as good as it gets in international relations." [84] Furthermore, to the surprise of many observers, the European Union agreed to institute trading mechanisms for greenhouse gases—a move they hoped would gain the support of Canada, Japan, and Russia.

In hopes of appeasing his increasingly voluble critics, in February 2002 Bush announced a domestic plan that relied on $4.6 billion in tax credits over five years to encourage businesses to take voluntary measures that would reduce the "carbon intensity" (the ratio of greenhouse gases to gross domestic product) of the economy by 18 percent over ten years. In announcing the plan, the president made it clear that economic growth was his primary concern, in part because a thriving economy would provide the resources to invest in clean technologies. Eileen Claussen pointed out that the administration's carbon intensity targets were consistent with the trend the nation was already on and therefore represented little improvement. (In fact, if the U.S. economy grew at 3 percent a year during that period, as predicted, total greenhouse gas emissions would rise.) At the same time, Myron Ebell of the Competitive Enterprise Institute warned that the administration's acknowledgement of climate change as a problem started the nation "down a dark path" toward mandatory emissions reductions.[85]

Climate Change Science Solidifies

For the next few years, as international negotiations over ratifying the Kyoto Protocol proceeded, climate science continued to evolve. Even as scientists investigated new aspects of the climate system, they grew more confident in their belief that human-caused greenhouse gas emissions were causing global warming. Supporting evidence continued to mount: for example, the warmest year on record since the 1860s was 1998, followed by 2002, 2003, and 2004, according to the UN World Meteorological Association.[86] An August 2004 update of federal climate research featured new computer simulations in which the rise in global temperatures since 1970 could be explained only by human influences, primarily rising emissions of greenhouse gases.[87] The following year researchers found the source of an error in satellite readings of atmospheric temperature trends that skeptics had used to dispute the global warming hypothesis; once corrected, temperatures in the tropics became consistent with climate change models' predictions. Moreover, scientists could find no credible evidence to support skeptics' alternative hypothesis that solar variation, rather than human activity, could explain the observed warming.[88]

The impacts of rising temperatures continued to manifest themselves more quickly than scientists had anticipated, particularly in the polar regions where nonlinear processes were causing ice to melt more rapidly than expected. For example, in February 2002 a 1,250-square-mile section of the Antarctic Peninsula's Larsen B ice shelf began splintering, and within a month it was gone. Studies of marine algae found in core sediment suggested that the Larsen B had been intact since it formed more than 10,000 years ago. Apparently, ice was flowing into the sea faster than scientists had expected: loss of coastal ice shelves was accelerating the flow of inland glaciers; in addition, water from summertime ponds percolating through cracks to the base was acting as a lubricant, facilitating the slide of glacial ice over the earth below.[89]

The Arctic was showing the effects of global warming as well. In September 2003 researchers reported that the largest ice shelf in the Arctic had shattered, and a massive freshwater lake behind it had drained away.[90] Then, in fall 2004 a comprehensive four-year study of Arctic warming confirmed that the buildup of greenhouse gases was contributing to profound environmental changes in the region, including sharp retreats of glaciers and sea ice and thawing of permafrost. This rapid melting, combined with increasing precipitation, exacerbated scientists' fears about the impact of additional fresh water on the ocean current that transports heat to the North Atlantic. According to scientist Wallace Broecker of Columbia University's Lamont-Doherty Earth Observatory, if that global conveyor belt—which is driven by cold, salty water that sinks to the bottom and flows south—shuts down, the climate at northern latitudes may shift abruptly, rather than gradually.[91]

Scientists also continued to document faster-than-expected impacts of global warming on species and biodiversity. According to two studies reported in *Nature* in January 2003, global warming was forcing species around the world to move into new ranges or alter their habits in ways that could disrupt ecosystems. Such large changes in response to a mere 1 degree temperature increase disturbed some researchers. "It's really pretty frightening to think what we might see in the next 100 years," said Dr. Terry Root, a Stanford ecologist and lead author of one of the studies.[92] A January 2004 article in *Nature* predicted that rising global temperatures could cause the extinction of one-quarter of the world's plant and animal species.[93]

In addition to detecting the consequences of global warming, scientists were refining their understanding of the interactions between carbon sources and sinks. For example, a study published in *Nature* in March 2004 suggested that changes in the Amazon rainforest appeared to make it less capable of absorbing CO_2 than once believed. The study revealed that trees were growing and dying at faster rates than twenty years earlier, and scientists attributed this change to rising CO_2 levels. Similarly, a study published in *Nature* in September 2004 described an experiment that confirmed the hypothesis that presumed carbon sinks, such as the Arctic tundra, may actually generate net CO_2 increases, as higher temperatures lead to more decomposition and leaching in the soil, the combination of which produces more CO_2 than new plants take up.[94]

While media coverage of these scientific findings helped buttress the precautionary arguments of environmentalists, scientists tried to enhance their impact by publicizing the high level of agreement and concern in the scientific community. In October 2003, 1,000 scientists around the country signed a "state of climate science" letter affirming the claims of the IPCC and the National Research Council that anthropogenic climate change, driven by emissions of greenhouse gases, was already underway and was likely responsible for most of the observed warming of the past fifty years and that they expected the earth to warm 2.5 degrees to 10.5 degrees Fahrenheit over the course of the twenty-first century, depending on future emissions levels and climate sensitivity. Adding to the chorus, in late December 2003 the prestigious American Geophysical Union followed the American Meteorological Society in adopting the official position that human-caused greenhouse gas emissions were causing global warming.

In an effort to persuade the public that U.S. citizens would be victims, not beneficiaries, of global warming, some activist scientists also undertook a campaign to portray its local impacts. For example, in fall 2004 the Union of Concerned Scientists released a city-by-city analysis for California that included dire forecasts for San Francisco and other major metropolitan areas. (The group conducted similar analyses for other regions, such as the Great Lakes, as well.) *Science* published a study in October 2004 suggesting that a warmer climate could exacerbate the severity and duration of western droughts.[95] And an EPA-commissioned study released in February 2005 concluded that by the end of the twenty-first century global warming could raise sea levels enough that a heavy storm would send flood waters into Boston's downtown waterfront, the financial district, and much of the Back Bay.[96]

OUTCOMES

The accumulating scientific evidence made little impression on the Bush administration, which continued to argue that the unsubstantiated threat of global warming did not warrant action that would cripple the economy. In June 2002 the White House sent a climate report to the UN that acknowledged the role of fossil fuel burning in global warming but did not propose any major changes in U.S. policy. Some vocal Republicans in Congress backed the administration's view, and in August 2003 efforts by Sen. John McCain, R-Ariz., and Sen. Joseph Lieberman, D-Conn., to force a vote on their bill to limit greenhouse gas emissions (S 139, the Climate Stewardship Act) prompted a furious resumption of the climate change debate. Representing the views of skeptics, Sen. James Inhofe, R-Okla., gave a two-hour speech in which he said, "With all of the hysteria, all of the fear, all of the phony science, could it be that manmade global warming is the greatest hoax ever perpetrated on the American people? It sure sounds like it." [97] (The Senate ultimately defeated the McCain-Lieberman bill by a vote of 55 to 43. A second effort, in June 2005, failed by an even larger margin, 60-38.) U.S. negotiators continued to impede international action as well: at the COP 10 meeting in December 2004, the U.S. delegation blocked efforts to undertake anything beyond limited, informal talks on ways to slow down global warming. In justifying the U.S. position, delegation leader Paula Dobriansky said, "Science tells us that we cannot say with any certainty what constitutes a dangerous level of warming, and therefore what level must be avoided." [98]

Despite continued obstruction by the U.S. government, in mid-February 2005 the Kyoto Protocol went into effect, thanks to Russia's ratification late in 2004. Europe began implementing a cap-and-trade system to meet its commitment to reduce CO_2 emissions 8 percent below 1990 levels by 2012. Furthermore, even though the federal government refused to budge on the issue, a host of states were acting to address climate change. By 2005 twenty-eight states had plans to reduce their net greenhouse gas emissions. California, Minnesota, Oregon, New Jersey, Washington, Wisconsin, and the New England states had launched initiatives to curb their CO_2 output. Other states, including Texas and Colorado, had established requirements that utilities achieve a certain percentage of their portfolio using renewable energy sources—measures that, although not framed as climate change policies, promised substantial reductions in CO_2 emissions. Georgia, Nebraska, North Dakota, and Wyoming were investigating methods for sequestering carbon in agricultural soils by promoting no-till farming methods. Other state programs included fuel efficiency mandates for state fleets and tax credits for energy conservation and the purchase of fuel-efficient vehicles.[99] Local governments were getting on the bandwagon as well: in February 2005 Seattle mayor Greg Nickels announced a campaign to get U.S. cities to adopt the terms of the Kyoto Protocol. Nickels aims to recruit 140 cities, to equal the 140 countries that have signed the treaty.[100]

Adding to the pressure on the federal government, many businesses were coming out in support of mandatory greenhouse gas emissions reductions. An August 2004 *Business Week* cover story reported that "consensus is growing—even among businesspeople—that they must act fast to combat climate change, and many companies are now preparing for a carbon-constrained world." [101] Companies were setting greenhouse gas reduction targets, improving energy efficiency, increasing the production and use of renewable energy, improving waste management, investing in carbon sequestration technologies and developing energy-saving products.[102] Furthermore, according to Michael Northrop, co-chair of the Climate Group, a coalition of companies and governments set up to share stories about the benefits of acting on climate change, "It's impossible to find a company that has acted and found no benefits."[103] DuPont boasted that it had cut its greenhouse gas emissions by 65 percent since 1990, saving hundreds of millions of dollars in the process; Alcoa was aiming to cut its emissions by one-quarter by 2010; General Motors was investing millions to develop hydrogen-powered cars that do not emit CO_2; and General Electric was anticipating a growing market for wind power and more energy-efficient appliances. BP developed an internal carbon-trading strategy that prompted a companywide search to find the lowest-cost reductions; the result was a 10 percent reduction in emissions at a savings of $650 million over three years. Similarly, New York utility Consolidated Edison had saved $5 million by fixing natural gas leaks.[104]

Meanwhile, scientists' admonitions were becoming even more urgent. Atmospheric carbon concentrations continued to rise. In 2004 they reached 379 ppm, the highest level ever recorded. U.S. greenhouse gas emissions also went up. The Energy Information Administration reported in January 2004 that U.S. CO_2 emissions increased by 0.7 percent in 2003, down from a 1 percent annual rate of increase since 1990. Although total emissions in 2003 were only slightly higher than they had been in 2000, they were 13.4 percent higher than in 1990. Furthermore, three countries—China, India, and the United States—were planning to build 850 new coal-fired plants, which together would pump up to five times as much CO_2 into the atmosphere as Kyoto plans to reduce.[105] At the same time, it was beginning to appear that limiting global warming to below 2 degrees Celsius, and thereby avoiding the worst consequences of climate change, would entail preventing atmospheric concentrations of CO_2 from reaching 450 ppm, not 550 ppm, as policymakers had hoped. According to a study by Swiss scientist Malte Meinschausen released in February 2005, 450 ppm is the level at which there is just a fifty-fifty chance that the global average temperature rise will not exceed 2 degrees Celsius. Attaining a 450 ppm concentration would require reducing the world's greenhouse gas emissions to between 30 percent and 50 percent of 1990 levels by 2050. And, as Norwegian scientist Steffen Kallbekken points out, delays in cutting back those emissions will make meeting targets more difficult, as much deeper yearly cuts will be required.[106]

CONCLUSIONS

Domestic opposition has hampered efforts to build the groundswell of support necessary to force American national leaders to pursue climate change policies. Opposing greenhouse gas reductions is a powerful coalition of oil and coal producers and fossil fuel–dependent industries that have deep pockets and strong, long-standing ties to elected officials. This coalition has lobbied intensely to ensure that members of Congress and the administration are aware of their position. They have also undertaken a costly public relations campaign in which they wield a dire threat: economic collapse. As they define the problem, the certain economic costs of acting vastly outweigh the highly uncertain and potentially negligible risks of inaction. The extensive efforts by opponents of climate change policies to undermine the credibility of mainstream scientists and elevate the views of conservative economists illuminate the importance of problem definition in American politics—not only in bringing about policy change but in preventing it.

At the same time, proponents of climate change policies are at a disadvantage, not just because they have fewer resources but also because they have a difficult case to make. The climate system is complex and uncertain; the villains of the climate change story are ordinary Americans; and any crisis associated with climate change is likely to occur in the (politically) distant future. Recognizing their situation, proponents of climate change policies have adopted new approaches. They have lobbied at the state level, where the fossil fuel-based coalition is less entrenched. They have also tried to disrupt alliances among economic interests in the United States in a variety of ways, some of them confrontational and others more conciliatory. They have used boycotts and shareholder resolutions to raise CEOs' concern about their corporate image. In addition, they have formed partnerships with businesses to encourage voluntary greenhouse gas emissions reductions. Abetting their efforts is a growing chorus of scientists, who have become unusually vocal. As Princeton economist Robert Socolow observes, the experts who do ice core research or work with climate models are "going out of their way to say, 'Wake up!' This is not a good thing to be doing."[107]

For business the motives for reducing emissions voluntarily and supporting mandatory emissions limits are varied. Scientists' growing certainty makes emissions limits appear inevitable, and savvy executives, such as BP's John Browne, recognize that acting early enhances their reputation and may get them a seat at the table when regulations are designed. Furthermore, state-level policies raise concerns among industries about diverse regulations and create an incentive to press for uniform national CO_2 rules. (Similarly, for multinationals, implementation of the Kyoto Protocol means they will face carbon constraints in other countries, so regulatory harmonization makes sense.) As a result, a growing number of prominent businesspeople have come out in favor of federal greenhouse gas limits. For example, in early December 2004 James Rogers, CEO of the electric utility Cinergy Corp., announced his support for the goals of the McCain-Lieberman bill, which would force major industrial sectors to cut their greenhouse gas emissions to 2000 levels by 2010. And in early February 2005 a Shell Oil economist told senators that climate change is a "wild card" that could shape energy markets and governance worldwide, so it would be prudent to take steps to reduce CO_2 emissions sooner rather than later.[108]

QUESTIONS TO CONSIDER

- Why has the United States resisted efforts to forge international agreements on CO_2 emissions reduction policies, and why is the European Union's position so different?
- What do you think the prospects are for a shift in the U.S. position on policies to prevent or mitigate the damage from climate change, and why?
- Should Americans be concerned about the pace at which the U.S. government is responding to this issue, or is a go-slow approach preferable?

Notes

1. Statement of Dr. James Hansen, Director, NASA Goddard Institute for Space Studies, Greenhouse Effect and Global Climate Change, Hearing Before the Committee on Energy and Natural Resources, U.S. Senate, 100th Cong., 1st sess., on the Greenhouse Effect and Global Climate Change, Part 2 (June 23, 1988).
2. Norman J. Vig, "Introduction," in *The Global Environment: Institutions, Law, and Policy,* ed. Norman J. Vig and Regina S. Axelrod (Washington, D.C.: CQ Press, 1999).
3. Ian H. Rowlands, "Classical Theories of International Relations," in *International Relations and Global Climate Change,* ed. Urs Luterbacher and Detlef Sprinz (Cambridge: MIT Press), 43–65.
4. Stephen Krasner, quoted in Vig, "Introduction," 4.
5. Helen Milner, *Interests, Institutions, and Information: Domestic Politics and International Relations* (Princeton: Princeton University Press, 1997), 9–10.
6. Robert D. Putnam, "Diplomacy and Domestic Politics: The Logic of Two-Level Games," *International Organization* 42 (Summer 1988): 434.
7. Darrell M. West and Burdett A. Loomis, *The Sound of Money: How Political Interests Get What They Want* (New York: Norton, 1999).
8. See, for example, Dewitt John, *Civic Environmentalism: Alternatives to Regulation in States and Communities* (Washington, D.C.: CQ Press, 1994); Daniel A. Mazmanian and Michael E. Kraft, *Toward Sustainable Communities: Transition and Transformation in Environmental Policy* (Cambridge: MIT Press, 1999).
9. Judith A. Layzer, "Deep Freeze: How Business has Shaped the Legislative Debate on Climate Change," in *Business and Environmental Policy,* ed. Michael E. Kraft and Sheldon Kamieniecki (Cambridge: MIT Press, forthcoming).
10. John Houghton, *Global Warming: The Complete Briefing,* 2d ed. (New York: Cambridge University Press, 1997).
11. Ian Rowlands, *The Politics of Global Atmospheric Change* (New York: Manchester University Press, 1995); Matthew Paterson, *Global Warming and Climate Politics* (New York: Routledge, 1996).
12. Roger Revelle and Hans E. Suess, "Carbon Dioxide Exchange Between Atmosphere and Ocean and the Question of an Increase of Atmospheric CO_2 During the Past Decade," *Tellus* 9 (1957): 18–27.
13. President's Science Advisory Committee, *Restoring the Quality of Our Environment: Report of the Environmental Pollution Panel* (Washington, D.C.: The White House, 1965), 126–127.
14. National Academy of Sciences, *Carbon Dioxide and Climate: A Scientific Assessment* (Washington, D.C.: National Academy of Sciences, 1979).
15. Enduring cooperation among meteorologists began with the First International Meteorological Conference in 1853. Twenty years later, the International Meteorological Organization (IMO) was established. After World War II, the IMO turned

into the World Meteorological Organization, and the latter began operating in 1951. See Paterson, *Global Warming*.

16. Quoted in William W. Kellogg, "Predictions of a Global Cooling," *Nature*, August 16, 1979, 615.

17. Stephen Seidel and Dale Keyes, *Can We Delay a Greenhouse Warming? The Effectiveness and Feasibility of Options to Slow a Build-Up of Carbon Dioxide in the Atmosphere* (Washington, D.C.: U.S. Environmental Protection Agency, September 1983).

18. World Meteorological Organization, *Report of the International Conference on the Assessment of the Role of Carbon Dioxide and of Other Greenhouse Gases in Climate Variations and Associated Impacts, Villach, Austria, 9–15 October*, WMO Publication no. 661 (Geneva: World Meteorological Association, 1986).

19. Quoted in Michael Molitor, "The United Nations Climate Change Agreements," in *The Global Environment*, 221.

20. A framework convention is a broad but formal agreement; a protocol contains more concrete commitments. Both must be signed and ratified by participating nations.

21. Molitor, "The United Nations Climate Change Agreements."

22. Quoted in Paterson, *Global Warming*, 37.

23. Quoted in Michael Weisskopf, "Bush Says More Data on Warming Needed," *Washington Post*, April 18, 1990, 1.

24. Quoted in Molitor, "The United Nations Climate Change Agreements."

25. IPCC Working Group I, *Climate Change: The IPCC Scientific Assessment*, ed. J. T. Houghton, G. J. Jenkins, and J. J. Ephraums (New York: Cambridge University Press, 1990).

26. Rowlands, *The Politics of Global Atmospheric Change*, 79.

27. John Hunt, "U.S. Stand on Global Warming Attacked," *Financial Times*, August 30, 1990, 4; Rowlands, *The Politics of Global Atmospheric Change*.

28. For the complete text of the FCCC, go to www.unfccc.de.

29. Steven Greenhouse, "Officials Say U.S. Is Unlikely to Meet Clean-Air Goal for 2000," *New York Times*, March 30, 1995, 6.

30. Bert Bolin, "Report to the Ninth Session of the INC/FCCC" (Geneva: IPCC, February 7, 1994), 2.

31. IPCC Working Group I, *Climate Change 1995: The Science of Climate Change*, ed. J. T. Houghton et al. (New York: Cambridge University Press, 1996), 4.

32. Ibid.

33. Stuart Eizenstadt, Under Secretary of State for Economic, Business, and Agricultural Affairs, Statement before the Senate Foreign Relations Committee, 105th Cong., 2d sess., February 11, 1998.

34. Quoted in Daniel Sarewitz and Roger A. Pielke Jr., "Breaking the Global-Warming Gridlock," *Atlantic Monthly*, July 2000, 57.

35. Ross Gelbspan, *The Heat Is On: The High Stakes Battle over Earth's Threatened Climate* (New York: Addison-Wesley, 1997).

36. To estimate the influence of greenhouse gases in changing climate, researchers run models for a few (simulated) decades and compare the statistics of the models' output to measures of the climate. Although observations of both past and present climate confirm many of the predictions of the prevailing models of climate change, at least some of the data used to validate the models are themselves model outputs. Moreover, the assumptions and data used to construct GCMs heavily influence their predictions, and those elements are themselves selected by scientists who already know what they expect to find. See Steve Rayner, "Predictions and Other Approaches to Climate Change Policy," in *Prediction: Science, Decision Making and the Future of Nature*, ed. Daniel Sarewitz, Roger A. Pielke Jr., and Radford Byerly Jr. (Washington, D.C.: Island Press, 2000), 269–296.

37. Michael L. Parsons, *The Truth Behind the Myth* (New York: Plenum Press, 1995); Patrick J. Michaels, *Sound and Fury: The Science and Politics of Global Warming* (Washington, D.C.: Cato Institute, 1992).

38. S. Fred Singer, "Benefits of Global Warming," *Society* 29 (March–April 1993): 33.

39. William K. Stevens, "At Hot Center of the Debate on Global Warming," *New York Times*, August 6, 1996, C1.

40. Thomas Gale Moore, "Why Global Warming Would Be Good For You," *Public Interest* (Winter 1995): 83–99.

41. Thomas Gale Moore, *Climate of Fear: Why We Shouldn't Worry About Global Warming* (Washington, D.C.: Cato Institute), 1–2.

42. Warren T. Brookes, "The Global Warming Panic," *Forbes*, December 25, 1989, 98.

43. Quoted in Gale E. Christianson, *Greenhouse: The 200-Year Story of Global Warming* (New York: Penguin Books, 1999), 258.

44. U.S. Council of Economic Advisors, *Economic Report of the President* (Washington, D.C.: U.S. Government Printing Office, February 1990), 214.

45. Moore, *Climate of Fear*, 2.

46. Rowlands, *The Politics of Atmospheric Change*, 139.

47. William R. Cline, *Global Warming: The Economic Stakes* (Washington, D.C.: Institute for International Economics, 1992), 1–2.

48. Rowlands, *The Politics of Atmospheric Change*, 137.

49. John J. Fialka, "Clinton's Efforts to Curb Global Warming Draws Some Business Support, But It May Be Too Late," *Wall Street Journal*, October 22, 1997, 24.

50. Craig Trumbo, "Longitudinal Modeling of Public Issues: An Application of the Agenda-Setting Process to the Issue of Global Warming, *Journalism & Mass Communication Monograph* 152 (August 1995).

51. Frank Loy, Undersecretary for Global Affairs, Statement Before the Committee on Foreign Relations and the Committee on Energy and Natural Resources, U.S. Senate, 106th Cong., 2d sess., September 28, 2000.

52. Quoted in William K. Stevens, "Greenhouse Gas Issue: Haggling Over Fairness," *New York Times*, November 30, 1997, 6.

53. Quoted in Molitor, "The United Nations Climate Change Agreements," 219–220.

54. Quoted in ibid., 220.

55. John H. Cushman Jr., "U.S. Says Its Greenhouse Gas Emissions Are at Highest Rate in Years," *New York Times*, October 21, 1997, 22.

56. John H. Cushman Jr., "Why the U.S. Fell Short of Ambitious Goals for Reducing Greenhouse Gases," *New York Times*, October 20, 1997, 15.

57. Quoted in Christianson, *Greenhouse*, 255.

58. Ibid.

59. Quoted in James Bennet, "Warm Globe, Hot Politics," *New York Times*, December 11, 1997, 1. The protocol takes effect once it is ratified by at least fifty-five nations; the terms become binding on an individual country only after its government ratifies the treaty.

60. John H. Cushman Jr., "Industrial Group Plans to Battle Climate Treaty," *New York Times*, April 26, 1998, 1.

61. William K. Stevens, "Science Academy Disputes Attacks on Global Warming," *New York Times*, April 22, 1998, 20.

62. John H. Cushman Jr., "New Policy Center Seeks to Steer the Debate on Climate Change," *New York Times*, May 8, 1998, 13.

63. Andrew C. Revkin, "The Tree Trap," *New York Times*, November 26, 2000, 16.

64. Interlaboratory Working Group, *Scenarios of U.S. Carbon Reductions: Potential Impacts of Energy Technologies by 2010 and Beyond* (Berkeley and Oak Ridge: Lawrence Berkeley National Laboratory and Oak Ridge National Laboratory, September 1997), Rept. No. LBNL-40533 and ORNL-444.

65. Council of Economic Advisors, *The Kyoto Protocol and the President's Policies to Address Climate Change: Administration Economic Analysis* (Washington, D.C.: Executive Office of the President, July 1998).

66. Robert Mendelsohn et al., "Introduction," in *The Impact of Climate Change on the United States Economy*, ed. Robert Mendelsohn and James E. Neumann (New York: Cambridge University Press, 1999), 15.

67. Bert Bolin, "The Kyoto Negotiations on Climate Change: A Science Perspective," *Science*, January 16, 1998, 330–331.

68. William K. Stevens, "March May Soon Be Coming in Like a Lamb," *New York Times*, March 2, 1999, 1.

69. John Noble Wilford, "Open Water at the Pole Is Not so Surprising, Experts Say," *New York Times*, August 29, 2000, C1.

70. Loy, Statement.

71. By employing prudent land use practices, the United States argued, parties can "sequester" CO_2—that is, they can store it in wood and soils, thereby preventing its release into the atmosphere. Critics were dubious about heavy reliance on forests to curb CO_2, however, pointing out that while forests currently do offset about one-quarter of the world's industrial CO_2 emissions, research at the Hadley Center in the United Kingdom indicated that many of the recently planted forests would, by the middle of the twenty-first century, begin releasing carbon back into the atmosphere. Moreover, they noted, during the same period, warming was likely to increase the amount of carbon released by soils, particularly in the peatland forests of the northern latitudes.

72. Andrew C. Revkin, "Treaty Talks Fail to Find Consensus in Global Warming," *New York Times*, November 26, 2001, 1.

73. Quoted in Andrew C. Revkin, "Odd Culprits in Collapse of Climate Talks," *New York Times*, November 28, 2000, C1.

74. "Climate Panel Reaffirms Major Warming Threat," *New York Times*, January 23, 2001, D8.

75. "Paradise Lost? Global Warming Seen as Threat," *Houston Chronicle*, February 20, 2001, 1.

76. Kilimanjaro has lost 82 percent of the icecap it had in 1912. In the Alps, scientists estimate 90 percent of the ice volume of a century ago will be gone by 2025. See Eric Pianin, "U.N. Report Forecasts Crises Brought On By Global Warming," *Washington Post*, February 20, 2001, 6.

77. James Glanz, "Droughts Might Speed Climate Change," *New York Times*, January 11, 2001, 16.

78. Quoted in Douglas Jehl and Andrew C. Revkin, "Bush, in Reversal, Won't Seek Cuts in Emissions of Carbon Dioxide," *New York Times*, March 14, 2001, 1.

79. Joseph Kahn, "Energy Efficiency Programs Are Set for Bush Budget Cut," *New York Times*, April 5, 2001, 16.

80. Douglas Jehl, "U.S. Rebuffs European Plea Not to Abandon Climate Pact," *New York Times*, April 4, 2001, 14.

81. Darren K. Carlson, "Scientists Deliver Serious Warning About Effects of Global Warming," Gallup Poll Releases (January 23, 2001).

82. Edmund L. Andrews, "Frustrated Europeans Set Out to Battle U.S. on Climate," *New York Times*, July 16, 2001, 3.

83. Katharine Q. Seelye and Andrew C. Revkin, "Panel Tells Bush Global Warming Is Getting Worse," *New York Times*, June 7, 2001, 1.

84. Quoted in Andrew C. Revkin, "Deal Breaks Impasse on Global Warming Treaty," *New York Times*, November 11, 2001, Sec. 1, 1.

85. Quoted in "White House Plan Marks Turf Amid Already-Contentious Debate," *E&E Daily*, February 15, 2002.

86. "Doubts Linger as Kyoto Takes Force This Week," *Greenwire*, February 14, 2005.

87. Andrew C. Revkin, "Computers Add Sophistication, but Don't Resolve Climate Debate," *New York Times*, August 31, 2004.

88. Peter Foukal, Gerald North, and Tom Wigley, "A Stellar View on Solar Variations and Climate," *Science*, October 1, 2004, 68–69.

89. By contrast, core sediment revealed that the Larsen A ice shelf, which disintegrated in the mid-1990s, had been open water 6,000 years ago. See Kenneth Chang, "The Melting (Freezing) of Antarctica," *New York Times*, April 2, 2002, D1; Andrew C. Revkin, "Study of Antarctic Points to Rising Sea Levels," *New York Times*, March 7, 2003, 8.

90. Usha Lee McFarling, "Arctic's Biggest Ice Shelf, a Sentinel of Climate Change, Cracks Apart," *Los Angeles Times*, September 23, 2003, Sec. 1, 3.

91. Wallace S. Broecker, "Thermohaline Circulation, the Achilles Heel of Our Climate System: Will Man-Made CO_2 Upset the Current Balance?" *Science*, November 28, 1997, 1582–8.

92. Quoted in Andrew C. Revkin, "Warming Is Found to Disrupt Species," *New York Times*, January 2, 2003, 1.

93. "Rising Temps Could Kill 25 Percent of World's Species, Scientists Say," *Greenwire*, January 8, 2004.

94. "CO_2 May be Changing Structure of Amazon Rainforest—Study," *Greenwire*, March 11, 2004; "Study Finds 'Carbon Sinks' May Actually Generate More CO_2," *Greenwire*, September 24, 2004.

95. Andrew Freedman, "Warming May Lead to Western 'Megadroughts,' Study Says," *Greenwire*, October 8, 2004.

96. Susan Milligan, "Study Predicts City Flood Threat Due to Warming," *Boston Globe*, February 15, 2005, 1.

97. Quoted in Andrew C. Revkin, "Politics Reasserts Itself in the Debate Over Climate Change and Its Hazards," *New York Times*, August 5, 2003, F2.

98. Quoted in Larry Rohter, "U.S. Waters Down Global Commitment to Curb Greenhouse Gases," *New York Times*, December 19, 2004, 16.

99. Barry Rabe, *Statehouse and Greenhouse: The Emerging Politics of American Climate Change Policy*, (Washington, D.C.: Brookings Institution Press, 2004).

100. "Cities Organizing to Reduce Greenhouse Gas Emissions," *Greenwire*, February 22, 2005.

101. John Carey, "Global Warming," *Business Week*, August 16, 2004.

102. Carbon sequestration is the long-term storage of carbon in forests, soils, geological formations, and other carbon sinks. See Pew Center on Global Climate Change, "Climate Change Activities in the United States: 2004 Update." Available at www.pewclimate.org.

103. Quoted in Carey, "Global Warming."

104. Carey, "Global Warming"; "Enviro Study Highlights Business Efforts to Reduce GHGs," *Greenwire*, October 26, 2004.

105. Mark Clayton, "New Coal Plants Bury Kyoto," *Christian Science Monitor*, December 23, 2004.

106. Jenny Hogan, "Only Huge Emissions Cuts Will Curb Climate Change," *New Scientist*, February 3, 2005.

107. Elizabeth Kolbert, "The Climate of Man—III," *New Yorker*, May 9, 2005, 55.

108. "Cinergy Says It Supports Mandatory GHG Reductions," *Greenwire*, December 2, 2004; Ben Geman, "Climate Change Is Energy 'Wild Card,' Industry Economist Says," *Greenwire*, February 4, 2005.

Recommended Reading

Gelbspan, Ross. *The Heat Is On: The High Stakes Battle over Earth's Threatened Climate.* New York: Addison-Wesley, 1997.

Houghton, John. *Global Warming: The Complete Briefing,* 2d ed. New York: Cambridge University Press, 1997.

Michaels, Patrick J. *Sound and Fury: The Science and Politics of Global Warming.* Washington, D.C.: Cato Institute, 1992.

Paterson, Matthew. *Global Warming and Climate Politics.* New York: Routledge, 1996.

Victor, David G. *The Collapse of the Kyoto Protocol and the Struggle to Slow Global Warming.* Princeton: Princeton University Press, 2001.

Weart, Spencer R. *The Discovery of Global Warming.* Cambridge: Harvard University Press, 2003.

Web Sites

http://unfccc.int/2860.php (UNFCCC site)
www.ipcc.ch (IPCC site)
www.epa.gov/globalwarming (EPA site)

CHAPTER 12

Trade Versus the Environment:
Dolphins, Turtles, and Global Economic Expansion

In the summer of 2005, ten major U.S. environmental groups adopted a unified position against the Central American Free Trade Agreement being debated in Congress. They emphasized the potential negative impacts of trade on the environment and argued that trade agreements should be designed to enhance, not impede, environmental protection. Environmentalists' concerns about trade were not new: for years they had complained bitterly that unfettered economic globalization threatened nations' ability to institute environmentally protective regulations, which can impede the free flow of goods, services, and capital. To illustrate the flaws in the international trading regime, environmentalists often cited two prominent examples: the tuna/dolphin dispute of the late 1980s and the shrimp/turtle conflict of the late 1990s. According to environmentalists, in both of these cases, trade officials condemned U.S. laws restricting imports from countries that did not use environmentally protective seafood harvesting techniques and thereby limited U.S. ability to use trade leverage to bring about global environmental improvements. Free trade advocates countered that unilateral measures of the kind that were struck down not only dampen global economic expansion but also, in the long run, impede environmental protection.

To support their positions, advocates on both sides drew on competing theoretical arguments rooted in fundamentally different values. According to those with a cornucopian worldview, trade liberalization enhances material prosperity, which in turn leads to greater environmental protection. The claim that liberalizing trade brings about economic growth dates back to the work of nineteenth-century British economist David Ricardo, who argued that trade encourages each nation to specialize in those activities in which it has a comparative advantage. If each nation focuses on what it can do most economically and exports its surplus while importing what it no longer produces, overall efficiency and productivity—and therefore wealth—increase. In the 1990s economists extended the argument with the claim that, although a country's environmental degradation may rise sharply during the early stages of development, it is likely to decrease as a country becomes wealthier because its businesses will adopt cleaner technologies and shift away from environmentally destructive activities, and its citizens will demand more environmental protection.[1] Although mainstream economists generally endorse this view, which is known as the "environmental Kuznets curve" hypothesis, scholarly studies offer limited empirical support for it, and a growing number are finding that in practice the relationship between economic growth and the environment is ambiguous.[2]

A contrasting belief more commonly held among environmentalists is that it is impossible for the world to grow its way out of poverty and environmental degradation, and free trade only hastens the world's already alarming environmental decline. Proponents of this argument point out that, although trade may result in economic growth, GDP (gross domestic product) is hardly a valid measure of progress or national well-being.[3] In any case, as economist Herman Daly explains, "The regenerative and assimilative capacities of the biosphere cannot support even the current levels of resource consumption," much less the enormous increases needed to produce higher levels of growth worldwide.[4] He adds that unregulated international commerce threatens to undermine existing and future efforts at environmental protection because it exposes domestic companies to competition from lower-cost producers and therefore creates incentives for them to resist protective regulations. Similarly, free trade creates incentives for heavily polluting companies to move their operations to developing countries where regulations are less stringent and therefore compliance is less expensive; fear of losing a competitive advantage may even prompt countries to compete for dirty industries. The evidence to support this hypothesis—alternately known as the "race to the bottom," "pollution haven," and "competition for laxity"—is also limited: most empirical investigations have found that the marginal costs of pollution abatement are relatively small and so are not a major influence on corporations' location decisions.[5]

Political scientist David Vogel proposes a third possibility: trade liberalization may result in harmonization of environmental regulations upwards of—what he calls the "California effect." According to this view, nations perceive environmental regulations as a source of competitive advantage, not disadvantage, because domestic businesses can comply with them more easily, and nations with large domestic markets can force their trading partners to meet their standards in order to continue doing business. Vogel notes, however, that there is nothing automatic about the California effect; rather, it depends on "the preferences of wealthy states and the degree of economic integration among them and their trading partners." [6] More specifically, trade liberalization is most likely to strengthen environmental protection when the most powerful in a group of economically integrated nations has an influential domestic constituency for stronger regulatory standards.[7]

Clearly, the California effect can arise only if the international trade regime allows environmentally protective nations to limit imports from countries that do not enforce regulations comparable to their own—precisely the issue in the tuna/dolphin and shrimp/turtle cases. But trade liberalization advocates oppose such flexibility out of concern that environmental regulation is simply a disguise for rules that protect domestic industries, a phenomenon they call "green protectionism." Some of the most vocal opponents of using trade restrictions to enforce environmental protection are developing countries' trade representatives, who accuse developed nations of "eco-imperialism" and contend that their domestic industries lack the resources to comply with strict environmental regulations. As scholars such as Vogel have observed, debates between environmentalists and free traders over whether a particular environmental regulation constitutes protectionism turn on a small number of questions: What is acceptable evidence of environmental harm, and who bears the burden of proof? Is the regulation prompted by genuine environmental concern or by an impulse to protect a domestic industry? Can governments legitimately enforce regulations that aim to protect resources that are outside their jurisdiction? If so, must regulators adopt the least trade-restrictive approach possible? And should they be allowed to dictate the process by which a product is produced or harvested, as opposed to just its content?

Further disagreements arise over whether, even if it is permitted, trade leverage is an effective means of bringing about international cooperation. Proponents of using trade leverage claim that historically it has produced positive environmental results, while detractors argue that in a "post-hegemonic" world only noncoercive measures are likely to work.[8] One approach many environmental organizations have endorsed, in part to circumvent debates over the appropriateness of using trade policy to influence manufacturing and harvesting processes in other countries, is eco-labeling. This practice, which aims to give consumers more information, rests on the theory that many will choose the product that was produced in a more environmentally friendly way or that contains more environmentally benign ingredients. Although eco-labeling schemes are growing in popularity, it is unclear how effective they are in terms of yielding environmental protection: their effectiveness depends heavily on both consumers' education and their willingness to pay to advance environmental values. Moreover, although labeling schemes are traditionally voluntary, the trade representatives of developing countries object that they constitute *de facto* barriers to trade because they require substantial investments in raw materials, new production processes, testing, and certification.

BACKGROUND

In 1947, when world leaders signed the General Agreement on Tariffs and Trade (GATT), their goal was to restore international economic stability. Protecting the global environment was not on the agenda. To promote trade across national borders, which was viewed as an essential feature of a stable and prosperous system, signatories agreed to comply with a series of rules for the treatment of domestic and imported goods and services. These rules established three basic principles: nondiscrimination among nations, minimal government restraints on the movement of goods and services, and agreement on the conditions of trade within a multilateral framework.[9] To these ends, Article I of GATT spells out the "most favored nation" principle, which prohibits applying different tariffs for the same product to different members, and Article III states the "national treatment" principle, which requires contracting parties to treat foreign and domestic products equally if they have met tariff and other import requirements.[10] To address the problem of nontariff trade barriers—rules that discriminate among products explicitly on the basis of national origin of the product or firm—Article XI prohibits the use of "quotas, import or export licenses, or other measures" to restrict imports or exports.

Although GATT's overall aim is trade liberalization, Article XX provides for exceptions to this broad mandate. Article XX's introductory clause, the chapeau, allows for the adoption and enforcement of discriminatory trade laws provided they are not applied arbitrarily, do not amount to unjustifiable discrimination between countries where the same conditions prevail, and are not simply disguised restrictions on international trade. Among the particular exceptions allowed under Article XX are measures "necessary to protect human, animal or plant life or health" (paragraph b) and those "relating to the conservation of exhaustible natural resources if such measures are made effective in conjunction with restrictions on domestic production or consumption" (paragraph g).

During the first four decades of GATT, trade representatives from member countries evinced little interest in the impact of the agreement's rules on environmental protection. In 1971, in preparation for the United Nations' 1972 Conference on the Human Environment, the GATT Secretariat developed a report that expressed concern about the potentially harmful impact of environmental policies on international trade. At that point, GATT officials established the Working Group on Environmental Measures and International Trade, but the group—which was to be convened at the request of GATT members—did not meet once in the ensuing two decades. During the Tokyo Round, which concluded in 1979, negotiators again said little about the environment; they did, however, develop the Agreement on Technical Barriers to Trade. Known as the "Standards Code," this agreement said that no country should be prevented from taking measures to protect the environment as long as there was no discrimination in the preparation, adoption, and application of technical regulations and standards.

Despite trade officials' reluctance to address the issue, over time, questions began to arise as to whether national environmental, health, and safety regulations—which often have a discriminatory effect if not a discriminatory intent—should be struck down as nontariff barriers to trade. Immediately, battle lines were drawn between environmentalists and free traders, both of whom quickly recognized that, "just as the definition of discrimination has important implications for the way American civil rights laws are enforced, so does the definition of a nontariff barrier have important consequences for both trade and regulatory policies." [11] Although the philosophical differences between the two sides were clear, prior to 1991 GATT dispute resolution panels had addressed formal challenges to national environmental regulations only three times and had not confronted the most divisive issues. Two of these cases involved disputes between the United States and Canada over fishery policies; in the third, Canada, the European Community, and Mexico challenged the excise tax provisions of the United States' Superfund amendments of 1986. In each case, the panels ruled that GATT signatories could impose whatever conservation, quality control, taxes, or advertising restrictions they wished, provided they applied those rules equally to imported and domestic goods.[12] Because they addressed relatively minor policy concerns, these decisions did not provoke widespread examination of GATT's ability to handle environmental challenges.

THE CASE

In 1991, however, the simmering controversy over trade and the environment boiled over when Mexico appealed a U.S. embargo on tuna caught using methods that kill dolphins. The case laid bare the fundamental disagreement between free traders and environmentalists over whether unregulated trade ultimately benefits or harms the environment. To advance their beliefs, each side tried to furnish the authoritative definition of a nontariff barrier to trade: trade liberalization advocates argued for a narrow interpretation of the exceptions to GATT's nondiscrimination provisions, while environmentalists pressed for a more expansive one. The tuna/dolphin decisions, which condemned U.S. policy, reflected trade officials' overriding concern with promoting economic growth and their strong distaste for unilateral environmental protection measures. But the rulings in a subsequent case, over whether the United States was justified in restricting imports of shrimp from nations that do not minimize harm to sea turtles, reflected trade officials' increasing sensitivity to the salience of environmentalism in the world's most powerful countries. The shrimp/turtle decision demonstrated a continuing preference for multilateral agreements, but it also incorporated a broader view of the valid exceptions to GATT prohibitions. The decision, which allowed nations to impose unilateral import restrictions if they were engaged in good-faith efforts to reach multilateral agreements, only intensified the debate over the utility of trade leverage as a means of spurring international cooperation.

The Tuna/Dolphin Dispute

In the early 1990s the tuna/dolphin controversy raised the visibility of the trade-versus-environment conflict and put it squarely on the American political agenda; in doing so it revealed major differences among domestic actors as to the pros and cons of using trade leverage to accomplish environmental goals. But the problem that provoked the controversy had arisen decades earlier, when U.S. fishers discovered that in the 5 million to 7 million square mile area of the Pacific west of Central and South America known as the Eastern Tropical Pacific (ETP), tuna tend to swim below dolphins for reasons that scientists do not understand. In 1959 U.S. fishers invented the practice of "dolphin setting," which involves using dolphins to locate schools of tuna and encircling both fish and dolphins with mile-long, 600-foot-deep nets called purse seines. As fishers draw the nets closed, some dolphins jump over the top, but many do not and instead become trapped and drown. Fishers quickly recognized that this technique—made possible by the development of a synthetic net that would not rot in tropical water and a hydraulically driven power block to haul the net—was the most economically efficient way to catch tuna in the ETP.[13] Scientists estimate that during the 1960s tuna fishing boats in the ETP, nearly all of which were American owned, killed between 350,000 and 500,000 dolphins each year. In the late 1960s government biologist William Perrin published two articles drawing attention to the practice of using dolphins to catch tuna in the ETP. His observations in turn provoked environmentalists to initiate a campaign to raise public awareness of the problem.

The Marine Mammal Protection Act. By 1972 scientists and environmentalists had generated sufficient public outrage about the destruction of dolphins and other marine mammals in the course of commercial fishing to persuade Congress to pass the Marine Mammal Protection Act (MMPA), whose purpose is to preserve whales, dolphins, porpoises, manatees, sea otters, polar bears, walruses, seals, and sea lions. To that end the MMPA required the Commerce Department's National Marine Fisheries Service (NMFS, pronounced "nymphs") to maintain "optimum sustainable populations" of marine mammals, issue permits for their incidental take in the course of commercial fishing operations, and ensure that any permitted take "be reduced to insignificant levels approaching a zero mortality and serious injury rate." [14] The law also mandated that U.S. boats fishing in the ETP carry on-board observers, comply with gear and practice standards, and stay within fleetwide mortality limits established by NMFS. In recognition that these measures put U.S. fishers at a competitive disadvantage, the law also required the State Department and NMFS to ban commercial fish (or products from fish) that have been caught with technology that results in the incidental death or injury of ocean mammals in excess of U.S. standards.

The law granted the U.S. tuna industry a two-year grace period to develop procedures for reducing dolphin mortality, but even after that time had elapsed the NMFS issued only a general industrywide permit to the American Tunaboat Association requiring them to maintain special gear and keep detailed records of their activities. In 1976, in response to a court order (*Committee for Humane Legislation v. Richardson*, 1976), NMFS finally issued a permit containing an annual quota for U.S. fishers in the ETP of 78,000 dolphins per year. The agency also promulgated specific gear and practice standards and placed observers on one-third of U.S. vessels. After the regulations were issued, dolphin mortality attributable to U.S. boats—which had already declined from 350,000 in 1972 to 166,000 in 1975, thanks to the adoption of backdown procedures and Medina panels—dropped dramatically to below 20,000 by 1980 (see Figure 12-1).[15] In 1981, after several rounds of debate and litigation, the NMFS issued the tunaboat association a five-year permit with an annual incidental take quota of 20,500.

Figure 12-1 Dolphin Mortality from U.S. Vessels in the ETP

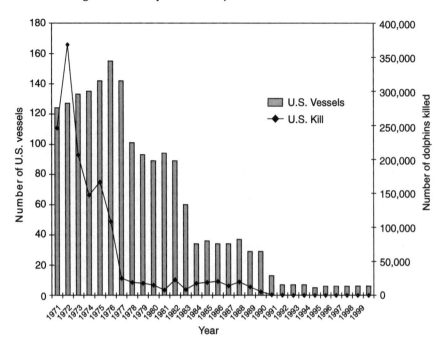

Sources: Inter-American Tropical Tuna Commission and NOAA Fisheries.

As the United States tightened its restrictions on tuna fishing, however, American fishers began working under foreign flags or leaving the ETP altogether, in order to avoid the regulations, and foreign fleets became a larger proportion of the boats operating in the region. Recognizing the growing importance of the foreign fleets, in 1979 the Inter-American Tropical Tuna Commission (IATTC) instituted a dolphin conservation program that aimed to get voluntary reductions in dolphin mortality. The program put observers on one-third of IATTC members' boats and initiated research on dolphin safety gear and the tuna/dolphin interaction. But despite the tuna commission's efforts, dolphin mortality began rising again: by 1984 fleets from Mexico, Panama, Venezuela, and the Pacific island nation of Vanuatu were killing more than 100,000 dolphins a year, and by 1986 that number had risen to 133,000.[16]

In its 1984 reauthorization of the MMPA, Congress statutorily extended the tunaboat association's permit indefinitely in hopes of quelling the recurrent disputes between environmentalists and fishers over the permit process. At the same time, however, Congress was concerned that, by not holding foreign fleets to U.S. standards, NMFS was jeopardizing not only dolphins but also the competitiveness of U.S. fleets. So the 1984 MMPA amendments established

Figure 12-2 Dolphin Mortality from Foreign Vessels in the ETP

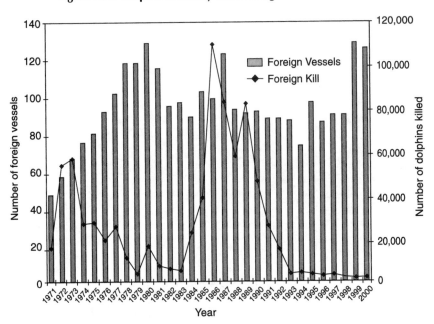

Sources: Inter-American Tropical Tuna Commission and NOAA Fisheries.

more precise standards for dolphin kills by non-American fleets: they allowed tuna caught in the ETP to be imported into the United States only if the government of the originating country could demonstrate it had implemented a dolphin protection program "comparable" to that of the American fishing fleet and had achieved an incidental kill rate "comparable" to that of the United States. The amendments also prohibited imports of tuna from intermediate countries that had purchased the fish from nations whose fleets exceeded the MMPA's dolphin mortality standards. Between 1984 and 1987, however, NMFS did not issue any formal rules to implement the import prohibition, even though newly available observer data revealed that dolphin kills by foreign fleets were higher than previously believed and continued to mount (see Figure 12-2).

Impatient with NMFS's inaction, in January 1988 a coalition of U.S. environmental groups led by the Earth Island Institute (EII) and the Humane Society launched a boycott of canned tuna in hopes of persuading the major American importers to stop buying tuna caught with purse seine nets. The coalition also began lobbying Congress to phase out purse seine fishing altogether. U.S. fishers applauded efforts to limit imports: at congressional hearings on reauthorizing the MMPA, fishers emphasized the loss of competitive advantage they suffered because foreign fleets were exempted from dolphin protection requirements, and environmentalists and fishers both pointed out the futility of ignoring foreign fleets' activities, which were responsible for 75 percent of dolphin deaths in the late 1980s.[17] To bolster their case, environmentalists showed members of Congress a film surreptitiously made by biologist Sam LaBudde while he was aboard a Panamanian tuna fishing vessel. The film depicted dolphins "shrieking in panic as they fought against the net and gasped for air. Some that were still alive were dragged into a power block that was used to haul in the net [and they] were crushed to death." [18] Although Congress declined to take the draconian step of phasing out purse seining, the 1988 amendments to the MMPA did tighten the restrictions on incidental take of dolphins in the ETP by requiring the secretary of commerce to ban imports from countries whose fleets exceeded 1.25 times the average incidental kill rate of the U.S. fleet by 1990. The amendments similarly tightened the conditions for imposing a secondary embargo on intermediate countries to prevent tuna "laundering." Congress believed that the import bans would protect dolphin populations, encourage foreign fleets to adopt dolphin-safe practices, and protect U.S. fishers from unfair competition from foreign nations that saved money by engaging in environmentally harmful practices.[19]

The Dolphin-Safe Label. Environmentalists' efforts to raise the salience of the tuna/dolphin issue bore fruit not just in Congress but among consumers. In April 1990, after a prolonged boycott, the three big U.S. tuna canning companies announced they would no longer sell tuna harvested by purse seine techniques. (The tuna caught in the ETP is yellowfin. It is sold as "light meat" and by the early 1990s accounted for about 20 percent of retail tuna sales in the United States.[20]) Heinz (Starkist), with a 36 percent share of the U.S. canned tuna market in 1989, made its announcement first, and the other two—Van Camp (Chicken of the Sea) and Unicord (Bumble Bee), which accounted for another 34 percent of the market combined—quickly followed suit.[21] According to journalist Anthony Ramirez, Heinz chairman Anthony O'Reilly attributed the company's decision to both concern within the corporation and widespread public awareness of the issue. The final catalyst for Heinz was a marketing survey that detected a jump in awareness of the dolphin issue among consumers from 50 percent to 60 percent and an increase in the level of concern from six to seven on a scale of one to ten.[22]

Pleased with the canners' announcement but concerned that smaller companies would label their tuna "dolphin safe" even though it was caught using purse seine nets, environmentalists lobbied Congress to enact the Dolphin Protection Consumer Information Act. This law, which passed in late November 1990, required companies selling tuna under a "dolphin safe" label to demonstrate their product was caught using methods that did not kill dolphins; in other words, tuna sold in the United States could not display the "dolphin-safe" label if it was harvested using purse seine nets deployed on dolphins. The major tuna processors, all of whom had already committed to selling only dolphin-safe tuna, testified in support of the bill. And, although small canners,

Mexican fishers, and the remaining U.S. fishers in the ETP bitterly opposed it, they lacked the political clout to oppose the big three canners.[23]

The GATT Challenge

According to legal scholar Richard Parker, the effect on foreign fleets of the embargo threat contained in the 1988 amendments to the MMPA was "electric." By the late 1980s IATTC research, based on newly abundant observer data, had identified a host of conditions for reducing dolphin mortality that were all under the control of a ship's captain and crew.[24] Armed with this knowledge, the tuna commission had held dozens of workshops, disseminated educational literature, and offered technical assistance to captains and crew. Participation by fishers in the IATTC's outreach program had been meager, but it increased dramatically after the passage of the 1988 amendments.[25] As a result of changes in the fishing practices of foreign fleets, total dolphin mortality in the ETP again began to decline: half as many dolphins were killed in 1990 as in 1989. Mexico, which had the largest fleet in the ETP, modified its tuna fishing regulations and reduced the number of dolphins killed from 49,000 in 1988 to 16,000 in 1991. Furthermore, the Mexican fleet reduced the average number of dolphins killed in each purse seine set from 15 to 1.85.[26]

As environmentalists pointed out, however, the Mexican kill rate still exceeded the U.S. rate (which was nearly zero largely because only eleven U.S.-registered vessels were still fishing in the ETP).[27] Yet the commerce secretary still had not issued the comparability findings required by the 1988 amendments and had made no effort to ban any imports, so in August 1990, in response to a lawsuit by EII, Judge Thelton E. Henderson issued a preliminary injunction against the importation of tuna from Mexico and four other countries fishing in the ETP (*Earth Island Institute v. Mosbacher*, 1990). Judge Henderson pointed out that under the NMFS's approach, which delayed imposing an embargo until it had assessed each nation's kill rate at the end of 1989, dolphins continued to be killed and American fishers bore a competitive burden. "The continued slaughter and destruction of these innocent victims of the economics of fishing constitutes an irreparable injury to us all," the judge wrote.[28]

A day after the judge's order, NMFS made positive findings for Mexico, Venezuela, and Vanuatu, thereby allowing the embargo on them to be lifted. But EII immediately challenged the agency's calculations for Mexico, and the issue went back to court. In October Judge Henderson agreed with EII that Mexico had, in fact, exceeded U.S. standards for dolphin mortality, and he required the Commerce Department to impose a primary embargo. After a series of legal skirmishes, the Ninth Circuit Court of Appeals upheld the embargo against Mexico, which took effect on February 22, 1991.[29] Then, in late March, the embargo was broadened to include Panama and Vanuatu. In response to these court rulings, the Bush administration's State Department— concerned about jeopardizing negotiations over the North American Free Trade Agreement (NAFTA)—reluctantly began enforcing the embargo.

The Mexican government regarded the U.S. tuna embargo as typical of efforts by developed nations to protect themselves from growing competition from developing nations. On January 25, 1991, it asked a GATT panel to deem the U.S. embargo a protectionist measure in violation of GATT rules. In legal terms, Mexico claimed the import prohibition was inconsistent with three GATT articles: XI (the general prohibition on quantitative restrictions), XIII (discretionary import rules), and III (like products). Mexico also challenged the MMPA's secondary embargo provision under Article XI. In response, the United States asked the panel to find the embargoes consistent with a provision of Article III that permits "internal regulations enforced at the time of importation" or, alternatively, justified as an exception under Article XX(b) and (g). Mexico's lawyers replied that Article XX exceptions apply only to animals within the territory of the nation imposing the restrictions. They suggested that, if the United States wanted to protect dolphins caught by the Mexican fishing fleet or in Mexican territorial waters, it should not act unilaterally, but negotiate an international agreement or add the dolphin species being killed to the Convention on International Trade in Endangered Species.

In May and June of 1991 the three-person GATT dispute resolution panel held hearings on the case, and more than a dozen countries—including Australia, Canada, Japan, Norway, and the entire European Community—submitted statements supporting Mexico's position. In early September the panel ruled that both the primary and secondary tuna embargoes imposed by the United States violated GATT. The panel agreed with Mexico that the measures neither regulated the sale of tuna nor prescribed fishing techniques that would affect the content of tuna as a *product*, either of which would have been allowed as internal regulations under Article III. Instead, the U.S. measure regulated the *process* by which tuna is produced, which—the panel ruled—is inconsistent with GATT's "national treatment" requirement. The panel then turned to the exceptions in Article XX—the "heart of the opinion." [30] It found that Article XX(b) and (g) did not provide exceptions because they applied only to production or consumption within one's borders. In addition, the panel held that, even if Article XX did allow for extrajurisdictional actions, the MMPA's direct embargo provisions would not qualify because they were not "necessary." According to the panel, the United States had not demonstrated it had exhausted all reasonable alternatives. Nor had it presented compelling evidence that its restrictions on foreign fleets—which were based on calculations that were both unpredictable and unfair to other countries—were primarily aimed at conserving dolphins.[31] (Mexico had also challenged the consumer information act, but the panel upheld that law on the grounds that the labeling provision did not limit access to the U.S. market because any advantage it conveyed resulted from consumer preferences.) The panel emphasized it was not trying to discourage environmental protection but was merely trying to ensure that such measures were consistent with trade agreements that nations had signed.

Environmentalists were outraged by the GATT panel's decision, which they believed defined nontariff trade barriers far too broadly and the exceptions to

GATT prohibitions too narrowly. An article in *Greenpeace* magazine said: "The GATT ruling sets a dangerous precedent. It paves the way for similar challenges of other national or international laws aimed, at least in theory, at protecting the Earth and its creatures." [32] David Phillips of EII said the decision showed that "In the 1990s, free trade and efforts to protect the environment are on a collision course." [33] Well aware of the issue's salience among their environmentally conscious constituents, 64 senators and 100 representatives wrote to President George H. W. Bush criticizing the panel's ruling, expressing their unwillingness to weaken the MMPA, and demanding that GATT be made compatible with American environmental laws.[34]

Free traders, by contrast, applauded the panel's decision, and, although the decision provoked controversy in the United States, the other GATT members overwhelmingly endorsed it. GATT's 1992 annual report and a World Bank report on trade and environment, issued shortly after the tuna/dolphin decision, defended the reasoning of the dispute panel. The GATT report, written principally by prominent trade economist Jagdish Bhagwati, articulated the environmental Kuznets curve hypothesis that economic development is more likely than trade restrictions to lead to environmental protection. Using a slippery slope argument, the report rejected tampering with GATT's nondiscrimination principle and asserted that unilateral trade restrictions would result in anarchy similar to that of the 1930s. It urged developed countries to use persuasion and incentives, not ultimatums and coercion, to change the behavior of developing countries. The World Bank report, *International Trade and the Environment*, drew similar conclusions but added that it would be irrational for countries to harmonize their environmental regulations, because doing so would undermine comparative advantage and because countries value the environment differently depending on their level of development and other considerations.[35]

Tuna/Dolphin Round Two: Another GATT Challenge. According to GATT rules, a dispute panel ruling was binding only if the General Council officially adopted it, and, despite pressure from the other members of GATT, the United States managed to persuade the Mexican government to forgo asking the council to adopt the tuna/dolphin decision. In return the United States began bilateral negotiations with Mexico in hopes that the two countries could settle the dispute in a way that would not jeopardize congressional approval of NAFTA. Eventually, the two sides agreed that Mexico would reduce its dolphin kills in exchange for efforts by the State Department to get the embargo against Mexico lifted by trying to persuade environmentalists that lifting the ban would save dolphin in the long run. Mexico immediately began publicizing its ten-point plan to reduce dolphin kills in an effort to resuscitate its image.[36]

Environmentalists continued to press for full implementation of the Marine Mammal Protection Act, however, and in September 1991 they filed suit against the commerce secretary for failing to enforce the secondary embargo required under the law. In January 1992 the court rendered its opinion: without mentioning GATT or the tuna/dolphin dispute, Judge Henderson required the commerce secretary to ban imports from the twenty-seven countries that were shipping tuna from Mexico, Vanuatu, and Venezuela to the United States (*Earth Island Institute v. Mosbacher*, 1992).[37] In the following months NMFS began to enforce the secondary embargo. Again U.S. exertion of trade leverage produced a reaction: According to Richard Parker, the embargoes galvanized a public dialogue about dolphin mortality, as well as prompting research and training programs, in both Venezuela and Mexico.

Although the European Union (EU) supported the goal of reducing dolphin mortality in the ETP, its members were fed up with U.S. unilateralism, and in late 1992 it appealed to a GATT dispute resolution panel on behalf of Spain and Italy, which, along with Costa Rica and Japan, were subject to the secondary embargo. The arguments reprised those made in the previous tuna/dolphin dispute: the United States contended its secondary embargo was an allowable exception under Article XX because it was intended to protect an "exhaustible natural resource" and was not discriminatory because it had been imposed in conjunction with resources on domestic production and consumption. The EU responded that the American interpretation of Article XX was so broad that it would allow any nation to place environmental labels on discriminatory trade measures.

In June 1994 the second GATT dispute panel found the intermediate embargo to be GATT inconsistent, but its reasoning narrowed the definition of a nontariff trade barrier considerably. Unlike the first tuna/dolphin panel, the second panel concluded that dolphins *are* an exhaustible resource; moreover, it acknowledged that there are circumstances under which a nation can use trade restrictions to influence environmental practices outside its jurisdiction—specifically to protect a global resource pursuant to an international agreement. But the panel nevertheless found the embargo was neither "related" to nor "necessary" for the conservation of exhaustible natural resources because it was not aimed directly at countries with harmful fishing practices. And the panel emphasized its continuing opposition to imposing such rules unilaterally.[38]

Tuna/Dolphin Round Three: A Challenge to the Dolphin-Safe Label. Although the second tuna/dolphin decision (which was never formally adopted) was relevant in terms of GATT jurisprudence, it made little difference for tuna fishing and dolphins because developments in U.S. domestic politics were already changing the international dynamic. Specifically, Greenpeace and four other moderate environmental groups—the Environmental Defense Fund, the World Wildlife Fund, the National Wildlife Federation, and the Center for Marine Conservation—had broken ranks with EII and its allies and initiated a dialogue among members of the IATTC. Members of the dissident coalition had been persuaded to change their position by commission scientists' data showing that alternative fishing techniques used in the ETP—setting on schools of small tuna or on floating logs—although safer for dolphins, caught

Table 12-1
Estimates of Bycatch in 10,000 New Sets in
Three Modes of Fishing Used in the Eastern Tropical Pacific

Species	Type of Set		
	School	Log	Dolphin
Dolphins	8	25	5,000
Small tunas	2,430,000	130,080,0	70,000
Mahi mahi	2,100	513,870	100
Sharks	12,220	139,580	—
Wahoo	530	118,660	—
Rainbow runner	270	30,050	—
Billfish	1,440	6,540	520
Sea turtles	580	1,020	100

Source: Richard W. Parker, "The Use and Abuse of Trade Leverage to Protect the Global Commons: What We Can Learn from the Tuna-Dolphin Conflict," Georgetown *International Environmental Law Review* 12 (Fall 1999), 1–122.

large numbers of juvenile tuna and killed a host of other marine species (see Table 12-1). According to Traci Romine of Greenpeace, members of the organization did some soul-searching when they learned of the bycatch problem and concluded that as environmentalists their concerns were broader than just marine mammals.[39] In addition, they acknowledged that even though U.S. laws had prompted major changes in developing countries' fishing practices, they still worried that the combined economic impacts of the embargoes and the labeling law were too severe. As a worldwide operation with chapters in many developing countries, Greenpeace was sensitive to the need to provide viable economic alternatives for communities in those places and to maintain strong relationships.[40]

As a result of the negotiations instigated by the dissenting environmental groups, in June 1992 the tuna commission member governments—including the United States, Mexico, Vanuatu, and Venezuela—signed the nonbinding Agreement for the Reduction of Dolphin Mortality in the Eastern Pacific Ocean, known as the La Jolla Agreement. This pact aimed to reduce dolphin mortality in the ETP to less than 5,000 by 1999. Although many regarded the La Jolla Agreement as promising, four months later Congress—heavily influenced by EII's persuasion campaign—passed the International Dolphin Conservation Act, which authorized the secretary of state to negotiate an international agreement to establish a global moratorium on dolphin setting and provided for an embargo of up to 40 percent of a nation's fish exports to enforce compliance.[41] If the United States failed to negotiate such an agreement, the law capped U.S. dolphin mortality at 1,000 for 1992 and required it to approach zero by 1999. Moreover, the law banned the sale of non–dolphin-safe tuna after June 1994, regardless of whether any country signed on to the moratorium.

Although the dolphin conservation law undermined the La Jolla Agreement, the tuna commission worked to keep the pact together, and, as a result, dolphin mortality in the ETP declined steeply.[42] Despite their best efforts, however, Mexico and Venezuela continued to find themselves excluded from the U.S. market: they were subject to the U.S. embargoes because they had not attained the same mortality rate as the tiny U.S. fleet, and their tuna was not eligible for the dolphin-safe label because they continued to use dolphin sets. Still convinced that, in the long run, negotiations would produce better results than coercive measures, the five environmental groups that had orchestrated the La Jolla Agreement initiated another round of multilateral negotiations. Those discussions, which included Ecuador, Mexico, and Venezuela—the largest purse seine fleets operating in the ETP—yielded the Declaration of Panama. Signed by the United States and eleven other nations, the declaration was a binding treaty that called on the State Department to seek changes in U.S. laws that would lift the tuna embargoes for all participating countries and to redefine "dolphin safe" to include tuna caught in dolphin sets that resulted in zero mortality. In return, the fishing nations committed to (1) instituting an international mortality limit of 5,000 dolphins immediately; (2) meeting even more restrictive per-stock limits than those contained in the La Jolla Agreement based on the U.S. zero mortality rate goal; (3) strengthening the IATTC's role in monitoring dolphin mortality and conducting research on and managing populations of tuna, dolphins, and other marine life; (4) taking steps to reduce or eliminate all bycatch taken in the fishery; and (5) maintaining oversight of the program by environmental, industry, and national scientific advisory groups.[43]

By this point the U.S. environmental community was deeply split over the treaty and in particular over its provision to redefine the dolphin-safe label. Defenders of the Panama Declaration pointed out that with dolphin mortality so reduced, NMFS and IATTC scientists, as well as an expert panel convened by the National Academy of Sciences, all agreed that current mortality was sustainable; with the exception of the two depleted dolphin populations, Atlantic spotted dolphins and eastern spinner dolphins, all stocks were below the zero mortality rate goal the MMPA required U.S. fisheries to achieve. In defense of relaxing the standard, they noted the label implied that no dolphins were killed during the fishing process, yet because there were virtually no observers on boats outside the ETP there was no way of knowing about dolphins killed on so-called "dolphin-safe" trips. (Only 13 percent of the so-called dolphin-safe tuna that entered the United States came from the ETP, and the rest came from unobserved trips around the world.) This group also pointed out that a failure to relax the dolphin-safe label would prompt participants in the fishery to switch to methods, such as log- and school-sets, that resulted in high catches of juvenile tuna and large bycatch of other marine species.[44]

But the more adamant environmentalists and animal rights groups led by EII defended the existing dolphin-safe labeling criteria and were determined to eliminate dolphin setting altogether. They pointed out that scientists remained perplexed as to why two of the depleted dolphin populations had remained low since the mid-1980s, even though mortality had declined substantially. Scientists had offered several plausible explanations for the lack of an observable recovery. One was that dolphin populations may grow slowly, and because mortality had been below 5,000 only since 1993, insufficient time may have passed to detect a recovery. But an alternative explanation, the one environmentalists were inclined to believe, was that dolphins suffer stress during the seining process, and the stress hinders their recovery. Many scientists suspected that repeated chase and capture of dolphins imposed short-term and long-term stress that was reducing the fertility and life spans of adults, and that young dolphins separated from their mothers also fared poorly. Sam LaBudde captured the sentiment of many hard-line environmentalists when he said, "Our basic premise is that it's an unacceptable method of fishing. It should never have been invented in the first place, and it's got to end." [45]

In August 1997, after an intense debate between these two factions, Congress formalized most features of the Panama Declaration in the International Dolphin Conservation Program Act. According to the new legislation, once an international agreement was in place, the United States would lift its embargoes, the total and per-stock mortality limits would become legally binding, and the emphasis of management and research would be broadened to include bycatch other than dolphins. [46] Congress did *not* endorse redefining the dolphin safe label, however. Instead, it required NMFS to carry out preliminary studies on the status of dolphin populations and the effect of stress on their recovery. More particularly, the law required the commerce secretary and NMFS to work with the Marine Mammal Commission and the IATTC to undertake population abundance studies and three specific stress studies to determine whether encirclement by purse seine nets was harming any dolphin stocks in the ETP. Based on this information, the law required the commerce secretary to make an initial finding by 1999 as to whether encirclement had a "significant adverse impact" on depleted dolphin populations. If not, then the dolphin-safe label could be redefined provisionally to include dolphin sets in which dolphins were not killed. If by 2002 further studies continued to show no effect, the redefinition would become permanent. [47]

Throughout the following year, participating nations negotiated the Agreement on the International Dolphin Conservation Program, a binding multilateral treaty among the major fishing nations that went into force in 1999. By this time, dolphin mortality had fallen to fewer than 3,000 per year, so the pressure on the Clinton administration from Mexico to lift the embargoes was intense. [48] On April 29, 1999, Commerce Secretary Richard Daley announced the department was provisionally broadening the definition of dolphin-safe tuna to include fish caught by encirclement. Environmental groups opposed to the redefinition immediately filed suit, however, and the following April the district court for Northern California set the secretary's finding aside under the Administrative Procedures Act on the grounds that it was an abuse of discretion and not in accord with the law (*Brower v. Daley*, 2000). Judge Henderson pointed out that Secretary Daley had failed to undertake the congressionally mandated stress studies. He added that the evidence that *was* available, although preliminary, pointed to the conclusion that encirclement *did* have significant adverse impacts on dolphins. Henderson also chastised Daley for giving undue weight to trade considerations in making his initial finding. The Ninth Circuit Court of Appeals subsequently affirmed the lower court's ruling, saying if it condoned the approach Daley had taken,

> the Secretary could deliberately drag his feet in commencing studies or while conducting studies and then conclude there was insufficient evidence to warrant finding a significant adverse impact on the ETP dolphin stocks. Similarly, the Secretary could limit the studies' breadth and then discover that there was insufficient evidence to warrant finding a significant adverse impact on the ETP dolphin stocks.[49]

Although EII prevailed in the labeling dispute, it fared less well in its efforts to keep the United States from dropping the tuna embargoes. At the end of 2001 the Court of International Trade dismissed a lawsuit brought by environmentalists and animal rights groups challenging the implementation of the international dolphin conservation program in the ETP. Judge Judith Barzilay agreed with NMFS that the dolphin conservation program was achieving the goal of conserving dolphin populations affected by the tuna purse seine fishery, thereby opening the way for Mexico to export tuna to the United States.[50] Even after the United States officially lifted its embargo, however, entrance to the U.S. market remained blocked to all tuna caught with dolphin sets because of the labeling issue. Exasperated, the Mexican government threatened to appeal the labeling requirement to the World Trade Organization (WTO), the successor to GATT.[51]

Meanwhile, after being rebuffed by the courts, NMFS expanded its dolphin research program significantly, and in September 2002 it synthesized the results in a peer-reviewed report. In addition, in November NMFS convened two expert panels to review the available evidence: one panel considered the effects of stress and other indirect effects on dolphin populations, and the other examined the effects of ecosystem changes on dolphin populations. And Donald Evans, President George W. Bush's commerce secretary, solicited public input on the final science report, as well as comments from the Marine Mammal Commission and the IATTC.

On December 31, 2002, NMFS director William Hogarth announced a final finding that "the tuna purse seine industry practice of encircling dolphins to catch tuna has no significant adverse impact on dolphin populations in the Eastern Tropical Pacific." [52] Based on this finding, Hogarth explained, the secretary was redefining the term *dolphin-safe*, as allowed under the 1997 dolphin conservation act. In justifying his determination, Hogarth acknowledged the hard work by U.S. and international fishers to create a sustainable tuna fishery and the importance of international cooperation and support to its continuance. He also cited the absence of conclusive scientific evidence of harm. According to journalist Christopher Marquis, however, some former NMFS scientists who were involved in preparing the science report said their superiors had shut down their investigations into dolphin stress over the past decade. Moreover, four of the five independent experts hired to review the study expressed concern about Secretary Evans's ruling and said the data did not support it. They felt the implications of the study were clear.[53] The department immediately faced a barrage of criticism, and Evans agreed to delay imposing the rule relaxing the dolphin-safe standard in exchange for an agreement by environmentalists not to seek an injunction.

Evans ultimately stood by his finding, however, and environmentalists proceeded to challenge it in court, again alleging violations of the Administrative Procedures Act. On April 10, 2003, Judge Henderson enjoined the secretary from changing the standard because the plaintiffs had shown a likelihood of success on the merits. As in the previous case, the judge found that the best available evidence, although not conclusive, was "suggestive of a significant adverse impact," and he expressed concern that once again the secretary's decision reflected concerns about trade policy rather than the scientific evidence. The judge noted that Congress, after weighing the arguments about international cooperation, had nevertheless set an explicitly science-based standard for changing the dolphin-safe label.

After more than a year of delay, the Commerce Department finally provided the full administrative record for the case, thereby allowing the judicial proceeding to move forward. The court found the record provided

> compelling corroboration of this Court's preliminary observations in its ruling on Plaintiff's Motion for Preliminary Injunction. It reflects an agency that (1) continued to drag its feet on conducting critical mandated research, (2) continued to ignore the fact that the best scientific evidence that *was* available, while not conclusive, pointed to the fishery as the cause of the dolphins' failure to recover as expected, and (3) compromised the integrity of its finding by allowing trade policy considerations to infect the decision-making process.[54]

Once again, Judge Henderson declared the commerce secretary's finding to be arbitrary, capricious, and an abuse of discretion, and he ordered that the original dolphin-safe label stand. The commerce secretary appealed the lower court's decision to the Ninth Circuit, where it remained in summer 2005.

The Shrimp/Turtle Case

As the battle over the tuna embargo and the dolphin-safe label played out, a second controversy erupted—this one over U.S. efforts to restrict imports of sea turtles caught in shrimpers' nets. The dispute eventually reached GATT's successor, the World Trade Organization. The WTO dispute panel, although it ruled against the United States, went even further than the second tuna/dolphin panel in narrowing the definition of a nontariff barrier to trade by expanding the exceptions. Its decision reflected the organization's sensitivity to the increasing salience in developed nations of concerns that trade rules jeopardized environmental protection. The decision did not ameliorate environmentalists' antipathy toward the WTO, however; nor did it resolve domestic tensions over the use of trade leverage to achieve environmental goals.

Introducing the World Trade Organization. The context for the shrimp/turtle case differed substantially from that of tuna/dolphin. The Uruguay Round that began in 1986 had culminated in the January 1, 1995, formation of the WTO, which subsumed GATT and included a new mechanism for settling disputes.[55] The Dispute Settlement Understanding established a compulsory and binding dispute settlement mechanism consisting of a first level of panel reports subject to appeals to the newly created Appellate Body. The panels and the Appellate Body make recommendations to WTO members sitting as the Dispute Settlement Body, which formally adopts their reports. A consensus is required to reject a recommendation—a sharp break with the old GATT system, in which any member, including the losing party, could veto a dispute panel's recommendations.

The preamble to the agreement establishing the WTO mentions sustainable development, but overall reflects the cornucopian values that underpin the organization:

> [R]elations in the field of trade and economic endeavor should be conducted with a view to raising the standards of living, ensuring full employment and a large and steadily growing volume of real income and effective demand, and expanding the production of trade in goods and services, while allowing for the optimal use of the world's resources in accordance with the objective of sustainable development, seeking both to protect and preserve the environment and to enhance the means for doing so in a manner consistent with their respective needs and concerns at different levels of economic development.[56]

In order to both assuage environmental constituencies in developed countries and appease commercial interests in developed and developing nations that were concerned about the threat environmental measures posed to free trade, the WTO created the Committee on Trade and Environment. The committee's charge was to identify the relationship between trade measures used for environmental purposes and the multilateral trading system and make recommendations for modifications in the provisions of the latter.[57]

The committee has accomplished little, however, because no consensus exists either among or within states as to the appropriate relationship between trade and the environment. As a result, the WTO's approach to resolving trade/environment conflicts has been developed largely through jurisprudence. The

WTO's first environmental dispute arose in 1995, when Venezuela and Brazil challenged the United States' reformulated fuel regulations under the 1990 Clean Air Act Amendments. The Appellate Body in that case confirmed that clean air is an "exhaustible natural resource" and noted that the WTO agreement "is not to be read in clinical isolation from public international law." But the decision in the reformulated gas case, which found the U.S. rule discriminatory and therefore GATT-inconsistent, provoked only mild criticism. By contrast, the shrimp/turtle case, which came before a dispute settlement panel in 1998, rekindled all the passion the tuna/dolphin case had ignited earlier in the decade.

Origins of the Shrimp Import Ban. Like the tuna/dolphin dispute, the shrimp/turtle controversy originated as a domestic issue, and the imposition of stringent domestic regulations prompted a coalition between fishers and environmentalists in favor of import restrictions. U.S. efforts to protect sea turtles began with a recognition that these marine reptiles, which have survived since the age of the dinosaurs, had become endangered in the space of several decades in the late twentieth century. "At one time the world's oceans were brimming with turtles," reports journalist Leslie Burdick. "Centuries ago, ships' logs said the Caribbean was so full of them one could be guided toward an island by the clacking of their shells knocking together." [58] According to turtle expert Jim Richardson, earlier in the twentieth century "you couldn't row a boat in front of nesting beaches. Turtles would kick the oars out of the oarlocks." [59] In the second half of the twentieth century, however, sea turtle numbers declined precipitously. On Mexico's Rancho Nuevo Beach, 40,000 Kemp's ridleys nested in a single day in the 1940s, whereas only 400 to 500 nested there by the 1980s; in places where people hunted them for food, wild turtles had disappeared altogether. In the 1970s the United States listed five of the world's remaining seven sea turtle species as endangered or threatened under the Endangered Species Act (ESA). One of those, the Kemp's ridley, was among the world's twelve most endangered species.

Also in the 1970s scientists identified shrimping as a major cause of sea turtle mortality: sea turtles swim in temperate and tropical waters and forage in the same habitats as some commercially valuable shrimp species. Shrimp trawls, which are towed across the ocean bottom, catch turtles, which may drown because they need to surface once an hour to breathe. Environmentalists claimed that 150,000 sea turtles were dying worldwide in shrimp nets each year.[60] Looking for ways to solve this problem in response to the ESA listings, in the 1970s NMFS began developing a prototype turtle excluder device (TED). TEDs are simple, relatively inexpensive, easy-to-operate modifications to shrimp trawls: they consist of grates installed in the back of a trawl that allow shrimp through but force turtles along a barrier to an opening in the top or bottom of the net. TEDs cost between $50 and $400 and, used properly, can exclude up to 97 percent of turtles caught in trawls while losing only about 6 percent of the shrimp catch.[61]

In the early 1980s NMFS initiated a voluntary program of TED use, but shrimpers refused to adopt the device, so in 1987, after several years of lobbying by environmentalists and scientists, the agency issued regulations under the ESA requiring shrimpers in the southeastern United States to use TEDs on their vessels during part of the year. The regulations immediately provoked a firestorm from shrimpers: commercial fishing groups challenged the regulations in court and appealed to their congressional representatives for help.[62] After two years of delay, however, the courts upheld the regulations, and in July 1989 they took effect. Shrimpers promptly staged massive protests, blockading Texas ports and threatening violence if the rules were not changed or reversed. The Commerce Department temporarily suspended the regulations in response to fishers' complaints that the devices were inconvenient, dangerous, and expensive to operate. Environmentalists immediately challenged the moratorium in court, and U.S. district court judge Thomas Hogan, pointing out that the Commerce Department appeared to have given in to "mob rule," ordered the commerce secretary to draft temporary measures that would effectively protect turtles.[63] The agency then responded by issuing an interim requirement that allowed shrimpers to simply pull their nets up every 105 minutes and release the dazed turtles.

That requirement was unlikely to pass legal muster, however, because an internal memo by NMFS scientists had already concluded that "the only reasonable and prudent alternative which will allow shrimping to continue without jeopardizing the continued existence of identified [listed] turtle species is full implementation of the [turtle excluder device] regulations." [64] So in September 1990 NMFS finally issued rules requiring the use of TEDs on large offshore shrimp trawlers during part of the year and in specific areas of the Southeast, and in October those regulations went into effect. Fishers continued to protest that the regulations would disable them economically and to complain that condominiums, beach traffic, and poaching posed more severe threats to turtles than shrimp fishing. But a May 1990 National Academy of Sciences report undercut their claims: it found that shrimp trawlers were by far the leading cause of turtle deaths at human hands, blaming them for at least 11,000 turtle deaths per year—and probably as many as 44,000. In support of its conclusions, the panel noted that the number of dead turtles washed ashore on nearby beaches increased when shrimp fisheries opened and decreased when they closed. In addition, loggerhead populations had increased where there was minimal shrimp trawling and decreased where it was frequent.[65] The report noted that shrimp trawling kills ten times as many sea turtles as all other human activities combined; it endorsed the TED requirement and provided the strongest evidence to date in favor of the regulations.[66] (In December 1992 NMFS expanded the TED requirements to year-round use in all inshore and offshore waters in the Gulf and Atlantic. The new regulations also instituted tough enforcement measures, which NMFS periodically had to employ to keep shrimpers from defecting.)

Recognizing that the TED requirements were here to stay, shrimpers went to their congressional representatives to ask them to provide a "level playing field" with foreign shrimpers who furnished more than 80 percent of the U.S. shrimp supply. The Concerned Shrimpers of America and the Louisiana Shrimp Association testified before Congress that low-cost imports had depressed shrimp prices in the United States and that import controls were necessary to stimulate a recovery of the domestic industry.[67] In response, Congress enacted Section 609 of P.L. 101-162, the annual funding authorization for the Departments of Justice, State, and Commerce, which was codified in a note to the ESA. The Turtle-Shrimp Law, as Section 609 became known, required the State Department, in consultation with the commerce secretary, to (1) initiate or modify bilateral or multilateral sea turtle protection agreements and (2) establish a ban on wild shrimp imports unless exporting nations could certify they were caught using sea turtle protection practices comparable to those used in the United States or that its fishing environment did not pose a threat to sea turtles.

Implementing the Ban and the WTO Challenge. As in the tuna/dolphin case, the executive branch interpreted its legislative mandate conservatively. NMFS began by identifying those countries whose commercial fishing operations might harm sea turtle species that were found in U.S. waters. To do this, the agency convened a panel of experts who determined that about seventy countries had shrimp trawling operations where sea turtles were present and had exported to the United States in the preceding two years. The State Department decided to apply the law only to fourteen countries in Central and South America, however, reasoning that the turtles that actually swim in U.S. waters migrate through the Gulf of Mexico, the Caribbean Sea, and into the South Atlantic Ocean. The State Department also assumed that, to comply with the law's requirement that exporting countries achieve an average rate of incidental take comparable to that of the United States, they would have to adopt TEDs. It issued a set of guidelines for making the transition to TEDs and allowed for a three-year phase-in period. Between 1991 and 1994, with the help of training from NMFS, nine of the fourteen countries made progress in adopting TED laws and phasing in their use; these nine were certified. Two others, Guatemala and Costa Rica, were able to get certified because their shrimp fisheries operated in the deep, cold waters of the Pacific, and three countries—Trinidad and Tobago, French Guiana, and Surinam—did not participate because they did not export shrimp to the United States.

Meanwhile, in 1992 the Sea Turtle Restoration Project, a coalition of environmental and animal welfare organizations led by EII, had filed suit in federal court to challenge the State Department's guidelines limiting the application of the Turtle-Shrimp Law only to countries in the Caribbean/Western Atlantic region. The jurisdiction of the case was eventually moved to the Court of International Trade, which in 1995 ruled in favor of the plaintiffs. The judge chastised the implementing agencies and compelled the United States to require that *all* wild shrimp imported into the United States be caught using TEDs or a comparable method, notwithstanding questions related to conflicts between the Turtle-Shrimp Law and GATT.[68] This ruling automatically increased the number of countries affected from fourteen to the seventy originally identified by NMFS. In doing so it also promised to raise the price of shrimp, which domestic shrimpers appreciated.

In May 1996 the State Department reluctantly began enforcing the Turtle-Shrimp Law, but, rather than embargoing shrimp from nonconforming countries, it allowed shrimp to be imported on a shipment-by-shipment basis. (That is, it allowed shipments from nonconforming countries if the shrimp in that shipment were caught using nets equipped with TEDs.) In October, however, the Sea Turtle Restoration Project won a court ruling in the international trade court disallowing that practice, so the rule reverted to requiring that all shrimp from a country that exported to the United States had to be harvested using TEDs. A month later the United States held consultations with India, Malaysia, Pakistan, and Thailand, but failed to reach a resolution, and in January 1997 the four countries challenged the law before the WTO. The plaintiffs charged that the Turtle-Shrimp Law violated three GATT articles: XI, which prohibits one member nation from imposing quantitative restrictions on imports and exports from other member nations; XIII, which establishes the like treatment rule; and I, which contains the most favored nation provision.

In hopes of influencing the political context for the decision, the Sea Turtle Restoration Project placed ads in the *New York Times*, the *Washington Post*, and the *International Herald Tribune* alerting the public to the threat the WTO posed to the ESA, democracy, and national sovereignty. The group also tried to raise questions about conflicts of interest among members of the dispute panel, as the panelists came from countries that had previously been embargoed by the United States under the Turtle-Shrimp Law or had signed on as interested parties in the dispute. Environmentalists believed they had a stronger case for their narrow definition of what constitutes a nontariff barrier to trade in the shrimp/turtle dispute than they had in the tuna/dolphin case: an amicus brief submitted to the dispute panel by the World Wildlife Fund pointed out that the UN had classified all five turtle species involved as threatened with extinction; the U.S. import ban complied with international law requiring states to protect endangered species; and TEDs were cheap and effective. Furthermore India, Malaysia, and Pakistan had all rebuffed U.S. efforts to secure a multilateral deal on TEDs.

Environmentalists' optimism notwithstanding, in April 1998 the WTO dispute panel concluded that the Turtle-Shrimp Law was inconsistent with GATT Article XI and could not be justified under Article XX. To reach its conclusions, the panel began by examining the U.S. law under the chapeau of Article XX and found that the import restrictions constituted "arbitrary and unjustifiable" discrimination among countries. Having decided the measure violated the chapeau, the panel did not even consider whether it qualified as an exception under XX(b) or (g). The panel also affirmed that environmental protection policies should be tailored to fit the particular development and environmental conditions in each country and that multilateral negotiations were the preferred means of achieving environmental goals.[69] (Because of its finding that the Turtle-Shrimp Law violated Article XI, the panel did not address the complainants' argument about Articles I and XIII.)

The United States appealed the panel's ruling, and in October the Appellate Body (AB) reversed much of the lower panel's decision. In particular, the AB took issue with the dispute panel's analysis. Instead of beginning with the chapeau, as the dispute panel had, the AB started by determining whether the Turtle-Shrimp Law qualified as an Article XX exception and *then* considered whether it was discriminatory. In legal terms, the AB found the import ban imposed by the United States *was* provisionally justified under Article XX(g) for two reasons. First, living creatures can be "exhaustible resources"; this phrase, although originally intended to apply to minerals, must be interpreted in light of contemporary concerns. And, second, the U.S. measure was "related to the conservation of exhaustible natural resources" because the means connected specifically to the purpose and the scientific evidence strongly affirmed the evidence between shrimp trawling and sea turtle mortality.[70] On the other hand, the AB found that the import ban failed to meet the requirements of Article XX's chapeau, which requires exceptions to be nondiscriminatory. In particular, trade officials objected to the State Department's failure to take local circumstances into account by demanding that countries adopt the same policies and practices as the United States; they also objected to the State Department's failure to hold multilateral negotiations before imposing the ban; and they found fault with the U.S. decision to give the fourteen Caribbean and Western Atlantic nations three years to phase in TEDs and others only four months.

Essentially, the AB ruled that a unilateral trade restriction to promote environmental objectives was permissible under GATT rules as long as it was implemented in ways that were not arbitrary or discriminatory. In addition, the AB made a set of nonbinding commitments that aimed to defuse environmentalists' ire:

> We have not decided that the protection and preservation of the environment is of no significance to the Members of the WTO. Clearly, it is. We have not decided that the sovereign nations that are Members of the WTO cannot adopt effective measures to protect endangered species, such as sea turtles. Clearly, they can and should.[71]

Despite these concessions, environmentalists were not mollified. Charles Aden Clarke of the World Wildlife Fund said the ruling "denies individual countries the right to restrict trade even when species . . . are endangered and the complainant countries have signed international environmental agreements to protect them." [72] David Schorr, director of the fund's sustainable commerce program, said the WTO "is simply not competent to decide issues that require a mature balance between liberalized trade and other legitimate policy goals." He also said the AB ruling revealed "the profound bias of the WTO against environmental policies and in favor of 'free trade' at any cost." [73]

Many prominent environmentalists urged the Clinton administration to reject the panel's ruling, which the Dispute Settlement Body adopted in November 1998, and work to modify WTO rules. To their dismay, however, the State Department accepted the ruling and adjusted its regulations to allow shrimp imports from countries without sea turtle protection programs on a shipment-by-shipment basis. (By this point, such an approach was legally acceptable because in June 1998, two months after the original WTO panel ruling, the U.S. Court of Appeals for the Federal Circuit had overturned the international trade court's ruling against the shipment-by-shipment guidelines on the grounds that Judge Acquilino had no jurisdiction to issue it because EII had withdrawn its motion.[74]) The State Department also began negotiating a sea turtle conservation agreement with the governments of Southeast Asia and the Indian Ocean region and stepped up its technical training program in those countries. Nevertheless, in October 2000 Malaysia again appealed to the WTO, saying the United States had not dropped its ban and therefore continued to be in violation of GATT. To the surprise of many observers, however, on June 15, 2001, the WTO panel ruled against Malaysia, finding that the U.S. implementation of its sea turtle protection law was fully consistent with WTO rules and complied with the earlier recommendations of the AB. Two weeks later, eight countries—including Malaysia and the United States—signed an agreement to voluntarily protect sea turtles in the Indian Ocean. And on October 22 the AB affirmed the compliance panel's decision.

OUTCOMES

Since the early 1990s environmentalists clearly have had a powerful impact on the international definition of nontariff trade barriers. Although they continue to express a preference for multilateral agreements and to insist on tailoring policies to the conditions of individual countries, trade officials' tolerance for unilateral, trade-restrictive measures to protect the earth's living resources has increased. Furthermore, the particular measures at issue— the U.S. bans on tuna and shrimp imports—have prompted environmental improvements: in the 1990s dolphin mortality in the ETP dropped precipitously and remains low; and turtle bycatch in shrimp fisheries is declining in most parts of the world. Nevertheless, overall bycatch in fisheries worldwide remains an enormous environmental problem, and the debate over how best to reduce it rages on.

The WTO and the Environment

According to legal scholar Louise DeLaFayette, the 2001 AB report in the shrimp/turtle case confirmed a "revolution in WTO jurisprudence heralded in 1998 by the original Appellate Body Report." [75] DeLaFayette argues that the

AB applied an "evolutionary approach" to Article XX by interpreting the phrase "exhaustible natural resources" consistent with its contemporary meaning in international law, to include living natural resources in danger of extinction. She adds that the shrimp/turtle case appears to have established the following principles:

- The interpretation of Article XX and the GATT in general must be guided by the objects and purposes set out in the preamble, including those of environmental protection, conservation of natural resources, and sustainable development.
- Article XX of the GATT *can* be used to justify trade-restrictive measures taken in order to protect the environment, provided the measures are applied in a nondiscriminatory manner and are not used only to protect national industries.
- There is no limit in Article XX(g) on the location of the natural resources to be protected. Therefore such resources may include those beyond the national jurisdiction of the state imposing the restriction, as long as there is a "sufficient nexus" with such resources within that state's jurisdiction.
- There is no exclusion of trade-restrictive measures based on process and production methods, which are not even mentioned in Article XX.
- The chapeau of Article XX requires only two conditions be met to justify trade-restrictive measures: (1) application of the measure must not involve arbitrary or unjustified discrimination, and (2) the measure must not be used as a cover for the protection of national industries.
- Discrimination can arise not only by applying different measures to countries where the same conditions prevail, but also by imposing exactly the same policy or measure on countries where different conditions prevail.
- The discrimination resulting from such rigidity is heightened by unilateral imposition of restrictions on imports and should be avoided, if possible, by negotiating multilateral agreements with all exporting countries. (It is not necessary to have concluded such an agreement, however, but only to have entered into and continued good faith efforts to reach international consensus.)[76]

The shrimp/turtle ruling, and the principles enunciated above, outraged free trade advocates. For example, Alan Oxley, a former ambassador from Australia to GATT and a panelist on the second tuna/dolphin panel, contends that "the endorsement of unilateral trade sanctions is fundamentally contrary to the philosophical basis of the GATT." [77] Like most free traders, he invokes a historical rationale: after World Wars I and II trade sanctions came to be regarded as the precursors to formal declarations of war. Oxley is also dismissive of the WTO's ability to make judgments about the importance and effectiveness of environmental measures; the organization's expertise, he points out, is in facilitating international trade. And he worries that allowing import restrictions based on attitudes within importing countries undermines the principle of comparative advantage. Other critics accuse the Appellate Body of trying to legislate changes in GATT and circumvent the WTO policymaking process.

Dolphins, Sea Turtles, and Other Bycatch

In addition to gaining some legitimacy within the WTO, import restrictions have prompted substantial environmental improvements. Dolphin mortality in the ETP plummeted in the early 1990s, and since the late 1990s has remained below 2,000, although the failure by the Atlantic spotted and eastern spinner dolphins to recover continues to perturb scientists. The situation for sea turtles is a bit more complicated, however.

Between 1990, when the TED rules went into effect, and 2002, the annual mortality of Kemp's ridley turtles was cut in half. As a result, federal biologists reported finding more than double the number of Kemp's ridley sea turtle nests on Texas beaches in 2000 than in 1999. Kemp's ridley nesting levels overall increased from between 700 and 800 annually in the mid-1980s to more than 6,000 in 2000.[78] In February 2003 the NMFS published new rules requiring larger openings for TEDs to allow larger turtles to escape. (The agency had known since 1999 that nearly 90 percent of the dead turtles on South Carolina beaches were too large to escape through the existing devices.) With the new rules, officials expected annual deaths of leatherbacks and loggerheads to decline dramatically.[79]

On the other hand, in August 2003 the Florida Fish and Wildlife Conservation Commission reported that the number of sea turtle eggs being stolen from Florida beaches had risen dramatically—probably to meet rising demand from Latin American and Caribbean culture and cuisine in southeast Florida—and Florida loggerheads, which had been gaining in population, appeared to be declining.[80] Furthermore, in early 2004 NMFS reported that sea turtle populations were crashing in Mexico, where nesting along the Pacific Coast had declined at an annual rate of 22 percent during the previous twelve years, and in Malaysia, where the sea turtle population was 1 percent of what it had been in the 1950s. The main culprit in the collapse is harvesting of eggs and adult turtles.[81] And skirmishes continued over efforts to regulate turtle bycatch in the longline swordfish fishery off Hawaii and the scallop fishery off the coast of New England.

Furthermore, although regulators have made progress in particular fisheries, marine mammal bycatch worldwide continues to be a serious problem. In the summer of 2003 the International Whaling Commission published a report claiming that as many as 300,000 porpoises, dolphins, and whales die each year in fishing gear entanglement—making that the leading cause of death among the cetacean group of mammals.[82] In June 2005 the World Wildlife Fund released a scientific report that contained a similar figure.[83] Experts note that bycatch threatens the productivity of the world's marine ecosystems. But they acknowledge that addressing the issue is complicated by the fact that, although scientists have developed a variety of relatively simple practices to reduce bycatch, many developing countries lack the political will to require such practices and choose instead to maximize their target catches at lowest cost. Fishers in developed countries in turn resist stricter regulations because they worry about being unable to compete with cheap foreign imports. And when developed countries do impose strict regulations, fleets often simply move elsewhere or reflag their vessels, just as the Americans did in the ETP. Enforcement of regulations is further complicated by the fact that most fishers simply dump their bycatch at sea and do not keep precise records.

CONCLUSIONS

For many environmentalists the positive impacts of import bans and eco-labeling for dolphin and sea turtle populations suggest that allowing developed countries to impose unilateral trade restrictions may be a critical element of protecting global resources. But the use of trade leverage to achieve environmental goals remains controversial. Many critics, including most WTO members, accuse the United States of green protectionism and eco-imperialism and believe that, in any case negotiated, multilateral solutions are more effective than coercive unilateral approaches.[84] On the other hand, trade leverage has indisputably prompted major change—not just in the policies of developing countries but in their discourse, perceptions, and practices.[85] So perhaps, as Richard Parker observes, the more serious questions are what form trade leverage should take and when to use it.

Many commentators also chastise environmentalists for their unrelenting criticism of the WTO and their failure to recognize the evolution in its jurisprudence toward a narrower definition of nontariff trade barriers and a broader view of the exceptions. For example, political scientists Elizbeth DeSombre and J. Samuel Barkin write, "The WTO's rules on environmental exceptions, clearly articulated throughout the past decade, should be seen not as favoring trade over the environment, but as a check on bad or incompetent legislation."[86] But political theorist Robyn Eckersley responds that the international trade regime is far more powerful and cohesive than any multilateral environmental accord and that concerns about running afoul of the WTO cast "a long shadow" over the negotiation and implementation of such accords.[87] Concerns about the dominance of trade over the environment have provoked some observers to propose creating a global environmental organization. Others have suggested more modest reforms: amendments to GATT to create specific exceptions for multilateral environmental accords or an expansion of the WTO or the UN to police the environment.

But such developments are unlikely without a stronger global consensus on environmentalism, and developed countries have done little to convince developing countries that environmental protection need not be detrimental to their economic aspirations.[88] One reason is that internal differences within the developed nations—and particularly within the United States, where antienvironmental and proliberalization forces exert a great deal of influence—prevent them from providing strong, unified leadership on behalf of the environment. In the absence of such leadership, voluntary schemes like eco-labeling are likely to continue to proliferate.

QUESTIONS TO CONSIDER

- To what extent should developing countries be allowed to have less stringent environmental regulations than developed countries, in the interest of fairness?
- To what extent should countries concern themselves with environmental degradation beyond their borders, and why?
- What do you believe are the best mechanisms to bring about improvements in environmental protection internationally, and why?

Notes

1. Jagdish Bhagwati, "The Case for Free Trade," *Scientific American*, November 1993, 42–49.
2. Kevin P. Gallagher, *Free Trade and the Environment: Mexico, NAFTA, and Beyond* (Stanford: Stanford University Press, 2004). According to the environmental Kuznets curve hypothesis, environmental degradation may increase sharply at early stages of economic development, but beyond a certain level of per capita income it begins to decline. The hypothesis gets its name from an 1955 article by economist Simon Kuznets in which he depicted the relationship between income inequality and levels of income as an inverted U-shaped curve. In 1993 G. M. Grossman and A. B. Krueger posited a similar relationship between environmental degradation and income levels. See G. M. Grossman and A. B. Krueger, "Environmental Impacts of a North American Free Trade Agreement," in *The Mexico-U.S. Free Trade Agreement*, ed. P. Garber (Cambridge: MIT Press, 1993), 13–56.
3. GDP conceals ecological, social, and other costs while counting as positive expenditures on prisons and cleanup of hazardous waste dumps. See Ted Halstead and Clifford Cobb, "The Need for New Measurements of Progress," in *The Case Against the Global Economy and for a Turn Toward the Local*, ed. Jerry Mander and Edward Goldsmith (San Francisco: Sierra Club Books, 1996), 197–206.
4. Herman Daly, "The Perils of Free Trade," *Scientific American*, November 1993, 54.
5. Gallagher, *Free Trade and the Environment*. According to David Vogel and Robert Kagan, globalization has produced *neither* policy convergence nor a race to the bottom; instead, its impacts appear to differ for developed and developing countries. See David Vogel and Robert A. Kagan, "Dynamics of Regulatory Change: How Globalization Affects National Regulatory Policies," in *Dynamics of Regulatory Change*, ed. David Vogel and Robert A. Kagan (Berkeley: University of California Press, 2004), 1–41.
6. David Vogel, *Trading Up: Consumer and Environmental Regulation in a Global Economy* (Cambridge: Harvard University Press, 1995), 5.
7. Other scholars have since refined the conditions under which a "race to the top" is likely to arise. See Vogel and Kagan, "Dynamics of Regulatory Change."
8. Richard W. Parker, "The Use and Abuse of Trade Leverage to Protect the Global Commons: What We Can Learn From the Tuna-Dolphin Conflict," *Georgetown International Law Review* 12 (Fall 1999): 1–122.

9. Don Mayer and David Hoch, "International Environmental Protection and the GATT: The Tuna/Dolphin Controversy," *American Business Law Journal* 31 (1993): 187–244.

10. According to the "most favored nation" clause in Article I: "an advantage, favour, privilege or immunity granted by any contracting party to any product originating in or designed for any other country shall be accorded immediately and unconditionally to the like product originating in, or destined for, the territories of all other contracting parties." According to the "national treatment" clause in Article III: "products of the territory of any contracting party imported into the territory of any other contracting party shall not be subject, directly or indirectly, to internal taxes or other charges of any kind in excess of those applied, directly or indirectly, to like domestic products."

11. Vogel, *Trading Up*, 14.

12. U.S. Congress, Office of Technology Assessment, *Trade and Environment: Conflicts and Opportunities*, OTA-BP-ITE-94 (Washington, D.C.: U.S. Government Printing Office, May 1992); Vogel, *Trading Up*.

13. National Research Council, *Dolphins and the Tuna Industry* (Washington, D.C.: National Academy Press, 1992).

14. 16 U.S.C. Sec. 1371(a)(2).

15. Vogel, *Trading Up*. Backdown, which was developed around 1960, works as follows: when about two-thirds of the purse seine has been brought aboard the ship and the dolphins are at the far back end of the net from the ship, the captain reverses the power, causing the back of the corkline at the back of the net to be pulled underwater and pass below the dolphins, which are mostly at the surface. Crew in speedboats are stationed at the dolphin release area to make sure they get out and prevent tuna from escaping. The Medina safety panel is an area of finer mesh at the back of the net that prevents dolphin entanglement. See Alessandro Bonanno and Douglas Constance, *Caught in the Net: The Global Tuna Industry, Environmentalism, and the State* (Lawrence: University Press of Kansas, 1996).

16. Mayer and Hoch, "International Environmental Protection and the GATT."

17. Parker, "The Use and Abuse of Trade Leverage." The proportion of U.S.-registered vessels in the ETP had declined from more than 90 percent in the early 1960s to 32 percent in 1988. Between 1981 and 1988 the number of U.S.-registered vessels in the ETP declined from ninety-seven to forty; during the same period Mexico, Venezuela, and Vanuatu combined added eighty-four new boats. By 1988 ships registered in Latin American countries accounted for half of all tuna caught in the region.

18. Ian Anderson, "Millions of Dolphins Butchered in Tuna Nets," *New Scientist*, March 17, 1988, 28.

19. *EII v. Mosbacher*, (1990) 746 F. Supp. 964.

20. Mayer and Hoch, "International Environmental Protection and the GATT."

21. Dale D. Murphy, *The Structure of Regulatory Competition: Corporations and Public Policies in a Global Economy* (New York: Oxford University Press, 2004).

22. Anthony Ramirez, " 'Epic Debate' Led to Heinz Tuna Plan," *New York Times*, April 16, 1990, D1.

23. Murphy, *The Structure of Regulatory Competition*.

24. IATTC staff found that dolphin mortality was associated with sets on large herds of tuna or dolphins, sets in areas where dolphin had not been chased before, sets that finished after dark, sets in strong subsurface currents that cause nets to canopy and collapse, gear malfunctions and misalignments, lack of crewmen in a raft in the backdown channel to help release dolphins, and longer (slower) sets. See Parker, "The Use and Abuse of Trade Leverage."

25. Parker, "The Use and Abuse of Trade Leverage."

26. Vogel, *Trading Up*.

27. Ibid.

28. Quoted in Associated Press, "Judge Orders Tuna Import Ban Over Dolphin Kill," *New York Times*, August 30, 1990, 21.
29. Mayer and Hoch, "International Environmental Protection and the GATT."
30. John P. Manard Jr., "GATT and the Environment: The Friction Between International Trade and the World's Environment—the Dolphin and Tuna Dispute," *Tulane Environmental Law Journal* 5 (May 1992): 373–428.
31. Ibid.
32. Quoted in Mayer and Hoch, "International Environmental Protection and the GATT," 190.
33. Quoted in Vogel, *Trading Up*, 114.
34. Ibid.
35. Peter Passell, "Economic Scene: Whose Rules?" *New York Times*, February 19, 1992, D2; Vogel, *Trading Up*.
36. Bonanno and Constance, *Caught in the Net*.
37. Keith Schneider, "Balancing Nature's Claims and International Free Trade," *New York Times*, January 19, 1992, D5.
38. Marlo Pfister Cadeddu, "Turtles in the Soup? An Analysis of the GATT Challenge to the United States Endangered Species Act Section 609 Shrimp Harvesting Nation Certification Program for the Conservation of Sea Turtles," *Georgetown International Environmental Law Review* 11 (Fall 1998): 179–207.
39. Parker, "The Use and Abuse of Trade Leverage."
40. Ibid.
41. Apparently, prior to negotiating the La Jolla Agreement, Mexican and Venezuelan officials had indicated to State Department negotiators they would support a moratorium on dolphin sets beginning in 1994 in exchange for a lifting of the U.S. embargo in 1992, and this agreement formed the basis for legislation introduced by Rep. Gerry Studds, D-Mass., in the summer of 1992. See Parker, "The Use and Abuse of Trade Leverage."
42. Ibid.
43. Michael Scott, "The Tuna-Dolphin Controversy," *Whalewatcher*, August 1998. Michael Scott is a senior scientist with the Dolphin Programme of the Inter-American Tropical Tuna Commission.
44. Ibid.
45. Quoted in Kenneth Brower, "The Destruction of Dolphins," *Atlantic*, July 1989, 58.
46. Scott, "The Tuna-Dolphin Controversy."
47. U.S.C. 16 Sec. 1385.
48. W. F. Perrin, B. Wursig, and J. G. M. Thewissen, eds., *Encyclopedia of Marine Mammals* (San Diego: Academic Press, 2002), 1269–73.
49. *Brower v. Evans* 2000; 257 F.3d 1058.
50. Katie O'Connell, "Tuna-Dolphin Update," *Whales Alive!* Vol. XI, No. 2, April 2002.
51. "Mexico Will Take Steps Next Week If USA Won't Comply," *Whales Alive!* April 11, 2002. Available at http://csiwhalesalive.org/csi02202.html.
52. "Commerce Department Determines No Significant Adverse Impact of Fishing on Dolphin Populations," Press Release, NOAA 01-168, December 31, 2002.
53. Christopher Marquis, "Rule Weakening Definition of 'Dolphin Safe' Is Delayed," *New York Times*, January 10, 2003, A20.
54. *Earth Island Institute v. Evans*, 2004; No. C 03-0007 TEH.
55. The WTO replaced GATT as an international organization, but GATT still serves as the WTO's umbrella treaty for trade in goods.
56. See www.wto.org/english.
57. Gregory C. Shaffer, "The Nexus of Law and Politics: The WTO's Committee on Trade and Environment," in *The Greening of Trade Law*, ed. Richard H. Steinberg (Lanham, Md.: Rowman & Littlefield, 2002), 81–111.

58. Leslie Burdick, "Sea Turtles Swim for Survival," *Christian Science Monitor*, August 29, 1989, 12.

59. Quoted in ibid.

60. Anne Swardson, "Taking the Turtle Test on World Trade," *Washington Post*, August 19, 1998, C9.

61. Charles A. Oravetz, "Development of Turtle Excluder Devices (TEDs) and their Potential Applicability to ASEAN Nations," Southeast Fisheries Science Center, National Marine Fisheries Service, 2001. Available at www.arbec.com.my/sea-turtles/art32julysept01.htm.

62. Legislators from the Gulf Coast states helped postpone the regulations by delaying the ESA reauthorization and adding amendments mandating a National Academy of Sciences study of the sea turtle problem and the impact of TEDs. See Cadeddu, "Turtles in the Soup?"

63. William Booth, "Amid Threats, U.S. Not Ensuring Turtles' Safety," *Washington Post*, July 19, 1989, A3.

64. Quoted in William Booth, "U.S. to Enforce Rules Protecting Sea Turtles," *Washington Post*, September 6, 1989, A4.

65. National Research Council, *Decline of the Sea Turtles: Causes and Prevention* (Washington, D.C.: National Academy of Sciences, 1990).

66. John Lancaster, "Study Blames Shrimpers for Sea Turtle Deaths," *Washington Post*, May 20, 1990, A10.

67. Gustavo Grunbaum, "Dispute Settlement and U.S. Environmental Laws," in *The Greening of Trade Law*, 51–80.

68. *Earth Island Institute v. Christopher* 1995; 913 F. Supp. 599.

69. Cadeddu, "Turtles in the Soup?"

70. Varamon Ramangkura, "Thai Shrimp, Sea Turtles, Mangrove Forests and the WTO: Innovative Environmental Protection Under the International Trade Regime," *Georgetown International Environmental Law Review* 15 (Summer 2003): 677–708.

71. World Trade Organization, "United States—Import Prohibition of Certain Shrimp and Shrimp Products," *Report of the Appellate Body*, October 12, 1998, 75.

72. Quoted in John Zarocostas, "U.S. Loses Appeal on Saving Sea Turtles," *Journal of Commerce Week*, October 14, 1998.

73. Quoted in Danielle Knight, "Environmentalists Protest WTO Ruling on Shrimp Nets," Inter Press Service, October 13, 1998.

74. Cadeddu, "Turtles in the Soup?" In 2003 the Supreme Court declined to grant plaintiffs' petition for writ of certiorari. See Sean D. Murphy, "Unsuccessful Challenge to Department of State Shrimp-Turtle Guidelines," *American Journal of International Law* 97 (July 1, 2003).

75. Louise DeLaFayette, "WTO—GATT—Trade and Environment—Import Restrictions—Endangered Species," *American Journal of International Law* 96 (July 1, 2002): 685–692.

76. Ibid.

77. Alan Oxley, "Implications of the Decisions in the WTO Shrimp Turtle Dispute," February 2002. Available at www.tradestrategies.com.au.

78. Eryn Gable, "NMFS Changes Requirements for Shrimping Gear," *Greenwire*, February 24, 2003; "Kemp's Ridley Numbers Improving in Texas," *Greenwire*, July 2, 2002.

79. Gable, "NMFS Changes Requirements."

80. "Poachers Stealing More Eggs off Florida Beaches," *Greenwire*, August 2, 2002; Gable, "NMFS Changes Requirements."

81. Natalie M. Henry, "Enviros Ask Judge to Protect Turtles, End Longlining in Pacific," *Greenwire*, November 4, 2003; Michael Burnham, "New Techniques Reduce Sea Turtle Deaths, Feds Say," *Greenwire*, January 6, 2004.

82. Otto Pohl, "Challenge to Fishing: Keep the Wrong Species Out of its Huge Nets," *New York Times*, July 29, 2003, F3.

83. Allison A. Freeman, "Nets Kill Hundreds of Dolphins, Whales Daily—Report Says," *Greenwire*, June 9, 2005.

84. See, for example, Abram Chayes and Antonia Handler Chayes, *The New Sovereignty: Compliance With International Regulatory Agreements* (Cambridge: Harvard University Press, 1995); J. Owen Saunders, "Trade and Environment: The Fine Line Between Environmental Protection and Environmental Protectionism," *International Journal* XLVIII (Autumn 1992): 723–750.

85. Parker, "The Use and Abuse of Trade Leverage."

86. Elizabeth R. DeSombre and J. Samuel Barkin, "Turtles and Trade: The WTO's Acceptance of Environmental Trade Restrictions," *Global Environmental Politics*, February 2002, 18.

87. Robyn Eckersley, "The Big Chill: The WTO and Multilateral Environmental Agreements," *Global Environmental Politics*, May 2004, 24–50.

88. Eric Neumayer, "The WTO and the Environment: Its Past Record is Better Than Critics Believe, But Future Outlook is Bleak," *Global Environmental Politics*, August 2004, 1–8.

Recommended Reading

Bhagwati, Jagdish. *In Defense of Globalization*. New York: Oxford University Press, 2004.

Gallagher, Kevin P. *Free Trade and the Environment: Mexico, NAFTA, and Beyond*. Stanford: Stanford University Press, 2004.

Mander, Jerry, and Edward Goldsmith. *The Case Against the Global Economy: And for a Turn Toward the Local*. San Francisco: Sierra Club Books, 1996.

Sampson, Gary P., and W. Bradnee Chambers, eds. *Trade, Environment, and the Millennium*, 2d ed. New York: United Nations University Press, 2002.

Vogel, David. *Trading Up: Consumer and Environmental Regulation in a Global Economy*. Cambridge: Harvard University Press, 1995.

Web Sites

www.wto.org (WTO site)
www.iattc.org/HomeENG.htm (Inter-American Tropical Tuna Commission site)
www.earthisland.org (Earth Island Institute site)
www.seaturtles.org (Sea Turtle Restoration Project site)

CHAPTER 1 3

Backlash

Wise Use, Property Rights,
and the Antienvironmental Movement

In 1995 a reaction against environmentalism that had been growing in scale and intensity since the late 1980s found expression in Congress with the ascension of the Republican Party. Antienvironmentalists across the country had stepped up their battles against environmental regulations, and their efforts had culminated in several legislative proposals: bills to compensate property owners whenever government regulations reduced the value of their property; a revamped Clean Water Act that dramatically curtailed the preservation of wetlands; and a revised Endangered Species Act (ESA) that virtually dismantled endangered species protection. Congress ultimately did not pass any of the major antienvironmental legislation proposed in the mid-1990s, in part because environmentalists mobilized rapidly to raise public awareness and resist these incursions. Although it retreated, the antienvironmental movement did not disappear; its persistence has left members of Congress, agency personnel, and environmental activists circumspect and prompted them to consider new strategies to achieve their long-term goals.

The antienvironmental backlash of the 1990s was not unprecedented; the West has a long history of antienvironmental and antigovernment activism. This backlash was more effective than its predecessors, however, in part because it was led by politically sophisticated policy entrepreneurs. When a talented entrepreneur adopts an issue, he or she can significantly increase the probability that Congress will consider and approve a policy innovation.[1] To have an impact, a policy entrepreneur must invest resources—time, energy, and skill—in softening up policymakers and the public and then linking solutions to problems when a chance to do so arises.[2] A savvy entrepreneur knows how to identify problems, network in policy circles, shape the terms of debate, and build coalitions.[3] Among the entrepreneur's challenges is the need to craft messages and policy goals that are sufficiently idealistic to appeal to the true believers but not so extreme that they repel potential supporters.[4]

To succeed in bringing about legislative policy change, entrepreneurs must create a situation in which a majority of lawmakers believe they can get credit—or at least avoid punishment—for their position. They must believe, in other words, that the issue is salient to their constituents. One way advocates convince politicians of an issue's salience is by mobilizing their grassroots: it is difficult for politicians to ignore an organized and vocal contingent of the electorate because such mobilization reflects intense concern. On the other hand, politicians find it hard to reconcile the deeply held preferences of a narrow group of loyal party activists and the more centrist views of the general electorate on salient issues.[5] Therefore, politicians also use other cues, such as polling data, to assess their vulnerability on an issue.

The information generated by polls can be misleading, however. Polling results often contain internal contradictions; for example, a single poll may show overwhelming support for environmental preserves, such as wilderness areas and wild and scenic rivers, while simultaneously revealing a ferocious mistrust of government in all its forms.[6] In addition, polls are notoriously poor at detecting the amount of immediate, personal interest people have in an issue. With occasional exceptions, the environment ranks low as Gallup's "most important problem"; in fact, it was mentioned by only 1 percent of those surveyed in January 1995 and 2 percent in 2000.[7] But, because salience measures, such as the most important problem question, are headline-sensitive, they are untrustworthy guides to how the public will respond to particular policy proposals.[8]

Politicians can try to placate vociferous constituents while avoiding the salience trap by concealing their choices, thereby making it difficult for voters to trace responsibility for a policy.[9] Alternatively, they can reduce the visibility of policies by attaching them as riders to larger bills. Or leaders can use their control over the legislative calendar to move a bill quickly and avoid giving the opposition time to mobilize. By the same logic, however, opponents of policy change can thwart such maneuvers by raising their visibility. Defenders of the status quo also can take advantage of institutional differences between the House, which is often more responsive to short-term changes in public sentiment, and the Senate, which tends to react more cautiously. (State-level representation makes the Senate slower to adjust to demographic shifts, and Senate procedures make it easier for a minority to block change.) Finally, the president can obstruct policy change by using the formidable veto. Because a two-thirds majority in both chambers is required to override a presidential veto, the mere threat of a veto is often enough to discourage members of Congress from pursuing a policy. At a minimum, a veto threat is likely to limit how far Congress is willing to diverge from the president's preferred policy.[10]

In addition to pressing for legislative change, challengers can opt for more direct means to upset the status quo—by litigating or getting an initiative on a state's ballot. In court, challengers can argue that agencies have overstepped their constitutional bounds or exceeded their statutory mandate. For antienvironmentalists, the U.S. Constitution's Fifth Amendment guarantee that government cannot "take" property without just compensation has been fertile ground for appealing environmental regulations.[11] Antienvironmentalists have also used ballot initiatives that rest on the same "takings" logic to require governments to compensate landowners when regulations devalue their property. Critics charge that such "direct democracy" is just another opportunity for wealthy special interests to promote their agendas.[12] But supporters say ballot initiatives provide citizens the opportunity to check overreaching or unresponsive legislatures.[13] Regardless of the form it takes, a backlash can have potent political effects: even if it fails to win lawsuits, pass new laws, or overturn old legislation, a backlash can persuade advocates, administrators, and lawmakers to retreat from their ambitious reform agendas, adopt new, more conciliatory approaches, and consider alternative policy tools.

BACKGROUND

After a brief honeymoon in the late 1960s and early 1970s, environmentalism began to encounter resistance. By the late 1970s and early 1980s several local organizations had formed to repel changes in national forest logging regulations, federal wilderness designations, and restrictions on landowners living in or near national parks.[14] Among the first of these organized efforts was the Sagebrush Rebellion of the late 1970s (see chapter 7). The energy behind that movement, which consisted primarily of ranchers disgruntled by Carter administration efforts to rehabilitate the western range, dissipated with the election of President Ronald Reagan, who was sympathetic to its aims and whose administration itself was antigovernment and antienvironmental. But in the late 1980s and the 1990s an environmental movement, reinvigorated by its opposition to Reagan-era policies, in turn breathed new life into antienvironmentalism.

Reagan Administration Policies

The Reagan administration temporarily defused the emerging antienvironmental backlash by holding new environmental legislation at bay and undertaking a series of administrative reforms to reduce the burden of existing regulations on industry and private property owners. Immediately after his inauguration, President Reagan—who had campaigned on an antigovernment platform—created the Task Force on Regulatory Relief to review environmental regulations. He then issued Executive Order 12291, which required all federal agencies to conduct (and the Office of Management and Budget to oversee) a cost-benefit analysis on any proposed regulations and to refrain from promulgating those regulations unless the benefits outweighed the cost. Reagan also issued the little noticed but symbolically important Executive Order 12630, which required a "takings impact analysis" of most regulations, in order to discourage the enactment of government rules affecting private property.

Among the most effective of Reagan's efforts to blunt the effect of environmental regulations was the installation of development advocates James Watt and Anne Gorsuch (later Burford) as secretary of Interior and EPA administrator, respectively. These senior officials proceeded to reorganize their agencies and reinterpret environmental laws to make them more consistent with the president's antiregulatory agenda.[15] Gorsuch, a former Colorado legislator and a corporate attorney who specialized in challenging federal regulations, virtually halted enforcement of the Comprehensive Environmental Response, Compensation, and Liability Act of 1980—known as the Superfund Act. Her activities eventually provoked a congressional inquiry, and in 1984 she and twenty other appointees resigned in hopes of sparing the president further embarrassment. Watt was the former president of the Mountain States Legal Foundation, which sues the government on behalf of private landowners and public lands resource users. Watt favored rapid development and disposal of public lands and justified his approach before Congress by saying that he saw no point in preserving lands because he did "not know how many future generations we can count on before the Lord returns." [16]

Reagan's outspoken appointees provoked a backlash of their own, however: environmental groups saw an explosion in membership and sharp increases in donations. National polls taken throughout the 1980s indicated that Reagan had greatly overestimated the level of public support for trimming environmental regulations.[17] The resurgence of environmentalism in turn gave new impetus to antienvironmental activism. Beginning in the late 1980s, shortly after the election of President George H. W. Bush, antienvironmental policy entrepreneurs united two main forces, the wise use and the property rights movements.

The Wise Use Movement

The wise use movement gained widespread recognition after the 1988 Multiple Use Strategy Conference in Reno, Nevada, where veteran political activists Ron Arnold and Alan Gottlieb brought together under a single banner a disparate array of groups whose common objective was to remove environmental restrictions from public lands. Dubbing the amalgamation the wise use movement, Arnold and Gottlieb prepared an agenda that included developing oil and gas reserves in the Arctic National Wildlife Refuge; eliminating restrictions on wetlands development; opening all public lands, including national parks and wilderness areas, to mineral and energy production; redesignating 70 million of the 90 million acres of the National Wilderness Preservation System for motorized trail travel, limited commercial development, and commodity use; instituting civil penalties against anyone who legally challenged economic action or development on federal lands; and recognizing private rights to mining claims, water, grazing permits, and timber contracts on federal lands.[18]

A small number of umbrella organizations, most headquartered in the West, began to coordinate wise use activities. Among those organizations were the Blue Ribbon Coalition, which represented some 500,000 off-road vehicle users; Gottlieb and Arnold's Center for the Defense of Free Enterprise, whose overarching goal was to promote and defend an unfettered capitalist economy; the Western States Public Lands Coalition; and its subsidiary, People for the West! (PFW), formed by mining companies in 1989 to improve their industry's public image.[19] Some of these organizations were industry fronts, such as the Marine Preservation Association, whose fifteen oil company members defined marine preservation as the promotion of petroleum and energy company interests.[20] Others, including PFW, were financed almost entirely by the industries that benefited from their activities: in 1992, 96 percent of PFW's $1.7 million budget came from corporate donors, led by NERCO minerals, Cyprus Minerals, Chevron, and Heclo Mining. Twelve of the group's thirteen directors were mining executives, and its chairman, Bob Quick, was the national director of state legislative affairs for the Asarco Mining Company.[21]

But the wise use movement boasted a citizen following as well. Although critics downplayed its grassroots membership, Arnold claimed that the wise use mailing lists reached more than 3 million people, of which 1 million actively participated in meetings and wrote letters to legislators.[22] Among the state and local groups that made up the wise use movement's base were the California Desert Coalition, formed in 1986 to oppose the California Desert Protection Act; the Shasta Alliance for Resources and Environment, which was concerned with northern California resource management policies; and the Oregon Lands Coalition, whose members—including agricultural, ranching, and timber interests—counted among their primary goals limiting federal protection for endangered species. A 1993 study commissioned by the Wilderness Society reported that these groups

> are apparently genuinely grassroots. That is: they [comprise] local individuals addressing local concerns who joined with other individuals, groups, and funders as a matter of common concern. It is true that special interests have in many cases fostered local Wise Use groups . . . but it is foolish to lay this movement solely at the doorstep of Exxon, Georgia Pacific, or Kawasaki. Real people have perceived a real threat. The national Wise Use movement is attempting to give these grassroots groups coherence; it did not give them life.[23]

Don Judge, an executive secretary for the AFL/CIO who battled the wise use movement in Montana, pointed out that, although big business interests exploited the suffering of local people to further their own aims, they found a receptive audience: "You cannot destroy entire communities without getting a backlash," said Judge, "and whenever there's a backlash of emotion, there's always somebody with a lot of money that manipulates that emotion to their benefit." [24]

The wise use movement also subsumed officials from the county supremacy movement, which arose in 1989 when Catron County, New Mexico, passed an ordinance asserting its authority to veto federal environmental protection regulations, defining federal grazing permits as private property rights, and authorizing the county sheriff to arrest federal or state officials trying to enforce federal statutes. More than thirty-five counties subsequently passed similar statutes. The main impetus for the county movement was the perception that eastern elites were trying to impose their policy preferences on westerners, who had an entirely different culture. The rallying cry of the county supremacy movement was that easterners were waging a "war on the West." Two clearinghouses were established in 1989 to coordinate the activities of the county movement: the Utah-based National Federal Lands Conference and the Coalition of Arizona/New Mexico Counties for Stable Economic Growth, based in Catron County.

The Property Rights Movement

A second component of the antienvironmental coalition was the property rights movement, the bulk of whose membership lay east of the Mississippi. Chuck Cushman, head of the American Land Rights Association, was a prime mover and, like Arnold and Gottlieb, was a skillful policy entrepreneur. Portraying himself as leading a holy crusade against environmentalists, Cushman used his organizational skills and shrewd political mind to unify the disparate grievances of landowners. Cushman's own organization, the National Inholders Association, defended the rights of those who owned land within the boundaries of national parks. He forged alliances with other major property rights groups, such as the Washington, D.C.-based Defenders of Property Rights, which wanted to "bring about a sea change in property rights law through strategically filed lawsuits and groundbreaking property rights legislation." [25]

The property rights movement's fundamental tenet was that property rights are paramount, and property owners ought to be compensated when government regulation devalues it. Advocates based this claim on the Fifth Amendment to the Constitution, which guarantees compensation for property taken by eminent domain. In 1995 one of the most outspoken proponents of unfettered private property rights, Nancie Marzulla, president of Defenders of Property Rights, testified before the Senate Judiciary Committee: "Today, environmental regulations destroy property rights on an unprecedented scale," she said. "Regulations designed to protect coastal zone areas, wetlands, and endangered species habitats, among others, leave many owners stripped of all but bare title to their property." [26] Marzulla contended that the focus on property rights emerged as individuals began to feel the impact of burgeoning federal and state environmental regulations on their day-to-day lives. She pointed out that the property rights movement gained momentum in the 1980s in response to wetlands policy revisions, endangered species protection efforts, public park and greenway expansions, scenic river corridors, land-use planning, zoning laws, and growth management plans, and the movement gained steam in the early 1990s.[27]

A hotbed of property rights activism was the Adirondack State Park in New York, where some residents began mobilizing in 1990 to prevent the state legislature from approving a sweeping new planning law for the area. The 6-million-acre park, which is enshrined in the state's constitution as a place that "shall be forever kept as wild forest land," is more than 50 percent privately owned. In 1971, in hopes of preventing rampant development in the park after Interstate 87 reached it in the 1960s, Gov. Nelson Rockefeller established the

Adirondack Park Agency (APA) to regulate land use in the region. In the late 1980s Gov. Mario Cuomo's Commission on the Adirondack Park in the 20th Century generated an ambitious land-use plan for the park, to be administered by the APA. The negative reaction to the proposal among some local residents was intense; for example, one vocal representative of the Adirondack Solidarity Alliance told a crowd at a rally, "The APA will take all of our private property. The APA will be a total dictator. Adirondacks will be forced to live in concentration camps working as slave laborers for APA." [28]

THE CASE

In 1991, 400 wise use and property rights groups joined forces to form the Alliance for America, an umbrella organization whose overarching goal was to eliminate environmental regulations affecting both private and public lands. The coalition was only loosely coherent, but it boasted an impressive mailing list and network of members that it could mobilize in response to perceived threats. Unifying these groups were their members' cornucopian values of human supremacy over nature, individual freedom and economic growth, and technology as the solution to environmental problems. A small number of sophisticated policy entrepreneurs devised the movement's two-pronged strategy, which entailed crafting dual messages—one to appeal to hardcore activists and the other to attract mainstream support—and challenging environmentalism in the legislative, administrative, and judicial arenas simultaneously.

Using Ideas to Mobilize Support

Antienvironmental policy entrepreneurs mobilized followers with powerful ideas expressed in skillfully crafted rhetoric. Most observers credit Ron Arnold with sparking the wise use movement in 1979 with a series of articles in *Logging Management Magazine* in which he called for an activist movement to defeat the environmental movement. Arnold appropriated the phrase "wise use" from conservationist Gifford Pinchot because it was both headline-friendly and rich with symbolism.[29] Adopting the stock-in-trade of their adversaries, antienvironmental groups quickly became expert at mounting grassroots campaigns. In 1988 Arnold advised resource companies to stop defending themselves and let citizens get out in front "because citizens' groups have credibility and industries don't." [30] To enhance their populist image, wise use groups began holding rallies, sponsoring petition drives, and launching T-shirt and bumper sticker campaigns. The broader Alliance for America initiated an annual "Fly In for Freedom," which brought local wise use and property rights activists to Washington, D.C., to convey their beliefs directly to members of Congress.

Arnold, Gottlieb, Cushman, and others attracted supporters by defining environmental regulations rather than environmental damage as the problem, using potent symbols and metaphors. In doing so, they were careful to craft separate messages for hard-core true believers and average citizens. Speaking to activists, antienvironmental leaders used incendiary rhetoric to depict a conspiracy among elitist environmentalists, government officials, and the media to take away citizens' rights. For example, Arnold told his followers, "We are sick to death of environmentalism and so we will destroy it. We will not allow our right to own property and use nature's resources for the benefit of mankind to be stripped from us by a bunch of eco-fascists." [31] But in their public campaigns antienvironmental leaders generally adopted a more moderate tone, framing environmental regulations as putting the environment ahead of jobs in order to tap into working people's economic anxieties. For example, promotional literature for People for the West! read, "Don't allow Congress to lock us out of all 730 million acres of public lands. . . . People will lose jobs, rural communities will become ghost towns, education for our children will suffer, and state and local governments will forfeit critical income for police, fire protection, roads, and social services." [32]

To mobilize followers, antienvironmental leaders also employed populist rhetoric, tapping into the powerful American dread of government tyranny. Pamela Neal, executive director of the Public Lands Council, which represented 31,000 cattle and sheep ranchers, argued, "It was free enterprise and private property rights that created America and made this nation great. Instead of protecting that independence, the government is making us servants of an environmental movement that I can only liken to socialism." [33] Ron Arnold described environmentalists as "part of an elite, part of the Harvard Yard crowd in three-piece suits and expensive shoes that is destroying the middle class." [34] By contrast, according to Arnold, the wise use movement represented ordinary citizens: "The environmental movement is the establishment now, and now we are the rebels coming to tear them down. Now they're Goliath and we're David, and we intend to put the stone in their head." [35] Painting environmentalists as extremists, Chuck Cushman characterized preservationism as "a new pagan religion" whose members "worship trees and animals and sacrifice people." [36] Wise use and property rights advocates portrayed themselves as moderates, seeking a balance between human activities and the preservation of nature.

Among the most effective public relations tools were anecdotes that depicted the government as the villain and private property owners, ranchers, loggers, and miners as innocent victims. Some of the most often repeated stories were the following:

- In 1986 Gaston Roberge, a retired businessman from Scarborough, Maine, was on the verge of selling his 2.8-acre lot in Old Orchard Beach to a developer for $440,000. When federal officials heard about the deal, however, they declared the Roberge property a wetland under the Clean Water Act, and therefore required him to get a special permit before it could be developed. After the buyer changed his mind about the purchase, Roberge launched an expensive legal battle that resulted, nearly ten years later, in a $338,000 settlement with the Justice Department.[37]

- One snowy September night, Montana rancher John Shuler thought he saw a grizzly bear outside his house. Grabbing his rifle, he raced outside to find three bears devouring his sheep herd. When he fired a warning shot in the air, a fourth bear emerged and turned to attack him. In fear for his life, Shuler shot and killed the bear, thereby taking an endangered species, a crime for which the Environmental Protection Agency (EPA) fined him $4,000.[38]

- Taiwanese immigrant Taung Min-lin bought a 723-acre parcel of California scrub land in 1990, intending to farm it. As it turned out, his land was home to three endangered species: the Tipton kangaroo rat, the blunt-nosed leopard lizard, and the San Joaquin kit fox. In February 1994 state and federal agents raided Lin's farm, carted off his tractor, and filed criminal charges against him for violating the Endangered Species Act.[39]

- In 1990 the government fined Paul Tudor Jones II $1 million, required him to make a $1 million contribution to an environmental group, and sentenced him to eighteen months probation after he filled wetlands on his Maryland property as part of an effort to create a private wildlife refuge. Jones's project manager, marine engineer William Ellen, refused to settle his case and was charged with five felony counts of knowingly filling wetlands and sentenced to six months in prison.[40]

Antienvironmentalists did not rely on anecdotes alone, however. Bolstering their credibility were a host of conservative think tanks that underwrote public relations campaigns and helped to build an intellectual foundation for the movement. These organizations generated studies, op-eds, and briefing papers in support of two primary lines of argument: there is no scientific certainty on which to base environmental regulations, and environmental regulations harm the economy and impinge on individual liberty. The Heritage Foundation led the charge against natural resource management agencies and environmental legislation, holding an annual conference at which directors of business-sponsored "public interest" law firms assembled and devised strategies. In 1990, coinciding with the twentieth anniversary of Earth Day, the foundation issued a report on "eco-terrorism"; it singled out the environmental movement as "the greatest single threat to the American economy." [41]

The Cato Institute, another Washington, D.C.-based libertarian think tank, promoted "free-market environmentalism" while downplaying the dangers associated with environmental problems. A 1993 Cato publication entitled *Apocalypse Not* argued that "much of the modern environmental movement is a broad-based assault on reason and a concomitant assault on freedom." [42] The Science and Environmental Policy Project, founded in 1990 by the Reverend Sun Myung Moon-funded Washington Institute for Values in Public Policy and subsequently allied with Virginia's George Mason University, also held conferences and seminars aimed at discrediting arguments that ozone depletion, global warming, acid rain, pesticide exposure, and toxic waste exposure pose real or potential threats to human health.[43]

Legal Theory and Litigation

In addition to their public relations campaign, antienvironmentalists developed a sophisticated legal capacity in hopes of emulating the successes of the environmental movement. The Center for the Defense of Free Enterprise disseminated antienvironmental literature and maintained its own legal defense fund.[44] The Pacific Legal Foundation, founded in 1973, was the first business-sponsored "public interest" law firm; by the mid-1990s there were twenty-three of them.[45] The Mountain States Legal Foundation, made famous by its president, former Interior secretary James Watt, filed legal actions all over the West contesting federal regulatory actions. The Competitive Enterprise Institute, the Federalist Society, the Washington Legal Foundation, and others also litigated pro bono on behalf of businesses opposing environmental laws and regulations.

The county supremacy movement made legal theory the centerpiece of its resistance to federal environmental regulations. The movement asserted the autonomy of counties by passing ordinances that defied federal hegemony over land within county borders, instead granting county officials decision-making power over those lands. Their authors based the legitimacy of such ordinances on three legal theories. First, they contended that the Constitution gives the federal government authority only over lands it legally owns—that is, land within Washington, D.C., defense facilities, and other "needful buildings." Second, they argued that the federal government had retained land in new territories only with the understanding that it would eventually divest itself of this land and return it to the states. Third, county commissioners pointed out that the National Environmental Policy Act requires the federal government to cooperate with state and local governments to "preserve important historic, cultural, and other aspects of our natural heritage." County supremacy advocates defined their culture as one that favored resource extraction.[46]

Although it was eager to test these legal theories in court, the county supremacy movement was not particularly successful. In January 1994 a state court judge ruled a Boundary County, Idaho, ordinance illegal, saying it violated the supremacy clause of the U.S. Constitution. Judge Lloyd George of the U.S. district court made a similar ruling in 1996, when he overturned a Nye County, Nevada, ordinance and affirmed the right of the federal government to own and administer public lands in the state.[47]

Like the county supremacists, property rights advocates relied heavily on legal theory and litigation to advance their policy goals. Their primary legal claim was that regulatory actions that reduced the value of property constituted takings, as defined by the Fifth Amendment. That claim gained credibility with the publication in 1985 of a book, *Takings: Private Property and the Power of Eminent Domain,* by the University of Chicago's libertarian law professor,

Richard Epstein. Epstein argued that under the Fifth Amendment the government must pay property owners whenever environmental regulations, health and safety rules, or zoning laws limit the value of their property.[48]

The courts were more hospitable to property rights than to county supremacy arguments. Although the idea of regulatory takings dates back to the nineteenth century, the Supreme Court accepted few regulatory takings cases after the 1930s. In the 1980s, however, the Court began to reconsider property rights claims, which were arising in greater numbers in response to the spate of new federal environmental laws. In 1987 the Court ruled in *First English Evangelical Lutheran Church v. County of Los Angeles* that where a government land-use regulation is successfully challenged, the landowner is eligible to collect damages. (Previously, governments could satisfy courts simply by removing the regulatory hurdle.)[49] Another California case (*Nollan v. California Coastal Commission*, 1987) sparked a trend in jurisprudence that was closely watched by property rights advocates and environmentalists alike. The plaintiffs in this case lived on the coast and wanted to replace their 504-square-foot bungalow with a new house nearly twice as large as the original. The Coastal Commission agreed to grant them a permit if they would allow public access to the beach in front of their property. The Nollans contended that there was no relationship between that requirement (known as an exaction) and their request, and the Supreme Court agreed. Court watchers regarded this as the first major land-use case in the modern era in which a property owner prevailed against the government on a takings issue.[50]

Between 1992 and 1995 property rights advocates were successful in two more important Supreme Court cases. First, the Court backed a claim by South Carolina beachfront property owner and developer David Lucas (*Lucas v. South Carolina Coastal Commission*, 1992). In 1986 Lucas bought two lots on a barrier island off South Carolina for $1 million. Two years later the state passed the Beachfront Management Act, which prohibited development in areas vulnerable to erosion. In 1992 the Court held that, because Lucas had suffered a total loss of property value as a result of a law passed after he purchased the land, he should receive financial compensation. More generally, the Court ruled that compensation is required when legislation deprives an owner of "all economically beneficial or productive use" of his property.[51]

Second, in a case brought by Oregonians in Action, a property rights group partly financed by timber companies, the Court ruled 5–4 in *Dolan v. City of Tigard* (1994) in favor of a plumbing supply store owner. The city had refused to grant Florence Dolan a permit to expand her store unless she turned over 10 percent of her property for a public bicycle path. In this case, the Court said that zoning officials may impose exactions only if they are related to the proposed development or are "roughly proportional" to any harms the development may cause. Again, this case indicated a willingness on the part of the Court to overturn state and local regulations it found unduly burdensome for landowners.

Despite these highly publicized victories, there was no strong judicial shift in favor of takings claims, and legal scholars continued to puzzle over their significance. As many commentators noted, the cases cited above were exceptional and involved extreme circumstances. (This is not surprising; legal activists always look for clear winners in their effort to establish a new precedent.) Nevertheless, plaintiffs continued to file lawsuits claiming takings under a variety of circumstances.[52] At a minimum, they hoped that landowners' increasing propensity to challenge land-use regulations, combined with the judiciary's apparent willingness to hear such cases, would deter state lawmakers from enacting protective rules or at least force them to conduct more explicit cost-benefit calculations before doing so.[53] To improve their prospects in the long run, in 1992 a Montana-based group called FREE (Foundation for Research on Economics and the Environment) began hosting week-long, all-expense-paid seminars for judges on property rights and the environment at resorts in Montana.[54]

Another legal tactic antienvironmentalists began using is what two University of Denver professors labeled SLAPPs—strategic lawsuits against public participation. Such lawsuits, employed primarily by developers and corporations, were powerful deterrents because they could bankrupt those who attempted to use administrative or legal procedures to obstruct development. For example, in West Virginia, the DLM Coal Corporation filed a multimillion-dollar libel action against Rick Webb and his nonprofit environmental group after the organization requested an EPA hearing on pollution of rivers by mine runoff and published an editorial in its newsletter criticizing strip mining. In Squaw Valley, California, a developer filed a $75 million suit against stunt skier Rick Sylvester for speaking out and writing letters to the editor against a planned development. And in Louisville, Colorado, a developer sued local activist Betty Johnson for unlimited damages after she organized a petition drive for a growth moratorium.[55] The goal of such suits was not necessarily to win and collect damages but rather to intimidate potential critics and stifle dissent; although 83 percent were dismissed before reaching trial, they cost defendants tens of thousands of dollars, as well as tremendous amounts of time and energy.[56]

Harassment and Intimidation

In addition to lobbying, legal activism, and political campaigns, the antienvironmental movement exhibited a more sinister side: federal officials were threatened, terrorized, and occasionally physically harmed when they tried to enforce environmental laws. In the summer of 1994 Dick Carver, commissioner of Nye County, Nevada, used a bulldozer to open a closed Forest Service logging road while an armed crowd cheered him on. "All it would have taken was for [the forest ranger] to draw a weapon," Carver later bragged, "and 50 people with sidearms would have drilled him." [57] In Catron County, Nancy and Clyde Brown wrote an open and threatening letter to the U.S. Fish and Wildlife Service: "I think bureaucrats better back off before someone gets seriously hurt. Who among you would want to loose [*sic*] your life for a bird . . . or a microscopic minnow?" [58] And shortly after the Fish and Wildlife Service reintroduced wolves into Yellowstone National Park, one of the radio-collared animals was found shot to death next to a partially eaten calf on the ranch of seventy-four-year-old rancher Eugene Hussey. When Fish and Wildlife agents came to investigate, Sheriff Brett Barsalon forced them to retreat, telling them to leave Hussey alone and threatening to "go to Plan B" if they did not. (A veterinary medical examiner found that the calf was already dead at the time the wolf scavenged its carcass and had probably been moved to the site—presumably to lure the wolf.)

In *War Against the Greens*, journalist David Helvarg relays a host of incidents in which environmental activists were victims of terror tactics. For example, after Ellen Gray, director of the Pilcuk Audubon Society in Everett, Washington, finished testifying at a county council hearing in favor of a land-use ordinance to protect local streams and wetlands, a man stood up in front of her with a noose and said, "This is for you." In Eureka Springs, Arkansas, Greenpeace USA's director of toxics research Pat Costner returned home to find her house burned to the ground. Arson investigators found abundant evidence that the fire had been set. In 1992 there were several attacks on Diane Wilson, a shrimper protesting the expansion of a Taiwanese-owned plastics plant near her home in Seadrift, Texas. Assailants shot at her mother-in-law, who lived on her property, as well as at her dog (which was hit). Her boat was sabotaged and almost sank.

According to Helvarg, the late 1980s and early 1990s saw

> a startling increase in intimidation, vandalism, and violence directed at grassroots environmental activists. Observers of this trend have documented hundreds of acts of violence, ranging from vandalism, assaults, arsons, and shootings to torture, rape, and possibly murder, much of it occurring in rural and low-income communities. Simple acts of intimidation—phone harassment, anonymous letters, and verbal threats of violence—may number in the thousands.[59]

Jacqueline Vaughn Switzer, who offers a balanced assessment of the antienvironmental movement in her 1997 book *Green Backlash*, suggests that environmentalists exaggerate the extent of antienvironmental militancy. Even if it attracted few adherents, however, the radical fringe served a purpose: it drew attention to the cause while rendering mainstream antienvironmental activists moderate by comparison. (Earth First! has played a parallel role for the environmental movement.)

The Legislative Response to Antienvironmentalism

Events in Congress in the early 1990s reflected the success of antienvironmentalists at defining environmental *regulations*, rather than environmental harms, as the problem. Riding the coattails of Bill Clinton and Al Gore, the Democratic-controlled 103d Congress initiated an ambitious environmental agenda, but the session turned out to be a bust for environmentalists. Only one major environmental bill—the California Desert Protection Act—passed during this period, while Republicans and conservative Democrats foiled efforts to reauthorize Superfund, the Clean Water Act, and other major environmental laws. Antienvironmental forces also derailed a bill to elevate the EPA to a cabinet-level department in early 1994.

Having stymied environmentalists in the 103d Congress, their opponents saw an opportunity to advance their own agenda after the 1994 elections, which resulted in Republican majorities in the House and Senate.[60] As part of their campaign, Republican leaders had devised the "Contract with America," which—although it did not mention environmental regulations explicitly—included three planks that curbed the federal government's ability to impose environmentally protective rules: one cut unfunded mandates to states and localities; another required federal agencies to conduct cost-benefit analyses and risk assessments before promulgating regulations; and a third mandated that government reimburse property owners for reductions in their property values that result from regulations.

After the Republican victory, Thomas L. Bliley Jr., chairman of the House Commerce Committee, summarized the party's position: "The American people sent us a message in November, loud and clear: Tame this regulatory beast. Our constituents want us to break the Feds' stranglehold on our economy and to get them out of decisions that are best left to the individual." [61] Majority Whip Tom DeLay of Texas announced that the goal of GOP regulatory reform was to "make sure that American small business and the American taxpayer don't become the next endangered species." [62] When asked by a reporter if there was any government regulation he would retain, DeLay—who compared the EPA to the Gestapo—responded: "I can't think of one." [63]

The House leadership then selected Don Young, a virulently antienvironmental Alaskan, to chair the Resources (formerly Natural Resources) Committee. "I'm the one in charge now," Young gloated. Environmentalists "are going to have to compromise. . . . If not, I'm just going to ram it down their throats." [64] Young, who in December 1994 described environmentalists as a "self-centered bunch, the waffle-stomping, Harvard-graduating, intellectual bunch of idiots," proceeded to stock his committee with conservative Republican freshmen.[65] Although Republican leaders in the Senate promoted proenvironmental John Chafee of Rhode Island to the chairmanship of the Environment and Public Works Committee, they loaded his committee with antienvironmental members as well.[66]

Pursuing Policy Change Through the Budget. The primary vehicle for congressional efforts to roll back environmental protection was the budget. By attaching antienvironmental riders to the fiscal 1996 omnibus spending bill, sponsors hoped to sidestep debate and avoid galvanizing environmentalists. Among the numerous antienvironmental measures added to the spending bill in 1995 were provisions to:

- impose a moratorium on new listings under the Endangered Species Act;
- transfer responsibility for the newly created Mojave National Preserve from the preservation-oriented National Park Service to the more commodity-oriented Bureau of Land Management;
- institute a ninety-day moratorium on proposed grazing regulations that the cattle and sheep industries opposed;
- curtail the ecological assessment of the Columbia River Basin;
- dismantle Energy Department conservation programs;
- increase the harvest from the Tongass National Forest in Alaska; and
- open up the Arctic National Wildlife Refuge to oil drilling.

Environmentalists responded by launching a campaign to mobilize their movement's grassroots, stimulating e-mails, phone calls, and letters to members of Congress in opposition to the riders. Their efforts paid off: fifty-one Republicans joined a majority of Democrats in approving (212–206) an amendment deleting the antienvironmental riders.[67] In a subsequent vote, the Republican leadership managed to persuade enough members to reinstate the riders, but in mid-November 1995 President Clinton vetoed the omnibus budget act, citing the antienvironmental riders as the main reason. The ensuing week-long shutdown of the federal government focused public attention on the riders—precisely what their sponsors had hoped to avoid—and empowered opponents of the measures. Although stopgap spending bills reopened the government, Clinton held firm, and Congress ultimately was compelled to drop most of the antienvironmental provisions to get a budget passed.

Protecting Private Property Rights. In addition to attaching riders to the budget, antienvironmentalists in the 104th Congress pursued another, slightly more visible line of attack. In March 1995 the House passed the Private Property Rights Act, which entitled property owners to receive compensation for any "measurable" reduction in the value of their property resulting from environmental restrictions on otherwise lawful use of it.[68] To receive compensation, a property owner would submit a written request within ninety days of notice of a final government action limiting the property use. Within 180 days, the agency would have to offer to pay the property owner for any reduction in the property's value. A property owner could reject the agency's offer and request binding arbitration.[69] One sign of the property rights movement's effectiveness at raising the salience of its concerns was that more than a third of House Democrats joined Republicans in passing the measure, even as most acknowledged that it would halt many regulations at their inception.

Property rights legislation fared less well in the Senate, however. An effort to attach property rights riders to the spending bill stalled. Majority Leader Bob Dole, R-Kan., got thirty-one cosponsors for a companion to the House bill but failed on three back-to-back cloture votes to bring his measure (S 343) to a vote.[70] And, although the Judiciary Committee approved a bill (S 605) similar to Dole's, it too was quashed by the threat of a filibuster.

Antienvironmentalists pushed property rights measures in state legislatures as well. All fifty states considered measures in the early 1990s, and, by the end of 1995, eighteen legislatures had passed laws requiring regulators to consider the effects of new regulation on property owners. Most of these laws required state governments to conduct a takings impact assessment before proposing regulatory action, but some also included compensation provisions.[71] In 1995 Florida passed the nation's toughest law: it set up an expedited review of land-use disputes between government and landowners and entitled landowners "inordinately burdened" by government action to compensation.[72] Although state legislatures were eager to pass takings laws, voters seemed less enthusiastic. For example, in 1995 the Washington State legislature approved a takings bill that came to it in the form of an initiative financed by the timber and building industries.[73] But the bill's passage prompted a proenvironmental backlash, in which 10,000 volunteers rounded up more than twice the number of signatures necessary to prevent its implementation by putting it on the ballot as a referendum.[74] Washington voters rejected the referendum by a three-fifths majority, even though takings-bill supporters outspent the opposition two to one.[75] A year earlier, relatively conservative Arizona voters had rejected by the same margin a measure that would have required state or local officials to consider whether any new regulation violated private property rights.

Voters' resistance to property rights legislation was almost certainly the result of a campaign by an unlikely alliance of environmentalists, some commercial interests, civil rights groups, children's groups, and organizations representing cities, states, and churches. The coalition developed a coherent set of arguments against property rights legislation, alerting voters to the possibility that the takings impact assessment process and compensation requirements would severely limit government's ability to regulate in the public interest. (A particularly shrewd point the coalition used to divide the right was that government would not be able to zone out pornography.) The coalition also pointed out that implementing compensation rules would create a bureaucratic and legal morass and would cost governments millions of dollars annually.[76] Citing a University of Washington study, the coalition noted that economic impact assessments alone could cost local governments between $305 and $986 million a year, and could eat up from 10 percent to 50 percent of the budget of large jurisdictions such as Seattle's King County.[77]

Dismantling Wetlands Protection. Aside from writing bills to guarantee private property rights, House Republicans also tried to revise the Clean Water Act to drastically reduce protection for the nation's wetlands.[78] Federal wetlands regulation had been controversial since the 1970s, when Section 404 of the Clean Water Act of 1972 authorized the EPA and the Army Corps of Engineers to regulate the discharge of dredged or fill materials into "navigable waters." Because wetlands regulations were a particular object of antienvironmentalists' wrath, congressional leaders in the 104th Congress wasted no time in crafting bills to dismantle them. In spring 1995 Bud Shuster, R-Penn., chairman of the House Transportation and Infrastructure Committee, introduced a radical set of revisions to the Clean Water Act (HR 961), including provisions to restrict federal wetlands protection and compensate landowners whose property values declined more than 20 percent as a result of federal regulations. Shuster's bill required federal agencies to delineate the nation's wetlands and categorize them as Type A, B, or C, in declining order of "ecological importance." It limited land-use activities only on Type A wetlands and allowed no more than 20 percent of any county to be designated Type A.[79] In April the House Transportation Committee approved HR 961, 42–16.

The House bill ignited a firestorm among scientists and environmentalists, who were furious because regulated industries such as International Paper, as well as industry groups like the Chemical Manufacturers Association, had helped draft the legislation.[80] Robert Perciasepe, a top water quality official from the EPA, called the bill "a program of counterfeit wetlands protection," saying that it "propose[d] scientifically unsound methods of identifying wetlands that the Association of State Wetlands Managers estimates would eliminate some 60 to 80 percent of the nation's wetlands from regulatory protection, including large parts of the Everglades and the Great Dismal Swamp." [81]

One day before the House opened debate on the bill, the National Academy of Sciences (NAS) released a congressionally mandated report, written by seventeen prominent wetlands experts, laying out the scientific consensus on wetlands delineation. The report maintained that the approach outlined in the House bill, with its insistence on narrow, quantitative definitions, was unscientific for a host of reasons. For example, the House bill required that a wetland be saturated for twenty-one consecutive days in the growing season, even though the NAS report contended that a wetland may experience periodic saturation for shorter periods, in the root zone of plants rather than at the surface, and not necessarily in the months between the spring thaw and the autumn frost. Moreover, the report noted, a uniform definition of wetlands cannot take into account the wetness of a wetland relative to its surrounding landscape. Areas that would be considered only marginal wetlands in the Northeast, for example, may constitute critical riparian areas in the arid West.[82]

When the chairman of the NAS committee, William M. Lewis Jr., called the House bill's requirements "arbitrary," Rep. Jimmy Hayes, D-La., who wrote the wetlands provisions, responded that the academy was meddling in politics by releasing its report the day before debate on the bill was scheduled to begin. Hayes pointed out that whether to protect wetlands was at heart a *political* decision to be made by Congress, not one that could be dictated by science.[83] To those, such as Maryland Republican Wayne Gilchrest, who argued that wetlands deserved special protection, Hayes responded that the property rights of individuals were more important than protecting ecologically worthless wetlands.[84] Echoing the rhetoric of property rights advocacy groups, Hayes called the decision a "vote on the distinction between the rights of individuals and the arrogance of power and government." [85]

As expected, on May 16, 1995, the House passed the Clean Water Act rewrite by a vote of 240 to 185. With forty-five conservative Democrats voting for the bill and thirty-four moderate Republicans voting against it, however, the volume of crossover voting troubled supporters of the legislation. Moreover, the revolt against the Republican leadership spurred by Rep. Sherwood Boehlert, R-N.Y., attracted widespread media coverage, making senators leery of the potential political fallout. In the end, the Senate refused to adopt a similar measure, and President Clinton vowed to veto any such bill.

Endangered Species Act Reform. Like wetlands regulations, endangered species protection became a favorite object of antienvironmentalists' derision in the late 1980s and early 1990s, particularly after the spotted owl debacle (see chapter 8). It was not surprising, then, that the 104th Congress chose the ESA as its third major target. When it passed the ESA virtually unanimously in 1973, Congress did not anticipate its impact; most supporters viewed it as a way to protect national icons such as the bald eagle, the grey whale, and the grizzly bear. In fact, early on the ESA did provide a means to support "charismatic megafauna": more than two-thirds of the species on the list in 1973 were birds and mammals. By the mid-1990s, however, the number of listed species had jumped from 114 to 1,516; moreover, nearly two-thirds of listed species were plants, and there were almost as many protected invertebrates as birds and mammals combined.[86] Opponents of the act multiplied as it became an ever more formidable tool—"the pit bull of environmental laws"—in the hands of environmentalists.[87]

By the time the ESA came up for reauthorization in 1992, demands for reform were escalating. In an effort to deflect criticism of the act and head off more permanent legislative revisions, the Clinton administration began proposing administrative changes to increase the law's flexibility. Among the administration's proposals were rules exempting small landowners from regulations and requiring independent scientific peer review of all listing decisions. The administration also adopted a series of innovative practices in hopes of salvaging the act. For example, it began allowing developers to pay a fee for destroying habitat and then using the money raised to purchase other tracts of habitat or buy permanent conservation easements from private landowners.[88] And it espoused cooperative regional conservation plans, such as the one built around the endangered California gnatcatcher in San Diego (see chapter 16).

ESA reform sponsors Richard Pombo, R-Calif., in the House and Dirk Kempthorne, R-Idaho, in the Senate were unmoved by the Clinton administration's gestures. Early in the legislative session, Chairman Young named revamping the ESA his top legislative priority and said he was certain he had the votes to bring a tough bill to the House floor. He boldly predicted that the House would finish its work on the ESA by August. To ensure his plan's success, Young created an endangered species task force and named Pombo, a conservative rancher and vocal property rights advocate, chairman. In doing so, he undercut New Jersey Republican Jim Saxton, the moderately proenvironmental chairman of the Resources Subcommittee on Fisheries, Wildlife and Oceans, which normally has jurisdiction over endangered species.

In mid-March Pombo began holding hearings in which anti-ESA speakers told their stories and presented their recommendations for revising the law. As in the wetlands debate, anti-ESA proponents' arguments relied heavily on rhetoric and anecdote. Environmentalists countered by distributing "fact sheets" purporting to tell the true stories behind the anecdotes. They posted emergency alerts on their Web sites and sent e-mail bulletins to members asking them to contact their senators and representatives to oppose the ESA rewrites. Scientists spoke out on behalf of the act. They pointed out that many plants and animals were in dire need of its protection, noting that more than 950 domestic species and more than 560 foreign species were listed as endangered or imminently threatened with endangerment; that thousands of others were candidates for listing; and that nearly two-thirds of all mammals were either listed or candidates for listing, along with 14 percent of birds, 12 percent of plants, and 10 percent of fish. While acknowledging its flaws, Dennis D. Murphy, president of the Society for Conservation Biology, argued that the ESA was "the most effective tool in the tool kit for preserving this country's biological diversity." [89]

Scientists' pleas notwithstanding, in May 1995 Sen. Slade Gorton, R-Wash., unveiled his own version of the ESA (S 768), which—to environmentalists' dismay—was written largely by lawyers representing the industries most affected by the law. The Gorton bill required federal officials to take economic and social considerations into account when deciding whether to restrict land use to protect a species; it required a cost-benefit analysis on proposed conservation measures; and it restricted the definition of "harm" to those actions that directly resulted in the death of an animal or plant. Gorton's bill also abolished the government's principal method of enforcing the ESA on private property: fines or imprisonment for those who destroy the habitat of an endangered species. Gorton trumpeted that his proposal did not "undo everything that's been done [under the ESA]. But I suspect it would end up having that effect." [90] But neither Gorton's bill nor alternative ESA bills introduced by Senator Kempthorne or Sen. Harry Reid, D-Nev., made much progress.

Like its Senate counterpart, the House ESA revision (HR 2275) proposed in September 1995 by Young and Pombo narrowed the definition of "harm" to those actions that killed or injured an endangered or threatened species. To protect species' habitat, the bill required federal officials to enter into cooperative management agreements with landowners, provide compensation to landowners when a regulatory action caused a property to lose more than 20 percent of its value, or provide financial incentives to encourage conservation. The Young-Pombo measure failed to move beyond approval (27–17) by the House Resources Committee, however. Ironically, although Pombo's hearings had garnered favorable publicity among the ESA's critics, they had also alarmed environmental activists and delayed any legislative action until the fall, by which time the antienvironmentalists had lost momentum. Further complicating matters, activists on the right began criticizing the Young-Pombo bill for not going far enough. The so-called Grassroots ESA Coalition, an alliance of property rights and wise use groups, preferred repealing the act altogether and replacing it with a voluntary wildlife management scheme. As Rob Gordon, executive director of the National Wilderness Institute, a free-market conservation group, remarked: "There are some fundamentally different worldviews on the Endangered Species Act within the [Republican] party. That makes it real difficult to horse trade." [91]

Although they were unable to accomplish their goal of substantially revising the ESA, congressional Republicans were able to achieve some significant legislative victories. Backed by constituents who feared the identification of more species requiring protection, Congress withdrew funding for the National Biological Service. Congress also imposed a moratorium on new endangered species listings and critical habitat designations until December 31, 1996, or until the act was reauthorized, whichever came first.

OUTCOMES

Antienvironmentalists scored some victories in 1995, but environmentalists responded adroitly to legislative attacks by rallying their grassroots base and spurring legislative defenders to action. In spring 1995, at the height of the antienvironmental legislative push, environmentalists took advantage of the twenty-fifth anniversary of Earth Day to launch a $2 million radio and television campaign that generated a blizzard of letters, e-mails, and faxes to members of Congress emphasizing mainstream support for environmental protection.[92] Perceiving Republicans' antienvironmental stance as a liability in the 1996 elections, congressional Democrats lambasted their colleagues in the press. By summer 1995 the Republican Party's unanimity had dissolved, as moderate Republicans such as New Jersey's Jim Saxton, New York's Sherwood Boehlert, and Rhode Island's John Chafee began to challenge the party's antienvironmental initiatives. In late 1995 House Speaker Newt Gingrich granted that the party's conservative wing had mishandled the environmental issue all spring and summer.[93] Sen. John McCain, R-Ariz., warned that "polls indicate that the environment is the voters' number one concern about continued Republican leadership of Congress" because Republicans were viewed as "too eager to swing the meat axe of repeal when the scalpel of reform is what's needed." [94] Even more worrisome to Republicans, polls indicated that voters, by a margin of more than two to one, had more confidence in Democrats than Republicans to protect the environment, and 55 percent of Republicans said they did not trust their own party to protect their environment.[95]

By the end of 1995 moderate Republicans had persuaded fellow party members to back off, and in early 1996 Congress authorized the president to lift the moratorium on listing endangered species, which he did in late April. In March 1996 Gingrich appointed a task force on the environment, chaired by adversaries Boehlert and Pombo, in hopes of reconciling the ideological and regional differences that had riven the party. By mid-May 1996 supporters of property rights legislation in Congress were also on the defensive. Republican staff members announced that they were canceling plans to bring Senator Dole's bill to the Senate floor because it could not muster even the majority of votes needed to save face, much less the sixty needed to break an anticipated filibuster.[96] Also in mid-May the task force released a one-page "vision statement and principles," which it billed as a blueprint for the party's new environmental agenda. In September 1996 a chastened Congress proceeded to approve a fiscal 1997 appropriations bill that contained relatively few antienvironmental riders. Many of those originally included were dropped after the administration expressed its unwavering opposition.[97]

Recognizing the clout of environmentalists in his electoral coalition and hoping to establish a legacy, in 1996 President Clinton launched an environmental counteroffensive. He devoted an unusually long time in his State of the Union address to environmental issues and drew loud cheers and applause when he derided Republicans' efforts to roll back federal regulations. Then, in the midst of his reelection campaign, Clinton established a 1.7-million-acre national monument in the red rock country of southern Utah, using authority granted under the Antiquities Act of 1906. In November the EPA proposed strict new standards for airborne particulates and ground-level ozone, a move strongly opposed by coal-fired utilities, carmakers, and petroleum refiners. In December the Army Corps of Engineers decided to phase out over two years Reagan-era regulations enabling fast-track approval for property owners to drain wetlands smaller than ten acres. Then, on December 13 the administration terminated the two-year-old and much-reviled timber salvage program (see chapter 8) two weeks before it was due to expire. Republicans' objections to the president's actions were muted. As Rep. Henry Bonilla, R-Texas, pointed out, "We just can't charge ahead in the way we did in the last few years. In the [public relations] battle, we have been defeated." [98]

The antienvironmental movement was down but not out, however. In 1999 Jeff Ruch, executive director of Public Employees for Environmental Responsibility, claimed, "Though the flamboyant challenges to the federal government of the mid-1990s abated after the shock of the Oklahoma City bombing in 1995, the number of reported death threats, discoveries of pipe bombs, arsons of buildings, and other incidents against the Forest Service and . . . the Bureau of Land Management keeps rising." [99] Using greater savvy in drawing up their bills, and abandoning their confrontational tone, opponents of strict environmental protection regulations forged ahead in the 105th and 106th Congresses (1997–2000). In September 1998 a coalition of prominent environmental groups tried to draw public attention to the antienvironmental activity quietly taking place in Congress by taking out a full-page ad in the *New York Times* labeling the 105th Congress the "worst ever" with respect to the environment. The ad lambasted Congress for being on the verge of passing nearly seventy antienvironmental riders, more than twice as many as the 104th Congress had attached to appropriations bills. President Clinton continued to use his veto power to hold off the most damaging of these for the remainder of his term, but with the advent of the more conservative Bush administration in 2001, antienvironmentalists hoped their legislative fortunes would rebound.

They have not been disappointed. President Bush made his priorities clear from the outset by appointing timber industry lobbyist Mark Rey to be the nation's top forestry official; James L. Connaughton, a former power company lobbyist, as chairman of the Council on Environmental Quality; and Gale Norton, formerly of the conservative Mountain States Legal Foundation, to the post of Interior secretary. The president created an energy task force led by Vice President Dick Cheney and consisting almost entirely of representatives of the utility, oil, and gas industries. Not surprisingly, the task force recommended (and the Interior Department has granted) greater access to energy resources on the public lands and outer continental shelf.

In addition, the administration relaxed Clean Air and Clean Water Acts rules in a variety of ways. For example, the EPA rewrote the New Source Performance Review rule to allow old, coal-fired plants to modernize without installing state-of-the-art pollution controls. The EPA also eliminated a rule that prevented coal companies from burying Appalachian streams under waste from mountaintop mining. The administration's approach to forest management included abandoning a Clinton-era rule to expand protection of roadless areas; the Bush administration allowed loggers to cut old-growth trees in the name of fire prevention. The Fish and Wildlife Service has dramatically curtailed enforcement of the ESA, adding fewer than ten species a year to the endangered species list, compared to sixty-five per year under Clinton and fifty-nine per year under George H. W. Bush. And it has designated only half of the "critical habitat" recommended by its own scientists.[100] Finally, to the dismay of environmentalists, the president reneged on his campaign pledge to take action on global warming and instead ruled out mandatory CO_2 emissions reductions. Yet, despite heavy lobbying by environmental groups, Bush won reelection in November 2004, a result that has caused serious introspection among environmental leaders.

The antienvironmental backlash is evident at the state level as well. Environmentalists were stunned in November 2004 when 61 percent of Oregon voters approved Measure 37, a ballot initiative that requires state and local governments to compensate property owners, or forgo enforcement, when regulations reduce the value of their property. Because the measure is retroactive—that is, it applies to land purchased prior to the imposition of land-use controls in the last three decades—environmentalists worry that it threatens to undermine Oregon's much-vaunted planning regime, which is the nation's most progressive. Particularly ominous was the fact that a majority of voters in Multnomah County, home to the city of Portland, approved the initiative (see chapter 17). Emboldened by the success of Measure 37, in early 2005 critics of Washington State's current land-use policies began exploring the possibility of filing a similar ballot proposition.

CONCLUSIONS

The antienvironmental movement that gathered steam in the late 1980s and culminated in the mid-1990s was, in part, "a desperate effort to defend the hegemony of the cultural and economic values of the agricultural and extractive industries of the rural West." [101] It employed a wide array of tactics to enhance its impact on policymaking at the state and national levels. Its leaders brought together an explosive coalition of westerners advocating unrestricted access to federal lands and easterners concerned with private property rights, integrating them under the banner of individual freedom. Although heavily backed by industry, antienvironmental leaders appealed to citizens by reframing environmental policies as the way elitist environmentalists impose their values and preferences on other Americans. They publicized compelling stories of heroes, victims, and villains that drew on longstanding American values of community autonomy and antipathy toward the federal government. Even more remarkable, they appropriated the staple tactics of the environmental movement, from grassroots organizing to nationalizing policy conflict to filing lawsuits. And then they lambasted environmentalists for causing controversy and gridlock. On occasion, the antienvironmental movement took the monkey-wrenching of environmental extremists to a new level, using violence and intimidation against environmental researchers and activists, as well as federal officials trying to implement environmental regulations.

Antienvironmentalists were sufficiently vocal by the mid-1990s to convince congressional Republicans that they could get electoral credit by rolling back environmental laws. Believing they were responding to powerful national sentiment, antienvironmental members of Congress were taken aback when the public reacted with hostility to their efforts. It appears that many Republicans in the 1990s fell into the "salience trap," assuming that, because people did not mention the environment as the nation's most important problem in polls, that the environmental consensus had dissolved. In fact, throughout the early 1990s, an annual survey conducted by Roper Starch Worldwide and Times Mirror Magazines consistently showed that more than three-quarters of Americans viewed themselves as active environmentalists or sympathetic to the environmentalist cause.[102] A majority of Americans also expressed their willingness to sacrifice economic growth for environmental protection.[103] A 1995 *Time*/CNN poll found that 63 percent of those questioned opposed any reduction in protection for endangered species; 59 percent opposed the expansion of logging, mining, or ranching on public lands; and fully two-thirds were against opening the Arctic National Wildlife Refuge to oil and gas exploration.[104] In the summer of 1995 Republican pollster Frank Lutz, one of the architects of the Contract with America, conceded, "The public may not like or admire regulations, may not think more are necessary, but [it] puts environmental protection as a higher priority than cutting regulations." [105]

Latent public opinion alone would not have been sufficient to prevent change, however. Environmentalists had to respond to the antienvironmental backlash by mobilizing supporters; showing that public opinion needs to be activated and brought to the attention of politicians to have an impact. To enhance their influence, environmentalists formed alliances with a variety of groups, from the National League of Cities to the United Mine Workers of America, to defeat antienvironmental legislation. Just as antienvironmentalists associated environmentalism with communism, environmentalists linked their foes with the religious right and militant militia groups in the West. They publicized violent incidents and demonized wise use leaders in an attempt to dilute the movement's appeal to moderates. They also exposed antienvironmentalists' tactics of attaching riders to spending bills and hustling legislation through Congress with minimal debate.

Such a reactive strategy is unlikely to be sufficient in the long run, however. The persistence and periodic successes of the antienvironmental movement suggest that the "environmental consensus" is neither deep nor reliable in the face of tradeoffs with other core values. Conservatives have been effective at persuading ordinary people they are bearing the costs of regulation, while environmentalists have done less well at showing people how they benefit from such regulations. As William Cronon, an environmental historian at the University of Wisconsin, admonishes environmentalists:

> We fool ourselves if we imagine that these new antienvironmental threats or their underlying cultural causes will simply go away. We need to figure out why certain kinds of antienvironmental arguments—about property rights, about excessive government regulation, about state interference with private liberty—are resonating with the public today more than 15 years ago. That means we have to look carefully at what our enemies are saying to find out what's right about it.[106]

Many environmentalists have, in fact, been reassessing the traditional approaches to environmental protection in the 1990s in response to the backlash those regulations engendered. They have considered a host of approaches to addressing environmental problems—from incentive-based policies to community-based decision making to ecosystem management—all of which are changing the dynamics of environmental politics.

QUESTIONS TO CONSIDER

- How strongly held do you think American environmental values are, and why do you believe this?
- Are the concerns of wise use and property rights advocates justified? Why do you think their arguments resonate so widely?
- Should the antienvironmental backlash prompt environmentalists to reexamine their goals and strategies? If so, what sorts of approaches should environmentalists be considering?

Notes

1. Michael Mintrom and Sandra Vergari, "Advocacy Coalitions, Policy Entrepreneurs, and Policy Change," *Policy Studies Journal* 24 (1996): 420–434.
2. John W. Kingdon, *Agendas, Alternatives, and Public Policies*, 2d ed. (New York: Addison-Wesley Educational Publishers, Inc., 1995); Carol S. Weissert, "Policy Entrepreneurs, Policy Opportunists, and Legislative Effectiveness," *American Politics Quarterly* 19 (April 1991): 262–274.
3. Michael Mintrom, "Policy Entrepreneurs and the Diffusion of Innovation," *American Journal of Political Science* 41 (July 1997): 738–770.
4. Jane J. Mansbridge, *Why We Lost the ERA* (Chicago: University of Chicago Press, 1986).
5. Lawrence R. Jacobs and Robert Y. Shapiro, *Politicians Don't Pander: Political Manipulation and the Loss of Democratic Responsiveness* (Chicago: University of Chicago Press, 2000).
6. Timothy Egan, "The 1994 Campaign: Western States," *New York Times*, November 4, 1994, 29.
7. Everett Carll Ladd and Karlyn H. Bowman, *Attitudes Toward the Environment: Twenty-Five Years After Earth Day* (Washington, D.C.: AEI Press, 1995); Deborah Guber, *The Grassroots of a Green Revolution* (Cambridge: MIT Press, 2003).
8. Robert Cameron Mitchell, "Public Opinion and the Green Lobby: Poised for the 1990s?" in *Environmental Policy in the 1990s*, ed. Norman J. Vig and Michael E. Kraft (Washington, D.C.: CQ Press, 1990), 81–99.
9. R. Douglas Arnold, *The Logic of Congressional Action* (New Haven: Yale University Press, 1990).
10. Keith Krehbiel, *Pivotal Politics: A Theory of U.S. Lawmaking* (Chicago: University of Chicago Press, 1998).
11. The Fifth Amendment reads: "No person shall ... be deprived of life, liberty, or property, without due process of law; nor shall private property be taken for public use, without just compensation."
12. See, for example, Peter Shrag, *Paradise Lost: California's Experience, America's Future* (New York: New Press, 1998); David Broder, *Democracy Derailed: Initiative Campaigns and the Power of Money* (New York: Harcourt Brace, 2000); Richard Ellis, *Democratic Delusions* (Lawrence: University Press of Kansas, 2002).
13. David Schmidt, *Citizen Lawmakers: The Ballot Initiative Revolution* (Philadelphia: Temple University Press, 1989).
14. Jacqueline Vaughn Switzer, *Green Backlash: The History and Politics of the Environmental Opposition in the United States* (Boulder: Lynne Rienner Publishers, 1997).
15. Norman J. Vig, "Presidential Leadership: From the Reagan to the Bush Administration," in *Environmental Policy in the 1990s*, 33–58.
16. Quoted in Philip Shabecoff, *A Fierce Green Fire: The American Environmental Movement* (New York: Farrar, Straus, and Giroux, 1993), 208.
17. Mitchell, "Public Opinion and the Green Lobby." William Ruckelshaus, Gorsuch's replacement at EPA, acknowledged that the administration had misread its mandate on the environment, confusing the public's wish for improving the way government pursued the goals of protecting the environment and public health with a desire to change the goals themselves. See Philip Shabecoff, "Ruckelshaus Says Administration Misread Mandate on the Environment," *New York Times*, July 27, 1983, 1.
18. Alan Gottlieb, ed., *The Wise Use Agenda* (Bellevue, Wash.: Free Enterprise Press, 1989).
19. Margaret Kriz, "Land Mine," *National Journal*, October 23, 1993, 2531–4.
20. Sandra K. Davis, "Fighting Over Public Lands," in *Western Public Lands and Environmental Politics*, ed. Charles Davis (Boulder: Westview Press, 1997), 11–31.
21. Samantha Sanchez, "How the West Is Won," *American Prospect*, March–April 1996, 37–42; Will Nixon, "Wising Up to Wise Use," *E Magazine*, September/October 1992, 34.

22. Kate O'Callaghan, "Whose Agenda for America," *Audubon*, September-October 1992, 80–91.
23. Macwilliams Cosgrove Snider, *The Wise Use Movement: Strategic Analysis and the Fifty State Review* (Washington, D.C.: Environmental Working Group, March 1993), 27.
24. Quoted in O'Callaghan, "Whose Agenda," 84.
25. Nancie G. Marzulla, "The Property Rights Movement: How It Began and Where It Is Headed," in *Land Rights: The 1990s Property Rights Rebellion*, ed. Bruce Yandle (Lanham, Md.: Rowman and Littlefield, 1995), 22.
26. Quoted in Kenneth Jost, "Property Rights," *CQ Researcher*, June 16, 1995, 516.
27. Marzulla, "The Property Rights Movement."
28. Will Nelson, "Fear & Loathing in the Adirondacks," *E Magazine*, September/October 1992, 28–35.
29. Thomas A. Lewis, "Cloaked in a Wise Disguise," in *Let the People Judge: Wise Use and the Private Property Rights Movement*, ed. John Echeverria and Raymond Booth Eby (Washington, D.C.: Island Press, 1995), 13–20.
30. Quoted in Sanchez, "How the West Is Won."
31. Quoted in Marla Williams, "Save the People!" *Boston Globe*, January 13, 1992.
32. Quoted in O'Callaghan, "Whose Agenda," 84.
33. Quoted in Williams, "Save the People!"
34. Ibid.
35. Quoted in Switzer, *Green Backlash*, 197.
36. Quoted in O'Callaghan, "Whose Agenda," 84.
37. Keith Schneider, "Fighting to Keep U.S. Rules from Devaluing Land," *New York Times*, January 9, 1995, 1.
38. Ann Reilly Dowd, "Environmentalists Are on the Run," *Fortune*, September 19, 1994, 91–92, 96–100.
39. Jost, "Property Rights."
40. Karol J. Ceplo, "Land Rights Conflicts in the Regulation of Wetlands," in *Land Rights*, 103–149.
41. Quoted in David Helvarg, *The War Against the Greens* (San Francisco: Sierra Club Books, 1997), 20.
42. Ben Bolch and Harold Lyons, *Apocalypse Not: Science, Economics, and Environmentalism* (Washington, D.C.: Cato Institute, 1993).
43. Helvarg, *The War Against the Greens*.
44. Phil Brick, "Determined Opposition: The Wise Use Movement Challenges Environmentalism," *Environment*, October 1995, 16–20, 36–41.
45. Some experts have questioned whether such firms rightly qualify for nonprofit status as "public interest" charities. One law professor who examined 132 cases brought by the Pacific Legal Foundation found that 70 of them were invalid by the terms of the IRS requirements and another 16 were questionable. See Helvarg, *The War Against the Greens*.
46. Switzer, *Green Backlash*.
47. Mark Dowie, "The Wayward West," *Outside*, November 1995, 59–67, 152–154; Timothy Egan, "Court Puts Down Rebellion over Control of Federal Land," *New York Times*, March 16, 1996, 1.
48. Richard A. Epstein, *Takings: Private Property and the Power of Eminent Domain* (Cambridge: Harvard University Press, 1985).
49. Jonathan Walters, "The Property Rights Bust," *Governing*, June 1999, 38–41.
50. Karen Curran, "Judge's Decision to Have Impact on Property Owners," *Boston Globe*, March 12, 1995, 1.
51. Joseph L. Sax, "Property Rights and the Economy of Nature: Understanding Lucas v. South Carolina Coastal Commission," *Stanford Law Review* 45 (May 1993): 1433–55; see also James R. Rinehart and Jeffrey J. Pompe, "The Lucas Case and the Conflict Over Property Rights," in *Land Rights*, 67–101.

52. Although it is a less-visible forum, plaintiffs also pursued claims in the U.S. Court of Federal Claims. See Switzer, *Green Backlash*.

53. Rinehart and Pompe, "The Lucas Case."

54. Ruth Marcus, "Issues Groups Fund Seminars for Judges," *Washington Post*, April 9, 1998, 1.

55. Helvarg, *War Against the Greens*.

56. Ibid.

57. Quoted in Dowie, "The Wayward West," 64.

58. Ibid. See also Richard Lacayo and Michael Riley, "This Land Is Whose Land?" *Time*, October 23, 1995, 68–71.

59. Helvarg, *War Against the Greens*, 13.

60. Nearly half of the seventy-three new members of the House received a zero rating for 1995 from the League of Conservation Voters.

61. Quoted in Bob Benenson, "GOP Sets the 104th Congress on New Regulatory Course," *Congressional Quarterly Weekly Report*, June 17, 1995, 1693–1701.

62. Quoted in Scott Allen, " 'Contract' Reframes Issue of Environment's Worth," *Boston Globe*, February 6, 1995, 25.

63. Quoted in Allan Freedman, "Accomplishments, Missteps Mark Congress' Record," *Congressional Quarterly Weekly Report*, October 12, 1996, 2918–22.

64. Quoted in Margaret Kriz, "Out of the Wilderness," *National Journal*, April 8, 1995, 864.

65. Ibid.

66. They staffed the committee with eight members whose League of Conservation Voters scores were less than 25 percent and League of Private Property Rights scores were over 80 percent. See ibid.

67. Freedman, "Accomplishments, Missteps."

68. The law defined property as land, any interest in land, and any proprietary water right.

69. Allan Freedman, "Property Rights Bill Advances but Faces Uncertainty," *Congressional Quarterly Weekly Report*, December 23, 1995, 3884–5.

70. Allan Freedman, "GOP Trying to Find Balance After Early Stumbles," *Congressional Quarterly Weekly Report*, January 20, 1996, 151–153.

71. Neal R. Pierce, "Takings—The Comings and Goings," *Congressional Quarterly Weekly Report*, January 6, 1996, 37.

72. Walters, "The Property Rights Bust."

73. Because the initiative was not originated by the state government, the Washington measure could not be amended by the legislature or vetoed by the governor. The only recourse for opponents was to gather 90,000 signatures within ninety days of legislative approval.

74. A referendum allows the voters to consider a disputed law directly, whereas an initiative allows voters to put the matter before the legislature. See Louis Jacobson, "Land-Rights Battle with Fresh Twists," *National Journal*, October 14, 1995, 2537–40.

75. Switzer, *Green Backlash*.

76. Timothy Egan, "Unlikely Alliances Attack Property Rights Measures," *New York Times*, May 15, 1995, 1.

77. Jacobson, "Land-Rights Battle."

78. The term "wetlands" encompasses a variety of shallow water, periodically flooded, and high-groundwater environments. Wetlands perform a host of ecological functions: they store flood waters by absorbing overflow waters during excessively wet periods and gradually releasing water as a river or stream recedes; they filter sediments and pollutants out of the water supply; and they replenish groundwater systems and provide critical habitat for fish and wildlife, including nearly half of all federally listed threatened and endangered species. By the early 1990s, when the antienvironmental movement was gaining steam, the nation had lost more than

half of its original wetland endowment, with only about 95 million acres of wetlands remaining in the lower forty-eight states, and was continuing to lose about
250,000–300,000 acres of wetlands each year, or about thirty acres an hour, to development and cultivation. See Dianne Dumanoski, "Heavy Toll Seen if 'Drier' Wetlands Are Developed," *Boston Globe*, December 10, 1991, 1; Jon Kusler, "Wetlands
Delineation: An Issue of Science or Politics?" *Environment*, March 1992, 6–11, 29–37;
and Douglas A. Thompson and Thomas G. Yocom, "Uncertain Ground," *Technology
Review*, August/September 1993, 20–29.

79. Bob Benenson, "Clean Water Law Revisions Mark Arrival of New Era," *Congressional Quarterly Weekly Report*, April 8, 1995, 1018–9.

80. John H. Cushman Jr., "Industry Helped Draft Clean Water Law," *New York Times*,
March 22, 1995, 1.

81. Quoted in John H. Cushman Jr., "House Panel Backs Easing of U.S. Water Standards," *New York Times*, March 30, 1995, 21.

82. John H. Cushman Jr., "House and Science Panels Clash on Wetlands Fate," *New
York Times*, April 7, 1995, 30.

83. Ibid.

84. John H. Cushman Jr., "Scientists Reject Criteria for Wetlands Bill," *New York Times*,
May 10, 1995, 1.

85. Quoted in John H. Cushman Jr., "Crossing Lines on Pollution Bill Clouds Future of
Environmental Issues," *New York Times*, May 15, 1995, 12.

86. Margaret Kriz, "Caught in the Act," *National Journal*, December 16, 1995, 3090–4.

87. Donald Barry of the World Wildlife Fund, quoted in Timothy Egan, "Strongest U.S.
Environment Law May Become Endangered Species," *New York Times*, May 26,
1992, 1.

88. John H. Cushman Jr., "Babbitt Seeks to Ease Rules in Bid to Rescue Imperiled
Species Law," *New York Times*, March 7, 1995, C4; William K. Stevens, "Future of
Endangered Species Act in Doubt as Law Is Debated," *New York Times*, May 16,
1995, C4.

89. Quoted in Stevens, "Future of Endangered Species Act."

90. Quoted in Timothy Egan, "Industries Affected by Endangered Species Act Help a
Senator Rewrite Its Provisions," *New York Times*, April 13, 1995, 20.

91. Quoted in Kriz, "Caught in the Act."

92. Michael Satchell, "A New Day for Earth Lovers," *U.S. News & World Report*, April
24, 1995, 58–61.

93. David S. Cloud and Jackie Koszczuk, "GOP's All-or-Nothing Approach Hangs on
a Balanced Budget," *Congressional Quarterly Weekly Report*, December 9, 1995,
3709–15.

94. John McCain, "Nature Is Not a Liberal Plot," *New York Times*, November 22, 1996,
31.

95. John H. Cushman Jr., "G.O.P. Backing Off From Tough Stand over Environment,"
New York Times, January 26, 1996, 1.

96. Margaret Kriz, "Taking Issue," *National Journal*, June 1, 1996, 1200–4.

97. Freedman, "Accomplishments, Missteps."

98. Quoted in Allan Freedman, "GOP Cautious on Easing Rules Despite Clinton's For-
ays," *Congressional Quarterly Weekly Report*, January 18, 1997, 168–170.

99. Jeff Ruch, "Nature's Guardians Still Face Disrespect," *New York Times*, December
22, 1999, 27.

100. Douglas Jehl, "On Environmental Rules, Bush Sees a Balance, Critics a Threat,"
New York Times, February 23, 2003, Sec. 1, 1; Juliet Eilperin, "Endangered Species
Act's Protections are Trimmed," *Washington Post*, July 4, 2004, A01; Emily Cousins,
Robert Perks, and Wesley Warren, *Rewriting the Rules: The Bush Administration's
First-Term Environmental Record* (Washington, D.C.: Natural Resources Defense
Council, 2005).

101. Ralph Maughan and Douglas Nilson, "What's Old and What's New About the Wise Use Movement" (Idaho State Department of Political Science, April 23, 1993); www.nwcitizen.com/publicgood/reports/maughan.htm.
102. Benenson, "GOP Sets the 104th Congress on a New Regulatory Course"; Ladd and Bowman, *Attitudes Toward the Environment*.
103. Benenson, "GOP Sets the 104th Congress on a New Regulatory Course"; Gallup Poll, April 22, 1995. Ladd and Bowman challenge the results of questions asking respondents to choose between economic growth and environmental protection. They point out that many Americans do not believe there is a tradeoff between growth and the environment. They also note that people are reluctant to support environmental protection in their own community if it means that jobs will be lost as a result. See Ladd and Bowman, *Attitudes Toward the Environment*, 23–27.
104. Benenson, "GOP Sets the 104th Congress on a New Regulatory Course."
105. Quoted in Margaret Kriz, "Drawing a Green Line in the Sand," *National Journal*, August 12, 1995, 2076.
106. Quoted in Kriz, "Taking Issue."

Recommended Reading

Echeverria, John, and Raymond Booth Eby, eds. *Let the People Judge: Wise Use and the Private Property Rights Movement*. Washington, D.C.: Island Press, 1995.
Helvarg, David. *The War Against the Greens*. San Francisco: Sierra Club Books, 1997.
Switzer, Jacqueline Vaughn. *Green Backlash: The History and Politics of Environmental Opposition in the United States*. Boulder: Lynne Rienner, 1997.
Yandle, Bruce, ed. *Land Rights: The 1990s Property Rights Rebellion*. Lanham, Md.: Rowman and Littlefield, 1995.

Web Sites

www.ewg.org (Environmental Working Group site)
www.cato.org (Cato Institute site)
www.heritage.org (Heritage Foundation site)

CHAPTER 14

Market-Based Solutions

Acid Rain and the Clean Air Act Amendments of 1990

The Clean Air Act of 1970 was the federal government's first serious step toward reducing the nation's air pollution (see chapter 2). In 1977 Congress amended the Clean Air Act and scheduled it for reauthorization in 1981. But President Ronald Reagan opposed any action on the bill, and legislators were deeply divided on the issue of acid rain.[1] As a result, the act languished in Congress throughout the 1980s. Finally, after a decade of stalemate, Congress and the administration of President George H. W. Bush agreed on a clean air plan that included as its signature provision an innovative allowance trading approach to reducing emissions that cause acid rain. The regulations required by the Clean Air Act Amendments of 1990 took effect in 1995 and aimed by the year 2000 to cut in half emissions of sulfur dioxide (SO_2), acid rain's main precursor.

This case illustrates the importance of regional concerns in Congress. The desire to protect local or regional economic interests is a powerful reason to resist making environmental policy more protective. The regional emphasis of Congress is particularly pronounced in this case because acid rain is a transboundary problem: those who bear the environmental burden of its effects are in a different region from those who cause it. As previous cases have made clear, the organization and procedures of Congress provide its members with many ways of resisting the imposition of direct, visible economic costs on their constituents: authorizing subcommittees can delete legislative provisions during markup; committee chairs can prevent a bill from reaching the floor, as can a majority of committee members; and legislative leaders, such as the Speaker of the House or the Senate majority leader, can refuse to schedule a vote on a bill. Even if a bill does reach the floor, its opponents may attach enough hostile amendments to cripple it, or, in the Senate, a minority can filibuster it.

Because it is relatively easy to block policy change, leadership is essential to the passage of major new laws. The president sets the legislative agenda and therefore plays a pivotal role in initiating policy change and mobilizing legislative supporters. The president has numerous political resources—including political favors as well as popularity and prestige—that can be deployed to assemble a legislative coalition. Executive-legislative branch rivalry is intense, however, so presidential backing is rarely sufficient; even when the same party controls the White House and Congress, skilled leaders in the House and Senate are also necessary to shepherd a policy through the cumbersome legislative process. Like the president, congressional leaders have a variety of resources at their disposal—from the authority to set the agenda to the ability to distribute rewards for cooperation. At least as important, however, are their reputations, personal negotiating skills, and the relationships they have built with fellow members of Congress.

In a legislative contest, science can play a critical, if indirect, role. While opponents of environmentally protective regulations typically emphasize scientific uncertainty and call for more research in hopes of delaying change, proponents of those policies rely on scientific evidence to buttress their claims of environmental harm and the need for prompt government action. If environmentalists have managed to persuade the public that a problem is serious and warrants remediation, a legislative leader is more likely not only to adopt the issue but also to succeed in recruiting allies. The more widely accepted a causal story for a salient problem, the less credible opposing positions become.[2] Moreover, such stories provide rank-and-file members with handy explanations for their positions that they can give constituents.[3]

International pressure can also affect legislative dynamics. Because pollutants emitted in the United States precipitate in Canada, the Canadian government, as well as Canadian scientists and environmentalists, pushed to get acid rain onto the U.S. policy agenda and then actively tried to influence policy. According to one observer, the issue "overshadowed almost all other elements of the bilateral relationship" between the United States and Canada.[4] Although they had little direct effect on the legislative process, the Canadians provided a steady stream of reliable information to, and publicity for, the proregulation side, which in turn helped to shape public and elite views about the need for controls.

Finally, policy entrepreneurs can facilitate the passage of new legislation by furnishing leaders with a novel solution that transforms the political landscape by broadening supportive coalitions or breaking up opposing ones. In this case, the allowance trading mechanism proposed for acid rain helped break the legislative logjam by appealing to conservatives who believe such market-based approaches are superior to conventional approaches in two respects. First, market-based policy instruments allow polluters who can clean up cheaply to do more and those for whom cleanup is costly to do less, which in theory reduces overall pollution to the desired level at a minimum total cost. Second, market-based tools create incentives for businesses to create and adopt new technologies and to continue reducing pollution beyond the target level because they save money by doing so.[5] The allowance trading mechanism also divided opponents by promising benefits to polluters that could clean up cheaply and then sell their allowances. If proponents of policy change can devise an attractive coalition-building solution, they are more likely to be able to capitalize on the political momentum unleashed when an opportunity presents itself.

BACKGROUND

Scientists began documenting the effects of acid rain more than 100 years ago. Robert Angus Smith, a nineteenth-century English chemist, was the first to detect the occurrence of acid precipitation. He coined the term "acid rain" and conducted extensive tests of its properties, but his research was largely ignored. Similarly, work by ecologist Eville Gorham on the causes of acid precipitation and its consequences for aquatic systems in the 1950s and 1960s "was met by a thundering silence from both the scientific community and the public at large." [6] But in the late 1960s Swedish soil scientist Svante Odén rekindled scientific interest in acid rain. Integrating knowledge from the scientific disciplines of limnology, agricultural science, and atmospheric chemistry, Odén developed a coherent analysis of the behavior of acid deposition over time and across regions. He hypothesized that acid precipitation would change surface water chemistry, lead to declines in fish populations, reduce forest growth, increase plant disease, and accelerate materials damage.[7]

Odén's research laid the groundwork for conclusions unveiled at the 1972 United Nations Conference on the Human Environment in Stockholm. At the conference, a group of Swedish scientists presented a case study demonstrating that acid precipitation attributable to SO_2 emissions from human-made sources—primarily industrial processes and utilities—was having adverse ecological and human health effects. These findings, in turn, prompted further efforts to identify the causes of acid deposition and to document its direct and indirect impacts on the environment.

Acid Rain Gets on the U.S. Agenda

Growing scientific concern about acid rain was a primary factor in getting the problem on the U.S. political agenda. In 1975 the U.S. Forest Service sponsored an international symposium on acid rain and forest ecosystems, and shortly thereafter Professor Ellis Cowling, a Canadian expert, testified at a congressional hearing on the need for more funding to study the phenomenon. In 1977 President Jimmy Carter's Council on Environmental Quality suggested that the United States needed a comprehensive national program to address acid rain. This argument gained momentum in the executive branch, and in 1978 Carter began to take steps toward that goal by establishing the Bilateral Research Consultation Group on the Long-Range Transport of Air Pollution to conduct a joint investigation with Canada. Calling acid precipitation "a global environmental problem of the greatest importance," the following year the president asked Congress to expand funding for research and to investigate possible control measures under the Clean Air Act.

Fueling environmentalists' interest in acid rain policy, a series of reports in 1978, 1979, and 1980 by the International Joint Commission, which had been created to address U.S.-Canada water quality issues in the Great Lakes, suggested that, if not controlled, acid rain could render 50,000 lakes in the United States and Canada lifeless by 1995, destroy the productivity of vast areas of forest, and contaminate the drinking water supplies of millions of people.[8] In addition, the Bilateral Research Consultation Group issued two reports, in October 1979 and November 1980, which together comprised the first comprehensive statement of scientific knowledge about acid rain and its likely effects in eastern North America. One of the group's major findings was that at least 50 percent of Canada's acid deposition originated in the United States, whereas only 15 percent of acid rain in the United States came from Canada.[9]

The Carter Administration Responds

The concern among environmentalists and high-level Canadian officials generated by these reports created pressure on the United States to do something about acid rain. In 1980 President Carter signed the U.S.-Canada memorandum of intent to negotiate an agreement on transboundary air pollution. He also approved the Acid Precipitation Act of 1980, which established the Interagency Task Force on Acid Precipitation and charged it with planning and implementing the National Acid Precipitation Assessment Program, a comprehensive research program to clarify the causes and effects of acid rain.

Impatient for a more substantial policy response, Canadian and U.S. advocates of acid rain controls appealed directly to the Environmental Protection Agency (EPA) to regulate acid rain-causing emissions under the Clean Air Act. Although Carter's EPA administrator Douglas Costle conceded that government intervention was warranted, he also expressed concern about the political risks, noting that "in an election year, it is best to keep your head down" rather than embark on a new environmental regulation program.[10] In the administration's final days, Costle acknowledged that U.S. emissions were contributing significantly to acid rain over sensitive areas of Canada, and he laid the groundwork for the next EPA administrator to invoke Clean Air Act Section 115, under which the EPA can require states to reduce the impact of air pollution on foreign countries.

THE CASE

In the early 1980s the topic of acid rain moved from the relative obscurity of scientific inquiry into the political spotlight. Despite the president's commitment to research, during the Carter administration few Americans considered acid rain a policy problem. Yet in 1983 a Harris poll found that nearly two-thirds of those questioned were aware of acid rain and favored strict controls on SO_2 emissions.[11] By this time acid rain had also become a serious foreign policy issue between the United States and Canada, and environmentalists had begun pressuring members of Congress to introduce controls as part of the Clean Air Act reauthorization. But President Reagan and powerful members of Congress opposed such measures, and for nearly a decade they used their political resources to thwart them.

The Emerging Scientific Consensus on Acid Rain

By the early 1980s scientists knew that the precursors to acid rain, SO_2 and nitrogen oxides (NO_x), were released by a variety of natural mechanisms, such as volcanic eruptions, lightning, forest fires, microbial activity in soils, and biogenic processes, but that industrial activity that relied on burning fossil fuels was spewing these substances into the air in quantities that dwarfed nature's output. They estimated that in 1980 the United States emitted about 27 million tons of SO_2 and 21 million tons of NO_x; that the thirty-one states east of the Mississippi River emitted about 80 percent of that SO_2 (22 million tons) and two-thirds of the NO_x (14 million tons); that nearly three-quarters of the SO_2 emitted east of the Mississippi came from power plants; and that forty enormous coal-fired plants clustered in the Midwest and the Ohio and Tennessee Valleys—a single one of which emitted about 200,000 tons of SO_2 a year—were responsible for almost half of the region's SO_2 emissions.[12]

Furthermore, scientists were beginning to recognize that, because these enormous plants had smokestacks as high as the tallest skyscraper, their SO_2 emissions traveled hundreds or even thousands of miles downwind, turning to acid and falling to earth along the way. Therefore, more than 50 percent of the acid sulfate in the Adirondacks of New York came from midwestern sources; about 20 percent came from the large metal smelters in Ontario, Canada; and less than 10 percent originated in the Northeast. Although the sources of NO_x were more diverse than those of SO_2, scientists estimated that more than half of all NO_x emissions also came from the smokestacks of power plants and industrial sources. Automobiles, as well as other forms of transportation, were the second major source of NO_x.

Scientists were also gaining confidence in their understanding of the consequences of acid rain, particularly for aquatic systems. They knew that healthy lakes normally have a pH of around 5.6 or above; that when a lake's pH drops to 5.0, its biological processes begin to suffer; and that at pH 4.5 or below, a lake is generally incapable of supporting much life. Because precipitation in the eastern United States had an average pH of 4.3, that region's lakes and streams whose soils lacked alkaline buffering had become highly acidic.[13] Lakes at high altitudes appeared to be particularly sensitive to acid rain because, surrounded only by rocky outcroppings, they tended to be poorly buffered. Furthermore, researchers discovered that when water ran off snow or ice or during snowmelt, high-altitude lakes received a large pulse of acid capable of killing fish and other aquatic life outright.[14]

Scientific understanding of the impacts of acidification on terrestrial ecosystems, particularly evergreen forests, was more uncertain, and researchers had only a sketchy understanding of the complex interaction between acid rain and other pollutants. Since the 1960s scientists had observed a massive decline in many forests in parts of Europe and the eastern United States, particularly in high-elevation coniferous forests. For example, in sites above 850 meters in New York's Adirondacks, the Green Mountains of Vermont, and the White Mountains of New Hampshire, more than half of the red spruce had died. At lower elevations, researchers had documented injury to hardwoods and softwoods. This loss of forest vitality could not be attributed to insects, disease, or direct poisoning because it was occurring in stands of different ages with different histories of disturbance or disease. Pollution was the only known common factor affecting all of them. In spite of the dimensions of forest decline, however, scientists had been unable to establish a firm causal link between acid rain and forest damage—although all the hypotheses to explain failing tree health in the United States and Europe implicated acid rain, if not as a lethal agent then as a major stress. Laboratory and field studies showed that acid deposition could damage leaves, roots, and microorganisms that form beneficial, symbiotic associations with roots; impair reproduction and survival of seedlings; leach nutrients such as calcium and magnesium from soils; dissolve metals such as aluminum in the soil at levels potentially toxic to plants; and decrease a plant's resistance to other forms of stress, including pollution, climate, insects, and pathogens.[15]

Scientists were also learning about acid rain's adverse effects on soils, and they had ascertained that although the forests in the Northeast and Canada grow on naturally acidic soils, acid rain can still damage these soils. The explanation for this is that most of the important ions in soil are positively charged—hydrogen (acidity); calcium and magnesium (nutrients); and aluminum, lead, mercury, and cadmium (heavy metals)—and are thus bound to the negatively charged surface of large, immobile soil particles. But acid deposition depletes the ability of soil particles to bind positively charged ions and thus unlocks the acidity, nutrients, and toxic metals.[16] Even in lakes that had not begun to acidify, the concentration of calcium and magnesium in the water was increasing with time, suggesting that these nutrients were being leached from surrounding soils.

In addition to its ecological impacts, scientists suspected that acid rain damaged human health, directly or indirectly. They had determined that once acid rain dissolves mercury, lead, cadmium, and other toxic metals in the environment, it transports them into drinking water supplies and thereby into the food chain. In addition, some reports suggested that downwind derivatives of SO_2, known as acid aerosols, posed respiratory health threats to children and asthmatics in the eastern United States. Finally, studies showed that particles of acid sulfate scattered light and reduced visibility, creating a haze that was most pronounced in summer but was present in all seasons. In the eastern United States, visibility was about twenty-five to forty miles absent pollution; it declined to as little as one mile during pollution episodes.

Resistance to Acid Rain Controls in the Reagan Administration

The emerging scientific consensus notwithstanding, upon taking office in 1981, President Reagan made his opposition to acid rain controls clear. Neither he nor the members of his administration believed the benefits of mitigating acid rain outweighed the costs of regulating generators of SO_2 and NO_x. David Stockman, head of the Office of Management and Budget (OMB) during Reagan's first term, expressed the administration's cornucopian view when he queried: "How much are the fish worth in those 170 lakes that account for four percent of the lake area of New York? And does it make sense to spend billions of dollars controlling emissions from sources in Ohio and elsewhere if you're talking about a very marginal volume of dollar value, either in recreational terms or in commercial terms?" [17] But administration officials were rarely so forthright about their values; instead, they continued to contest the science and cite scientific uncertainty as a rationale for delay in formulating a policy to reduce SO_2 and NO_x emissions.

In June 1981 the National Academy of Sciences (NAS) released a comprehensive study of the effects of acid rain and other consequences of fossil fuel combustion. The report's authors concluded that "continued emissions of sulfur and nitrogen oxides at current or accelerated rates, in the face of clear evidence of serious hazards to human health and to the biosphere, will be extremely risky from a long-term economic standpoint as well as from the standpoint of biosphere protection." [18] The NAS called for a 50 percent reduction in the acidity of rain falling in the Northeast. The Reagan administration, while not actually disputing the NAS's scientific findings, labeled the report as "lacking in objectivity." In October 1981 the EPA issued a press release reiterating the administration's position that "scientific uncertainties in the causes and effects of acid rain demand that we proceed cautiously and avoid premature action." [19]

In 1982 the EPA released its own "Critical Assessment" of acid rain, a long-awaited, 1,200-page document that was the combined effort of fifty-four scientists from universities and research institutes around the country. The report's findings clearly indicated a link between human-made emissions in the Midwest and dead and dying lakes and forests, materials damage, and human health effects in the eastern and southeastern United States and southeastern Canada. But high-level, politically sensitive EPA administrators downplayed the report, refusing to draw inferences from it or employ the models proposed in it.

Then, in February 1983 the United States and Canada released the results of the bilateral study initiated by President Carter in 1980. The two countries had hoped to reach a consensus, but they deadlocked over a major section of the report dealing with the effects and significance of acid rain. In an unusual move that reflected high-level opposition to acid rain controls in the United States, the two nations issued separately worded conclusions:

> The Canadians concluded that reducing acid rain "would reduce further damage" to sensitive lakes and streams. The U.S. version omitted the word "damage" and substituted "chemical and biological alterations." The Canadians concluded that "loss of genetic stock would not be reversible." The U.S. version omitted the sentence altogether. The Canadians proposed reducing the amount of acid sulfate deposited by precipitation to less than 20 kilograms of acid sulfate per hectare per year—roughly a 50 percent reduction—in order to protect "all but the most sensitive aquatic ecosystems in Canada." The United States declined to recommend any reductions.[20]

The Reagan White House decided not to have the U.S.-Canada report peer reviewed by the NAS as originally planned and instead hand-picked a scientific panel to review it. To the administration's dismay, however, its own panel strongly recommended action, saying, "It is in the nature of the acid deposition problem that actions have to be taken despite the incomplete knowledge. . . . If we take the conservative point of view that we must wait until the scientific knowledge is definitive, the accumulated deposition and damaged environment may reach the point of irreversibility." [21] Although the panel delivered its interim conclusions well in advance of the House Health and Environment Subcommittee hearings on acid rain, the White House did not circulate them. Instead, administration officials testified before the subcommittee that no action should be taken until further study was done.

It appeared that administration obstruction might end when William Ruckelshaus, a respected environmentalist and the original head of the EPA, assumed leadership of the beleaguered agency in 1983. Although Ruckelshaus described acid rain as one of the "cosmic issues" confronting the nation and named it a priority, it quickly became apparent that the administration had no intention of pursuing acid rain regulation. By August 1984 the White House still had not released the report prepared by its expert panel, leading some members of Congress to question whether the administration was suppressing it. Gene Likens, director of the Institute of Ecosystem Studies of the New York Botanical Gardens and a member of the panel, expressed his irritation in an interview with the *Boston Globe:*

> I have been concerned for some time that the Administration is saying that more research is needed because of scientific uncertainty about acid rain. I think that is an excuse that is not correct. You can go on exploring scientific uncertainty forever. We must do something about acid rain now. Clearly in this case, it was an economic consideration that was most important to the Reagan Administration because of the cost of fixing the problem.[22]

When a spokesman for the White House attributed the delay to panel chairman William Nierenberg, director of the Scripps Institute of Oceanography, he retorted: "Let me say that somebody in the White House ought to print the damn thing. I'm sick and tired of it. What we said in effect was, as practicing scientists, you can't wait for all the scientific evidence." [23]

The administration not only refused to release the panel's conclusions but went so far as to alter important passages of an EPA report entitled "Environmental Progress and Challenges: An EPA Perspective," moderating statements about the urgency of environmental problems. The OMB deleted a sentence referring to the findings of a recent NAS report on the adverse effects of acid rain and replaced a sentence on EPA's intent to establish an acid rain control program with one that simply called for further study of the problem.[24]

Congressional Divisions in the Reagan Years

While the White House dawdled, a coalition of environmental lobbyists urged legislators to pass comprehensive Clean Air Act revisions that included provisions to reduce acid rain. Richard Ayres, cofounder of the Natural Resources Defense Council, was the leading policy entrepreneur for the Clean Air Coalition, an umbrella organization of environmental and other lobbies trying to link SO_2 and NO_x control policies to the acid rain problem. The coalition counted among its allies the Canadian Coalition on Acid Rain, the first registered Canadian lobby in the United States to work for a nongovernmental, nonbusiness citizens' organization and a vocal participant in the U.S. policy debate.[25] At the same time, however, a unified coalition of utilities, industrial polluters, the eastern and midwestern high-sulfur coal industry, the United Mine Workers (UMW), and public officials from eastern and midwestern coal-producing states made its opposition to acid rain controls known to Congress.

In the face of intense lobbying, members of the House and Senate split over three central issues, all of which involved the regional allocation of costs and benefits. First, how much and how quickly should polluters have to reduce SO_2 emissions?[26] Proposals generally called for reductions of between 8 million and 12 million tons of SO_2 emissions from 1980 levels, the bulk of which would have to be made by the midwestern states that burned large quantities of high-sulfur coal.[27] Second, what means should polluters be able to use to reduce SO_2 emissions? Allowing utilities to switch from high-sulfur to low-sulfur coal would be the most cost-effective solution for some, but members from high-sulfur coal–producing states such as Illinois, Kentucky, Pennsylvania, and West Virginia feared major job losses if fuel switching became widespread. On the other hand, requiring all generators to install scrubbers was unacceptable to western states already using low-sulfur coal. The third and most contentious issue was who would pay for the proposed reduction in SO_2 emissions. One financing model employed the "polluter pays" principle; the second included subsidies for the regions bearing the greatest share of the cleanup costs. Midwestern representatives opposed "polluter pays," but western and southern states disliked cost-sharing because they neither caused nor suffered from the effects of acid rain.

Congressional leaders sympathetic to opponents of regulation capitalized on a membership sharply divided along regional lines to foil efforts at acid rain legislation. The Senate Energy Committee—led by senators from coal-mining states, such as Wendell Ford, D-Ky., and Richard Lugar, R-Ind.—opposed acid rain controls. By contrast, in the relatively liberal Senate Environment and Public Works Committee, with members from eastern states affected by acid rain, Robert Stafford, R-Vt, and George Mitchell, D-Maine, introduced bills to curtail emissions of acid rain precursors with a variety of financing provisions, and the Environment Committee repeatedly endorsed these proposals.[28] But in each session Majority Leader Robert Byrd, D-W.Va., representing a state that produces high-sulfur coal, was able to block consideration of the bills on the Senate floor.

Similar regional divisions stymied efforts in the House. The Energy and Commerce Committee annually debated but failed to approve bills to distribute the costs of emissions reductions across electricity users nationally. On several occasions, the committee's powerful chairman, John Dingell, D-Mich., made deft use of his parliamentary power to scuttle clean air legislation because he feared it would include more stringent automobile emissions standards. In 1984 the Energy Committee's Health and Environment Subcommittee's chairman, Henry Waxman, a liberal California Democrat, teamed up with Gerry Sikorski, D-Minn., and 125 others to sponsor a major acid rain bill. The Waxman-Sikorski measure established a goal of a 10 million ton reduction in SO_2 and a 4 million ton reduction in NO_x and distributed the cost nationally by creating a fund financed by a one mill (one-tenth of a cent) federal tax per kilowatt hour of electricity used. But insurmountable political divisions among the constituencies of the Health and Environment Subcommittee killed the measure; environmentalists, supported by recreation interests from New England and New York and by the Canadian government, demanded more stringent restrictions than the bill provided, while coal miners and utilities refused to support any action at all.

As Congress debated, abundant media coverage raised the salience of acid rain: the media propelled the term "acid rain" into common currency, portrayed it as a serious problem, and linked large coal-fired power plants to the death of pristine lakes and forests in the Northeast. The media also suggested that a looming catastrophe could be averted with cuts in SO_2. Reporting on acid rain by the major newspapers—the *New York Times, Washington Post, Boston Globe, Chicago Tribune,* and *Los Angeles Times*—remained steady throughout the 1980s, peaking at 216 articles in 1984 and ranging from 129 to 144 articles per year through 1988. As important as the number of stories, the coverage largely adopted a precautionary tone. Between 1974 and 1981, 72 percent of the articles on acid rain conveyed the idea that it was harmful. Even after the antiregulation forces mobilized, coverage remained largely favorable to environmentalists: 51 percent of the articles published between 1982 and 1985 depicted acid rain as dangerous, while 44 percent were neutral. And 62 percent of those issued between 1986 and 1988 had a proregulation slant, while 31 percent were neutral.[29] Surveys suggested that constant media coverage of the issue had raised public concern. According to a 1986 review of existing polls, by the mid-1980s the North American public was aware of acid rain as an environmental problem and, although their understanding of it was limited, regarded it as a serious problem. Most believed that concrete actions should be taken to address it and were willing to pay for abatement measures.[30]

Prospects for Controls Improve in the Bush Administration

During the Reagan years, interests that opposed reauthorization of the Clean Air Act were able to rest assured that they had friends in high places, both in Congress and the White House. As the Reagan administration drew to a close, however, several factors combined to give hope to proponents of acid rain controls. First, in 1987 the House got a rare chance to vote on clean air legislation: Representative Dingell, who had been bottling up Clean Air Act revisions in committee, sponsored legislation to extend clean air deadlines into 1989 as a way to take the urgency out of producing a new clean air bill before the 1988 elections.[31] But the Dingell amendment lost, 162–247. Instead, the House backed a proenvironmental amendment pushing the deadlines only to August 1988, thereby keeping the heat on Congress to write a new clean air law. Waxman and others interpreted the vote to mean that they had the support to pass clean air legislation if only they could get it out of committee and onto the floor.[32] In the Senate the prospects for clean air legislation improved as well when Byrd stepped down as majority leader and was succeeded by George Mitchell, a determined advocate of acid rain controls.

Perhaps most important, presidential candidate George H. W. Bush made reauthorizing the Clean Air Act a centerpiece of his election campaign. Bush and his advisers hoped to capitalize on a proenvironmental backlash against the Reagan years: memberships in environmental groups had exploded during the 1980s, and public opinion polls revealed that a large majority of Americans considered themselves environmentalists.[33] Furthermore, acid rain control was especially important to Canadian prime minister Brian Mulroney, a confidante of Bush.[34] Reflecting these influences, in a speech in Detroit, candidate Bush repudiated the Reagan administration approach, saying "the time for study alone has passed." He went on to offer a detailed plan "to cut millions of tons of sulfur dioxide emissions by the year 2000." [35] Although his position on many issues ultimately disappointed environmentalists, Bush did follow through on his campaign promise to offer revisions to the Clean Air Act. Soon after taking office, he assembled a team of advisers to craft a White House version of what would become the Clean Air Act Amendments of 1990.

An Innovative Allowance Trading Plan. The Bush team spent most of its time working on the acid rain details of the Clean Air Act reauthorization bill, and these provisions proved to be the most innovative part of the president's proposal. The group selected a system of allowance trading combined with a nationwide cap on total SO_2 emissions designed by Dan Dudek of the Environmental Defense Fund. This market-based mechanism, which environmental policy entrepreneurs had been softening up in the policy community for more than a decade, aimed to reduce SO_2 emissions by 10 million tons by the year 2000. Utilities could meet their emissions allowance using any of a variety of methods, or they could purchase allowances from other plants and maintain the same level of emissions. The plan was founded on a simple premise: the federal government should not dictate levels of pollution control required of individual companies as it had done in the more conventional regulations of the 1970 Clean Air Act. Rather, it should limit total emissions and distribute tradable allowances to all polluters, thereby creating incentives for individual companies to reduce their own pollution at lowest cost.

Politically, the allowance trading system had several advantages over more conventional approaches. It satisfied President Bush's preference for market-based regulatory solutions. Moreover, because it was designed by the Environmental Defense Fund and had been floating around the environmental community for some time, the White House thought the emissions-trading scheme was unlikely to arouse the ire of environmentalists. In addition, the plan created a strong coalition of supporters that included the clean coal–burning western states (whose utilities would not be forced to install scrubbers or subsidize acid rain controls), eastern and western producers of low-sulfur coal (for which demand was likely to accelerate), Republican advocates of less government interference in the market (for whom a trading system satisfied both efficiency and individual liberty concerns), and the northeastern states affected by acid deposition. Within this alliance, different groups had concerns about the details of the plan. In particular, representatives of western states worried that their utilities, which were already relatively clean, would not be able to obtain allowances that could facilitate economic growth in their states and that most of the allowances would be concentrated in the Midwest.

Those who stood to lose the most under the White House plan and consequently mobilized to oppose it were the UMW, with its strong presence in high-sulfur coal mines, and the midwestern utilities that traditionally relied on high-sulfur coal. The UMW argued that the bill would force major coal purchasers to shift to low-sulfur coal, jeopardizing thousands of coal-mining jobs. Midwesterners contended that the Bush plan was skewed against them: nine states responsible for 51 percent of the nation's SO_2 emissions were going to have to accomplish 90 percent of the reduction and bear 73 percent to 80 percent of the cost—in the form of higher electricity bills—in the first phase of the plan.

The Bush Plan in the Senate. In short, when Bush presented his plan to Congress, the battle lines were already drawn. In the Senate, Majority Leader Mitchell realized that most of the resistance to clean air legislation would come from outside the Environment and Public Works Committee because the regional balance of the committee clearly favored supporters of acid rain controls: of its sixteen members, five were from New England, two were from New York and New Jersey, and four others were from the Rocky Mountain states that produce low-sulfur coal. Furthermore, Sen. Max Baucus, D-Mont., had assumed the chairmanship of the Environmental Protection Subcommittee upon Mitchell's ascension to majority leader, and he had consistently supported clean air legislation—in part because Montana produces and uses low-sulfur coal, which many utilities would adopt under a market-based system. The ranking minority member of the subcommittee, John Chafee, R-R.I., also had a strong environmental record; moreover, his state had low per capita SO_2 emissions and therefore had little to lose from stringent acid rain controls. So the committee was able to mark up and approve (15–1) the president's clean air bill with relative ease. The controversy arose later, in the full Senate.

It took ten full weeks from its introduction on January 23, 1990, for the Senate to pass the Clean Air Act Amendments. During that time, the chamber worked continuously on the bill, virtually to the exclusion of all other business. The lengthy process was unusual for a complex and controversial proposal in at least one respect: there was no extended talk or procedural delay on the Senate floor; rather, Senator Mitchell presided over most of the debate behind closed doors in his suite. Commented Sen. Tom Daschle, D-S.D., "In my [12] years in Congress, I have never seen a member dedicate the attention and devotion to an issue as George Mitchell has done on clean air. He has used every ounce of his energy to cajole senators and come up with imaginative solutions." [36] As majority leader, Mitchell was both a persistent advocate of clean air legislation and a pragmatist: he wanted a clean air bill, and he knew that he would have to strike deals to get one. As a result, he often antagonized environmentalists, who hoped for greater regulatory stringency and less compromise than Mitchell was willing to tolerate. For example, despite objections from some major environmental groups, Mitchell and Baucus embraced the emissions-trading system devised by the Bush team in exchange for White House acceptance of changes in other parts of the bill.

Although there was clear momentum in the Senate in favor of reaching agreement on the clean air bill, the Appalachian and midwestern senators, led by Senator Byrd, were not ready to give up their fight to diffuse the region's acid rain cleanup costs. With extensive help from his aide, Rusty Mathews, Byrd crafted a formula that won the approval of coal-state senators: he proposed to give midwestern power plants bonus emissions credits to encourage them to adopt scrubbers rather than low-sulfur coal. An informal head count revealed that the Senate would not support Byrd's plan, however, and he was forced to scramble to salvage something from the acid rain debate. Mathews came up with another alternative: giving the heaviest polluters extra credits in Phase I to help them buy their way out of the cleanup effort. Eventually, Byrd and his cosponsor, Sen. Christopher Bond, R-Mo., were able to persuade Mitchell and others to accept this modification, known as the Byrd-Bond amendment, in exchange for their support on the acid rain provisions of the bill, and on April 3 the Senate passed its version of the Clean Air Act Amendments by a vote of 89 to 11.

Acid Rain Controls in the House. The decade-long rivalry between Waxman and Dingell continued to dominate the clean air debate in the House Energy and Commerce Committee. Dingell had chaired the full committee since 1979, and Waxman had chaired the Health and Environment Subcommittee since 1981. To augment his influence and counteract Waxman, Dingell had worked assiduously with House Speaker Jim Wright, D-Texas, to recruit sympathetic members to Energy and Commerce. By 1990, one-third of the committee's members were from the industrial heartland—the Midwest had nine seats, and the Appalachian coal states another seven—and only two were from New England. Nevertheless, when the Bush administration presented its proposal, Dingell took the advice of some important allies in the House (most notably Majority Whip Tony Coelho, D-Calif.) and from his wife Debbie Dingell, a General Motors executive, that delay and defensive tactics would no longer succeed, and he would have to get on the bandwagon if he wanted to avoid blame for inaction. According to one Democratic aide, "Dingell always knew that he could delay action for a time, but that he then would have to fight for the best deal he could get." [37]

Dingell had assigned Waxman's Environment Subcommittee responsibility for marking up most of the clean air package but had strategically referred the two most controversial titles of the bill, acid rain and alternative fuels, to the Subcommittee on Energy and Power chaired by Philip Sharp, D-Ind., who had long opposed acid rain legislation in hopes of protecting Indiana's old and dirty utilities. In November 1989 Sharp told reporters he planned to dramatize his concerns about the administration's proposal by stalling the acid rain provisions in his subcommittee. Two of Sharp's midwestern allies on the committee, Edward Madigan, R-Ill., and Terry Bruce, D-Ill., publicly criticized Chairman Dingell for failing to deliver on a promise to help solve their cost-sharing problems. In an effort to patch things up, Dingell unveiled a plan to enroll support among the "cleans"—predominantly western states—for a cost-sharing program that would relieve some of the burden on the midwestern "dirties." [38]

The protracted recalcitrance of the utility lobby and its supporters in the House had not earned them many friends, however, and the midwestern contingent was unable to persuade members from other states to accept their cost-sharing proposals. The utilities also had increased their vulnerability to tough controls by stubbornly insisting throughout the 1980s that there was no acid rain problem and refusing to provide members of Congress and their aides with information on their operations. Making matters worse for the utilities, the Bush plan had fractured the antiregulation coalition: midwestern representatives were split between those who favored giving utilities flexibility in reducing their emissions and those who wanted to protect high-sulfur coal miners and therefore preferred a scrubber mandate. The utilities themselves were divided depending on their energy source and the extent to which they had already engaged in pollution control in response to stringent state laws. In particular, the heavily polluting utilities and those that had already begun to clean up—such as those in Minnesota, New York, and Wisconsin—could not resolve their differences.

To facilitate negotiations among members of this fractious group, nearly all of the committee meetings were conducted behind closed doors and often at night. Like Mitchell in the Senate, Dingell hoped to spare rank-and-file lawmakers the constant pressure to serve constituent demands by freeing them from the speechmaking and position-taking associated with public hearings on controversial legislation.[39] The "dirties" and "cleans" finally agreed on a compromise in which midwestern utilities got more time to reduce emissions, additional emissions credits, and funds to speed development of technology to reduce coal emissions. Members from the "clean" states extracted some concessions as well: they obtained greater flexibility for their utilities under the trading system, and they got all the permits the midwesterners initially had been reluctant to give them. The Energy and Commerce Committee completed its drafting of the clean air legislation on April 15, 1990, and the full House passed its version of the bill on May 23 by a vote of 401 to 21.

Reconciling the House and Senate Bills. Following Senate and House passage of their separate versions of the clean air bill, all that remained was to reconcile the differences in conference committee. The House conferees controlled most aspects of the conference committee bill, but the Senate prevailed on the acid rain provisions.[40] (Its version of those provisions was more coherent and closer to the original Bush administration plan.) Despite their failures in the House and Senate chambers, midwestern representatives still hoped to extract some relief from the conference committee. Representative Sharp and his colleagues worked during the final days to salvage aid to their region, requesting additional allowances to ease the pain for coal-fired utilities that would be hardest hit by the new rules. The midwesterners among the House conferees settled on a proposal to give some additional credits to Illinois, Indiana, and Ohio utilities each year until 1999. After 2000, ten midwestern states would get a small number of extra allowances each year.[41]

When they presented the plan to a group of pivotal House and Senate conferees, however, the reaction was unenthusiastic. Rep. Dennis Eckart, D-Ohio, then took the plan to Senator Mitchell, who agreed to support it in exchange for a few concessions. In the end, said Eckart, Mitchell broke the impasse by convincing the skeptics to pacify the Midwest. In the process, the midwesterners lost on some other demands, including a provision in the House bill that would have protected high-sulfur coal mining jobs by requiring utilities to install pollution control devices rather than switching to low-sulfur coal.[42]

In general, despite the extra allowances granted to some midwestern utilities, the acid rain provisions represented a big loss for the Midwest and the old, dirty generating units. The final bill, according to one veteran Washington lobbyist, "proved the axiom that divided industries do badly on Capitol Hill." [43] (House conferees did manage to extract from the Bush administration a concession on displaced worker assistance, even though the president had threatened to veto the bill if it included unemployment benefits to workers who lost jobs as a result of the law.) Once the conferees had resolved or agreed to abandon the remaining issues, the final package had to pass the House and Senate. Reflecting the momentum behind the law and the skills of the legislative leaders who had shepherded it through the legislative process, the six days of debate that followed were perfunctory. The House passed the clean air conference report 401–25 on October 26, and the Senate passed it 89–10 the following day. President Bush signed the Clean Air Act Amendments into law on November 15, 1990.

Implementing the Acid Rain Provisions

Title IV of the 1990 Clean Air Act Amendments (CAAA) required a nationwide reduction in SO_2 emissions by 10 million tons—roughly 40 percent from

1980 levels—by 2000. To facilitate this reduction, Title IV established a two-phase SO_2 allowance trading system under which the EPA issues each utility a certain number of allowances, each of which permits its holder to emit 1 ton of SO_2 in a particular year or any subsequent year.[44] A utility that generates more emissions than it receives allowances for may reduce its emissions through pollution control efforts or may purchase allowances from another utility. A utility that reduces its emissions below the number of allowances it holds may trade, bank, or sell its excess allowances. (Anyone can hold allowances, including utilities, brokers, environmental groups, and private citizens.) Title IV also mandated a 2 million ton reduction in NO_x emissions by 2000. To achieve this reduction, the law required the EPA to establish emissions limitations for two types of utility boilers by mid-1992 and for all other types by 1997. Finally, Title IV required all regulated utilities to install equipment to monitor SO_2 and NO_x emissions continuously to ensure compliance.

EPA Rulemaking Under Title IV. For opponents of acid rain regulations, the implementation of Title IV was the last remaining opportunity to subvert the goal of reducing SO_2 and NO_x emissions. They were gratified when, less than a year and a half after signing the much-heralded Clean Air Act Amendments, President Bush instituted the Council on Competitiveness headed by Vice President Dan Quayle. The council was driven, in Quayle's words, by "the desire to minimize regulations and to make regulations as unburdensome as possible while meeting the requirements of the statutes." [45] Bush wanted to retreat from the most onerous commitments of the act because, with a reelection campaign imminent, he needed to accommodate his allies in the Republican Party and in the business community. Efforts to derail the program were largely unsuccessful, however, and on January 15, 1991, the EPA issued a report delineating the dozens of deadlines the agency would have to meet to comply with the new law. By summer 1991 the agency had resolved most of the major SO_2 rulemaking issues; the following December it published its proposed rules for notice and comment; and by early 1993 it had promulgated its final SO_2 regulations.[46]

Vigorous and supportive congressional oversight helped to ensure that the regulatory process stayed on track. Because committee Democrats wanted to take credit for the act as the 1992 presidential and congressional races neared, high-ranking members of the authorizing committees monitored Clean Air Act implementation zealously. In April 1992 Waxman wrote an angry *New York Times* editorial chiding the Bush administration for failing to issue the regulations necessary to carry out the act. Even Dingell joined Waxman in this effort. Having thrown his support behind the law, Dingell was not going to let the White House undermine it, so he made sure the EPA had the wherewithal to write rules under the CAAA. One manifestation of this support was the agency's ability to increase its FY1992 acid rain staff from fifteen to sixty-three.

In addition to congressional oversight, the statute itself encouraged compliance because it contained clear guidelines and strict penalties for failure by the agency to put SO_2 regulations in place, a feature that reflected Congress's determination to make the act self-enforcing. Waxman explained that "the specificity in the 1990 Amendments reflects the concern that without detailed directives, industry intervention might frustrate efforts to put pollution control steps in place. . . . History shows that even where EPA seeks to take strong action, the White House will often intervene at industry's behest to block regulatory action." [47]

A comparison between the statutory provisions for NO_x and SO_2 reveals the importance of statutory design for effective implementation. Although the EPA required utility boilers to meet new NO_x emissions requirements, there was no emissions cap, so overall emissions continued to rise. Moreover, the NO_x provisions did not contain a hammer: NO_x limitations did not apply unless rules were actually promulgated, so there was considerable incentive for regulated sources to delay and obstruct. In fact, the NO_x rule was delayed by a court challenge and was not finalized until early 1995. (NO_x reductions began in 1996 and were increased in 2000.) According to one EPA analyst, "Poor statutory construction [for NO_x regulation] has cost the environment in terms of delayed protection, has cost the industry in terms of burner reconfiguration expenditures, and has cost the public, who ultimately pays the capital, administrative, and litigation expenses." [48]

The Emissions-Trading System. Between 1991 and 1992 the EPA issued all 182 Phase I permits for SO_2, certified the continuous monitoring systems that utilities had installed and tested, and developed an emissions tracking system to process emissions data for all sources. The SO_2 trading system's first phase required 263 units in 110 coal-fired utility plants (operated by sixty utilities) in twenty-one eastern and midwestern states to reduce their SO_2 emissions by a total of approximately 3.5 million tons per year beginning in 1995. The EPA allocated allowances to utilities each year based on a legislative formula.[49] The agency provided some units with bonus allowances, the subject of so much congressional haggling: for example, high-polluting power plants in Illinois, Indiana, and Ohio got additional allowances during each year of Phase I that they could sell to help generate revenues to offset cleanup costs. To appease clean states, the EPA also allowed plants to receive extra allowances if they were part of a utility system that had reduced its coal use by at least 20 percent between 1980 and 1985 and relied on coal for less than half of the total electricity it generated. Additional provisions gave clean states bonus allowances to facilitate economic growth.

Phase II, which began in 2000, tightened emissions limits on the large plants regulated in Phase I and set restrictions on smaller, cleaner coal-, gas-, and oil-fired plants. Approximately 2,500 units in 1,000 utility plants were brought under the regulatory umbrella in Phase II, during which the EPA issued 8.95 million allowances for 1 ton of SO_2 emissions each to utilities annually. To avoid penalizing them for improvements made in the 1980s, Title IV permitted the cleanest plants to increase their emissions between 1990 and 2000 by roughly 20 percent. Thereafter, they were not allowed to exceed their 2000 emission levels. The EPA did not allocate allowances to utilities that began operating after 1995; instead, it required them to buy into the system by purchasing allowances. This ensured that overall emissions reductions would not be eroded over time.

Once it set up the system, the EPA's ongoing role in allowance trading became simply to receive and record allowance transfers and to ensure at the end of each year that a utility's emissions did not exceed the number of allowances held. Each generator has up to thirty days after the end of the year to deliver to the EPA valid allowances equal to its emissions during the year. At that time, the EPA cancels the allowances needed to cover emissions. If a generator fails to produce the necessary allowances, the EPA can require it to pay a $2,000-per-ton excess emissions fee and offset the excess emissions in the following year. Because the excess emissions fee is substantially higher than the cost of complying with the law by purchasing allowances, the market is likely to enforce much of the emissions reductions.

The EPA also maintains a reserve of 300,000 special allowances that it can allocate to utilities that develop qualifying renewable energy projects or institute conservation measures. The agency is establishing the reserve by reducing Phase II allowances by 30,000 annually between 2000 and 2009. In addition, the EPA is considering other mechanisms to promote the use of conservation and renewable energy. Furthermore, the EPA maintains a reserve of allowances for auctions and sales by withholding 2.8 percent of the total allowances each year. (Auctions and sales are open to anyone and are conducted by sealed bid.)

OUTCOMES

On March 29, 1993, the Chicago Board of Trade held the first of three SO_2 allowance auctions. The auction reaped $21 million and attracted more participants than most observers had expected.[50] The EPA managed to sell the allowances it was offering at prices ranging from $130 to $450, with an average price of $250. Over the next four years, allowance prices declined from $180 to $159 to $132 and finally to $68 in 1996; by mid-1997 allowance prices had risen again to between $90 and $100; they hovered around $140 in 2000; and between 2001 and 2004 they ranged from $150 to $200.[51]

The Economic Impacts of Title IV

To some observers, the lower-than-expected allowance prices suggested that utilities were investing more heavily in emissions reduction than projected and anticipated having more allowances than they needed in 1995, when emissions limits would be tightened. Others worried that such low prices might cause utilities that had planned to install pollution control devices to reconsider because it might prove cheaper simply to buy more allowances. Indeed, one utility that bid in the first auction, the Illinois Power

Company, stopped construction on a $350 million scrubber and began making private deals to stockpile permits that it intended to use between 1995 and 2000.[52] But a 1996 Resources for the Future report suggested that, although most were not trading allowances, utilities had in fact cut pollution.[53] (The study found that the bulk of EPA-cited trades were record-keeping changes in which utilities consolidated ownership.)

Utilities were cutting their emissions because it had become substantially cheaper to do so. By allowing utilities to choose how to achieve compliance, Title IV created a dynamic marketplace in which pollution control alternatives competed directly with one another, prompting price cuts and innovation among coal marketers, railroads, and scrubber manufacturers. Fuel switching and blending with low-sulfur coal was the compliance option of choice for more than half of all utilities. But the most important factor accounting for lower compliance costs, according to study author Dallas Burtraw, was the nearly 50 percent reduction in transportation costs for moving low-sulfur coal from the Powder River Basin to the East.[54] As a result of these savings, by 2001, 10 million tons of SO_2 emissions had been eliminated at one-fifth to one-tenth the original cost estimates put forth by Congress and the EPA.[55]

The Ecological Impacts of Title IV

Assessments of Title IV have revealed some impressive and unexpected accomplishments beyond low compliance costs. According to the EPA, SO_2 emissions from Phase I utilities were down to 5.4 million tons in 1996, or 35 percent below that year's cap of 8.3 million tons.[56] By 2003 SO_2 emissions from all sources covered by Title IV were 10.6 million tons, down from 15.7 million tons in 1990, when the act was passed. Total SO_2 emissions declined from 23.1 million tons in 1990 to 18.6 million tons in 1995 and to 15.8 million tons in 2003 (see Table 14-1).[57] Moreover, the U.S. Geological Survey (USGS) found that in 1995, sixty-two sites in the mid-Atlantic and Ohio River Valley regions experienced, on average, a 13.8 percent decline in sulfur compounds and an 8 percent drop in hydrogen ions. The authors attributed this "greater-than-anticipated" decline to the implementation of Phase I of the CAAA.[58] Similarly, reports from the Adirondacks in 2000, 2002, and 2003 showed declining sulfur levels in many of the regions' lakes.[59]

Assessments of the act's ecological impacts have been less sanguine, however; between 1996 and 2005 scientists realized that the reductions mandated in Title IV would not be sufficient to stem the ecological damage done by acid rain. A report released in April 1996, based on more than three decades of data from New Hampshire's Hubbard Brook Forest, suggested that the forest had not bounced back as quickly as expected.[60] "Our view and that of soil scientists had been that soils were so well buffered that acid rain didn't affect them in any serious way," said ecologist Gene Likens, commenting on the report.[61] Even though the deposition of acid had abated, its effects lingered. Vegetation in the Hubbard Brook Experimental Forest had nearly stopped growing since

Table 14-1
Sulfur Dioxide (SO₂) and Nitrogen Oxide (NOₓ) Emissions

Year	(SO$_2$)		(NO$_x$)	
	Total	Title IV Sources	Total	Title IV Sources
1980	25.9	17.3	27.1	NA
1985	23.3	16.1	25.8	NA
1990	23.1	15.7	25.5	NA
1995	18.6	11.8	25.0	5.8
1996	18.4	12.5	24.8	6.0
1997	18.8	12.9	24.7	6.0
1998	18.9	13.1	24.3	6.0
1999	17.5	12.4	22.8	5.5
2000	16.3	11.2	22.6	5.1
2001	15.9	10.6	21.5	4.7
2002	15.4	10.2	21.1	4.5
2003	15.8	10.6	20.5	4.2
2004		10.3		3.8

Source: Environmental Protection Agency.

1987, and the pH of many streams in the Northeast remained below normal. Researchers speculated, and subsequent evidence confirmed, that years of acid deposition had depleted the soil's supply of alkaline chemicals and that the soil was recovering only gradually.[62] A second likely cause of the slow comeback of Hubbard Brook was that, because NOₓ emissions had not declined significantly (see Table 14-1), nitrates continued to acidify the rain falling in the Northeast.

The Hubbard Brook findings were consistent with the observations of plant pathologist Walter Shortle of the U.S. Forest Service. In fall 1995 Shortle's group had reported in the journal *Nature* that, because acid rain was no longer sufficiently neutralized by calcium and magnesium, it was releasing aluminum ions from minerals into the soil, where they are toxic to plants.[63] Another study, conducted in the Calhoun Experimental Forest in South Carolina, confirmed that acid rain dissolves forest nutrients much faster than was previously believed.[64] And in October 1999 the USGS concurred that, while sulfur levels in rain and streams were declining, the alkalinity of stream water had not recovered.[65]

A 1999 National Acid Precipitation Assessment Program report summarizing the research on acid rain affirmed that, although the 1990 CAAA had made significant improvements, acid precipitation was more complex and intractable than was thought when that law was passed. The authors noted that high-elevation forests in the Colorado Front Range, West Virginia's Allegheny Mountains, the Great Smoky Mountains of Tennessee, and the San Gabriel

Mountains of Southern California were saturated or near saturated with nitrogen; the Chesapeake Bay was suffering from excess nitrogen, some of which was from air pollution; high-elevation lakes and streams in the Sierra Nevada, the Cascades, and the Rocky Mountains appeared to be on the verge of chronically high acidity; and waterways in the Adirondacks were becoming more acidic, even as sulfur deposits declined.[66] The report concluded that if deposits of sulfur and nitrogen were not reduced, these sensitive forests, lakes, and soils would continue to deteriorate. According to Jack Cosby, a University of Virginia environmental scientist, "It's been the near consensus of scientists that the Clean Air Act amendments haven't gone far enough." [67]

A study conducted by ten leading acid rain researchers and published in the March 2001 issue of *Bioscience* further verified that acid rain's effects continued to be felt. Although acid rain had decreased 38 percent since controls were implemented, 41 percent of lakes in the Adirondacks and 15 percent of lakes in New England were either chronically or periodically acidic, largely because the buffering capacity of surrounding soils had been depleted.[68] The authors also noted that research since 1990 had clarified how acid deposition was harming the region's forests: acid fog and rain depletes calcium, an important plant nutrient, from spruce needles, leaving them susceptible to freezing; acid rain also mobilizes aluminum, which interferes with maple tree roots' ability to take up nutrients. According to Gene Likens: "The science on the issue is clear. Current emission control policies are not sufficient to recover sensitive watersheds in New England." [69] The article claimed an 80 percent reduction in SO_2 would be necessary to restore the region's soils, lakes, and streams within twenty-five years.

Acid rain's effects were also becoming apparent in the Southeast. Impacts there took longer to manifest themselves because southern soils are generally thicker than northern soils and so had absorbed more acid. Once the soils were saturated, acid levels in nearby waters began to skyrocket. Even in the West, acid rain was attracting attention, as scientists studying spruce trees in the Rockies found that trees downwind of populous areas showed high levels of nitrogen and low ratios of magnesium in their needles.[70] And researchers were beginning to observe additional consequences of acid rain: ornithologists at Cornell University charged that acid rain was implicated in the decline of the wood thrush and other northeastern bird species. They argued that by depleting the soil of calcium, acid rain caused the number of earthworms, millipedes, slugs, and snails to plummet, leaving females and chicks calcium deficient.[71]

New Research Spurs Calls for More Controls

In response to new findings about acid rain's lasting ecological impacts, in the late 1990s pressure began mounting for strict NO_x emissions controls. In November 1997 the EPA called for new state air pollution plans to cut the NO_x emissions of utilities and other large sources in the states east of the Mississippi by 85 percent. Over the protests of midwestern governors and power plant executives, the EPA in 1998 ordered twenty-two states in the East and Midwest to reduce emissions of NO_x by an average of 28 percent, mainly during the summer.[72] The following year Sen. Daniel Patrick Moynihan, D-N.Y., proposed new legislation to cut SO_2 by 50 percent more than required by the 1990 amendments, reduce NO_x 70 percent by 2005, and establish an NO_x trading scheme similar to the one created for SO_2. But the bill attracted minimal support in Congress, where some members thought the government had done enough to address the issue.[73] In 2000 New York officials and environmental groups seized on a GAO report showing that nitrogen levels continued to rise in Adirondack waterways as ammunition for their case that Congress needed to tighten acid rain controls.[74] But officials representing midwestern utilities remained adamant that further regulations were unnecessary, pointing out that it was too early to evaluate the impacts of existing NO_x reductions, which had taken effect in 1996 and were tightened in 2000. Furthermore, although most scientists supported policies to reduce NO_x, some were dubious about proposals that focused only on utility emissions, pointing out that much of the nitrogen in the atmosphere comes from motor vehicle emissions.[75]

While Congress wrestled with the issue, proponents pursued tighter controls on another front with greater success. In September 1999 New York attorney general Eliot Spitzer announced his intention to sue seventeen southern and midwestern power plants, as well as several utilities in New York State, to force them to reduce their acid rain–causing emissions. Spitzer employed a novel argument under the New Source Review (NSR) rule of the Clean Air Act: that power companies had expanded and upgraded their old plants sufficiently to be considered new plants for regulatory purposes.[76] In November Connecticut attorney general Richard Blumenthal said he would follow Spitzer's lead and sue sixteen coal-fired power plants. The EPA, also emulating Spitzer, filed lawsuits against fifty-one companies across the country. By the end of 2000, the tactic appeared to be bearing fruit: in November 2000 the Virginia Electric Power Company signed a landmark $1.2 billion settlement in which it agreed to cut SO_2 and NO_x emissions from its eight coal-burning plants by 70 percent, or 252,000 tons per year, within twelve years.[77] A month later, the Cinergy Corporation of Cincinnati reached a settlement with the EPA in which it agreed to spend $1.4 billion over twelve years to cut SO_2 from its ten coal-burning plants in Kentucky.[78]

In 2001, however, President George W. Bush disavowed the Clinton administration's litigation strategy and instead began exploring ways to relax the NSR rule to give utilities more flexibility to enhance their plants without adding pollution controls. After the administration published five revised NSR rules in the *Federal Register* on December 31, 2002, nine northeastern states immediately filed suit. The lawsuit challenged four of the new provisions, each of which would allow plants to increase their emissions without penalty. In their press release, the attorneys general framed the issue in stark terms, portraying corporate polluters as the villains and public health (rather than lakes and forests) as their main concern. Spitzer said, "This action by the Bush

Administration is a betrayal of the right of Americans to breathe clean, healthy air." Maine attorney general G. Steven Rowe said, "Our national government should be looking out for the health of the American people, rather than the corporate financial interests of dirty power plants." [79] Undaunted, in August 2003 the administration finalized an additional NSR rule, which said that pollution upgrades would be required only if companies spent more than 20 percent of the replacement cost of the entire plant—an extremely generous standard. Once again, the state attorneys general filed suit. In June 2005 the D.C. Court of Appeals sided with the Bush administration's EPA on the first set of rules, and the second case has yet to be resolved.[80]

On a parallel track, because the Clean Air Act was up for reauthorization in August 2002, the administration began promoting its "Clear Skies" legislative initiative. First introduced in early 2002, Clear Skies established a 2.1 million ton cap on NO_x by 2009 and a 1.7 million ton cap by 2018. For SO_2, the plan called for a 4.5 million ton cap by 2010 and a 3 million ton cap by 2018. The initiative failed repeatedly to get out of the Senate Environment and Public Works Committee, however, because a small number of Republicans agreed with environmentalists that it would achieve less than the existing Clean Air Act, which generally requires any region that does not meet federal air standards to reach those goals within five years, and because it failed to address CO_2 emissions (see chapter 11). Stymied in Congress, EPA administrator Mike Leavitt in December 2003 unveiled the Clean Air Interstate Rule (CAIR), which established by administrative fiat a regime similar to that in Clear Skies but applicable only to the twenty-eight eastern states. The administration said that the emissions-trading scheme established under CAIR, which became final in March 2005, would yield a 73 percent reduction in SO_2 emissions and a 61 percent drop in NO_x emissions by 2015. Most environmentalists applauded the new rule, but in July 2005 a handful of environmental groups filed a lawsuit challenging language in the rule's preamble that would limit the government's ability to reduce emissions in the future. At the same time, industry filed a dozen lawsuits arguing that the EPA overstepped its authority in making the rule.[81]

CONCLUSIONS

The acid rain case provides a vivid example of the interaction between science and politics in environmental policymaking. Critics of the 1990 Clean Air Act Amendments point out that Congress had virtually completed work on the bill before the multimillion dollar National Acid Precipitation Assessment Program report, commissioned by President Carter ten years earlier, had even been released. (The assessment program had released drafts of the report, however, and its major findings were already well established.) More important, just as opponents of acid rain controls justified their position on the grounds of scientific uncertainty, proponents of acid rain controls used the scientific consensus throughout the 1980s to build a compelling political story that raised the issue's salience. By generating support among voters, advocates created incentives for leaders to appropriate the issue. Hoping to capitalize on widespread public concern in the United States and Canada, 1988 presidential candidate Bush promised to address the acid rain problem.

When Bush was elected and George Mitchell became majority leader of the Senate, the advocates of acid rain controls saw an opportunity to link the environmental problem to a market-based solution. Such an approach changed the political dynamics of the issue because it was palatable to many conservatives and westerners. The emissions-trading scheme also helped to break up the formidable coalition of utilities that had been monolithic in their opposition to regulations. (The strategy worked in part because environmentalists had lobbied successfully for the state-level acid rain laws that had prompted some power plants to clean up.)

After a decade of delay, the CAAA passed by overwhelming majorities in both chambers, making manifest both the power of well-placed opponents to maintain the status quo against a popular alternative and the importance of legislative leaders in facilitating a successful policy challenge. President Bush's imprimatur on the new bill contrasted sharply with the Reagan administration's obstruction and was critical to attracting Republican support. Congressional leaders, particularly Mitchell and Dingell, brokered deals within the emissions-trading system that were crucial to building a majority coalition. Their willingness to hold meetings behind closed doors, away from the scrutiny of lobbyists, was particularly decisive.

As it turns out, the emissions-trading program has brought about greater reductions in SO_2 emissions at lower costs than expected—illustrating the pitfalls of cost projections, which typically fail to account for the market's dynamic response to regulation. Ironically, subsequent scientific research suggests that further emissions controls, particularly for NO_x, will be needed to address the acid rain problem. In the absence of further cooperation from a conservative Congress to promote more stringent acid rain legislation, proponents of tighter controls have pursued their goals in court. The younger president Bush has not endorsed this approach, however. Instead, his administration has focused on providing polluters with greater flexibility to reduce their costs. In defending his approach, Bush explains that Republicans need to be able to say, "Our party has led to reasonable, sane environmental policy." [82]

QUESTIONS TO CONSIDER

- Critics often cite acid rain regulations as evidence of misplaced environmental priorities, saying the 1990 National Acid Precipitation Assessment Program report made clear that acid rain does not pose a serious threat. Do you agree with this critique? Why, or why not?
- Has science played a sufficient role in the development of U.S. acid rain policy? If not, why not, and how might its impact be increased?

• Why do proponents believe emissions-trading programs are more effective, economically and ecologically, than uniform emission limitations? Can you think of any drawbacks to the emissions-trading approach?

Notes

1. Acid rain is the common term that describes all forms of acid precipitation as well as dry deposition of acid materials. It occurs when sulfur and nitrogen combine with oxygen in the atmosphere to produce sulfur dioxide (SO_2) and nitrogen oxides (NO_x). Within hours or days, these pollutants spontaneously oxidize in the air to form sulfate and acid nitrate, commonly known as sulfuric and nitric acids. These acids usually remain in the atmosphere for weeks and may travel hundreds of miles before settling on or near the earth in rain, snow, mist, hail, or in dry form. Scientists measure the relative acidity of a solution on a logarithmic potential hydrogen (pH) scale. While all types of precipitation are somewhat acidic—"pure" rainfall has a pH of about 5.6—in industrial regions, the pH of rain is often around 4.0 and can drop as low as 2.6. A neutral substance has a pH value of 7.0. An acidic substance has a pH of less than 7.0, whereas an alkalinic one has a pH of greater than 7.0. Furthermore, because the pH scale is logarithmic, a full pH unit drop represents a tenfold increase in acidity.
2. Judith A. Layzer, "Sense and Credibility: The Role of Science in Environmental Policymaking" (Ph.D. diss., Massachusetts Institute of Technology, 1999).
3. John W. Kingdon, *Congressmen's Voting Decisions*, 3d ed. (Ann Arbor: University of Michigan Press, 1989).
4. Alan Schwartz, quoted in Leslie R. Alm, *Crossing Borders, Crossing Boundaries: The Role of Scientists in the U.S. Acid Rain Debate* (Westport, Conn.: Praeger, 2000), 8.
5. Robert N. Stavins, "Market-Based Environmental Policies," in *Public Policies for Environmental Protection*, 2d ed., ed. Paul R. Portney and Robert N. Stavins (Washington, D.C.: Resources for the Future, 2000), 31–76.
6. Ellis B. Cowling, "Acid Precipitation in Historical Perspective," *Environmental Science & Technology* 16 (1982): 111A–122A.
7. Ibid. At the same time, Ontario government researchers were documenting lake acidification and fish loss in a wide area surrounding Sudbury and attributing those effects to SO_2 emissions from the Sudbury smelters. This work was suppressed by the Ontario government, however. See Don Munton, "Dispelling the Myths of the Acid Rain Story," *Environment* 40 (July-August 1998): 4–7, 27–34.
8. Paul Kinscherff and Pierce Homer, "The International Joint Commission: The Role It Might Play," in *Acid Rain and Friendly Neighbors*, rev. ed., ed. Jurgen Schmandt, Judith Clarkson, and Hilliard Roderick (Durham: Duke University Press, 1988), 190–216.
9. Marshall E. Wilcher, "The Acid Rain Debate in North America: 'Where You Stand Depends on Where You Sit,'" *The Environmentalist* 6 (1986): 289–298.
10. Quoted in Philip Shabecoff, "Northeast and Coal Area at Odds Over Acid Rain," *New York Times*, April 19, 1980, 22.
11. James L. Regens and Robert W. Rycroft, *The Acid Rain Controversy* (Pittsburgh: University of Pittsburgh Press, 1988).
12. Roy Gould, *Going Sour: The Science and Politics of Acid Rain* (Boston: Birkhauser, 1985).
13. Only 5 percent to 10 percent of the water in a lake comes from rain that has fallen directly on the lake; most of the water is runoff from the surrounding watershed and has been neutralized by the alkaline soil.

14. Acidity can kill fish in several ways: by interfering with their salt balance, by caus-ing reproductive abnormalities, by leaching aluminum into the lake at levels toxic to fish gills, or by killing the organisms on which they feed.

15. Gould, *Going Sour*; Office of Technology Assessment, *Acid Rain and Transported Air Pollutants: Implications for Public Policy* (Washington, D.C.: Office of Technology Assessment, 1984); U.S. GAO, *An Analysis of Issues Concerning Acid Rain*, GAO/ RCED-85-13 (December 1984), 3.

16. Gould, *Going Sour.*

17. Quoted in Regens and Rycroft, *The Acid Rain Controversy*, 85.

18. National Research Council, *Atmosphere-Biosphere Interactions: Toward a Better Under-standing of the Ecological Consequences of Fossil Fuel Combustion* (Washington, D.C.: National Academy Press, 1981).

19. Quoted in Gould, *Going Sour*, 30.

20. Ibid., 32.

21. Quoted in ibid., 33.

22. Quoted in Michael Kranish, "Acid Rain Report Said Suppressed," *Boston Globe*, August 18, 1984, 1.

23. Quoted in ibid.

24. Philip Shabecoff, "Toward a Clean and Budgeted Environment," *New York Times*, October 2, 1984, 28.

25. Alm, *Crossing Borders, Crossing Boundaries.*

26. Congress focused on SO_2 emissions because scientists believed SO_2 was the pri-mary culprit in acid rain (accounting for more than two-thirds of the acidity) and because it was the simplest—both technically and politically—to address.

27. The heaviest sulfur-emitting states in the proposed acid rain control region were Florida, Illinois, Indiana, Kentucky, Missouri, Ohio, Pennsylvania, Tennessee, West Virginia, and Wisconsin. These states accounted for two-thirds of the SO_2 emitted by the thirty-one states east of the Mississippi. See Steven L. Rhodes, "Superfund-ing Acid Rain Controls: Who Will Bear the Costs?" *Environment*, July-August, 1984, 25–32.

28. Two of the more prominent proposals were reported out of the Environment Com-mittee in 1982 and 1984 (S 3041). Both required a 10 million ton reduction in SO_2 emissions in the thirty-one states east of the Mississippi. Both allowed fuel switch-ing. In 1985 Senator Stafford introduced the Acid Rain Control Act, which divorced the issue from the Clean Air Act revisions and contained provisions similar to those in S 3041.

29. Aaron Wildavsky, *But Is It True? A Citizen's Guide to Environmental Health and Safety Issues* (Cambridge: Harvard University Press, 1995).

30. Keith Neuman, "Trends in Public Opinion on Acid Rain: A Comprehensive Review of Existing Data," *Water, Air & Soil Pollution* 31 (December 1986): 1047–59.

31. George Hager, "The 'White House' Effect Opens a Long-Locked Political Door," *Congressional Quarterly Weekly Report*, January 20, 1990, 139–144.

32. Richard Cohen, *Washington at Work: Back Rooms and Clean Air*, 2d ed. (Boston: Allyn and Bacon, 1995).

33. For example, Cambridge Reports found the percentage of people who said the amount of government regulation and involvement in environmental protection was "too little" increased from 35 percent in 1982 to 53 percent in 1988. A series of polls conducted by the *New York Times*/CBS News asked a national sample of Amer-icans whether they agreed with the following statement: "Protecting the environ-ment is so important that requirements and standards cannot be too high, and con-tinuing environmental improvements must be made regardless of cost." In 1981, 45 percent said they agreed with this statement. By the end of Reagan's first term, this proportion had increased to 58 percent and in 1988, shortly before he left office, had climbed to 65 percent. Between 1980 and 1989 membership in the major, national

environmental groups grew from 4 percent (Audubon) to 67 percent (Wilderness Society) annually; the Sierra Club nearly tripled in size over the course of the decade. See Robert Cameron Mitchell, "Public Opinion and the Green Lobby: Poised for the 1990s," in *Environmental Policy in the 1990s*, ed. Norman J. Vig and Michael E. Kraft (Washington, D.C.: CQ Press, 1990), 81–99.

34. Marc K. Landy, Marc J. Roberts, and Stephen R. Thomas, *The Environmental Protection Agency: Asking the Wrong Questions from Nixon to Clinton*, exp. ed. (New York: Oxford University Press, 1994).

35. Quoted in Norman J. Vig, "Presidential Leadership and the Environment: From Reagan and Bush to Clinton," in *Environmental Policy in the 1990s*, 2d ed., ed. Norman J. Vig and Michael E. Kraft (Washington, D.C.: CQ Press, 1994), 80–81.

36. Quoted in Cohen, *Washington at Work*, 96.

37. Ibid., 82.

38. The clean states wanted assurances that they would get credit for earlier emissions reductions and would be allowed to expand their utility capacity if needed without busting tight emissions caps. They also did not want to foot the bill for other states' cleanup.

39. Cohen, *Washington at Work*.

40. Alyson Pytte, "Clean Air Conferees Agree on Industrial Emissions," *Congressional Quarterly Weekly Report*, October 20, 1990, 3496–8.

41. In Phase I, Illinois, Indiana, and Ohio utilities each got 200,000 extra allowances per year; in Phase II, ten midwestern states got 50,000 extra allowances each year.

42. Alyson Pytte, "A Decade's Acrimony Lifted in Glow of Clean Air," *Congressional Quarterly Weekly Report*, October 27, 1990, 3587–92.

43. Quoted in Cohen, *Washington at Work*, 128.

44. These allowances are like checking account deposits; they exist only as records in the EPA's computer-based tracking system, which contains accounts for all affected generating units and for any other parties that want to hold allowances.

45. Quoted in Cohen, *Washington at Work*, 211.

46. Brian McLean, "Lessons Learned Implementing Title IV of the Clean Air Act," 95-RA120.04 (Washington, D.C.: U.S. Environmental Protection Agency, 1995).

47. Quoted in Landy et al., *The Environmental Protection Agency*, 290.

48. McLean, "Lessons Learned," 9.

49. For example, in Phase I, an individual unit's allocation was the product of a 2.5-pound SO_2 per million BTU emission rate multiplied by the unit's average fuel consumption between 1985 and 1987.

50. Barnaby J. Feder, "Sold: The Rights to Air Pollution," *New York Times*, March 30, 1993, B1.

51. Munton, "Dispelling the Myths"; Raymond Hernandez, "Albany Battles Acid Rain Fed by Other States," *New York Times*, May 2, 2000, A1; www.epa.gov/airmarkets/trading/SO_2market/alprices.html.

52. Feder, "Sold."

53. Dallas Burtraw, "Trading Emissions to Clean the Air: Exchanges Few but Savings Many," *Resources*, Winter 1996, 3–6.

54. Dallas Burtraw, "Utilities Cut Pollution, But Few Trade Allowances," *Environmental Science & Technology* 29 (1995): 547A.

55. Eryn Gable, "Acid Rain Recovery Requires Patience, Experts Say," *Greenwire*, June 3, 2002.

56. Cited in U.S. GAO, *Air Pollution: Overview and Issues on Emissions Allowance Trading Programs*, GAO/T-RCED-97-183 (July 1997).

57. Environmental Protection Agency, "Acid Rain Program 2005 Progress Report," September 2005.

58. James A. Lynch, Van C. Bowersox, and Jeffrey W. Grimm, "Trends in Precipitation Chemistry in the United States, 1983–1994: An Analysis of the Effects in 1995 of

Phase I of the Clean Air Act Amendments of 1990, Title IV," USGS Report 96-0346 (Washington, D.C.: U.S. Geological Survey, 1996).

59. U.S. GAO, *Acid Rain: Emissions Trends and Effects in the Eastern United States,* GAO/RCED-00-47 (March 2000); "Acid Rain Compounds Decrease in N.Y. Lakes," *Greenwire,* September 20, 2002; "Lakes Less Acidic—Study," *Greenwire,* April 15, 2003.

60. G. E. Likens, C. T. Driscoll, and D. C. Buso, "Long-Term Effects of Acid Rain: Response and Recovery of a Forest Ecosystem," *Science,* April 12, 1996, 244–246.

61. Quoted in Jocelyn Kaiser, "Acid Rain's Dirty Business: Stealing Minerals from Soil," *Science,* April 12, 1996, 198.

62. William K. Stevens, "The Forest that Stopped Growing: Trail Is Traced to Acid Rain," *New York Times,* April 16, 1996, C4. A series of studies by Dr. Lars Hedin and six colleagues, published in 1994 in the journal *Nature,* found that reductions in the release of alkaline particles offset the cuts in sulfates by 28 percent to 100 percent. See William K. Stevens, "Acid Rain Efforts Found to Undercut Themselves," *New York Times,* January 27, 1994, 14.

63. Gregory B. Lawrence, Mark B. David, and Walter C. Shortle, "A New Mechanism for Calcium Loss in Forest-Floor Soils," *Nature,* November 9, 1995, 162–165.

64. Daniel Markewitz et al., "Three Decades of Observed Soil Acidification in the Calhoun Experimental Forest: Has Acid Rain Made a Difference?" *Soil Science Society of America Journal* 62 (October 1998): 1428–39.

65. "Good News-Bad News Story for Recovery of Streams from Acid Rain in Northeastern U.S.," USGS News Release, October 4, 1999.

66. James Dao, "Federal Study May Give New York Allies in Acid Rain Fight," *New York Times,* April 5, 1999, B1.

67. Quoted in ibid.

68. Charles T. Driscoll et al., "Acidic Deposition in the Northeastern United States: Sources and Inputs, Ecosystem Effects, and Management Strategies," *Bioscience* 51 (March 2001): 180–198; Kirk Johnson, "Harmful Effects of Acid Rain Are Far-Flung, A Study Finds," *New York Times,* March 26, 2001, B1.

69. Quoted in Tim Breen, "Acid Rain: Study Finds Little Improvement in Northeast," *Greenwire,* March 26, 2001.

70. Kevin Krajick, "Long-Term Data Show Lingering Effects from Acid Rain," *Science,* April 13, 2001, 196–199.

71. "Acid Rain in Northeast May Cause Population Decline—Report," *Greenwire,* August 13, 2002.

72. John H. Cushman Jr., "U.S. Orders Cleaner Air in 22 States," *New York Times,* September 25, 1998, 14. Apparently, new selective catalytic reduction (SCR) equipment reduced NO_x emissions by more than 90 percent at some coal-fired plants, prompting the demand that they be used year-round, instead of only during the summer months when ground-level ozone is most likely to form. Critics of this plan warned that SCR increases sulfur trioxide production and emission of sulfuric acid aerosol. See "Coal-Fired Plants Continue Use of SCR Units to Reduce Emissions," *Greenwire,* August 19, 2004.

73. Dao, "Federal Study."

74. James Dao, "Acid Rain Law Found to Fail in Adirondacks," *New York Times,* March 27, 2000, 1.

75. Ibid. Because stationary sources reduced their NO_x emissions in the 1980s, by 1998 on- and off-road vehicles and engines accounted for 53 percent of NO_x emissions.

76. The 1970 Clean Air Act grandfathered old plants but imposed strict emissions standards on new plants. The 1977 CAA amendments established the New Source Review permitting process, which requires existing sources that make substantial modifications to install updated pollution controls. To avoid this requirement, many utilities began making significant upgrades but characterizing them as routine maintenance.

77. Richard Perez-Pena, "Power Plants in South to Cut Emissions Faulted in Northeast Smog," *New York Times,* November 16, 2000.

78. Randal C. Archibold, "Tentative Deal on Acid Rain Is Reached," *New York Times,* December 22, 2000, 2.

79. "Nine States Sue Bush Administration for Gutting Key Component of Clean Air Act," Press Release, Office of New York State Attorney General Eliot Spitzer, December 31, 2002.

80. Throughout the rulemaking period, plaintiffs continued to file lawsuits under the old rule. Those suits yielded contradictory results, suggesting that ultimately the matter is likely to come before the Supreme Court.

81. Darren Samuelsohn, "Industry Files 12 Lawsuits Against EPA's CAIR Rule," *Greenwire,* July 12, 2005.

82. Quoted in Samuel Goldreich, "Hill Weighs Competing Plans for New Air Pollution Limits," *CQ Weekly,* February 22, 2003, 448–449.

Recommended Reading

Alm, Leslie. *Crossing Borders, Crossing Boundaries: The Role of Scientists in the U.S. Acid Rain Debate.* Westport, Conn.: Praeger, 2000.

Cohen, Richard. *Washington at Work: Back Rooms and Clean Air,* 2d ed. Boston: Allyn and Bacon, 1995.

Gould, Roy. *Going Sour: Science and Politics of Acid Rain.* Boston: Birkhauser, 1985.

Regens, James L., and Robert W. Rycroft. *The Acid Rain Controversy.* Pittsburgh: University of Pittsburgh Press, 1988.

Web Sites

http://bqs.usgs.gov/acidrain/index.htm (U.S. Geological Survey site)
www.epa.gov/rgytgrnj/programs/artd/air/acidrain/acidrain.htm (EPA's acid rain site)
http://nadp.sws.uiuc.edu (National Atmospheric Deposition Program site)
www.rff.org (Resources for the Future site)
www.hubbardbrook.org (Hubbard Brook Research Foundation site)

CHAPTER 15

Ecosystem-Based Solutions

Restoring the Florida Everglades

The Everglades is a freshwater marsh encompassing the area from Lake Okeechobee south to the tip of Florida.[1] It is one of the flattest and most extensive wetland ecosystems in the world. In its natural form, the Everglades is a slow-moving river between forty and seventy miles wide and only a few feet deep. It is bordered to the east by the Atlantic Coastal Ridge, now a highway, and to the west by the Big Cypress Swamp. Once a thriving habitat for wading birds, alligators, and a host of other species, the Everglades has been deteriorating since the 1940s, when the federal government began work on a vast hydrologic project designed to make the area more hospitable to settlers and farmers. It was not until 1988, however, that serious political attention turned to the issue of damage to the Everglades. That year the U.S. attorney general for South Florida filed a lawsuit against the state for failing to enforce its own water quality laws. In 2000, after a lengthy planning process that included citizens, industry, and representatives of more than a dozen federal, state and local agencies, Congress, the president, and Florida's governor enthusiastically approved a plan to restore the Everglades. But five years later the nation's largest-ever ecological restoration was still stuck on the drawing board, mired in disagreements over how to implement it.

Like the spotted owl and New England fisheries cases, the Everglades story highlights the role of litigation as a catalyst for more protective environmental policy within a subsystem that evolved to promote economic development. Lawsuits can increase the likelihood that policy will become more protective in several ways. First, a lawsuit can force participants in a dispute to reveal the values that underpin their positions. Such exposure favors advocates of protective policies because development-oriented practices—which directly benefit private interests—are more difficult to justify publicly. In addition, by requiring agencies to document the rationale for their decisions, lawsuits prompt the creation of scientific information on which advocates can build a case for more protective policy. And finally, lawsuits can raise the visibility of an environmental problem by attracting media coverage, thereby providing protection advocates an opportunity to define it in ways that raise its salience. As we know from previous cases, if environmentalists succeed in drawing national attention to a problem, they have a better chance of overwhelming local economic interests, particularly in the legislative arena, because aspiring political leaders are more likely to seek recognition by attending to the problem. Such leadership is critical to overcoming resistance to policy change and ending stalemate.

This case also introduces the idea of ecosystem restoration. Notwithstanding its attractiveness as a concept, ecosystem restoration raises a variety of thorny questions about means, ends, and evaluation. First, given that human beings have fundamentally altered virtually every ecosystem on earth, what should be the target of a restoration—the ecosystem's presettlement state? If that is not feasible, what previous configuration of plants, animals, and ecological processes should be reproduced? Second, how should the restoration be accomplished? Should planners rely on technology and intensive management to control natural systems, or should they devise approaches that allow nature to run its course and require human development to be compatible with it? Third, what are the appropriate criteria for measuring success? Ecologists recognize that revitalizing an ecosystem involves reestablishing ecological functions and processes, not just native species, making the question of how to monitor performance extremely complicated.[2]

Beyond the conceptual demands, ecosystem restoration poses logistical challenges as well. It requires comprehensive planning that considers the many interactions among ecosystem elements and functions. It is difficult to create the scientific basis for this kind of planning, however, because the highly specialized disciplinary structure of scientific inquiry and the emphasis on reductionist approaches typically yields disparate research projects rather than integrated assessments. Planners, therefore, must create institutions and incentives to encourage interdisciplinary studies and syntheses of existing data. Moreover, although comprehensive planning may be ecologically sensible, the holism it requires is hard to reconcile politically with the fragmented jurisdictions of government agencies and inconsistent with the kinds of piecemeal, incremental solutions to which the American political system is best suited. Efforts to facilitate interagency cooperation typically encounter a welter of obstacles, among the most daunting of which is managers' desire to protect their autonomy.[3] A related impediment to cooperation is agencies' incompatible missions and standard operating procedures.

The Everglades case also illuminates how a changing scientific understanding of ecosystem functioning has affected policy and politics. Popular ecological notions of balance, carrying capacity, and the stability of natural systems underpinned the environmental laws of the 1970s.[4] But more up-to-date environmental thinking recognizes the complexity of population and ecosystem dynamics and the consequent need to expect surprises. It now appears, says ecologist Daniel Botkin, that "change [is] intrinsic and natural at many scales of time and space in the biosphere." [5] In light of this new perspective, ecologists have developed an approach called "adaptive management," which involves treating management as an experiment and revising practices according to lessons learned.[6] But the experimental and flexible approach environmental scientists now commonly recommend are anathema to many elected officials who are reluctant to dispense authority to administrative agencies without imposing strict accountability measures. Adaptive management also troubles some environmentalists who worry that administrative flexibility creates opportunities for development interests to regain control of policy once public attention has shifted.

BACKGROUND

The Everglades originally covered 9,000 square miles, originating in a series of lakes and streams south of Orlando and extending more than 200 miles to Florida Bay. Two hundred years ago, the Everglades' headwaters overflowed during the spring and summer rains. Streams and sloughs carried water to Lake Okeechobee, which overflowed its banks. From there, a slow-moving sheet migrated across a gently sloping sawgrass plain over a period of many months. Moving at a rate of only twenty feet per day, the sheetflow eventually reached the twenty-mile-wide depression of the Shark River Slough, which is the entrance to the modern Everglades National Park.[7] Finally, the water drained into the mangrove forests and salt marshes of Florida Bay. Historically, an average of 4 million acre-feet of water a year flowed southward, and 1 or 2 million acre-feet reached the Bay and the Gulf of Mexico. This hydrologic regime—combined with the region's frequent droughts, fires, and hurricanes—produced a mosaic of plant communities, which in turn sustained a variety of endemic wildlife.[8]

The Central and Southern Florida Project

Efforts to "reclaim" the Everglades for development date back about 160 years. (Ironically, "reclaiming" a wetland means filling it or otherwise drying it out to make it habitable for humans.) In the 1840s Florida's first state legislature called the Everglades "wholly valueless" and asked the U.S. Congress for help draining it.[9] There followed a century-long series of failed attempts at reclamation. But after a succession of dry spells between 1931 and 1945—including one of the worst droughts in Florida's history—two fierce hurricanes hit the Everglades in 1947, dropping 100 inches of rain and inundating 90 percent of southeastern Florida. These events were the catalyst for congressional approval of the Central and Southern Florida (C&SF) Flood Control Project, a billion-dollar hydrologic scheme proposed by the U.S. Army Corps of Engineers. The governor approved the plan in February 1948, and the following year the legislature formed the C&SF Flood Control District to act as the federal government's local partner on flood control. Although they were in the minority, detractors expressed their disapproval of the project. For example, in her much-admired paean entitled *The Everglades: River of Grass*, Marjory Stoneman Douglas described the ecosystem's subtle beauty and unique natural history and warned against tampering with it. And ironically, even as it launched the nation's most ambitious plumbing project, Congress was simultaneously designating the Everglades National Park, comprising the southwestern section of the Everglades, in recognition of its biological importance.[10]

Despite this apparent contradiction, development interests prevailed, and over the next twenty years, the Corps of Engineers dug, widened, or deepened 978 miles of canals; built 990 miles of levees; installed 212 tide gates, floodgates, and other control structures; and built 30 pumping stations to drain water from potential farmland (see Map 15-1).[11] The corps began by establishing a perimeter levee through the eastern portion, blocking the sheetflow so that lands east of the levee would be protected from flooding. The levee, which was about 100 miles long, became the westward limit of agricultural, residential, and other land development for the lower east coast from West Palm Beach to Homestead; it severed 16 percent of the Everglades from its interior.[12] Farmers cleared the 1,000-square-mile area south of Lake Okeechobee and north of the Everglades National Park for agriculture. The Everglades Agricultural Area (EAA), as this swath is known, encompasses about 27 percent of the historic Everglades. The corps designated for water conservation the acreage between the EAA and the park, bounded by the eastern perimeter levee and an incomplete western levee at the edge of the Big Cypress Swamp. It then divided that reservation into three wetland impoundments called water conservation areas (WCAs), which together comprise nearly one-third of the historic Everglades. The northernmost of these, WCA1, eventually became the Arthur R. Marshall Loxahatchee National Wildlife Refuge, managed by the U.S. Fish and Wildlife Service. Federal engineers built levees to separate the WCAs and interconnecting canals and water structures to regulate their water supply.

In another triumph for development interests, cattle ranchers and landowners succeeded in getting the C&SF Project to include plans to straighten areas of the meandering, 103-mile-long Kissimmee River. Over the objections of the Fish and Wildlife Service and the Florida Game and Fresh Fish Commission, both of which argued that the project would seriously disturb the region's ecology, that endeavor got under way in the early 1960s.[13] When the corps sliced a 56-mile-long channel (C-38) down the middle of the river, it destroyed 80 percent of the surrounding marshes and 90 percent of the duck population. Water levels in the aquifer dropped, and the amount of nutrients flowing into Lake Okeechobee jumped, resulting in severe eutrophication.[14]

Hydrological modification continued at a brisk pace through the decade. In 1963 the corps dug drainage canal C-111 along Everglades National Park's eastern boundary and completed L-29, a levee and canal along the north boundary of the park delineating the southern edge of WCA3. The early 1960s were a time of drought in South Florida, and the new levee choked off what little water was arriving from the north. Compounding the pressures on the ecosystem were two major new highways, Alligator Alley and the Tamiami Trail, that spanned the width of South Florida and blocked the southward flow of water. In addition, developers excavated 183 miles of canals outside the Big Cypress Preserve, which borders the park to the west, to facilitate construction of an enormous real estate boondoggle named The Golden Gate Estates. The

Map 15-1 Central and South Florida Flood Control System

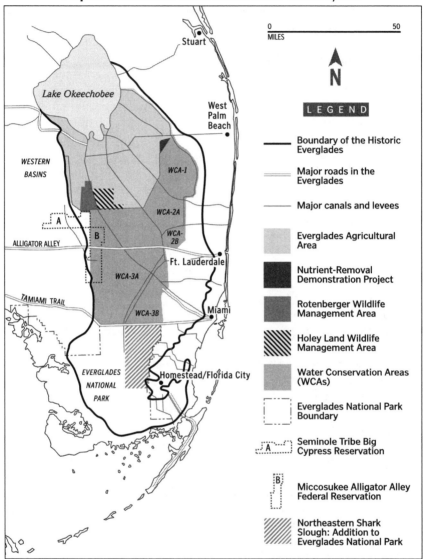

Source: Thomas E. Lodge, *The Everglades Handbook* (Delray Beach, Fla.: St. Lucie Press, 1994).

Note: The Miccosukee Indians have interests in lands bordering the Tamiami Trail in much of WCA-3a.

canals lowered the water table by more than two feet and discharged 1.6 billion gallons of fresh water annually into the Ten Thousand Islands estuary.[15]

By the late 1960s, Everglades National Park had been deprived of its water supply and appeared to be dying of thirst. Frantic park officials begged for more water, but to no avail; the corps and the district refused, arguing that water had to go first to people, not animals. Following the drought of 1970–1971, the worst in forty years, reports from the park claimed that 90 percent of the wading birds had disappeared and that alligators and panthers, as well as other plant and animal species, were critically endangered. The environmental stresses on South Florida were becoming apparent in other ways as well: as periodic muck fires raged, soil subsided at more than an inch a year, and salt water intruded into freshwater supplies.

Environmentalists Mobilize

As the park's crisis approached, South Florida's environmentalists—backed by a small group of the state's prominent scientists—mobilized to resist two major development proposals. They achieved their first triumph in 1969, when they convinced President Richard Nixon to call a halt to the Cross-Florida Barge Canal project. Within the year they scored another stunning victory with the defeat of the Big Cypress jetport proposal. These engagements shattered the exclusive South Florida water "subgovernment"—a once-impermeable network of government agencies, congressional committees, and private interests oriented toward development.[16] As a result of these two major controversies, Florida's environmentalists gained political stature, and in 1970 they used their clout on behalf of Everglades National Park, successfully petitioning Congress for a law requiring the corps to release a minimum of 315,000 acre-feet of water annually into the parched park.[17]

Buoyed by these successes, environmentalists began to lobby the state of Florida for a comprehensive new land and water management policy. A groundswell of public support for environmental protection bolstered their efforts; Floridians, according to pollster Patrick Caddell, were becoming much more interested in "quality of life," and issues such as growth, overpopulation, pollution, and water shortages had become highly salient.[18] Also encouraging were changes in the state government, including a legislative overhaul, the election of a conservationist governor, and the passage of a new constitution.[19]

In response to the state's budding environmentalism, in 1972 the legislature enacted a series of land and water management reforms. Among the most critical for the Everglades was the Water Resources Act of 1972, which transformed the Central and South Florida Flood Control District into the South Florida Water Management District (SFWMD) and vested in it responsibility for water supply and quality. In addition, the Florida Environmental Land and Water Management Act ensured "a water management system that will reverse the deterioration of water quality and provide optimum utilization of [the state's] limited water resources" and allowed the governor to designate "areas of critical state concern." [20] Three years later, in 1975, the Florida legislature consolidated control over water quantity and quality, as well as drinking water standards, in the Department of Environmental Regulation and required the new agency to supervise the state's five water management districts' preparation of state water plans.

THE CASE

Although the state's new laws promised to enhance its capacity to incorporate environmental values into water management, development interests remained firmly entrenched in the day-to-day operations of the C&SF Project's elaborate water distribution system. As a result, the Everglades continued to show unmistakable signs of distress. Recognizing this, in the early 1980s environmentalists capitalized on a series of environmental disasters to challenge Everglades policy. Unable to raise the issue's salience with a public relations campaign, environmentalists turned to another venue, the courts, where they had greater success. Having finally drawn public attention to the Everglades' ecological health, however, environmentalists faced a daunting challenge: getting agreement among the myriad federal, state, and local stakeholders on their real objective—an ambitious ecosystem-scale restoration.

The Save Our Everglades Campaign

A succession of environmental crises opened a window of opportunity for protective Everglades policies in the 1980s. In the late 1970s, large algae blooms appeared on the already troubled Lake Okeechobee. Scientists attributed the problem to nitrogen and phosphorous flowing from dairy farms along the Kissimmee River and the backpumping of nutrients from the EAA to the south of the lake. To clean up the lake, the SFWMD required the EAA to stop pumping its water into it. So instead, the EAA began diverting the wastewater through the Everglades National Park by way of the water conservation areas, despite park and refuge scientists' warnings that this practice would cause a host of ecological problems. Scientists at the Loxahatchee National Wildlife Refuge were hardly surprised, therefore, when in 1981 they noticed an excess of phosphorous in the system and a corresponding change in the mix of plants: cattails were crowding out the native sawgrass. Then, in 1980–1981, a yearlong drought dried out much of the Everglades muck, resulting in lightning-sparked wildfires that sent clouds of noxious smoke billowing over Miami, Fort Lauderdale, and the Palm Beaches. An underground wedge of salt water moved inland, tainting some freshwater supplies and threatening others. [21]

Capping this series of disasters, in 1983 torrential rains struck the state, and the corps opened the floodgates into the park, deluging it with three and a half times the minimum amount of water set by Congress in 1970. During what is usually the dry season, 5 billion gallons flowed into the park daily. [22] The influx devastated wading bird nesting and inundated alligator habitat. At the same time, commercial and recreational fishermen began to complain about the degradation of the Florida Bay, where fish populations were plummeting. With its mixture of salt and fresh water and vast mangrove forests, the area had once been one of the world's most productive fish hatcheries; by the early 1980s, however, murky patches of algae were blooming on its surface.

Prompted by scientific concern about South Florida's ecological future, a coalition of sixty environmental groups, commissions, and municipalities mobilized to launch a political campaign that aimed to transform the water management priorities of South Florida from fostering economic development to repairing the Everglades ecosystem. With participation estimated at 250,000, the coalition was the largest ever to gather around a single environmental issue in the state.[23] Acting as a policy entrepreneur was Gov. Bob Graham, who in 1983 announced his "Save Our Everglades" initiative. In an effort to redefine the Everglades problem to emphasize ecology rather than urban water supply, Graham linked human survival with the ecosystem's health, saying that the region faced "an awesome truth. Our presence here is as tenuous as that of the fragile Everglades. The complicated ecosystems that support delicate swamp lilies and great blue herons are the source of our water." [24] After declaring his intent to save the Everglades, Graham dispatched staff around the state to settle environmental disputes, began lobbying for protective legislation, instituted reforms in several main agencies, and—perhaps most important— appointed five new, environmentally oriented board members and a new executive director to the SFWMD.[25]

Despite Graham's strong backing, environmentalists had difficulty raising the salience of the Everglades' ecological problems. Observers attributed the public's inattention to the elusiveness of the landscape's splendor. Bruce Babbitt described the challenges of generating passion about a wetland, saying "there aren't any glaciers in the Everglades, there aren't any grizzly bears, there aren't any 500-foot waterfalls. We've been a little slow in expanding our image of parks to include equally important but more subtle kinds of ecosystems." Patti Webster, an environmental activist, agreed. "Getting people interested in saving the manatee isn't a problem, but getting them to love a swamp is a real challenge," she said. Even those who lobbied on behalf of the park pointed out that it could be a brutal place. As one park ranger noted, "The temperature gets up to 95 degrees with 100 percent humidity, and there are thunder and lightning storms like I've never imagined, and every day the mosquitoes are so thick you can't breathe. It's miserable." [26]

Making matters worse, during much of the 1980s the National Park Service— environmentalists' prime ally in recruiting public and political support—was incapable of generating the scientific information and expertise that might have helped to document and dramatize the Everglades' problems. As noted in chapter 9, from its inception in 1916 the National Park Service has struggled with its schizophrenic mandate to preserve scenery and wildlife unimpaired for future generations while also providing for tourism. The service's ongoing preoccupation with attracting visitors detracted from its ability to manage the parks with ecological sensitivity and to develop scientific capabilities, and for decades the agency ignored pleas from outsiders to improve the scientific basis for park management.[27] In 1976, however, a prominent Florida Republican named Nathaniel Reed convinced Congress to establish the South Florida Research Center within the Everglades National Park. The center's scientists began studying historic water records, installing a network of water gauges, monitoring rainfall, and systematically examining the parks' wildlife and vegetation. By the early 1980s, their studies were yielding sobering results. For example, upon completion of a ten-year study, park scientist James Kushlan reported that high water was flooding alligator and woodstork nesting sites and threatening those species. But, as Kushlan recalls, "The Superintendent told me he did not even want to read my study. If he read it he would have to design a management plan to satisfy it, and manipulation of water levels was a lot more risky than doing nothing." [28] According to Park Service critic Alston Chase, the superintendent suppressed the study, and shortly thereafter the chief of the research center issued an order prohibiting all center scientists from publishing the results of their work. Frustrated with those restrictions, Kushlan and several of his colleagues left the service for university positions.

Resisting the Everglades Rescue. The Save Our Everglades initiative not only lacked broad public support and powerful institutional allies but also faced formidable opposition from the sugar industry, which wielded tremendous political clout in both the state legislature and the U.S. Congress. Since the eighteenth century, Congress had provided the sugar industry with generous subsidies and highly restrictive import quotas.[29] Despite the industry's exploitative labor practices and environmental abuses, the Florida legislature was also deferential to sugar, in part because of the legislature's traditional rural bias and its recognition of the economic potency of the industry, but also because sugar executives provided their allies with generous campaign contributions.[30]

In addition to its legislative connections, the sugar industry maintained strong ties to the SFWMD, which by the 1980s was a wealthy, powerful, and highly professionalized entity with broad policymaking authority. Although the SFWMD's initial purpose was flood control, the Florida Water Resources Act of 1972 had made Everglades protection part of its mandate.[31] In the early 1980s, with its broader mission and under the influence of environmentally oriented board members appointed by Governor Graham, the SFWMD began to acquire a more progressive reputation. Overall, however, the agency continued to be more attentive to the demands of economic development interests than to long-term ecological considerations; top management still consisted of development-oriented engineers; and standard operating procedures aimed to facilitate the region's economic growth.

The sugar industry was also an important client of the Corps of Engineers, the federal agency that—in partnership with the SFWMD—was responsible for managing South Florida's water supply. From its inception in 1802, the corps had been a versatile organization but one primarily oriented toward economic development; since 1850 its main responsibility had been to build, maintain, and operate flood control and other water development projects to facilitate farming and real estate development. In 1936 Congress established a national flood control policy and gave the corps even greater authority over this area. Finally, in 1938 and 1941 Congress removed certain local participation and approval requirements from the corps' authorizing statute, "paving the way for the Corps to become the engineer consultants and contractors of the U.S. Congress." [32]

Although the corps was the nation's premier development organization, it began to incorporate environmental concerns into its standard operating procedures in the 1970s after the passage of the National Environmental Policy Act. By the end of the decade the agency had made a habit of consulting advisory boards composed of planning and environmental professionals and a range of interest groups. In addition, all the agency's offices had a distinct unit whose primary purpose was to provide environmental input into planning. Nevertheless, in the mid-1980s, the corps was still regularly denying the SFWMD the permits it needed to undertake Everglades restoration and was widely seen as impeding such efforts. [33] It also routinely dispensed permits to developers who wanted to fill wetlands across the state.

The Government's Response. The Save Our Everglades campaign was ineffectual when pitted against the well-heeled team of the SFWMD and the corps, who were abetted by a Florida legislature that was reluctant to antagonize wealthy development interests. Governor Graham nevertheless continued to promote environmental initiatives and, as a result, did accomplish some noteworthy policy changes. At Graham's behest, the state continued to fine-tune its planning and growth management apparatus—although it did so without directly confronting the sugar industry on the Everglades issue. Most important, in 1987 the legislature approved SWIM, the Surface Water Improvement and Management Act, requiring the water districts to develop plans to prevent and reverse degradation of the state's waters. SWIM also set targets for the amount of phosphorous entering Lake Okeechobee and established a technical advisory council to study the effects of phosphorous on the WCAs and other areas south of the lake. Finally, the act specified that water management districts "shall not divert water to . . . the Everglades National Park in such a way that state water quality standards are violated [or] that nutrients in such waters adversely affect indigenous vegetation communities or wildlife." [34]

Although the district expressed its commitment to devise and implement a SWIM plan, the prospects for bringing about major changes in the Everglades regime appeared bleak. Newly elected governor Bob Martinez had appointed five new SFWMD board members, including several with close ties to the sugar industry and vegetable growers. In any case, SWIM plans by themselves do not mandate particular actions, and neither the state nor the district was taking serious steps to change the hydrologic regime. As one highly respected former SFWMD board member put it, the district was "drifting" on the issue of water quality in 1988 and was not giving it adequate attention.[35]

Mounting Evidence of Ecosystem Decline

By the late 1980s scientists had formulated a clear picture of how land-use and water management practices in South Florida had damaged the Everglades ecosystem. They understood that the extensive network of canals, levees, and pumps had dramatically altered the balance among the four main hydrologic variables that govern the region's ecological health: the timing of water releases, the distribution of the water flow, the amount of water released, and the water quality. As a result of the changes to the system, sixty-eight species of plants and animals were threatened or endangered. Among the species in trouble were the Florida panther, the West Indian manatee, the southern bald eagle, the Cape Sable sparrow, the brown pelican, the indigo snake, and several varieties of sea turtle. Endemic plants, tropical trees, and rare orchids were disappearing as well.

Perhaps most alarming was the steep decline in the population of wading birds: by the late 1980s the historic giant rookeries of the southern Everglades were gone, and, although new rookeries had appeared in the WCAs north of the park, they were small and appeared unstable. Biologist John Ogden noted that by 1989, the number of nesting wood storks, an indicator species, had dropped 80 percent from its already-reduced level in the 1960s.[36] The birds' decline was closely related to changes in the hydroperiod—that is, the timing and quantity of water flowing into the Everglades. Historically, the birds synchronized their nesting with slow-moving dry fronts. They started nesting in November or December and raised their young during the subsequent dry season, when the receding water along the wetlands' edge left behind shallow pools of water filled with prey. Hydrological modifications had disrupted the normal cycle, however, leaving deeper pools that dried out more slowly and creating abrupt shifts between wet and dry periods, so in many years the nesting season was virtually nonexistent.[37]

Another of the Everglades' keystone species, the American alligator, had also suffered from alterations in the hydroperiod, although the effects of those changes initially were masked because the population had rebounded after the federal Endangered Species Act eliminated poaching.[38] Having survived since the age of the dinosaurs, alligators were adaptable and willing to use human-made canals for breeding. Nevertheless, they suffered when too much water flooded their nests early in the wet season. As the alligators dwindled, wading birds could no longer rely on the alligator holes and trails that once enhanced their habitat by providing a home for prey that would repopulate the adjacent marshes during the rainy season.[39]

Scientists were piecing together the causes of some other disturbing trends in the region as well, particularly in Florida Bay. Located between the Everglades National Park and the Florida Keys, the bay is a large, shallow, coastal lagoon that contains numerous islands fringed with mangroves and mud shoals. Signs of decline appeared in Florida Bay in the 1970s and accelerated in the 1980s. About fifteen square miles of seagrass died in the bay's western half between 1987 and 1990, and about ninety square miles were damaged. The coral reef in the Florida Bay—the only such reef in the continental United States—was deteriorating rapidly. And scientists were documenting spectacular declines in the populations of the bay's wading seabirds, sponges, and mangrove trees. Fish and shellfish were so scarce that in 1985 park officials banned commercial fishing in the bay altogether.

The Lawsuit

Activated by scientists' concern and frustrated with the intransigence of the SFWMD and the corps, environmentalists began to explore legal avenues through which to change government priorities. They were having difficulty finding a legal toehold when the newly appointed acting U.S. attorney for South Florida, Dexter Lehtinen, called them into his office to ask which environmental problem his office ought to tackle next. Environmentalists responded that the decline of the Everglades was the single most important issue facing the state.[40] Lehtinen proposed suing the state in federal court for failing to enforce its own water quality laws by allowing the EAA to pump water into the Loxahatchee National Wildlife Refuge without obtaining a permit from the SFWMD and thereby inflicting a nuisance on the refuge and the park.[41] Recognizing that Lehtinen was better positioned to mount a legal challenge than they were, environmentalists dropped their own legal exploration and, at Lehtinen's invitation, joined the Justice Department's suit.[42]

The lawsuit further polarized environmental and development interests, which were already antagonistic, and for three years the parties were at an impasse. Although a resolution was elusive, the environmental coalition took advantage of the publicity surrounding the lawsuit to promote its cause. The coalition used the scientific evidence relating phosphorous levels to the Everglades' decline as a basis for a compelling causal story: they pointed out that the EAA lay directly in the path of the region's historic sheetflow and thereby severed the connection between Lake Okeechobee and the park, and that sugar cane fields—which occupied the bulk of the EAA—were responsible for most of the phosphorous flowing into the Everglades.[43] It was not difficult to portray sugar executives as greedy and dishonest: they were making enormous profits while reaping millions annually in government subsidies.[44] Moreover, they were notorious for their exploitative labor practices and close connections to the political establishment. Although sugar was the main villain in the story, environmentalists had far wider ambitions: according to Assistant Attorney General Richard Stewart, "Agricultural pollution was . . . only the opening wedge in a much larger issue. It was really a question of changing the culture of the district, the state, and the industry."[45]

Naturally, once environmentalists went public with their attack on sugar, the industry retaliated in kind, hoping to minimize the groundswell of public support for restoration and defuse antipathy toward "big sugar." Industry executives began by asserting that the cattails in the refuge and the park were neither as extensive nor as voracious as environmentalists contended, and they cited alternative explanations for the presence of cattails, emphasizing natural factors such as fire, hydroperiod changes, and sediments from Lake Okeechobee. Once it became clear that phosphorous was in fact the prime culprit, they began marshalling scientific evidence to refute environmentalists' claim that runoff from cane fields was primarily responsible for the high phosphorous levels. To enhance their credibility, the EAA hired Curtis Richardson, a Duke University wetlands expert, and the Florida Sugar Cane League retained a respected Florida scientist who held a position on the board of the Florida Wildlife Federation.[46] These experts pointed out that growing sugar cane requires relatively little fertilizer and that cane does not have to be replanted annually, so it causes less erosion than other crops. They added that sugar was not the EAA's only source of phosphorous and was a relatively benign one at that.[47]

Settling the Lawsuit. The sugar industry's counterattack notwithstanding, environmental activists' efforts were beginning to bear fruit. Even before the lawsuit, the U.S. Congress—which had been apathetic about Florida's environmental problems throughout much of the 1980s—had taken its first big step toward Everglades restoration by passing the 1989 Everglades National Park Protection and Expansion Act, which authorized the purchase of more than 107,000 acres east of the park. The goal of the acquisition was to enable the park to regain 55 percent of the natural water flow to the Shark River Slough, a flow that had been reduced 90 percent by the corps.[48] Everglades restoration had also become Florida's premier environmental issue: gubernatorial challenger Lawton Chiles, a Democrat, made the lawsuit a central point of contention in his campaign, ridiculing Martinez's passivity and pointing out that millions of dollars were being wasted on legal fees. Chiles pledged to reach a settlement and subsequently won the election partly on the strength of that commitment.

The combination of Governor Chiles's leadership and environmentalists' ongoing campaign advanced the cause of Everglades restoration toward a tipping point. On his first day in office, Chiles delivered a speech at the annual meeting of the Everglades Coalition and told the gathering that, as commander in chief of the state's environmental programs, he would settle the Everglades lawsuit within six months.[49] Although his initial effort—a summit involving environmentalists, state and district officials, and the sugar industry—was a flop, Chiles proceeded to operate on other fronts. He asked Carol Browner, his secretary of the Department of Environmental Regulation, to take the lead in negotiations with the Justice Department. And he appointed five environmentally oriented members to the SFWMD board.

As part of the settlement effort, industry and government scientists met to try to establish the scientific parameters of the dispute. Once they sat down

together, the scientists were able to agree fairly easily on the level of phosphorous that would be harmful to the Everglades: approximately 10 ppb (parts
per billion). The scientists also converged on the idea that building a large,
artificial wetland to filter the water draining from the EAA would help solve
the water quality problem. The more challenging (and politically loaded)
question was how large a wetland would be necessary to bring EAA waters
down to an acceptable standard?[50]

While scientists worked to resolve the technical questions, environmentalists turned the sugar industry's continuing intransigence to their advantage,
using the delay to build their case in public and the legislature. They added
economic arguments to their arsenal of justifications for Everglades restoration, enlisting hotel and dive shop owners in the Keys, as well as sport and
commercial fishermen from Florida Bay. Tom Martin, director of the National
Audubon Society's Everglades campaign, revealed the extent to which environmentalists were willing to appropriate their opposition's arguments when
he said: "It's become clear that the economic health of South Florida is tied to
its environmental health. South Florida's economy is based on growth. . . .
Saving the Everglades isn't just for the birds. It's jobs." [51] Environmentalists
also pursued urban interests, recognizing that the more than 5 million people
living along the state's Gold Coast relied for clean water on the Biscayne
Aquifer, which—as environmentalists pointed out—depended on a healthy,
functioning Everglades.

Recognizing the Everglades' increasing popularity, Florida legislators got
on the restoration bandwagon. In addition to appropriating matching funds to
buy land for conversion to wetlands, in the spring of 1991, the legislature
unanimously passed a critical bill: the Marjory Stoneman Douglas Act, which
rendered moot several of the issues in the lawsuit. The act specified numerical
standards for the quality of water passing through the EAA pumps, required
the SFWMD to apply to the Department of Environmental Regulation for permits for those pumps, and directed the district to make farmers get permits for
water draining off their lands. The act also required the district to prepare a
SWIM plan "to bring facilities into compliance with applicable water quality
standards and restore the Everglades hydroperiod." [52] Finally, the law authorized the SFWMD to condemn land and build artificial wetlands, thereby facilitating the restoration.

Shortly thereafter, the governor broke the legal impasse that had stymied
negotiators for three years by stipulating in court that the water flowing into
the Everglades was polluted. Over a two-month period following Chiles's
concession, the scientific task force agreed that at least 34,700 acres of artificial
wetlands (at an estimated cost of $400 million to build) would be necessary to
purify water flowing into the park.[53] On July 8, six months after Chiles took
office, the parties to the lawsuit submitted a thirty-page settlement to district
court judge William Hoeveler, who approved it nine months later, after rejecting a slew of appeals by the sugar companies. Under the 1992 consent decree,
the state of Florida agreed to implement a water quality restoration plan by

building artificial filtration marshes, imposing best management practices[54] on farms, and requiring agricultural runoff to meet an interim phosphorous limit of 50 ppb and a long-term limit of 10 ppb.

For environmentalists, however, the consent decree was only a first step because the quality of the water flowing into the Everglades was only part of the problem. Disruption of the hydroperiod remained to be addressed. (Although both the consent decree and the Marjory Stoneman Douglas Act referred to restoring the Everglades hydroperiod, neither provided specifics on how the restoration would be done.) Moreover, although the court, the federal government, the state, and the SFWMD were amenable to the consent decree, the sugar industry—which had not been a formal party to either the lawsuit or the settlement—was not. The industry was willing to implement the best management practices set forth by the SFWMD, but it resisted the more expensive remedy of building artificial wetlands. In spring 1992 the industry launched a public relations campaign to denigrate the settlement as unreasonable and unfair. When sugar executives made it clear that they were prepared to spend millions on court battles, Florida officials and the Justice Department felt compelled to embark on another round of negotiations.

Isolating the Sugar Industry. This time, any interested parties—including both the sugar industry and environmentalists—were invited to join the talks. Like the discussions leading up to the original settlement, the second round of negotiations involved a technical group, whose job was to devise a science-based plan to address the water quality and hydroperiod problems in the Everglades. Like its predecessor, the technical group reached agreement on the range of acceptable phosphorous levels fairly easily and by early 1993 had also come up with a plan to create artificial wetlands and simultaneously improve the hydroperiod. The technical group's proposal, known as the Mediated Technical Plan, subsequently became the basis for the debate over who would pay for the restoration.

Throughout the discussions, while privately exploring alternatives to artificial wetlands for reducing the flow of phosphorous off its lands, publicly the sugar industry tried to minimize its financial culpability by maintaining that phosphorous was not a serious problem and that, in any case, sugar was not the culprit behind its elevated levels. As late as July 1993, a Flo-Sun company spokesman said, "It's not true that cattails are caused by phosphorous—it's because of flooding." [55] J. Nelson Fairbanks, president of U.S. Sugar, continued to adhere to the theory that phosphorous was already in the water when it entered the cane fields from Lake Okeechobee or that it seeped up from underground. Fairbanks suggested that, because the Corps of Engineers had built the C&SF system, it should have to fix it. Sugar industry executives also resorted to economic and equity arguments: U.S. Sugar's executive vice president of operations, Robert Buker, commented that "the deal that was struck will bankrupt South Florida." [56]

The sugar industry was increasingly isolated in its stance, however; recognizing that momentum for restoration was building, the SFWMD and the corps had both joined the prorestoration coalition. The SFWMD had begun developing a "natural systems" model to quantify the actual water level and flow in the primeval Everglades. And the corps, once perceived as the primary obstacle, had taken the lead on devising an Everglades restoration plan. (Even its harshest critics were impressed with the corps' alacrity, although many attributed its chameleon-like shift to its ability to spot and take advantage of lucrative, budget-enhancing opportunities rather than to a genuine philosophical transformation.)

Federal Leadership Propels the Cleanup Plan Forward

In 1993 a series of personnel changes—this time at the federal level—opened another political window of opportunity for proponents of Everglades restoration. By appointing environmentally oriented officials to head the EPA, Interior, and other departments and agencies, President Bill Clinton dramatically changed the climate for environmental protection in Washington. Although Clinton's EPA administrator, Carol Browner, recused herself from the Everglades dispute because of her former role, she encouraged Clinton's proenvironment Interior secretary, Bruce Babbitt, to be a policy entrepreneur on the issue.[57] In addition to these executive-branch changes, several congressional shifts had major consequences for the Everglades: Democrat George Miller of California took over the chairmanship of the House Interior Committee, and two new members of Congress from South Florida—both advocates of Everglades research and restoration—obtained positions on the House Appropriations Committee.

Shortly after he was appointed, Secretary Babbitt—hoping to make resolution of the Everglades a national model of ecosystem-level environmental problem solving—invited his top assistants, as well as important state officials and executives from Flo-Sun and U.S. Sugar, to come to Washington, D.C., and settle their differences. In July 1993 a jubilant Babbitt held a press conference to proclaim that the parties had reached a tentative agreement to split the costs of implementing the Mediated Technical Plan (devised as part of the second round of settlement negotiations): the agricultural community would pay 50 percent of the plan's estimated $700 million cost over twenty years; the federal government would pay 8 percent; and the state of Florida would pitch in the remaining 42 percent.[58] The basic agreement, known as the Statement of Principles, involved a combination of best management practices and nearly 40,000 acres of stormwater treatment areas, or artificial wetlands. The sugar executives agreed to withdraw their lawsuits so that the details of the plan could be worked out.

Some environmentalists were cautiously optimistic about the deal Babbitt had brokered, but others were outraged. For many environmentalists, the principle was clear: the sugar industry had polluted the Everglades and it, not the taxpayers, ought to pay to clean it up. Audubon's Joe Browder denounced Babbitt for compromising on the Everglades. Others questioned whether the plan entailed a real, long-term obligation on the part of the sugar industry because the new deal was, in many respects, less ambitious than the 1992 consent decree: it called for only as many acres of wetlands as necessary to reduce the concentration of phosphorous in the water entering the park to 50 ppb, whereas the 1992 settlement had included a second-phase target of 10 ppb.[59] Just months after the agreement was announced, opposition from environmental groups had crystallized: nineteen national and state-level organizations wrote to Secretary Babbitt asking that 70,000–120,000 acres of EAA land be set aside for wetlands and requesting additional treatment for any water brought into the Everglades to restore the hydroperiod if it was below water quality standards.

Laying the Groundwork for a Restoration Plan. Thanks to the visibility of the water quality lawsuit and its settlement, environmentalists were able to build support for a more comprehensive restoration—an idea that, beginning in the early 1990s, moved forward alongside the cleanup plan. To facilitate interagency coordination among the numerous federal entities whose cooperation would be required to restore the Everglades ecosystem, as well as to build the scientific capability and credibility that would be necessary for this unprecedented enterprise to succeed, Secretary Babbitt established the South Florida Ecosystem Restoration Task Force, composed of assistant secretaries from six federal agencies and representing ten bureaus.[60] The task force charter, signed in September 1993, set forth the goal of establishing a science program that could furnish the interdisciplinary studies and syntheses necessary for a complex, ecosystem-scale restoration. To accomplish this, the task force created the South Florida Management and Coordination Working Group, headed by Dick Ring, superintendent of the Everglades National Park, who proceeded to designate three subgroups to coordinate the research agenda for South Florida.

In parallel with the Interior Department's efforts, the corps' C&SF Project Comprehensive Review Study, or Restudy, authorized by Congress as part of the 1992 Water Resources Development Act, also adopted a multiagency, cooperative approach to planning the restoration effort. Congress hoped that by incorporating all the stakeholders, the corps' planning effort could gain widespread support, which would reduce the likelihood that any individual agency or organization would subsequently undermine the project.[61] A collaborative approach was also intended to enhance the production and flow of information. Taking advantage of many sources of expertise in the system, the Restudy team included civil engineers, hydraulic engineers, cost engineers, biologists, ecologists, resource managers, community planners, economists, geographic information system specialists, and real estate experts.

As the reconnaissance phase of the corps-led Restudy got under way, the Interior Department task force's science subgroup was already at work on the scientific underpinning of a restoration plan. In late November 1993 the sub-group released a draft report that stunned opponents of Everglades restoration. The report, which was the second integrated assessment of the region's ecological characteristics, drew heavily on the results of a 1989 symposium, at which scientists first tried to synthesize existing knowledge about the ecosystem. It affirmed scientists' belief that the goal of the restoration should be to "recover and sustain the major defining ecological characteristics of the pre-drainage South Florida wetland systems over as large an area of the remaining wetlands as possible." [62] It also outlined many of the tenets that scientists believed should ground the restoration effort. Foremost among those principles was that "hydrologic restoration is a necessary starting point for ecological restoration." [63] To that end, the report proposed permanently flooding 195,000 of the 450,000 acres under cultivation in the EAA. The remainder of the EAA, the report suggested, should be under water 60 percent of the time. The timing of the report's release, just days before the final meeting of the sugar industry, farmers, and federal and state officials to sign an agreement on the cleanup plan, was a public relations disaster, and within weeks a furious sugar industry had withdrawn its support for the fragile Everglades cleanup deal.[64]

The sugar industry proceeded to file thirty-six lawsuits challenging the state's plans to implement the water quality improvement plan, and a court date was scheduled for April 25, 1994. Preempting the trial, however, on April 15, the Florida legislature passed another major statute, the Everglades Forever Act. The new law put an end to the sugar industry's legal maneuvering by stipulating the need for Everglades cleanup and hydroperiod remediation, asserting the suitability of the cleanup program as a remedy for those problems, and condoning the Statement of Principles (negotiated by Babbitt) as a basis for remediation. It went beyond the Statement of Principles by incorporating suggestions from the environmental community to improve on the Mediated Technical Plan. The Everglades Forever Act enabled restoration of the ecosystem to begin in earnest by requiring the state to administer a $700 million Everglades cleanup that included a water treatment system, extensive research and monitoring, and a regulatory program.[65] Most important, the act mandated a substantial financial contribution from agriculture, thereby aborting what promised to be a series of time-consuming administrative and judicial proceedings instigated by the sugar industry.

Although the Everglades Forever Act eliminated some potential legal hurdles to making water quality improvements, proponents of a comprehensive restoration still faced many additional impediments. To bolster public support, the Corps of Engineers and the SFWMD held workshops to gather public comments on the Restudy. They held three rounds of large public meetings in 1993 and 1994, with up to 700 people at each, and they made plans for smaller focus group sessions to discuss specific issues in subsequent years. In addition, in March 1994 Governor Chiles appointed a forty-two-member citizens group called the Commission for a Sustainable South Florida. From the outset the commission members agreed that "The human community is dependent on the surrounding natural system for public health, safety and welfare; continued economic vitality; and enhanced quality of life." [66] Two years later the assemblage of homeowners, builders, sugar and citrus growers, business leaders, tribal officials, water managers, and environmentalists unanimously endorsed their preferred alternative from among the set of options prepared by the corps. The option they chose rested on an elaborately engineered system of collecting and storing the water that was currently being shunted to tide during the wet season and distributing it to various constituencies in dry periods. They regarded their choice as a "win-win" solution; the idea was that, by "expanding the pie," they could avoid making tradeoffs between ecological health and water supply for human use.

The governor's commission's seal of approval, combined with growing public support for the restoration, in turn enhanced the prospects for political backing. Because Florida was the nation's fourth most populous state and therefore a pivotal source of Electoral College votes, it had become the focus of both Democratic and Republican presidential campaigns. Given its burgeoning popularity within the state and nationally, the Everglades restoration became an obvious source of political credit-claiming as the 1996 presidential race heated up. Between 1994 and 1996, Congress came up with nearly $5 million annually to buy land for buffer areas around the park; moreover, at the instigation of Republican presidential candidate Bob Dole, the Senate Agriculture Committee inserted into the 1996 omnibus farm bill $200 million for the Everglades.[67] Not to be outdone, Vice President Al Gore—on behalf of President Clinton—officially endorsed the restoration project in February 1996 and proposed going well beyond the terms of the 1994 Everglades Forever Act by adding $500 million over the next several years to the $100 million the federal government had already committed to the Interior Department's Everglades Restoration Fund.[68]

In addition to providing monetary support, in October 1996 Congress affirmed its backing for the planning portion of the restoration with Section 528 of the Water Resources Development Act of Corps to provide "a proposed comprehensive plan for the purpose of restoring, preserving, and protecting the South Florida ecosystem." [69] The law required the Corps of Engineers to develop the plan in cooperation with the SFWMD and in consultation with the South Florida Ecosystem Restoration Task Force, and to submit it to Congress by July 1, 1999. It allowed the corps to begin implementing restoration projects as deemed necessary by the corps, the state of Florida, and the task force, and it authorized appropriations of $75 million from 1997 to 1999 to carry out such projects. Once sold on the restoration, a bipartisan Congress endorsed it again the following year, appropriating $269 million for fiscal year 1998 and $221 million for fiscal year 1999.

The Restoration Plan. In October 1998, after five years of study, the corps unveiled a draft of its $7.8 billion plan, the Comprehensive Everglades Restoration Plan (CERP). Far more extensive than the cleanup requested by the plaintiffs in the original lawsuit or subsequently devised under the Everglades Forever Act, CERP covered 18,000 square miles from the northern edge of the Kissimmee River drainage near Orlando to Florida Bay along the Keys. Its fundamental goal was to "get the water right"—that is, to deliver the right amount of water, of the right quality, to the right places at the right times. To this end, the plan proposed to remove 240 miles of levees and canals and create about 30,000 acres of wetlands—in addition to the more than 40,000 acres already under development—that would filter urban and agricultural run-off before discharging it into the Everglades. Because it was premised on "expanding the pie," the new approach was heavily engineered: the corps intended to create eighteen reservoirs and 333 underground aquifer storage and recovery wells and to build a system for reusing wastewater, all of which would allow it to retain in the system over 90 percent of the 1.7 million acre-feet of water per year that was currently being pumped into the ocean. Engineers also planned to add nearly 500 miles of new canals and levees on the periphery of the system to facilitate the elaborate process of transporting water from one place to another to restore the region's historic water depths, if not its historic flows. Finally, the plan promised to employ adaptive management because, although scientists assumed that restoring the hydrologic regime would lead to healthier biological communities, they were uncertain about how the much-compromised Everglades would actually respond to changes in the water regime.

Although CERP was announced with great fanfare, opponents of restoration were hardly vanquished. Opponents generated dire predictions of the economic impact of the project: the Florida Citizens for a Sound Economy calculated that residents would lose nearly 3,000 jobs and pay about $120 per household per year in taxes and water fees.[70] (By contrast, the corps estimated that its plan would *create* between 3,900 and 6,800 jobs.) Meanwhile the sugar industry was working behind the scenes to undermine the plan.[71] As the public turned its attention elsewhere, allies of the sugar industry slipped two bills through the Florida state legislature in spring 1998. The first bill gave the legislature direct oversight over the corps; the second made it more expensive for the federal government to acquire land for the restoration. Environmentalists breathed a sigh of relief when Governor Chiles vetoed both bills, calling them "a poison pill" that would jeopardize the state-federal partnership.[72]

In addition to trying to subvert the restoration, the sugar industry, as well as dairy farmers and other growers, made every effort to shape the plan. While environmental groups (and Interior's science subgroup) supported taking more land out of the EAA, sugar executives successfully lobbied the corps to seek alternative approaches.[73] What land the sugar industry did relinquish was not actually lost but rather swapped with the federal government for land bought from a willing seller. Furthermore, instead of building a large reservoir on sugar lands, CERP relied on expensive, underground storage systems for water around Lake Okeechobee and created a reservoir north of the lake. Although these storage wells—known as Aquifer Storage and Recovery, or

ASR, technology—had been used in Florida since 1983, the new plan proposed employing it at a much larger (and untested) scale: engineers would inject water into wells as deep as 1,400 feet, where in theory it would sit bubble-like in the brackish Floridan Aquifer. Environmentalists worried that under-ground chemical reactions would increase concentrations of heavy metals and other contaminants in the water; that the composition of water stored in one area could, when transported, be harmful to plants and animals in another; and that pressure created by pumping might fracture rock layers, potentially allowing the salty Floridan to infiltrate the freshwater Biscayne Aquifer.[74]

Even as development interests tried to gut CERP, scientists assailed it from the other side. Park officials criticized the proposal for meeting the demands of urban water users without giving the park and Biscayne Bay the water they needed to survive. In a December 1998 report, Park Service scientists said that their consensus opinion was that there was "insufficient evidence to substan-tiate the claims that [CERP] will result in recovery of a healthy, sustainable ecosystem. Rather, we find substantial, credible evidence to the contrary." [75] In response to the criticisms of park officials, the corps began looking into cap-turing billions of gallons of urban runoff and diverting it to wells, reservoirs, and filter marshes. Using this and other sources, engineers thought they could get another 112 billion gallons per year for the park and bay. Many had con-cerns about this remedy, however: urban runoff is polluted, and drainage changes would likely exacerbate problems with the timing of water delivery to the park.

Some environmentalists were critical of the plan as well. Breaking with the Everglades Coalition, which endorsed CERP, the Sierra Club objected to the plan's emphasis on engineering, rather than natural, solutions and asked that it be reviewed by an independent panel of nationally known scientists. A group of eminent ecologists agreed with the Sierra Club and Park Service's positions and in late January 1999 sent a letter to Secretary Babbitt charging the corps' plan had deep, systemic failings.[76] As ecologist Stuart Pimm pointed out, "There is very little restoration, and most of it doesn't come for the next 25 years." Pimm argued the approach embodied in the plan was fundamen-tally flawed because it relied heavily on technological solutions and therefore retained the fragmentation and compartmentalization of the Everglades as well as "the notion that the entire system can be managed in perpetuity" by humans.[77] In hopes of deflecting further criticism, the South Florida Ecosys-tem Restoration Task Force decided unanimously in February 1999 (and the SFWMD agreed) to submit the restoration plan for review to an indepen-dent panel assembled by the National Academy of Sciences. (They insisted the academy team keep its focus narrow, however, and adamantly refused to allow them to consider issues such as population growth in the region.)

After months of incorporating public comment and tinkering, in April 1999 the corps released the Final Integrated Feasibility Report and Programmatic Environmental Impact Statement for CERP. In an effort to address charges that the original plan contained insufficient ecological restoration, the revised version proposed to complete many core environmental projects in less than a decade, thereby more than doubling the pace of the draft plan. Under the new, accelerated schedule, forty-four of sixty-eight projects would be finished by 2010. By that time, according to the plan, the corps would have removed enough barriers that water would flow in a broad sheet through state-owned marshes from southern Palm Beach County to the Everglades National Park. About 130,000 acres of reservoirs would be completed, and urban and agricultural runoff would be cleansed by 28,000 new acres of stormwater treatment areas.[78] Under the new plan, 80 percent of the water that was captured and stored would go to the Everglades, which would give the system half of the expanded water supply. Although some environmentalists were pleased with the corps' responsiveness, others continued to disparage the agency's clear preference for imposing solutions that involved intensive engineering and management, rather than simply removing obstacles and letting nature take its course.

Approving the Restoration Plan. Despite apparently broad agreement on the restoration's goals, CERP's concrete details not only provoked environmentalists and sugar executives but also laid bare tensions between the federal government and the state of Florida. On July 1, 1999, the Clinton administration presented its ten-volume, 4,000-page restoration plan to Congress, which planned to hold hearings on the report before incorporating it into the 2000 Water Resources Development Act. To the chagrin of state, municipal, and agricultural interests, the administration had modified the plan to include more water for the park, an expanded role for the Interior Department in South Florida water management decisions, and a pledge to make ecosystem restoration, not urban water supply, its priority. Many in Congress supported these changes and were concerned about ensuring the primacy of the federal government's interest in promoting ecological rehabilitation, not local economic development. Exacerbating congressional skepticism, in May 1999 Florida's newly elected Republican governor, Jeb Bush, approved a sugar industry-supported bill, similar to those that Governor Chiles had vetoed, requiring the state's Department of Environmental Protection to review any restoration work before Congress authorized money for it and resurrecting the use of a state condemnation law that could drive up the purchase price of some land by one-third or more. In the same session, a bill authorizing $100 million per year in state bond money died, and the legislature failed to appropriate any funds for restoration.

Congressional debates over funding the restoration reflected legislators' wariness about the state's commitment as well as their unease about granting the Corps of Engineers broad discretion to carry out adaptive management. In 1999 both the House and the Senate recommended large cuts in funding from the $150 million requested by the Interior Department for restoration work in 2000 to $90 million (Senate) and $114 million (House). Members of appropriations committees in both chambers cited a General Accounting Office report released that April, which found that interagency feuds had already raised costs as much as $80 million and delayed for more than two years restoration projects that were then under way.[79] Ultimately, on October 22, 1999, Congress passed an appropriations bill that allocated only $10 million to Everglades restoration, and even that was conditional on a binding agreement to provide specific volume, timing, location, and duration of water flows to guarantee an "adequate and appropriate" water supply to South Florida's natural areas "to ensure a restored ecosystem." [80] The House Appropriations Committee also requested an annual report on how federal funds were spent and a detailed plan of how restoration would be done.

The following year, as the presidential campaign heated up, Vice President Gore staked his claim to environmentalists' votes in Florida and nationally by backing an Everglades bill that required the governor and the president to sign a binding agreement assuring the water produced by the project would be available to the ecosystem first; restrained the corps' propensity for construction by requiring congressional scrutiny of all new building projects; and required an independent scientific panel to oversee corps activity.[81] In September the major interests in the restoration reached a compromise that bought them together in support of the Senate version of the water resources act, which authorized $1.4 billion for CERP's first ten projects and four related Everglades projects. In late September, the Senate passed the bill, 85–1; in October the House passed it, 394–14; and President Clinton signed it on December 11. In recognition of the issue's salience, in May 2000 Governor Bush signed the Everglades Restoration Investment Act, a bill that committed the state to spending $2 billion over ten years on the restoration project.

OUTCOMES

The momentum behind the restoration spurred substantial land acquisitions. By 2005 the state of Florida had acquired 207,000 acres for CERP—representing 51 percent of the land expected to be needed—using $800 million in state funds, $259 million in federal funds, and $32 million in local funds.[82] Efforts to improve water quality as part of the court-mandated cleanup plan also produced results. Between 1995 and 2002, by following best management practices recommended by the district, farmers reduced their phosphorous discharge by 56 percent. Newly constructed filtration marshes cut phosphorus concentrations in cane field runoff from 64 ppb to less than 30 ppb.[83] In 2004 the SFWMD released a report saying that cleanup measures had removed 1,400 tons of phosphorus since the program began in 1994. Water management practices seemed to be paying off as well. The corps reported that it had enhanced conditions within the Shark River Slough substantially by restoring a more natural hydrologic regime. Researchers reported that during 2002 they found more wading birds' nests in the Everglades than in any year since 1940, and 2004 was another banner year. Although they attributed the increase primarily to favorable weather, ecologists pointed out that better water management also helped; in particular, water managers were no longer releasing huge amounts of water into the system during dry periods. (They cautioned, however, that ibises fared well, but other species—woodstorks, roseate spoonbills, and snowy egrets—continued to struggle.)

On the other hand, within a year of CERP's approval, the fragile consensus that had facilitated its passage had unraveled; as a result, controversy surrounded the corps' regulations for implementing CERP, and disagreements delayed construction projects. The debate over the corps' programmatic regulations, demanded by environmentalists and members of Congress to ensure the project's accountability, reprised all of the arguments that preceded congressional authorization of restoration plans. When the corps released the first draft of the rules, environmentalists immediately charged the agency with ignoring congressional intent by asserting too much authority for itself vis-à-vis the Interior Department, giving insufficient emphasis to ecological restoration, and failing to specify measurable performance goals. Environmentalists regarded the revised rules, issued in November 2003, as an improvement but still problematic: although the rules gave the Interior Department a coequal role in developing performance goals, they retained its subordinate position on the science team; they created a process for establishing interim goals but did not make performance targets legally enforceable; and they did not explicitly retain the water allocation in the original authorization, according to which 80 percent of the water gained by the project should benefit the ecosystem. The corps defended its approach, saying it needed the rules to be flexible in order to engage in adaptive management.

The corps' credibility dwindled even further, as critical "foundation" projects fell behind schedule.[84] For example, the Modified Water Deliveries Project, or Mod Waters—which, although not a part of CERP, is pivotal to the overall restoration—had been stalled since the early 1990s over the acquisition of land in the so-called 8.5-Square-Mile Area, and during that time the project's total price had quadrupled. In hopes of jump-starting Mod Waters, the corps announced in August 2002 that it would suspend work on CERP's Decompartmentalization and Sheetflow Enhancement Project, which is supposed to follow Mod Waters, unless Congress acted to fund the 8.5-Square-Mile-Area buyout. Congress responded by approving a partial buyout of the area, and in early 2004 the corps began demolishing the seventy-eight homes targeted. Still undecided in fall 2005 was how the corps would move water across the Tamiami Trail: environmentalists and scientists advocated building a 10.7-mile skyway, but the corps preferred the substantially cheaper alternative of two shorter bridges.

Disagreements over the water quality plan increased tensions between the state and federal governments. In 2003 the state legislature revamped the Everglades Forever Act to give the state and the sugar industry more time to reduce phosphorous levels—a change that promised to save millions of dollars but could cause irreversible ecological damage. Furthermore, a new phosphorous rule issued by the Environmental Regulatory Commission, a politically appointed board, was also controversial: like the revised law it seemed to dilute cleanup standards by averaging phosphorous measurements from dozens of monitoring stations across broad areas over a five-year period—an approach that could easily mask highly polluted hot spots.[85] Skepticism about the state's commitment to environmental protection exacerbated federal officials' reluctance to contribute financially to the restoration.

A lack of federal funding hampered crucial restoration projects, and, for every day of delay, speculation and development pressures drove land acquisition costs higher. (By 2005 the plan's estimated cost had risen to $10.5 billion, largely as a result of higher land prices.) On October 16, 2003, Florida officials broke ground on the first construction project of CERP. The Southern Golden Gates Hydrologic Restoration Project, otherwise known as the Picayune Strand, involves plugging 83 canals and removing 227 miles of roads on 55,000 acres of a failed development project. By 2005 the state had acquired most of the land for the project and plugged two miles of the seven-mile-long Prairie Canal; project officials were preparing to tear down 130 houses and deal with 68 acres of land polluted by agricultural chemicals.[86] Congress had not contributed its share of the funding, however, held up by bickering over the Water Resources Development Act. Further complicating matters, under its "no new start" program, Congress was preventing the corps from undertaking any new projects until it had cleared its backlog. Nor had Congress contributed to the $1.2 billion Indian River Lagoon project, which aims to restore 145 square miles of estuary and is one of the core ecological elements of CERP.

Impatient with the delays that dogged the plan, in mid-October 2004 Governor Bush announced a plan to accelerate CERP by shifting much of the power over the restoration from the federal to the state government. The governor's plan, dubbed Acceler8, aimed to finish eight major projects by 2010, with the state shouldering the entire $1.5 billion cost (in addition to the $200 million per year of state money pledged for CERP). Environmentalists were enthusiastic about the prospect of moving more quickly and hoped that the initiative would jolt the flagging restoration back to life. They pointed out, however, that most of the projects included in Acceler8 were more beneficial to water users than to the ecosystem.

CONCLUSIONS

Like the New England fisheries and spotted owl cases, the Everglades case reveals how environmentalists have used litigation to change the political dynamics of an environmental issue. For years, the ecological decline of the Everglades was apparent, yet agricultural interests—particularly the sugar industry—were sufficiently ensconced within state and federal policymaking institutions to resist efforts to revive the ecosystem. At the state level, sugar executives had strong, long-standing ties with members of the legislature, a relationship whose effects had been magnified by the historic malapportionment of state legislators to rural areas. The sugar industry had also fared well in the U.S. Congress, discreetly obtaining subsidies that enabled it to remain more than competitive with Caribbean growers. And sugar was a force within the state and federal agencies responsible for allocating water in South Florida; their well-established ties had developed into a symbiotic relationship in which sugar interests had an assured water supply at the expense of the environment.

The Department of Justice's novel legal argument—that the state had failed to enforce its own water pollution laws in South Florida—was less important than the way the lawsuit transformed the politics of Everglades restoration. Above all, the litigation simultaneously created a host of opportunities for environmentally oriented press coverage and fractured the alliance among the corps, the SFWMD, and the sugar industry. From environmentalists' perspective, the lawsuit served a third, critical function: reaching a technical agreement entailed assembling the disparate scientific research on Everglades water quality into a coherent consensus, which in turn provided a firm foundation for a compelling political story in which the villainous sugar industry had heedlessly destroyed one of the nation's most precious wetlands. That story, in turn, raised the salience of Everglades decline. While campaigning for governor, Lawton Chiles then capitalized on the issue's popularity. He promised to settle the suit and, once in office, felt obligated to resolve the issue; his imprimatur further enhanced public support for the restoration. The growing national salience of the issue subsequently made it the object of competition for credit between presidential candidates as well as among members of both parties in Congress.

Thanks to the political feedback sparked by the lawsuit, the Everglades controversy ultimately yielded a restoration plan that was more ambitious than anything the initial plaintiffs could have imagined. Once the federal government had assembled a team of scientists and given them some leeway to craft an integrated, holistic portrait of the ecosystem, the possibility of getting a genuinely comprehensive plan increased dramatically. Moreover, by collaborating with stakeholders and coordinating the activities of all the agencies that would be affected by such a plan, the corps dramatically increased the prospects for agreement on its goals and broad outlines. That consensus rested on "expanding the pie," however, which in turn meant embracing a technologically oriented, heavily managed approach to restoration. Furthermore, collaborative planning did not ensure that the project would experience smooth sailing once approved. Obstacles to interagency cooperation continue to arise: aside from the sheer logistical complexity of implementing the plan, each agency has its own mission and standard operating procedures and jealously guards its turf.

The restoration has also been slowed by disharmony between the federal and state governments, which are funding and administering the plan jointly. Federal-state tension in part reflects differences in political incentives: federal officials can get credit for responding to environmental concerns, but, at the state level, the pressure to serve agricultural, commercial, and municipal interests is intense. Throughout the process of formulating a restoration plan, sugar and other development interests made it clear that they would do whatever was necessary to stymie it if their demands were not met. Aside from holding up the plan in court, they can wait out environmental interests—whose political clout relies heavily on public attention and support—and then go back to the legislature, where they wield credible threats of the state's economic demise.

Federal resistance to funding the restoration project also reflects the incompatibility between the requirements of adaptive management and the demands of accountability. The overriding problem is that the approach described by the corps—recapturing billions of gallons of water that currently flow into the Atlantic, storing it in reservoirs or underground wells, and pumping it out as needed—is purposefully broad and flexible. Because administrators want to be able to adjust the system in response to new information, the restoration plan is nothing more than a roadmap with details to be worked out and adjustments to be made as the project proceeds. But, traditionally, Congress authorizes corps projects only after seeing a precise blueprint, and legislators worry that if they grant the corps too much latitude the project's ecological goals will be subverted in favor of development interests. Environmentalists applaud congressional insistence that ecological goals be paramount, but the accountability Congress demands may undermine the experimentation and adaptation on which the plan's ultimate success depends.

The restoration's long-term viability faces additional threats as well. The gravest of these is the pressure for development that will accompany South Florida's booming population, which is expected to double to 12 million by 2050. Massive population growth could exacerbate political pressures to divert water from the ecosystem to water users, a concern for scientists and environmentalists who are already worried that the plan is biased in favor of development and will not succeed in restoring the Everglades. Even as the government undertakes restoration projects, development in Southwest Florida is decimating large tracts. According to developer Al Hoffman, South Florida's runaway development is inevitable: "There's no power on Earth that can stop it!" [87] Certainly, curbing growth requires a political will that few state governments have demonstrated, and, as a result, urban sprawl has become a priority for American environmentalists who recognize that fragile ecosystems, such as the Everglades, depend on their vigilance.

QUESTIONS TO CONSIDER

- Should the federal government spend $4 billion or more to support the Everglades restoration? Why, or why not?
- What might environmentalists do to maintain or increase public support for the Everglades restoration over its projected twenty-year lifetime?
- Is restoring an ecosystem's ecological health a legitimate goal? If so, what are likely to be the most significant political obstacles to achieving it?

Notes

1. A marsh is a wetland dominated by low, herbaceous (nonwoody) vegetation; in a swamp the dominant plants are trees.
2. Daniel J. Simberloff et al., "Regional and Continental Conservation," in *Continental Conservation: Scientific Foundations of Regional Reserve Networks*, ed. Michael Soule and John Terborgh (Washington, D.C.: Island Press, 1999), 65–98.
3. Craig Thomas, *Bureaucratic Landscapes: Interagency Cooperation and the Preservation of Biodiversity* (Cambridge: MIT Press, 2003).
4. Dan Tarlock, "Environmental Law: Ethics or Science?" *Duke Environmental Law and Policy Forum* 7 (Fall 1996): 193–223.
5. Daniel B. Botkin, *Discordant Harmonies: A New Ecology for the Twenty-First Century* (New York: Oxford University Press, 1990), 9.
6. C. S. Holling, ed., *Adaptive Environmental Assessment and Management* (New York: John Wiley, 1978); Kai N. Lee, *Compass and Gyroscope: Integrating Science and Politics for the Environment* (Washington, D.C.: Island Press, 1993).
7. The limestone plate that underlies South Florida decreases in elevation by only 5.3 meters over the Everglades' entire 100-mile span. See C. S. Holling, Lance H. Gunderson, and Carl J. Walters, "The Structure and Dynamics of the Everglades System: Guidelines for Ecosystem Restoration," in *Everglades: The Ecosystem and Its Restoration*, ed. Steven M. Davis and John C. Ogden (Delray Beach, Fla.: St. Lucie Press, 1994), 741–767.
8. David McCally, *The Everglades: An Environmental History* (Gainesville: University Press of Florida, 1999).
9. Alan Mairson, "The Everglades: Dying for Help," *National Geographic*, April 1994, 2–35.
10. Congress had actually authorized the park in 1934, but some of the land (850,000 acres donated by the state of Florida) was not forthcoming until the mid-1940s. The park, which comprises less than one-quarter of the historic freshwater Everglades, was dedicated in 1947.
11. "Development of the C&SF Project." Retrieved from http://restudy.org/history.htm.
12. Thomas E. Lodge, *The Everglades Handbook* (Delray Beach, Fla.: St. Lucie Press, 1994).
13. Ranchers and landowners persuaded Sen. Spessard Holland, D-Fla., to include the Kissimmee flood control works in the corps' 1948 Comprehensive Plan, and Congress approved this phase of the project in the Flood Control Act of 1954. Nothing was done, however, until a series of floods prompted renewed calls for action. The corps then proposed a $31-million project to channelize the Kissimmee River and build control structures to regulate its flow. The project was completed in 1971. See Nelson Manfred Blake, *Land into Water—Water into Land* (Tallahassee: University Presses of Florida, 1980).
14. Eutrophication occurs when water becomes rich in mineral and organic nutrients, causing plant life, especially algae, to proliferate, thereby reducing the dissolved oxygen content of the water and killing native organisms.
15. Lodge, *Everglades Handbook*.
16. Robert S. Gilmour and John McAulay, "Environmental Preservation and Politics: The Significance of 'Everglades Jetport,' " *Political Science Quarterly* 90 (Winter 1975–1976): 719–738.
17. Reflecting the Everglades' national appeal, Sen. Gaylord Nelson, D-Wis., and Sen. Edmund Muskie, D-Maine, sponsored the measure over the opposition of Sen. Spessard Holland, D-Fla. The bill required the C&SF Project to deliver to the park 315,000 acre-feet of water or 16.5 percent of total water deliveries, whichever was less.
18. Blake, *Land into Water*.

19. In 1967 the Florida legislature had begun redistricting in accordance with the 1962 Supreme Court ruling that legislative malapportionment was unconstitutional. The impact of the legislative overhaul was magnified by the election of environmentally oriented governors—Claude Kirk in 1966 and Reuben Askew in 1970. Enhancing the impact of these electoral changes, the state adopted a progressive new constitution in 1968.
20. Florida Environmental Land and Water Management Act, F. S. 380–021.
21. Jeffrey Kahn, "Restoring the Everglades," *Sierra,* September–October 1986, 40–43.
22. Kevin Hansen, "South Florida's Water Dilemma: A Trickle of Hope for the Everglades," *Environment,* June 1984, 14–20, 40–42.
23. Included in the network were the Florida Wildlife Federation, Friends of the Everglades, the Florida Audubon Society, the Coalition to Repair the Everglades, Defenders of the Environment, and the Everglades Protection Association. See Rose Mary Mechem, "In Florida, the Grass is No Longer Greener," *National Wildlife,* October–November 1982, 51–55.
24. Quoted in Kahn, "Restoring the Everglades," 41–42.
25. The district has a nine-member, unpaid board, with members serving four-year terms.
26. Quoted in Mairson, "Everglades," 7, 10.
27. Alston Chase, *Playing God in Yellowstone* (New York: Harcourt Brace, 1987).
28. Quoted in ibid., 252.
29. In the 1700s sugar was regarded the way oil is now: as central to national security. Once supportive policies were established, they were difficult to dislodge in the absence of a major public challenge. The Agriculture and Food Act of 1981 restricted sugar imports and provided domestic producers loans of 18 cents per pound of raw sugar.
30. In 1981 sugar accounted for $600 million of the EAA's $700 million revenues. See Hansen, "South Florida's Water Dilemma." Sugar companies are regularly among the top contributors to Florida's state and federal politicians. See, for example, Center for Responsive Politics, "The 1990 Farm Bill," www.opensecrets.org/pubs/cashingin_sugar/sugar05.html.
31. It is worth noting that the SFWMD's predecessor, the Central and South Florida Flood Control District, spearheaded the campaign to stop the South Florida jetport in 1969.
32. Jeanne Nienaber Clarke and Daniel C. McCool, *Staking Out the Terrain,* 2d ed. (Albany: State University of New York Press, 1996), 21.
33. For example, in 1983, after the corps released billions of gallons of water into the park, research director Gary Hendrix, notified the SFWMD that wildlife populations had sunk so low that only swift emergency action to restore the park's wet and dry seasons would give them a fighting chance at recovery. The district endorsed a plan for distributing water more equally throughout the park during floods, but the corps would agree only to a more conservative approach. In 1985, after Congress authorized a two-phase, five-year experimental water release program, the district began to experiment with using existing technologies to try to mimic the area's natural water flow patterns. The revised flow was an improvement, but insufficient to remedy the park's problems.
34. Surface Water Improvement and Management Act, F.S. 373-4595 (2)(a)(1).
35. Dewitt John, *Civic Environmentalism: Alternatives to Regulation in States and Communities* (Washington, D.C.: CQ Press, 1994).
36. Norman Boucher, "Smart as Gods," *Wilderness,* Winter 1991, 11–21.
37. Lodge, *Everglades Handbook.*
38. The alligator poaching industry flourished in the 1960s, as the state of Florida curtailed legal alligator hunting. Poaching began to decline only after the 1973 placement of the alligator on the federal endangered species list because the law imposed stiff penalties for poaching.

39. Frank J. Mazzoti and Laura Brandt, "Ecology of the American Alligator in a Seasonally Fluctuating Environment," in *Everglades: The Ecosystem and Its Restoration*, 485–505.

40. John, *Civic Environmentalism*.

41. The central legal issue was whether the state needed permits for the pumps at the southern edge of the EAA and, if so, what were the proper standards for phosphorous in the water passing through those pumps. The Justice Department initially chose to litigate the suit in federal court on the grounds that the nuisance created by the state's failure to regulate victimized two federal entities: the Everglades National Park and the Loxahatchee Wildlife Refuge.

42. The environmental groups that signed on as plaintiffs in the suit included the Wilderness Society, the Florida Wildlife Federation, the Florida and National Audubon Societies, the Sierra Club Legal Defense Fund, and the Environmental Defense Fund. See John, *Civic Environmentalism*.

43. In 1991 sugar cane occupied 457,000 acres of the EAA, more than seven times the acreage occupied by all other agricultural commodities. The number of acres in the EAA devoted to sugar cane had doubled since the 1970s.

44. The Wilderness Society commissioned a study to estimate the value of those public subsidies and used the results to further galvanize public sentiment against the industry.

45. Quoted in John, *Civic Environmentalism*, 155.

46. John, *Civic Environmentalism*.

47. Water from cane fields contains about 75 to 120 ppb (parts per billion) of phosphorous; by comparison, industry experts pointed out, a sample of effluent from a municipal sewage treatment plant contained 100 ppb of phosphorous; a sample of drinking water from Tallahassee contained 80 ppb of phosphorous; and rain over the Everglades occasionally contained as much as 60 to 70 ppb of phosphorous. Park scientists replied that the normal level of phosphorous in the park is only 7 to 14 ppb. See ibid.

48. Mairson, "The Everglades." The surprise was that approximately 60 percent of the land targeted for acquisition was owned by 10,000 individuals, most of them absentee landlords, who had purchased the property through the mail.

49. John, *Civic Environmentalism*.

50. Efforts to reach agreement on this question were hampered by lawyers' refusals to release critical information to the group. See ibid.

51. Quoted in Margaret Kriz, "Mending the Marsh," *National Journal*, March 12, 1994, 593.

52. Marjory Stoneman Douglas Everglades Protection Act, F. S. 373-4592 (3) (a) (1).

53. *United States v. SFWMD et al.*, Case No. 88-1886-civ-Hoeveler, *Settlement Agreement*, Appendix B.

54. For dairy farms, best management practices include installing drains to carry away water from where cows stand and drop manure. For sugar cane farms, they include letting storm water stand in fields rather than draining it off, so that the soil does not dry out and oxidize, leaving high concentrations of phosphorous to be swept up in a pulse during the next heavy rainfall. Another best management practice for sugar cane and other fruit and vegetable crops is to fertilize more precisely, applying chemicals to the roots of crops rather than spreading them in swaths across entire fields.

55. Quoted in Ben Barber, "Trouble in Florida's 'River of Grass,' " *Christian Science Monitor*, July 9, 1993, 3.

56. Quoted in William Booth, "Everglades Accord Indicative of EPA Designee's Approach," *Washington Post*, January 11, 1993, 4.

57. John, *Civic Environmentalism*.

58. The present value of the plan was $465 million; the estimated value over the life of the project was $700 million.

59. John, *Civic Environmentalism.*
60. Participants included representatives of the Interior Department (the National Park Service, Fish and Wildlife Service, and U.S. Geological Survey), the Commerce Department (the National Marine Fisheries Service), the Army Corps of Engineers, the EPA, the Department of Agriculture, and the Department of Justice.
61. In addition to the federal agencies involved in the task force, the Restudy included representatives of the state of Florida, the SFWMD, county and local governments, and the Miccosukee and Seminole tribes.
62. John Ogden, quoted in National Research Council, *Science and the Greater Everglades Ecosystem Restoration* (Washington, D.C.: National Academy Press, 2003), 21.
63. The Science Subgroup of the South Florida Management and Coordination Working Group, *Federal Objectives for the South Florida Restoration,* November 1993, 1.
64. Tom Kenworthy, "Administration, Sugar Industry Talks on Everglades Restoration Deadlock," *Washington Post,* December 17, 1993, 17.
65. However, the Everglades Forever Act also pushed the target date for achieving 10 ppb of phosphorous from 2002, as the 1991 settlement had required, to 2006. See the Everglades Forever Act, F. S. 373-4592 (1994).
66. Governor's Commission for a Sustainable South Florida, "The Initial Report," 1995. Available at www.state.fl.us/everglades/gcssf/gcssf-reports.html.
67. John H. Cushman Jr., "Panel Agrees on Overhaul of Farm Aid," *New York Times,* March 22, 1996, 1.
68. John H. Cushman Jr., "Clinton Backing Vast Effort to Restore Florida Swamps," *New York Times,* February 18, 1996, 1.
69. Water Resources Development Act of 1996, P.L. 104-303 sect. 528 (b)(l)(A)(i).
70. Robert P. King, "Business Group Rips Everglades Restoration Plan's Costs," *Palm Beach Post,* November 10, 1998, B1.
71. An analysis by the Center for Responsive Politics showed that in the three election cycles between 1994 and 1998, the Fanjul family donated $575,000 to campaigns for federal offices, and their sugar companies contributed at least $843,000 to the Democratic and Republican national committees. Over the same period, the U.S. Sugar Corp. donated $584,000 to national committees, while employees gave $276,000 to federal candidates. See James C. McKinley Jr., "Sugar Industry's Pivotal Role in Everglades Efforts," *New York Times,* April 16, 1999, 1.
72. Jan Hollingsworth, "Environmentalists Fear Law Will Sap Everglades Plan," *Tampa Tribune,* May 7, 1999, 1.
73. McKinley, "Sugar Industry's Pivotal Role."
74. Curtis Morgan, "Water Plan Goes Underground," *Miami Herald,* February 2, 2001, 1B.
75. Quoted in Tony Reichhardt, "Everglades Plan Flawed, Claim Ecologists," *Nature,* February 11, 1999, 462.
76. Ibid. The signatories were Stuart Pimm of the University of Tennessee, Paul Ehrlich of Stanford, E. O. Wilson of Harvard, Gary Meffe of the University of Florida, Peter Raven of the Missouri Botanical Garden, and Gordon Orians of the University of Washington.
77. Quoted in William K. Stevens, "Everglades Restoration Plan Does Too Little, Experts Say," *New York Times,* February 22, 1999, 1.
78. Cyril T. Zaneski, "Army Corps Plans to Double Pace of Everglades Restoration," *Miami Herald,* March 29, 1999, 1.
79. U.S. GAO, "South Florida Ecosystem Restoration: An Overall Strategic Plan and a Decision-Making Process Are Needed to Keep the Effort on Track," GAO/RCED-99-121, April 22, 1999.
80. Craig Pittman, "Glades Funding Restriction Irks State Officials," *St. Petersburg Times,* October 23, 1999, 5B.
81. Cyril T. Zaneski, "Senators Plan Jumpstart for $7.8 Billion Everglades Restoration," *Congress Daily/A.M.,* June 27, 2000.

82. U.S. Army Corps of Engineers, "Central and Southern Florida Project Comprehensive Everglades Restoration Plan 2005 Report to Congress," Draft, August 23, 2005.
83. Michael Grunwald, "When in Doubt, Blame Big Sugar," *Washington Post*, June 25, 2002, 9.
84. CERP builds on the successful completion of a set of foundation projects that predate the restoration plan: the Kissimmee River Restoration Project, the Modified Water Deliveries to the Everglades National Park Project, the Modifications to the C-111 Project, the Critical Restoration Projects, the C-51/STAE-1E Project, and the State of Florida's Everglades Construction Project.
85. Curtis Morgan, "Fight over Florida Everglades Far from over Despite Revised Water Law," *Miami Herald*, July 22, 2003.
86. Tasha Eichenseher, "Managers Fear State-Federal Funding Imbalance May Jeopardize Restoration Effort," *Land Letter*, May 5, 2005.
87. Quoted in Michael Grunwald, "Growing Pains in Southwest Fla.," *Washington Post*, June 25, 2002, 1.

Recommended Reading

Davis, Steven M., and John C. Ogden, eds. *Everglades: The Ecosystem and Its Restoration*. Delray Beach, Fla.: St. Lucie Press, 1994, 741–767.
Lodge, Thomas E. *The Everglades Handbook*. Delray Beach, Fla.: St. Lucie Press, 1994.
McCally, David. *The Everglades: An Environmental History*. Gainesville: University Press of Florida, 1999.

Web Sites

http://everglades.fiu.edu/Library/index.html (Florida International University site)
http://serc.fiu.edu (Florida International University's Southeast Environmental Research Center site)
www.sfwmd.gov (SFWMD site)

CHAPTER 16

Local, Collaborative Problem Solving

Using Habitat Conservation Plans to
Save Southern California's Endangered Landscape

In the early 1990s, five Southern California counties embarked on a last-ditch effort to save the region's remaining natural habitat while allowing development to continue. This unprecedented undertaking was perhaps the largest, most complete conservation planning exercise ever attempted.[1] It involved devising regional landscape maps and then negotiating among developers, landowners, and local, state, and federal government officials to agree on a long-term plan to preserve swaths of undisturbed natural areas. And it attempted this "smack in the middle of some of the most expensive, desirable, and booming real estate in America." [2] President Bill Clinton's Interior secretary, Bruce Babbitt, touted the San Diego program as marking "the beginning of a new chapter in American conservation history." [3] Even as many are heralding such local, collaborative efforts, however, critics are challenging their effectiveness.

The decision to experiment with collaborative, ecosystem-scale planning in California was a response to frustration with conventional mechanisms for endangered species protection. Environmentalists and conservation biologists recognized that the Endangered Species Act (ESA), with its focus on individual species, is a clumsy and inadequate tool for protecting entire ecosystems. It is typically invoked only once a species and its habitat are in such dire condition that they may not recover. Its parcel-by-parcel implementation often exacerbates, rather than reduces, habitat fragmentation. And it makes no provision for buffer areas or landscape linkages that, although perhaps not occupied by a listed species, may be crucial to its long-term survival.[4] In any case, the Fish and Wildlife Service (FWS) lacks the political clout, manpower, and funding to enforce the ESA on private land, where many endangered species reside. Developers resent the ESA as well because it creates uncertainty in planning, can jeopardize a project's financing, and sometimes imposes costly delays on projects after substantial investments have been made. And many on both sides dislike the contentious, litigious politics that has accompanied implementation of the law.

Advocates, experts, and government officials have converged on local, collaborative environmental problem solving as an alternative to species-by-species conservation. Proponents of such approaches believe they enable "citizen leaders from government and business to mobilize their deep concern for a place close to home and turn that concern into creative and far-reaching

436

cooperative ventures." [5] In theory, local collaboration has two advantages over top-down, adversarial policymaking. First, if communities have sufficient technical information and the capacity to absorb that information, they will craft solutions that are environmentally superior to the one-size-fits-all prescriptions generated by conventional regulatory processes.[6] Second, if communities are allowed to make meaningful decisions, and all stakeholders are involved in the process from the outset, collaborative decision making should bring about voluntary compliance because "programs are more likely to be implemented successfully if they are supported and owned by affected groups." [7] In short, proponents believe that by changing the process by which decisions are made, local, collaborative approaches can produce environmentally protective solutions that endure.

Although it has been widely endorsed, the concept of local, collaborative environmental problem solving has also prompted vigorous challenges. Some critics have questioned whether such approaches actually foster meaningful citizen participation and whether civic environmentalism places an excessive burden on citizens, who are disadvantaged relative to development interests.[8] Others fear that arrangements granting equal status to citizens and scientists weaken the influence of science on policy and wonder whether collaboration yields genuine environmental protection.[9] In short, it remains to be seen whether local, collaborative environmental problem solving actually yields the anticipated procedural and substantive benefits in practice.

To evaluate such novel processes, it is important to assess not only the content of the plan that results, but also the extent to which it is implemented. As noted in the Everglades case (chapter 15), scientists continue to emphasize the need for experimentation and adaptation; policies to protect ecosystems must be sufficiently flexible, they argue, to accommodate surprises and incorporate new information and scientific learning.[10] But such flexibility leaves plans and programs vulnerable at the implementation stage: as political scientists Aaron Wildavsky and Jeffrey Pressman observe, implementation in our federal system is inherently hazardous because most programs must clear myriad decision points, any one of which can delay or even halt program activity altogether.[11] Even when broad agreement exists on a program's goals, the more entities—from federal and state agencies to local government officials—that have to sign on for a program to work, the less chance it has of achieving its stated goals. Environmentalists are especially concerned about plans that rely on local governments, which are particularly susceptible to economic development interests.

BACKGROUND

A mosaic of coastal sage scrub (CSS)—a distinctive mix of sage and other low-growing, drought-tolerant shrubs that is found nowhere else in the United States—once spread across 2.5 million acres from Ventura County to San Diego. Between 1940 and 1995, however, Southern California's population quintupled to 17.5 million, growing at a rate twice that of Bangladesh.[12] The seemingly endless demand for Southern California real estate that accompanied this boom produced skyrocketing land values, with lots ranging from $200,000 to $3 million per acre.[13] As a result of its burgeoning agricultural, commercial, and residential development, the FWS estimated that by 1991 the region had lost more than 85 percent of its original CSS habitat, leaving only between 343,000 and 444,000 acres.[14] The remaining patches, many of which had been degraded by human activities and fire, were highly fragmented across five Southern California counties—Los Angeles, Orange, Riverside, San Bernardino, and San Diego—although most of them (125,000–150,000 acres) were in San Diego.

Similar degradation had occurred in the region's chaparral, grassland, and riparian habitats.[15] The rapid disappearance of habitat in turn had driven hundreds of the region's small mammals, birds, and plants to the brink of extinction. With more than 200 species considered imperiled, San Diego was the nation's only hot spot for endangered fish, mammals, and plants.[16] The situation was exacerbated by the fact that 80 percent of CSS was privately owned, and endangered species tend to fare worse on private land than on federally owned land.[17]

Protecting Endangered Species on Private Land

The main vehicle for protecting species and habitats on both public and private lands is the federal ESA, which requires the FWS—or, for marine species, the National Marine Fisheries Service—to identify and publish lists of species that are endangered (in imminent danger of going extinct) or threatened (likely to become endangered in the foreseeable future). Anyone can petition the FWS to list a species. Once a petition is submitted, however, the agency must decide whether a listing is warranted based solely on the available scientific evidence. After deciding to list a species as endangered or threatened, the agency is supposed to designate critical habitat and develop a recovery plan.[18] Section 7 of the ESA, the provision of the act that historically has been most controversial, prohibits the destruction or adverse modification of critical habitat by actions carried out, funded, or authorized by a federal agency (see chapter 13).

More recently, however, Section 9 of the ESA has come under attack. Section 9 prohibits the "take" by any party, public or private, of species listed as endangered. The act defines "take" as "harass, harm, pursue, hunt, shoot, wound, kill, trap, capture, or collect, or attempt to engage in any such conduct," and the FWS has interpreted this phrase as empowering the federal government to prosecute landowners who destroy a species or its habitat. In the more than thirty years since passage of the ESA, however, the federal government has been reluctant to take action against private property owners. The Department of Justice rarely prosecutes people for killing a species and even less frequently penalizes those who destroy its habitat.[19] Between 1990, when the FWS listed the northern spotted owl as a threatened species, and 1997, the Justice Department did not prosecute a single company for destruction of spotted owl habitat, and the FWS lost the few civil actions it filed. The Interior Department went to court only twice to block logging activities that threatened spotted owls.[20]

The FWS was not shirking; rather, it was vastly understaffed and underfunded for the chore of implementing the ESA. In the early 1990s it had 210 enforcement agents nationwide, with 175 in the field, and they were enforcing several other laws in addition to the ESA.[21] It was also extremely difficult to get a conviction for damaging habitat. In the absence of a "corpse," prosecutors had to show that habitat destruction inevitably would have killed or injured a species or created a significant likelihood of injury. Therefore, according to David McMullen, director of law enforcement for the FWS's West Coast region: "If I say I want someone prosecuted for shooting a bald eagle, no problem. But if I want a person prosecuted for cutting near a bald eagle nest, the U.S. attorney is much less inclined to take the case. That's true even though the permanent harm that is done from harvesting too close to a bald eagle nest is far greater than the harm done by shooting a single eagle." [22]

Moreover, members of Congress put immense pressure on the FWS to ignore ESA violations on private land, thereby undermining the agency's enforcement capability. Even those who supported the act worried that legal action against property owners would agitate opponents of the ESA and galvanize their sympathetic congressional representatives. These concerns were justified: in the late 1980s and early 1990s the backlash against the ESA mounted, and efforts to dilute or repeal the act gained momentum in Congress (see chapter 13). In Southern California, frustration with the ESA ran high following restrictions to protect the Stephens Kangaroo Rat in Riverside County in the late 1980s. T-shirts emblazoned with a picture of a rat being smashed by a mallet and the words "Kangaroo Rat Whackers Association" proliferated; farmers applied rodenticide to their fields and refused to leave them fallow, all to prevent the endangered rats from taking up residence on their property.[23]

A Policy Innovation: Habitat Conservation Plans

Finding itself stymied in its efforts to protect species on private land, the FWS was intrigued by the concept of habitat conservation plans (HCPs) that emerged in the early 1980s. The agency actually approved a prototype HCP in 1980 in the absence of any statutory authorization. It had used the novel approach to resolve a conflict over developing the habitat of three rare species of butterfly—particularly the federally listed Mission Blue and Callippe Silverspot butterflies—on the San Bruno Mountain in San Francisco. After lengthy negotiations, a consortium comprising the primary landowner and developer, environmental groups, and local, state, and federal officials came up with a management plan that allowed some destruction of butterflies but also reserved large swaths of the mountain as protected habitat.[24] The plan also provided for the establishment and funding of long-term habitat management and restoration. The FWS was not certain that it had the legal authority to approve such deals, however, and was therefore reluctant to make HCPs common practice, so in 1982 the real estate lawyers who had brokered the San Bruno deal acted as policy entrepreneurs and persuaded Congress to amend the ESA to provide for HCPs.[25]

The 1982 amendments included Section 10(a), under which a landowner can negotiate a deal with the FWS that allows him to destroy some portion of a listed species' habitat as long as he has prepared a satisfactory HCP that explains how he will "mitigate" the loss. More precisely, the amendments require HCPs to specify the impact that would result from a take, the steps that would be taken to minimize and mitigate such impacts, the funding that would be available to implement those steps, the alternative action considered by the applicant and reasons such alternatives were rejected, and other measures the Interior secretary may require as "necessary and appropriate" for purposes of the plan. The FWS may grant a Section 10(a) "incidental take permit" only if the take will be incidental to an otherwise lawful activity; the applicant will minimize and mitigate the impacts of the take; and the take will "not appreciably reduce the likelihood of survival and recovery of species in the wild."

Although the 1982 amendments did not mandate a specific process for devising HCPs, a common approach soon emerged. First, the federal government appoints a steering committee made up of representatives of major stakeholders: the environmental community, landowners, developers, and local, state, and federal resource management agencies. The committee then hires consultants to prepare background biological and land-use studies. The plans themselves usually create habitat preserves using a variety of mechanisms, including fee-simple acquisitions or dedication by the landowner in exchange for development rights elsewhere. In addition, HCPs generally include provisions for habitat management, ecological restoration, and ongoing research and monitoring. They may also involve predator and exotic species controls as well as land-use regulations. Finally, HCPs may offer financial incentives to landowners who preserve habitat, including tradable credits that the landowner can sell to someone else who must mitigate for development in another location, or they may set up a system in which developers pay a set per-acre price to the city or county, which then uses the money to buy conservation land. Controversy surrounding HCPs most often arises over the amount of habitat preserved, the boundaries and configuration of the proposed reserves, the means of financing plans, and which entities will oversee the administration of the plan.[26]

THE CASE

In the early 1990s, within the national context of ineffectual enforcement of the ESA on private land, an incipient backlash against endangered species protection, and the recent emergence of HCPs, Southern California faced an impending collision between environmentalists and developers over a small songbird called the coastal California gnatcatcher. A scientist had inadvertently laid the foundation for this "train wreck" by providing credible scientific evidence that environmentalists could use to make claims—both in agencies and in the courts—under the ESA. Perceiving the potential costs associated with an ESA listing of the gnatcatcher, development interests mobilized. Instead of pursuing adversarial politics in venues where they had fared poorly under the act in the past, however, one developer took a new tack and proposed collaborative, ecosystem-scale planning—a solution that had been floating around the environmental policy community for some time. Proponents of the collaborative planning approach hoped to redefine the problem as species *and* jobs rather than species *versus* jobs.[27] They hoped that redefinition, in turn, would facilitate a new kind of politics—one in which developers and environmentalists work cooperatively rather than competitively to devise a "win-win" solution.

The Coastal California Gnatcatcher

The story began, unremarkably, in 1979, when UCLA biology graduate student Jonathan Atwood was casting around for a dissertation topic that would enable him to do his research locally. Atwood took on the task of sorting out the various species of *Polioptila*, a genus of small songbirds native to the Southwest whose classification scheme was imprecise.[28] In the course of his research, Atwood found that, contrary to what ornithologists previously believed, the black-tailed gnatcatcher and the California gnatcatcher could not mate with one another and therefore should be considered distinct subspecies. He also observed that the coastal California gnatcatcher (*Polioptila californica californica*) made its home exclusively among the low-elevation (below 300 meters) coastal sage scrub and used chaparral, grasslands, and riparian areas for dispersal and foraging.[29] Atwood pointed out that, as its habitat became increasingly fragmented, the gnatcatcher had become more vulnerable to parasitism and nest predation, and therefore extinction. In 1989 the American Ornithologists Union concurred with Atwood's findings and officially designated the coastal California gnatcatcher as a distinct subspecies. The implications of this designation were profound: if the bird was a subspecies that relied for its survival on low-elevation CSS, then it was a promising candidate for endangered species listing.[30] (In fact, in 1980 Atwood had conducted a gnatcatcher census for the California Department of Fish and Game and estimated its population at fewer than 2,000 breeding pairs. At that time, he had recommended adding the bird to state and federal ESA lists and halting development in CSS.[31])

Although Atwood published his research in the journal *Ornithological Monographs* in 1988, the gnatcatcher remained a relatively obscure bird until 1990, when some of Atwood's former UCLA classmates informed him that development in Southern California threatened the gnatcatcher with extinction.[32] As environmental consultants to California developers, they felt they could not sound alarms about the bird and its disappearing habitat without jeopardizing their own livelihoods, but they encouraged Atwood, who was working at the Manomet Bird Observatory in Massachusetts, to petition the FWS to list the bird as endangered under the ESA. With the help of the Natural Resources Defense Council (NRDC), Atwood proceeded to gather data on and generate projections of Southern California's growth prospects. He concluded that "nearly all areas where California gnatcatchers are currently distributed are expected to be destroyed within 20 years as a result of intensive urban development." [33] Backed by a seventy-two-page status review of the bird and letters of support from the American Ornithologists' Union, the International Council for Bird Preservation, and the National Audubon Society, in December 1990 the Manomet Bird Observatory and the NRDC requested that the FWS list the bird under an emergency rule.[34] They sent a similar packet to the state of California and asked it to list the bird under the California Endangered Species Act as well.

Developers React to Efforts to List the Gnatcatcher

The prospect that the FWS might list the gnatcatcher prompted some of Southern California's most profitable and influential developers to begin seeking ways to avert the listing, which could temporarily derail construction on thousands of acres of prime real estate and block the installation of crucial infrastructure—from highways to water-reclamation projects to sewer lines. The region's developers were already intimately familiar with the ESA, having had two formative experiences in the 1980s—with the Least Bell's Vireo and the Stephens Kangaroo Rat—and having observed the conflagrations in the northern part of the state over the spotted owl.[35] Moreover, it was clear that not only the gnatcatcher but also a host of other CSS-obligate species were candidates for listing, so the potential for regulatory delays was enormous.

One approach developers could adopt was to generate public opposition in hopes of intimidating the California Department of Fish and Game and the FWS so that they would refrain from listing the bird.[36] To this end, some builders launched a public relations campaign to frame the listing petition as an attack on private property rights and an effort by no-growth extremists to stymie all development in the region. In a handbill advertising informational lunches about the proposed listing in Orange County, the hard-line Building Industry Association of Southern California (BIA) characterized the gnatcatcher as "Your Worst Nightmare." [37] Portraying opponents of listing as moderates and advocates of balance, Mark Ellis Tipton of the National Homebuilders Association said: "There is a place in society for protecting the gnatcatcher, but it has to be with a proper relationship to mankind. I see people in California living in garages and cardboard boxes and abandoned cars. Now who's more important? These people and their children, or ecological preserves?" Defining quality of life in a way that stressed cornucopian, rather than environmental, values, Tipton argued: "When you destroy the quality of life to protect an endangered species, it doesn't make sense. You're going to stop water reclamation [projects]; you'll stop hospitals; you'll have lawsuits." The consequences of a listing, he claimed, would be cataclysmic: "When that lesser quality of life shows up, you're going to have a revolution." Tipton characterized environmentalists as the elite and their policy goals exclusionary, saying: "I look at most of the resumes of the Sierra Club, and they're doctors and lawyers, and they have got great big houses and they don't want anybody else to have them." [38]

California's New Conservation Planning Process

A more moderate group of landowners, including some of the largest holders of CSS, formed the Alliance for Habitat Conservation, and they chose a different route to head off the ESA listing.[39] In particular, the Irvine Company—a massive and sophisticated developer—hoped to capitalize on a window of opportunity opened by the election of Republican governor Pete Wilson to link its preferred solution to the newly defined problem of saving endangered species while allowing development.[40] Irvine vice president Monica Florian urged Wilson to create a state-level program that would facilitate conservation planning by stakeholders based on principles developed by a scientific panel. In theory, this approach would enable communities to set aside some acreage for conservation while continuing to allow development according to specified rules. Because it would preserve enough land that species could persist, proponents reasoned, there would be no reason to invoke the ESA.

Collaborative, ecosystem-scale planning promised a win-win solution by addressing the concerns of environmentalists and developers simultaneously: it would provide landowners and developers with greater certainty about what they could do with their land while also making possible the kinds of ecosystemwide reserves that conservation biologists prefer. Governor Wilson immediately perceived the proposal's broad political appeal, and in April 1991 he unveiled the Natural Community Conservation Planning (NCCP) program, the framework of which had been crafted by scientists from the Department of Fish and Game and the FWS, staff from the Nature Conservancy, and Irvine Company executives. In announcing the program, Wilson said that environmental problems for too long had been stalled by the "tactic of confrontation." The NCCP, he said, would inaugurate a "new era of consensus" based on "good faith efforts at mutual accommodation." [41] The legislature was dubious about the program, however, so to demonstrate its viability the state Resources Agency chose Southern California for a test run.

The first step in the pilot project was to establish an advisory committee of experts—the Scientific Review Panel—to create scientific guidelines for reserve design, species conservation, and adaptive management that cities and counties could use in developing their long-range conservation plans. The panel's more subtle purpose was to provide a credible underpinning for the program and avert the usual technical squabbles that so often derail regulatory efforts. To ensure the panel's views would be authoritative, NCCP administrators staffed it with five eminent conservation biologists and geographers—Reed Noss, Dennis Murphy, Peter Broussard, Michael Gilpin, and John O'Leary—all of whom were nationally known and familiar with the local ecology.

The Scientific Review Panel, however, soon found itself deeply frustrated in its efforts to develop guidelines for building viable preserves. Its efforts were complicated by the fact that CSS is an extraordinarily variable ecological community, and mapping it is open to a wide range of interpretations. Furthermore, developers who had information about species on their land obstinately refused to hand it over to government scientists. The panel was limited to identifying potentially imperiled species (they found ninety-six) and providing a set of general tenets to guide reserve design. They came up with the following principles:

- Conserve target species throughout the planning area. Species that are well distributed across their native ranges are less susceptible to extinction than are species confined to small portions of their ranges.
- Preserve larger reserves containing large populations of the target species; they are better than small blocks containing small populations.
- Keep reserve areas close to one another.
- Keep habitat contiguous because less fragmentation is better than more.
- Link reserves with corridors. Such linkages function better when the habitat within them resembles the preferred habitat of target species.
- Make sure reserves contain a diversity of physical and environmental conditions.
- Protect reserves from encroachment by human disturbance.[42]

After concluding that it was "not able to produce scientifically defensible guidelines for long range planning purposes," [43] given the inadequacy of the existing database, the Scientific Review Panel strongly recommended that the state convene a new panel to study three target species: the coastal California gnatcatcher, the San Diego Cactus Wren, and the Orange-Throated Whiptail Lizard. The research program the panelists envisioned would entail six tasks: mapping the biogeography of CSS; monitoring trends in biodiversity in the region; gathering information on the dispersal abilities of CSS species and landscape corridor use; conducting a viability analysis; collecting data on particularly sensitive CSS-associated species; and acquiring baseline data on genetic variability in target species. State resource agencies did not pursue these tasks, however.

The FWS Moves to List the Coastal California Gnatcatcher

As the Scientific Review Panel was embarking on its work, the FWS and the state of California were simultaneously reviewing the biological data on the coastal California gnatcatcher in response to the listing petitions. On August

30, 1991, in a move that delighted developers and incensed environmentalists, the California Fish and Game Commission announced that it would not make the gnatcatcher a candidate for the California endangered species list. Designating the bird as a candidate would have afforded it temporary protection and, more important, spurred exhaustive studies of its status that could serve as the basis for advocacy to limit future development in the region.

The no-list decision, in which the commissioners disregarded the advice of their own staff, followed an impassioned plea by Undersecretary of Resources Michael Mantell, on behalf of Governor Wilson, against making the bird a candidate on the grounds that doing so would lead to more "polarization and confrontation between the two sides." [44] The commission's decision may have been influenced by continuing efforts by some developers to frame gnatcatcher protection as a major economic risk; for example, a BIA-sponsored study released a week earlier projected that protecting the gnatcatcher would cost the region 212,000 jobs and $20 billion in business activity and earnings. Furthermore, developers had told the commission that more than 100 square miles of CSS were already protected as open space in the region (although commission staff recognized that much of that acreage was high-elevation and therefore unsuitable for the coastal California gnatcatcher).[45] Immediately after the commission announced its decision, the NRDC filed a lawsuit on the grounds that the panel did not follow the provisions of California's endangered species act and that its decision "virtually guarantees that the California gnatcatcher will continue toward extinction." [46]

Unfortunately for developers, one week after the Fish and Game Commission's announcement, the FWS concluded that proposing the bird for listing as an endangered species under the normal (but not the emergency) procedures *was* warranted based on the available science. In 1990 Atwood had estimated that no more than 2,500 breeding pairs of coastal California gnatcatchers remained in the United States. Moreover, the FWS found clear evidence of the impending threats to gnatcatcher habitat: of about 19,000 acres of CSS below 300 meters in elevation in coastal Orange County, only 36 percent was preserved; another 21 percent was approved or proposed for development, and 43 percent was of uncertain status. San Diego County in particular had lost much of its CSS: between 1980 and 1990 San Diego's human population increased by 600,000, and most of the growth occurred on or near the coast, where CSS historically predominates.[47]

The agency published a proposed rule on September 17, 1991, at which point an extended period of public comment began. During this interval, which the agency extended twice in response to political pressure, the FWS received 770 reactions to the proposed rule, more than half of which opposed the listing. Listing opponents hired experts to mount a sophisticated methodological challenge to the scientific basis for concern about the bird and its habitat. Specifically, they argued that the coastal California gnatcatcher and its northern nominate subspecies were not valid taxa.[48] They based this assertion on Atwood's appendix to the listing petition, which amended the conclusions of his doctoral dissertation. In his 1990 status report, Atwood divided the California gnatcatcher into three subspecies rather than two, as he previously had, thereby making the condition of *Polioptila californica californica* appear even more dire. Although this change was comprehensible to scientists—it was actually a return to an earlier classification scheme—it looked highly suspicious to developers.[49] FWS taxonomists independently evaluated Atwood's modification in response to these objections, however, and concluded that the coastal California gnatcatcher is a valid subspecies whose range extends only to Baja California, Mexico.

Opponents of the listing also criticized Atwood's statistical analysis, but here too the FWS found Atwood's procedures and methods "well within the norm for systematic/taxonomic reviews of geographic variation in birds." Independent scientific reviewers concluded that "all readily available pertinent specimen material was used, population samples were assembled properly, all important variable morphological characteristics were examined, and statistical treatments were appropriate." [50] The FWS was similarly unpersuaded by consultants' reports suggesting that scientists had underestimated the amount of available gnatcatcher habitat or that they had overestimated the loss of CSS habitat since 1940. (A study commissioned by developers put the figure at 65 percent since 1900, a figure considerably lower than the 85 percent claimed by the FWS.)

In a last-ditch bid to get the FWS to change its position, in November 1991 developers requested Atwood's data to assess whether his switch from two species to three was justified. When Atwood declined to turn over his data, developers insisted that the FWS halt the listing process until he complied. The FWS refused, and a coalition of developers and public transportation agencies filed suit in November 1992. The judge dismissed the suit, however, because the agency had not actually made a decision to list the bird.[51]

The FWS was particularly adamant because, notwithstanding assurances by developers that the CSS already was adequately protected, local governments were continuing to approve construction projects in the face of FWS requests for greater scrutiny. Between 1989 and 1993 urban and agricultural development had destroyed 3,600 acres of CSS in Orange County and 2,400 acres in San Diego County, most of it located below 300 meters. Another 8,000 acres of gnatcatcher habitat was vulnerable to proposed or approved construction projects.[52] Not only was the gnatcatcher's habitat deteriorating rapidly, but no regulatory mechanisms were in place to protect it. It was not listed under the federal or California ESA, and local and county ordinances did not have sufficiently stringent standards to protect the bird—or the ordinances were easily changed, or both.

Even areas that had been designated as open space were vulnerable to changing land-use decisions. The FWS documented numerous instances in which construction projects during the 1990s made no effort to mitigate habitat losses, and county agencies ignored the FWS's notifications that the projects they were approving failed to disclose the presence of gnatcatchers, even though the birds were candidates for federal listing. In one incident, which occurred just prior to the FWS proposal to list the bird, the San Marcos City Council allowed a San Diego developer to clear hundreds of acres of prime gnatcatcher habitat despite a FWS request to hold off until its own biologists could review mitigation measures ordered by the city. The city council approved the bulldozing of CSS even though it had not yet approved the final development plans.[53] With development interests clearly holding sway in local decision making, by the early 1990s pressure was mounting on the FWS to list the gnatcatcher as endangered in the hopes of saving the last remaining vestiges of CSS habitat.

The Marriage of the ESA and NCCP

While the FWS analyzed its listing proposal—a process that ultimately took eighteen months—the state of California moved ahead with its NCCP program. The stated goal of the NCCP act, which the California legislature passed in October 1991, was to provide "for the regional or areawide protection and perpetuation of diversity, while allowing compatible and appropriate development and growth." [54] The act created a process in which developers, environmentalists, and local officials could meet, under the auspices of the Department of Fish and Game, to develop a regional wildlife preserve and accompanying development guidelines. By contrast with the ESA, the NCCP allowed for the creation of reserves *before* species were on the brink of extinction, and it was ecosystem- rather than species-based. The pilot project for NCCP divided the 6,000-square-mile CSS region of Southern California into eleven subregions, each of which was required to come up with its own plan.

Aside from generating conservation guidelines and a research protocol, however, the inchoate NCCP did not make much headway. It had little structure, no funding, and minimal support; it did not specify the criteria habitat reserves needed to meet, nor did it provide incentives for property owners to enroll their land, and initially the region's landowners and developers had little enthusiasm for the program. By late 1993 only thirty-nine private landowners had enrolled.[55] Federal agencies, which managed some of the most intact CSS habitat in the region, were unable to enroll their land in the NCCP because no legal mechanism enabled them to do so. Governor Wilson's appointees, who were supposed to recruit local officials to implement the program, were not particularly sympathetic to environmental concerns and did not promote the program as effectively as they might have.[56] Even the Irvine Company, which had originally backed the program, threatened to drop out if environmentalists pursued the gnatcatcher listing. Environmentalists refused to back down, however, concerned that in the absence of a listing they would have little leverage against developers.

In an effort to jumpstart the NCCP, in late 1993 the Wilson administration—whose appointees had lobbied aggressively to keep the coastal California gnatcatcher off state and federal lists—reversed itself and threw its support behind federal listing of the bird.[57] The governor changed his position after working out an arrangement with the FWS to list the bird as threatened rather than endangered, as the agency had originally intended, and to issue a special rule allowing for a series of HCPs to be negotiated under the auspices of California's NCCP program.[58] Plans prepared under the program differed from HCPs negotiated under the ESA in a couple of respects: HCPs were required for compliance with the ESA, whereas participation in the NCCP program was voluntary; HCPs were created to deal with listed species, whereas the NCCP program was designed to prevent listings. The Special Rule for the Coastal California Gnatcatcher, published in December 1993, linked the two processes, however: it delegated authority for enforcement and development approval to the California Department of Fish and Game, and it specified that incidental take due to development activities in an approved NCCP plan would not be considered a violation of the ESA. A habitat plan devised under the special rule would serve as both an NCCP and an HCP (hereafter NCCP/HCP). In announcing the special rule for the gnatcatcher, Interior Secretary Babbitt underscored the imperative for such innovations with a slew of metaphors, saying: "We need to find common ground, to find parallel tracks that show the compatibility of environmental protection and economic development. . . . If we don't, we'll run ourselves right off a cliff." [59]

The marriage of the ESA and the NCCP created several powerful new incentives for landowners to enroll in the program. First, the creation of an NCCP/HCP promised to streamline the regulatory process: once the FWS was satisfied that an NCCP/HCP would save enough habitat, it would issue a blanket permit allowing local governments to approve development on habitat outside the preserves. Without this rule, landowners would have to navigate a labyrinth of federal permitting and review procedures for each new housing development or road in gnatcatcher habitat. Once the rule was in place, landowners who chose to participate in the NCCP would only have to go through a single permit application process, an advantage that was touted as "one-stop shopping." By contrast, those who chose not to participate would have to craft a separate HCP or undergo a Section 7 consultation and then demonstrate that the plan they formulated was consistent with NCCP/HCP. The special rule offered an additional incentive to landowners as well: participants were allowed to destroy 5 percent of CSS within each subregion during the NCCP/HCP development process. And a final feature—added in early 1994—made the NCCP process almost irresistible: once a plan was developed, even if species covered by it were later listed by the ESA, participating landowners were not responsible for any additional conservation requirements; instead, public authorities would have to finance measures not included in the original plan—a controversial provision that became known as the "no surprises" policy.

Although NCCP/HCPs promised to eliminate layers of regulatory review and compliance, the process of devising them threatened to be arduous. Each separate subregional plan would have to be approved by a host of municipal and county officials; to implement a subregional plan each municipality would have to enact zoning changes, come up with ways to mitigate habitat loss, and create mechanisms for funding the acquisition of land. The prospect did not dampen the enthusiasm of the program's most vocal cheerleader, however: "It is admittedly going to be a long and complicated and sometimes frustrating process," Secretary Babbitt conceded. "But the alternatives are all worse. The alternative is a train wreck that results in stalemate and no development, and a decade of litigation like we've had in the forests of the Pacific Northwest." [60]

The NCCP's objective of eliminating adversarial politics notwithstanding, as the process moved forward, advocates on both sides tried their luck in court, and in 1994 two lawsuits threatened to derail the NCCP experiment. In May U.S. district court judge Stanley Sporkin ordered the FWS to remove the bird from its list of threatened species. Although its original lawsuit had been thrown out, the BIA of Southern California and the Orange County Transportation Agencies had reinstated their suit after the FWS made its final listing decision, on the grounds that the agency had failed to make public all the data it relied on in declaring the gnatcatcher threatened. The ruling was only a temporary setback, however; Atwood immediately submitted his data to the FWS, and the agency made it publicly available. A second judicial ruling in 1994 threatened to unravel the program as well: California's Third District Court of Appeals found in favor of the NRDC, which had contested the state's refusal to list the gnatcatcher. The court ordered the Fish and Game Commission to reconsider its decision, a move that prompted outrage and threats to withdraw from the program among developers who wanted no more complications. Although environmentalists pressed the commission to list the gnatcatcher (concerned that the Republican Congress would dismantle the federal ESA and leave the bird unprotected), it again declined, and the NCCP/HCP process went forward.

The San Diego Multiple Species Conservation Program

In December 1996 the FWS and the California Department of Fish and Game approved what the Clinton administration hailed as its showpiece example of local, collaborative environmental problem solving: the San Diego Multiple Species Conservation Program (MSCP) plan.[61] Officially adopted in 1997 by the San Diego City Council and the County Board of Supervisors, the MSCP carved out a 172,000-acre habitat preserve from a 582,000-acre portion of southwestern San Diego County. The plan purported to protect 62 percent of the remaining CSS (70,700 of 117,500 acres) and 54 percent of all habitat types in one of the most densely populated and fastest-growing areas of the United States; it was touted to benefit eighty-five species of animals and plants and twenty different habitats.[62]

Formulating the Plan. The original impetus for the San Diego MSCP actually preceded the NCCP program. The Clean Water Department of the San Diego Metro Waste District initiated an HCP process in 1990, in response to a lawsuit by the EPA charging that the city was improperly treating its sewage. To get a permit under the Clean Water Act, the city needed to upgrade and expand its sewerage system, but doing so entailed construction in endangered species habitat. The FWS recommended that the city prepare an HCP to satisfy the mitigation demands that would be raised during the permitting process.[63]

In 1991 the city of San Diego established a small, industry-dominated citizen advisory committee to begin crafting an HCP but quickly realized that it would need to broaden participation to include environmentalists if it wanted to have any credibility. The resulting group, which became the MSCP Working Group, had twenty-nine members, including representatives of the FWS, the Department of Fish and Game, officials from the city and county of San Diego and ten other municipal jurisdictions, developers, environmentalists, and representatives of several special districts. Shortly into its deliberations, the Working Group recognized that it needed a chair who would be perceived as both neutral—that is, not affiliated with developers or environmentalists—and highly qualified. They settled on Karen Scarborough, the president of the San Diego-based Citizens Coordinate for the Century Three (C3), a moderate environmental group. Scarborough was a fortuitous choice: shortly after becoming chair of the Working Group, she took a position in Mayor Susan Golding's office as a land-use and environmental policy analyst, which gave her even more authority as a leader.[64] Moreover, Scarborough turned out to be a committed and talented policy entrepreneur. The group also selected Jim Whalen, a moderate developer, to be its vice chair, and it hired environmental and financial consultants to enhance its technical capacity.

Early on, the city recognized that it would need a portrait of the region's biological resources as well as its political and private property boundaries to serve as a foundation for planning decisions. Led by Ogden Environmental and Energy Services Co., Inc., a local consulting firm, staff from various regional and municipal offices assembled data gleaned from aerial photos, satellite images, field surveys, and existing maps and environmental impact reports. Biologists then developed a model to evaluate the quality of the region's habitat depending on its vegetation, the presence of sensitive species, soil types, connectivity, and other features. In a third step, planners used geographic information systems to create habitat maps, as well as maps reflecting current and planned land uses, ownership, and economic value. By overlaying the land-use maps on the biological resource maps, they were able to conduct a "gap analysis" that identified areas in the region most at risk of development.[65]

The mapping exercise showed that the MSCP study area—which is bordered by Mexico to the south, national forest lands to the east, the Pacific Ocean to the west, and the San Dieguito River Valley to the north—contained 315,940 acres of undisturbed habitat, of which almost two-thirds was privately owned. The gap analysis revealed that only 17 percent of the 202,757 acres of biological core and linkage areas was preserved for biological open space as of 1994, and that these areas were widely distributed and often unconnected.[66] Existing general and community plans had designated much of the remaining habitat in the MSCP study area for low density residential uses (39 percent) and less than one-third (29 percent) for parks or open space.[67] The task of the Working Group, then, was to devise a reserve that preserved as much of the core biological resource areas and linkages as possible, maximizing inclusion of public lands and lands already conserved as open space, while sharing costs equitably among landowners and not "unduly" limiting development.

The group initially considered three alternatives: a builder-initiated plan to focus exclusively on the gnatcatcher and protect 85,000 acres (the Coastal Sage Scrub alternative); an environmentalist-supported plan to set aside 179,000 acres (the Biologically Preferred alternative); and a middle-ground plan (the Multiple Habitats alternative), also generated by developers, that relied almost exclusively on preserving existing parcels of public land and adding thin linkages among them. Negotiations centered on how much land to reserve, whether to draw a firm line around the habitat preserve, how many species to cover, what assurances to give landowners regarding the amount of land designated as preserve, how to allocate the financial responsibilities of involved parties, how to achieve equity between large and small landholders, and how to allocate the contribution of federal and state governments to land acquisition funds.[68] Negotiations were complex and arduous because so many landowners—and such inordinately valuable real estate—were involved; nevertheless, most participants characterized the Working Group's monthly meetings as generally "civil and friendly." [69] According to Scarborough, over the course of resolving a number of issues, members of the group came to trust one another and their commitment to the innovative effort to conduct ecosystem-scale planning strengthened.[70] This commitment turned out to be vital because in 1993 the city of San Diego prevailed in the lawsuit over its sewage treatment. Although the ruling eliminated the original impetus for the MSCP, Mayor Golding, a moderate Republican, remained firmly committed to the planning process. Along with the imprimatur of Secretary Babbitt, Golding's backing was crucial to maintaining the plan's political momentum.[71]

Although trust developed among most participants, some environmentalists expressed concern that the planning process was not sufficiently inclusive. From the beginning, Working Group meetings were public, with time reserved for public comment, but some found that forum intimidating, and few members of the public attended those meetings. Interested parties were more likely to attend public hearings that were held in the evening and on weekends. Although these hearings were better attended and more participatory than the Working Group meetings, it was not always clear whether or how public input was subsequently incorporated into Working Group decisions.[72] Moreover, some of the most delicate and potentially contentious decisions, such as whether to grant incidental take authorization for certain species, were made outside of the larger group in subcommittees or closed-door meetings between city and county representatives and resources agencies.[73] Finally, although representation in the group was broad, some environmental and private property rights groups felt marginalized.[74]

Furthermore, the Working Group was unable to resolve the most contentious issues it faced. After the group failed several times to reach consensus on a plan delineating reserve boundaries, in spring 1994 Mayor Golding proffered a fourth option that represented a compromise between developers' and environmentalists' preferred approaches. The mayor's alternative was not a map but a series of preservation targets: 155,000–165,000 acres of habitat that would encompass 70 percent to 80 percent of the biological core areas, as well as 50 percent to 60 percent of the corridors, and would provide coverage for nearly sixty priority species.[75] After quickly settling on the mayor's alternative, the Working Group set about developing standards for each subarea plan. The new idea was that the subareas would develop their plans, adhering to guidelines developed by the Working Group, and the result would add up to a coherent preserve network.

As the Working Group struggled to reconcile the objectives of each of the subareas covered by the plan, several episodes provoked the ire of environmentalists. The cities of San Diego and Chula Vista each approved large-scale developments in critical habitat; in two cases, permits were issued over the objections of the FWS, which noted that the projects were inconsistent with the MSCP. The FWS threatened to reject the entire plan if the third project, locating a University of California satellite in Otay Valley, went forward, so the Working Group simply eliminated the area from the reserve design. Moreover, environmentalists contended that once subarea plans had been incorporated into the MSCP, the level of habitat protection offered was diminished considerably: buffer zones were narrower than some alternatives in the original plan had envisioned; several core habitat areas were designated for low-density residential development; a future road was slated to run through the Otay area; and the FWS raised the list of species ostensibly covered by the plan from fifty-seven to eighty-five, even though the scientific basis for the increase was unclear.[76]

Approving the MSCP. Despite these setbacks and disagreements, after nearly four years of negotiations, in May 1995 the Working Group presented its draft MSCP plan, along with an environmental impact statement prepared by the FWS, for public review and comment. The 172,000-acre habitat preserve was to be assembled through conservation of 82,000 acres that were already in public ownership, more than half of which was held by localities, private contributions of 63,000 acres to comply with development regulations and mitigate impacts of development outside the preserve, and public acquisition of about 27,000 acres of private land from willing sellers. (Local governments were to acquire half of that land, and the state and federal governments would acquire the remainder.) The Working Group had decided on a "soft-line" reserve, known as the Multi-Habitat Planning Area. Although the plan delineated the general boundary of the reserve, it did not specify precisely which lands were to be protected; instead, as noted above, local jurisdictions were supposed to make decisions about individual development projects in conformance with the plan's habitat protection guidelines.

Emerging from a deliberative effort that had received little media coverage, the MSCP entered the arena of electoral politics, where rhetoric and framing assumed much larger roles. To enhance the prospects for the plan's approval, the city of San Diego launched a publicity blitz featuring public hearings and mass mailings in the spring of 1995. The state's largest bank, the Bank of America, threw its weight behind the plan, warning that unchecked urban sprawl would delay the state's economic recovery and destroy its quality of life.[77] Despite efforts to publicize the MSCP, however, the public did not seem to understand it, so the officials and scientists who had developed the plan asked the Nature Conservancy to come up with a more effective sales pitch. In fall 1996 the Nature Conservancy—in collaboration with Stoorza, Ziegaus, and Metzger, California's biggest public relations firm—embarked on a campaign to gain public acceptance of the MSCP. Entitled the Naturelands Project, the public outreach and education effort was intended to tap into existing values in order to generate enthusiasm about the plan. Recognizing that the average Californian was no longer susceptible to the doomsday rhetoric traditionally employed by environmentalists, the project sought instead to ascertain what San Diegans *did* care about and craft a message that reflected those values.[78]

Decision Resources, the company hired to acquire information on San Diegans' values, discovered that an overwhelming percentage of the region's residents—even those who did not consider themselves environmentalists— placed a high value on quality of life (an admittedly vague concept). More specifically, surveys suggested that San Diegans cared deeply about their chaparral- and sagebrush-covered hillsides and the region's other environmental features. In recognition of these findings, the Naturelands Project focused on building the equivalent of "brand loyalty" for quality of life in San Diego. The campaign included billboards, public service announcements, and corporate comarketing. To gain visibility, the Nature Conservancy wooed a host of celebrities, including Robert Redford, to serve on the project.[79]

Apparently, the offensive paid off: in March 1997, after a six-hour session before a standing-room-only crowd, the San Diego City Council unanimously approved the MSCP. Many at the meeting expressed satisfaction with the plan: the San Diego office of the BIA, the San Diego Chamber of Commerce, the Sierra Club, the Audubon Society, and the League of Conservation Voters all endorsed it.[80] The plan was not without its detractors, however. Of continuing concern to many scientists and environmentalists was the "no surprises" clause that freed landowners from financial responsibility for additional conservation measures. Critics also lamented that, even though it provided stronger development curbs than otherwise would have existed in the region's smaller municipalities, the MSCP supplanted the city of San Diego's stronger restrictions, a charge that the creators of the plan rejected.[81] Jim Peugh, former president of the San Diego chapter of the Audubon Society, did not believe the plan supported the recovery of endangered species. "Our grandkids are going to think we were really stupid at some point," he said, "and we'll work to make this stronger."[82] Skeptics also pointed out that the region was likely to have trouble raising the funding necessary to implement the plan fully. And some elected officials, small landowners, and antitax advocates characterized the plan as a waste of money and an infringement on private property rights.

Despite critics' objections, the city's endorsement of the MSCP promised to pave the way for its adoption by the other subareas covered by the plan. With its outsized political clout, the city of San Diego had taken the lead in developing the plan, even though it controlled only one-third of the 172,000-acre preserve. It had spearheaded the process both because its sewer system was the impetus and because it controlled the most valuable real estate and faced the most contentious development battles. By gaining the city's approval, the MSCP had surmounted its biggest potential hurdle. Still, potential stumbling blocks remained, the largest of which was that the approval of San Diego County—which controlled the other major chunk of habitat—was not assured. In particular, Bill Horn, chairman of the San Diego County Board of Supervisors, had been outspoken in his opposition to the plan, dubbing it the "Multiple Stolen and Confiscated Property" plan.[83]

Implementing the Plan. After considerable lobbying by backers, in October 1997 the San Diego County Board of Supervisors voted 4–1 to approve the MSCP. Although the vote was a triumph, the plan still faced a host of additional veto points; it awaited the approval of and, more important, implementation by, ten additional local jurisdictions. To comply with the plan, each jurisdiction, or subarea, had to create a plan consistent with the MSCP that would then need to be approved by the Department of Fish and Game and the FWS.[84] (The MSCP itself is just a framework. It is the area plans, together with the implementing agreements, that are the basis for ESA take permits.) Each subarea plan must specify how the recipient of a take authorization will conserve habitat and contribute to the MSCP preserve, using, in part, the existing land-use-planning and project-approval processes. Subarea plans also contain conservation targets, mitigation standards, and measures to ensure development is consistent with habitat preservation. And they contain mechanisms to avoid or minimize project impacts on the preserve, as well as preserve management plans. Each local jurisdiction must incorporate its subarea plan into its policies, land-use plans, and regulations; any development project a local jurisdiction approves has to be consistent with the subarea plan. The implementing agreement, a binding contract signed by the local jurisdiction (or other take authorization holder) and the wildlife agencies, specifies the responsibility of each of the parties and the remedies to be imposed if participants fail to live up to the agreement.

While subareas struggled to devise their plans, developers were finding that the MSCP had not created regulatory certainty or eliminated project-by-project review because environmentalists continued to challenge individual projects on the grounds that they were inconsistent with the spirit of the MSCP. And environmental groups—even those that had supported the MSCP—became more critical and suspicious as they watched individual development projects go forward. They described the development proposal for Carmel Mountain as an early test of the plan's capacity to protect endangered wildlife and habitat. Pardee Homes, a major San Diego builder, had proposed developing Carmel Mountain in the early 1990s, to the consternation of environmentalists, who touted the site's status as home to numerous endangered plant communities, including the extremely rare southern maritime chaparral, and one of the last remaining coastal mesas in Southern California.[85] Given the laxity of existing laws and regulations, environmentalists hoped the MSCP would enhance protection of Carmel Mountain, because early habitat evaluation maps indicated it was a core biological resource area. Instead, after extensive negotiations with Pardee, the city proposed a compromise plan that allowed the company to develop much of the site while doing its mitigation elsewhere. In response, local environmentalists came up with a competing plan to acquire 150 acres of the most sensitive land on Carmel Mountain—the mesa top. After a vigorous public relations campaign by Pardee squelched that option, the mayor's office convened a stakeholder group to devise a solution it could present to the city council. Eventually, the participants struck a deal in which Pardee traded permission to develop less-sensitive land at another site in exchange for protecting the mesa top. In 1998 the city council adopted a modified version of the stakeholders' agreement that protected 150 acres of the mesa top while allowing intensive development on the rest of the site. Although some saw this plan as the best that could be hoped for given the context, others complained that the whole point of the MSCP was to make more innovative solutions possible.

A second major controversy arose in 1998, when the city of San Diego allowed Cousins Market Centers to bulldoze seventy acres of wetland habitat in the northern part of the city. Audubon's Jim Peugh charged that local authorities abused their discretion in allowing the project to proceed. The land clearance destroyed sixty-five of the site's sixty-six rare vernal pools, which were habitat to dozens of species, including the endangered San Diego fairy shrimp. Fourteen environmental groups sued the city of San Diego, the Army Corps of Engineers (which issued the permit), and the FWS over the Cousins decision, pointing out that the MSCP implementing agreement required the city to avoid vernal pool impacts "to the maximum extent practicable." [86] Michael Beck, a county planning commissioner and director of the Endangered Habitats League, responded that the MSCP itself was not the problem; rather, the plan gave local elected boards such as the San Diego City Council tremendous discretion.[87]

On the other hand, supporters of the MSCP pointed out that the program also boasted successes. For example, in the early 1990s developers had won approval to build 27,000 homes on Mount San Miguel, but, after environmentalists persuaded the federal government to acquire some of the land, the developer scaled back his proposal. The area became the center of the new San Diego National Wildlife Refuge, which currently comprises approximately 8,000 acres and is projected to encompass 50,000 acres by 2008. Similarly, a successful effort to prevent the construction of ninety-two houses on a site east of

San Diego yielded the 2,600-acre Crestridge Ecological Preserve. According to the program's boosters, this and other land acquisition projects would never have occurred without the MSCP.

OUTCOMES

By the fall of 2005, five subarea plans had been approved, including Chula Vista's in January 2005; one (Coronado) awaited approval by the wildlife agencies; and three were not yet complete. (Three cities—Imperial Beach, Lemon Grove, and National City—had withdrawn from the process altogether.) It is difficult to estimate total habitat acquisitions and losses or money spent under the MSCP because no single agency compiles such data for the entire program. As of December 2004, however, the City of San Diego had conserved 32,528 acres toward its 52,012-acre goal, including 22,141 baseline (already publicly owned) acres. The county had conserved—through acquisition, dedication of easements, and protection of baseline land—61,472 acres of its 98,739-acre goal.[88]

As expected, funding for the acquisition of private land necessary to build the reserve system has been a major stumbling block. Over thirty years, the MSCP was projected to cost a total of $540 million to $650 million, of which localities would bear $262–$360 million.[89] Each year since the MSCP plan was approved, the state has appropriated money for the purchase of habitat land; furthermore, California voters approved bond initiatives in 2000 and 2002, both of which promised money for land acquisition in Southern California. The federal government has awarded grants of between $2 million and $6 million annually from the Land and Water Conservation and ESA funds. Local governments have struggled to raise their share of funds, however, and they have yet to establish a dedicated funding source as required under the plan. In November 2004 San Diego County voters approved a $14 billion sales-tax renewal measure (TransNet) that earmarked $850 million for environmental spending, but it is unclear how much of that will go to the MSCP.

The shortage of money has affected not only land acquisition but also the ability of jurisdictions to manage and monitor the land they have set aside for conservation.[90] As a result, managers struggle to keep illegal trash dumpers and off-road vehicle riders off preserves, control weeds and invasive plants, and assess the status of species ostensibly protected by the plan. Making manifest the precariousness of San Diego's habitat conservation efforts, in fall 2003 wildfires charred 775,000 acres in Southern California, including about 390,000 acres in San Diego County—nearly 15 percent of the county's total land area. The blaze destroyed about 71,000 acres of coastal sage scrub.[91] Scientists predicted the area would take many years to recover, and environmentalists urged caution in opening up any of the remaining land to development given the fires' uncertain biological consequences.

Although no one can yet say whether the MSCP—in combination with the other NCCP/HCPs being developed as part of Southern California's pilot project—will protect the region's biological diversity, researchers have released critical evaluations of the NCCP program and HCPs more generally that raise doubts. In May 1997 the NRDC—which has followed the NCCP/ HCP process closely since its inception—released the first comprehensive assessment of the program. The study, entitled "Leap of Faith," identified a host of problems with the process, including inadequate scientific review of plans, poor and insecure funding to implement plans, and undefined or inadequately enforced regulatory standards. The NRDC recommended the following reforms: requiring independent scientific consultation and review of planning decisions and reserve design; setting clear standards for reserve design, including buffer zone specifications and infrastructure restrictions; scaling back blanket assurances to landowners; creating secure funding sources; and ensuring that the NCCP program does not interfere with enforcement of other environmental laws, such as the Clean Water Act. A year later, the National Center for Ecological Analysis and Synthesis released a study of 208 HCPs that underscored the concern that HCPs did not follow consistent standards and concluded that, even when good science was available, political or economic considerations often trumped it in decision making. The study recommended that the FWS institute basic standards for HCPs and require peer review of plans by independent scientific experts.[92] In response to these and other critiques, in 2000 the California legislature amended the NCCP to enhance both scientific oversight and public participation in NCCP development. Similarly, the Clinton administration proposed modifying HCP rules to require measurable biological goals and objectives, mandate a monitoring program based on science, and create flexible systems of managing reserves that can adjust as more is learned. These modifications were never formally adopted, however, and a 2005 investigation by the *Seattle Post-Intelligencer* concluded that "many of the nation's habitat plans have serious shortcomings that tip the scales in favor of development over endangered species." [93]

Even as the state and federal governments were responding to these critiques of the NCCP and HCP processes, several changes in the regulatory context threatened to undermine the programs. After seven years of legal battles, in October 2000 the FWS released court-mandated critical habitat designations for the gnatcatcher. The designation, which comprised 513,650 acres of habitat, imposes an additional layer of government on major developments in the region—precisely what the NCCP sought to avoid. Although the FWS grandfathered existing NCCP/HCPs, it could not exempt future HCPs, and developers contend that the designation eliminated incentives for them to participate in the NCCP process.[94] Further exasperating developers, environmentalists sued the FWS for exempting existing NCCP/HCPs from critical habitat designation. A second hurdle appeared in December 2003, when U.S. District Court judge Emmet Sullivan ruled that the FWS had violated the Administrative Procedures Act by promulgating the "no surprises" policy without giving prior notice or meaningful opportunity for public participation. In early 2005, after Judge Sullivan again ordered the agency to stop issuing HCPs containing such clauses, the agency reissued a slightly modified version of the rule in order to allow HCPs to proceed. Karen Scarborough conceded that the lawsuits are a setback, saying, "We had hoped to change the environmentalist vs. builder paradigm." [95]

CONCLUSIONS

According to conservation biologist Dennis Murphy, "The goal of the Endangered Species Act is unrealizable. Recovering species that only need public lands may be possible, but on private lands only heroic efforts will be able to sustain species that will inevitably decline. That's a reality." [96] Many environmental groups, including the Nature Conservancy, the World Wildlife Fund, and Environmental Defense, eschew Murphy's pessimism, however, and see NCCP/HCPs as a promising solution to the quandary of preserving species on private land. One observer eloquently suggests that

> although it will be some years before it is known whether the plans have been successful at sustaining the biodiversity of Southern California ecosystems, the plans faithfully incorporate the concepts that inspired their creation and offer a potent response to a difficult environmental challenge. They are unprecedented in breadth and scale, unique in approach and technique, and unsurpassed in their capacity to protect wildlife and natural habitats and to harmonize environmental and economic goals for the region.[97]

The potential advantages of NCCP/HCPs over more conventional regulatory approaches to habitat protection are evident. For landowners and developers, NCCP/HCPs promise to streamline the regulatory process and provide certainty. For conservation biologists, NCCP/HCPs promise to generate information about species and habitats and offer an ecosystem-level approach to habitat conservation, rather than a species-by-species approach. For environmentalists, NCCP/HCPs promise to provide a mechanism for acquiring habitat that might not otherwise be protected and, in theory at least, establish funds for management and monitoring of habitat preserves. And for regulators, NCCP/HCPs promise to reduce regulatory conflict while facilitating more innovative, tailor-made solutions to the problems of individual regions.

Not surprisingly, however, detractors argue that in practice NCCP/HCPs have not achieved all that their boosters hoped. One set of concerns is procedural: critics have expressed reservations about the policy consequences of devolving habitat preservation decisions to the local level. Environmentalists are concerned that for municipal officials, development—which generates prosperity in the short-run—is almost always a more attractive option than habitat preservation. This feature of local governments may undermine efforts to preserve habitat in the long run, especially if—as in Southern California— local jurisdictions have primary responsibility for implementing plans. As one scientist commented after the Cousins Market incident: "Personally, I believe the [MSCP] is a setback because, as I understand it, you are basically handing the enforcement of the Endangered Species Act over to the San Diego city council, and they have no track record for conservation, in particular for vernal pools." [98] Furthermore, although collaborative processes are intended to defuse conflict among stakeholders, questions about who is a stakeholder and how to incorporate "the public" into decision making remain; groups on both sides of the MSCP complain that they were excluded from the process. Moreover, it was conflict—more precisely, the threat of litigation over ESA regulations, which could have halted development altogether—that brought landowners and developers to the table in Southern California. In any case, the lawsuits that have accompanied the implementation of the MSCP make it clear that the plan has eliminated neither conflict nor the fundamental value differences between environmentalists and cornucopians.

A second set of concerns is substantive. Above all, many environmentalists and scientists have serious doubts about the scientific basis for NCCP/HCPs. Enthusiasts point out that in a collaborative working group, scientists collect and interpret information jointly with citizens, who become quasi-experts by imitation.[99] Critics of the NCCP/HCP process, however, suggest that working groups have disregarded science when it was politically or economically inexpedient. They point out that, although the state of California assembled a prestigious team of scientists to develop the overarching conservation principles to which NCCP plans would adhere, scientists subsequently played only a minor role in the process: they had little input into subregional decisions about where to draw boundaries, and no peer review panel was formed to evaluate the final MSCP. In his careful assessment of the MSCP, Daniel Pollak concludes, "it appears the decisions [to issue incidental take permits] did not employ a clear methodology or well-defined criteria, and relied on uncertain assumptions." [100] In short, because collaboration promotes compromises that are dictated by nonscientific concerns, NCCP/HCPs are unlikely to be ideal from the perspective of wildlife and habitat protection.

Scientists and environmentalists also remain dubious about the no surprises policy embedded in the MSCP. Proponents of the policy insist that it constitutes a powerful incentive for developers to negotiate, noting that prior to the no surprises rule the FWS had approved only fourteen HCPs in the decade from 1983 to 1992. By contrast, as of fall 2005, more than 435 HCPs covering near 40 million acres had been finalized.[101] The no surprises rule does not preclude additional mitigation measures; rather, it ensures that "where additional requirements are needed, the financial burden of those requirements will fall on the public, not the private landowner or business." [102] But environmentalists and scientists point out that the biological world is inherently uncertain, as is our understanding of it, and they doubt the wisdom of a policy that effectively locks in plans for fifty years or more. They contend that the no surprises rule gives business the assurances it wants at the expense of government's ability to respond to new information.

A related worry concerns the extent to which the monitoring and adaptive management—that is, continuous collection of data on species and habitats, as well as refinement of management techniques in response to new information—

will actually occur under the MSCP. The Scientific Review Panel made clear that "areas designated as reserves are . . . unlikely to be self-sustaining (that is, provide for natural, dynamic ecosystem processes) or to be capable of maintaining viable populations without active management." [103] The design of the MSCP's habitat reserve network and the issuance of incidental take permits were premised on adaptive management; such practices are critical because the plan's designated reserves lie in the middle of or on the fringes of densely populated urban and suburban areas. Yet the funding of both research and reserve monitoring and management remain tenuous; moreover, coordination of those activities within or across MSCP jurisdictions is generally lacking.

To remedy this failing, the U.S. Geological Survey and the Department of Fish and Game are developing an integrated monitoring data warehouse that, ideally, would provide synthesized information that could be used for adaptive management.[104] The agencies are also experimenting with remote sensing technology, which could provide an inexpensive way to monitor the health of preserves. But, although committed participants are making heroic efforts, as journalist Robert McClure observes, nearly twenty-five years after the birth of HCPs, many still worry that they are "helping to push creatures to the brink of extinction." [105]

QUESTIONS TO CONSIDER

- Are HCPs, the current mechanisms of choice for dealing with endangered species on private lands, likely to defuse conflict over preserving species habitats and landscapes? Why or why not?
- Are such approaches likely to accomplish their conservation goals? Or are they, as some environmentalists suggest, simply a way that developers can circumvent the strict requirements of the ESA?

Notes

1. Reed F. Noss, Michael A. O'Connell, and Dennis D. Murphy, *The Science of Conservation Planning: Habitat Conservation Plans Under the Endangered Species Act* (Washington, D.C.: Island Press, 1997).
2. Oliver Houck, quoted in Daniel Pollak, *The Future of Habitat Conservation? The NCCP Experience in Southern California* (Sacramento: California Research Bureau, California State Library, June 2001), 4.
3. Quoted in Terry Rodgers, "City Affirms Plan to Save Area Wildlife, Interior Secretary Calls Large-Habitat Action Magnificent," *San Diego Union-Tribune*, March 19, 1997, A1.
4. Thomas S. Reid and Dennis D. Murphy, "Providing a Regional Context for Local Conservation Action," *Bioscience (Supplement)* 45, 3 (June 1995): S-84–S-90.
5. Deborah S. Knopman, M. Susman, and Marc K. Landy, "Civic Environmentalism: Tackling Tough Land-Use Problems with Innovative Governance," *Environment* 41 (December 1999): 26.
6. Dewitt John, *Civic Environmentalism: Alternatives to Regulation in States and Communities* (Washington, D.C.: CQ Press, 1994); Knopman et al., "Civic Environmentalism"; and Philip Brick, Donald Snow, and Sarah Van De Wetering, *Across the Great*

Divide: Explorations in Collaborative Conservation and the American West (Washington, D.C.: Island Press, 2001).

7. Julia M. Wondollek and Steven L. Yaffee, *Making Collaboration Work: Lessons from Innovation in Natural Resource Management* (Washington, D.C.: Island Press, 2000), 23.

8. See, for example, Jacqueline Savitz, "Compensating Citizens," in *Beyond Backyard Environmentalism,* ed. Charles Sabel et al. (Boston: Beacon Press, 2000), 65–69; Matthew Wilson and Eric Weltman, "Government's Job," in *Beyond Backyard Environmentalism,* 49–53; and Steven L. Yaffee et al., *Balancing Public Trust and Private Interest: Public Participation in Habitat Conservation Planning* (Ann Arbor: School of Natural Resources, University of Michigan, 1998).

9. See, for example, B. C. Bingham and B. R. Noon, "Mitigation of Habitat 'Take': Application to Habitat Conservation Planning," *Conservation Biology* 11 (1995): 127–139; F. Shilling, "Do Habitat Conservation Plans Protect Endangered Species?" *Science* 276, June 13, 1997, 1662–3; and Peter Kareiva et al., *Using Science in Habitat Conservation Planning* (Washington, D.C.: American Institute of Biological Sciences, 1999).

10. See, for example, Lance H. Gunderson, C. S. Holling, and Stephen S. Light, eds., *Barriers and Bridges to the Renewal of Ecosystems and Institutions* (New York: Columbia University Press, 1995).

11. Jeffrey L. Pressman and Aaron Wildavsky, *Implementation*, 3d ed. (Berkeley: University of California Press, 1983).

12. Charles Mann and Mark Plummer, "California vs. Gnatcatcher," *Audubon*, January–February 1995, 29–38, 100–104.

13. Ibid.

14. U.S. FWS, "Special Rule Concerning Take of the Threatened Coastal California Gnatcatcher," *Federal Register*, 58 CFR 16742 (March 30, 1993).

15. Chaparral is a community of shrubby plants adapted to dry summers and moist winters. Riparian habitats are areas of stream- and riverside vegetation.

16. A. D. Dobson et al., "Geographic Distribution of Endangered Species in the United States," *Science* 275, January 24, 1997, 650–653.

17. U.S. FWS, "Endangered and Threatened Wildlife and Plants: Determination of Threatened Status for the Coastal California Gnatcatcher," *Federal Register*, 50 CFR Part 17 (March 30, 1993). Half of all ESA-listed species make their homes exclusively on nonfederal land, most of which is privately owned. For listed species found only on private land, the ratio of declining to improving is 9:1, whereas the ratio is 1.5:1 for listed species found entirely on federal land. See Noss et al., *The Science of Conservation Planning.*

18. Critical habitat is defined as areas that contain "physical or biological features (I) essential to the conservation of the species, and (II) which may require special management considerations or protection." See P.L. 93-205, 16 U.S.C. 1531 et seq. § 4(b)(2). The 1978 amendments to the ESA allow the FWS to take economic considerations into account when designating critical habitat.

19. According to the FWS, fifty-three charges were filed against individuals or corporations for killing endangered species, destroying their habitat, or poaching for specimen collectors between October 1988 and September 1992. Thirty-three were convicted of criminal charges and six of civil charges. Fines and civil penalties totaled about $60,000, and offenders served 1,347 days in jail. See Maura Dolan, "Nature at Risk in a Quiet War," *Los Angeles Times*, December 20, 1992, 1.

20. In the first case, against Anderson and Middleton Logging Company of Washington, the FWS later dropped the charges and bought the threatened stand of 1,000-year-old trees for $3.5 million. In the second case, involving the Oregon Coast Range, the FWS fined International Paper Company $92,000 for illegally clear-cutting 300 acres of critical owl habitat between 1991 and 1996. In an out-of-court settlement, IP agreed to contribute $47,000 to the Nature Conservancy and $25,000

to help fund a database for tracking owls. The company admitted to no wrong-doing, however. See Kathie Durbin and Paul Larmer, "The Feds Won't Enforce the ESA," *High Country News,* August 4, 1997.

21. Dolan, "Nature at Risk."
22. Quoted in Durbin and Larmer, "The Feds Won't Enforce the ESA."
23. Dolan, "Nature at Risk."
24. Ecologists believed that preserving 2,000 of the landowner's 3,500 acres would be sufficient to ensure the long-term survival of the two federally listed butterfly species. See Timothy Beatley, *Habitat Conservation Planning: Endangered Species Protection and Urban Growth* (Austin: University of Texas Press, 1994).
25. Ironically, twenty-five years later the watershed San Bruno agreement is in a predicament: its funding mechanism turned out to be inadequate, so it lacks the money to manage the preserve, and invasive species are crowding out the endangered butterflies' preferred plants. See Robert McClure, "Pioneer Conservation Plan Falls Short," *Seattle Post-Intelligencer,* May 3, 2005, online.
26. Timothy Beatley, "Habitat Conservation Plans: A New Tool to Resolve Land Use Conflicts," *Land Lines,* September 1995.
27. Craig W. Thomas, *Bureaucratic Landscapes: Interagency Cooperation and the Preservation of Biodiversity* (Cambridge: MIT Press, 2003).
28. The coastal California gnatcatcher (*Polioptila californica californica*) was originally described in 1881 as a distinct subspecies. A subsequent analysis conducted in 1926 suggested that *P. californica* was actually three subspecies of the black-tailed gnatcatcher (*P. melanura*), which is widely distributed throughout the deserts of the southwestern United States and Mexico. In 1988, however, Atwood challenged the prevailing classification scheme, contending that *P. californica* was distinct from *P. melanura* based on differences in its behavior and its ecological niche. See U.S. FWS, "Endangered and Threatened Wildlife."
29. Ibid.
30. Under the ESA, the FWS may determine a species or subspecies to be endangered or threatened if one or more of the following is true: its habitat or range is threatened with or undergoing destruction or curtailment; it is being overused for commercial, recreation, scientific, or educational purposes; it is experiencing high rates of disease or predation; existing regulatory mechanisms are inadequate to protect it; and/or other natural or manmade factors are affecting its continued existence.
31. Mann and Plummer, "California vs. Gnatcatcher."
32. Ibid.
33. Quoted in ibid., 24.
34. The FWS had received similar petitions in September 1990 from the Palomar Audubon Society and the San Diego Biodiversity Project.
35. Thomas, *Bureaucratic Landscapes.*
36. Although the FWS is allowed to take only scientific considerations into account in deciding whether to list a species, in practice its decisions have reflected economic and political concerns. See Richard Tobin, *The Expendable Future: U.S. Politics and the Preservation of Biological Diversity* (Durham: Duke University Press, 1990).
37. Terry Rodgers, "Catching Gnats—and Flak," *San Diego Union-Tribune,* May 4, 1991, 1.
38. Quoted in David L. Coddon, "What Price Progress? Tiny Gnatcatcher Hatches a Conflict that Won't Go Away," *San Diego Union-Tribune,* September 6, 1991, F1.
39. In a letter to California Resource Agency head Douglas Wheeler, Irvine Company vice president Monica Florian made clear that the company's goal was to avert state or federal listing of the gnatcatcher. See Ralph Frammolino, "Irvine Co. Tries to Forestall Bid to Protect Bird," *Los Angeles Times,* April 25, 1991, A1.
40. In the mid-1990s the Irvine Company owned two hotels, eighteen shopping centers, 5.2 million square feet of industrial property, a six-square-mile technology center,

and 62,000 acres of "amazingly valuable" real estate. See Mann and Plummer, "California vs. Gnatcatcher."

41. Quoted in Mann and Plummer, "California vs. Gnatcatcher," 48.
42. California Department of Fish and Game and California Resources Agency, "Southern California Coastal Sage Scrub Natural Communities Conservation Planning: Draft Conservation Guidelines" (August 1993). Available at www.dfg.ca.gov/nccp.
43. Quoted in Pollak, *The Future of Habitat Conservation?* 13.
44. Quoted in Drew Silvern, "Protected Status for Gnatcatcher Is Turned Down," *San Diego Union-Tribune*, August 31, 1991, 1. The three against listing were all California businessmen appointed by former Republican governor George Deukmejian. The dissenting vote was cast by a Wilson appointee and former director of the Nature Conservancy.
45. Ibid.
46. Quoted in Marla Cone, "Endangered Status Denied for Gnatcatcher," *Los Angeles Times*, August 31, 1991, 1.
47. U.S. FWS, "Endangered and Threatened Wildlife."
48. If the bird is not a valid subspecies, then it is part of a larger group whose habitat extends over more territory. Such a finding, in turn, changes the calculus of whether the bird is endangered.
49. Mann and Plummer, "California vs. Gnatcatcher."
50. U.S. FWS, "Endangered and Threatened Wildlife."
51. The courts can rule only on a final decision.
52. U.S. FWS, "Endangered and Threatened Wildlife."
53. Drew Silvern, "Bird Loses More Land While Fate is Debated," *San Diego Union-Tribune*, October 13, 1991, B1.
54. The NCCP Act of 1991 (AB 2172). For a summary of the act's legislative history, see Daniel Pollak, *Natural Community Conservation Planning (NCCP): The Origin of an Ambitious Experiment to Protect Ecosystems* (Sacramento: California Research Bureau, California State Library, March 2001).
55. Marla Cone, "U.S. Begins Experiment to Save Songbird," *Los Angeles Times*, December 9, 1993, 3.
56. Thomas, *Bureaucratic Landscapes*.
57. Craig Thomas contends that the Wilson administration approached the FWS behind the scenes, in order to be able to deflect blame for the federal regulations while providing the necessary incentives to increase participation in the NCCP. See ibid.
58. Under Section 4(d) of the ESA, the FWS can issue special regulations for a threatened (but not endangered) species that are deemed "necessary and advisable to provide for the conservation of such species." Section 6 allows the ESA to delegate enforcement of the rule to states.
59. Quoted in Michael Jasny, *Leap of Faith: Southern California's Experiment in Natural Community Conservation Planning* (Washington, D.C.: Natural Resources Defense Council, 1997), 4.
60. Quoted in Cone, "U.S. Begins Experiment."
61. This plan was Southern California's second NCCP/HCP. The first, approved in July 1996, was Orange County's Central-Coastal Plan, which set aside 37,380 acres out of a 209,000-acre planning area. See Noss et al., *The Science of Conservation Planning*.
62. Wildlife experts believe there are more endangered species in the region covered by the plan than in any other location in the country. See Frank Clifford, "San Diego OKs Conservation Plan," *Los Angeles Times*, October 24, 1997, 3.
63. Because of its origins, the boundaries of the MSCP reflect the boundaries of the Metropolitan Sewerage System.
64. Michael McLaughlin, director of land-use planning at the San Diego Association of Governments, personal communication, March 30, 2001.

65. Janet Fairbanks, "Room to Roam: Why the San Diego Region Is Considered a National Model for Habitat Conservation," *Planning* 60 (January 1994): 24–26.
66. Core areas are defined as "areas generally supporting a high concentration of sensitive biological resources which, if lost or fragmented, could not be replaced or mitigated elsewhere." See Multiple Species Conservation Program, "MSCP Plan," August 1996, www.sannet.gov/mscp.
67. Ibid.
68. Jennifer Merrick, "The San Diego Multiple Species Conservation Plan," in *Improving Integrated Natural Resource Planning: Habitat Conservation Plans*, October 14, 1998, National Center for Environmental Decision-Making Research, www.ncedr.org/casestudies/hcp/sandiego.htm.
69. Ibid.
70. Karen Scarborough, MSCP Working Group Chair, personal communication, May 20, 2001.
71. McLaughlin, personal communication; Scarborough, personal communication.
72. Merrick, "The San Diego Multiple Species Conservation Plan."
73. Ibid.; McLaughlin, personal communication.
74. Merrick, "The San Diego Multiple Species Conservation Plan."
75. Allison Rolfe, "Mapping the MSCP Process: Habitat Conservation Planning in the San Diego Region" (masters thesis, San Diego State University, Spring 2000).
76. Raising the number of listed species covered reduces the likelihood of further conservation measures in the future. See Jasny, *Leap of Faith*.
77. Emmet Pierce and Terry Rodgers, "Four Years of Biological Surveys and Quiet Negotiations by Builders, Conservationists, and Planners Are Nearing a Climactic Conclusion," *San Diego Union-Tribune*, June 11, 1995, H1.
78. Emmet Pierce and Terry Rodgers, "Environmentalists Will Try Soft Sell," *San Diego Union-Tribune*, November 14, 1996, 1.
79. Ibid.
80. Marla Cone, "San Diego Approves Broadest Conservation Plan in U.S.," *Los Angeles Times*, March 19, 1997, 1.
81. Scarborough, personal communication.
82. Quoted in Cone, "San Diego Approves."
83. Ibid.
84. Not only local jurisdictions but also special purpose agencies, regional public facility providers, and utilities were all preparing subarea plans.
85. Rolfe, "Mapping the MSCP Process."
86. Vernal pools are small, isolated pools that retain water on a seasonal basis and serve as nurseries for a variety of frogs, salamanders, and other species.
87. Steve LaRue, "Environmental Groups in Region Assail Habitat Management Plan," *San Diego Union-Tribune*, January 4, 1999, B3.
88. City of San Diego, "2004 MSCP Annual Public Workshop Summary Report," June 18, 2005; County of San Diego, "MSCP Annual Report 2004," May 2005. In addition, the city had conserved an additional 1,946 acres adjacent to the preserve, and the county had acquired 14,546 acres outside the boundary.
89. Ibid. Municipalities can raise money in a variety of ways, including a benefit assessment by a regional park or open space district, a habitat maintenance assessment, an ad valorem property tax, or a sales tax increase.
90. The plan's management costs were estimated at $4.6 million per year for local governments and $2 million annually for federal and state governments. See Pollak, *The Future of Habitat Conservation?*
91. Tony Davis, "Fires Take Toll on San Diego's Wildlife," *High Country News*, December 22, 2003.
92. Deborah Schoch, "New Approach to Protecting Fragile Habitats Criticized," *Los Angeles Times*, July 20, 1998, 3.

93. Robert McClure and Lisa Stiffler, "A License to Kill: Flaws in Habitat Conservation Plans Threaten the Survival of Scores of Species," *Seattle Post-Intelligencer*, May 3, 2005, 1.

94. Seema Mehta, "Wide Swaths of Southland Called Vital to Bird, Shrimp," *Los Angeles Times*, October 18, 2000, 1.

95. Scarborough, personal communication.

96. Quoted in Paul Larmer, "The Real Problem is Lack of Time," *High Country News*, August 4, 1997.

97. Marc J. Ebbin, "Is the Southern California Approach to Conservation Succeeding?" *Ecology Law Quarterly* 24 (November 1997): 696.

98. Quoted in LaRue, "Environmental Groups in Region."

99. Charles Sabel, Archon Fung, and Bradley Karkkainen, "Beyond Backyard Environmentalism," in *Beyond Backyard Environmentalism*, 3–46.

100. Pollak, *The Future of Habitat Conservation?*

101. For updated information on HCPs, see http://endangered.fws.gov/hcp/index.html.

102. Noss et al., *The Science of Conservation Planning*, 63.

103. Quoted in Pollak, *The Future of Habitat Conservation?* 46.

104. Keith Greer, "Habitat Conservation Planning in San Diego County, California: Lessons Learned after Five Years of Implementation," *Environmental Practice*, 6, 3 (September 2004): 230–239.

105. McClure and Stiffler, "A License to Kill."

Recommended Reading

Mann, Charles, and Mark Plummer. "California vs. Gnatcatcher." *Audubon*, January–February 1995, 29–38, 100–104.

Noss, Reed, Michael A. O'Connell, and Dennis D. Murphy. *The Science of Conservation Planning: Habitat Conservation Plans Under the Endangered Species Act*. Washington, D.C.: Island Press, 1997.

Pollak, Daniel. *The Future of Habitat Conservation? The NCCP Experience in Southern California*. Sacramento: California Research Bureau, California State Library, June 2001.

Web Sites

www.dfg.ca.gov/nccp (California Department of Fish and Game site)
http://ceres.ca.gov (California Environmental Resources Evaluation System site)
www.sandiego.gov/mscp/plansum.shtml (City of San Diego site)

CHAPTER 17

Making Tradeoffs

Urban Sprawl and the Evolving System of Growth Management in Portland, Oregon

On November 3, 2004, Portlanders woke to stunning news: the day before, by a 60–40 margin, Oregon voters had approved a ballot initiative that threatened to unravel the state's thirty-year-old growth-management regime—a system that had made metropolitan Portland a worldwide model of urban livability. Ten years earlier the curmudgeonly urbanist James Howard Kunstler had written in *The Geography of Nowhere* that Portland "seems to defy the forces that elsewhere drag American urban life into squalor and chaos.... Intelligent planning, plus a little geographical luck" has created a city whose residents "deserve to feel proud." [1] In 1997 political writer Alan Ehrenhalt remarked: "Every week of the year, somebody arrives in Portland, Oregon, from far away, wanting to know the secrets of big-city livability. And invariably they fall in love and return home proclaiming that they have seen a glimpse of urban life as it ought to be lived in the century to come." [2] And as recently as 2001, historian Carl Abbott wrote that metropolitan Portland was noteworthy "for a political culture that treats land use planning, with its restrictions on private actions, as a legitimate expression of the community interest." [3] Even as Abbott penned that phrase, however, a rebellion in Oregon had already begun, and the forces of privatism were undermining the state's apparent consensus on growth management. This chapter tells two stories, then: the first describes the evolution of Portland's unique growth management experiment; the second describes both the sources and implications of the backlash against it.

At the heart of this case is the issue of urban sprawl. As architect Jonathan Barnett points out, even as many older cities and suburbs are declining, other suburbs—as well as rural counties—are choking on new development. As close-in suburbs become disillusioned by the environmental, aesthetic, and social costs of new growth, they tighten their restrictions, forcing development even farther out. This "leapfrog" process in turn puts corporate offices out of commuting range of city residents. In response, people move still farther from the city, spreading the urbanizing area even more. According to Barnett, "A series of perfectly reasonable decisions by companies and individuals becomes an immensely destructive mechanism, ripping up the landscape to produce scattered, inefficient development, and splitting the metropolitan area into a declining old city and a self-sufficient, but fragmented, new city." [4] The cumulative result is a landscape in which

Cul-de-sac subdivisions accessible only by car—separated from schools, churches, and shopping—spread out from decaying cities like strands of a giant spider web. Office parks and factories isolated by tremendous parking lots dot the countryside. Giant malls and business centers straddle the exit ramps of wide interstates where cars are lined up bumper to bumper. The line between city and country is blurred. Green spaces are fragmented. Only a remnant of natural spaces remains intact.[5]

Its detractors point out that, aside from its aesthetic drawbacks, sprawl has serious environmental costs: it eliminates wetlands and forests, alters water courses and runoff patterns, disrupts scenic vistas, destroys and fragments wildlife habitat, and damages air and water quality. Sprawl also has severe economic and social consequences: communities become more segregated by income, and—as noted in chapter 5—urban disinvestment reduces opportunities for the poor. In 1998 Vice President Al Gore tried to elevate sprawl to the top of the national political agenda as part of his early primary campaign for president. In speeches around the country the vice president told a nostalgic story of decline that captured many Americans' discomfort with unchecked development:

> From the desert Southwest to the forested Northeast, from the most pristine snowfields of Alaska, to the loveliest hollows of the Carolinas—thickets of strip development distort the landscape our grandparents remember. Acre upon acre of asphalt have transformed what were once mountain clearings and congenial villages into little more than massive parking lots.[6]

Gore briefly succeeded in raising the political profile of urban sprawl in the late 1990s. But public concern about the issue originated decades earlier, in the early 1970s, as the impacts of the rapid postwar suburbanization manifested themselves. In response, some states adopted policies to redirect public and private investment away from infrastructure and development that spreads out from already-built areas. Hawaii enacted the first state-level growth management law in the 1960s, and since then nine states—Vermont (1970 and 1988), Florida (1972, 1984, and 1986), Oregon (1973), New Jersey (1986), Maine (1988), Rhode Island (1988), Georgia (1989), Washington (1990), and Maryland (1992 and 1997)—have passed laws that aim to regulate the rate and location of growth.[7] Early growth management policies included constraints on intensity of development through zoning limitations on subdivisions, design and capacity standards for lots and buildings, requirements for adequate impact fees, reductions in the supply of land open for development, and restrictions on where development is permitted.[8] In the 1990s the term "smart growth" came into vogue to describe a more proactive and comprehensive growth management approach designed specifically as an antidote to sprawl. Among the crucial elements of smart growth are creating walkable cities; establishing fast, efficient public transportation systems; and locating dense, mixed-use development at transit nodes (see Box 17-1).

Box 17-1 Smart Growth Goals and Principles

- Preserve, if not advance, public goods such as air, water, and landscapes.
  Prevent further expansion of the urban fringe.
  Use a systems approach to environmental planning.
  Preserve contiguous areas of high-quality habitat.
  Design to conserve energy.
- Minimize, if not prevent, adverse land-use impacts (effects on others).
  Prevent negative externalities between land uses.
  Separate auto-related land uses from pedestrian-oriented uses.
- Maximize positive land-use impacts; for example, neighborhood schools create synergy.
  Achieve job/housing balance within three to five miles of development.
  Design street network with multiple connections and direct routes.
  Provide networks for pedestrians and bicyclists as good as the network for motorists.
  Incorporate transit-oriented design features.
  Achieve an average net residential density of six to seven units per acre (clustering with open space).
- Minimize public fiscal costs.
  Minimize cost per unit of development to provide public facilities and services.
  Channel development into areas that are already disturbed.
- Maximize social equity.
  Balance jobs and housing within small areas; provide accessibility to work, shopping, leisure; offer socioeconomic balance within neighborhoods.
  Provide for affordable single-family and multifamily homes for low- and moderate-income households.
  Provide life-cycle housing.

Source: Adapted from Arthur C. Nelson, "How Do We Know Smart Growth When We See It?" in *Smart Growth: Form and Consequences*, ed. Terry S. Szold and Armando Carbonell (Washington, D.C.: Island Press, 2002), 83–101.

Planners support state-level growth management laws but are virtually unanimous in believing that implementation cannot be left to local governments. They argue that only regional planning can curb the relentless spread of sprawl and its attendant problems of urban decay, traffic congestion, and suburbanization. They point out that local governments tend to pursue their own best interests, not the common good, even though the results of one town's decisions directly affect its neighbors. Furthermore, as planning expert Dennis Gale points out, the cumulative effect of thousands of incremental land-use decisions by local governments can result in net impacts equal to or exceeding those resulting from the kinds of larger projects that are typically regulated under state laws—"death by a thousand cuts."[9] Even if a municipality does enact growth controls, some research suggests that such measures do little to change outcomes because localities lack the political will to enforce them.[10] In any case, many planners are critical of local efforts to control growth, which they believe simply shift growth to places without such controls and are frequently used to exclude "undesirable" populations.

Scholars and practitioners also have converged on the notion that land-use planning and management cannot succeed without the support of citizens, and some even contend that citizens, not planning experts, ought to be the wellspring of such policies. For example, policy analyst Debra Knopman argues for engaging "a broad band of citizens in the business of solving their own problems." [11] Similarly, John Turner and Jason Rylander assert, "Land use planning is about people developing a sense of place and then deciding what their communities should look like in the future." [12] The environmental consensus these authors imagine will underpin such efforts may be elusive, however. Notwithstanding the rhapsodic and persuasive writing of authors such as Daniel Kemmis about the unifying power of shared geography, the same place can—and clearly does—evoke different meanings to different people. Recognizing this, competing advocates in the growth management debate have engaged in a fierce struggle to persuade Americans to see the good life as they do. For one side, urban sprawl jeopardizes not only the environment but the very connections to a community that make life worthwhile, and some limits on development are a price worth paying to protect those values. For the other side, sprawl is simply a reflection of Americans' desire for a house with a yard, and government policies to address it threaten every individual's freedom to pursue a better life. Given this divide, it is not surprising that, just as fans of growth management cite Portland as an exemplar, critics tout it as a prime example of overbearing and unrepresentative government run amok.

BACKGROUND

Journalist David Goldberg depicts Portland as "among the nation's most livable cities, lacking the blight of so many central cities while offering a broad array of vibrant urban and suburban neighborhoods." He attributes this outcome to the fact that "citizens of all stripes have a say in making the plans everyone will live by." [13] As Abbott observes, however, Portland's contemporary image contrasts sharply with its persona in the 1950s and 1960s.[14] According to Henry Richmond, cofounder of the environmental group 1000 Friends of Oregon, prior to 1970 Portland was anything but vibrant: "There was no street life. The Willamette River was polluted. There weren't a lot of jobs. . . . Public transportation was poor." [15] Similarly, community activist Steven Reed Johnson describes Portland in the 1950s as a "strikingly dull and derivative city, only a restaurant or two above a logging town." [16] The city, he says, was run by white men, and the rare instances of citizen involvement consisted of discussions among well-known elites.

Portland's politics underwent a dramatic transformation, however. Between 1969 and 1973, the average age of Portland City Council members dropped by nearly fifteen years, as civic leadership shifted from men in their sixties and seventies to men and women in their thirties.[17] During the same period, the number of advocacy organizations in the city rose from 31 to 184.[18] The first outward sign of this "revolution" was a protest on August 19, 1969, when about 250 people gathered for a picnic in the median strip of Harbor Drive, a freeway that separated the city from the waterfront. The goal of the protest was to generate support for a proposal (that eventually succeeded) to tear down the highway and replace it with a waterfront park. A second indication of the sea change under way in Portland was the 1972 release—after three years of collaborative work by business owners, planners, and citizens—of the Portland Downtown Plan. The plan rejected conventional urban redevelopment orthodoxy and instead responded to overwhelming public sentiment in favor of "a pedestrian atmosphere with interesting and active streets." [19] It provided for new parks and plazas, high-density retail and office corridors, improved mass transit, and pedestrian-oriented street design.

Environmental concern and a growing willingness to adopt innovative approaches extended beyond Portland's city limits. By the early 1970s the state of Oregon had acquired a reputation as an environmental leader by cleaning up the Willamette River, banning flip-top beverage containers, requiring a deposit on beer and soft drink cans and bottles, and setting aside 1 percent of its highway revenues for bike path construction. As planning scholar John DeGrove explains:

> Oregonians seemed to feel that the state enjoyed a special place in the world by virtue of its natural features and that these should be protected. The beauties of a wild and rugged coast, the pastoral valley stretching for a hundred miles between mountain ranges, and the rugged sagebrush and timber areas of eastern Oregon all were seen by many residents of the state as a precious and valuable heritage that made the state different from most other places.[20]

Denizens of the 100-mile-long Willamette Valley, which runs from Portland to Eugene and is home to 70 percent of the state's population, were especially disconcerted by the symptoms of sprawl and determined not to repeat the mistakes made by California, where a natural paradise was rapidly disappearing. For some Oregonians, rampant coastal development was also disturbing: throughout the 1960s developers erected condominiums, high rises, and amusement parks along the seacoast, prompting Mark Hatfield, the Republican governor, to dub the coastal Lincoln City "the 20 miserable miles." [21] Others worried that the loss of rural land presaged the demise of Oregon's rich agricultural heritage.

Alarmed by the appearance of new houses encroaching on farmland, in 1971 newly elected Republican legislator and dairy farmer Hector MacPherson of Linn County became a champion of statewide planning. He joined forces with Portland Democrat Ted Hallock and Republican governor Tom McCall in a campaign to link Oregon's problems to a new statewide planning law. While MacPherson and Hallock recruited potential allies inside and outside the legislature, McCall used his formidable rhetorical powers to evince Oregonians' environmental concern. In 1972 the governor made national news with a speech in which he declaimed:

> There is a shameless threat to our environment . . . and to the whole quality of life—[that threat] is the unfettered despoiling of the landscape. Sagebrush

subdivisions, coastal "condomania," and the ravenous rampage of suburbia in the Willamette Valley all threaten to mock Oregon's status as the environmental model for the nation. We are in dire need of a state land use policy, new subdivision laws, and new standards for planning and zoning by cities and counties. The interests of Oregon for today and in the future must be protected from the grasping wastrels of the land.[22]

With overwhelming support from the Willamette Valley, in 1973 the legislature passed Senate Bill (SB) 100, a land-use planning law that required each of Oregon's 241 cities and 36 counties to prepare a comprehensive plan that was consistent with a set of statewide goals and provided legal support for zoning and other local regulations.[23] In addition, the law created a new entity, the seven-member Land Conservation and Development Commission (LCDC), as well as an administrative agency (confusingly named the Department of Land Conservation and Development) staffed with professionals to serve it. The law also established a process by which the commission would monitor local plans for accordance with state goals and gave the LCDC the authority to revise nonconforming plans. To formulate the state's planning goals, the newly established LCDC embarked on a massive statewide citizen engagement initiative, mailing out more than 100,000 invitations for residents to attend workshops in thirty-five locations. Approximately 10,000 people participated in these workshops, simultaneously helping devise the system's goals while getting a "crash course" in land-use planning.[24]

In late 1974, with the public process complete, the LCDC adopted fourteen statewide planning goals (later expanded to nineteen), several of which are particularly critical to metropolitan planning: Goal 5 emphasizes setting aside open space; Goal 10 promotes the provision of affordable housing; Goal 11 aims to ensure the orderly development of public facilities and services; and Goal 12 involves the development of regional transportation systems. But two goals in particular formed the backbone of the state's growth management system: Goal 3, which promotes farmland preservation by requiring counties to zone productive land exclusively for agricultural use, and Goal 14, which directs local governments to establish urban growth boundaries that separate rural from "urbanizable" land. As journalist Rebecca Clarren explains, the system's founders hoped that by establishing such ground rules they could create an "ideal Oregon, a place where small towns could remain small, urban areas would hum with efficiency, and farms and forests would surround cities in great ribbons of green."[25]

THE CASE

In 1975 the LCDC began implementing its new planning framework and immediately encountered pockets of resistance, particularly in rural areas. This reaction was not surprising: forty-nine of the sixty Willamette Valley legislators had supported SB 100, but only nine of the thirty legislators from rural counties had voted to adopt it. In 1976 and 1978 the law's detractors tried to repeal it using ballot initiatives (voters defeated the measures, 57–43 percent and 61–39 percent, respectively). In addition to trying to roll back the law, rural officials simply refused to implement it. By 1981 about 1.6 million acres of prime farmland in the Willamette Valley had been zoned exclusively for farm use, but a study by 1000 Friends of Oregon revealed that this designation carried little weight with local officials: of the 1,046 actions taken by twelve county governments dealing with applications for residential development in farm zones, 90 percent were approved, and 81 percent of those were "illegal." [26] In 1982 opponents took yet another stab at repealing SB 100 through the initiative process, failing again after an appeal from the terminally ill former governor McCall. (A fourth effort, in 1984, did not even garner enough signatures to get on the ballot.)

A sluggish economy in the 1980s alleviated some of the pressure to relax SB 100 and gave the LCDC some breathing room to work on enhancing local implementation and increasing the law's legitimacy in rural areas. During this period, planners laid the foundations of the Portland metropolitan area's growth management system. They altered the region's transportation options dramatically by ripping up the waterfront freeway and replacing it with a park, tearing down parking garages, ramping up bus service, and building light rail. In addition, they established an urban growth boundary (UGB) and worked to coordinate local comprehensive planning by communities inside and outside of it. All of this was done in consultation with the region's citizens through a variety of mechanisms designed to both incorporate their views and garner their support. Beginning in the late 1980s, however, a booming regional economy increased the demand for housing and prompted building and real estate interests to begin pressing policymakers to expand the UGB and relax development rules. Over the course of the 1990s, even as the fruits of Portland's growth management system manifested themselves, a full-fledged campaign aimed at undermining support for it was taking shape. Ultimately, that movement led to the passage of a ballot initiative that substantially loosened the government's control over development in metropolitan Portland and the state as a whole.

Regional Planning in the Portland Metropolitan Area

To carry out its responsibilities under SB 100, the Portland metropolitan area created a unique entity: the country's only elected regional government, the Metropolitan Service District (known as Metro), which oversees land-use matters for three counties and twenty-four municipalities. The seeds of Metro were sown in the 1957, with the establishment of the Metropolitan Planning Commission, whose purpose was to get a share of federal funds for regional planning. Ten years later that organization evolved into the Columbia Region Association of Governments, a weak and underfunded coalition of five counties and thirty-one municipalities. In May 1978 Portland area voters approved the merger of this association and the existing Metropolitan Service District (which was established in the early 1970s to manage solid waste disposal and the Washington Park Zoo) into the new entity, Metro, whose jurisdiction covers 460 square miles in three metropolitan Portland counties: Clackamas, Multnomah, and Washington. Metro assumed responsibility for establishing and managing the UGB for the region's 24 cities and urbanized parts of those counties. In 1979 voters elected the first Metro Council, consisting of twelve members chosen from districts and an executive officer elected at large.

Metro's first major task was to designate the Portland region's UGB, and in 1979 it drew a line around a 364-mile (232,000-acre) territory. During most of the 1980s Metro did not engage in much planning for managing development either within or outside the boundary; rather, it focused on transportation planning, selecting sites for landfills, managing the solid waste and recycling system, and approving and coordinating local comprehensive plans. But in the late 1980s, as the economy rebounded, challenges began to emerge that demanded a response from Metro. According to planning professor Ethan Seltzer, inside the UGB communities were experiencing the symptoms of sprawl development, from traffic congestion to disappearing open space. Outside the boundary, speculation on rural land was ubiquitous, and high-end mansions were springing up in rural residential zones. Furthermore, there was little clarity about where the boundary might expand, creating uncertainty for farmers, elected officials, and local service providers. A study commissioned by the state and conducted by ECONorthwest, a land-use planning and economic consulting firm, confirmed that inappropriate development was occurring both inside and outside Portland's UGB.

To address these concerns, Metro began developing a set of regional urban growth goals and objectives (RUGGOs) that would underpin an overall regional growth management plan. In late 1991, following an intensive public participation process, Metro adopted its new RUGGOs. The first major goal spelled out how regional planning would be done; when Metro would exercise its powers; and what role citizens, jurisdictions, and organized interests would play in the planning process. To advance this goal, Metro established a regional Committee for Citizen Involvement and a Regional Policy Advisory Committee. The second major goal concerned urban design and incorporated specific objectives for the built and natural environments and growth management. Parallel to the RUGGO process, Metro developed the Regional Land Information System, a geographical information system that links a wide range of public records to a land parcel base map. The object was to provide a database to support land-use planning and management throughout the region. In particular, Metro hoped the database would enable planners to develop overlays linking landscape characteristics to environmental planning and would facilitate citizen involvement by making possible real-time depictions of land-use policy choices.[27]

Apparently affirming Metro's movement toward more aggressive regional planning, in 1990 statewide voters approved a constitutional amendment allowing the agency to function under a home rule charter, and in 1992 voters in the metropolitan area adopted such a charter. The charter retained the independently elected executive, reduced the number of councilors from twelve to seven, added an elected auditor (for accountability), established a standing system of policy advisory committees (to professionalize the council), reiterated Metro's broad mandate, clarified and strengthened its planning powers, and declared urban growth management to be the agency's primary responsibility.[28] (In 2000 voters revised the charter to provide for six councilors elected by districts, a council president elected at large, and an appointed administrator.)

As its new charter was being debated, Metro was undertaking an even more ambitious endeavor, the Region 2040 Planning Project, to give concrete form to the vague conceptions articulated in the RUGGOs. More specifically, the project sought to specify the extent and location of future UGB expansion; identify the major components of the regional transportation system; designate a hierarchy of places, from downtown Portland to the outlying neighborhoods; and integrate a system of greenspaces into the urban region.[29] As part of the Region 2040 project, Metro made an explicit effort to engage citizens: it held public hearings and workshops, publicized the effort on cable TV and the news media, mailed more than 25,000 newsletters to households, and made hundreds of presentations to local governments and civic organizations.

After this exhaustive public process, Metro established a set of alternative scenarios for the region's development. The agency then disseminated more than a half million copies of a publication outlining the tradeoffs involved in different strategies, prompting 17,000 citizen comments and suggestions. From these responses planners gleaned that participating citizens generally favored holding the existing UGB in place, retaining the emphasis on greenspace preservation and transit-oriented development, reducing traffic and encouraging alternative travel modes, increasing density within the UGB, and continuing public education and dialogue.[30] Consistent with these preferences, the final Metro 2040 Growth Concept that emerged in December 1994 called for very little UGB expansion in the ensuing fifty years and instead encouraged higher density, mixed-used centers around light rail stations. Following a series of public hearings, Metro formally adopted the 2040 Growth Concept, and in December 1996 the state acknowledged its consistency with applicable land-use laws, goals, and rules.

Metro's planning push culminated in 1997 with the adoption of the Regional Framework Plan. The threefold purpose of the plan was to allocate a projected 500,000 new residents by 2017, unify all of Metro's planning activities, and address ten regional planning concerns—such as management and adjustment of the UGB, the transportation system, and greenspaces—in ways consistent with the Region 2040 Growth Concept. In essence, the plan was a composite of regional functional plans that would be implemented through a combination of local actions and Metro initiatives.[31]

Transportation Planning

Achieving the quality-of-life goals articulated in Metro's planning documents rested heavily on improving the region's transportation system and in particular on decreasing residents' dependence on cars. In 1991 the LCDC adopted the controversial Oregon Transportation Planning Rule (TPR) to try to get people out of their cars. The TPR set the ambitious statewide goal of reducing the number of per capita vehicle miles traveled (VMT) by 10 percent in twenty years and 20 percent in thirty years. To instigate movement toward this goal, the TPR mandated that local governments provide bikeways and pedestrian paths, designate land for transit-oriented development, and require builders to link large-scale development with transit. It also directed local governments and metropolitan planning organizations to produce their own transportation plans within four years.

The TPR was largely the product of a sustained campaign by 1000 Friends of Oregon and other environmental groups to integrate land use and transportation and create a compact, dense urban area that would be hospitable to bicyclists and pedestrians, rather than cars.[32] But local officials' attempts to implement the TPR immediately provoked hostility from big-box retailers, homebuilders, and commercial developers, who bitterly opposed efforts to reduce the number of parking spaces and dictate street connectivity. In response to these complaints, the LCDC relaxed the deadline for adopting ordinances to comply with the TPR and convened a group of stakeholders to amend the rule. That process yielded a more flexible approach and scaled back building orientation and street connectivity requirements.[33]

Despite the LCDC's adjustments, however, a scheduled review of the TPR in the mid-1990s revealed continuing reluctance by some planners to use VMT per capita as a measure of reliance on cars and strong opposition among builders to mechanisms such as regulating the parking supply. The consulting firm that conducted the review—Parsons, Brinckerhoff, Quade, and Douglas— recommended tempering the TPR's VMT-reduction goal and further increasing the rule's flexibility by shifting the emphasis from regulating the supply of parking spaces to adjusting the price and location of parking.[34] In 1998, in partial conformance with this advice, the LCDC decreased the VMT target from a 10 percent reduction to 5 percent for all the metropolitan planning organizations in the state except Metro, for which it retained a slightly higher goal. Moreover, the rule allowed planners to develop alternative approaches to reducing automobile reliance in place of the VMT target—although any alternative had to be approved by the LCDC.[35]

In 2000 Metro issued an updated version of its TPR that reflected changes in the state's plan. Metro's plan took advantage of the TPR's flexibility to propose an alternative to a VMT standard: instead it set non–single-occupancy vehicle mode share targets—that is, targets for the percentage of trips taken by individuals traveling alone in cars (as opposed to by bicycle or transit, on foot, or by carpool)—ranging from 42 percent to 67 percent for various parts of central Portland. Although it created performance standards against which to measure progress, Metro allowed local jurisdictions to figure out how they would meet the targets. Metro's plan also recommended doubling the existing transit service to accommodate an expected 89 percent increase in ridership by 2020. And it included a regional parking policy, which required cities and counties to regulate the amount of free, off-street parking for most land uses. Finally, Metro required local governments to implement its Green Streets program, which was designed to improve regional and local street design and connectivity and minimize the environmental impacts of transportation choices (in particular, the impact on stream habitat for endangered salmon and steelhead). Although Metro's approach remained deeply controversial in the region, environmentalists applauded the council's efforts to integrate transportation and land use and to reduce the metropolitan area's dependence on the automobile.[36]

The city of Portland completed its own transportation plan in 2002. Unlike the region's other cities, Portland decided to retain the 10 percent parking reduction target set in the original TPR. The city was well positioned to achieve this goal thanks to thirty years of investment in a sophisticated system of bus, light rail, bicycle, and pedestrian transit. In 1969 the legislature had begun the process by establishing the Tri-County Metropolitan Transportation District (Tri-Met), which immediately took over the failing Rose City Transit system and a year later subsumed the suburban bus lines. On taking office in 1973 Mayor Neil Goldschmidt had made transit a core element of his urban revitalization strategy by shifting investment from highways to public transportation.

Consistent with its new emphasis, in 1975 the city canceled plans to build the Mount Hood Freeway, a five-mile connector highway between I-5 in the center of Portland and I-205 through the eastern suburbs. Three years later the city completed the transit mall, a central feature of the Downtown Plan that dedicated two north-south streets through the heart of downtown to buses. To encourage ridership Tri-Met made buses along the mall (and everywhere else within the city's inner freeway loop) free. In 1986 the city inaugurated its 15-mile Eastside light rail line (the Metropolitan Area Express, or MAX), and it opened the 18-mile Westside line in 1998. Although voters balked at financing a north-south line, a spur line to the airport began running in 2001, thanks to a substantial contribution from Bechtel Corporation, which owns an industrial park along the line. And builders completed a scaled-down six-mile North Portland line in 2004. The city also built the first modern streetcar system in North America, connecting downtown and Portland State University to the Pearl District and trendy Northwest neighborhoods. To complement its efforts at reducing auto dependence through mass transit, the city also adopted a Bicycle Master Plan in 1996 and a Pedestrian Master Plan in 1998. By 2001 the city had more than doubled the amount of bikeways (off-street paths, on-street lanes, and bicycle boulevards) from 111 miles to 228 miles.[37]

Development Rules

In addition to enhancing transit, the Portland region's smart-growth approach relied on combining infill and density in urban areas with strict protection of open space and rural land rich in natural resources. As the growth management regime evolved, the number of regulations burgeoned, and development rules became more complex and detailed. For example, to protect rural areas, Metro issued regulations that prevented a developer from building a destination resort on prime forestland, within three miles of high-value farmland, or anywhere in the 300,000-acre Columbia River Gorge National Scenic Area. Planners devised numerous restrictions on homebuilding in rural areas as well: they divided rural property into eight categories based on characteristics, such as soil depth and quality, slope, and erosion, and zoned about 16 million acres of farmland for exclusive farm use. Any house built on high-value farmland has to qualify as a farm dwelling, a temporary hardship shelter, or a home for relatives helping out on the farm. In addition, as of 1994 the property must have yielded $80,000 in annual gross farm income over the previous three-year period. Such measures reduced the market value of agricultural land dramatically: in 2000 ECONorthwest estimated that residentially zoned land inside the UGB was worth about $150,000 an acre, while property outside the boundary zoned for farm or forest sold for about $5,000 per acre.[38] But farmers and owners of forestland got enormous property tax breaks in return; farmland was assessed at as little as 0.5 percent of the value of land where development was encouraged.[39]

Outside the UGB, developers had to show their land was worth little for forestry or farming and was easily supplied with services, and that comparable land was not available inside the boundary, but inside the UGB, the burden of proof rested on opponents of development. For example, the LCDC developed housing rules that required every jurisdiction to zone at least half its vacant residential land for attached single-family homes or apartments, and it prohibited suburbs from adopting exclusionary zoning to block construction of affordable housing. To encourage dense development, Metro established aggressive housing targets for jurisdictions within the UGB. And to attract development near transit stops, Metro and other taxing districts, as well as many individual jurisdictions, created tax abatements and other incentives. As a result of these policies, in 1998 and 1999, 50 percent of new housing starts in the metropolitan area were apartments and attached dwellings, up from 35 percent in the 1992 to 1995 period.[40]

In addition to putting in place measures to encourage infill, the city of Portland enacted a variety of rules that aimed to maintain neighborhood aesthetics and protect natural resources. In the early 1990s city planners devised a system of environmental overlays designed to prevent development in areas with the highest resource values and to ensure environmentally sensitive development in conservation zones. As the decade wore on, the city enacted standards that required developers to landscape foundations and preserve or plant trees when building new housing in single-family zones. Street standards became progressively tougher, so that by the late 1990s every new Portland street had to have sidewalks, a tree strip, and street trees. And in 1999 the city council voted unanimously to outlaw new garage-front "snout houses" that had proliferated in response to the city's efforts to promote infill. The new rules specified that the garage cannot dominate the front of the house; the main entrance has to be close to the street; and the street-facing side of the house must meet specific standards for window and door space. The aim, planners said, was to ensure that houses make "more connection to the public realm." [41]

The Results of Planning

As a result of its formidable growth management regime, by the late 1990s Portland was defying many of the trends occurring nationally. While development was gobbling up farm- and forestland around the country, Oregon's losses were modest. According to Agriculture Department figures, even at the height of the economic boom of the 1990s, Oregon yielded rural land to development at a slower rate than the national average. [42] And while most of the nation's major metropolitan areas were spreading out during the 1970s and 1980s, Portland remained compact: on average, the populations of Boston, Chicago, Cleveland, Detroit, New York, Philadelphia, St. Louis, and Washington, D.C., increased by 3.4 percent from 1970 to 1990, while their urbanized areas increased by 38.9 percent. [43] Metropolitan Cleveland's population declined by 8 percent between 1970 and 1990, but its urban land area increased by a third. Cities whose populations increased spread at an even faster rate: metro Chicago's population grew 4 percent between 1970 and 1990, but its metropolitan area expanded 46 percent. During the same period, metropolitan Los Angeles's population grew 45 percent, and its developed land area expanded 300 percent. [44] Metropolitan Denver, which is often compared to Portland, expanded its developed area from 300 to 530 square miles between 1970 and 1997, a 77 percent increase. By contrast, Portland's 364-square-mile developed metropolitan area grew by fewer than 5 square miles between 1979 (when the UGB was put in place) and 1997. [45]

Portland's pattern of housing development was also unusual compared to other U.S. cities. In 1999 the Brookings Institution reported that Portland was one of the few places in the nation where new housing construction was increasing faster within the central city than in the larger metropolitan region. [46] Portland was also building smaller, more dense housing units. When Metro drew the growth boundary in 1979, lot size for the average new single-family detached house in the metro area was 13,200 square feet. By the mid-1990s it was down to 8,700 square feet. Whereas the median size lot for single-family homes sold in the United States in 1990 exceeded 9,000 square feet, Metro encouraged builders to average 6,700 square feet or build multifamily units. [47] Furthermore, in 1985 attached homes accounted for 3 percent of units in the city of Portland; a decade later that figure was 12 percent. [48] In 1994 Portland was building new houses at a density of five dwellings per acre; by 1998 that figure was eight dwellings per acre—higher than the 2040 Plan target.[49] Even as it increased density and infill, Portland worked to save oases of green throughout the city: between the 1995 passage of a $135.6 million bond initiative and 2001, Metro acquired nearly 8,000 acres of greenspace.[50]

Portland's downtown businesses were thriving as well, despite the city's concerted effort to limit driving. Between 1973 and 1993 the amount of office space in downtown Portland nearly tripled, and the number of downtown jobs increased by 50 percent. Nevertheless, the volume of cars entering Portland's downtown remained the same.[51] Rather than driving, many workers relied on mass transit: by the mid-1990s Tri-Met's radial bus and rail system carried 30 percent to 35 percent of the city's commuters into downtown Portland, roughly twice the proportion in comparable cities like Phoenix or Salt Lake City.[52] Furthermore, according to the 2000 Census, Portland ranked in the top five among sixty-four U.S. cities with a population of 250,000 or more in the percentage of workers that commute by bicycle. Counts of cyclists crossing the main bridge with bicycle access into downtown went up 143 percent from 1991 to 2001, outpacing population growth for that period. The 2000 Census also showed that the Portland metropolitan area had more people walking to work than in most regions of a similar size: more than 5 percent of workers in the city of Portland got to their jobs on foot.[53] In short, "Downtown Portland's landscaped streets, light rail system, innovative parks, and meticulously designed new buildings have transformed what was once a mediocre business district into a thriving regional center."[54]

The combination of dense housing, efficient public transportation, and a lively downtown made Portland a national model of smart growth and New Urbanism.[55] Beginning in the mid-1970s and continuing through the 1990s, Portland consistently made the lists of the top ten places to live and the best-planned cities in the United States. In 1975 the prestigious Midwest Research Institute rated 243 cities on their economic, political, environmental, social, and health-and-education qualities, and Portland was the only city rated as "outstanding" in all categories. In spring 1980 the *Chicago Tribune* profiled a dozen American cities and described Portland as "largely free of graffiti, vandalism, litter, street gangs, Mafiosi, racial tensions, desolate slums, choking pollution, crooked politicians, colonies of freaks, phony social climbers, and those legions of harassed men whose blood pressure rises whenever the Dow Jones average dips a few points."[56]

The accolades continued to roll in over the next two decades, as a spate of books cited Portland as a city worth imitating, and complimentary articles abounded. Writing in 1997 in the *Denver Post*, journalist Alex Katz said:

> Swirling with street life and commerce, Portland is best seen at afternoon rush hour, when office workers pour out of buildings and into taverns and coffeehouses. Buses roar up and down the narrow streets by the dozen. Light-rail trains whisk by, carrying commuters to the east-side suburbs.

What's particularly striking about central Portland is its residential and retail density—unlike downtown Denver, which is pockmarked with surface parking lots and boarded up buildings. Portland's density creates a lively retail climate, and the presence of pedestrians makes the downtown streets feel safer.[57]

And after *Money* magazine named Portland the "best place to live in the U.S." in 2000, a British visitor wrote admiringly:

Portland is a delight. Walking through the city's bustling streets on a sunny day, it is easy to forget that one is in the most car-dominated country on the planet. The streets are lined with trees ablaze in green and gold. Sculpture and fountains distract the eye and please the soul. Safe and direct pedestrian crossings at every junction make walking easy and quick for people in a hurry. For those with time to spare, benches, street cafes and pocket parks provide places for reflection and relaxation. The traffic is slow and light. The pavements are wide and clean. There is not a guard railing to be seen.[58]

Institutionalizing Civic Engagement in Portland

A host of observers have attributed the longevity of Portland's unusually stringent growth management regime to the participation and buy-in of the region's uniquely engaged citizenry. The number of advocacy groups in Portland, which increased sixfold in the early 1970s, continued to grow—to 222 in 1985 and 402 in 1999.[59] Neighborhood associations, which originated in Portland in the 1940s, thrived under Mayor Goldschmidt after he created the Office of Neighborhood Associations in 1974. This office provided funding and technical training to members and thereby "legitimized direct democratic action at the grassroots level by allowing neighbors to directly influence city policies." In addition the city created a host of citizen advisory committees and task forces: the number of citizen advisory committees grew from twenty-seven in 1960 to fifty-six in 1972; the number of task forces jumped from five in 1960 to twenty-five in 1972. By 1986 there were twenty-three bureau advisory committees that engaged citizens in the everyday business of city agencies. As longtime Portland activist Steve Johnson explains, the city "created an open-door policy that changed the expectation of citizens' relationship to their government." [60]

According to political scientist Robert Putnam, the responsiveness of Portland's leaders to the surge in citizen activism produced a virtuous circle of "call and response," that resulted in "a positive epidemic of civic engagement." This pattern contrasted sharply with what was happening in most other American cities, where, after a great deal of political activity in the 1960s and early 1970s, "the aging baby boomers left the streets, discarded their placards, gave up on politics, and slumped onto the couch to watch television. In Portland, by contrast, the ranks of civic activists steadily expanded as Portlanders experienced a resurgence of exuberant participation in local affairs." [61] Abbott says the result was an unusually inclusive and civil political dialogue:

> The openness of civic life in Portland is the basis for an emphasis on team play. Public life takes place around a big table. Some of the seats are reserved for elected officials and heavy hitters from the business community. But anyone can sit in who accepts the rules (politeness is important) and knows how to phrase ideas in the language of middle class policy discussion (the goal is to do "what's good for the city"). Once an organization or interest group is at the table, or on the team, it has an opportunity to shape policy outcomes. [62]

As Johnson notes, however, during the 1990s the tone of citizen activism changed, and some of Portland's civic engagement was directed at stopping growth control and preventing the increases in density prescribed by Metro. For example, in Oak Grove, a blue-collar suburb with large lots, homeowners successfully resisted a plan for a dense, transit-oriented "town center." They preferred parking their boats alongside their houses to strolling to a café along pretty sidewalks. Similarly, leaders in the Multnomah Village section of southwest Portland blanketed the streets with signs opposing what they said was city officials' heavy-handed attempt to increase the area's population by 20 percent—changes that would deprive single parents of an affordable place with yard space for their kids. Resisters in these and other low-density neighborhoods claimed they were being targeted, while wealthy areas escaped planners' push. [63] Meanwhile, residents in the more affluent suburbs, such as Milwaukie, West Linn, and Tigard, feared the environmental costs and socioeconomic diversification associated with compact growth. West Linn City Council member John Jackley complained about Metro planners' disdain for suburbs and their apparent desire to impose their "urban village" concept on unwilling residents. Similarly, the mayor of Tigard defended the large-lot, upscale developments and "lifestyle opportunities" that Tigard provided. [64]

Trouble in Paradise: Measures 7 and 37

Neighborhood resistance to density increases was only one manifestation of long-standing divisions over the state's growth management program. As Oregon's economy boomed through the 1990s, a coalition of homebuilders, real estate brokers, the Oregon Association of Counties, Safeway and other large retail companies, as well as the conservative group, Oregonians in Action, began to complain bitterly about Portland's UGB—and particularly the rules limiting rural development. Bill Moshofsky, leader of Oregonians in Action captured the essence of these groups' sentiment:

> Instead of a planning tool, the urban growth boundaries have become a Berlin Wall to restrict growth to a high-density model. The whole thing is, they want Oregon to look like Europe. The screws have been tightened year by year. . . . Property rights have been swept under the rug. And the

high density is going to reduce the quality of life. People will be crowded together, living on small lots. The land supply will be so limited that housing costs will become unaffordable.[65]

To garner support for their position among the public, growth management opponents claimed Portland's boundary had raised home prices—more precisely, that the price of a buildable acre of land inside the UGB had tripled in the two years prior to 1996 and that land prices had gone from 19 percent below the national average in 1985 to 6 percent above it in 1994. Defenders of the UGB retorted that high demand was the primary cause of the price increase, noting that land prices were rising in many western cities that lacked growth boundaries. They observed that Portland house prices rose 26 percent between 1992 and 1996, while Denver's increased 44 percent during the same period; house prices rose 25 percent between 1994 and 1996 in Salt Lake City, compared to Portland's 19 percent.[66] Not surprisingly, building interests were not persuaded.

After several failed legislative efforts to rewrite the planning laws to accommodate developers' concerns, in 2000 the conflict came to a head with the passage of Measure 7, a ballot initiative written by Oregonians in Action that required state and local governments to compensate landowners whose property values were affected by regulation or, if they could not find the money, to waive the rules. The Oregon Supreme Court struck down Measure 7 in 2002 on the grounds that it contained multiple constitutional changes that should have been voted on separately. But the measure's approval by 53 percent of voters, including both rural and urban residents, sent a chill through the state's environmental establishment. Although polls by 1000 Friends of Oregon and the League of Conservation Voters consistently showed support at a rate of two to one for the state's land-use planning system, the proponents of Measure 7 clearly had tapped into some latent dissatisfaction with the rules. As journalist Rebecca Clarren commented:

> While Oregon's land-use system was born with huge public support, over half the state's current population wasn't around when it was created. For many newcomers, the regulations are confusing and restrictive. Even many long-time Oregonians say that a system that began with clear goals has grown into a bureaucratic snarl, and that the rules have become onerous and arbitrary.[67]

In hopes of defusing conflict and reducing the impetus to overhaul the system, in early 2002 Metro took 18,000 acres of land—an area equal to more than 7 percent of the existing boundary—and designated it as "urban reserves" eligible to be incorporated into the UGB. Metro also addressed complaints about a shortage of industrial land by identifying a small number of "regionally significant industrial areas," which would be reserved for industries that provided "family wage" jobs. Opponents of growth management were not mollified, however, and they became even more determined after legislative efforts to craft a compromise reform fell apart over how to finance a compensation system.

In 2004 Oregonians in Action spearheaded another initiative campaign, and this time they carefully crafted a measure to avoid a constitutional challenge. Measure 37, which got onto the November 2004 ballot, created a state law that allowed property owners to petition to be excused from state or local land-use rules put in place after they bought their land or be paid for any decrease in their land's market value as a result of those rules. The measure gave the government 180 days to make a decision, or the rule would be waived automatically. As the battle over Measure 37 heated up in the fall of 2004, the rhetorical battle lines were sharply drawn. Proponents offered a handful of potent anecdotes that emphasized the unfairness of the planning system and the burdens its regulations imposed on ordinary folks:

- According to one story, Barbara and Gene Prete bought twenty acres in 1990, envisioning a horse barn and farmhouse in the shadow of the mountains. When they got ready to move from Los Angeles to Sisters in 1995, however, they got bad news: a new Oregon rule required them to produce $80,000 in farm goods a year if they wanted to build their house. The Pretes became chief petitioners for Measure 37, which they said would bring "justice" to property owners.[68]
- According to a second story, Connie and Steve Bradley were unable to rebuild the run-down house on their family's property because it had been abandoned for more than a year and so reverted to its farming designation. Connie Bradley said she trusted Oregonians to preserve their landscape and liked Measure 37 because it put power back into the hands of the people (and took it out of the hands of bureaucrats).[69]
- By far the most effective story, however, featured Dorothy English, a ninety-one-year-old widow who recorded a radio ad that was played constantly in the weeks leading up to the election. English told of a series of battles with the state over subdividing 20 acres of land, which she bought in 1953, into residential lots. Her punch line was, "I've always been fighting the government, and I'm not going to stop."[70]

Defenders of the growth management system, led by 1000 Friends of Oregon, responded to these stories by saying that Measure 37 would create uncertainty, bankrupt local governments, and dismantle the state's planning system. They raised the specter of factories and big-box stores mixed in with houses and farms. Although opponents of Measure 37 outspent proponents four to one, the initiative passed with 61 percent of the vote—even carrying Multnomah County, the "epicenter of planning," by a slim majority.[71] Explanations for the measure's passage abounded. Some said voters did not appreciate its full implications; others pointed to its straightforward and appealing title ("Governments Must Pay Owners, or Forgo Enforcement, When Certain Land Use Restrictions Reduce Property Values"), the power of the anecdotes told during the campaign, and the opposition's failure to convey the success of the state's planning system. Some observers said that the sheer comprehensiveness of Oregon's growth management system made it especially vulnerable. The puzzling fact remained that, when polled, Oregonians said they either supported or strongly supported land-use regulations in the same proportions by which voters passed Measure 37.[72]

OUTCOMES

By mid-August 2005 more than 2,000 Measure 37 claims were in the pipeline across the state.[73] Washington County was overwhelmed with claims, which were coming in at a rate of between fifty and sixty a month. In Clackamas County filings had shot up in April, May, and June, as county commissioners steadily waived zoning regulations in response to claims. The majority of the claims were for relatively small developments, between one and a handful of homes, but even those cumulatively threatened the very death-by-a-thousand-cuts result that Oregon's planning framework was devised to avoid. And some claims promised much more substantial short-run impacts. One proposal in Clackamas County for a subdivision of fifty-two houses that was approved in late March would undo years of planning for the rolling hills and farmland of the Stafford Triangle between Tualatin, Lake Oswego, and West Linn. Another, in scenic Hood River County, would convert 210 acres of pear orchard land into housing. Farmer John Benton, who was asking for $57 million or permission to build as many as 800 houses, told listeners at a hearing on his application that Oregon legislators should "quit trying to be social engineers and let the market forces and the good people of this state realize their potential." [74]

There was some variation in the process cities and counties used to handle Measure 37 claims, but, in the vast majority of cases, officials felt they had little choice but to approve virtually every claim. In some instances they supported the applications, but in many they felt hamstrung by Measure 37's clear language and lacked resources to compensate landowners rather than waive the rules. Some county commissioners also bemoaned the fact that the law contained no provisions for involving neighbors in the process of deciding the appropriate uses of property, a dramatic reversal of Oregon's status quo.

Although environmentalists were alarmed by the increasing number of Measure 37 claims, county approval was just the first step. Most proposals had to clear state review, and the state's early rulings—which denied some requests and attached strings to others—suggested that development under Measure 37 would not be as simple as applicants had hoped. Most claimants also had to get land-use and building approvals typical of any subdivision, and developments outside the UGB needed clearance for new wells and septic systems. Complicating matters even further, banks were skittish about financing Measure 37 properties because it was unclear whether development rights were transferable to new owners. (The state attorney general issued an advisory letter in February saying that in his opinion any change in zoning under Measure 37 was *not* transferable.)

As local and state officials grappled with claims, the legislature worked on revising the law. The central questions were how to set up a compensation system for landowners and whether to make development rights transferable. The bill that got the most interest from both Democrats and Republicans established a compensation system in which applicants who got permission to develop their land would have to pay the property tax that had been forgiven when the land was zoned for agriculture, forestry, or habitat protection, and that money would be used to pay off other claimants. The bill also limited the potential for large-scale subdivisions in exchange for making small-scale development easier. Even this proposal foundered, however. Fundamental philosophical differences over the importance of ensuring private property rights versus limiting development divided legislators, and the highly visible controversy surrounding the issue discouraged compromise. The 2005 legislative session ended without a resolution, and the issue remained to be decided case by case within individual jurisdictions. Meanwhile, Dave Hunnicutt—executive director of Oregonians in Action and a prime mover behind Measure 37—was crafting initiatives that targeted suburban housing density requirements and restrictions on rural road construction.

As Oregonians struggled to implement Measure 37, its impact spread well beyond the state's borders. Emboldened by the measure's success, property-rights activists in other western states began planning ballot initiatives of their own. In Washington State, rural property owners mobilized to challenge the state's Growth Management Act and the regulations counties had adopted to comply with it. Hopeful advocates from Alaska, California, Colorado, Idaho, Maine, North Carolina, South Carolina, and Wisconsin contacted Oregonians in Action for strategic advice on getting similar measures passed.[75]

Property rights activists' euphoria was short-lived, however. In mid-October 2005, in response to litigation brought by 1000 Friends of Oregon and several agricultural groups, Judge Mary James of the Marion Circuit Court ruled that Measure 37 violates the state constitution because it grants special privileges and immunities, impairs the legislative body's plenary power, suspends laws, and violates the separation of powers. The judge also ruled the measure violates substantive and procedural due process guaranteed by the U.S. Constitution. Vowing to appeal the ruling, Hunnicutt called it "another kick in the face to the citizens of [the] state who want nothing more than protection of their right to use their land as they could when they bought it, to Dorothy English and Gene and Barbara Prete, and to all those people who have bought property over the years, only to have the State of Oregon change the land use rules and take away their rights." [76]

CONCLUSIONS

The debate over Oregon's growth management system in general, and Measure 37 in particular, captures many of the most important elements of contemporary environmental politics. Activists are divided by genuine value differences. For proponents of Measure 37, the belief in unfettered private property rights trumps any interest in conserving a particular landscape for the common good. They believe property owners have a right to a return on their investments and that the housing market, not lines on a map, should determine where people live.[77] The measure's opponents, by contrast, believe that some restrictions on individual freedom are worth the benefits. As Robert Liberty, former president of 1000 Friends of Oregon and a member of the Metro board, says: "Quality of life is something that is shared. A golf course is not. A four-car garage is not. One of the best things about the planning process is that it makes a better community for everyone, regardless of income." [78]

The public's views are much more ambiguous and therefore susceptible to framing. Many environmentalists believe that the defenders of the status quo in Oregon made tactical mistakes in characterizing their position, but that the state's residents fundamentally support growth management. They point out that Measure 37's backers chose their words carefully; they did not challenge the system itself but rather criticized the rules, which they called irrational and unfair, and its administrators, whom they described as elitist and out of touch with the people. This strategy enabled them to play on the public's ambivalence: many Oregonians seem to want to avoid the effects of sprawl without having to comply with the rules government has employed to achieve that result.

Public opinion is probably even more complicated, however. Notwithstanding the fervent convictions of smart-growth advocates, it is unclear how many people really dislike sprawl and even less obvious that the public will readily accept density as an alternative. Certainly, a vocal coalition opposing growth control, led by Samuel Staley of the Reason Public Policy Institute, challenges the idea that middle-class Americans will (or should) trade their lawns, gardens, and privacy for housing in dense urban neighborhoods. As journalist Tim Ferguson writes, "A nation in love with truck-size sport utility vehicles is unlikely to embrace the housing equivalent of an Escort." [79] Whereas antisprawl advocates blame misguided government policies, such as traditional zoning laws and highway subsidies, opponents of growth management insist that the market—and in particular Americans' passionate desire for a spread-out, car-centered way of life—has shaped the American landscape.[80] Economist J. Thomas Black of the Urban Land Institute adds that changes in the workforce complicate housing decisions: jobs are often in different suburbs, and a close-in address does not work; moreover, close-in housing is often expensive once renewal/gentrification begins and the economy is booming.[81]

Environmentalists and other smart-growth advocates remain hopeful, however: they point out that even as opponents of growth management seem to be gaining momentum, in the 2004 elections, voters in red and blue states alike approved smart-growth measures and voted to tax themselves to expand transit options and set aside open space. Nationally, 80 percent of the more than thirty transit funding measures passed, for a total value of $40 billion. Voters in 111 communities in twenty-five states passed ballot measures to invest $2.4 billion in protecting parks and open spaces, a success rate of 76 percent, according to the Trust for Public Land. Even in conservative Colorado, Montana, and Utah, candidates ran and won on smart-growth platforms. David Goldberg argues, "Though it was little noted in the political coverage, the desire to address growth issues was one of the few arenas that transcended partisanship in this era of polarized discourse." [82]

QUESTIONS TO CONSIDER

- What are the strengths and weaknesses of using ballot initiatives to decide the fate of Oregon's land-use planning system?
- What might supporters of the growth management system in Oregon have done differently if they wanted to head off a property rights challenge?
- Do you think it is reasonable for cities, towns, and regions to impose requirements and restrictions on its citizens to avert urban sprawl? Why, or why not?

Notes

1. Quoted in Carl Abbott, *Greater Portland: Urban Life and Landscape in the Pacific Northwest* (Philadelphia: University of Pennsylvania Press, 2001), 5.
2. Alan Ehrenhalt, "The Great Wall of Portland," *Governing Magazine*, May 1997, 20.
3. Abbott, *Greater Portland*, 6.
4. Jonathan Barnett, "Shaping Our Cities: It's Your Call," *Planning*, December 1995, 13.
5. John Turner and Jason Rylander, "Land Use: The Forgotten Agenda," in *Thinking Ecologically*, ed. Marion R. Chertow and Daniel C. Esty (New Haven: Yale University Press, 1997), 60.
6. Albert Gore, remarks delivered to the Brookings Institution, September 1998; cited in John Carlisle, "The Campaign Against Urban Sprawl: Declaring War on the American Dream," *National Policy Analysis #239* (Washington, D.C.: National Center for Public Policy Research, April 1999).
7. The growth management literature distinguishes between policies that aim to *control*—that is, limit—growth and those that aim to *manage*—that is, shape, but not limit—growth. I use the term "growth management" in this chapter because virtually no U.S. policies actually seek to impose limits on growth. See Gabor Zovanyi, *Growth Management for a Sustainable Future: Ecological Sustainability as the New Growth Management Focus for the 21st Century* (Westport, Conn.: Praeger, 1998).
8. Wim Wievel, Joseph Persky, and Mark Senzik, "Private Benefits and Public Costs: Policies to Address Suburban Sprawl," *Policy Studies Journal* 27 (1999): 96–114.
9. Dennis E. Gale, "Eight State-Sponsored Growth Management Programs: A Comparative Analysis," *Journal of the American Planning Association* 58 (1992): 425–439.
10. Kee Warner and Harvey Molotch, *Building Rules: How Local Controls Shape Community Environments and Economics* (Boulder: Westview Press, 2000).
11. Debra S. Knopman, "The Trouble With Sprawl," 1999. Retrieved on May 19, 2000, from www.intellectualcapital.com/issues.
12. Turner and Rylander, "Land Use," 74.
13. David Goldberg, "The Wisdom of Growth," *Sacramento Bee*, December 12, 2004, E1.
14. Carl Abbott, *Portland: Planning, Politics, and Growth in a Twentieth-Century City* (Lincoln: University of Nebraska Press, 1983).
15. Quoted in Alan Katz, "Building the Future," *Denver Post*, February 9, 1997, 1.

16. Steven Reed Johnson, "The Myth and Reality of Portland's Engaged Citizenry and Process-Oriented Governance," in *The Portland Edge*, ed. Connie P. Ozawa (Washington, D.C.: Island Press, 2004), 103.
17. Abbott, *Portland: Planning, Politics, and Growth.*
18. Johnson, "The Myth and Reality."
19. Abbott, *Portland: Planning, Politics, and Growth*, 220.
20. John M. DeGrove, *Land, Growth & Politics* (Washington, D.C.: Planners Press, 1984), 235.
21. Rebecca Clarren, "Planning's Poster Child Grows Up," *High Country News*, November 25, 2002.
22. Quoted in DeGrove, *Land, Growth & Politics*, 237.
23. In 1969 Oregon had adopted SB 10, a precursor to SB 100 that mandated that all counties and cities develop land-use plans that met ten state goals, but few local governments had taken steps to implement the law, and the state had not enforced it.
24. Johnson, "The Myth and Reality."
25. Clarren, "Planning's Poster Child Grows Up."
26. The approvals were "illegal" in that they did not provide sufficient findings of fact to allow a judgment as to whether the exception was justified. See DeGrove, *Land, Growth & Politics.*
27. Ethan Seltzer, "It's Not an Experiment: Regional Planning at Metro, 1990 to the Present," in *The Portland Edge*, 35–60; John M. DeGrove, *The New Frontier for Land Policy: Planning and Growth Management in the States* (Cambridge, MA.: Lincoln Institute of Land Policy, 1992).
28. Seltzer, "It's Not an Experiment."
29. Ibid.
30. Ibid.
31. Ibid. A functional plan addresses a narrow set of concerns associated with an issue of regional significance. Although Metro's charter gave it functional planning authority, the agency never used it prior to the mid-1990s.
32. Sy Adler and Jennifer Dill, "The Evolution of Transportation Planning in the Portland Metropolitan Area," in *The Portland Edge*, 230–256.
33. Ibid.
34. Parsons, Brinckerhoff recommended the less-ambitious VMT goal in part because even Metro's sophisticated transportation planning effort did not promise to achieve the original objective.
35. Adler and Dill, "The Evolution of Transportation Planning."
36. Ibid.
37. Ibid.; Abbott, *Greater Portland.*
38. R. Gregory Nokes, "Study Sees Billions in Boundary Costs if Measure Passes," *Oregonian*, October 17, 2000, 1.
39. Felicity Barringer, "Property Rights Law May Alter Oregon Landscape," *New York Times*, November 26, 2004, 1.
40. Abbott, *Greater Portland.*
41. Timothy Egan, "In Portland, Houses are Friendly. Or Else," *New York Times*, April 20, 2000, F1.
42. Hal Bernton, "Oregon Slows Sprawl to a Crawl," *Oregonian*, December 8, 1999, A01.
43. Wievel, Persky, and Senzik, "Private Benefits and Public Costs."
44. Turner and Rylander, "Land Use."
45. Katz, "Building the Future."
46. Gordon Oliver, "City Outpaces Region in Growth of New Housing," *Oregonian*, December 14, 1999, 1.
47. Ehrenhalt, "The Great Wall"; Tim Ferguson, "Down With the Burbs! Back to the City!" *Forbes*, May 5, 1997, 142–152.
48. Ehrenhalt, "The Great Wall."

49. Abbott, *Greater Portland.*
50. Seltzer, "It's Not an Experiment."
51. Marcia D. Lowe, "Alternatives to Sprawl: Shaping Tomorrow's Cities," *The Futurist,* July-August 1992, 28–34.
52. Abbott, *Greater Portland.*
53. Adler and Dill, "The Evolution of Transportation Planning."
54. Barnett, "Shaping Our Cities."
55. New Urbanism is a movement initiated by architects that aims to restore many of the principles of traditional urban design, particularly the emphasis on pedestrian movement and comfort, instead of vehicular mobility: front doors rather than garages face the street; on-street parking is allowed; tightly spaced houses with small front yards abut the sidewalk; neighborhood shopping is within walking distance; public parks and squares are designed to foster neighborly gatherings. In short, "The multiple components of daily life—workplace, residence, shopping, public space, public institutions—are integrated, after 50 years of sorting, separating, and segregating functions and people." See Roberta Brandes Gratz and Norman Mintz, *Cities Back from the Edge: New Life for Downtown* (Washington, D.C.: Island Press, 1998), 327–328.
56. Paul Gapp, "Portland: Most Livable—'But Please Don't Stay,' " *Chicago Tribune,* April 2, 1980, 1.
57. Alan Katz, "Developing the Future," *Denver Post,* February 10, 1997, 1.
58. Ben Plowden, "A City Ablaze in Green and Gold," *New Statesman,* January 8, 2001.
59. Johnson, "The Myth and Reality"; Robert D. Putnam, Lewis M. Feldstein, and Don Cohen, *Better Together: Restoring the American Community* (New York: Simon and Schuster, 2003).
60. Johnson, "The Myth and Reality," 109, 110.
61. Putnam, Feldstein, and Cohen, *Better Together,* 244.
62. Abbott, *Greater Portland,* 151.
63. Johnson, "The Myth and Reality"; Ferguson, "Down With the Burbs!"
64. Abbott, *Greater Portland.*
65. Quoted in Alan Katz, "Developing the Future."
66. Ehrenhalt, "The Great Wall"; Katz, "Developing the Future." Deborah Howe suggests that those who attribute Portland's housing price increases to market constraints should explain the 80 percent increase in homeowner-reported values during the 1970s, before the UGB was established. See Deborah Howe, "The Reality of Portland's Housing Market," in *The Portland Edge,* 184–205.
67. Clarren, "Planning's Poster Child Grows Up."
68. Laura Oppenheimer, "Initiative Reprises Land Battle," *Oregonian,* September 20, 2004, B01.
69. Laura Oppenheimer, "Property Compensation Fight: People on Both Sides," *Oregonian,* October 7, 2004, 4.
70. Quoted in Barringer, "Property Rights Law."
71. The measure won in all thirty-five of the state's counties except Benton County, which encompasses Corvallis and Oregon State University. See Laura Oppenheimer, "Land-Use Laws on Turf that Is Uncharted," *Oregonian,* November 4, 2004, 1.
72. Laura Oppenheimer and James Mayer, "Poll: Balance Rights, Land Use," *Oregonian,* April 21, 2005, C01. Respondents in a poll by the Oregon Business Association and Portland State University's Institute of Portland Metropolitan Studies said they value property rights more than farmland, the environment, or wildlife habitat, and 60 percent chose individual rights over responsibility to their community. On the other hand, two-thirds said growth management makes Oregon a more desirable place to live, and respondents strongly favored planning over market-based decisions and wanted to protect land for future needs instead of using it now for homes and businesses.

73. Laura Oppenheimer, "Battle Intensifies over Oregon's Property Rights Law," *Oregonian*, August 13, 2005.

74. Quoted in Blaine Harden, "Anti-Sprawl Laws, Property Rights Collide in Oregon," *Washington Post*, February 28, 2005, 1.

75. Barringer, "Property Rights Law."

76. "Marion County Judge Overturns Measure 37," press release, Oregonians in Action, October 14, 2005.

77. James Mayer, "Planners Brace for Growth Battle," *Oregonian*, August 12, 1990.

78. Quoted in Barringer, "Property Rights Law."

79. Ferguson, "Down With the Burbs!"

80. Christopher R. Conte, "The Boys of Sprawl," *Governing Magazine*, May 2000, 28.

81. Ferguson, "Down With the Burbs!"

82. Goldberg, "The Wisdom of Growth."

Recommended Reading

Abbott, Carl. *Greater Portland: Urban Life and Landscape in the Pacific Northwest*. Philadelphia: University of Pennsylvania Press, 2001.

Ozawa, Connie P. *The Portland Edge*. Washington, D.C.: Island Press, 2004.

Robbins, William G. *Landscapes of Conflict: The Oregon Story, 1940–2000*. Seattle: University of Washington Press, 2004.

Web Sites

www.metro-region.org (Metro site)
www.friends.org (1000 Friends of Oregon site)
www.oia.org (Oregonians in Action site)

CHAPTER 18

Conclusions

Politics, Values, and Environmental Policy Change

Having read the preceding cases, you do not expect that just because some-one has identified an environmental problem and even figured out how to fix it, the government will necessarily address the problem or adopt the most "rational" solution. As the framework laid out in chapter 1 made clear, policymaking is not a linear process, in which government officials recognize a problem, deliberate based on all the available information, and select the optimal solution. Rather, policymaking consists of a series of engagements among advocates trying to get problems addressed in the venue they believe will be most hospitable to their concerns and in ways that are consistent with their values. Advocates of policy change struggle to create a context in which their definition of a problem dominates the debate, while awaiting a window of opportunity to push their preferred solution. But defenders of the status quo have a crucial advantage: in American politics, it is much easier to prevent change than to enact it.

THE STRENGTH OF THE STATUS QUO

One of the features of the American environmental policymaking process that stands out most starkly in the preceding cases is the remarkable persist-ence of the status quo. The prevailing policy may be shielded by the president, well-situated members of Congress, or the agencies that administer it. The president can block change using a veto or veto threat or, more subtly, by simply failing to put forth a policy proposal and arguing instead for more research. Highly placed members of Congress can rebuff attempts to change policy as well: committee chairs can decline to send a bill to the floor; majority leaders in either chamber can refuse to schedule a vote on a bill. In the Senate, a minority can filibuster legislation; in the House, the majority party can use multiple referral, amendment-friendly rules, and other parliamentary maneu-vers to derail a bill. Agencies can weaken a legislative mandate by delaying implementation or interpreting a statute in ways that are inconsistent with the apparent intent of Congress.

The strength of the status quo manifests itself plainly in cases involving natural resources on public lands, where environmentalists have faced enor-mous resistance to reforms aimed at introducing their values into management practices. In natural resource policymaking, narrow, relatively homogeneous subsystems that are biased in favor of development historically have been extremely difficult for competing interests to penetrate. Although timber policy has become noticeably more environmentally protective in response to advocates' efforts, mining and grazing policies on public lands retain vestiges of century-old routines. As the case of snowmobiles in Yellowstone National Park makes clear, even the national parks—which are relics of the preservationist impulse—struggle with a history of accommodation to commercial development. The fact that existing policies resist change does not benefit development interests exclusively, however; as the Arctic National Wildlife Refuge and backlash cases make clear, the tenacity of the status quo can occasionally work in favor of environmentalists. The point is that history shapes current politics and policy, making some outcomes more likely and others less so.

The strength of the status quo means not only that institutionalized interests have an advantage in policy debates, but also that policies tend to lag behind advances in the scientific understanding of the natural world. Many of the environmental policies passed in the 1970s, which continue to shape decision making, reflect ecological notions of stability and balance that were anachronistic among practicing scientists even then. For example, the Endangered Species Act focuses on conserving individual species and their habitats, even though conservation biologists for decades have advocated preserving diversity at all levels of biological organization. Critics also charge that, because of their initial design, many environmental laws are inefficient or counterproductive. Economists have disparaged the Superfund Act, for example, for diverting millions of dollars to what most public health professionals agree are relatively low-risk toxic dump sites. Although neither the Endangered Species Act nor the Superfund Act is perfectly "rational" from many experts' point of view, both have stubbornly resisted reform—not just because some economic interests benefit from the laws as written but because environmentalists recognize that, once they are opened up for reconsideration, they are vulnerable to being weakened or rescinded altogether.

LEGISLATIVE POLICY CHANGE

Given the fragmentation of American politics—among both the levels and branches of government—and hence the numerous opportunities to stymie a challenge, dislodging the status quo requires a formidable effort. In legislative policymaking, two elements are crucial to challengers' success: a large, diverse coalition and the backing of influential leaders. Therefore, advocates define problems in ways they hope will both inspire leadership and facilitate coalition-building. They are more likely to succeed in proffering the authoritative problem definition if they can tell a story that features loathsome villains, sympathetic victims, a simple causal relationship between them, and an imminent crisis.

The Importance of Building Coalitions

As the backlash case reveals, one way that opponents of the status quo have tried to circumvent the arduous process of changing policy in Congress is by attaching riders to appropriations and omnibus budget bills. More commonly, however, proponents of fundamental policy change must assemble a broad supporting coalition. To build such a coalition, advocates have learned they must join forces with groups that may have different values but similar objectives. For example, environmentalists worked with tuna canners to press for the Dolphin Protection Consumer Information Act, which established standards for dolphin-safe labels. Environmentalists have also allied with hazardous waste cleanup firms to resist changes in the Superfund law; gas, solar, and geothermal power companies, as well as insurance firms, are cooperating with environmentalists to press for cuts in greenhouse gas emissions; labor unions and municipal governments have taken the side of environmentalists in opposing legislation to compensate property owners when regulation reduces the value of their land because they believe such laws will severely compromise government's ability to protect public (and workers') health and safety.[1]

Keeping such pragmatic "Baptist and bootlegger" coalitions together is no mean feat; in fact, it is difficult to maintain the cohesiveness of even a more homogeneous union. For environmentalists, it is hard to craft approaches that are palatable to mainstream interests without alienating the true believers that form the activist core. Moreover, when the vague ideas and symbols that bind members of an alliance together are translated into practical policies, rifts and factions often develop. For example, a schism appeared during climate change negotiations at the Hague in 2000, when some environmental groups supported a plan to allow the United States to get credit toward its carbon dioxide (CO_2) emissions limits for forests, which absorb CO_2, while others opposed such a deal because they felt it allowed the United States to evade its responsibility for cleaning up its share of pollution. Similarly, environmentalists disagree over whether trade restrictions are an appropriate way to get developing countries to stop encircling dolphins while catching tuna. Although it is easier to maintain cohesiveness among economic interests, those bonds can also be broken. In the acid rain case, for example, unity among utilities dissolved once some figured out how to clean up and so had an incentive to support limits on sulfur dioxide (SO_2) emissions. In the climate change case, business interests have diverged on the question of whether mandatory limits on CO_2 emissions are desirable. The dissolution of coalitions renders them vulnerable, creating opportunities for their opponents.

The Crucial Role of Leadership

Even if advocates succeed in building a supportive coalition, legislative majorities large enough to enact policy change do not simply arise spontaneously in response. Rather, one feature that emerges powerfully from the cases is the importance of individuals and, more particularly, of leaders, in bringing about policy change. Just as well-placed individuals can block reform, talented leaders can greatly increase the likelihood of policy change by facilitating coalition-building, brokering solutions to apparently intractable conflicts, and shepherding solutions through the decision-making process. For example, after nearly a decade of stalemate over acid rain, Sen. George Mitchell's skillful and dogged micromanagement of negotiations over the Clean Air Act Amendments of 1990 proved indispensable to the policy's passage. By conducting negotiations in private, away from the glare of the media and the demands of special interests, Mitchell was able to wring concessions from holdouts and forge an agreement among parties that for a decade had refused to bargain. Similarly, the Clinton administration's highly publicized backing of the Everglades restoration and the San Diego Multispecies Conservation Program made it possible to enact far more protective solutions than might otherwise have emerged. Compare the outcome of those cases with that of the Arctic National Wildlife Refuge case, where for years public squabbling among competing interests, unmediated by leadership, stymied efforts to pass a comprehensive energy policy bill.

Leaders need not be "true believers." The stringency of the Clean Air and Clean Water acts of the early 1970s reflect the efforts of President Richard Nixon and presidential hopeful, Sen. Edmund Muskie, to trump one another and thereby gain the kudos of environmentalists. Twenty years later, presidential candidate George H. W. Bush promised to be "the environmental president" in hopes of undermining support for Democrat Michael Dukakis, and one result was the Clean Air Act Amendments of 1990. Neither Nixon nor Bush was an environmentalist; both were trying to garner political credit by capitalizing on the salience of environmental issues that advocates had worked so hard to create.

Nor are elected officials the only people who can make a difference in policymaking; policy entrepreneurs outside government can also be effective. Ralph Nader's organization spurred Senator Muskie to propose more ambitious clean air and water laws than he originally intended. Karen Scarborough's skilled facilitation of the San Diego habitat conservation program yielded a plan that protects more coastal sage scrub than might otherwise have been saved; without her, the process might have collapsed altogether. Dexter Lehtinen's flamboyant decision to launch a dubious lawsuit in the Everglades started in motion a chain of events whose result no one could have predicted. Ron Arnold, Alan Gottlieb, and other antienvironmental policy entrepreneurs employed powerful rhetoric to throw a wrench into the environmental juggernaut and thereby prompt a wholesale reevaluation of the movement's tactics and goals. More recently, David Hunnicutt of Oregonians in Action launched an initiative campaign that threatens to turn Oregon's land-use planning process on its head.

Using Information to Define Problems

Critical to advocates' success in building coalitions and inspiring leadership is their ability to devise and disseminate a compelling definition of the environmental problem. Although conventional tactics, such as lobbying legislators and donating money to political campaigns, remain important means of influencing policy, scholars have recognized the importance of strategically defining problems in determining the outcome of policy contests. For environmentalists, those efforts entail framing scientific information in ways that emphasize the risk of inaction. When protection advocates succeed in translating the scientific explanation of a problem into a compelling definition of the problem, as they did in the Everglades, spotted owl, and other cases, they are much more likely to attract support.

Among the attributes of problem definition that emerge from the cases is the political power of scientific explanations and predictions. According to a rational view of policymaking, "If predictive science can improve policy outcomes by guiding policy choices, then it can as well reduce the need for divisive debate and contentious decision making based on subjective values and interests." [2] As should be clear from the cases in this book, however, science cannot provide such a definitive, value-free basis for policy: scientific explanations are inherently uncertain because natural systems are not "closed" or static and therefore may respond to perturbations in fundamentally unpredictable ways. Scientists' ability to measure environmental phenomena is also limited—by time, money, and inability to control for complex interactions among variables in the real world. Scientists' explanations and predictions therefore reflect experts' assumptions and extrapolations, which in turn hinge on their values. Although they do not provide an objective basis for policymaking, scientific explanations do furnish the elements of environmentalists' causal stories. Science-based stories that feature loathsome villains (such as large chemical companies), innocent victims (ideally children or fuzzy animals), and a simple connection between them are more likely to get sympathetic media coverage and therefore to prompt public concern. Examples abound: environmentalists have succeeded in generating public alarm about dolphins, turtles, owls, and caribou—all of which are charismatic species. They have less to show for their efforts to provoke public alarm about declining rangelands.

As any experienced advocate will tell you, another crucial attribute of stories that succeed in garnering public (and hence political) attention is an impending crisis. The cases of Love Canal and Rocky Flats illustrate the impact that dramatic events can have on the public, particularly if advocates manage to interpret dramatic events in ways that reinforce their policy position. In the Love Canal case, advocates pounced on scientific studies identifying chemicals in the air and soil and health effects to buttress their claims that their neighborhood was contaminated; journalists were their allies in this endeavor because of their propensity to focus on human interest stories and health risks. In the Rocky Flats case, media revelations of government and contractor misappropriation of funds, errors and carelessness in disposing of waste, and concealment of waste management practices all enhanced advocates' efforts to create public anxiety about the plant. Opponents of the plant in turn drew on those stories to reinforce their definition of the plant as an environmental and public health threat rather than a critical building block of the national security edifice.

Further buttressing environmentalists' efforts to define a problem is the support of scientists, who may have identified the problem in the first place. Periodic scientific bulletins serve as focusing events, keeping media—and therefore public and elite—attention trained on the issue. Scientific consensus reports, particularly if they are crafted by prestigious bodies such as the National Academy of Sciences, bolster the credibility of science-based stories. And individual scientists, acting as knowledge brokers, can be particularly compelling proponents of policy change. The impact of activist scientists is especially obvious in the Rocky Flats, acid rain, and climate change cases, but it is evident in most of the other cases as well.

Ultimately, for advocates of policy change to prevail, they must not only define a problem but also furnish a solution that is consistent with their definition of the problem, as well as viable in terms of the budget and the political mood.[3] While waiting for a window of opportunity to open, policy entrepreneurs soften up their pet solutions. For example, the concept of emissions trading was in the pipeline for more than two decades before it was finally incorporated into legislation to curtail acid rain. During that period, economists were expounding on the benefits of using market-based mechanisms to solve environmental problems in textbooks, classrooms, and scholarly and popular journals. Similarly, the Everglades restoration plan and San Diego habitat conservation program reflect ideas about adaptive, ecosystem-scale management that had been circulating among conservation biologists for nearly a decade.

Even linking a ready-made solution to a compelling definition of the problem does not guarantee success, however, because opponents of policy change have devised a host of tactics to counter challenge. Recognizing the importance of science to environmentalists' problem definition, opponents try to undermine the information and ideas on which protection advocates base their claims. The climate change case provides an especially vivid example of this tactic: the fossil fuel industry funds contrarians, who challenge the scientific consensus on global warming, as well as conservative think tanks and foundations, which disseminate these counterclaims. In addition, opponents of regulation try to shift attention to the costs of policies proposed to address environmental concerns. Like scientific predictions of environmental outcomes, cost projections are highly uncertain and—as is clear in the owl and acid rain cases—tend to overestimate the expense of complying with new regulations.[4] The reason, in part, is that such forecasts rarely take into account the accidents and unpredictable events of the future, technological innovations, or the market's response to regulation. Furthermore, like scientific projections, they are heavily shaped by modelers' assumptions. Nevertheless, cost projections can be persuasive when interpreted as providing certainty about the future, particularly when—as in the owl case—they portend economic and social disaster.

Finally, opponents of protective regulations have become adept at crafting and disseminating persuasive stories of their own. Development advocates have defended the prerogatives of ranchers and fishers by portraying them as iconic Americans. These heroic figures survive thanks to their rugged individualism and hard work and would prosper but for the interference of overweening bureaucrats. Similarly, both the backlash and Portland cases reveal the power of symbolic anecdotes in which average Americans suffer when government infringes on their private property rights.

ADMINISTRATIVE POLICY CHANGE

Although observers tend to focus on legislation, another avenue for major policy change in the American political system is administrative decision making. Managers have enormous discretion to interpret their typically vague statutory mandates, and agencies' missions, standard operating procedures, and past interactions with client groups and congressional overseers constrain day-to-day decision making. As a result, as the cases in this volume make abundantly clear, simply changing the law is rarely enough to prompt a substantial shift in administrative behavior. Upon confronting this reality, environmentalists have frequently turned to the courts. The "adversarial legalism" that results has, in turn, prompted efforts to try alternative approaches, such as grassroots mobilization and collaborative problem solving.

The Courts

The courts have always been the forum for resolving intractable value conflicts; it is therefore not surprising that environmentalists and cornucopians find themselves so frequently making their cases before a judge. At the beginning of the modern environmental era, environmentalists filed lawsuits to prod the fledgling Environmental Protection Agency to write regulations under the Clean Air and Clean Water Acts. Subsequently, they used the National Environmental Policy Act, the National Forest Management Act, and other laws in the spotted owl case to redirect federal land management priorities. Efforts to control overfishing of cod, flounder, and haddock in New England were failing until a lawsuit filed by the Conservation Law Foundation forced the National Marine Fisheries Service to institute more protective rules. A lawsuit against the state of Florida spurred action in both the state legislature and Congress to restore the Everglades. And litigation compelled the National Marine Fisheries Service to implement a legally mandated export ban on tuna caught using dolphin sets.

Lawsuits can have direct and indirect effects. They can prompt administrative policy change directly by narrowing the range of options an agency may consider and precluding the status quo altogether. They may have less immediate but equally potent impacts if they raise an issue's visibility and thereby facilitate reframing or result in the intervention of elected officials or their appointees. Another underappreciated impact of lawsuits is the generation of new information, which in turn can form the basis for efforts to institute new policies.

Observing the success of environmentalists in court during the 1970s, those who oppose environmental regulations also began resorting to litigation to achieve their ends. Property rights advocates made skillful use of the courts in the 1990s to revise the legal interpretation of the takings clause of the Fifth Amendment. Snowmobilers persuaded a sympathetic federal judge to prevent a ban on using snowmobiles in Yellowstone National Park from taking effect. Since the 1980s it has been common for both industry and environmental groups to sue the Environmental Protection Agency over the same decision, with one litigant claiming the regulation is too strict and the other arguing that it is too lenient. By contrast with many other nations whose political cultures are less litigious, in the United States, jurisprudence—and the adversary relationships it fosters—has been a defining feature of environmental politics.

Local and Ecosystem-Scale Collaboration

In an effort to avert the wave of lawsuits that seems to accompany every new environmental law or regulation, agencies have been experimenting with negotiated rulemaking, mediation, and other consensus-building procedures. Many advocates on both sides have endorsed collaborative environmental problem-solving as an alternative to more conventional, top-down regulatory decision making. Since the early 1990s a huge variety of place-based collaborative endeavors have emerged, particularly in the West, from citizen-led watershed protection programs to government-sponsored planning efforts. These initiatives have fostered novel solutions to formerly intractable problems such as grazing on public lands, forest management, and watershed restoration. Their proponents contend that such approaches yield outcomes that are both more environmentally protective and more durable than those produced by the conventional, adversarial approach.

Critics, however, point out that win-win solutions are not always possible and that compromise is often scientifically indefensible. They have raised concerns about the long-term accountability of such approaches as well as the extent to which they shift the burden of environmental regulation from government to citizens. Critics have suggested that collaborative efforts exclude stakeholders with "extreme" views and avoid tackling the most contentious issues in order to gain agreement. And they have questioned whether consensus is, in fact, an appropriate goal. In any case, even the most ardent fans of collaboration acknowledge that involving stakeholders in program design is not a panacea. As efforts to restore the Everglades show, numerous institutional barriers to cooperation exist among agencies as they try to implement collaborative plans. The gnatcatcher case reveals, in addition, that ordinary obstacles—such as a lack of funding or sustained political will—can impede that attainment of vague planning goals. Finally, as both cases make clear, as long as fundamental value differences persist, advocates are likely to challenge the results of collaborative processes in hopes of bringing about an outcome more consistent with their preferences.

ACKNOWLEDGING THE ROLE OF VALUES

A primary objective of this book is to identify patterns that help us understand the politics of environmental issues without obscuring the uniqueness of each case. I posited at the outset that two elements of American environmental politics remain relatively constant across the cases: advocates in environmental policy contests are almost always deeply divided over values, and how those values translate into political choices depends heavily on the way a problem is defined in terms of science, economics, and risk. Direct discussions of competing values are rare, however, in part because, although its adversaries caricature environmentalism as an effort by elites to impose their values on society, public opinion polls suggest that most Americans sympathize with the general aims of the environmental movement. Even its critics concede that environmentalism is becoming "the lens through which we look at our relationship to nature." [5]

At the same time, survey and behavioral evidence on American environmentalism is contradictory and suggests deep inconsistencies in people's attitudes and beliefs. Efforts to address issues such as climate change and urban sprawl expose the tensions latent in American environmentalism. Americans claim to value the natural environment, but most appear unwilling to relinquish their energy-consuming lifestyles—a reality that is underscored by the proliferation of SUVs and pickup trucks in U.S. cities and suburbs. Although individual behavior is clearly at the root of many of our environmental problems, political stories that cast ordinary citizens as the villains have fared poorly in the American political context. Similarly, stories that suggest direct human health effects have galvanized the public more consistently than those involving ecological decline.

In short, our commitment to environmental protection remains ambiguous, as does our willingness to sacrifice on behalf of healthy natural systems. Our aversion to making tradeoffs, in turn, enables opponents of environmental regulations to frame issues in ways that emphasize costs or inconvenience to individuals or that emphasize other core values—such as freedom, national security, or economic growth—and thereby stymie efforts to amass support for protective policies. For some, the patterns that emerge from these cases may suggest that the prospects for genuine change in our approach to environmental protection are poor. But an alternative interpretation is possible: the Dudley Street Neighborhood case, for example, shows that the synthesis of environmental goals with other social values can yield extraordinary results. Efforts in the West to find common ground among ranchers and local environmentalists suggest that, at least under some circumstances, concern about the future of a particular place may trump mutual distrust; practical agreements may emerge even in the face of underlying value differences. Recent empirical evidence on the sources of human well-being offers fertile ground for those who hope to persuade Americans to consider alternatives to the single-minded pursuit of economic growth.[6]

Most important, political science, like ecology, is not a predictive science: as is true of the natural world, the patterns we identify in human affairs are probabilistic and subject to change. New people and new ideas can affect the process in dramatic and unexpected ways. Therefore, the lessons of past experience should not limit but rather should liberate both professional activists and concerned citizens who wish to challenge the status quo.

Notes

1. For a critical view of such coalitions, see Jonathan H. Adler, "Rent Seeking Behind the Green Curtain," *Regulation* 4 (1996): 26–34; Michael S. Greve and Fred L. Smith, *Environmental Politics: Public Costs and Private Rewards* (New York: Praeger, 1992).
2. Daniel Sarewitz and Roger A. Pielke Jr., "Prediction in Science and Policy," in *Prediction: Science, Decision Making, and the Future of Nature*, ed. Daniel Sarewitz, Roger A. Pielke Jr., and Radford Byerly Jr. (Washington, D.C.: Island Press, 2000), 17.
3. John Kingdon, *Agendas, Alternatives, and Public Policies*, 2d ed. (New York: Harper-Collins, 1995).
4. For example, in the late 1970s the chemical industry predicted that controlling benzene emissions would cost $350,000 per plant, but, by substituting other chemicals for benzene, chemical manufacturers virtually eliminated pollution control costs. In 1993 carmakers estimated that the price of a new car would rise $650 to $1,200 as a result of regulations limiting the use of chlorofluorocarbons, yet in 1997 the actual cost was between $40 and $400 per car. Prior to the passage of the 1978 Surface Mining Control and Reclamation Act, estimates of compliance costs ranged from $6 to $12 per ton of coal, but in fact costs were in the range of $.50 to $1 per ton. See Eban Goodstein, "Polluted Data," *The American Prospect*, November-December 1997. Available at www.prospect/print/V8/35/goodstein-e.html.
5. Charles T. Rubin, *The Green Crusade: Rethinking the Roots of Environmentalism* (Lanham, Md.: Rowman and Littlefield, 1998).
6. See, for example, Richard Layard, *Happiness: Lessons From a New Science* (New York: Penguin Press, 2005); Andrew C. Revkin, "A New Measure of Well-Being from a Happy Little Kingdom," *New York Times*, October 4, 2005, C1.

Index

About the Author

Judith A. Layzer is assistant professor of environmental policy in the Department of Urban Studies and Planning at the Massachusetts Institute of Technology. She earned a PhD in political science at MIT. After four years at Middlebury College in Vermont she returned to MIT, where she teaches courses in science and politics in environmental policymaking, ecosystem management, and public policy.

Layzer's research focuses on several aspects of U.S. environmental politics. Her overarching concern is with the way environmental problems get defined and in particular with how advocates use scientific ideas and information to tap into Americans' environmental values. Ongoing research explores the impact of science-based stories on environmental politics and policymaking. Another project investigates the extent to which collaborative, ecosystem-scale management initiatives affect political dynamics and yield promised environmental benefits. A third project examines the relationships among business interests, conservative ideas, and U.S. environmental policy.

Layzer is an athlete as well as a scholar. In addition to having finished five Boston marathons, she shares nine national championship titles and one world championship trophy with her teammates on Lady Godiva, Boston's premier women's Ultimate Frisbee team.